PRIVATE LAND CLAIMS
IN
MISSOURI

1834

United States:

House of Representatives Document #1178
Twenty-third Congress – First Session

Heritage Books
2024

HERITAGE BOOKS
AN IMPRINT OF HERITAGE BOOKS, INC.

Books, CDs, and more—Worldwide

For our listing of thousands of titles see our website
at
www.HeritageBooks.com

Published 2024 by
HERITAGE BOOKS, INC.
Publishing Division
5810 Ruatan Street
Berwyn Heights, MD 20740

International Standard Book Number
Paperbound: 978-0-7884-9402-4

23D CONGRESS.] No. 1173. [1ST SESSION.

PRIVATE LAND CLAIMS IN THE STATE OF MISSOURI.

COMMUNICATED TO THE HOUSE OF REPRESENTATIVES FEBRUARY 5, 1834.

GENERAL LAND OFFICE, *January* 18, 1834.

SIR: The report of the recorder and commissioners, under the provisions of the acts of Congress of the 9th of July, 1832, and March 2, 1833, for the final adjustment of private land claims in Missouri, upon such claims as, in their opinion, are entitled to be placed in the *first* class, specified by the act of 1832, has been sent to this office, but the voluminous character of the report preventing this office from making copies thereof for the two Houses of Congress within a reasonable time, I have this day transmitted the original report to the Senate, with a request that it may be placed in the possession of the House of Representatives whenever the Senate shall have acted upon the subject.

I have been induced to send the report to the Senate from the fact that one of the commissioners appointed to investigate those claims is now a member of that honorable body.

It being very important that this office should be in possession of the *originals* of all the reports upon private land claims, I have to request that the report herein mentioned may be returned after the final action of Congress thereon.

With great respect, sir, your obedient servant,

ELIJAH HAYWARD.

The Hon. SPEAKER *of the House of Representatives.*

PRIVATE LAND CLAIMS IN MISSOURI.

TWENTY-THIRD CONGRESS—FIRST SESSION.

IN THE HOUSE OF REPRESENTATIVES OF THE UNITED STATES, *June* 30, 1834.

On motion of Mr. ASHLEY:

Resolved, That the report of the recorder and commissioners for the adjustment of land titles in Missouri, under the acts of July 9, 1832, and March 2, 1833, be referred to the Secretary of the Treasury, and that he be directed to report his opinion as to the validity of the several claims contained in said report to the next session of Congress, and that said report be printed.

RECORDER'S OFFICE, ST. LOUIS, MO., *November* 27, 1833.

SIR: In pursuance of the act of Congress entitled "An act for the final adjustment of land claims in Missouri," and of the act supplementary thereto, of March 2, 1833, the undersigned recorder and commissioners beg leave to lay before you, for the decision of Congress, the result of their examination.

In the report now submitted the board have included only such claims as appear to be entitled to confirmation, and to be placed in the first class. They reserved their decision upon those claims which seemed to be destitute of merit, in law or equity, under the laws, usages, and customs of the Spanish government, for their final report to Congress We were influenced to take this course from the belief that we were authorized, by the terms of the act, which provide that the lands contained in the second class shall not be subject to sale until the final report of the recorder and commissioners shall have been made. This view of the subject was the more readily adopted from the fact that, during the almost entire existence of the board, the cholera has prevailed to such an extent as to prevent, in a great measure, the appearance of the claimants, or their witnesses, before the board. Under such circumstances ordinary justice not only to the claimants, but to the government itself, seemed to require that the greatest indulgence should be given which the law could possibly extend.

Before entering into an examination of the claims the board came to the determination of settling such general principles as might be found to be applicable, and which should be not only their guide in the decisions to be made, but the basis of the report which they are required to submit.

These principles or general propositions will be found embodied in the form of resolutions in the paper marked A, which accompanies this report, and to which you are referred.

The tabular form has been adopted as the most convenient mode of presenting each claim, including the evidence produced in support of it. But, as it is made the duty of the board not only to present the claims as they have been submitted, but also to "*state the authority and power under which they were granted, by the French or Spanish governors, commandant, or sub-delegate,*" they will do so as succinctly as the nature of the case will permit.

For the purpose of arriving at correct conclusions upon the merits of the claims reported, we have availed ourselves of all the sources of information accessible to us. We have consulted not only all the authorities and proofs within our reach on the subject of the French and Spanish laws, usages, and customs, but have also attentively considered the acts of Congress heretofore passed on the subject, and the construction which has been given to them.

By a reference to the various acts of Congress relative to the incomplete French and Spanish claims in Louisiana, it will be seen that the confirmations which have been made of those titles have not been donations or gratuities on the part of our government, but, on the contrary, were predicated upon a right vested in the grantee, or those claiming under him, and founded upon the laws, usages, customs, and practice of the government under which the claims originated. These acts and confirmations might, therefore, have been considered as conclusive, as far as they went, of those laws, usages, customs, and practice; and, consequently, that every claim of a similar character should be confirmed, or placed in the first class, would be the reasonable and natural inference. Without, however, going this length, the board felt it to be their duty, whenever a principle protective of a claim was furnished by those acts, to give it effect, unless some law, usage, or custom of the government which originated the claim should be found to be inconsistent with their provisions.

Among the claims examined we found that many of them have been excluded from confirmation upon grounds which have since been abandoned by Congress; or upon grounds which have been taken by former commissioners to whom the claims were submitted, and from whose decision there was no appeal; or lastly, upon grounds which, although justified perhaps by the letter of those acts, were evidently opposed to their spirit and intention. No claim, by the act of 1807, could be confirmed which contained a lead mine or salt spring; and, consequently, a class of claims whose merits, in every other particular, were admitted, were rejected for that reason. This objection, although at the date of the act considered sound, it seems has long since been abandoned. By the act of 1824, and those subsequent to it, no such exception is made. A meritorious claim, therefore, although containing a lead mine or salt spring, was entitled, intrinsically, to as favorable consideration in 1807 as in 1824, and in justice, it would seem, should never at any time have been excluded from confirmation.

Again, by the act of 1814, it is provided "*that in every case where it shall appear by the report of the commissioners, register, or recorder, that the concession, warrant, or order of survey under which the claim is made contains a special location, or had been actually located or surveyed* (within the Territory of Missouri) *before the 10th day of March*, 1804, *by a surveyor* duly authorized by the government making such grant, the claimants shall be and are hereby confirmed in their claims; provided that no claim adjudged fraudulent, nor a greater quantity than a league square, nor the claim of any person who has received, in his own right, a donation grant from the United States in said Territory, shall be confirmed."

Now, if those claims, coming directly within the provisions of the act just alluded to, were entitled to be confirmed, and were actually confirmed, we would reasonably conclude, from the same views, that the claims now reported, especially such as are within a league square, are entitled to protection from principles established not only by the acts of 1807 and 1814, but by other acts of Congress; for we are not able to perceive the difference in merit or character which has confirmed some and rejected others, which were evidently intended by Congress should be confirmed.

By a parity of reasoning the authority of the Spanish sub-delegate officers in Upper Louisiana to grant lands, not only to the quantity of 7,056 arpents, or a league square, but even to the extent of 27,000 arpents, it would seem, has been established by Congress. In several cases Congress confirmed claims to land exceeding 7,056 arpents, based upon *mere permission to occupy* given by the lieutenant governor. The case of the Vallés and others for the *Mine la Motte* tract, believed to contain 27,000 arpents, and that of the Shawnee Indians, who inhabited a considerable tract of country in the former districts of St. Genevieve and Cape Girardeau, who removed from their situation in the United States by invitation of the Spanish government, through their agent, Louis Lorimier, to use them against the aggressions of foreign or domestic enemies in the province of Upper Louisiana, is another and a strong instance illustrating the view here taken on this point.

By several acts of Congress, also, concessions by the lieutenant governor to various individuals have been confirmed to the extent of 7,056 arpents out of a larger quantity of from 15,000 to 20,000 arpents, including the original grant. From this the board would conclude that, in thus ratifying those concessions, Congress has settled the question of the power of the granting officer to make them. Because they would reasonably suppose that, if the authority was not possessed, the grant would have been void *in toto*, as it would have been a usurpation on the part of the officer, and a flagrant violation of his duty, to make grants to such an extent. Such a concession should be regarded as a whole, and its validity or invalidity settled accordingly.

When we ascend beyond the various acts of Congress passed upon the subject of these claims, and seek for their grounds of confirmation under the laws, usages, customs, and practice of the government and of the authorities at New Orleans acting in obedience to them, as we are required by the law under which we act, we find nothing in those laws, usages, customs, or practice which would justify the idea that Congress, in extending its protection to these claims, has transcended the bounds of propriety and of justice. On the contrary, a close and (as far as we could) a thorough investigation of the subject has brought our minds to the conclusion that, with the exception of the act of 1824, and those acts amendatory of and supplementary to it, the laws of Congress passed in relation to these claims have not been sufficiently comprehensive. Impressed with this belief, we cannot but think that those acts which limit confirmations within a league square, those which exclude claims which contain lead mines or salt springs, and those which require either a special location or a survey previous to March 10, 1804, have not had sufficiently in view the rights of the claimants as founded upon the laws, usages, customs, and practice of the French and Spanish authorities, and as protected by the treaty of cession and the law of nations.

Breckenridge, in his "Views of Louisiana," speaking of these claims, says, page 143: "It is a subject on which the claimants are feelingly alive. This anxiety is a tacit compliment to our government, for, under the former, their claims would scarcely be worth attention. The general complaint is, the want of sufficient liberality in determining on the claims. There is, perhaps, too great a disposition to lean against the larger concessions, some of which are certainly very great; but when we consider the trifling value of lands under the Spanish government, there will appear less reason for this prepossession against them. For many reasons it would not be to the honor of the United States that too much strictness should be required in the proof or formalities of title, particularly of a people who came into their power without any participation on their part, and without having been consulted." In compliance with the provision in the act which requires the commissioners *to state the authority and power under which each claim was granted by the French or Spanish governor, commandant, or sub-delegate*, we would refer, for proof of the same, to—

1st. The usage and practice of the lieutenant governors and sub-delegates in Upper Louisiana from the earliest period to the last concession granted in that province.

2d. To the usage and practice of the governors general and the intendant general at New Orleans.

3d. To the Spanish laws and royal ordinances on the subject of grants of lands belonging to the royal domain in all its colonial possessions in the western hemisphere.

That the usage and practice have been consistent with the presumption of lawful power in the officers who made grants is, in our opinion, demonstrated and sustained by all the evidence, oral and written, to which we have had access. It is to be observed that the lieutenant governor and the other sub-delegates in Upper Louisiana have almost universally originated the claim or concession. The cases are few in which the original grant emanated from the governor general, and scarcely constitute exceptions to the general practice, since, even in those few cases, the survey was to be made under the immediate sanction of the subordinate provincial authority.

Not a single case has been discovered in which the exercise of the power to grant by the lieutenant governor has been questioned; nor where a complete title has been refused by the governor general, or intendant, at New Orleans, upon the ground of the want of power in the lieutenant governor or sub-delegate to make the grant; nor have we found that any was ever refused on the ground that the granting officer had transcended his powers. On the contrary, in the complete titles which have come to our knowledge, the inchoate or primary concession is recognized as legal and valid, and, with the survey, forms the foundation of the formal or complete title. It is a fact worthy of notice that all the lieutenant governors in Upper Louisiana, from the first to the last, exercised this power of making grants, varying in the number of the arpents according to the prayer of the petitioner and the circumstances of the case. Every grant, as far as we have been able to ascertain, made by the French authorities prior to the treaty of Fontainbleau in 1762, by which Spain acquired possession of Louisiana, and, indeed, all such as were made prior to the year 1767, the time when Spain was put in possession of the country, were subsequently recognized by the Spanish authorities. The right to make such grants by the French authorities was never questioned. From that period to the date of the purchase of the country by the American government there was a continual and uninterrupted exercise of the granting of lands by lieutenant governors and sub-delegates, and no complaint was ever uttered by the French or Spanish government for this use of authority. The proclamation made by the Spanish commissioners at New Orleans the 18th of May, 1803, in the presence of the American authorities, upon delivering the province of Louisiana to the French republic, explicitly assures the people, who were then about to pass into the hands of a new sovereign, of protection in their rights, by announcing "*that all concessions, or property of any kind soever, given by the governors of these provinces, be confirmed, although it had not been done by his Majesty.*" These facts alone are sufficient, in our opinion, to authorize the conclusion that those officers who made grants in Upper Louisiana had the power so to do, and did act within the pale of their authority. It would be a very rash and violent presumption to suppose that a succession of provincial officers, regularly pursuing the same course for nearly half a century in the granting of lands, were, in every step taken and every act done, usurping power and violating not only the mandates of an arbitrary despotism, but also the laws, usages, customs, and practice of the government under which they acted. And it would be an unreasonable inference to be deduced from these facts that, because the sovereign has nowhere given his *express assent* to such proceedings, they were therefore illegal and void. We are happy to find that we are sustained in these views by the opinion of the Supreme Court of the United States in the case of the United States against Arredondo. These are the words of the court: "The grants of colonial governors, before the revolution, have always been, and yet are, taken as plenary evidence of the grant itself, as well as authority to dispose of the public lands. Its actual exercise, without any evidence of disavowal, revocation, or denial by the King, and his consequent acquiescence and presumed ratification, are sufficient proof, in the absence of any to the contrary, (subsequent to the grant,) of the royal assent to the exercise of his prerogative by his local governors. This or no other court can require proof that there exists in every government a power to dispose of its property; in the absence of any elsewhere, we are bound to presume and consider that it exists in the officers or tribunal who exercise it by making grants, and that it is fully evidenced by occupation, enjoyment, and transfers of property, had and made under them, without disturbance by any superior power, and respected by all co-ordinate and inferior officers and tribunals throughout the State, colony, or province where it lies."—(6th Peters's Rep., p. 728.)

We find that all the complete grants, eighteen only of which have come to our knowledge, were based on grants made by the subordinate authorities. Subsequent to the 1st of December, 1802, no complete title could be made, as appears from the letter of the intendant, Morales, to the lieutenant governor of Upper Louisiana, of the same date, stating that the office was closed on account of the death of the assessor, and directing that no applications for complete titles should be made till further orders. No order, so far as we know, was given; nor does it appear that the office was ever reopened previous to the treaty of cession.

The difficulties attending the making of titles complete were many and great. The expenses in procuring a complete title at New Orleans were enormous and considered as extortionate. Stoddart, in his "Sketches of Louisiana," a book to which we particularly refer as shedding much light on this subject, says that it "was necessary that a concession should pass through four, and in some instances seven, officers before a complete title could be procured; in which the fees exacted, in consequence of the studied ambiguity of the thirteenth article, frequently amounted to more than the value of the lands." Besides, the difficulties of intercourse between the posts in Upper Louisiana and New Orleans were so great that few were willing to encounter them, especially as the formalities of a complete title seemed in the minds of the people to vest no more right than was acquired when incomplete.

From the closest scrutiny that we have been able to make, the quality and the location of the land were the principal concern; but little importance was attached to the fact that the title was incomplete. And why should it have been otherwise when the governor general unquestionably well knew the constant and invariable practice of the lieutenant governors in granting lands, and never, so far as we know, either ordered or required that the concessions should be taken to New Orleans for his signature before they could be considered as passing titles? These incomplete grants could be, and were, sold for debts, did pass by devise, and were transferable at the will of the concessionary; and it is notorious that these several modes of disposing of them were resorted to and adopted as the fixed practice of the country. The governor general, as the superior of the lieutenant governor or sub-delegate, must be presumed to have known the acts of his inferior and the ordinary customs of the country; and if such practices and customs were contrary to law the supposition is that he would have prohibited them for the future. There was no regulation or law that we have been able to find in the researches which we have made which required that the grantee should apply within any given time to have his grant made complete. It would seem that he was at perfect liberty to consult his own convenience. Indeed, the royal domain was distributed in such a liberal manner, and for such worthy purposes, that it appears the people were entirely satisfied with the assurance of property contained in the grant made by the lieutenant governor. The objects contemplated by these grants were the improvement of the country, the increasing of population, and also they were given as rewards and as compensation for services rendered. We have not been able to find a single instance of the sale of the royal domain in Upper Louisiana, from the first establishment of the post of St. Louis, in 1764, to the 10th of March, 1804. A proposal to purchase was made by Bartholomew Cousin on the 5th of March, 1800, at a price to be fixed by the intendant general, but it does not appear that it was ever acted on. The first sale of land that was ever made in Upper Louisiana by the sovereign of the soil was, from all the information in our possession, made by the government of the United States.

The regulations of O'Reily, Gayoso, and Morales, in the opinion of the board, had no effect in changing the practice in the distributing of the royal lands, nor were ever considered as a new code different from the one already existing as the settled law of the Spanish American dominions. Those by Gayoso evidently had reference to new settlers coming from foreign countries, and, as regards Spanish subjects, were disregarded by himself, as appears by a complete title granted by him to one Regis Loisel, of St. Louis, described in the grant as a merchant. By his regulations no grants were allowed to merchants. As respects the laws of O'Reily, Stoddart, in his Sketches of Louisiana, pages 251 and 252, says, that "it may be doubted whether the land laws of O'Reily ever operated in Upper Louisiana. They bear date nearly three months before the Spaniards took possession of that part of the country, at which time there existed only a few miserable huts in it; the first settlements commenced only four years before." Again, he says: "Indeed, the regulations contained in them were totally inapplicable to that part of the country, and the Spanish authorities there always conceded lands on principles not derived from them."

The same author, speaking of the laws of Morales, says, page 252: "It is believed that these laws were never in force; certain it is that they were never carried into effect. The reason for the first is, that the great clamor raised against them in all parts of the province induced the governor general and cabildo to draw up a strong protest against them and to lay it before the King. The consequence was that Morales was removed from office, though he was afterwards reinstated merely to assist in transferring the possession of the country to the French republic. The reason for the second is, that the assessor died soon after they were promulgated, which totally deranged the tribunal of finance, and rendered it incapable of making or confirming land titles." The board cannot therefore believe, if they were ever so intended, that these laws had the effect to supplant the laws, usages, customs, or practice of the Spanish government in the province of Upper Louisiana, as they were then known to the people and recognized and acted upon by those in power. The general code of the Spanish land laws in Louisiana seemed to have grown into gradual though silent operation, originating from the circumstances of the country, and accommodating itself to the necessities and condition of the people. They were resorted to as the country required their application and became ripe to receive them, and furnished the rules of action and decision for all the subordinate civil authorities of the province.

So peculiarly connected with the circumstances of the country was the administration of the law, that Stoddart, page 250, advances the opinion that the lieutenant governors had a *discretionary power* in the making of grants. "For," says he, "they always exercised it, and it is difficult to presume that they would contravene the known laws of their superiors without instructions to that effect. In all their concessions they were regulated by the wealth and importance of the settlers." He adds: "The governor general at first imposed considerable restrictions on the commandant relative to the concession of lands, but he afterwards found it necessary to be more liberal than even the land laws of O'Reily." In July, 1789, he wrote to the commandant at New Madrid as follows: "Notwithstanding the instructions heretofore sent you, more or less front or depth may be given, according to the exigency of the ground, *as likewise a greater or less quantity of land, agreeably to the wealth of the grantee.*" In the claims which have been examined, and are now submitted for the supervision of Congress, we noticed the fact as remarkable, that grants prior to 1789 differed from those subsequent to that period, not only as regards quantity, but also the terms of the grant, those subsequent generally containing a much larger quantity and being more liberal to the concessionary.

In a colony so partially organized, and under such circumstances, it would seem unreasonable to call for the *precise* written authority under which each officer acted, or to require that the particular law or ordinance of the Spanish government under which any act or series of acts was done should be *specially exhibited.* It is sufficient that nothing in these laws, usages, customs, or practice is inconsistent with, or repugnant to, the royal ordinances of the King.

The Spanish laws which we have consulted, and to which we beg leave to refer Congress as calculated to throw some light upon the subject, are to be found in the *Recopilacion de leyes de las Indias;* the royal ordinance of October 15, 1754, by Ferdinand VI; that of 1786, by Charles III, and the royal letters to Morales of October 22, 1798. Also, we would here again refer to the "Sketches of Louisiana," written by Mr. Amos Stoddart, who was the first civil and military commandant in Upper Louisiana after the country was taken possession of by the American government. The board have, with great attention, consulted this author, and have relied with unhesitating confidence on his statements. Coming to the country, as he did, immediately after the treaty of cession, to take command of the country as a civil officer of the American government when the Spanish officers were many of them still in the province, and the laws, usages, customs, and practice, as exercised and applied under the Spanish government, although it had just ceased to exist, were still fresh in the minds of the people, with the Spanish records in his possession, he must have known as facts what he has stated as such, and if fraud had been practiced, of all other times, it must then have been discovered.

The laws authorizing grants of land for the purposes of settlement and population are to be found in White's Compilation, pages 34, 35, 38, and 39. Those relating to grants of lands as rewards for services, or as pure graces, "mercedes," will be found in the same work, pages 30, 35, and 41. The earliest of the first class of laws bears date in 1513. The first law of the second class was made in 1542; the former twenty-one years, the latter fifty years after the discovery of the New World by Columbus.

The grants of land for services rendered were of a liberal character, and we are bound to believe had the sanction of the sovereign, as we know of no objection having been urged to the usage. The practice seems to have originated from the liberal views of the Emperor Charles, in his decree of 1542, which ordains that the viceroys of Peru and New Spain, and the governors of the provinces under their authority, *grant such rewards, favors, and compensation as to them may seem fit.* This decree, recognized successively by Philip II in 1588, in 1614 by Philip III, and in 1628 by Philip IV, was finally incorporated by Charles II, in 1682, into the *Recopilacion de leyes de los Reynos de las Indias.*

Thus it manifestly appears, by the laws and authorities above recited and referred to, that it was the duty of the provincial authorities not only to grant and distribute the royal lands in the King's name for the purposes of settlement and population, but that it was specially enjoined upon them to grant lands as rewards for services.

The royal ordinances of 1754 and 1786 have been carefully examined, and nothing has been found in them to limit the power conferred on the authorities in the *Recopilacion*. An order of Philip V, of November 24, 1735, which required confirmation by the crown, was revoked by the ordinance of 1754, which authorized the *audiencias* to issue the confirmations in the King's name, and, when the sea intervened, or they were in distant provinces, empowered the governors, with the assistance of the other officers mentioned, to issue complete titles.

By the eighty-first article of the ordinance of 1786, intendants in the kingdom of New Spain were made exclusive judges of grants of lands, and referred them for their government to the various laws on the subject in the *Recopilacion*, and to the ordinance of 1754, which is appended to the eighty-first article.—(See White's Compilation, pp. 54, 55, 56, 57, and 58.) The ordinance of 1786, so far as it vested in the intendants the power to grant lands, was for the first time declared to be in force in Louisiana by the royal order of October 22, 1798, to be found in White's Compilation, p. 218.

In the enacting part of the ordinance of 1754 it is to be observed that the King speaks of "mercedes," rewards, as contemplated by it. This ordinance does not specifically mention the laws of the Emperor Charles, of the 2d, 3d, and 4th Philip, and of Charles II, who compiled and promulgated the *Recopilacion;* but it does not therefore follow that they were repealed, or in any manner altered, as respects the power given by those laws to the subordinate authorities in the Spanish American dominions to grant lands as rewards or graces, "mercedes," for services rendered the government. Nor have we discovered anything in this ordinance to lead us to the opinion that a mere sale of lands, with a view to revenue, was the object of the government, or that the far more useful and wise policy of settlement and population, as developed in the *Recopilacion*, was intended to be abandoned.

It would extend this report beyond reasonable limits to enter at large into a detail of the circumstances and state of Louisiana to show that the Spanish land system then observed and practiced upon was expedient and applicable to that part of the Spanish American dominions. The importance of population and settlement in that province, arising from its contiguity to the North American republic on the one side and its great exposure to numerous and formidable Indian nations on the other, were certainly great inducements for the establishment of those laws, usages, customs, and practice which we find did most certainly prevail. These causes and circumstances, instead of narrowing the power to grant, given by the code of Indies, must rather have been a sufficient reason for widening its range and facilitating its exercise.

In forming an opinion as to what would have been the fate of the claims submitted and now reported, "if the government under which they originated had continued in Missouri," the view here taken of the laws, usages, customs, and practice of the Spanish government in the province of Louisiana, and the spirit and policy which they disclose, have led us to the conclusion that those claims which we have examined, and which are now reported to Congress, would have received the sanction of the governor general at New Orleans, and been perfected into complete titles. Laying aside every other consideration, the practice alone which universally prevailed of regarding these grants as private property by the government in both Upper and Lower Louisiana, would have strongly inclined the board to regard them in a favorable light. It is a matter of recorded history that inchoate concessions, even such as were unlocated, unsurveyed, and having nothing special in their character, were the objects of sale, transfer, inheritance, and devise.

That they were sold under execution for debt, included in the inventories of persons deceased intestate—in short, that they were regarded by the inhabitants and public authorities, to all intents and purposes, as any other available property, satisfactorily appears from the claims heretofore confirmed, and from those examined by the board and now submitted for the consideration of Congress. Some were even adjudicated upon by the governor general at New Orleans. May it not then be inferred that the government which would adjudicate upon and sell under execution an inchoate concession, and complete the title in favor of the purchaser, would, *a fortiori*, unless fraud were shown, perfect that into a complete title, if required, which was in the hands of the original grantee?

In the claims reported, it will be seen that some have been recommended for confirmation which were never surveyed. The fact that such grants were regarded by the inhabitants and authorities of the country as property, also induced the board, from that custom, to look upon it in the same light; and as we have not discovered that any condition appears ever to have been implied as to the time within which a complete title was to be applied for, so the same view holds good as to the time when the land should have been located or surveyed. Nor was it possible, in the nature of things, that the inhabitants could have anticipated a change of government. A survey, besides, as appears from evidence brought before us, and which is now submitted with this report, was accompanied with great expense and difficulty. The cost for surveying a league square was near six hundred dollars. Besides, it was impossible to obtain surveys of all concessions: first, because of the scarcity of surveyors; secondly, because of the presence of hostile Indians on the lands granted. We are unwilling to suppose that the Spanish government, had it still continued, would, under such circumstances, have declared the grant void for the want of a survey on or previous to March 10, 1804. This date is mentioned because, by the act of 1814, a survey previous to it is made an indispensable prerequisite to confirmation. It appeared, therefore, to be no valid objection to the confirmation of a grant, in the opinion of the board, that it had not been surveyed either before or after March 10, 1804, because, previous to that date and even subsequent to it, it was almost impossible to make surveys, and by the act of Congress passed March 26, 1804, such survey was prohibited under heavy penalties.

The same view of the subject has brought the board to the conclusion that where no improvement or cultivation upon land included within an incomplete grant, although located or surveyed previous to the 10th of March, 1804, has been made, it should work no injury to the grantee, because that act specially forbade any improvement, suspended his rights, and deprived him of all practical benefit of his land until it should be confirmed. This construction of the act was taken by Mr. Madison, the President of the United States, who, in his proclamation of December 12, 1815, prohibited all occupation of unconfirmed lands, and ordered the proper officers of the United States to drive off those who should enter upon them. In the examination of these claims by the board, most carefully made, we have looked with an eye particularly directed to the question of their *bona fide* character. At the same time that we have labored with an anxious scrutiny to detect fraud, we have been careful not gratuitously to presume its existence. On this head we have been governed by the well-settled principle, recognized by every enlightened nation, that fraud must be proved, and not presumed. In the luminous decision given by the Supreme Court of the United States in the Arredondo claim, this view of the subject is ably laid down and sustained. "Fraud (say the court) is not to be presumed, but ought to be proved by the party who alleges it; and if the motive and design of an act was to be traced to an honest source equally as to a corrupt one, the former ought to be preferred." With such sound principles, sustained not only by the voice of society, but by the decision of the highest judicial tribunal in the country, we have endeavored to conform our opinions; and it is but justice to declare that, in the examination of the claims reported, no proof of fraud has been made.

Some claims are reported and submitted for the consideration of Congress which rest alone upon a mere grant. There was no survey, and, as far as we know, no cultivation. From the most mature reflection that we have been enabled to bestow on this class of claims, the conclusion was forced upon our minds, from the circumstances and condition of the country, and from the customs and practice of the inhabitants and civil authorities, that such should be recommended for confirmation. In the first place, the grant was made and signed by an officer of the existing government, whose acts we are bound to presume were in accordance with his powers, and sanctioned by the sovereign will, as contained and expressed in the laws, customs, usages, and practice of the country.

Secondly. They were regarded as vesting a right so far indefeasible, that they were subject to the adjudication of the civil authorities; were so adjudged upon; were made liable to public sale for debt; were transferable in the ordinary transactions of life; could be inherited, and were capable of being devised.

Thirdly. By a reference to the testimony of Baptiste Vallé, senior, Frémon Delauriere, and others, which accompanies this report, it will be seen that it was both dangerous and difficult, on account of the Indians and the scarcity of surveyors, to make surveys. The difficulty of making cultivation, habitation, or improvement, arose from the same causes. Indeed, the inhabitants found it a matter of no small concern and difficulty to protect themselves from the Indians without encountering the dangers which would arise from excursions into the woods. Breckinridge, in his "Views of Louisiana," bears testimony (page 138) that but "a few troops were kept up in each district throughout the province, and were too inconsiderable to afford much protection to the inhabitants."

Fourthly. There being no limited time within which a survey should be made, the change of government prevented the execution of it under the French and Spanish governments, and our laws, after the existence of those governments, prohibited it.

Fifthly. If such, for the want of survey and cultivation, by the laws, usages, customs, and practice of the Spanish government, were void, they would, by those same laws, usages, customs, and practice, have been reannexed to the domain. Whenever a grantee became delinquent as to any of the conditions or requisitions contained in his grant, such land so granted was reannexed to the royal domain. Stoddart (p. 247) says: "The same formality and solemnity were observed in the annexation of lands to the domain as when they were granted or conceded. All annexations were declared by an ordinance of Louis XV, in 1743, to be null and void, and of no effect, *unless they were judicially decreed*. The same principle obtained under the Spanish authorities, and they deemed it obligatory." That such was the law, custom, or usage, and so practiced by the authorities of the country, is fully established by reference to the "Livre Terrein," now in the office of the recorder of land titles, in which we have instances of this method of "judicially decreeing" an annexation to the domain of such lands as had been forfeited for a non-fulfilment of the terms of the grant.

Sixthly. Such grants bear, in their terms, the character of vesting a fee-simple in the grantee; they seem to have been so petitioned for, and were so granted. If such a title could not have been passed by the grant, it would be unreasonable to suppose either that it would have been so requested or so granted. It must be admitted that they were acquainted with their own laws and customs; and allowing them only a small degree of regard and obedience to the same, it is nothing more than a fair presumption that what was asked for and what was granted was legitimate and proper.

In the claim of Bernard Pratte for 800 arpents, to be found among those examined and recommended for confirmation, it will be seen that a transfer of it was made before the grant was located, all of which was sanctioned by the lieutenant governor himself.

In 1779 land was granted by Ferdinand de Leyba to one John Saunders, upon express condition that said Saunders should cultivate it one year from the date of the grant. Before the expiration of the year Saunders sold the land, and his assignee made or proved no cultivation. In 1793 Zenon Trudeau, lieutenant governor, made a decree in favor of the claimant against one Joseph Hortez, who claimed the same as his property. Who will say that Trudeau, the lieutenant governor, in this proceeding, violated the laws and customs of the country, and that this was an act of usurpation? There is certainly much more in the history of the country, during the time the French and Spanish governments existed in Louisiana, to prove that it was in accordance with their laws and customs, than that it was a violation, and an act of usurped authority.

There is one claim reported which, seemingly, is at variance with the principle contained in the tenth resolution adopted by the board. It is the claim of Louis Bissonet for forty arpents. The grant was made in 1777 by Francisco Cruzat, in which there was an express condition that the land should be cultivated within a year from its date. No cultivation is shown until the year 1798. It was then claimed by, and cultivated as the land of, Louis Bissonet. Subsequently the same land was surveyed by Antoine Soulard, surveyor general of the province of Upper Louisiana under the Spanish government. Much reflection induced the board to recommend this claim for confirmation, because it was believed that although the condition was not proven to have been performed, yet the claim so long set up was a fair presumption that the condition had been fulfilled, and that if it had not, it would have been reannexed to the domain.

Having thus presented the views which we have of the question referred to the board by the act of July 9, 1832, we will now proceed to state in a few words the nature and grounds of the decisions made upon the claims submitted to them by virtue of the act of March 2, 1833, founded upon settlement and cultivation.

In deciding upon and applying the evidence submitted in support of these claims, we have observed the following rules:

1st. That under the act of 1833 only such claims, founded on settlement and cultivation, are cognizable as have been heretofore filed with the recorder.

2d. That all such claims as come within the provisions and requisitions of the act of Congress of

March 2, 1805, and the acts supplementary thereto, of April 21, 1806, March 3, 1807, and June 13, 1812, are entitled to confirmation.

The evidence in support of the claims herewith reported is spread upon the tabular statement of each of them, to which we beg leave to refer.

Before concluding, permit us to notice one or two subjects more, upon which we think it is proper that some suggestions should be made. In the examination of the question submitted to us, it was discovered that there were some cases which could not be noticed in consequence of their not having been filed within the time limited by the acts of Congress. The omission to file them arose from numerous causes; in some cases they were found to be in the hands of infant heirs; in other cases owned by the French or Spaniards, who, not knowing our language, were ignorant of our laws and of what was demanded under them. But most generally the omission to file them in proper time arose from the ignorance of the people that such a requisite was necessary to the validity of their claims. The first settlers of the country were daring men, who were scattered over a wide range of country, and whose sources of information of the proceedings of the government were few and difficult. Besides, by the act of March 2, 1805, section 4, it was not obligatory on the claimants to file notice of claim founded on any incomplete grant bearing date prior to the 1st day of October, 1800. The 4th section of the act of 1805 provides that every person claiming land "by virtue of an incomplete title bearing date subsequent to the 1st day of October, 1800, shall, before the 1st day of March, 1806, deliver to the recorder of land titles within whose district the land may be a notice in writing, stating the nature and extent of his claim, together with the plat of the tract or tracts claimed." The 5th section of the act of March 3, 1807, provides that "the time fixed by the act above mentioned, (the act of 1805,) and the acts supplementary thereto, be extended to July 1, 1808." Many of these claims deserve, perhaps, the favor which has been extended to those which have been filed.

From all that we can learn, some of these claims seem to possess intrinsic merit. We have been led to make these suggestions from the fact that these claims were recognized by the act of March 26, 1824, and the acts supplementary thereto, under which the United States district court of Missouri was authorized to adjudicate upon the French and Spanish unconfirmed land claims in said State. There are many claims depending on settlement and cultivation in the same situation, and arising from the same causes.

Upon the subject of conflicting claims, we have been unable to ascertain to what extent they exist. Having no *data* by which our exertions could be directed, we have labored pretty much in vain to find out in what cases they have taken place, although we caused a notice to be published, requesting in it adverse claimants to come forward and notify us of the fact, which notice is forwarded with the report. We are of the opinion, however, that they exist to a considerable degree. There are numerous cases of lands lying within these French and Spanish claims belonging to the individuals whose right or claim originated under the government of the United States; some depend upon purchases; some upon the law allowing pre-emption; some others upon New Madrid locations, and some again upon settlement rights which have been confirmed.

Most of these persons have been for a long time settled on their lands. Their claims being of a *bona fide* character, derived from the government of the United States, they went on to improve their lands, making for themselves and families comfortable homes, without any belief that they would ever be interrupted in their possessions. Should the claims reported by the board be confirmed by Congress in whole or in part, Congress will, in their wisdom, no doubt, notice the suggestion here made, and carve out such a course as will quiet the uneasiness and anxiety which are felt, by doing everything which even the most scrupulous demands of justice could require.

We deem it proper to state, before concluding, our apprehension that in some cases where French or Spanish grants have been held for a small quantity of land only the grants have been laid aside, and a claim set up by settlement right for 640 acres, a much larger quantity. It is difficult to discover or detect the imposition.

We would respectfully suggest that, in the event of the confirmation of this report, in whole or in part, a provision should be made confirming settlement rights, where they have sufficient merit, upon the condition that the person to whom it is confirmed had not previously held under a French or Spanish grant. It is due to the claims reported to say that no such suspicion attached to them. Nor will we say positively that we know of any case where such a course has been taken. We have ventured to make the suggestion from circumstances which authorize the belief that some such instances have occurred.

We now close this report by observing that the great number of claims originating under the French and Spanish governments arose from the condition of the country, from their want of population, and from their desire to have the lands speedily brought into a state of cultivation and improvement. For we find that France, in attempting to accomplish her great plan of permanently uniting the St. Lawrence with the Gulf of Mexico, held out inducements to emigration, with the view to form a permanent barrier against the encroachments of the English. Around her various military posts in this quarter colonies were planted, where, amid the vicissitudes of climate, at war with the elements and various Indian tribes, suffering every privation, they continued to flourish under the fostering care of the mother country. The same policy was pursued by the Spanish government. In recommending the claims of these people now presented to your notice, we do it on the grounds of their merit, the various laws, usages, customs, and practice of the different governments under which they originated, and, in our opinion, the great and immutable principle of justice.

All of which is most respectfully submitted.

ALBERT G. HARRISON.
L. F. LINN.
F. R. CONWAY.

ELIJAH HAYWARD, Esq., *Commissioner of the General Land Office.*

A.

Resolutions passed by the board of commissioners on the 30th October, 1833.

1st. *Resolved*, That it was the custom of both France and Spain, and formed a part of the policy of those nations in the settling of new countries, to appoint officers, whose business it was, by express regulations, to grant lands to all such of their subjects as might wish to settle in those countries, for the avowed purposes of improving and populating said countries.

2d. That all acts in relation to grants, concessions, warrants, and orders of survey, done and performed by the French and Spanish officers during the time those governments had possession of and exercised the sovereignty over the province of Upper Louisiana, ought to be considered as *prima facie* evidence of their right to do those acts and perform those duties, and ought to be held and considered binding on the government of the United States, inasmuch as the acts of the officers in said province were not only tolerated but approved by their superiors in power.

3d. That all grants, concessions, warrants, or orders of survey, made and issued by the French or Spanish officers in the late province of Upper Louisiana on or before the 10th day of March, 1804, where the same are not proved to be fraudulent, ought to be confirmed, provided the conditions annexed to the grant have been complied with, or a satisfactory reason given for not fulfilling the same.

4th. That O'Reily's instructions or regulations of 18th February, 1770, those of Gayoso of 9th September, 1797, and those of Morales of 17th July, 1799, were not in force in Upper Louisiana, except, perhaps, the provisions contained in those of Gayoso, which related to new settlers.

5th. That sub-delegates, in making grants, &c., were not limited by any known law or custom as to the quantity of arpents they should grant, except, perhaps, as to new settlers, and that such grants passed title, and that a survey was merely an incidental matter after the title had passed by the grant, so as to identify the land, that the grantee might take possession of it.

6th. That what are called incomplete grants by the custom and practice of the country were recognized as property capable of passing by devise, transferable from one to another, and were liable to be sold for debt.

7th. That those grants which are general in their terms pass as good a title as those which are more special, the difference being in the description of the land, and not in the title.

8th. That those officers of the French and Spanish governments whose names are signed to concessions must be presumed to have acted agreeably to powers vested in them by their sovereign, and that their acts are accordingly legal until the contrary is shown.

9th. That fraud is an affirmative charge, and, as relates to the French and Spanish claims, as well as in all other cases, must be proved, and not presumed.

10th. That in all cases where there are conditions to a grant, &c., if the grantee shows satisfactorily that he has been prevented from a fulfilment of the conditions by the act of God, by the act of law, by the enemies of the country, or by the act of the party making the grant, or any other sufficient cause, the grantee will be considered as absolved from the performance of the same, and the grant regarded as absolute.

A. G. HARRISON.
L. F. LINN.
F. R. CONWAY.

Private land claims.

The undersigned commissioners, appointed for the purpose of finally settling the private land claims in Missouri, would beg leave respectfully to notify all whom it may concern that the time of taking testimony is limited to the 9th of July next, after which period no new evidence can be received. From great age and infirmity many of the witnesses cannot attend at this place. One of the commissioners is authorized to proceed to the southern counties for the purpose of receiving testimony. He will give notice when and where he will be in attendance for that object.

There is another point to which they would call your attention. Many persons have bought lands from the government of the United States which had been covered by Spanish and French grants. Where this is the case the undersigned should be informed, that they may report the fact to Congress, which may have the effect of preventing embarrassment and litigation.

L. F. LINN.
A. G. HARRISON.
F. R. CONWAY.

St. Louis, *March* 21, 1833.

Editors of papers would confer a favor on the public by giving the above a few insertions.

A true copy of an advertisement published in the Free Press of March 28, 1833.

JULIUS DE MUN, *T. B. C.*

St. Louis, *November* 27, 1833.

Testimony of Charles Dehault Delassus.

Charles Dehault Delassus. He well knew Don Zenon Trudeau, formerly lieutenant governor of the late province of Upper Louisiana, whom deponent succeeded in the said government on the 28th of July, 1799; that all the lieutenant governors of Upper Louisiana were, in virtue of their offices as lieutenant governors, likewise sub-delegates; that the offices of lieutenant governor and sub-delegate were inseparable; that when deponent was commandant at New Madrid, in Upper Louisiana, he wrote to the Baron de Carondelet at New Orleans, the governor general, desiring to be excused from discharging the duties of sub-delegate, and that he received for answer, that since the commencement of the Spanish government in Louisiana the officers appointed by patent by the governor general (of which witness was one) were at the same time sub-delegates and military and political or civil officers; that the offices were inseparable; that there never was in Upper or Lower Louisiana a commission of sub-delegate specifically made to any officer; that the lieutenant governor of Pensacola was also sub-delegate in virtue of his office as lieutenant governor, without any other commission; that in Upper Louisiana there were but two patented officers who had the authority of sub-delegates—one at St. Louis and one at New Madrid; that the commandants at other ports, as at St. Genevieve, were called particular commandants; that the functions of a sub-delegate were the same before as after the appointment of the intendant at New Orleans in relation to the granting of lands, except that the sub-delegates on those subjects addressed themselves to the intendant, after his nomination, instead of the governor general, as previously they had done; that the practice in Upper Louisiana of the sub-delegate in relation to the granting of lands was, when a petition was presented to him for the purpose of obtaining a concession, if the sub-delegate considered that the petitioner possessed merits to entitle him to the concession, he granted the same, subject to the confirmation of the intendant, or, before his time, of the governor general; that in making a concession it was usual, in general, for the sub-delegate to make at the same time an order of survey, and more particularly since the appointment of Mr. Soulard, surveyor general, but that such orders of survey were not indispensable; that the grantee, however, in his (deponent's) opinion, without such order of survey, might proceed to have the survey made; that he knows no objection proceeding from the authorities at New Orleans to the usage or to the power of granting lands by the sub-delegates; that a petitioner for a concession of lands had a right of appeal from the refusal of the sub-delegates to the superior authority at New Orleans; that concessions made by deponent, as lieutenant governor, have been confirmed by the superior authority at New Orleans—by both the governor general and the intendant; that in no case within his knowledge has there been a less quantity confirmed than that originally granted; that he knows this to be the fact in relation to the grants made by his predecessor, Don Zenon Trudeau; that Don Zenon Trudeau is deceased; that he held his commission as lieutenant governor from the Baron de Carondelet; that this commission, as deponent believes, was in terms similar to the one which he himself held, and which he is ready to produce; that while lieutenant governor he kept no registry of concessions by him made; that he gave the concession to the petitioner, and that thereupon, as he believes, whether before or after the survey he knows not, the surveyor made a note or record of the concession; that matter did not concern deponent as lieutenant governor; that there was no mention made of any instructions by him received of the necessity of the registry of concessions. He knows of the existence of a book called the "Livre Terrein;" that when he was appointed lieutenant governor he believes he saw it; that he made no use of it; that it had not been made use for some time theretofore; that, as deponent believes, it had not been made use of from the time of the appointment of Soulard as surveyor general; that the Livre Terrein did not concern witness; that when a concession was made, and order of survey, there was no time limited within which a survey should have been made; that mineral lands were not reserved from sale by the Spanish government; that, on the contrary, the government encouraged the settlement of the country by miners, and the working of lead mines. The object of the government was to attract population by every means for the purposes of cultivation, and, above all, for the purpose of mining; that he was frequently at St. Louis during the government of Don Zenon Trudeau; that he was intimate with him, and frequently at his house during said time; that at various times when witness was at the house of Don Zenon Trudeau, he heard him mention a concession of 10,000 arpents of land which he (Trudeau) said he had made to Antoine Soulard, the petitioner; that one of the acquirements and talents of Mr. Soulard at that time must have been of great service to the government of Upper Louisiana; that he was, in fact, the right arm of the government at the time referred to, and that these remarks are true of Mr. Soulard in reference to the time at which deponent was lieutenant governor; that Soulard, during the last-mentioned period, continued to exercise the duties of the same office that he had done during the government of his predecessor, and without any fixed salary for either; that he saw the concession of which he has spoken in the possession of Mr. Soulard, on his table or among his papers; witness cannot say that he read the concession from beginning to end, but that it was the same concession of which he has already spoken; that the concession was in the usual form, for ten thousand arpents of land; that the requête or petition was in the handwriting of Soulard, and the whole of the decree or concession was in the handwriting of the lieutenant governor, Trudeau; that it was frequently the case that the concession was written by some person other than the governor for his signature; that he knew Santiago Rankin, and that he was the deputy of Soulard, the surveyor general; that Soulard had the power of appointing a deputy surveyor; the manner of appointing was by letter. The commission of Antoine Soulard, surveyor of all the districts of Illinois and New Madrid, of the date of February 3, 1795, marked A; the original official letter of Morales, the intendant, respecting Mr. Soulard's right to survey in the district of New Madrid, by himself or deputy, marked B; the official letter of Colonel Howard, recommendatory of Soulard, marked C; appointment of Soulard adjutant, marked D; the proclamation of Salcedo and Casa Calvo, marked E; the ordinance or regulations of Morales, marked F; the letter accompanying the same, marked G; the official letter of Delassus to Soulard, wherein he announces the death of the assessor at New Orleans, as made known to him by Morales, marked H; the letter from Casa Calvo to Colonel Delassus, acknowledging the receipt of the ordinance, &c., dated May 30, 1805, marked I; letter of Morales to Colonel Delassus, of August 26, 1799, in which witness is informed that the sub-delegates are independent of each other, marked K; the certificate of Gilberta Leonard and Don Manuel Armires, ministers of the royal treasury, in favor of Colonel Delassus, as former commandant at New Madrid and lieutenant governor of Upper Louisiana, dated 27th of June, 1805, marked L, are identified and proved by witness, and are indorsed and marked with the letters of the alphabet from A to L, inclusive; that he received six copies of the regulations of Morales, officially transmitted to him, as announced by the letter already referred to, upon the margin of which letter he noted, in Spanish, that the letter was answered and that the regulations were not to be complied with until further orders; that he did answer the letter of Morales, as noted in the margin thereof, and accompanied his answer with objections, a rough draught of which is herewith presented, marked M; that he knows that Morales received the letter and objections; at least that Morales made other communications to witness in answer to those made by him at the same time and through the same medium; that, as lieutenant governor, he had a right to suspend the execution of any order which to him appeared prejudicial to the interest of the King or people, until fresh instructions; that he received afterwards other letters and communications from Morales, referable to the department of sub-delegate, and that he never mentioned the subject of those regulations; that he does not remember to have caused those regulations to be published; that he gave no orders to his inferiors relative to the regulations of Morales, because he did not intend to obey them himself and had remonstrated against them. His acts in relation to the granting of lands, since the regulations of Morales, were approved, because he received the letter of approbation from the Marquis Casa Calvo, of the 30th May, 1805, marked N, heretofore offered, and because he thinks his acts or grants were confirmed; and because, if his acts had not been approved, he would have been informed thereof; that he is not certain whether any concession made by him was confirmed; he received from Morales answers to all his communications, except that objecting to the regulations. The practice in relation to the concessions of land in Upper Louisiana was to return the procés verbal and plat and concession to the party, and the governor below had no other means of knowing to whom lands had been conceded. Witness says he recollects one instance of receiving a note from the governor below, or from the intendant, either when he was governor here or at New Madrid, desiring to know whether a certain person, to whom he (witness) had made a concession, had the requisite qualifications; says he did not consider the regulations of Morales as obligatory upon him, but that if any person had made application to him for a grant, he would have made it as though the regulations had not been made. He says the regulations were not binding on him, because of the reasons mentioned in the objections heretofore offered in evidence. He has seen several ordinances of the King of Spain in relation to the granting of lands, but he does not recollect the date of them; the regulations of O'Reily were so old that they were not regarded; those which governed witness were those made by Carondelet. When he went to New Madrid to command, he found the regulations of Carondelet; he left them there when he came here to command. They had authority only in Upper Louisiana. Those regulations authorized the granting of lands according to the number of the family and means, and according to the object in view in granting. He consulted no ordinances of the King for his duties, but the orders and instructions of the governor, which were authoritative to him. He was likewise governed by the usage and customs of his predecessors. The quantity was not limited by any law or usage; he delivered a bundle of official letters which would clear up many things here. When he left Orleans to take command at Madrid, Carondelet told him in person what he afterwards wrote, that he wanted him to invite inhabitants from the United States, not hunters, but those who had families and great means. Those who would make settlements and bring other families, to grant them as much land as they want. While here as lieutenant governor he received the same instructions from Gayoso in writing. He was commandant at New Madrid from the year 1796 to 1799. Those papers, with others, he lost at Baton Rouge, on the revolution there. There was no other record of concessions except that kept by Soulard, who was obliged to keep such book.

The government below were aware of the manner in which Soulard's book was kept, and it always received the greatest approbation. He knows this by report generally, by what Soulard said to him, and by a letter received by Soulard. A Livre Terrein was kept before Soulard was appointed, but not after. Those instructions which he received from Carondelet were written, as well those he found at Natchez as those he received. They were particular to him. When publication of instructions or regulations was to be made, the governor directed it, and the manner. All the instructions which were official which he received he delivered to the commissioners at New Orleans. The instructions of Gayoso were official, and were delivered to the commissioners. It was not the duty of the lieutenant governor to keep any memorandum of concessions made. The vacant lands were seen, and those who had got titles were settled. He does not think Soulard rendered any account of the official acts done by him. He believes Soulard received instructions from the surveyor general as to the manner in which he should keep his books. But the surveyor was under the orders of the lieutenant governor. The surveyor general below had his district, and so had Soulard. The letter of the surveyor general to Soulard was rather a letter of friendly advice than of instructions. He, the witness, never received any commission of sub-delegate. He declined accepting the command at Pensacola, because the duties of sub-delegate were attached thereto, as he knew nothing about those. The instructions were by the King to the governor, and by the governor to him. He did not know the instructions to the governor from the King.

The regulations of O'Reily, Gayoso, and Morales were for the government of Upper Louisiana, and were delivered to the commissioners at New Orleans. He means by the word usage, the practice of his predecessors, because they were based upon the instructions. He may have added something to the usage of his predecessors, according to his instructions, where these may have required it. He never received orders to discontinue Livre Terrein. He found Mr. Soulard at St. Louis, as surveyor, and knows nothing of Livre Terrein. He thinks he delivered over every public document which was necessary or useful to the citizens of this country; he delivered them to Major Stoddart, an inventory of which he gave to Stoddart; one he kept, and the other he gave to the commissioners, Salcedo and Casa Calvo. He took with him only his official papers relative to his responsibility to his government. He took no book with him, nor anything, except his official instructions, which could relate to land titles. He left here March 10, 1804, and remained a governor two years at Baton Rouge, until 1810, previous to which time he was colonel of a regiment. In granting lands, they, the sub-delegates, were authorized to reward gratuitous services, secret, military, or civil, and were not limited as to quantity, because generally the governor had confidence in those he appointed, and because it was in virtue of the good will of his Majesty towards his subjects. He first derived intelligence of the treaty of 1803 from Lewis and Clark the fall or winter of 1803. Santiago, Rankin, and Madden were deputies in the spring of 1804. He does not know whether he made any concessions after the treaty of cession of 1803. He thinks information of the cession to France and to the United States came at the same time.

For the foregoing evidence and the documents therein referred to, the board refer to exhibit A, referred to by James H. Peck, judge of the district court of the United States for the district of Missouri, in his answer to the article of impeachment preferred against him by the honorable the House of Representatives of the United States, as printed by order of the Senate.

Testimony of Frémon Delauriere.

Charles Frémon Delauriere maketh oath and saith that he resided at St. Genevieve from the year 1796 until late in the year 1802; that he occupied the office of recorder (greffier) at that post; that in that capacity he read many letters addressed by the governor general, Baron of Carondelet, to M. François

Vallé, commandant of St. Genevieve, and to the Chevalier Dehault Deluzieres, commandant of New Bourbon; that in those letters the Baron of Carondelet particularly recommended to those two commandants to adopt all possible means of peopling their respective districts, by attracting foreigners to them by the gratuitous concessions of lands; to encourage agriculture, establishments of dairy and grazing, the making of salt, raising mineral, and erecting mills, by granting lands and privileges calculated to insure their success. That he also recommended to said commandants to induce, if possible, all the poorer inhabitants of the villages to settle on the lands instead of living in indolence and idleness; to give to each head of a family a quantity of land in proportion to the number of persons in the family; and to each unmarried man, who wished to make a settlement, as much land as they should consider proportioned to his means. That this deponent was employed by the aforesaid commandants, and particularly by the commandant of St. Genevieve, to persuade the inhabitants of the different villages to make those settlements; that the deponent himself drew up for them a great number of their petitions for grants of land; that a considerable number of those inhabitants availed themselves of the bounty of the government, some of them having located themselves in the neighborhood of the lead mines; some on the banks of the streams or rivers in the vicinity of St. Genevieve; that all of the inhabitants did not locate. This deponent further saith that when, towards the end of the year 1802, he delivered up the office of recorder, at St. Genevieve, to Mr. Francis Vallé, for the purpose of attending personally to the deponent's establishments on Salt river, there were in the possession of this deponent about forty concessions of land which had not been taken out of his office by their respective owners, of whom some were old inhabitants, and others new settlers, coming from different parts of the United States of America. This deponent saith that, at that time, there was only one deputy surveyor for the district of St. Genevieve and of New Bourbon, Madden still lives, and one for the district of Cape Girardeau, Mr. Bartholomew Cousin, since deceased; that the deputy surveyors for the remainder of the province of Upper Louisiana were few in number; and that the expense, difficulty, and danger of surveying at a distance from the posts was very great; that the fee payable to the surveyor was four cents per arpent, exclusive of the fee to the principal surveyor for the plat of survey, and exclusive, also, of the wages and support, while employed, of the axemen and chain-carriers; that to all these expenses was to be added that of travelling and choosing the location; that, in few instances, the value of the land at that day was equal to the expense attending the location and survey; that money was very scarce in the province at that date, and that the circulating medium or currency was in shaved deer skins; that very few of the grantees were moneyed persons, or able, conveniently, to pay the expenses of their respective locations; that this deponent, in the year 1803, resided at Salt river, where he carried on his salt-making establishment; that from the above point he addressed letters to his friends and acquaintances, as well at St. Louis as at other places, informing them of the advantages which the surrounding country for thirty or forty miles around presented; that on the report so made by this deponent, those amongst them who had not located their grants became desirous of locating them in this part of the province; that some of them came in person to this deponent, and others wrote to him on the subject; that this deponent showed to them that it would be impossible to effect their locations and surveys unless a number of them should join together for that purpose; that the Indians, (savages,) appeared determined to oppose and prevent all white settlements in that part of the country, having recently committed several murders; that at the salt works of the deponent they had massacred three men; that they had burned one Bouvet in his own house, and had killed one man at Cap aux Gres, and several other white men on Cuivre river; that this deponent informed the persons who consulted him that, inasmuch as there existed at or near Salt river and Cuivre river considerable tracts of excellent land, they ought, several of them, to co-operate in their locations, so as to include some of those tracts sufficient for the formation of several establishments contiguous to each other; that they would then be enabled to effect their surveys, and to make their settlements, by affording to each other material assistance and succor; that the difficulty of procuring surveyors, and the danger from the Indians, evidently compelled them to take this course; that this deponent believes that, from these considerations, the surveys of various large tracts, including a number of grants of eight hundred arpents each, located in connexion with each other, were made; and that, if such a mode of location had not been adopted, but very few surveys could have been effected in that part of the province. This deponent further saith that he believes that if there had been a sufficient number of competent surveyors, and if the difficulties, dangers, and expenses of locating had not been so great, the whole of the concessions issued by the authorities in Upper Louisiana would have been surveyed previous to the 10th March, 1804, the date of the taking possession of Upper Louisiana by the government of the United States. This deponent saith that, under the Spanish government, at all times within the knowledge of the deponent, and whilst he was an officer or subject of the King of Spain, previous to the cession of Louisiana to the United States, grants of land, whether located and surveyed, or unlocated or unsurveyed, whether special or general, were objects of sale, transfer, and inheritance, and were liable to be seized and sold for payment of debts due either to private creditors or to the King of Spain; that the unlocated concessions were often more valuable than those actually located and surveyed; that this deponent, from the opportunities and means of information presented to him in his office of recorder, (greffier,) at St. Genevieve, and afterwards of deputy surveyor, he considers himself well qualified to form an opinion of the value of lands and concessions, at that date, in Upper Louisiana.

FRÉMON DELAURIERE.

Sworn to and subscribed before me, Wilson Primm, a justice of the peace within and for the county of St. Louis, this eighteenth day of November, eighteen hundred and thirty-three.

WILSON PRIMM, *Justice of the Peace, St. Louis county.*

Albert Tison's testimony.

Albert Tison maketh oath and saith that he has been an inhabitant of this country since 1793, when he first arrived in the province of Upper Louisiana; that he is well acquainted with all that relates to the value of public land, and the surveying and locating of concessions or grants made thereof by the Spanish government previous to the 10th day of March, 1804; that the expenses and difficulty of obtaining surveys of said lands were very great, and that in few instances the land surveyed was worth or could be sold for the cost of survey and location; that the expense of surveying a square league was at least between five and six hundred dollars, without taking into the account the expense of choosing the location, which was often difficult, and even dangerous; that the number of practical surveyors was very small in the province of Upper Louisiana; that, for the first time, in 1795, a principal surveyor was appointed for Upper Louisiana, namely, Mr. Antoine Soulard; that, some time after, deputy surveyors were appointed for different districts, to wit: Mr. Story, for New Madrid, in or about 1798; Mr. James Madden, for St. Genevieve, in or about 1798; Mr. Bartholomew Cousin, in or about 1799 or 1800, for New Madrid; Mr. James Mackay, in or about the year 1796 or 1797. This deponent saith said Mackay was also commandant of the post of St. André and St. Charles, and, consequently, the range of his duty as deputy surveyor was very limited. This deponent saith the other deputy surveyors were appointed at intervals between 1799 and 1803, and that their names were as follows: James Rankin, H. —. Morison, John Ferry, and Frémon Delauriere. This deponent saith that there was also a deputy surveyor named Bouvet, who made a few surveys north of the Missouri, and who, about the end of the year 1802, or in the beginning of the year 1803, was taken and burnt to death by the Indians, on the Salt river, in the county now called Ralls county, in the State of Missouri. This deponent verily believes that if the expense, difficulty, and danger of surveying previous to the treaty of cession to the United States, on the 10th March, 1804, had not been so great, the whole of the grants of land made by the Spanish government would have been located and surveyed. This deponent saith that, in consequence of the scarcity of surveyors and the danger and difficulty of surveying, a party was obliged to wait sometimes as long as two years before he could have his survey executed. This deponent saith that he was himself driven off by the Indians in the month of December, 1803, while endeavoring to effect a survey in that part of the province included in Pike county, and in the neighborhood of Salt river. This deponent saith that he lived in the family of Lieutenant Governor Zenon Trudeau during two years and half, and was attached to the administration of Lieutenant Governor Delassus from the commencement to the end of his government in Upper Louisiana. That this deponent knows, from his own personal knowledge, that it was the custom of those lieutenant governors to date their concessions of land on the day of the date of the petition, or the day or two after said date, although in many cases the petitions had been dated and presented as far as two years or more previous to the issuing of the concession; that, in general, the lieutenant governor, Don Zenon Trudeau, wrote his grants himself, and that, in general, the grants signed by Lieutenant Governor Delassus were written by the principal surveyor, Antoine Soulard, or by other persons authorized to draw them up.

ALBERT TISON.

Sworn to and subscribed before me this nineteenth day of November, one thousand eight hundred and thirty-three.

PETER FERGUSON, *Justice of the Peace, county of St. Louis.*

Copy of a letter from Frémon Delauriere to Antoine Soulard, dated Saline, February 15, 1806.

My Dear Soulard: I avail myself of this opportunity to send you the returns of the surveys I have made. I start to-morrow to finish what remains, in spite of the alarms caused now and then by the Indians; but at all events we shall be five men, well armed, and I hope that we shall not be taken so unawares that we cannot defend ourselves; besides, it must be done, Indians or no Indians. In places so remote, and without direct communication with the settlements, I do not know when I shall be able—— [Here the paper is torn off and missing.]
yet about eight days' work, and it would be already done if I had not been obliged to come back on account of the Indians the first time I went to survey the Bay de Charles. By this same opportunity I write to Labeaume to send me a boat. If there is anything new in your quarter, let me know by that opportunity; you will confer an obligation on one who is always your friend and faithful deputy.

FRÉMON DELAURIERE.

Charles Frémon Delauriere's testimony in the case of François Saucier.

Charles Frémon Delauriere, being duly sworn, says that the survey already produced is one of those included among the surveys mentioned in the above letter; that the survey was executed at the time it bears date; that there was great difficulty and danger in executing surveys; that he was twice repulsed by the Indians, and that the third time he went up he could not execute several of the surveys, being prevented by Indians of the Sac and Fox nations, although he and his companions were well armed; that surveyors were very scarce, and it was difficult to procure any one to take a survey; that there was not half the number of surveyors necessary to execute the surveys that were then to be made.

Testimony of Colonel Baptiste Vallé in the case of Marie Louise Vallé Villars.

St. Genevieve, *Missouri, October* 23, 1832.

Colonel Baptiste Vallé, senior, personally appeared before Lewis F. Linn, one of the commissioners appointed finally to settle and adjust the land claims in Missouri, and authorized by the commissioners to receive testimony in this behalf. Said Vallé, being duly sworn, deposeth and said that he knew of a concession to Marie Louise Villars for seven thousand and fifty-six arpents of land on the waters of the Saline; that he knew of the intendant or governor of Lower Louisiana sending up instructions to the lieutenant governor of Upper Louisiana directing that the survey of Peyrouse should be run in such a way as to respect the concessions of Marie Louise Villars and François Vallé; that said concessions were given to the Rev. James Maxwell, vicar of Upper Louisiana, to take to New Orleans for the purpose of being laid before the intendant; that he understood and believes that they were either lost by the said Maxwell or left in some of the offices for confirmation.

Question by the commissioner. Do you know or believe that these concessions were antedated?

Answer. No.

Question by the commissioner. Have you any knowledge or reason to believe that any Spanish or French concessions were antedated?

Answer. No; for when I was in New Orleans, during the existence of the Spanish government, the Baron de Carondelet told me that if I wanted any lands in Upper Louisiana to make out a list, and he would grant them.

Question by the commissioner. Whilst you were at New Orleans, in your conversations with the Baron de Carondelet did you understand from him that the power to grant lands by the sub-delegates was denied?

Answer. No; on the contrary, when he pressed me to accept lands for myself and family, I informed him that the sub-delegates had given me and my family grants of land; to which he replied, "if you have not enough, ask for more."

J. BTE. VALLÉ.

Sworn to and subscribed the day and year first above written, before L. F. Linn, land commissioner.

L. F. LINN.

No. 1.—Gabriel Cerré, *claiming* 800 *arpents of land.*

To the Lieutenant Governor of Illinois:

Sir: Gabriel Cerré, merchant of this town of St. Louis, appears before you, and says that being desirous to establish a stock farm at the saline of Maramec, which is situated at about seven leagues from this said town, on the north bank of the above-mentioned river, therefore he humbly prays that you will condescend to grant to him the quantity of land which it is customary to grant to those who wish to establish stock farms in this province, and that the tract which he solicits for shall have its principal front on the aforesaid bank of said river, and the direction of its depth from the river to the hills of said saline; favor which he hopes to deserve of you.

CERRÉ.

St. Louis of Illinois, *October* 10, 1782.

Don Francisco Cruzat, lieutenant colonel of infantry, commandant and lieutenant governor of the western part of Illinois and its districts:

Cognizance being taken of the foregoing memorial, presented by Don Gabriel Cerré, an inhabitant of this town of St. Louis, dated October 10 of this present year, I have conceded to the said Gabriel Cerré, as a property belonging to him, his heirs, or assigns, a tract of land, of eight arpents front by forty in depth, at the saline of the river Maramec, situated at about seven leagues from this said town, on the north bank of the aforesaid river, having its first front on the bank of said river, and the direction of its depth to the hills of the aforesaid saline, that he may thereon establish the stock farm he solicits for, in the space of three years; and, in case he does not do it, said tract to remain incorporated to the royal domain, and also, at all times, to be subject to the public charges and others which it may please his Majesty to impose.

Given in St. Louis of Illinois, October 12, 1782.

FRANCISCO CRUZAT.

To Don Zenon Trudeau, lieutenant colonel by brevet, captain of the stationary regiment of Louisiana, and commandant of the western part of Illinois:

Sir: I have the honor humbly to represent to you that, having obtained from Mr. Francisco Cruzat (as is obvious by the title here annexed) a concession for eight arpents front by forty in depth, on the banks of the river Maramec, and having improved with success a saline that is thereon, having raised a great quantity of cattle and considerable crops, and not having been able at the time to have my boundaries fixed, as there was no surveyor, and now being desirous to have these things regulated, to avoid all difficulties which might take place henceforward, may it please you to order the surveyor of the government to fix my boundaries, and to deliver to me his certificate of survey. Having made a mature examination of the localities, I humbly pray also that you will grant to me twelve arpents more in front, which will make twenty arpents, and permit me to take my depth of forty arpents in following the course of the said river Maramec, as, at a distance from said river, the said lands are uninhabitable; and I do assure you that in this way it will carry prejudice to no one. Your petitioner will observe to you that, at this present moment, he has on said farm upwards of eighty horned cattle, a farmer, two negroes, and hired men who work there daily; he dares hope that, owing to your wishes to help industry, you will grant to him what he solicits; favor which he expects of your justice.

CERRÉ.

St. Louis, *January* 10, 1798.

The surveyor of this jurisdiction will set boundaries to the land of the petitioner in the same form as it is granted to him by his title, and will add to it the twelve arpents in front by forty in depth which he asks for to enlarge his farm, as it is obvious to me that they belong yet to the King's domain, and for which the petitioner shall have to solicit the concession from the governor general, as soon as said surveyor shall have delivered a plat and certificate of survey.

ZENON TRUDEAU.

A true translation.

JULIUS DE MUN.

No.	Name of original claimant.	Quantity, in arpents.	Nature and date.	By whom granted.	By whom surveyed, date, and situation.
1	Gabriel Cerré, by Pascal L. Cerré, as devisee.	800	Two concess'ns, one dated October 12, 1782, the other January 10, 1798.	F. Cruzat and Z. Trudeau.	James Rankin, February 27, 1806, and certified by Ant. Soulard, same date. On the Maramec, district of St. Louis.

Evidence with reference to the minutes and records.

August 30, 1806.—The board met pursuant to adjournment. Present: John B. C. Lucas, Clement B. Penrose, and James L. Donaldson, esqs.

Pascal Cerré, as devisee of Gabriel Cerré, claiming eight hundred arpents of land situate on the Maramec, district of St. Louis, produces a duly registered concession from Franqois Cruzat for eight by forty arpents, dated October 12, 1802, (1782,) together with an order of survey for the same, with an addition of twelve by forty arpents, to be included in the same survey, said order dated January 10, 1798, and signed Zenon Trudeau.

Auguste Chouteau, being duly sworn, says that the said Gabriel Cerré settled the said tract of land in the year 1782, and that the same has been actually inhabited and cultivated to this day. The board confirm to the said claimant the said tract of eight hundred arpents, as per the said concessions.—(See minutes No. 1, pages 512, 514, and 515.)

Friday, December 27, 1811.—Board met. Present: John B. C. Lucas, Clement B. Penrose, and Frederick Bates, commissioners.

Pascal Cerré, devisee of Gabriel Cerré, claiming eight hundred arpents of land.—(See book No. 1, page 514.) Concession from Cruzat, dated October 12, 1782. It is the opinion of Clement B. Penrose that this claim ought to be confirmed. It is the opinion of John B. C. Lucas that eight by forty arpents ought to be confirmed. Frederick Bates forbears giving an opinion.—(See minutes No. 5, pages 540, 544, and 545.)

October 5, 1832.—The board met pursuant to adjournment. Present: Lewis F. Linn and F. R. Conway, commissioners.

Pascal Cerré, claiming, as devisee of Gabriel Cerré, eight hundred arpents of land situate on the Maramec, district of St. Louis.—(See book No. 1, page 514, and book No. 5, page 544.)

The two original concessions being produced, (see Livre Terrein, No. 4, page 6,) one bearing date the 12th of October, 1782, signed by Francisco Cruzat, the other on the 10th of January, 1798, signed by Zenon Trudeau; was also produced a paper purporting to be the survey of the same, signed by James Rankin, deputy surveyor, and by Antoine Soulard, surveyor general.—(See book A, pages 532 and 533.)

M. P. Le Duc, having been duly sworn, saith that the signature to the first petition is the handwriting of Gabriel Cerré, and the signature to the concession is the handwriting of Francisco Cruzat; that the signature to the second petition is the handwriting of the said Gabriel Cerré, and the signature to the decree of concession is the handwriting of Zenon Trudeau; that the signatures to the aforesaid surveys are the handwriting of the said James Rankin and Antoine Soulard.

October 31, 1833.—The board met pursuant to adjournment. Present: L. F. Linn, A. G. Harrison, F. R. Conway, commissioners.

Gabriel Cerré, claiming 800 arpents of land, (see page 2 of this book.) The board are unanimously of opinion that this claim ought to be confirmed to said Gabriel Cerré, or his legal representatives, according to the concession.—(See book No. 6, page 286.)

L. F. LINN.
F. R. CONWAY.
A. G. HARRISON.

No. 2.—Pascal Cerré's *petition and concession.*

To Don Charles Dehault Delassus, lieutenant colonel, attached to the stationary regiment of Louisiana, and lieutenant governor of the upper part of the same province:

Pascal Leon Cerré, sub-lieutenant of militia, father of a family, and owner of several slaves, has the honor of representing to you that, having obtained yet no concessions, he would desire to enjoy the same favor as all the other inhabitants of the country, and participate to the bounties which his Majesty diffuses with generosity amongst all his subjects; consequently, and as owner of a great quantity of cattle, he would wish to establish a considerable stock farm, distant enough from our settlements not to give umbrage to anybody. To obtain his object he has the honor humbly to pray that you will have the goodness to grant to him, in full property, a league square of land in superficie, or seven thousand and fifty-six arpents, to be taken in two different places, situated as follows: the half of said quantity, or three thousand five hundred and twenty-eight arpents, to be taken at the place commonly known by the name of the great source of the river Maramec, at about three hundred miles from its mouth, so as to include the said sources; the other half, or three thousand five hundred and twenty-eight arpents, at some distance from the first, at the upper part of the headwaters of the Gasconade, and of those of the fork of the Maramec, known by the name of La Bourbeuse (Muddy.) The said tracts of land being only fit for the establishments projected by your petitioner, who hopes his fidelity, and that of all his family, to the government, will be titles, in your opinion, which will contribute to the fulfilment of the favor which he hopes to obtain of your goodness and justice.

St. Louis of Illinois, November 5, 1799.

P. L. CERRÉ.

A true translation.

JULIUS DE MUN.

St. Louis of Illinois, *November* 8, 1799.

Whereas the petitioner is one of the most ancient inhabitants of this country, whose known conduct and personal qualities are recommendable, and being convinced of the truth of what he exposes in his petition, I do grant to the petitioner the land which he solicits; and as it is situated in a desert where there is no settlement, and at a considerable distance from this town, he is not compelled to have it surveyed immediately, but as soon as some one settles on said place, in which case he must have it surveyed without delay; and Don Antonio Soulard, surveyor general of this Upper Louisiana, will take cognizance of this title for his own intelligence and government in the part which concerns him, so as to enable the interested, after the survey is executed, to solicit the title in due form from the intendant general of these provinces of Louisiana.

CARLOS DEHAULT DELASSUS.

Registered by order of the lieutenant governor, pages 15 and 16 of book No. 1, of titles of concessions.

SOULARD.

New Orleans, *April* 25, 1798.

Sir: Your letter of the 7th of last March has been delivered to me. Yes, sir, it is with pleasure that I have learnt by the letter which you have written to Mr. Zenon Trudeau on the subject of your journey to Canada, which letter has been forwarded to me, that you had returned to St. Louis. No one better than myself can feel how many inconveniences you must have experienced in this journey, and how many difficulties you had to surmount, and that it required nothing less than your intelligence and knowledge, your activity, firmness, and courage, to extricate you from the embarrassments into which your zeal for the service of the King, and your attachment to our government, precipitated you.

Penetrated with this conviction, and knowing how to appreciate your merit, your uncommon disinterestedness, and the services which you have rendered, and which, I am persuaded, you will always be disposed to render to the King, you will find me at all times ready to seize the occasion of testifying to you how much I do desire to be of some utility to you, and making it available in case of need.

With respect to the affair between you and Mr. Lorimier, of which a statement has been submitted to me by Mr. Zenon Trudeau, it is with very sensible pain that I see myself compelled to announce to you that my judgment upon it will not be, perhaps, exactly conformable to your wishes. The immutable principles of justice, whatever may be the interest I take in you in my inward thoughts, does not permit me to pronounce a decision different from that which will be officially communicated to you by the lieutenant governor, Don Zenon Trudeau. You have too sound an understanding, and too much discernment, not to comprehend that a public man ought never to suffer his affections or his feelings of private friendship to make him deviate from the path which his reason points to him as that of equity and impartiality. On all other occasions put my friendship to the test, and reckon on the attachment of him who has the honor to be, with all the consideration which is due to you on so many accounts,

Sir, your very humble and very obedient servant,

MANUEL GAYOSO DE LEMOS.

Monsieur Gabriel Cerré.

A true translation. JULIUS DE MUN.

No.	Name of original claimant.	Quantity, in arpents.	Nature and date of claim.	By whom granted.	By whom surveyed, date, and situation.
2	Pascal L. Cerré..	7,056	Concession dated the 8th November, 1799.	Charles Dehault Delassus.	To be surveyed in two parts or halves, the one on the Big Spring of the river Maramec, so as to include said spring, and the other at the fall of the forks of the Gasconade and those of the Maramec, called the Muddy.

Evidence with reference to the minutes and records.

September 15, 1806.—Pascal L. Cerré, claiming a tract of a league square, to be surveyed in two parts or halves, the one on the Big Spring of the river Maramec, so as to include said spring, and the other at the fall of the forks of the Gasconade and those of the Maramec, called the Muddy, produces a concession from Charles Dehault Delassus, dated the 8th November, 1799.

Anthony Soulard, being duly sworn, says that he wrote the aforesaid concession or decree of the lieutenant governor, but does not recollect if it was issued at the time it bears date; that a letter was addressed to Gabriel Cerré, the father of claimant, by the governor general, Gayoso de Lemos, dated April 25, 1798, "wherein he acknowledges the many services he has rendered to government, and his claim to the generosity of the same;" that the lieutenant governor, on seeing said letter, inquired of him in what manner he might reward him; that the said Gabriel Cerré replied that he was already advanced in years, and did not want for lands, having already a sufficiency of the same, but recommended his son, the claimant, who had not then received any grant for land, to the bounty of government; and further, that said claimant was, in the year 1798, the head of a family.—(See minutes No. 2, pages 30 and 31.)

Thursday, September 28, 1810.—Board met. Present: John B. C. Lucas and Clement B. Penrose, commissioners. Pascal L. Cerré, claiming one league square of land.—(See book No. 2, page 30.) It is the opinion of this board that this claim ought not to be confirmed.—(See book No. 4, pages 516 and 517.)

October 5, 1832.—The board met. Present: L. F. Linn and F. R. Conway. Pascal L. Cerré, claiming a tract of land of a league square, to be surveyed, &c.—(See book No. 2, page 30; book No. 4, page 516;

record book B, pages 512 and 513.) M. P. Le Duc, being duly sworn, saith that the signature to the petition is the handwriting of the claimant, and that the signature to the concession is the handwriting of Carlos Dehault Delassus.

The claimant also produces a paper purporting to be an original letter from Gayoso de Lemos, late governor of Louisiana, bearing date the 25th day of April, 1798. M. P. Le Duc saith that the signature to the said letter is the handwriting of said Gayoso de Lemos.—(See book No. 6, page 8.)

October 31, 1833.—The board met pursuant to adjournment. Present: L. F. Linn, A. G. Harrison and F. R. Conway, commissioners. Pascal L. Cerré, claiming 7,056 arpents of land.—(See page 8 of this book.) The board are unanimously of the opinion that this claim ought to be confirmed to said Pascal L. Cerré, or to his legal representatives, according to the concession.—(See book No. 6, page 287.)

L. F. LINN.
F. R. CONWAY.
A. G. HARRISON.

No. 3.—James Mackay, *claiming* 30,000 *arpents.*

To Don Charles Dehault Delassus, lieutenant colonel, attached to the stationary regiment of Louisiana, and lieutenant governor of the upper part of said province:

James Mackay, captain commandant of the settlement of St. André, of Missouri, has the honor to represent that during the years 1795 and 1796 he made (in consequence of the commission sent to him to this effect, by his excellency the Baron de Carondelet, governor general of these provinces, which document is here annexed) a voyage of discovery to the upper and unknown parts of Missouri, from which voyage he has brought memoirs, and particularly a map, such as never appeared before of this unknown part of the world; which papers he has himself delivered to his excellency Don Manuel Gayoso de Lemos, governor general of these provinces, who, in consequence of his services, has granted to him the rank he holds now, and that of commandant of St. André, with the permission to make choice of a considerable quantity of land in this Upper Louisiana, and the assurance, as a reward for his services, that he should be proposed to the King for a grade in the army; this could not be effected on account of the war. Therefore, your petitioner being willing to establish himself, and not having enjoyed any of the favors which have been promised to him, commandant, with a very small salary, of a settlement which gives him a great deal of occupations, he hopes of your justice that you will be pleased to grant to him, in full property for the establishment of farms, and considerable stock farms, thirty thousand arpents of land, in superficie, to be taken on the vacant lands of his Majesty's domain, in one or several parts, at his choice. The distance of said lands from the settlements, and their known little value, are reasons which will lessen, in your opinion, the importance of the favor which your petitioner expects of your justice, which favor cannot give him any hopes of utility but at a very remote time. Full of confidence in the informations which must have been given to you upon his services and conduct, by his excellency the governor general of these provinces, and by your predecessor, Don Zenon Trudeau, to whom your petitioner has delayed, by divers reasons, to submit his demand, he hopes to obtain the fulfilment of it, of your equity and justice.

JAMES MACKAY.

St. Louis, *October* 12, 1799.

St. Louis of Illinois, *October* 13, 1799.

Cognizance being taken of the foregoing petition presented by the captain of mounted dragoons of militia, James Mackay, commandant of the settlement of St. André of this dependency; being well satisfied of the truth of what he advances, and due regard being paid to the respectable recommendations which have been made to me of this officer by Don Manuel Gayoso de Lemos, ex-governor general of these provinces, and by my predecessor, Don Zenon Trudeau, I do grant, as a reward for his good services, for him, his heirs, or others that may represent his right, the land which he solicits, if it is not prejudicial to any person; and the surveyor, Don Ant. Soulard, shall put the petitioner in possession of the quantity of land which he asks for in different (various) parts of the royal domain; and when this is done, he shall draw a plat which he shall deliver to the party, with his certificate, that said party may use it to obtain the concession and title in due form from the intendant general, to whom alone corresponds, by royal order, the distributing and granting of all classes of lands belonging to the royal domain.

CARLOS DEHAULT DELASSUS.

Don Ant. Soulard, surveyor general of Upper Louisiana.

I do certify that on the 25th of May, of last year, (in consequence of the decree here annexed of the lieutenant governor and sub-delegate of the fiscal department, Don C. B. Delassus, dated October 13, 1799,) I have transported myself on the land of James Mackay, to survey it, according to his petition, for 30,000 arpents of land, of which quantity I have only measured 13,835 arpents, described in the above figurative plat, the interested party having desired it so, reserving to himself the right (as it is mentioned in his petition and ordered by a superior decree of the lieutenant governor) to choose the complement of his concession, in one or more parts, in the vacant lands of the royal domain; which measurement has been executed in presence of the proprietor and bordering neighbors, with the perch of Paris, of eighteen feet in length, as it is customary in this province of Louisiana, and without paying attention to the variation of the needle, which is 7° 30′ E., as is evident by the above figurative plat. This land is situated at about six miles west of the river Mississippi, eighteen to the northwest of St. Charles, and fifteen from the river Missouri, bounded as follows: to the north and east, by vacant lands of the royal domain; west, by lands of C. D. Delassus; and south, by lands of Adam Sonalt and vacant lands of the royal domain. In testimony whereof, I have given him the present, with the figurative plat here above, in which are indicated the dimensions, and the natural and artificial bounds which surround said land.

ANTONIO SOULARD.

St. Louis of Illinois, *March* 8, 1802.

New Orleans, *May* 20, 1799.

Sir: It is with great pleasure that I have received your letter, to which I should like to answer more at large, but I find myself so much overburdened with business that it is out of my power to entertain myself with you as long as I would wish; but a boat has just arrived to-day, which is to start back next week, and by it I shall write to you.

I see with pleasure the arrangements you have taken, opening roads and establishing good regulations of military and civil police, in the view of aggrandizing your post.

By this opportunity I particularly recommend you to Mr. Delassus.

Poor Evans is very ill; between us, I have perceived that he deranged himself when out of my sight, but I have perceived it too late; the strength of liquor has deranged his head; he has been out of his senses for several days, but, with care, he is doing better, and I hope he will get well enough to be able to send him to his country. I have proposed to court a very important project, in which you shall be employed.

Be assured that I am attached to you, and that I will not forget you.

I am, with esteem, your very humble servant,

MANUEL GAYOSO DE LEMOS.

Monsieur James Mackay.

My Dear Mackay: Mr. Jones, bearer of this, has come to my house by chance, an accident having happened to him before my door; and this gives me an opportunity of saying two words to you in answer to your letter of August 13, which has been a long while delayed in reaching me. I tell you, then, that I can certify that I have conceded to you a saline in the Missouri, but it is impossible for me to say neither the place of the said river nor the number of arpents for which the said concession was granted. I would fail in what I owe to myself, as well as to the tribunal before which you are to lay my affidavit, if I said differently, without having before my eyes the decree I have signed. A lapse of time, so long as the one that has passed since that transaction, does not leave, in the memory of a man so old as I am, the impression of things upon which he believed he never would have to think any more. Besides, and you know it well, business was transacted for a government which dispensed us with great formalities, which were considered as onerous to the inhabitants. Therefore I have not registered my decree relating to this saline, but it must have been done at the seat of the general government if the said decree has been approved of. I have been more fortunate in the affair concerning Mr. Williams. Why? Because he had some difficulties with Vincent Bouis, and that, on that very head, I wanted to justify my own conduct by an official letter, of which I have yet a copy. As I am to write to you very soon, and that for the present I have but a moment to dispose of, I confine myself to these few words, adding only that we always love you; that we do speak of you often and with pleasure, and but a few minutes ago my decrepit wife was saying, ha! if I could make the journey by land, like Mr. Jones, with what eagerness would I go and see those I love in Illinois! As to me, my friend, I say just as much. I see the end of my term approaching; my brother, who lately died at the age of 66 years, was the oldest person I have known in my family; not one has ever passed 60 years, and I am 59 and upwards.

My letter to Soulard could not contain loves and compliments to Mr. and Madame Chouteau; be you our interpreter near them; we love and cherish them more than ever. We say the same for you, your dear wife, and small family. All yours.

Your friend and servant,

ZENON TRUDEAU.

Captain James Mackay, *St. Louis.*

Truly translated. St. Louis, October 16, 1832. JULIUS DE MUN.

No.	Name of original claimant.	Quantity, in arpents	Nature and date of claim.	By whom granted.	By whom surveyed, date, and situation.
3	James Mackay, by his heirs.	30,000	Concession, October 13, 1799.	Carlos Dehault Delassus.	13,835 arpents, by Antonio Soulard, May 25, 1801, 18 miles northwest of St. Charles; 10,340 arpents, by Mackay, February 7, 1803, on a fork of Maramec, called Muddy; 5,280 arpents, by Mackay, December 20, 1804, on the Missouri; the two surveys by Mackay were recorded by Soulard, surveyor general, February 28, 1806.

Evidence with reference to the minutes and records.

July 22, 1806.—The board met agreeably to adjournment. Present: The honorable J. B. C. Lucas, Clement B Penrose and James L. Donaldson, esquires.

James Mackay, claiming 30,000 arpents of land, produces a concession from Charles D. Delassus, dated the 13th October, 1799; a survey of 13,835 arpents on the river Cuivre, taken May 25, 1801, and certified 8th March, 1802; a survey of 545 arpents, situated on same river, taken 29th December, 1802, and certified 28th February, 1806; another survey of 5,280 arpents, situate on the Missouri, taken the 20th December, 1804, and certified the 28th of February, 1806; and lastly, a survey of 10,340 arpents, taken the 7th February, 1803.

George Faillis, being duly sworn, says that, in the year 1799, one John Wealthy built a cabin on a small piece of land which he fenced in; that he lived on the same for about one year, when he made a present of his improvement to one Keitchley, who, having remained on it until Christmas of the year 1801, gave it to one Rhode, who afterwards gave it to witness; that the same was afterwards surveyed in by claimant, in consequence of a purchase from the said Rhode; that he, the witness, never heard of a concession for the said tract of land, and that the same was surveyed after his, the witness's, removal from the same; and, further, that the said small improvement was surveyed in the aforesaid tract of ——, on the ——.

The board reject this claim, and require further proof. Thereupon the said claimant produced a passport from Zenon Trudeau to him, as agent of the Commercial Company of the river Missouri, on a voyage of discovery up said river, undertaken by the orders of the Baron de Carondelet, and which was to last six years; and also a letter from Don Manuel Gayoso de Lemos, the intendant general at New Orleans, dated the 20th May, 1799, wherein he much approves of the conduct of claimant as commandant, commends the steps taken by him for the opening of roads and establishing good police regulation, both military and civil, with the view to the aggrandizement of his post; and informing him, further, that he has recommended him very particularly to the lieutenant governor of the province, Charles D. Delassus.—(See book No. 1, pages 415 and 416.)

July 31, 1807, 3 *o'clock*.—The board met agreeably to adjournment. Present: The honorable John B. C. Lucas, Clement B. Penrose and Frederick Bates, esquires.

James Mackay claiming 30,000 arpents of land. The agent of the United States objects to the aforesaid concession on the grounds of its being antedated, and otherwise fraudulent. He also objects to two surveys made on part of the aforesaid concession: one for 13,835, the other for 10,340, on the grounds aforesaid. Further proof is required of the party.—(See book No. 3, page 21.)

November 4, 1809.—Board met. Present: John B. C. Lucas, Clement B. Penrose, commissioners.

James Mackay claiming 30,000 arpents of land.—(See book No. 1, page 415; book No. 3, page 21.) It is the opinion of the board that this claim ought not to be confirmed.—(See book No. 4, page 186.)

October 5, 1832.—The board met pursuant to adjournment. Present: Lewis F. Linn and F. R. Conway, commissioners.

James Mackay's heirs, claiming 30,000 arpents of land.—(See book No. 1, page 415; book No. 3, page 21; book No. 4, page 186; record book B, pages 435, 436, and 437.) Produces a paper purporting to be a concession of the same, and certificates of surveys; one for 13,835 arpents, dated 8th March, 1802, the survey executed 25th May, 1801; another for 10,340 arpents, dated 28th February, 1806, survey executed the 7th of February, 1803, and signed by Antonio Soulard; and a third for 5,280 arpents, executed the 20th of December, 1804, and certified by Antonio Soulard, as received for record on the 28th of February, 1806. Also a paper purporting to be an original letter from Manuel Gayoso de Lemos, governor of Louisiana, to James Mackay, dated 20th May, 1799. Also a paper purporting to be an affidavit of Antonio Soulard, taken before F. M. Guyol, a justice of the peace for the county of St. Louis, dated the 5th December, 1817, authenticated on the 15th December, 1817, under the great seal of the Territory of Missouri, by Frederick Bates, exercising the government of said Territory. Also a paper purporting to be an original letter from Zenon Trudeau to said Mackay.

M. P. Le Duc, being duly sworn, saith that the signature to the decree of concession aforesaid is the handwriting of Lieutenant Governor Carlos Dehault Delassus; that the signature to the first survey is the handwriting of Antonio Soulard; that the signature to the survey of 10,340 arpents is the handwriting of Antonio Soulard; that the signature to the survey of 5,280 arpents is the handwriting of Antonio Soulard; that the signature to the said letter of M. Gayoso de Lemos is the handwriting of the said M. Gayoso de Lemos; that the signatures to the affidavit are the handwriting of Antonio Soulard, of F. M. Guyol, and Frederick Bates; that Antonio Soulard died about six or seven years ago; that the signature to the letter of Zenon Trudeau, above mentioned, is the handwriting of Zenon Trudeau.—(See book No. 6, pages 3 and 4.)

November 27, 1832.—The board met pursuant to adjournment. Present: Lewis F. Linn, F. R. Conway, commissioners.

In the case of James Mackay, claiming 30,000 arpents of land. Charles Frémon Delauriere, being duly sworn, saith that the signature to the original concession is in the proper handwriting of C. D. Delassus, and the signature to Mackay's petition is in the proper handwriting of said Mackay; that he was well acquainted with said Mackay; that he was an officer who stood very high in the estimation of the Spanish government, and was looked upon as a very useful man to the country; that he was commandant of St. André, and that the only salary he received as such was hardly sufficient to pay for the stationery; that he recollects his return from New Orleans, where it was understood he had been to make his report to the general government of his voyage of discovery in the western part of Upper Louisiana, towards the Pacific ocean; that he continued commandant of St. André till the cession of this country to the United States; that he acted also as deputy surveyor to Antonio Soulard.

Albert Tison, being duly sworn, saith that said James Mackay was also commandant of St. Charles; that said district of St. Charles comprehended then all the country north of the Missouri, with the exception of the small district of Portage des Sioux.

Charles Frémon Delauriere and Albert Tison prove the signature to the letter of Zenon Trudeau, heretofore presented in evidence in this case. Frémon Delauriere proves the handwriting of Manuel Gayoso de Lemos to a letter dated May 20, 1799; that he, said Delauriere, being a public officer, had occasion to see it often. He also proves the signature of Antonio Soulard to an affidavit dated December 5, 1817, and to three plats of surveys.—(See book No. 6, pages 53 and 54.)

June 15, 1833.—F. R. Conway, esq., appeared, pursuant to adjournment.

In the case of James Mackay, claiming 30,000 arpents of land, (see pages 3 and 53 of this book,) claimant produces a paper purporting to be an original commission, dated May 1, 1798, from Manuel

Gayoso de Lemos, then governor general of Louisiana, appointing James Mackay captain of the first company of militia in Missouri.—(See book 6, page 176.)

October 31, 1833.—The board met pursuant to adjournment. Present: L. F. Linn, A. G. Harrison, F. R. Conway, commissioners.

James Mackay, by his heirs, claiming 30,000 arpents of land.—(See page 3 of this book.)

The board, after a minute examination of the original papers, see no cause to entertain the belief that they are fraudulent or antedated, as urged against the confirmation by the United States agent before the former board. They are unanimously of opinion that this claim ought to be confirmed to said James Mackay, or his legal representatives.—(See book No. 6, page 287.)

L. F. LINN.
F. R. CONWAY.
A. G. HARRISON.

No. 4.—JACQUES ST. VRAIN, by J. SMITH, T., *claiming* 10,000 *arpents of land.*

To the Baron de Carondelet, knight of Malta, brigadier of the King's armies, governor general, vice patron of Louisiana and western Florida, and inspector of the troops in said provinces, &c.:

MY LORD: Jacques Ceran Delassus de St. Vrain, formerly an officer in the French royal navy, with all the respect due, has the honor to represent to you and says, that having been compelled to emigrate to the United States by circumstances unfortunately too well known; having lost his fortune and station, he has followed his family to St. Genevieve, and associated himself to its fate, which your generous goodness and protection has taken care to alleviate. The petitioner, since that period, has had the good fortune to render himself useful to the government which has given him such a kind reception, in doing all his efforts to show his zeal, his activity, and devotedness against a party of Frenchmen who had dared to threaten the Spanish possessions. The knowledge of mineralogy which the petitioner possesses has determined his father to yield up to him the contract he has made with the government for furnishing a certain quantity of lead; and in order to fulfil with more facility the conditions made by his father with the intendant, to satisfy the government, and to secure to himself a competency which may in future afford him an honorable existence, the petitioner prays you to grant to him and his heirs ten thousand arpents of land in superficie, with the special permission to locate them in separate tracts on various mines of whatever nature they may be, on mill seats, and, finally, on all places which may appear advantageous to his interest, without, however, being in the obligation to improve them, which at the present he could not do with success, as those several explorations would require great expenses, and because those lands are to be taken in places distant from the population and exposed to the incursions of the Indians. These are favors which the petitioner presumes to hope from your generous goodness and justice.

J. DE ST. VRAIN.

ST. GENEVIEVE, *November* 10, 1795.

NEW ORLEANS, *February* 10, 1796.

Granted.

EL BARON DE CARONDELET.

Truly translated, St. Louis, January 21, 1833, from book C, pages 336 and 337.

JULIUS DE MUN.

No.	Name of original claimant.	Quantity, in arpents.	Nature and date of claim.	By whom granted.	By whom surveyed, date, and situation.
4	Jacques St. Vrain, by his assignee, J. Smith, T.	10,000	Concession, 10th February, 1796.	The Baron de Carondelet.	

Evidence with reference to minutes and records.

August 30, 1806.—The board met agreeably to adjournment. Present: The honorable John B. C. Lucas, Clement B. Penrose, and James L. Donaldson, esquires. James St. Vrain, claiming 10,000 arpents of land, produces a concession by the Baron de Carondelet, dated at New Orleans, the 10th February, 1796, in these words: *Concedido.* The petition stating that the claimant may survey the said land in different tracts, of such size as may best suit him, when to him convenient, and wherever he may deem it most suitable to his interest, whatever may be the nature of the soil, either saline or mine land, mill seats, or other lands, provided the same be vacant.

Louis Labeaume, being duly sworn, says: Claimant being going down to New Orleans in the year 1797, he left his business and papers to the charge of the witness, and that the aforesaid concession was then among those papers left to his charge.

Auguste Chouteau, being duly sworn, says that he knows the handwriting of the Baron de Carondelet, having seen him write often, and that the signature to the said decree is his own handwriting. Anthony Soulard, being also duly sworn, says that the concession or decree aforesaid, to wit: *Concedido,* is in the handwriting of the secretary of government, but that the signature is the Baron de Carondelet's own handwriting.—(See book No. 1, page 514.)

December 27, 1811.—Board met. Present: John B. C. Lucas, Clement B. Penrose, commissioners.

John Smith, T., assignee of Jacques St. Vrain, claiming 10,000 arpents of land.—(See book No. 1, page 514.) Original papers not produced.

The record of the concession much compressed, thirty-three words are interlined with different ink;

the words Louis Labeaume, apparently the heading of said Labeaume's notice of claims, occupy one-third of the paper in the direction which four lines of the record of said concession stand in; so that two-thirds of the said paper, in the direction of the said lines, is covered on each side with the said four lines, and the remaining one-third in the middle is occupied by the said words Louis Labeaume. It appears from the records that John Smith, T.. claims under this concession, as follows: 1,000 arpents at a place called the New Diggins, about two miles from the Mine à Breton; a place known by the name of Mine à Robina, 300 arpents; on the branch above Renauld's mine, 300 arpents; 300 arpents, including Doyet's mines; 200 arpents on the first branch emptying into the mine fork on the south side, above its junction with Big river; 200 arpents, including a place called McKee's Discovery, about one and a quarter mile from the last-mentioned place; 50 arpents, including a mill seat on the second creek emptying into Big river, above the junction of the mineral fork on the west side. It is the opinion of a majority of the board that this claim ought not to be confirmed.

Frederick Bates, commissioner, forbears giving an opinion.—(See book No. 5, page 540.)

October 5, 1832.—The board met pursuant to adjournment. Present: Lewis F. Linn, F. R, Conway, commissioners. John Smith, T., assignee of Jacques St. Vrain, claiming 10,000 arpents of land.—(See book C, (record,) pages 336 and 337; book D, page 57, for deed. For testimony, see minutes, book No. 1, page 514; No. 5, page 540.)

The claimant files a paper purporting to be original depositions taken in the case of J. M. White, in the district court of the United States, in support of said claim; also, depositions taken in the case of Thomas A. Smith, guardian, against the United States.—(See book No. 6, page 6.)

October 9, 1833.—The board met pursuant to adjournment. Present: Lewis F. Linn, A. G. Harrison, F. R. Conway, commissioners.

In the case of St. Vrain, by John Smith, T., claiming 10,000 arpents of land.—(See page 6 of this book, No. 6.)

John Scott, aged about 51 years, being duly sworn, says that in the year 1810 he was employed by John Smith, T., as his agent and attorney, to attend at St. Louis with the concession to said St. Vrain, named in the deposition of Joseph Pratte, and to file the same for record with the recorder, and to attend to the claim before the board of commissioners; and for that purpose he had put in his hands and possession the original concession from the Baron de Carondelet to said St. Vrain for 10,000 arpents of land, together with the petition preceding the grant; and that both the petition and the grant were written in a fair, intelligible hand, entirely free and clear of all blots, erasures, and interlineations; and that he verily believes, if the record of the said petition and grant presents any other aspect than those of a fair, clear, and intelligible paper, it must be entirely owing to the mistake, negligence, or want of room or accuracy in the person who may have committed or placed the same of record.

The following testimony was taken before Lewis F. Linn, esq., on the 3d of May last:

STATE OF MISSOURI, *county of Perry:*

Jeseph Pratte, witness, aged about 59 years, being duly sworn as the law directs, deposeth and saith that he has had in his hands and possession, and frequently seen and examined, the original petition and grant aforesaid, from the Baron de Carondelet to said St. Vrain, both before and after the same was sold and transferred by said St. Vrain to John Smith, T., and that both the petition and the grant were written in a fair, intelligible hand, entirely clear of all blots, erasures, or interlineations; and that he verily believes, if the record of the said petition and grant presents any other aspect than that of a fair, clear, intelligible paper, it must be entirely owing to the mistake, negligence, or want of accuracy in the person who may have committed or placed the same of record.

JOSEPH PRATTE.

Sworn to and subscribed May 3, 1833.

L. F. LINN, *Commissioner.*

(See book No. 6, page 271.

October 31, 1833.—The board met pursuant to adjournment. Present: L. F. Linn, A. G. Harrison, F. R. Conway, commissioners. Jacques St. Vrain, by his assignee, John Smith, T., claiming 10,000 arpents of land.—(See page 6.) The board remark that they are satisfied that there existed such concession, which was presented to the former board, as appears from their minutes, and then no objections made to it; they are also satisfied that the interlineations, mentioned in said minutes as existing in the record of said concession, are merely the completing of words abbreviated by the recorder for want of room. The board are unanimously of opinion that this claim ought to be confirmed to said Jacques St. Vrain, or his legal representatives, according to the concession.—(See book No. 6, page 287.)

L. F. LINN.
F. R. CONWAY.
A. G. HARRISON.

No. 5.—DAVID DELAUNAY, *claiming* 800 *arpents.*

To Don Carlos Dehault Delassus, lieutenant governor of Upper Louisiana, &c.:

SIR: David Delaunay, Frenchman, formerly an inhabitant of the island of St. Domingo, has the honor of representing to you that the disasters which desolated his country obliged him at first to emigrate to the Spanish side of said island, where he found, as well as his countrymen, all the assistance which suffering humanity has the right to expect of a generous nation. A series of misfortunes obliged him to come to the American continent, where, a short time after his arrival, he heard of the advantages made by the Spanish government to foreigners who came to fix themselves in Louisiana; he believed in these reports so much more readily, having already experienced in his disasters the generous protection of this same government. Penetrated with this confidence which is inspired by favors, and desirous more than ever to identify himself to the Spanish nation in becoming a subject of his Majesty, he came to St. Genevieve of Illinois with his wife, where, having the project to form an establishment, he has the honor to supplicate you to grant to him a concession of 800 arpents in superficie, to be taken in a vacant place of his Majesty's domain.

Your petitioner presumes to offer to the government the assurance of his sincere fidelity, and hopes that this just statement of the events which have brought him here will be a sufficient title, in your opinion, sir, to obtain the favor which he solicits of your justice.

D. DELAUNAY.

St. Genevieve, *January* 15, 1800.

St. Louis of Illinois, *January* 18, 1800.

As it is evident that the petitioner has more than the means and number of hands *(populacion)* necessary to obtain the concession which he solicits, I do grant for him and his heirs the land which he petitions for, if it is not prejudicial to any one, and the surveyor, Don Antonio Soulard, shall put the interested in possession of the quantity of land which he asks for, in a vacant place in the royal domain; and when this is done, he shall draw a plat of survey which he shall deliver to the party with his certificate, to be used by him in obtaining the concession and title in form from the intendant general, to whom alone corresponds, by royal order, the distributing and granting all classes of land belonging to the royal domain.

CARLOS DEHAULT DELASSUS.

Don Antonio Soulard, surveyor general of the settlements of Upper Louisiana.

I do certify that a tract of land of 800 arpents was measured, the lines run and bounded, in favor and in presence of David Delaunay, with the perch of the city of Paris, of eighteen French lineal feet of the same city according to the agrarian measure of this province; which land is situated on the river Maramec, twenty miles southwest of St. Louis, bounded to the N.NE., E.SE., and S.SW. by vacant lands of the royal domain, and to the W.NW. by lands belonging to Gregoire Sarpy; which survey and measurement were executed without paying attention to the variation of the needle, which is 7° and 30′ east, as is evident by the figurative plat here above, in which are noted the dimensions and directions of the lines and other boundaries, &c.; which survey was executed by virtue of the decree of the lieutenant governor and sub-delegate of the fiscal department, Don Carlos Dehault Delassus, dated January 18, 1800, which is here annexed. In testimony whereof, I do give the present with the figurative plat above, drawn in conformity with the survey executed by the deputy surveyor, Don Juan Terrey, dated January 3, 1804, who signed the minutes, which I do certify.

ANTONIO SOULARD, *Surveyor General.*

St. Louis of Illinois, *April* 15, 1804.

Truly translated. JULIUS DE MUN.

No.	Name of original claimant.	Quantity, in arpents	Nature and date of claim.	By whom granted.	By whom surveyed, date, and situation.
5	David Delaunay.	800	Concession, January, 18, 1800.	Charles Dehault Delassus.	John Terrey, January 3, 1804; certified by Soulard, April 15, 1804. On the Maramec, district of St. Louis.

Evidence with reference to minutes and records.

May 2, 1806.—The board met agreeably to adjournment. Present: The Hon. J. B. C. Lucas, and Clement B. Penrose, esq. David Delaunay, claiming 800 arpents of land situate on the waters of the *river Renaud, district of St. Charles,* (Renaud's fork, a branch of the Maramec, district of St. Louis,) produces a concession from Charles D. Delassus, without any condition expressed in the same, dated the 8th (18th) January, 1800, and a survey of the same taken the 3d of January, and certified April 15, 1804.

Anthony Soulard, being duly sworn true answers to give, &c:

Question. Were you the surveyor of Upper Louisiana under the Spanish government?

Answer. Yes.

Question. Was it any part of the duties imposed on you by the Spanish law and the functions of your office to obey the orders of the lieutenant governor of the province, without any regard to their legality or illegality?

Answer. Yes; the lieutenant governor was accountable for it.

Question. From whom did you derive your appointment?

Answer. From the governor general of Lower Louisiana, Baron De Carondelet.

Question. Is that your handwriting? (showing him the aforesaid concession.)

Answer. I believe it is.

Question. Do you recollect when that was written, and is it your belief that it was written at the time it bears date?

Here the witness refused to answer; whereupon he was asked by the board whether he meant to give similar answers to the questions in all similar cases, and answered yes. The board not being still satisfied, required further proof of the date of the above concession, which not being adduced, they reject this claim.

The same, claiming 7,056 arpents of land situate in the district of St. Charles, produces a concession from Charles Dehault Delassus, without any condition expressed in the same, dated May 9, 1800, and a survey of the same, dated December 25, 1800, and certified January 20, 1804. The same questions were here put to Anthony Soulard, who gave the same answers. The board not being still satisfied, required further proof of the date of the above concession, which was not adduced. (This claim of 7,056 arpents was subsequently confirmed by F. Bates, recorder.—See Bates's Decisions, page 40.) James St. Vrain was, in the above two claims, sworn, who said that the above concessions were granted at the time they bear date; that Charles D. Delassus, his (the witness's) brother, informed him that he had been instructed by Gayoso to grant lands to such respectable French emigrants as should come to this country; that claimant arrived at St. Genevieve towards the latter end of 1799; that he (the witness) being then there with Delassus, the then lieutenant governor, this last informed him (the witness) that he wished much to have claimant at St. Louis, and requested of him (the witness) that he would endeavor to persuade claimant to go to that place, informing him at the same time that he had it in his power to do much for him, and that he would reward him in lands, having received orders to that effect.

The board are satisfied, from passports produced then, that claimant was, prior to his coming to this country, a Spanish officer, and was recommended as such. They reject this claim.—(See book No. 1, page 269.)

August 18, 1810.—Board met. Present: Clement B. Penrose and Frederick Bates, commissioners. David Delaunay, claiming 800 arpents of land.—(See book No. 1, page 269.) It is the opinion of the board that this claim ought not to be confirmed.—(See book No. 4, page 464.)

October 5, 1832.—The board met pursuant to adjournment. Present: Lewis F. Linn and F. R. Conway, commissioners. David Delaunay, claiming 800 arpents of land, (see book No. 1, page 269, and book No. 4, page 464; record book C, pages 247 and 248,) produces a paper purporting to be a concession from Carlos Dehault Delassus, dated January 18, 1800, and a survey of the same, taken January 3, 1804, certified April 15, 1804, and signed by A. Soulard, surveyor general.

M. P. Le Duc, duly sworn, saith that the signature to the said concession is the handwriting of C. D. Delassus; that the signature to the certificate of survey is the handwriting of A. Soulard.

October 31, 1833.—The board met pursuant to adjournment. Present: L. F. Linn, A. G. Harrison, F. R. Conway, commissioners. David Delaunay, claiming 800 arpents of land.—(See page 5 of this book.) The board are unanimously of opinion that this claim ought to be confirmed to said David Delaunay, or his legal representatives, according to the concession.—(See book No. 6, page 288.)

L. F. LINN.
F. R. CONWAY.
A. G. HARRISON.

No. 6.—Richard Caulk, *claiming* 4,000 *arpents.*

To Don Carlos Dehault Delassus, lieutenant colonel, attached to the stationary regiment of Louisiana, and commandant-in-chief of Upper Louisiana, &c.:

Richard Caulk, syndic of the settlement of St. André, formerly an inhabitant of the United States, settled on this side several years with his father-in-law, Lawrence Long, and having both of them concurred (at the desire manifested to them by your predecessor, Don Zenon Trudeau) to a large emigration to this side, has the honor of representing to you that in several cases he has been employed by the government in expeditions against the Indians; that he is the only one who, in his capacity of syndic, has always been charged with the command of the settlement of St. André in the absence of Captain Mackay, commandant of said settlement, and that, in consideration of his gratuitous services, that were often painful and onerous to your petitioner, your predecessor had made to him the promise of a large concession of land as a reward for his services, which fact is known by Captain Mackay.

Full of confidence in your justice, he hopes that you will be pleased to ratify said promise, as tending to prove the gratitude of the government towards a zealous subject who has been fortunate enough to give proofs of his zeal; therefore, he has the honor to supplicate you with respect to have the goodness to grant to him, in full property, four thousand arpents of land in superficie, to be taken in one or several parts of the vacant domain, at his choice. The petitioner having given proofs of his fidelity, can assure you that he desires sincerely to find the occasion of manifesting it at all times that his services may be of utility to the security of the country he inhabits, and to the good of the service of his Majesty.

RICHARD CAULK.

St. André, *November* 30, 1799.

Be it referred to the commandant-in-chief, with information that all that is exposed here above is true; and that the petitioner has rendered many services to the settlements on the frontiers of this country; and that he is worthy in every respect of the confidence and protection of the government, and of the favor which he solicits.

SANTIAGO MACKAY.

St. André, *November* 30, 1799.

St. Louis of Illinois, *December* 5, 1799.

Cognizance being taken of the above petition, and of the informations of the commandant of St. André, Captain Don Santiago Mackay, considering the circumstances of his character, and what he exposes being an excepted case, in virtue of his merits and of his good services I do grant to him and his heirs the land which he solicits, if it is not prejudicial to any one, and the surveyor, Don Antonio Soulard, shall put the interested in possession of the quantity of land he asks in one or two vacant places of the royal domain; and, this done, he will draw a plat, which he will deliver to the party, with his certificate, to serve him to obtain the concession and title in form from the intendant general, to whom alone corresponds, by royal order, the distributing and granting all classes of lands of the royal domain.

CARLOS DEHAULT DELASSUS.

A true translation. St. Louis, October 17, 1832.

JULIUS DE MUN.

No.	Name of original claimant.	Quantity, in arpents.	Nature and date of claim.	By whom granted.	By whom surveyed, date, and situation.
6	Richard Caulk.	4,000	Concession Dec. 5, 1799.	Carlos Dehault Delassus.	James Mackay, December 17, 1804; certified by Soulard October 30, 1805, on river Calumet.

Evidence with reference to minutes and records.

July 22, 1806.—The board met agreeably to adjournment. Present as before, to wit, J. B. C. Lucas, Clement B. Penrose, and James L. Donaldson, esquires. The same, to wit, Richard Caulk, claiming 4,000 arpents situate on the river Calumet, district of St. Louis, produces a concession from Charles D. Delassus, dated December 5, 1799, and a survey of the same, taken December 17, 1804, and certified October 30, 1805. James Mackay, being duly sworn, says that the aforesaid Thomas Caulk was for some years syndic of the Bonhomme settlement, in which capacity he received no compensation, and that he, the witness, verily believes that the aforesaid concession was granted him as a compensation for the same. The board require further proof, and reject this claim.—(See book No. 1, page 418.)

September 21, 1808.—Board met. Present: Hon. John B. C. Lucas, Clement B. Penrose, and Frederick Bates. Richard Caulk, claiming 4,000 arpents of land situate on the river Calumet, district of St. Charles. Laid over for decision.—(See book No. 3, page 259.)

June 12, 1810.—Board met. Present: John B. C. Lucas, Clement B. Penrose, commissioners. Richard Caulk, claiming 4,000 arpents of land.—(See book No. 1, page 418; book No. 3, page 259.) The board believe that there is a mistake made in the taking of the testimony of James Mackay in this claim; that the name of Thomas Caulk in said testimony was intended to have been Richard Caulk. It is the opinion of this board that this claim ought not to be confirmed.—(See book No. 4, page 376.)

October 5, 1832.—The board met pursuant to adjournment. Present: Lewis F. Linn and F. R. Conway, commissioners. Richard Caulk, claiming 4,000 arpents of land, (see record book C, pages 120 and 121; book No. 1, page 418; book No. 3, page 259; and book No. 4, page 376,) produces affidavit of James Mackay, sworn to before Jeremiah Connor, October 25, 1819; also an affidavit of Antoine Soulard, sworn to before F. M. Guyol, a justice of the peace, October 26, 1819; also the affidavit of Thomas Caulk, sworn to and subscribed before William Long, a justice of the peace, October 21, 1819; also an affidavit of Martin Wood, taken before Benjamin Cottle, a justice of the peace, September 28, 1819; also a paper purporting to be a concession, dated December 5, 1799, granted by Charles Dehault Delassus, and a survey made December 17, 1804, and certified October 30, 1805, by Antoine Soulard, surveyor general.

M. P. Le Duc, being duly sworn, saith that the signature to the decree of concession is the handwriting of C. D. Delassus, lieutenant governor; that the signature to the survey is the handwriting of Antoine Soulard, surveyor general of Louisiana; that the signatures to the affidavits of Mackay and Soulard are in their proper handwriting.—(See book No. 6, page 6.)

October 31, 1833.—The board met pursuant to adjournment. Present: L. F. Linn, A. G. Harrison, F. R. Conway, commissioners. Richard Caulk, claiming 4,000 arpents of land.—(See page 6 of this book.) The board are unanimously of opinion that this claim ought to be confirmed to said Richard Caulk, or his legal representatives, according to the concession.—(See book No. 6, page 288.)

L. F. LINN.
F. R. CONWAY.
A. G. HARRISON.

No. 7.—M. P. Le Duc, *claiming 7,044 arpents.*

To Don Carlos Dehault Delassus, lieutenant colonel in the armies of his Majesty, lieutenant governor of Upper Louisiana, dependencies, &c.:

Mary Philip Le Duc, who has had the honor, sir, to inspire sufficient confidence to the government as to be employed by Mr. Portill, and again, for the present, by yourself, both acting as heads of the said government, as well at New Madrid as at this post, since your arrival, having shown his zeal and attachment in doing the functions of interpreter of the English language, there being no one particularly appointed to that place, and it being known to you, sir, that he has made it his duty to fill said place without getting any remuneration, the petitioner presumes to pray you, sir, to be pleased to grant to him 15,000 arpents of land in superficie, to be taken on the left side of the Missouri, on a vacant place of his Majesty's domain, in the view of establishing, in process of time, a stock farm on the said lands, and to make thereon improvements corresponding to a farm; also, in the view to secure for the future a real estate, in order to maintain his numerous family, and which may shield him from adversities, which are too frequently experienced in the other branches of industry. The petitioner, having no other views but those of continuing to live as a peaceable and faithful subject of his Majesty, and be submissive to the generous government whose benevolence he has already experienced, hopes that you will do him the favor to take his demand into consideration in a manner favorable to the accomplishment of his wishes, pledging himself to have the necessary works done as soon as you will permit him not to be assiduously ready to interpret when, by your orders, he is required to do so.

M. P. LE DUC.

St. Louis of Illinois, *December* 30, 1799.

St. Louis of Illinois, *January* 7, 1800.

Considering that the petitioner has been a long time settled in this country, that his known conduct and personal merit are recommendable, being satisfied to evidence as to the truth of what he states in his petition, and that he possesses more than the means sufficient to improve the lands which he solicits, I do grant to him and his heirs the land which he solicits, in case it is not prejudicial to any one, and the surveyor, Don Antonio Soulard, shall put the interested in possession of the quantity of land he asks in the place indicated; and this being done * * * (here is an omission) * * * * the same to the party with his certificate, in order to serve to him to obtain the concession and title in form from the intendant general, to whom alone belongs, by royal order, the distributing and granting all classes of lands of the royal domain.

CARLOS DEHAULT DELASSUS.

Don Antonio Soulard, surveyor general of the settlements of Upper Louisiana.

I do certify that a tract of land of 15,000 arpents in superficie was measured, the lines run and bounded, in favor and in presence of Mr. Mary Philip Le Duc. Said measurement was taken with the perch of the city of Paris, of 18 French feet lineal measure of the same city, conformably to the agrarian measure of this province. Said lands are situated at about 65 miles to the north of St. Louis; bounded to the N.NW. by lands of Don Pedro Provenchere; S.SE. by lands of Don Pedro Janin; S. by land of Alberto Tison, and SE. by that of Lewis Delisle; E.NE. by land of David Delaunay, and E.SE. by that of Lewis Brazeau; S.SW. by land of André Landreville, and W. by that of Mrs. Widow Dubreuil. The said survey and measurement were executed without regard to the variation of the needle, which is 7° 30′, as it is evinced in the foregoing figurative plat, on which are noted the dimensions, courses of the lines, other boundaries, &c. Said survey was executed by virtue of the decree of the lieutenant governor and sub-delegate of the Royal Fisc, Don Carlos Dehault Delassus, dated 7th January, 1800, which is here annexed; and in order that the whole may be available according to law, I do give the present, with the foregoing figurative plat, drawn in conformity with the operations of survey, executed by the deputy surveyor, Mr. James Rankin, on the 18th February, 1804, who has signed on the minutes, which I do certify.

ANTONIO SOULARD.

St. Louis of Illinois, *March* 5, 1804.

Truly translated from record book C, page 444. St. Louis, January 17, 1833.

JULIUS DE MUN.

No.	Name of original claimant.	Quantity, in arpents	Nature and date of claim.	By whom granted.	By whom surveyed, date, and situation.
7	M. P. Le Duc.......	7,944	Concession for 15,000 arpents, January 7, 1800.	Carlos Dehault Delassus.	James Rankin, February 18, 1804; certified by Soulard, March 5, 1804, 65 miles north of St. Louis, district of St. Charles.

Evidence with reference to minutes and records.

May 3, 1806.—The board met agreeably to adjournment. Present: The Hon. John B. C. Lucas, Clement B. Penrose and James L. Donaldson, esquires. Marie P. Le Duc, claiming 15,000 arpents of land situate in the district of St. Charles, produces a concession from Charles D. Delassus, dated January 7, 1800, and a certificate of survey of the same, dated 5th March, 1804.

The board applies to this claim the questions put to Anthony Soulard, page 270, and his answers to the same.

Louis Labeaume, being duly sworn, says that claimant arrived in the country in the year 1792, and took his residence at New Madrid; that about the end of 1793 he was employed by government in the arrangement and regulating of the militia of that place; that he remained so for about twelve months, and never received any compensation for the same; that government was then in daily expectation of an attempt of the French to invade the country, and preparing to oppose them; that he afterwards was employed by government in writing and translating; that he never did receive any compensation for his services in that capacity; that witness, on his return from New Orleans in the year 1796, found said claimant in Charles D. Delassus's employ, the said Delassus being then commandant of New Madrid; that the said Delassus having come to St. Louis and taken the command of that post, claimant followed him, and was by him employed as his private secretary, for which witness believes he received some compensation, but cannot tell what it was.

Auguste Chouteau, being also sworn, says that he knew claimant in the year 1799; that he was then employed with the lieutenant governor, Charles D. Delassus, both on public and private business, and acted then as his interpreter; that Delassus sent him to New Madrid on public business; and, further, that the lieutenant governor, Delassus, informed him, the witness, prior to his, the claimant's, arrival at this place, that he would interfere with government in his favor.

Albert Tison, being also sworn, says that he knew the above claimant at New Madrid, when in the employ of Delassus; that claimant did, sometime towards the latter end of 1799 or the beginning of 1800, show him, the witness, a concession, which he informed him he had received from the lieutenant governor;

that a few days afterwards he again saw the said concession; that the quantity therein specified was that above claimed; and that he verily believes it the one showed him by claimant at the time above mentioned.

The board reject this claim; they are, however, satisfied that the concession is neither antedated nor fraudulent.—(See book No. 1, page 274.)

July 25, 1807.—The board met agreeably to adjournment. Present: The honorable John B. C. Lucas, Clement B. Penrose and Frederick Bates, esquires. Mary P. Le Duc produced a concession for 15,000 arpents of land from Charles D. Delassus, dated 7th January, 1800. On the suggestion of the agent of the United States that there had been an erasure in the above concession, this case was laid over, to enable the claimant to produce further proof.—(See book No. 3, page 11.)

October 8, 1808.—Board met. Present: The honorable Clement B. Penrose and Frederick Bates. Marie Philipe Le Duc, claiming 15,000 arpents of land, produces to the board the concession for the same before produced.

The board, on a re-examination of the erasure alleged to have been made in the concession, are of opinion that the same was given at the time it bears date, 7th January, 1800. Laid over for decision.—(See book No. 3, page 284.)

October 30, 1809.—Board met. Present: John B. C. Lucas, Clement B. Penrose, and Frederick Bates, commissioners. Mary P. Le Duc, claiming 15,000 arpents of land, situate in the district of St. Charles.—(See book No. 1, page 274; book No. 3, pages 11 and 284.) It is the unanimous opinion of the board that this claim ought not to be confirmed.—(See book No. 4, page 182.) *Nota.*—For the confirmation of 7,056 arpents out of these 15,000, see Bates's Decisions, page 38.

October 6, 1832.—The board met pursuant to adjournment. Present: Lewis F. Linn, F. R. Conway, commissioners. M. P. Le Duc, claiming 7,944 arpents of land, being the balance of 15,000 arpents granted for services, (see record book C, pages 443 and 444,) the quantity of 7,056 arpents of said claim having already been confirmed. In support of said claim, the claimant refers to the evidences produced before the late board of commissioners.—(See minute books No. 1, page 274; No. 3, pages 11 and 284; and book No. 4, page 182.) And for the confirmation aforesaid, see the report of the late recorder of land titles and the laws of Congress, 2d section of land laws, No. 290, pages 699 and 700.—(See book No. 6, page 8.)

March 12, 1833.—The board met pursuant to adjournment. Present: L. F. Linn, A. G. Harrison, commissioners. In the case of M. P. Le Duc.—(See page 8 of this book, No. 6.) Claimant produces a paper purporting to be an original concession from Carlos Dehault Delassus, dated 7th January, 1800. Also a plat of survey taken 18th February, and certified by A. Soulard 5th March, 1804. Charles Frémon Delauriere, being duly sworn, says that the signatures to the concession and plat of survey are in the respective handwriting of C. D. Delassus and of A. Soulard. Albert Tison, duly sworn, says the same.—(See book No. 6, page 113.)

November 1, 1833.—The board met pursuant to adjournment. Present: L. F. Linn, A. G. Harrison, F. R. Conway, commissioners. M. P. Le Duc, claiming 7,944 arpents of land, it being the balance of 15,000 arpents, of which 7,056 have been confirmed.

The board are unanimously of opinion that this claim of 7,944 arpents, being the balance of the said 15,000 arpents, ought to be confirmed to the said M. P. Le Duc, or his legal representatives, according to the concession. The board, after examining minutely the original concession produced in this case, see no cause to support the suggestion made by the agent of the United States, before the former board, of there being an erasure in the same.—(See book No. 6, page 288.)

L. F. LINN.
F. R. CONWAY.
A. G. HARRISON.

No. 8.—James McDaniel, *claiming* 1,800 *arpents.*

To Don Zenon Trudeau, brevetted lieutenant colonel, captain in the stationary regiment of Louisiana, and lieutenant governor of the western part of Illinois:

James McDaniel, formerly an inhabitant of the United States of America, and residing in this country since upwards of one year, has the honor to observe that he is temporarily established, with your permission, on a tract of land situated in the Pointe du Missouri (Missouri bottom;) that, considering his views of establishment, he has not thought the place fit for the object intended; therefore he supplicates you to grant to him, as you had already permitted him, a tract of land of 1,800 arpents in superficie, which he will select in a vacant place, where it shall not be prejudicial to any person. The petitioner presumes to expect this favor of your justice, and of the encouragement which every day you give to farmers.

JAMES McDANIEL.

St. Louis of Illinois, *February* 1, 1798.

St. Louis of Illinois, *February* 1, 1798.

The surveyor, Don Antonio Soulard, shall put the party interested in possession of the land he solicits, and afterwards shall make out a plat of his survey, in order to serve to solicit the concession from the governor, who shall be informed that the petitioner deserves the favor which he solicits.

ZENON TRUDEAU.

Truly translated. St. Louis, November 23, 1833.

JULIUS DE MUN.

No.	Name of original claimant.	Quantity, in arpents.	Nature and date of claim.	By whom granted.	By whom surveyed, date, and situation.
8	James McDaniel, by his assignee, James Mackay.	1,800	Concession, February 1, 1798.	Zenon Trudeau..	Anthony Soulard, —— 29, 1802; certificate by said Soulard, dated March 15, 1803, on River des Peres.

Evidence with reference to minutes and records.

St. Louis, December 16, 1813.—James Mackay, assignee of James McDaniel, claiming 1,800 arpents of land on River des Peres. Notice also a paper purporting to be a receipt of James L. Donaldson, late recorder of land titles, dated February 28, 1806; on which receipt the concession of said McDaniel is the 6th. Antoine Soulard, duly sworn, says that he has seen, held, and read, in 1798, a concession from Zenon Trudeau, late lieutenant governor, to James McDaniel for 1,800 arpents of land on River des Peres. Witness further states that he has a knowledge that the concession was entered by claimant with the late recorder for record.—(See recorder's minutes, page 80.)

St. Louis, June 2, 1818.—This day James Mackay, by Colonel Lawless, his attorney, as authorized by act of Congress of 20th April last, entitled "An act for the relief of James Mackay, of the Missouri," filed in this office a writing, purporting to be a warrant of survey or concession from Zenon Trudeau, lieutenant governor of the late Spanish province of Upper Louisiana, called western part of Illinois, bearing date February 1, 1798, for 1,800 arpents of land granted to James McDaniel, in the following words and figures, to wit, &c. Afterwards, to wit, on the 12th day of June, 1818, being the day assigned for the presentation of subordinate evidences, both written and oral, the said James Mackay appeared personally, accompanied by his attorney, and presented, in support of the claim, a writing, purporting to be a plat and field-notes of the said land on the River des Peres, in the following words and figures, to wit, &c. A writing, purporting to be a receipt of James L. Donaldson, late recorder of land titles, for sundry papers in relation to sundry claims of the said James Mackay, in which receipt there is found enumerated, among others, the first concession, or paper purporting to be a concession, to said James McDaniel; also deed from McDaniel to Mackay.—(Book B, page 433.) General Bernard Pratte, being duly sworn, says, after examining the concession to McDaniel, as above stated, that the body of concession, to wit, the requête and the decree, is in the handwriting of Antoine Soulard, and that the signature to the decree is in the proper handwriting of Zenon Trudeau, late lieutenant governor. Antoine Soulard, duly sworn, says that the requête was written by himself, (the witness,) and that he, the witness, saw the late lieutenant governor, Zenon Trudeau, subscribe his own proper name to the decree or order of survey. Witness further states that more than one year past, walking up the street with James Mackay, when near the tavern of Peebles, the said Mackay observed that he would go in and inquire for letters which he expected from his son. On coming out, he held in his hand a letter, which, when opened in presence of witness, was found to be anonymous, and to enclose the concession to James McDaniel for 1,800 arpents of land, and which concession has already been said to have been mislaid by the late recorder of land titles, or stolen from his office in the year 1806, which said letter is now presented by witness, and is in the following words and figures, &c.—(See recorder's minutes, page 163.)

October 6, 1832.—The board met pursuant to adjournment. Present: Lewis F. Linn and F. R. Conway, commissioners.

James McDaniel, by his assignee, James Mackay, claiming 1,800 arpents of land on River des Peres, (see record book E, page 358, recorder's minutes, pages 80, 163, and 164,) produces a paper purporting to be a concession from Zenon Trudeau, lieutenant governor, dated February 1, 1798; also a plat and certificate of survey of same, executed the 29th, (month not mentioned,) 1802, and certified by A. Soulard, March 15, 1803. Also a report made by Frederick Bates, late recorder of land titles, to Josiah Meigs, Commissioner of the General Land Office, together with the accompanying documents, marked A, B, C, D, and E. Also a paper purporting to be an original letter from Gabriel Long, dated October 29, 1818. M. P. Le Duc, duly sworn, saith that the signature to the concession above mentioned is the handwriting of Zenon Trudeau; that the signature to the survey above mentioned is the handwriting of A. Soulard; and that the signature to the letter above mentioned is the handwriting of Gabriel Long.—(See book No. 6, page 9.)

November 1, 1833.—The board met pursuant to adjournment. Present: L. F. Linn, A. G. Harrison, and F. R. Conway, commissioners.

James McDaniel, claiming 1,800 arpents of land.—(See page 9 of this book.) The board are unanimously of opinion that this claim ought to be confirmed to the said James McDaniel, or his legal representatives, according to the concession.—(See book No. 6, page 289.)

L. F. LINN.
F. R. CONWAY.
A. G. HARRISON.

No. 9.—Old Mine concession.

Don Carlos Dehault Delassus, lieutenant colonel of the stationary regiment of Louisiana, lieutenant governor of the western part of said province:

The undersigned inhabitants, of whom the greatest part are natives of the country, and the rest Canadians and Frenchmen, settled since several years at the place known by the name of Vieille mine, (Old mine,) situated on one of the forks of the river Renault, at the distance of sixty miles of the village of St. Genevieve, and at about nine miles of the village of Mine à Breton, have the honor of representing to you that their confidence in the reiterated promises of their chiefs, and in the generosity of the government, has kept them in such a state of security that they have delayed till this day to make the necessary demands to obtain the titles of the land they cultivate and improve since a number of years. The publication of your official note, dated May 18, of this year, addressed to the commandant of the post of St. Genevieve, by which we have learnt the retrocession of this colony to France, which news made us acquainted with the precarious state of our properties, and has caused us to take the step we are taking to-day before you, hoping of your justice that it will not belie in anything the long series of favors which have been accumulated upon us by the Spanish government, and that you will give us, in these last moments, a shining mark of your justice in condescending to acquiesce with our respectful representations. Therefore the thirty-one heads of families undersigned have the honor to supplicate you to have the goodness to grant to them, at the same place where they claim, a quantity of land corresponding to their population, according to the last regulation made on this subject by his lordship the late governor general of these provinces, Don Manuel Gayoso de Lemos, for the said quantity, corresponding to the number of individuals composing the said families, to be divided in equal portion to each of them, and to be allotted by chance according to the dispositions they shall take among themselves, with the approbation of their respective commandant, Don François Vallé, as well as with the surveyor of this Upper Louisiana. The said undersigned engaging themselves beforehand to assure you that no contest shall trouble the good harmony which reigns among them in the said division; to obtain which more surely, they hope that if you condescend to grant them their demands, you will be pleased to order the total survey of the quantity of land which will correspond to them, according to which a certificate of survey will be expedited, to serve to the said inhabitants to claim their title in form from whom it may concern. The said plat of survey shall have to be divided, according to the above-mentioned agreement, in as many equal portions, which shall all be numbered, and each of the said inhabitants will have to be put in possession of a figurative plat of the part of land which shall fall to him by lot, with the attestation of the surveyor, to serve to each of them as a proof of property; precautions which they believe they ought to take to be able to avoid henceforward difficulties which might take place among themselves.

The said undersigned inhabitants have the honor of reiterating their supplications, and of representing to you that this same concession was promised to them by your predecessors since a number of years, and that the great confidence they had in these same promises are the only wrongs they are guilty of; truth which can be attested to you by our worthy respective commandant, Don François Vallé, to whose information we do recommend ourselves with the same confidence, which causes us to believe that you will be pleased to grant to us the concession for the quantity of land corresponding to the totality of the population of the families of the undersigned, at the same place where they claim, to enjoy in full property the part which will fall to each by lot, and exercise their industry as well in agriculture as in digging lead mineral, which might be found on said land. The undersigned, having no other views but to live as peaceable and submissive farmers, presume with confidence to hope everything of your justice.

Charlean Bozé.	Louis Boyer, his ⋈ mark.
Hypolite Robert.	Louis Lacroix, his ⋈ mark.
Charles Robert, his ⋈ mark.	Bazil Vallé, his ⋈ mark.
Widow Colmant, her ⋈ mark.	J. Guibourd.
Maniche, his ⋈ mark.	François Thibaut, his ⋈ mark.
Blay, his ⋈ mark.	Jacob Boisse, his ⋈ mark.
Antoine Govereau, his ⋈ mark.	Jos. Bequet, his ⋈ mark.
Pierre Bte. Boyer, his ⋈ mark.	François Milhomme, his ⋈ mark.
Bernard Colmant, his ⋈ mark.	James Roxe.
Alexandre Duclos, his ⋈ mark.	N. Boilvin.
Amable Partnay, his ⋈ mark.	Jh. Pratte.
Joseph Boyer.	Pierre Martin, his ⋈ mark.
John Porter.	François Bte. Vallé.
Manuel Blanco.	P. Charles.
Bapt. Placet, his ⋈ mark.	Aug't Vallé.
Jean Robert, his ⋈ mark.	Amable Pasenute, his ⋈ mark.

St. Genevieve, *May* 25, 1803.

Be the present petition transmitted to the lieutenant governor, with information that the allegations of the petitioners are in all and every part conformable to the most exact truth; that they are worthy of obtaining the favor which they beg of your justice; that the tract of land they ask makes a part of his Majesty's domain; that the proposed settlement can be but advantageous to the country in general, and that the total population of the families of the undersigned is composed of the following number of individuals: heads of families, 31; women, 13; children, 72; slaves, 18. The knowledge I have acquired of the locality and of the character of the interested lead me to recommend them particularly to your justice, as I consider them worthy of obtaining from the government the favor they solicit for with respect.

FRANCISCO VALLÉ.

St. Genevieve, *May* 25, 1803.

St. Louis of Illinois, *June* 4, 1803.

Cognizance being taken of what is advanced in this memorial, dated May 25, of this year, supported by the information of the Captain Don Francisco Vallé, commandant of the town of St. Genevieve, and by his official note of same date. Considering the authenticity of the said informations, besides the fidelity and affection which these inhabitants have always manifested, so much so, that at all times they deserved praises from the authorities, and the miserable state in which the interested would find themselves, if, in these circumstances of effectuating the delivery of the colony, they had no title to prove the antiquity of their properties, I do grant to them in full property for them and their heirs, in the same place they inhabit and cultivate since many years, which properties were assigned to them by my predecessors, as follows: Four hundred arpents in superficie for each of the thirty-one families that have signed, which will make the quantity of twelve thousand four hundred arpents in superficie, which quantity shall be surveyed in a square form, if possible, and no one of these concessions shall be taken separately, but (the whole tract) shall be divided in thirty-one parts of 400 arpents each, which, after being surveyed, and figurative plats executed, shall be numbered and drawn by lot in presence of Don Francisco Vallé, or another officer commissioned by him to represent him at the said drawing, and the drawing of numbers shall begin by the first settled in said place, and will follow successively to the last one settled; and the surveyor general of this Upper Louisiana, Don Antonio Soulard, will execute the survey according to what is specified in this decree, and conforming himself to what is asked by the interested in the above petition, observing, as to what relates to the expediting of plats and certificates, that this concession must not be prejudicial to any other that has been already surveyed; and the said operations being done, and certificates of survey delivered to the interested, as I have been informed (by the intendant of these provinces, Don Juan Ventura Morales, in his official note dated December 1, of last year,) that, on account of the death of the assessor of the intendancy, the tribunal of land was shut until a new order is received, the said interested will have to wait for this new order to the said tribunal of the intendancy, (to which alone belongs, by order of his Majesty, the granting of all classes of lands belonging to the royal domain,) to obtain the title in form; in the meanwhile the interested will possess it quietly.

CARLOS DEHAULT DELASSUS.

A true translation of the original Old Mine concession.

JULIUS DE MUN.

Don Antonio Soulard, surveyor general of the settlements of Upper Louisiana.

I do certify that I have run the lines, measured and bounded a tract of land of twelve thousand four hundred arpents and forty perches in superficie, in favor and in presence of the thirty-one heads of families who have signed the petition here annexed; said tract to be hereafter divided in thirty-one concessions of four hundred arpents each, according to the tenor of the proprietors' petition, and to what is ordered by superior decree of the lieutenant governor; which lines of division have not been run on account of the taking of possession and of the order which has been forwarded to me by the captain of artillery of the United States of America, Amos Stoddart, first civil commandant of Upper Louisiana, intimating to me to suspend all sorts of operations of survey on said tract until I receive new orders; and as I am obliged, by my private agreement with the said settlers, to have their lands bounded and divided in thirty-one concessions of four hundred arpents each, according to their demand in the above-mentioned petition, and as it is ordered by the lieutenant governor, as soon as I shall be authorized by the government I will conclude faithfully the said operation. The foregoing survey has been executed with the perch of the city of Paris, of eighteen French feet, lineal measure, of the same city, according to the agrarian measurement of this province. Said land is situated at about fifty miles to the W.NW. of the post of St. Genevieve. Bounded as follows: to the north by lands of F. Tayon; south, in part by lands of Elias Bates, Augustin Chouteau, son of Don Pedro, and by vacant lands of the royal domain; to the east and west by said vacant lands of the royal domain. Said survey and measurement was executed without regard to the variation of the needle, which is 7° 30′, as is evident by the figurative plat here above, in which are noted the dimensions, directions of the lines, other boundaries, &c. Which survey was executed in virtue of the decree of the lieutenant governor and sub-delegate of the fiscal department, Don Carlos Dehault Delassus, dated June 4 of last year, here annexed. In testimony whereof I do give the present, with the figurative plat above, drawn in conformity with the survey, executed by the deputy surveyor, Don Thos. Maddin, dated February 3 of this present year, and signed by him on the minutes, which I do certify.

ANTONIO SOULARD, *Surveyor General.*

St. Louis of Illinois, *March* 15, 1804.

A true translation. October 17, 1832.

JULIUS DE MUN.

No.	Name of original claimant.	Quantity, arpents.	Nature and date of claim.	By whom granted.	By whom surveyed, date, and situation.
9	Alexander Duclos, by his assignees, John Smith, T. & Co., and thirty other claimants, each for 400 arpents.	420	Concession for 12,400 arpents, granted to thirty-one heads of families. June 4, 1803.	Carlos Dehault Delassus.	The 12,400 arpents by Thos. Maddin, Feb'ary 3, 1804. The 31 divisions by said Maddin, Dec. 20, 1805, certified by Soulard, Feb. 25, 1806.

Evidence with reference to minutes and records.

October 22, 1808.—Board met. Present: the Hon. Clement B. Penrose and Frederick Bates.

John Smith, T. & Co., assignees of Alexander Duclos, claiming 420 acres (arpents) of land situate as aforesaid (to wit, at the Old Mine, district of St. Genevieve,) produces as aforesaid, (to wit, a concession from Charles Dehault Delassus, lieutenant governor, as a special permission to settle to thirty-one inhabitants,) the same concession wherein Alexander Duclos is found to be one of the thirty-one inhabitants; also the plat aforesaid, in which plat said Duclos is No. 7. A deed of transfer from said Duclos to claimants, dated August 24, 1805.

Peter Boyer, sworn, says Alexander Duclos was settled in the village of Old Mines, and inhabited and cultivated a part of said tract of 12,400 arpents five years ago, and for three years. Laid over for decision.—(See book No. 3, page 313.)

December 21, 1811.—Board met. Present: John B. C. Lucas, Clement B. Penrose, and Frederick Bates, commissioners.

John Smith, T. assignee of Alexander Duclos.—(See book No. 3, page 314.) It is the opinion of

Clement B. Penrose, commissioner, that this claim ought to be granted, being embraced by the 2d section of the act of 2d March, 1805, and claims with as slight testimonies have been granted. It is the opinion of John B. C. Lucas, commissioner, that this claim ought not to be granted, because the testimony of Peter Boyer concerning the inhabitation and cultivation of Alexander Duclos is indefinite, and does not apply more to the part of the connected plat to which his claim refers than to any other part of the 12,400 arpents represented by the connected plat. Frederick Bates, commissioner, forbears giving an opinion.—(See book No. 5, page 530.)

October 5, 1832.—The board met pursuant to adjournment. Present: Lewis F. Linn and F. R. Conway, commissioners.

John Smith, T. & Co., assignees of Alexander Duclos, claiming 420 acres of land.—(See book No. 3, page 313; book No. 5, page 530; record book D, page 73.) Produces a paper purporting to be the original survey for 12,400 arpents, taken the 3d of February, and certified the 15th of March, 1804, signed Antoine Soulard, surveyor general; said survey not heretofore recorded.

M. P. Le Duc, duly sworn, saith that the signature to the aforesaid survey is the handwriting of said Antoine Soulard.

The said claimant also files a paper purporting to be original depositions taken in behalf of said claimant before the district court of the United States.

November 20, 1832.—The board met pursuant to adjournment. Present: Lewis F. Linn and F. R. Conway, commissioners.

Old Mine concession for 12,400 arpents of land.—(See book D, page 67, and following; record of survey, book D, page 73; for testimony see book 5, page 530.)

The following additional testimony was taken in the foregoing case, in compliance with a resolution of this board of the 10th of October last:

STATE OF MISSOURI, *county of St. Genevieve:*

The inhabitants of the Old Mine, 31 in number, and their heirs and representatives, each claiming 400 arpents of land, situated at a place called the Old Mine, in the former district of St. Genevieve, now the county of Washington. When Joseph Pratte, in his own right, and Joseph Pratte, under Antoine Govereau, and Walter Wilkinson, under Bazil Vallé, and Charles C. Vallé, in his own right, and François B. Vallé, in his own right, and St. Germine Beauvis, under Thomas Ross, and the heirs and legal representatives of Jacques Guibourg, and Bartholomew St. Germine, under Bte. Placet, produce the original concession, dated the 4th day of June, in the year 1803, granted on the petition of the said inhabitants, dated the 25th of May, 1803, and granted and signed by Charles Dehault Delassus, lieutenant governor of Louisiana. The claimants also produce general and particular plats of survey made according to law—made by the proper authorities under the Spanish and American governments. When Pascal Detchmendy, who is aged 71 years, being produced, and duly sworn as the law directs, deposeth and saith that he came to this country in the year 1796, and that he has remained in the country ever since; that he is well acquainted with the handwriting and signature of Charles Dehault Delassus, who was, at the date of this grant or concession, the lieutenant governor of Upper Louisiana; that he has frequently seen him write his name, and that the name and signature to the said concession, dated the 4th day of June, 1803, is the proper handwriting of the said Charles Dehault Delassus, and the body of the said concession is in the handwriting of Antoine Soulard, then surveyor general of Upper Louisiana. This deponent further states that he knows personally (for he was frequently on the land granted, as he traded to said place,) that the land conceded to each of the claimants here above stated was taken possession of by them in person, or by some person for them and for their use and in their behalf; and this deponent further says that he knows that the land aforesaid conceded to each individual was not only taken possession of as aforesaid, but that many of the tracts were actually inhabited and cultivated by the concessioners in person, or by some person for them or under them, from the date of the concession aforesaid till the present time; and this deponent further states that as early as the year 1797 he made application to Zenon Trudeau, who was then lieutenant governor of Upper Louisiana, for a grant of land at this very place, and that said Zenon Trudeau refused him the grant, stating as his reason for refusing that the said land was already promised to the said inhabitants of the Old Mine, and would be granted to them so soon as they should make the application in form; and this deponent further states that he knows that each of the original concessioners aforesaid were at the date of the concession aforesaid actual inhabitants and citizens of this country, and that the others, in general, continued inhabitants during their lives, and that the present claimants are all citizens and residents of this State; and this deponent further states that he has been informed from a source entitled to credit that Moses Austin asked for and wanted a grant for the same land aforesaid, and was refused by the Spanish authorities for the same reasons that this deponent was refused.

P. DETCHMENDY.

Sworn to and subscribed before me, the subscriber, Lewis F. Linn, one of the commissioners appointed to finally settle and adjust land claims in Missouri, this 29th day of October, 1832.

L. F. LINN.

[Translation.]

In the year 1800, on the 4th of January, I have supplied the ceremonies of baptism to Charles François Pierre Auguste Vallé, legitimate son of François Vallé, civil and military commandant of St. Genevieve, and of Marie Carpentier, his wife, born on the 5th of March of the preceding year, and sprinkled (ondoyé) the same day. The godfather has been Don Carlos Auguste Delassus, lieutenant governor of Illinois, the godmother, Miss Julia Vallé, who have signed with us.

MAXWELL, *Curate.*

I, the undersigned, priest officiating at the Old Mine, and being for the present in St. Geneviéve, certify that the above certificate of baptism of Charles François Pierre Auguste Vallé is a true copy faithfully extracted from the registers of the church of St. Genevieve.

Given and signed in St. Genevieve the 30th October, 1832, the curate of the said St. Genevieve, Rev. Mr. Dahmen, having declared to be unable to do it on account of sickness.

T. BOULLIER.

(See book No. 6, page 28, and following.)

July 1, 1833.—The board met pursuant to adjournment. Present: Lewis F. Linn, F. R. Conway, commissioners.

In the case of the Old Mine concession the following testimony was taken before L. F. Linn, commissioner:

St. Genevieve, *April* 29, 1833.

John Boullier, being duly sworn, deposes and says that, as curate of Joachin parish, (Old Mines,) he is well acquainted with some of the original claimants named in this concession, particularly with widow Coleman, and knows that she has 105 children and grandchildren, most of whom reside on the concession, and great many on that part which it is said, according to the numbers, belongs to her; also that he is well acquainted with Charlot Boyer and wife, and knows they have 97 children and grandchildren, nearly all residing on the concession, and several on that part which, according to the numbers, is said to belong to them; and, also, he knows well the widow of Jean Portais, and that she has 45 children and grandchildren, and most of whom reside on the concession, and that part which is said to belong to her according to the number; and, also, he likewise knows Bernard Coleman and wife, and they have 35 children and grandchildren, many of whom reside on the concession, and that he knows they are, generally, worthy, industrious, honest people, and that they have exerted themselves much, with their limited means, to build a church and preserve their religious privileges; that he verily believes if many of these old, respectable, and venerable people, relying on the justness and liberality of the government, were, at their advanced age, to be deprived of their lands, they would inevitably sink under so heavy a calamity.

J. BOULLIER.

Sworn to and subscribed day and date above written.

L. F. LINN, *Commissioner.*

(See book No. 6, page 208.)

Personally appeared before L. F. Linn, one of the commissioners appointed for the final adjustment of private land claims in Missouri, Thomas Maddin, aged 93 years, who, after having been sworn, deposes and says that he was deputy surveyor under the Spanish and American governments. Deponent says that he surveyed the tract of land called the Old Mine concession, granted to 31 heads of families; he surveyed the general survey in the year 1804, 3d of February. Deponent further states that, on the 22d of December, 1805, he run the division lines by running across the original survey, and marking a point on each division line, so that each individual might know his claim. Deponent further states that he run the special lines between claims marked in the plat at the request of the individuals interested, who paid him for the same. Deponent further states that at the time he heard of no complaints or dissatisfaction expressed by the claimants at the division as made, nor until lately. Deponent further states that it appeared to him understood between the claimants that, in the event of an individual who had made an improvement being thrown on a tract where there was no improvement, he was to be paid for his labor.

THOMAS MADDIN.

Subscribed to and sworn May 11, 1833.

L. F. LINN, *Commissioner.*

Personally appeared before L. F. Linn, one of the commissioners appointed for the final adjustment of land claims in Missouri, Charlot Boyer, who, after being duly sworn, deposes and says he came to the place now called Old Mines in the year 1801, and has continued to reside at the place ever since. Deponent says that he is 83 years of age. Deponent further states that Baptiste Vallé and C. H. F. Vallé (Auguste) never resided or cultivated land on the Old Mine concession. Deponent further states that he was well acquainted with Manuel Blanco; that he knew of said Blanco having settled on and improved a piece of land which was claimed by Elias Bates, and not embraced in the Old Mine concession. Deponent further states that said Blanco never resided or cultivated land in the Old Mine concession. Deponent further states that he was well acquainted with John Potel, who came to and resided on the Old Mine concession in the year 1801; that he commenced that year to build a house and barn, after which he began to open lands for cultivation. Deponent further states that John Potel, jr., resided in a house built on the same land, which house joins the one built by his father. Deponent further states that he was well acquainted with Pierre Martin, and knows that said Martin never resided on or cultivated land in the Old Mine concession. Deponent further states that he was well acquainted with Jacob Wise; that said Wise never resided on or cultivated in the Old Mine concession. Deponent further states that he was well acquainted with Alexander Duclos, who inhabited and cultivated land in the Old Mine concession. Deponent says he cannot recollect the time, but it was many years since, perhaps in 1803 or 1804. Deponent further says said tract of land, so inhabited and cultivated, lies near a place formerly inhabited by N. Hebert, in the Old Mine concession. Deponent further states that he was well acquainted with his nephew, Charles Robert, who inhabited and cultivated land in the Old Mine concession, which was a tract of land adjoining one inhabited and cultivated by Alexander Duclos, their houses being the width of one arpent apart. Deponent further states that he was well acquainted with Joseph Pratte; that said Pratte never resided on or cultivated land in the Old Mine concession. Deponent further states that he was well acquainted with Francis Maniche; that said Maniche built a house and cultivated a garden in the Old Mine concession; he does not recollect distinctly at what time, but it was many years since; same place is now inhabited by François Portel.

CHARLOT BOYER.
L. F. LINN, *Commissioner.*

Caledonia, *Washington county:*

Personally appeared before L. F. Linn, one of the commissioners appointed, &c., John Stewart, formerly deputy surveyor in Upper Louisiana, who, after being sworn, deposes and says that he came to this State and to this, now Washington, county in the month of November, 1800, and transacted business at and near the Old Mines in part of the years 1803 and 1804; and that he was well acquainted with the persons residing at that time in the Old Mine concession, and knows that Joseph Pratte resided in St. Genevieve, and never was to his knowledge an inhabitant of the Old Mines. Deponent further states that C. F. Auguste Vallé, alias Charles C. Vallé, was at that time very young and did not reside on the Old Mine concession. Deponent further states that Pierre Martin was a resident of Mine à Breton and never resident of the Old Mines, nor did he cultivate land on the same, to the best of his knowledge. Deponent further says he never knew or heard of Baptiste Vallé being an inhabitant of the Old Mine concession; he has always heard of his residence being in St. Genevieve. Deponent further states that Manuel Blanco resided on a piece of land belonging to Elias Bates adjoining the Old Mine concession; he never knew or heard of said Blanco residing on or cultivating land in the Old Mine concession. Deponent further states that Jacob Wise was a resident of Mine à Breton, and never an inhabitant of the Old Mine concession, to the best of his knowledge.

JOHN STEWART.

Sworn to and subscribed May 14, 1833.

L. F. LINN, *Commissioner.*

OLD MINE, *May* 11, 1833.

Personally appeared before L. F. Linn, one of the commissioners appointed, &c., Mr. John Trimble, who, after being duly sworn, deposes and says that he came to reside in Upper Louisiana, now the State of Missouri, in the year 1811; that he is acquainted with the general survey of the Old Mine concession, and knows that lots marked one and two on the plat of survey, and said to belong to the Vallés, had no appearance of habitation or cultivation up to the year 1817, when George Breckenridge built a cabin on the same and made no other improvements.

J. T. TRIMBLE.

Sworn to and subscribed May 11, 1833.

L. F. LINN, *Commissioner.*

(See book No. 6, pages 225, 226, 227, 228, and 229.)

October 18, 1833.—The board met pursuant to adjournment. Present: A. G. Harrison, F. R. Conway, commissioners. In the Old Mine case the following testimony was taken by F. R. Conway, esq.

This day personally appeared Jacque Bon before me, F. R. Conway, recorder of land titles, acting as a commissioner for the final adjustment of private land claims in Missouri, this 6th day of July, 1833, and being sworn, says that he is nearly 58 years of age, and that he is not interested for or against the part of the grant about which he deposes or gives testimony. He says he settled in the Old Mines in Washington county in the year 1801, and has resided there ever since; when he came there Charles Boyer, Bernard Coleman, John Potel, Joseph Boyer, John Polite, Polite Robert, P. Boyer, Louis Boyer, and Alexander Coleman resided there on small improvements, having been there but a short time on what was afterwards surveyed to 31 persons by Thomas Maddin about two years after this; that Boilvin came to this affiant and imformed him he was obtaining signatures to a petition in order to procure a concession for the land on which they were residing, agreeing, as this affiant then understood, that each of the settlers should have the improvement he had made, and that a village should be laid off on the land, and in this way obtained their consent to sign the petition. This affiant does not know who did sign or the number, but has been informed that 32 were obtained; but when or how the grant was obtained he does not recollect He heard about that time the names of some who had signed the petition were stricken off without their consent, and others added to the petition before the grant was obtained, or about that time. The grant No. 1 was granted to Baptiste Vallé, and No. 2 was granted to Charles, François, and Auguste Vallé, neither of whom ever lived on or cultivated the land either before or since the grant was obtained; No. 5 was granted to Pierre Martin, and No. 6 to Jacob Boise, neither of whom ever lived on or cultivated the land; No. 7 was granted to Alexander Duclos, and No. 8 was granted to Charles Robert, neither of whom ever lived on or cultivated his own land, they resided on the land granted to Jacob Boise near where N. G. Hebert resided; No. 9 was granted to Joseph Pratte, who never lived on or cultivated the land; No. 10 was granted to Francis Maniche, he never lived on or cultivated the land where his grant was made, he resided on the concession No. 4, as this affiant thinks; No. 11 was made to Amable Partenay, No. 12 to Joseph Blay, No. 13 to Francis Robert, No. 14 to L. Boyer, neither of whom lived on or cultivated the land granted to him, nor did any one of the persons to whom a grant was made at the Old Mines as numbered and surveyed by Thomas Maddin. This affiant assisted in making the survey of the exterior boundary, it was made by running all the lines but the closing line, this was not run, as this affiant believes; neither were the subdivision lines ever run by Thomas Maddin between each grant; he run across each and stuck posts about the centre of the tracts in 1805 or 1806, at the request of those interested; and should this grant be confirmed the improvements of those who did settle will be on the grants of others who never settled or improved. Several of those to whom a grant was made claimed land by settlement on the same place where they cultivated within the bounds of this survey, and some to whom a grant was made here got land in other places, of those claiming now Jacob Boise is one. This affiant knows that Alexander Duclos did not live on this tract more than two years at any time, nor did Robert live on this survey three years before he sold it. Both of these persons settled under Boyer (Joseph) who had the land enclosed, and they built in his enclosure, one of whom was his son-in-law and the other his nephew. Joseph Boyer lived on lot No. 6, granted to Jacob Boise, and Duclos and Robert lived to the south of him. Polite Robert and Francis Maniche both resided on grant No. 4, granted to John Potel; Maniche did not reside here more than one year. And further saith not.

his
JACQUE ⋈ BON.
mark.

Sworn to and subscribed before me the 6th day of July, 1833.

F. R. CONWAY.

John Trimble, being sworn, says that John Potel lives on lot No. 5, granted to P. Martin; he does not reside on the grant made to John Potel, jr., and N. P. Hiblard formerly resided on lot No. 6, granted to Jacob Boise. And further saith not.

JOHN TRIMBLE

Sworn to and subscribed before me the 9th day of July, 1833.

F. R. CONWAY.

Amable Partenay appeared this day before me, F. R. Conway, recorder of land titles, acting as a commissioner for the final adjustment of private land claims in Missouri, who, being sworn, saith, that while he resided in St. Genevieve he saw, in the possession of Francis Vallé, who was commandant, a petition for land at the Old Mines in Washington county; he offered to add thereto this affiant's name, and finally did do so, asking for 400 arpents of land, French measure. This affiant says this was in the year 1796 or 1797, as it was shortly before he moved to Potosi, in Washington county, which was in 1799. This petition contained the names of thirty-one persons Some time after he went to Potosi, he thinks in 1802 or 1803, he was informed that Moses Austin had a number of grants, and was going to survey them at the Old Mines; and when the surveyor went there to survey said Austin's claims, those who were interested and had settled there prevented him from making the survey, believing that they owned the land, or ought to have it, having petitioned for it. This affiant went immediately to St. Genevieve to look for the petition and grant, if any had issued on the petition that he had signed, but found neither a grant either there or at St. Louis. While at St. Louis the commandant, Delassus, informed this affiant he would prove that a petition had existed; he might obtain from Francis Vallé, the commandant at St. Genevieve, a copy of the first petition, and he would give a grant for the land. This affiant went back to St. Genevieve, and obtained certificates from different citizens there proving the existence, or that a petition had existed for this land to thirty-one petitioners or applicants. The said Francis Vallé directed his clerk to make out a petition, intended to be a copy of the original, according to the instructions of Delassus. Instead of this he left off the names of five, at least, who had been on the first petition, and put on five who were not on the first petition; and the said Vallé, as this affiant believes, presented this petition, and obtained the grant of 400 arpents to each of the thirty-one petitioners. The out boundary line of this survey was made by Thomas Maddin. This affiant had become bound to him for the payment of his fees, but he does not recollect at what time it was made, but not long after the grant was made; but he did not at that time run the division lines, but claimed his fees and sued for them, but could not recover them. Afterwards, in 1806 or 1807, as this affiant thinks, the said Maddin came back to finish the survey, and numbered them by a lottery drawn by two individuals; they were numbered from 1 to 31, both inclusive; to this several of the claimants objected, as they might lose their improvements, but it was done notwithstanding, and the survey was made by running across each grant about the middle from east to west. This affiant has no interest at this time; he has owned grants, but sold them without any recourse on him. This affiant is 67 years of age, and one among the first settlers in this part of the country.

AMABLE PARTENAY.

Sworn to and subscribed before me the 6th day of July, 1833.

F. R. CONWAY.

This day personally appeared Amable Partenay before me, F. R. Conway, recorder of land titles, acting as a commissioner for the final adjustment of private land claims in Missouri, who, being sworn, says that he has no interest in this claim, and that he is 67 years of age; he knows that Jacque Bon settled in the Old Mines in the year 1801, and has been cultivating a farm there ever since; he has been married for a number of years, but he does not know at what time; he still lives on said land, and has had possession ever since he first settled the land on which he lives. This affiant was among the first settlers in this part of the country.

AMABLE PARTENAY.

Sworn to and subscribed before me this 6th day of July, A. D. 1833.

F. R. CONWAY.

(See book No. 6, pages 376, 377, 378, 379, 380, 381, and 382.)

November 1, 1833.—The board met pursuant to adjournment. Present: L. F. Linn, A. G. Harrison, F. R. Conway, commissioners.

Old Mine concession for 12,400 arpents of land, granted to thirty-one heads of families.—(See page 5 of this book.)

The board are unanimously of opinion that this tract of 12,400 arpents ought to be confirmed to the thirty-one heads of families, or to their legal representatives.—(See book No. 6, page 289.)

Conflicting claims.

By letter dated October 2, 1833, Solomon Houk states to the board that he bought of the United States the SE. ¼ section 20, range 3 E., township 38 N., and that it appears on the plat at the land office that his purchase does not interfere with the Old Mine claim; but, by the lines of the said Old Mine claim, his said purchase would take off from 60 to 65 acres of the aforesaid Old Mine concession.

Peter Boyer, one of the concessioners in the above grant, claimed 639¾ acres and 12 poles as a settlement right, situated within the bounds of the survey made for the thirty-one inhabitants, upon which a report recommending the confirmation of the same was made by the recorder, Bates, November 1, 1815, and which is considered as confirmed by the Commissioner of the General Land Office, as per his letter to the recorder of land titles.

L. F. LINN.
F. R. CONWAY.
A. G. HARRISON.

No. 10.—David Cole, *claiming* 400 *arpents.*

To Mr. Zenon Trudeau, lieutenant governor and commandant in chief of Upper Louisiana:

David Cole (German) has the honor to expose that he is settled, with your agreement, on the north side of the Missouri, near a place called La Femme Osage, and on a vacant spot, where he has worked with his family since some time. He respectfully supplicates you to grant to him the property of four hundred arpents of land in such manner as to include his present establishment; favor which he expects of your goodness and justice.

DAVID his ⋈ mark. COLE.

St. Louis, *January* 23, 1798.

Inasmuch as the land solicited appertains to the King's domain, and is not prejudicial to any person, the surveyor of this jurisdiction, Don Antonio Soulard, shall put the petitioner in possession; so that, after having fixed boundaries, he may solicit the concession from the governor general.

ZENON TRUDEAU.

A true translation. St. Louis, October 18, 1832.

JULIUS DE MUN.

No.	Name of original claimant.	Quantity, arpents.	Nature and date of claim.	By whom granted.	By whom surveyed, date, and situation.
10	David Cole, by Jesse Richardson, assignee of James Mackay, who was assignee of said Cole.	400	Concession, January 23, 1798	Zenon Trudeau..	Jas. Mackay, February 15, (eighteen and five;) certified by Soulard, December 10, 1805; north side Missouri, thirty miles west of St. Louis.

Evidence with reference to minutes of records.

September 28, 1808.—Board met. Present: The Hon. Clement B. Penrose and Frederick Bates. Jesse Richardson, assignee of James Mackay, assignee of David Cole, claiming 430 arpents of land situate in the district of St. Charles, produces to the board a concession from Zenon Trudeau, lieutenant governor, to David Cole, for the same, dated January 23, 1798; a plat and certificate of survey, dated February 15, 1805, and certified December 10, 1805; a certified copy of a deed of transfer from David Cole to James Mackay, dated July 14, 1799; a deed of transfer from James Mackay to claimant, dated September 10, 1803. Laid over for decision.—(See book No. 3, page 268.)

June 14, 1810.—Board met. Present: John B. C. Lucas, Clement B. Penrose, and Frederick Bates, commissioners.

Jesse Richardson, assignee of James Mackay, assignee of David Cole, claiming 430 arpents of land.—(See book No. 3, page 268.) It is the opinion of the board that this claim ought not to be confirmed.—(See book No. 4, page 380.)

October 6, 1832.—The board met pursuant to adjournment. Present: L. F. Linn and F. R. Conway, commissioners.

David Cole, by his assignee, Jesse Richardson, assignee of James Mackay, (see book E, page 15, book No. 3, page 268, and book No. 4, page 380,) claiming 400 arpents of land. Produces a paper purporting to be a concession from Zenon Trudeau, dated January 23, 1798; also, a plat and certificate of survey, certified by Soulard, and dated December 10, 1805; also, an affidavit of James Mackay, taken before Jeremiah Connor, a justice of the peace for the county of St. Louis, dated October 21, 1818, authenticated by Frederick Bates, secretary, exercising the government of the Territory of Missouri, dated November 10, 1818.

M. P. Le Duc, duly sworn, saith that the signature to the said concession is the handwriting of Zenon Trudeau; that the signature to the above survey is the handwriting of Antoine Soulard.—(See book No. 6, page 9.)

July 24, 1833.—The board met pursuant to adjournment. Present: L. F. Linn, A. G. Harrison, and R. F. Conway, commissioners.

In the case of David Cole, claiming 400 arpents of land, (see page 9 of this book, No. 6,) the following testimony was taken before A. G. Harrison, one of the commissioners:

Isaac Vanlibber, sr., being duly sworn, says that in the year 1800 he, the witness, rented of David Cole a field in Darst bottom, on the Missouri river, consisting of three or four acres, which field witness put in corn that year and raised a crop on it; that said field had been cultivated the year preceding by said Cole; that said Cole had a cabin on said tract of land and lived there; that said place has been in cultivation ever since, and is the place where one Zachariah Moore now lives; that said place or tract of land was bounded by Joshua Dodson's claim, Joseph Hayne's, David Darst's, by my own, (the witness's,) William Hay's, Colonel Daniel Boon's, and by the Missouri river; that Darst's bottom is sometimes called Femme Osage bottom.—(See book No. 6, page 237.)

A. G. HARRISON, *one of the commissioners.*

Loutre Lick, *June* 26, 1833.

November 1, 1833.—The board met pursuant to adjournment. Present: L. F. Linn, A. G. Harrison, and F. R. Conway, commissioners.

David Cole, claiming 400 arpents of land.—(See page 9 of this book.) The board are unanimously of opinion that this claim ought to be confirmed to said David Cole or his legal representatives, according to the concession of 400 arpents, and not to the extent of 430 arpents shown by the plat of survey.—(See book No. 6, page 290.)

L. F. LINN.
F. R. CONWAY.
A. G. HARRISON.

No. 11.—John Bassy, *claiming* 1,600 *arpents.*

To Don C. Dehault Delassus, lieutenant governor of Upper Louisiana:

Sir: John Bessé has the honor to represent that, wishing to establish himself in this Upper Louisiana, where he has resided for some time, he has recourse to the kindness of the government, hoping that, on account of his numerous family, you will be pleased to grant to him a concession of sixteen hundred arpents of land in superficie, to be taken on vacant lands of H. M.'s domain, in the place which will appear most convenient to the interest of your petitioner, who presumes to expect this favor of your justice.

JOHN BASSY.

St. Louis, *January* 5, 1801.

Considering that the petitioner has long been settled in this country, and that his family is sufficiently large to obtain the quantity of land which he solicits, I do grant to him and his heirs the land he solicits, if it is not prejudicial to anybody; and the surveyor, Don Antonio Soulard, shall put the interested in possession of the quantity of land he asks, in a vacant place of the royal domain, and when this is executed he shall draw a plat, which he will deliver to the party with his certificate, to serve him to obtain the concession and title in form from the intendant general, to whom alone belongs, by royal order, the distributing and granting all classes of lands of the royal domain.

CARLOS DEHAULT DELASSUS.

St. Louis of Illinois, *January* 8, 1801.

Don Antonio Soulard, surveyor general of the settlements of Upper Louisiana.

I do certify that a tract of land of 1,600 arpents was measured, the lines run and bounded, in favor of Don Santiago St. Vrain, in presence of Mr. Alberto Tison, his agent, as appears by the above figurative plat. This said concession was bought last year by its present proprietor, from its primitive owner, as appears by the deed of sale which is deposited in the archives of this government. Said tract of land was measured with the perch of the city of Paris, of eighteen French feet, according to the agrarian measure of this province. Said land is situated at about fifty miles north of St. Louis, bounded north, south, and west by vacant lands of the royal domain, and east equally by lands of the royal domain and lands of Joseph Burns; which survey and measurement were made without regard to the variation of the needle, which is 7° 30′ east, as is evident by the above figurative plat, in which are noted the dimensions, direction of the lines, and other boundaries, &c.; this survey was done in consequence of the decree of the lieutenant governor and sub-delegate of the fiscal department, Don C. D. Delassus, dated January 8, 1801, which is here annexed. In testimony whereof, I do give the present with the above figurative plat, which was executed conformably to the operations done by the deputy surveyor, Don Santiago Rankin, on the 10th of February, 1804, and signed by him on the minutes; all which I do certify.

ANTONIO SOULARD, *Surveyor General.*

St. Louis of Illinois, *March* 20, 1804.

A true translation. St. Louis, October 18.

JULIUS DE MUN.

No.	Name of original claimant.	Quantity, arpents.	Nature and date of claim.	By whom granted.	By whom surveyed, date, and situation.
11	John Bassy, by his assignee, J. St. Vrain.	1,600	Concession, January 8, 1801.	Carlos Dehault Delassus.	James Rankin, February 10, 1804; certified by Soulard, March 20, 1804; 50 miles north of St. Louis, on Cuivre river.

Evidence with reference to minutes and records.

May 28, 1806.—The board met agreeably to adjournment. Present: the Honorable Clement B. Penrose, esq. The same, (James St. Vrain,) assignee of John Bassy, claiming 1,000 (1,600) arpents of land, situate as aforesaid, produces a concession from Charles Dehault Delassus to the said Bassy for 1,600, dated January 8, 1801; a survey of the same, dated February 10, and certified March 20, 1804; transfer of the same, dated September 3, 1803. The board cannot act.—(See book No. 1, page 303.)

August 17, 1811.—Board met. Present: Clement B. Penrose and Frederick Bates, commissioners. Jaques St. Vrain, assignee of John Bassy, claiming 1,000 arpents of land, and John Bassy, claiming 600 arpents of land.—(See book No. 1, page 303.) It is the opinion of the board that this claim ought not to be confirmed.—(See book No. 5, page 318.)

October 6, 1832.—The board met pursuant to adjournment. Present: L. F. Linn, F. R. Conway, commissioners. John Bassy, by his assignee, Jaques St. Vrain, claiming 1,600 arpents of land.—(See record book C, page 327; minutes No. 1, page 303, and No. 5, page 318.) Produces a paper purporting to be a concession from C. D. Delassus, lieutenant governor, dated January 8, 1801; also a plat and certificate of survey signed by Antoine Soulard, surveyor general, executed the 10th of February, and certified March 20, 1804. M. P. Le Duc, duly sworn, saith that the signature to the concession is the handwriting of

Carlos Dehault Delassus, and that the signature to the certificate of survey is the handwriting of Antoine Soulard.—(See book No. 6, page 10.)

November 1, 1833.—The board met. Present: L. F. Linn, A. G. Harrison, F. R. Conway, commissioners. John Bassy, claiming 1,600 arpents of land.—(See page 10 of this book.) The board are unanimously of opinion that this claim ought to be confirmed to said John Bassy, or to his legal representatives, according to the concession.—(See book No. 6, page 290.)

L. F. LINN.
F. R. CONWAY.
A. G. HARRISON.

No. 12.—Toussaint Cerré's concession for Paysa island.

To Don Charles Dehault Delassus, lieutenant colonel attached to the stationary regiment of Louisiana, and lieutenant governor of the upper part of same province:

Toussaint Cerré, father of a family, ancient inhabitant of this country, and residing at the village of St. Charles of the Missouri, has the honor to supplicate you (considering the difficulty of raising cattle in the neighborhood of the settlements; also, the scarcity of wood, which is diminishing every day,) to have the goodness to grant to him the concession of the great island of Paysa, distant about 18 miles from St. Louis, and six miles above the mouth of Missouri, and by its proximity belonging to the Spanish side, the main channel passing between the island and the American side, and in low water it being fordable from our side to the said island. The certainty of not being prejudicial to whomsoever, and the confidence which the petitioner has in your justice, makes him hope that you will accede to his demand in a manner advantageous to his views.

TOUSSAINT CERRÉ, his ⋈ mark.

St. Louis, *January* 15, 1800.

I sign as a witness: Auguste Chouteau.

St. Louis of Illinois, *January* 15, 1800.

Cognizance being taken of the contents of the foregoing petition, and being satisfied that the petitioner is of such a conduct and personal merit that he is recommendable among the ancient inhabitants of this country, and that the said island belongs to this side of the Mississippi, I do grant it to him in all its extents of width, length, and superficie, such as it now stands, for him and his heirs, to possess and enjoy, and dispose of it as their own property; provided it does not do prejudice to the territorial right of the United States of America, stipulated in article four of the treaty of amity, navigation, and limits, concluded between the two powers on the 27th October, 1795, and ratified the 25th of April, 1796. And Don Antonio Soulard, surveyor general of this Upper Louisiana, will take notice of this title for his intelligence and government in what concerns him; after which the petitioner shall have to solicit the title in form from the intendant general of these provinces of Louisiana, to whom alone corresponds, by royal order, the distributing and granting of all classes of lands of the royal domaim.

CARLOS DEHAULT DELASSUS.

Registered by order of the lieutenant governor, pages 9 and 10 of book No. 1 of the titles of concessions.

SOULARD.

A true translation: St. Louis, October 19, 1832.

JULIUS DE MUN.

No.	Name of original claimant.	Quantity in arpents.	Nature and date of claim.	By whom granted.	By whom surveyed, date, and situation.
12	Toussaint Cerré, by his assignee, Auguste Chouteau.	1, 220 75-100	Concession, January 15, 1800.	Carlos Dehault Delassus.	Wm. Millburg, (no date.) An island in the Mississippi, six miles above the mouth of Missouri river.

Evidence with reference to minutes and records.

September 13, 1808.—Board met. Present: The Hon. John B. C. Lucas, Clement B. Penrose, and Frederick Bates. Auguste Chouteau, assignee of Toussaint Cerré, claiming an island in the Mississippi, commonly called the Paysa island, about eighteen miles from St. Louis and six above the mouth of Missouri, produces to the board a concession from Don Carlos Dehault Delassus, lieutenant governor, for the the same, to Toussaint Cerré, dated January 15, 1800; a certified copy of a deed of conveyance from Toussaint Cerré to claimant, dated December 28, 1803. Laid over for decision.—(See book No. 3, p. 239.)

June 7, 1810.—Board met. Present: Clement B. Penrose and Frederick Bates, commissioners. Auguste Chouteau, assignee of Toussaint Cerré, claiming an island in the river Mississippi.—(See book No. 3, page 239.) It is the opinion of the board that this claim ought not to be confirmed.—(See book No. 4, page 369.

October 6, 1832.—The board met pursuant to adjournment. Present: L. F. Linn and F. R. Conway, commissioners. Toussaint Cerré, by the heirs of Auguste Chouteau, claiming an island in the Mississippi, the Paysa island.—(See record book B, page 55; minutes book No. 3, page 239; and book No. 4, page 369.) Produces a paper purporting to be a concession from Carlos Dehault Delassus, lieutenant governor, dated January 15, 1800; also a plat and certificate of survey, signed by William Millburg, without date. M. P. Le Duc, duly sworn, saith that the signature to the said concession is in the handwriting of Carlos Dehault Delassus, and that the signature to the said plat is the handwriting of said Millburg.—(See No. 6, page 10.)

November 1, 1833.—The board met pursuant to adjournment. Present: L. F. Linn, A. G. Harrison, and F. R. Conway, commissioners. Toussaint Cerré claiming an island.—(See page 10 of this book.) The board are unanimously of opinion that this claim ought to be confirmed to said Toussaint Cerré, or his legal representatives, according to the tenor of the concession.—(See book No. 6. page 291.)

L. F. LINN.
F. R. CONWAY.
A. G. HARRISON.

No. 13.—Auguste Chouteau, *claiming* 7,056 *arpents.*

To Don Zenon Trudeau, lieutenant colonel, captain of the stationary regiment of Louisiana, and lieutenant governor of the western part of Illinois:

Auguste Chouteau, merchant of this town, has the honor of representing to you that, having heard advantageous reports of several tracts of land situated along the Mississippi, at about 50 miles, more or less, from this town, and having sufficient means to establish a stock farm, (vacherie,) he has the honor to supplicate you to have the goodness to grant to him, in the same place above mentioned, one league square of land, or 7,056 arpents in superficie; said quantity has never been denied by the government, either in the lower or upper part of this colony, for the undertaking of such establishments; the petitioner having, besides, the project of establishing on said land a considerable farm, hopes that you will please to patronize him in his views, which cannot be but advantageous to the security of these settlements, and to the interior communications, in keeping off the Indians, who scatter themselves in our neighborhood at various seasons of the year, to lay waste the plantations too far distant from one another to lend themselves the necessary help in such cases.

Your petitioner, full of confidence, dares hope everything of your justice, as well as of the generosity of the government which you represent.

AUGUSTE CHOUTEAU.

St. Louis of Illinois, *January* 5, 1798.

St. Louis of Illinois, *January* 8, 1798.

Being well satisfied that the land solicited belongs to the royal domain, the surveyor, Don Antonio Soulard, shall put the interested person in possession of it, and shall draw a plat, with his certificate, in continuation, to serve in soliciting the concession from the governor general of the province, whom I inform that the petitioner finds himself in the circumstances which deserve this favor.

ZENON TRUDEAU.

Don Antonio Soulard, surveyor general of the settlements of Upper Louisiana.

I do certify that a tract of land of 7,056 arpents in superficie was measured, the lines drawn and bounded, in favor and in presence of Don Augustin Chouteau; which measurement was done with the perch of the city of Paris, of 18 French feet lineal measure of the same city, conformably to the agrarian measure of this province. Said tract of land is situated three miles west of the river Mississippi, and fifty-seven north of this town of St. Louis; bounded NW. ¼ N. by lands of Joseph Brazeau, SE. ¼ S., NE. ¼ E., and SW. ¼ W. by vacant lands of the royal domain; which survey and measurement were performed without regard to the variation of the needle, which is 7° 30′ E., as appears by the figurative plat here above, in which are noted the dimensions, direction of the lines, and other boundaries, &c. Said survey was executed in consequence of a decree of the lieutenant governor, Don Zenon Trudeau, dated January 8, 1798, here annexed. In testimony whereof I do give the present, with the foregoing figurative plat, drawn conformably to the survey executed by the deputy surveyor, Don Santiago Rankin, on the 20th December, 1803, signed by him on the minutes. All which I do certify.

ANTONIO SOULARD, *Surveyor General.*

St. Louis of Illinois, *December* 29, 1803.

A true translation. St. Louis, October 19, 1832.

JULIUS DE MUN.

No.	Name of original claimant.	Quantity, arpents.	Nature and date of claim.	By whom granted.	By whom surveyed, date, and situation.
13	Auguste Chouteau, by his heirs.	7,056	Concession, 8th January, 1798.	Zenon Trudeau.	James Rankin, December 20, 1803; certified December 29, 1803, by Soulard; three miles west of river Mississippi, and 57 miles north of St. Louis.

Evidence with reference to minutes and records.

November 2, 1811.—Board met. Present: John B. C. Lucas, Clement B. Penrose, and Frederick Bates, commissioners.

Auguste Chouteau, claiming 7,056 arpents of land, situate on the river St. Augustine, district of St. Charles, produces a concession from Zenon Trudeau, lieutenant governor, dated January 8, 1798; a plat of survey, dated December 20, 1803, certified December 29, 1803. It is the opinion of the board that this claim ought not to be confirmed.—(See book No. 5, page 395.)

October 8, 1832.—The board met pursuant to adjournment. Present: L. F. Linn, W. Updyke, F. R. Conway, commissioners.

Auguste Chouteau, by his heirs, claiming 7,056 arpents of land.—(See book of record D, pages 121 and 122; minutes book 5, page 395.) Produces a paper purporting to be a concession, dated January 8, 1798, from Zenon Trudeau, lieutenant governor; also a plat of survey executed the 20th of December, 1803, and certified December 29, 1803.

Pascal Corré, duly sworn, saith that the signature to the concession is the handwriting of Zenon Trudeau; that the signature to the plat of survey and certificate is in the handwriting of Antoine Soulard; that, in the year 1798, and long before that time, Auguste Chouteau was considered a man of large property; possessed of large herds of cattle of all descriptions; owned 50 or .60 slaves; in fact, was the richest man in Upper Louisiana.—(See book No. 6, page 12.)

November 1, 1833.—The board met pursuant to adjournment. Present: L. F. Lynn, A. G. Harrison, F. R. Conway, commissioners.

Auguste Chouteau, claiming 7,056 arpents of land.—(See page 12 of this book.) The board are unanimously of opinion that this claim ought to be confirmed to said Auguste Chouteau, or his legal representatives, according to the concession.—(See book No. 6, page 291.)

L. F. LINN.
F. R. CONWAY.
A. G. HARRISON.

No. 14.—*To Mr. Zenon Trudeau, lieutenant governor and commander-in-chief of the western part of Illinois, &c., &c.:*

Prays very humbly, Pierre Charles Dehault Delassus Deluziere, knight, &c., captain and commandant, civil and military, of the post of New Bourbon and dependencies, has the honor to submit that there being in his district an emigrant from the United States of America, very expert in the art of making maple sugar, and refining it after the method so advantageously practised in the Jerseys, he determined to look for a piece of land provided with maple trees, for the purpose of establishing a sugar manufactory thereon, and causing it to be worked according to the process used in the Jerseys; that he has found such a tract, situated on the south fork of the Saline river, containing about one hundred arpents in superficie, and such as it is designated in the foregoing plat, at the entrance to which he has caused to be marked, on the 10th December last, a white oak with the letters D. L. S., and three maples blazed on each side of it. Wherefore your suppliant addresses himself to you, sir, to the end that you may be pleased to grant to him, his heirs and assigns, in full property, the said tract, containing about one hundred arpents in superficie, for the purpose not only of establishing a manufactory of maple sugar thereon, but also of sending his cattle to graze there during the winters, inasmuch as there is a great deal of cane on said land; doing which the petitioner will not cease to pray for the precious conservation of your days.

DELASSUS DELUZIERE.

At New Bourbon of Illinois, *January* 2, 1798.

Cognizance being taken of the above petition, and of the request made by Mr. Pedro Delassus Deluziere, commandant of the post of New Bourbon, the surveyor, Don Anto. Soulard, will put the party interested in possession of it, (land asked for;) after which he shall make the procès verbal of his survey, in order to serve to solicit the title in form from the governor general of the province. The zeal which he (said petitioner) has manifested for the service of the King in all occasions in which he has been employed renders him worthy of receiving this favor.

ZENON TRUDEAU.

St. Louis of Illinois, *January* 20, 1798.

No.	Name of original claimant.	Quantity, arpents.	Nature and date of claim.	By whom granted.	By whom surveyed, date, and situation.
14	Pierre Delassus Deluziere.	100	Concession, January 20, 1798.	Zenon Trudeau.	On south fork Saline river, district of St. Genevieve.

Evidence with reference to minutes and records.

Sittings at St. Genevieve, June, 1806.

Peter D. Deluziere, claiming 100 arpents of land, situate on the Saline, produces a concession from Zenon Trudeau, dated the 20th January, 1798, and granting the same for sugar making.

Israel Dodge, being duly sworn, says that a sugar camp was established on said land in the year 1799. The board reject this claim.—(See book No. 2, page 25.)

September 28, 1810.—Board met. Present: John B. C. Lucas, Clement B. Penrose, commissioners.

Pierre Delassus Deluziere, claiming 100 arpents of land —(See book No. 2, page 25.) It is the opinion of the board that this claim ought not to be confirmed.—(See book No. 4, page 515.)

October 8, 1832.—The board met pursuant to adjournment. Present: L. F. Linn, W. Updyke, F. R. Conway, commissioners.

Pierre Delassus Deluziere, claiming 100 arpents of land.—(See record book B, page 515; minutes book No. 2, page 25, and book No. 4, page 515.) Produces a paper purporting to be a concession from Zenon Trudeau, dated 20th January, 1798.

Pascal Cerré, duly sworn, says that the signature to the concession is the handwriting of said Zenon Trudeau; states that he knew Deluziere as commandant of New Bourbon, and believes he was yet commandant of said place at his death.—(See book No. 6, page 13.)

November 1, 1833.—The board met pursuant to adjournment. Present: L. F Linn, A. G. Harrison, F. R. Conway, commissioners.

Pierre Delassus Deluziere, claiming 100 arpents of land.—(See page 13 of this book.) The board are unanimously of opinion that this claim ought to be confirmed to the said Pierre Delassus Deluziere, or his legal representatives, according to the consession.—(See book No. 6, page 291.)

L. F. LINN.
F. R. CONWAY.
A. G. HARRISON.

No. 15.—P. MÉNARD'S *concession.*

To Don Zenon Trudeau, lieutenant colonel, attached to the regiment of Louisiana, and lieutenant governor of the western part of Illinois:

The undersigned has the honor to state that being settled since several years in this country, and having as yet received no donation in land from the government, favor which is granted to all the other inhabitants; besides, the undersigned wishing to settle on a piece of land already cleared by one of the name of Berthiaume, who has abandoned to him the said improvement in presence of witnesses, the said undersigned hopes of your goodness that you will be pleased to grant to him the said piece of land, situated on the river La Pomme, (Apple creek,) as follows: twenty arpents in front, to begin at the mouth of said creek and ascending the Mississippi, by twenty arpents in depth.

The petitioner has the honor to represent, at the same time, that although this quantity appears considerable, there is not, however, in all, one hundred arpents of good land. The only real advantage resulting to him is an improvement already begun, and upon which there are some buildings. He hopes of your goodness that you will condescend to grant his demand, and he will never cease to pray for you.

PIERRE MÉNARD.

ST. LOUIS, *November* 5, 1798.

The four hundred arpents of land solicited, being situated in a vacant part, (of the domain,) and the petitioner having not yet obtained any land of the government, the surveyor of this jurisdiction, Don Ant. Soulard, will put him in possession, so that, after the survey is made, he may solicit the concession from the governor general.

ZENON TRUDEAU.

A true translation. St. Louis, October 22, 1832.

JULIUS DE MUN.

No.	Name of original claimant.	Quantity, arpents.	Nature and date of claim.	By whom granted.	By whom surveyed, date, and situation.
15	Pierre Ménard.	400	Concession, Nov. 5, 1798.	Zenon Trudeau.	

Evidence with reference to minutes and records.

May 25, 1806.—Board met. Present: John B. C. Lucas, Clement B. Penrose, and Frederick Bates, commissioners.

Peter Ménard, claiming 580 arpents of land, produces to the board a concession from Zenon Trudeau, lieutenant governor, for 400 arpents, dated November 5, 1798. Laid over for decision.—(See book No. 4, page 74.)

March 19, 1810.—Board met. Present: John B. C. Lucas, Clement B. Penrose, and Frederick Bates, commissioners.

Peter Ménard claiming 580 arpents of land.—(See book No. 4, page 74.) This claim is for 400 arpents, and not 580, as stated in the minutes referred to. It is the opinion of the board that this claim ought not to be confirmed.—(See book No. 4, page 298.)

October 9, 1832.—The board met pursuant to adjournment. Present: L. F. Linn, F. R. Conway, W. Updike, commissioners.

Pierre Ménard, claiming 20 arpents of land in front by twenty arpents in depth, on the river à la Pomme, (Apple creek.)—(See record book, page 25; book No. 4, pages 74 and 298.) Produces a paper purporting to be a concession from Zenon Trudeau to P. Ménard, dated November 5, 1798. Pascal Cerré, duly sworn, says that the whole concession and the signature to it is the handwriting of Zenon Trudeau.—(See book No. 6, page 15.)

November 2, 1833.—The board met pursuant to adjournment. Present: L. F. Linn, A. G. Harrison, F. R. Conway, commissioners.

STATE OF MISSOURI, *County of Cape Girardeau:*

Personally appeared before me, L. F. Linn, one of the commissioners appointed under the law for the adjustment of land claims in the State of Missouri, Jonathan Bois, who, being duly sworn according to law, deposeth and saith, that some time in the month of June, 1799, he was at the mouth of Apple creek and saw Berthiaume, who then resided there; he had two log-houses or cabins, and some cleared land under fence, a garden, &c. And further this deponent states that he was at the same place in the year 1804 or 1805, and the said Berthiaume (whose given name he does not recollect) still resided there.

JONATHAN BOIS.

Sworn to and subscribed October 17, 1833.

L. F. LINN, *Commissioner.*

William Russell, being sworn, deposeth and saith that in the year 1799 he was on the east bank of the Mississippi river, opposite to the mouth of Apple creek, on the west bank of the Mississippi; and, on inquiry, was told that a François Berthiaume resided there; and in the year 1802 he was at the mouth of Apple creek, and François Berthiaume still resided there, and had a small improvement, garden, &c., at the same place.

WILLIAM RUSSELL.

Sworn to and subscribed October 17, 1833.

L. F. LINN, *Commissioner.*

(See book No. 6, page 15.)

November 1, 1833.—The board met according to adjournment. Present: L. F. Linn, A. G. Harrison, F. R. Conway, commissioners.

Pierre Ménard claiming 400 arpents of land.—(See page 15 of this book.) The board are unanimously of opinion that this claim ought to be confirmed to the said Pierre Ménard, or his legal representatives, according to the concession.—(See book No. 6, page 292.)

Conflicting claims.

Kimmel and Taylor give notice to the board by two letters, dated November 3, 1832, and February 16, 1833, that the surveyor for the United States disregarded the original survey of the above claim, and made a fraction on the Mississippi, which fraction has been entered and paid by them. Said fraction numbered 1,097. They value their improvements, for the present, at $2,500; and in one year it will be worth $4,000, as they are continually improving. John Hays can certify to the above statement.

A. G. HARRISON.
L. F. LINN.
F. R. CONWAY.

No. 16.—FRANÇOIS SAUCIER'S *concession.*

To Don Charles Dehault Delassus, lieutenant colonel, attached to the stationary regiment of Louisiana, and lieutenant governor of the upper part of the same province:

Francis Saucier, appointed by your predecessor, Don Zenon Trudeau, commandant of the new settlement of Portage des Sioux, formerly an officer in the reformed French troops of the navy, and father of fifteen children, having not received to this date any concession from the government, and having been obliged to make great sacrifices to correspond to the confidence of your predecessor, when he (the petitioner) left the village of St. Charles, to go and take the command of that of Portage des Sioux, has the honor to supplicate you to have the goodness to grant to him, in full property, a concession of 8,800 arpents of land in superficie, which will be divided as follows: 600 arpents for each of his children, to the number of thirteen, under his charge, which makes 7,800 arpents, and 1,000 for him and his wife; this will complete the above stated quantity of 8,800 arpents, to be taken in vacant places of the domain, as follows: 1,000 arpents in the point formed by the rivers Mississippi and Missouri, to the eastward of the land of Lewis Labeaume; 1,000 arpents to the westward of the small lakes, distant about forty or fifty arpents from the village of Portage des Sioux; and finally the remaining quantity of 6,800 arpents, to be taken in a vacant place of the domain, at the choice of your petitioner, who hopes that you will be pleased to take his demand into consideration, and that his years, the numerous family which he has to maintain, and the laborious task he fills, without any renumeration from the government, will be strong motives in your opinion to obtain the justice which he presumes to deserve.

F. SAUCIER.

ST. LOUIS, *September* 10, 1799.

ST. LOUIS OF ILLINOIS, *September* 18, 1799.

Considering the numerous family of the petitioner, and examining the generous sacrifices made by him in order to answer the views of government, when he was appointed commandant for the new settlement of Portage des Sioux, where he commands and performs his duties with the greatest zeal, without enjoying the annual salary granted by his Majesty to all civil commandants of posts; as much for these motives as in consideration of his great age, I do grant to him and his heirs the land he solicits, if it is not prejudical to any person; and the surveyor Don Antonio Soulard shall put the interested party in possession of the quantity of eight thousand eight hundred arpents of land in superfice, solicited for, in the places indicated; which being done, he shall draw a plat of survey, to be delivered to the interested party, with his certificate, to enable him to obtain the concession and title in form from the intendant general, to whom alone corresponds the distributing and granting all classes of land of the royal domain.

CARLOS DEHAULT DELASSUS.

Registered by request of the interested party.—(Book No. 2, pages 21, 22, and 23, No. B.)

SOULARD.

The deputy surveyor, Don Santiago Mackay, will survey the quantity of six thousand eight hundred arpents of land, which remains to be taken to complete the total of the above title, in a vacant place of the domain called La Pointe Basse de la Rivière au Sel, (Salt River Bottom,) situated at least one hundred and eighty miles from this town; which tract of land is evidently in the domains of his Majesty, and consequently can be prejudicial to no one.

ANTONIO SOULARD.

St. Louis, *December* 5, 1803.

St. Louis, *March* 15, 1799.

I have already made known to you that several creole inhabitants of the neighboring American side had manifested to me the wish of forming a village at the place called La Portage des Sioux, situated above the Missouri, and at a little distance from Illinois river; considering this settlement as very advantageous in drawing to us a population analogous to the one wanted in this country, besides being almost in view of the military post which the Americans intend to form at the place called Paysa. This is an advantage which it is prudent to foresee, and which must be most important for the future. Furthermore, I do consider that this same settlement will be a respectable guard, which may put a stop to the depredations often committed by the nations of Indians of the rivers Illinois and Upper Mississippi, upon the plantations in the interior of the country. Owing to these considerations, and knowing that you enjoy the esteem and confidence of the people in question, that you know them, and have lived a long time with them, I do entreat you and recommend to you, in the name of government, to employ yourself in encouraging, silently, the said inhabitants to execute their project, and put yourself at their head, if it is possible to you, and act as their commandant, giving you all the facilities in my power to place them on the most convenient spot to form their village, and assign lands to them for cultivation, in proportion to the faculties of each of them, in such a manner as to collect the greatest number of people possible, giving to them, however, just what is necessary to live with ease and be forever contented.

Having no doubt, sir, after your verbal promise, that you will employ yourself to fulfill, for the greatest advantage of the government, what I propose to you, I have given orders to Mr. Antonio Soulard, commissioned surveyor, to be ready, at your first demand, to go with you on the spot where it is fit the village in question should be, to have the lines marked, and to execute two plats of survey, conformably, as much as possible, to the instructions he has received from me, for the one to be delivered to you; and the other to remain deposited in the archives of this government.

I think, sir, that if, as I hope, you succeed in accomplishing what I have proposed, you will have confidence in the generosity of a government which has never left without reward any services rendered. The service in question is important, and I do flatter myself that you will have but to congratulate yourself for having employed yourself in it.

May God keep you under his holy guard.

ZENON TRUDEAU.

Mr. François Saucier.

A true translation. St. Louis, October 23, 1832.

JULIUS DE MUN.

Survey.—Land of François Saucier, of six thousand eight hundred arpents in superficie, situated in the Salt river bottom, at about forty leagues northwest of St. Louis, surveyed December 26, 1805, having to carry the chain J. B. Taillon and Jos. Recollet, who were sworn as the law directs. First line south 45° west; the trees in the lines are marked F. S. Point of departure on the bank of the Mississippi, a lynn tree; at — arpents, entered in a prairie, about the middle of which are five or six oaks, 26 arpents; at 35 arpents, went through hills several arpents; at 40 arpents, a red oak; at 68 arpents, a white oak. Second line east 45° south, at 20 arpents, a nut tree; at 40 arpents, a lynn tree; at 50 arpents, crossed Salt river, running west ¼ northwest and east ¼ southeast; from 50 to 85 arpents, prairie; at 100 arpents, a white oak and little river of the Prairie Gras. Third line north 45° east, at 20 arpents, a white oak; at 46 arpents, crossed Salt river, a white oak; the river runs west-northwest and east-southeast. The little river of Prairie Gras (Fat Prairie) running almost as the line; at 68 arpents, near the Mississippi, a lynn tree. Fourth line north 45° west, to join the point of departure.

FRÉMON DELAURIERE, *Deputy Surveyor.*

Truly translated. St. Louis, November 2, 1833.

JULIUS DE MUN.

Saline, *February* 15, 1806.

My Dear Soulard: I avail myself of this opportunity to send you the returns of the surveys I have made. I start to-morrow to finish what remains, in spite of the alarms caused now and then by the Indians; but at all events we shall be five men, well armed, and I hope that we shall not be taken so unawares that we cannot defend ourselves; besides, it must be done, Indians or no Indians. In places

so remote, and without direct communication with the settlements, I do not know when I shall be able
forward the returns of
it shall be as soon as possible — [Here the paper is torn off and missing.]
log always un
can hardly ho
yet about eight days' work, and it would be already done if I had not been obliged to come back, on account of the Indians, the first time I went to survey tho Bay de Charles.

By this same opportunity I write to Labeaume to send me a boat. If there is anything new in your quarter let me know by that opportunity; you will confer an obligation on one who is always your friend and faithful deputy.

FRÉMON DELAURIERE.

Mr. ANTOINE SOULARD, *Surveyor General, St. Louis.*

Truly translated. St. Louis, November 2, 1833.

JULIUS DE MUN.

No.	Name of original claimant.	Quantity, in arpents.	Nature and date of claims.	By whom granted.	By whom surveyed, date, and situation.
16	François Saucier.	7,800, it being the balance of 8,800, of which 1,000 have been confirmed.	Concession, Sept. 18, 1799.	Carlos Dehault Delassus.	6,800 arpents by Frémon Delauriere, December 26, 1805, on Salt river bottom.

Evidence with reference to minutes and records.

May 2, 1806.—The board met agreeably to adjournment. Present: the Hon. John B. C. Lucas and Clement B. Penrose, esq.

François Saucier, claiming 8,800 arpents, situate on the Mississippi, district of St. Charles, produces a concession from Charles D. Delassus, without any condition expressed in the same, dated September 18, 1799; and a survey of 1,000 arpents, dated January 30, 1804, and certified February 15, 1804; and another survey of 1,000, dated May 1, 1805.

The same questions were here put to Anthony Soulard, (see David Delaunay, claiming 800 arpents,) who gave the same answers. It was further proved to the satisfaction of the board that claimant is the father of a family, composed of himself, wife, and about fifteen children; was commandant of the Portage des Sioux for about eight years, for which he received no other compensation than the perquisites of office, which were trifling and seldom paid; and further, that he claims no other land in his own name in the Territory but a farm of 400 arpents, now under cultivation. The board not being still satisfied, required further proofs of the date of the above concession, which were not adduced. The board reject this claim.—(See book No. 1, page 271.)

August 18, 1810.—Board met. Present: Clement B. Penrose and Frederick Bates, commissioners.

François Saucier, claiming 8,800 arpents of land.—(See book No. 1, page 271.) It is the opinion of the board that this claim ought not to be confirmed.—(See book No 4, page 464.)

October 9, 1832.—The board met pursuant to adjournment. Present: L. F. Linn, W. Updyke, and F. R. Conway, commissioners.

François Saucier, claiming 8,800 arpents of land, of which 1,000 arpents are confirmed.—(See minutes book, No. 1, page 271; No. 4, page 464; record book C, page 248. For confirmation of 1,000 arpents, see Bates's Decisions, page 41.)

Produces a paper purporting to be a concession from C. D. Delassus to François Saucier, dated September 18, 1799; also a survey of 6,800 arpents, (part of said concession,) executed December 26, 1805, and certified by Antoine Soulard on the 20th of December, 1817; also an original letter of Zenon Trudeau to F. Saucier, dated March 15, 1799.

Pascal Cerré, duly sworn, saith that the signature to the petition is the handwriting of François Saucier; that the signature to the concession is the handwriting of C. D. Delassus; that the signature to the survey is the handwriting of Frémon Delauriere, deputy surveyor; and that the signature to the certificate of survey is the handwriting of Antoine Soulard, surveyor general; that the signature to the above-mentioned letter is the handwriting of Zenon Trudeau.—(See book No. 6, page 15.)

March 13, 1833.—The board met pursuant to adjournment. Present: L. F. Linn, A. G. Harrison, commissioners.

In the case of François Saucier, claiming balance of 8,800 arpents of land, (see page 15 of this book, No. 6,) claimant produces a paper purporting to be a commission from Soulard, appointing Charles Frémon Delauriere his deputy surveyor; also, a paper purporting to be a letter from said Delauriere to A. Soulard, dated February 15, 1806, and receipt of same by Soulard, and signed by B. Cousins as witness. M. P. Le Duc and Albert Tison, being duly sworn, say that the signatures to the receipt are in the respective handwriting of A. Soulard and B. Cousins.

Charles Frémon Delauriere, being duly sworn, says that the survey already produced is one of those included among the surveys mentioned in the above letter; that the survey was executed at the time it bears date; that there was great difficulty and danger in executing surveys; that he was twice repulsed by the Indians, and that the third time he went up he could not execute several of the surveys, being prevented by Indians of the Sac and Fox nations, although he and his companions were well armed; that surveyors were very scarce, and it was difficult to procure any one to make a survey; that there was not half the number of surveyors necessary to execute the surveys that were then to be made.—(See book No. 6, page 118.)

November 2, 1833.—The board met pursuant to adjournment. Present: L. F. Linn, A. G. Harrison F. R. Conway, commissioners.

In the case of François Saucier, claiming 8,800 arpents of land, (see pages 15 and 118 of this book, No. 6,) the following affidavit of Soulard is to be incorporated, by order of the board, with the other testimony.

I hereby certify that Colonel Charles Dehault Delassus, heretofore lieutenant governor of the province of Louisiana, made a grant of eight thousand eight hundred arpents of land to Mr. Francis Saucier, formerly commandant of the establishment of Portage des Sioux. That said grantee made an application at my office, while I exercised the duties of special surveyor of the establishments of the province of Upper Louisiana, under the Spanish government, to have his land under said concession surveyed, which said survey was prevented from being made of the totality of said concession or land, by a variety of circumstances, which rendered said survey at that time inconvenient. That it is particularly within my knowledge that said Mr. Saucier, while formerly an inhabitant of the village of St. Charles, was invited by the late lieutenant colonel, Don Zenon Trudeau, predecessor of the lieutenant governor, Delassus, to quit his situation at said village, and to fix his residence at Portage des Sioux, in order that he might, by his influence, draw to that settlement as many inhabitants as possible. That he did comply with the invitation without consulting his interest, and that the post of Portage des Sioux, established by his efforts, remained under his command until the change of government, without producing to him the smallest emolument. I declare, also, that it is a matter of notoriety that Mr. Francis Saucier is a native of Louisiana. That his father, who was a captain in the troops of the French marine, was the officer under whose direction Fort Chartres was finished; that said François Saucier is the officer who was charged with the surrender of Fort Massac to the English; that he is the father of a family of twenty-two children; that he is poor, and almost eighty years of age; and that he has never obtained any other favor of the Spanish government than the concession heretofore mentioned, and a small quantity of land, being a part of the common field which the inhabitants of Portage des Sioux have a right to cultivate.

ANT. SOULARD.

St. Louis, *December* 19, 1817.

Territory of Missouri, *county and township of St. Louis, sct.*

Be it remembered, that on the nineteenth day of December, A. D. one thousand eight hundred and seventeen, before me, the undersigned, F. M. Guyol, one of the justices of the peace in and for the county and township aforesaid, personally appeared Antoine Soulard, who being duly sworn according to law, made oath that the above affidavit, by him made, contains the truth, the whole truth, and nothing but the truth. St. Louis, this day, month, and year above written.

F. M. GUYOL, *J. P.* [L. S.]

Frederick Bates, secretary, exercising the government of the Territory of Missouri.

To all whom it may concern: Be it known that F. M. Guyol is and was on the 19th instant a justice of the peace within and for the county of St. Louis, in the Territory of Missouri, regularly commissioned. In testimony whereof, I have hereunto affixed the seal of the Territory. Given under my hand, at St. Louis, the 23d day of December, A. D. 1817, and of the independence of the United States the forty-second.—(See book No. ——, page ——.)

FREDERICK BATES.

November 1, 1833.—The board met pursuant to adjournment. Present: L. F. Linn, F. R. Conway, A. G. Harrison, commissioners.

François Saucier, claiming 7,800 arpents of land, it being the balance of 8,800 arpents, of which 1,000 have been confirmed.—(See page —— of this book. For confirmation, see Bates's Decisions, p. 41.)

The board are unanimously of opinion that 7,800 arpents of land, being the balance of the said 8,800 arpents, ought to be confirmed to the said François Saucier, or his legal representatives, according to the concession.—(See book No. 6, page 292.)

L. F. LINN,
F. R. CONWAY.
A. G. HARRISON,

No. 17.—C. D. Delassus, *claiming* 30,000 *arpents.*

To Don Zenon Trudeau, lieutenant colonel in the royal army, captain of the regiment of infantry of Louisiana, lieutenant governor of the settlements of Illinois and dependencies, &c.:

Don Carlos Dehault Delassus, lieutenant colonel, attached to the regiment of infantry of Louisiana, and for the present civil and military commandant of the post of New Madrid and dependencies, &c, states to you, that having made a demand of a tract of land of the royal domain proportionate only to a part of his means, which tract you have granted to him in the year 1796, conformably to the orders of the governor, the Baron de Carondelet, dated the 8th of May, of the year 1793, he now solicits again your justice, that you may be pleased to grant to him, for the complement of his means, (conformably to the said orders,) the quantity of thirty thousand arpents in superficie on the vacant lands of the royal domain, that as soon as circumstances do permit, and the occupations of the royal service do not hinder him, which is the case at the present moment, he may cause them to be surveyed, and use them to establish, if possible, two manufactories, (one for making soap and the other for a tan-yard,) which, if he can succeed, besides being profitable to himself, will be of great utility to the public in procuring soap and leather much cheaper than at the present prices, having to bring them from Europe and in small quantities from the Americans.

May God preserve your life many years.

CARLOS DEHAULT DELASSUS.

St. Louis of Illinois, *February* 8, 1798.

St. Louis of Illinois, *February* 10, 1798.

Being satisfied that the land solicited is of the King's domain, the surveyor, Don Antonio Soulard, shall put the interested party in possession; after which, he will make a proces verbal of his survey, to serve in soliciting the concession from the governor general of the province, to whom I give information that the individual finds himself in circumstances that deserve this favor.

ZENON TRUDEAU.

I send you back the primitive titles of the concession granted to Mr. François Vallé, of St. Genevieve, who has retroceded it to Mr. Dodge, and of which he (Dodge) has ceded the half to Mr. Tardiveau, who has made a donation of it to you. I send it with the examination *(visa)* and approbation you desire.

By this opportunity I have written to Mr. Zenon Trudeau to grant to you the tract where you will have made the discovery of lead mines, with adjacent lands in sufficient quantity for the working of said mines; provided, however, they were not previously granted to others.

Your son-in-law and your son will have also, as you wish it, a plantation in such a part of Illinois as they will choose, and of an extent proportionate to the culture and establishments they propose to form. This will serve as an answer to your letter No. 3.

May God keep you under his holy guard.

EL BARON DE CARONDELET.

New Orleans, *May* 8, 1793.

Nota.—This is the translation of a copy of a letter written in French, and certified a true copy of the original in the records by M. P. Le Duc, recorder, on the 27th of February, 1806.

Land of Charles Dehault Delassus, of 30,000 arpents, situated on Salt river, at about three leagues above its mouth; surveyed on the 2d of January, 1806. Having to carry the chain, J. B. Taillon, Joseph Récolet, and F. Duchouquet, who have been sworn according to law. The line trees are marked C D.

First line S. 22½° E.—Point of departure a red oak, at 48 arpents a sycamore, at 60 arpents a red oak, at 80 arpents a red oak, at 100 arpents an elm, at 130 arpents an elm, at 150 arpents a honey locust.

Second line W. 22½° S.—At 20 arpents a black walnut; at 40 arpents a black walnut, small creek; at 70 arpents a hickory; at 90 arpents a lynn tree; at 120 arpents a red oak, pine fork; at 140 arpents a white oak; at 180 arpents a white oak; at 200 arpents a walnut tree.

(At some arpents to the south is the lick *(glaise sans dessein)* of B. Spencer.)

Third line N. 22½° W.—A walnut tree; at 5 arpents an elm; at 70 arpents a hickory; at 115 arpents a cottonwood tree, crosses Salt river; at 150 arpents a honey locust.

Fourth line E. 22½° N.—200 arpents to strike the point of departure.

FRÉMON DELAURIERE.

A true translation. St. Louis, October 24, 1832.

JULIUS DE MUN.

No.	Name of original claimant.	Quantity, in arpents.	Nature and date of claim.	By whom granted.	By whom surveyed, date, and situation.
17	Charles Dehault Delassus.	30,000	Concession, February 10, 1798.	Zenon Trudeau..	Frémon Delauriere, Jan. 2, 1806. On Salt river, three leagues above its mouth.

Evidence with reference to minutes and records.

October 10, 1808.—Board met. Present: The Hons. Clement B. Penrose and Frederick Bates.

Charles Dehault Delassus, claiming 30,000 arpents of land where the same may be found vacant, produces an official letter from the Baron de Carondelet to Dehault Delassus, father of claimant, stating that he had ordered Zenon Trudeau to grant to him a certain tract of land which he had requested, and also that a plantation sufficiently large for their cultivation and establishment should be granted to his son-in-law and son, dated May 8, 1793. Laid over for decision.—(See book No. 3, page 286.)

June 18, 1810.—Board met. Present: John B. C. Lucas, Clement B. Penrose, and Frederick Bates, commissioners.

Charles Dehault Delassus, claiming 30,000 arpents of land, (see book No. 3, page 286,) produces also to the board a concession for the same, dated February 10, 1798, from Zenon Trudeau, lieutenant governor. It is the opinion of the board that this claim ought not to be confirmed.—(See book No. 4, page 387.)

October 9, 1832.—The board met pursuant to adjournment. Present: L. F. Linn, W. Updyke, F. R. Conway, commissioners.

Charles Dehault Delassus, claiming 30,000 arpents of land, (see record book B, pages 515 and 516; book No. 3, page 286, and No. 4, page 387,) produces a paper purporting to be an original concession from Zenon Trudeau to C. D. Delassus, dated February 10, 1798; also a survey, executed January 2, 1806, signed by Frémon Delauriere.

Pascal Cerré, duly sworn, says that the signature to the petition is the handwriting of C. D. Delassus; that the signature to the concession is the handwriting of Zenon Trudeau; that the signature to the certificate of record of concession is the handwriting of Antoine Soulard; that the signature to the survey is the handwriting of Frémon Delauriere. Claimant refers to a letter which was offered in evidence under the claim of Pierre Delassus Deluziere, dated May 8, 1793, signed El Baron de Carondelet, and addressed to said Delassus.—(See book No. 6, page 16.)

November 27, 1832.—The board met pursuant to adjournment. Present: L. F. Linn, F. R. Conway, commissioners.

In the case of Carlos Dehault Delassus, claiming 30,000 arpents, (see page 16 of this book, No. 6,) Albert Tison and Charles Frémon Delauriere, being duly sworn, prove the handwriting of Carlos Dehault

Delassus to a petition dated February 8, 1798; also the handwriting of Zenon Trudeau to a decree of concession dated February 10, 1798. The above-named witnesses say that the claimant had no salary as lieutenant governor, and received but sixty dollars a month as his pay for his rank in the army; they also say that he acted as civil and military governor and judge; that his jurisdiction and command extended from Arkansas to the northern extremity of the Spanish possessions on the western side of the Mississippi; that he was highly considered by the Spanish government; and that his administration of the government of Upper Louisiana gave general satisfaction to the people under his command. Albert Tison states that Carlos Dehault Delassus was an officer in the European Spanish army; that by his good military conduct and the great bravery he showed in the several engagements wherein he fought he acquired great honor; that knowing the destitute circumstances of his father in this country, he was at his own request promoted from the Guard Wallon to the stationary regiment of Louisiana. The above-named Frémon Delauriere acknowledges his own handwriting to a plat and certificate of survey. The above papers have already been offered in evidence in this case.—(See book No. 6, page 56.)

March 13, 1833.—The board met pursuant to adjournment. Present: L. F. Linn, A. G. Harrison, commissioners.

In the case of C. Dehault Delassus, claiming 30,000 arpents of land, claimant refers the board of commissioners to the testimony given by C. F. Delauriere in the case of François Saucier, claiming 8,800 arpents of land.—(See book No. 6, page 118.)

March 15, 1833.—The board met pursuant to adjournment. Present: Lewis F. Linn, A. G. Harrison, F. R. Conway, commissioners.

In the case of Carlos Dehault Delassus, claiming 30,000 arpents of land. John Baptiste Vallé, being duly sworn, says that he is seventy-two years of age; that he was born in St. Genevieve; that under the Spanish government a concession, although not surveyed, was nevertheless considered as lawful property, transferable by sale or otherwise; that previous to 1800 the Spanish government had no other means of rewarding its officers or other persons for their services but by granting them lands; that to his knowledge it never happened that a grant made by a sub-delegate was ever refused by a governor general. The deponent has no doubt that Mr. Delassus, as being lieutenant governor, could have obtained any quantity of land he would have applied for. He further states that a grant obtained from a lieutenant governor was considered in this country as equivalent to a complete title; that when a concession for a stock farm (vacherie) was obtained, although it was not settled in due time, said concession was nevertheless considered as the property of the grantee, it being known there was imminent danger to settle such places on account of the Indians; that it was the policy of the government to encourage as much as possible those remote settlements; that to his knowledge the government never sold an arpent of land, even in Morales's time; that the regulations of O'Reily, Morales, and Gayoso, were never in force in this country. Witness further says that under the Spanish government the communication between this country and New Orleans was very difficult and very expensive, and that prevented people from sending their papers to said place, inasmuch as the approbation of the governor general was then considered as mere formality, and did not add, as they thought, any value to their concessions; that it was the custom to publish the regulations in the towns at the sound of the drum or at the church door, and that Morales, Gayoso, and O'Reily's regulations were never so published in St. Genevieve, where he, the deponent, was born and always lived; that he had several concessions, and never applied for the governor general's approbation, although he conversed on the subject in 1795 with the Baron de Carondelet, who told him that if he wanted more land to ask for it to the lieutenant governor. The deponent thinks it is probable that if the inhabitants had not thought their property secured by the treaty a number of them would have left the country and followed the Spanish government.—(See book No. 6, page 125.)

November 2, 1833.—The board met pursuant to adjournment. Present: L. F. Linn, A. G. Harrison, F. R. Conway, commissioners.

Charles Dehault Delassus, claiming 30,000 arpents of land.—(See pages 6, 16, 56, 118, and 125, of this book.) The board are unanimously of opinion that this claim ought to be confirmed to the said Charles Dehault Delassus, or his legal representatives, according to the concession.—(See book No. 6, page 293.)

L. F. LINN.
F. R. CONWAY.
A. G. HARRISON.

No 18.—F. Caillou, *claiming* 1,600 *arpents.*

To Don Charles Dehault Delassus, lieutenant colonel attached to the stationary regiment of Louisiana, and lieutenant governor of the same province:

François Caillou, one of the oldest inhabitants of this town, father of a family, wishes to make an establishment in this Upper Louisiana: therefore he has recourse to your goodness, praying that you be pleased to grant him sixteen hundred arpents of land in superficie, to be taken on the vacant lands of the King's domain, in a convenient place, where he may with advantage cultivate the land and raise all kinds of cattle. Favor which the petitioner presumes to expect of your justice.

his
FRANÇOIS ⋈ CAILLOU.
mark.

St. Louis, *January* 2, 1800.

St. Louis of Illinois, *January* 3, 1800.

Considering that the petitioner has been a long time settled in this country; that he is father of a family, and possesses sufficient means to improve the lands which he solicits, I grant to him and his heirs the land he solicits, provided it is not prejudicial to any person, and the surveyor, Don Antonio Soulard, shall put the party interested in possession of the quantity of land he asks for, on a vacant place of the royal domain; and when this is executed he shall make out a plat of his survey, delivering the same to said party, with his certificate, in order that it shall serve him to obtain the concession and title in form from the intendant general, to whom alone belongs, by royal order, the distributing and granting all classes of lands of the royal domain.

CARLOS DEHAULT DELASSUS.

Truly translated. St. Louis, November 1, 1833

JULIUS DE MUN.

IN THE TOWN OF ST. LOUIS OF ILLINOIS, *August* 12, 1800.

For want of a notary public in said town, before me, Don Carlos Dehault Delassus, lieutenant colonel and lieutenant governor of this Upper Louisiana, and in presence of the assisting witnesses, Don Josef Hortiz and Don Francisco Valois, personally appeared Francisco Caillou, an inhabitant of this same town, who, by these presents, declares and confesses to have this day sold, made over, transferred, and abandoned, as much for the present as forever, and promises to give full enjoyment and guaranty against all debts, dower, mortgage, inhibitions, substitutions, and generally against all whatsoever, to Don Augustin Chouteau, of this town, here present, who stipulates, accepts, and acquires for himself, his heirs, or others who may represent his right, a quantity of land of eleven hundred arpents in superficie, being a part of a concession granted to me, for one thousand six hundred arpents in superficie, by the lieutenant governor of this Upper Louisiana, dated January 3d of this present year. I do bind myself to put the above-named Augustin Chouteau in possession of the said eleven hundred arpents of land as soon as they shall be surveyed, and the figurative plat of survey be delivered to me; all which is done in consideration of the price and sum of one hundred and forty dollars, which the aforesaid purchaser has counted to me to my satisfaction; and, for the better securing the above-mentioned sum received by me, I do deliver to him the petition which I have presented to obtain the said land, below which is the decree of the aforesaid lieutenant governor. And the purchaser gives himself for contented and satisfied, without making any retention or reservation, making the acquisition according and conformably to the laws. In testimony whereof, the seller promises, &c., obliges himself, &c.; and not knowing how to sign, he made a cross for his mark, after lecture was made, and Don Augustin Chouteau, and assisting witness have signed with me, the aforesaid lieutenant governor. Date as above.

One cross for Francisco Caillou.
AUGUSTIN CHOUTEAU.

FRANCISCO VALOIS.
JOSEPH HORTIZ.

CARLOS DEHAULT DELASSUS.

Don Carlos Dehault Delassus, lieutenant colonel in the royal army, and lieutenant governor of this Upper Louisiana:

I do certify that the present copy is conformable to the original, which is deposited in the archives of this government under my command.

In testimony whereof, I do give these presents. Same date as above.

DELASSUS.

A true translation. St. Louis, October 20, 1832.

JULIUS DE MUN.

No.	Name of original claimant.	Quantity, in arpents.	Nature and date of claim.	By whom granted.	By whom surveyed, date, and situation.
18	François Caillou.	1, 600	Concession, January 3, 1800.	Carlos Dehault Delassus.	

Evidence with reference to minutes and records.

November 1, 1811.—Board met. Present: John B. C. Lucas, Clement B. Penrose, and Frederick Bates, commissioners.

Manuel Lisa, assignee of Francis Caillou, alias Cayou, claiming 500 arpents of land situate on the river Matis, district of St. Louis, produces a concession from Charles D. Delassus, lieutenant governor, to Francis Caillou, for 1,600 arpents, dated January 3, 1800, and three plats of survey, two of 400 arpents each, and one of 460 arpents, dated February 25, 1806. Francis Caillou claims 1,100 arpents of the above tract.

It is the opinion of the board that this claim ought not to be confirmed.—(See book No. 5, page 394.)

October 8, 1832.—The board met pursuant to adjournment. Present: Lewis F. Linn, William Updyke, F. R. Conway, commissioners.

François Caillou, claiming 1,600 arpents of land.—(See minute book No. 5, page 394; record book C, page 443.) Claimed under a concession from Carlos Dehault Delassus, said to be dated January 3, 1800.—(This concession is not produced.) Produces a deed certified by C. D. Delassus, dated August 12, 1800.

Pascal Cerré, duly sworn, saith that the signature to the certificate of the above deed is the handwriting of said Delassus.—(See book No. 6, page 13.)

November 27, 1832.—The board met pursuant to adjournment. Present: Lewis F. Linn, F. R. Conway, commissioners.

In the case of François Caillou, claiming 1,600 arpents of land, (entered October 8,) the original concession is produced.

M. P. Le Duc, being duly sworn, saith that the signature to the original concession is in the proper handwriting of Carlos Dehault Delassus.—(See book No. 6, page 53.)

November 2, 1833.—The board met pursuant to adjournment. Present: L. F. Linn, A. G. Harrison, F. L. Conway, commissioners.

François Caillou, claiming 1,600 arpents of land.—(See pages 13 and 53 of this book.) The board are unanimously of opinion that this claim ought to be confirmed to the said François Caillou, or to his legal representatives, according to the concession.—(See book No. 6, page 293.)

L. F. LINN.
F. R. CONWAY.
A. G. HARRISON.

No. 19.—THE SONS OF VASQUEZ, *claiming* 800 *arpents each.*

To Don Carlos Dehault Delassus, lieutenant governor of Upper Louisiana:

SIR: Benito, Antoine, Hypolite, Joseph, and Pierre Vasquez, all of them sons of Don Benito Vasquez, captain of militia of this town, brevetted by his Catholic Majesty, full of confidence in the generosity and benevolence of the government under which they are born, hope that you will be pleased to take into consideration the unfortunate situation in which they find themselves by the want of means of their family, which has been living for some time in distressed circumstances, and unable to give them the necessary education: therefore, wishing to procure to themselves in the course of time an independent existence, they think of forming an establishment which may one day insure their welfare. They flatter themselves, sir, that the services of their father will assure to them your protection, and the goodness of your heart will lead you to grant their demand; consequently, they supplicate you to grant to each of them eight hundred arpents of land in superficie, making altogether the quantity of four thousand arpents, which they wish to take in one or several places of the vacant lands of the King's domain, favor which your petitioners presume to hope of your justice.

BENITO VASQUEZ.
ANTOINE VASQUEZ.
HYPOLITE VASQUEZ.
JOSEPH VASQUEZ.
PIERRE VASQUEZ.

ST. LOUIS, *February* 16, 1800.

ST. LOUIS OF ILLINOIS, *February* 17, 1800.

After seeing the precedent statement, and the laudable motives which animate the petitioners, and considering that their family is one of the most ancient in this country, and worthy of all the benevolence of government, as much for their personal merit as on account of the services of the father of the petitioners, I do grant to said petitioners, for them and their heirs, the land which they solicit, if it is not prejudicial to any person, and the surveyor, Don Antonio Soulard, shall put the interested party in possession of the quantity of land asked for, in one or two vacant places of the royal domain; after which, he shall draw a plat which he shall deliver to the interested parties, with his certificate, to serve to them in obtaining the concession and title in form from the intendant general, to whom alone corresponds, by royal order, the distributing and granting all classes of lands of the royal domain.

CARLOS DEHAULT DELASSUS.

A true translation. St. Louis, October 27, 1832.

JULIUS DE MUN.

No.	Name of original claimant.	Quantity, in arpents.	Nature and date of claim.	By whom granted.	By whom surveyed, date, and situation.
19	The sons of Vasquez: Benito, Antoine Hypolite, Joseph, and Pierre Vasquez.	800 each.	Concession, 17th February, 1800.	Carlos Dehault Delassus.	

Evidence with reference to minutes and records.

August 25, 1806.—The board met agreeably to adjournment. Present: The Hon. John B. C. Lucas, and Clement B. Penrose, esq.

Rodolph Tillier, assignee of Benito Vasquez, junior, claiming 800 arpents of land situate in the district of St. Louis, produces a concession from Charles D. Delassus to the said Benito, Antoine, Hypolite, Joseph, and Pierre Vasquez, the children of Benito Vasquez, senior, for 800 arpents each, granted to them for the purpose of settling the said Benito Vasquez, junior, and educating his four younger brothers, who then were minors, and as a compensation for services rendered the Spanish government by Benito Vasquez, their father; said concession dated February 17, 1800; a survey of the aforesaid 800 arpents, dated February 27, 1806, and a deed of transfer of the same, executed by the aforesaid Benito Vasquez, junior, dated February 11, 1806. Hyacinthe St. Cir, being duly sworn, says that Benito Vasquez, senior, the father of the said Benito and brothers, told him, the witness, about five or six years ago, that he had received a concession for his children, of 800 arpents each; that the aforesaid Benito Vasquez, junior, was, at the time of obtaining said concession of the age of twenty-one years and upwards; that his father, who was a Spaniard by birth, was a confidential subject of the officers of government; that he acted for some time as commandant by interim, and witness believes never received any compensation for his services.

Charles Gratiot, being also duly sworn, says that the said Benito Vasquez, senior, is by birth a Spaniard; that he was the first militia captain, and acted sometimes as commandant by interim, and never received any pecuniary compensation for his services. The board reject this claim; they are satisfied that the said concession was granted at the time it bears date; they remark that the grant is expressly given to the children, as is said in the body of it, as a compensation for the public services of the father, and that they may locate and establish it, in two or three vacant places of the domain, when it shall be convenient.—(See book No. 1, page 491.)

May 22, 1808.—Board met. Present: Clement B. Penrose and Frederick Bates, commissioners.

Rodolph Tillier, assignee of Benito Vasquez, junior, claiming 800 arpents of land. Jacques Clamorgan, sworn, says that he knows that this land was given as compensation to Benito Vasquez, junior, for services rendered to the Spanish government by his father; that said Benito, the father, was a confidential person under said government, and a Spaniard by birth. Laid over for decision.

Antoine Vasquez claiming 800 arpents of the concession stated in the foregoing claim. Laid over for decision.

Hypolite Vasquez claiming 800 arpents of same concession. Laid over for decision.

Joseph Vasquez claiming 800 arpents of same concession. Laid over for decision.

Pierre Vasquez claiming 800 arpents of same concession. Laid over for decision.—(See book No. 4, page 67.)

September 22, 1810.—Board met. Present John B. C. Lucas, Clement B. Penrose, and Frederick Bates, commissioners.

Rodolph Tillier, assignee of Benito Vasquez, junior, claiming 800 arpents of land.—(See book No. 1, page 491; book No. 4, page 67.) It is the opinion of the board that this claim ought not to be confirmed. John B. C. Lucas, commissioner, declares that he does not concur in opinion with the former board in the present case, respecting the satisfaction which the said former board expresses, that the concession was issued at the time it bears date; (same decision on Antoine, Hypolite, Joseph, and Pierre Vasquez's claims.) (See book No. 4, page 502.)

October 9, 1832.—The board met pursuant to adjournment. Present: L. F. Linn, W. Updyke, F. R. Conway, commissioners.

The sons of Vasquez—Benito, Antoine, Hypolite, Joseph, and Pierre Vasquez—claiming 800 arpents of land each, under a concession dated 17th February, 1800, (see record book C, pages 474 and 475; book No. 1, page 491; No. 4, pages 67 and 502,) produces a paper purporting to be an original concession, dated 17th of February, 1800, from C. D. Delassus; also a plat of survey, dated 7th February, 1806, of 800 arpents.

Pascal Cerré, duly sworn, says that the signature to the concession is the handwriting of Delassus; that the signatures to the survey are in the handwriting of Mackay and Antoine Soulard.

November 2, 1833.—Board met pursuant to adjournment. Present: L. F. Linn, A. G. Harrison, F. R. Conway, commissioners.

The sons of Vasquez, each claiming 800 arpents of land, under a concession from Charles Dehault Delassus.—(See page 17 of this book.) The board remark that they can see no cause for entertaining the idea that the said concession was not issued at the time it bears date, as intimated in the minutes of the former commissioners. The board are unanimously of opinion that this claim ought to be confirmed to the said Benito, Antoine, Hypolite, Joseph, and Pierre Vasquez, or their legal representatives, according to the concession.—(See book No. 6, page 293.)

L. F. LINN.
F. R. CONWAY.
A. G. HARRISON.

No. 20.—Aaron Quick, *claiming* 800 *arpents of land.*

To Don Carlos Dehault Delassus, lieutenant governor of Upper Louisiana:

Sir: Aaron Quick has the honor to represent to you that, wishing to establish himself in the upper part of this province, where he has resided for some time, therefore he has recourse to the benevolence of this government, that you may be pleased to grant to him a concession of eight hundred arpents of land in superficie, to be taken along the river St. Ferdinand, bounded on one side by the land of E. Harington; on the other by the land of Ezechias Lard, adjoining on the two other sides to lands belonging to the King's domain. Favor which the petitioner presumes to hope of your justice.

AARON QUICK, his x mark.

St. Louis, *March* 19, 1801.

St. Louis of Illinois, *March* 20, 1801.

As we are assured that the petitioner has sufficient means to improve the lands he solicits for, I do grant to him and his heirs the land solicited by him, in case it does not carry prejudice to any person; and the surveyor, Don Antonio Soulard, shall put the interested in possession of the quantity of land asked by him, in a vacant place of the royal domain; and this being done, he shall draw a plat of survey which he shall deliver to said interested party, to serve to him to obtain (also with his certificate) the title in form from the intendant to whom alone corresponds, by royal order, the distributing and granting all classes of lands, &c.

CARLOS DEHAULT DELASSUS.

In my capacity of surveyor general of this Upper Louisiana, I do notify the interested party that the land described in his petition has already been taken, and that he must have an order from the lieutenant governor to obtain that the same quantity be measured for him in any other vacant part of the domain.

SOULARD.

St. Louis, *December* 17, 1803.

Having seen the above information, the interested may take the land mentioned in any other vacant part of the royal domain, being understood that it shall not be prejudicial to any person.

DELASSUS.

Translation of a certificate at the foot of the plat of survey, certified before Thomas F. Riddick, a justice of the peace

I do certify to all whom it may concern, that, at the above date, John Terrey was employed as my deputy surveyor, and that the said plat having been lost amongst other papers, the official return and registering could not take place before the delivery of the archives, to which I do certify in my ex-capacity.

ANTOINE SOULARD.

St. Louis, *March* 15, 1808.

Truly translated. St. Louis, December 3, 1832.

JULIUS DE MUN.

No.	Name of original claimant.	Quantity, in arpents.	Nature and date of claim.	By whom granted.	By whom surveyed, date, and situation.
20	Aaron Quick........	800	Concession March 20, 1801.	Carlos Dehault Delassus.	John Terrey, deputy surveyor, January 8, 1804; certified by Soulard, Mar. 15, 1808; Richwood, district of St. Genevieve.

Evidence with reference to minutes and records.

December 6, 1811.—Board met. Present: John B. C. Lucas, Clement B. Penrose, and Frederick Bates, commissioners.

Louis Labeaume, assignee of Albert Tison, assignee of Jacques St. Vrain, assignee of Aaron Quick, claiming 800 arpents of land, situate at Richwood, district of St. Genevieve, produces record of a concession from Delassus, lieutenant governor, to Quick, dated 20th March, 1801; record of a certificate from A. Soulard, that the land petitioned for is not vacant; record of a plat of survey, dated 20*th December*, 1803, (8th January, 1804;) certificate of survey from Soulard, dated 15th March, 1808; record of transfer from St. Vrain to Tison, dated 3d November, 1804.

It is the opinion of the board that this claim ought not to be confirmed.—(See book No. 5, page 484.)

October 9, 1832.—The board met pursuant to adjournment. Present: L. F. Linn, W. Updyke, F. R. Conway, commissioners.

Aaron Quick, claiming 800 arpents of land under a concession from C. D. Delassus, (see record book D, page 312; minutes book No. 5, page 484,) produces a paper purporting to be an original concession from Delassus, dated the 20th of March, 1801, with a certificate at the foot thereof, dated 18th December, 1803, signed A. Soulard, and an order at the foot of last-mentioned certificate, dated 20th December, 1803, and signed Carlos Dehault Delassus. Also produces a survey of 800 arpents, dated January 8, 1804, certified by Antoine Soulard the 15th of March, 1808.

Pascal Cerré, duly sworn, saith that the signatures to the above-mentioned papers are in the respective handwriting of Delassus and Soulard.—(See book No. 6, page 18.)

November 2, 1833.—The board met pursuant to adjournment. Present: L. F. Linn, A. G. Harrison, F. R. Conway, commissioners.

Aaron Quick, claiming 800 arpents of land.—(See page 18 of this book.)

The board are unanimously of opinion that this claim ought to be confirmed to the said Aaron Quick, or his legal representatives, according to the concession.—(See book No. 6, page 293.)

L. F. LINN.
F. R. CONWAY.
A. G. HARRISON.

No. 21.—Peter Chouteau, senior's, concession.

To Don Carlos Dahault Delassus, lieutenant colonel, attached to the stationary regiment of Louisiana, and lieutenant governor of the upper part of the same province:

Peter Choteau, lieutenant of militia and commandant of the fort of Carondelet in the Osage nation, has the honor to represent to you that formerly he obtained of Don Manuel Perez, lieutenant governor of this part of Illinois, a concession for a tract of land of 10 arpents in front by as many in depth, to be taken on the left side of the Missouri at about 20 arpents above St. Charles, upon which concession your petitioner has made all the preparatory works for the construction of a water grist mill which was to be built on the creek comprised in his concession. The lieutenant governor, Don Zenon Trudeau, was pleased to grant to your petitioner an augmentation to the said tract of 80 arpents in depth, all which is proven by the authentic documents necessary to this object.

The desire of profiting of the favor which the general government granted to all those who presented their titles to obtain their ratification caused your petitioner to address those same (above-mentioned documents) to a friend at New Orleans, to whom probably they have not been remitted, since he could not effectuate their presentation; the said original documents having not been registered in the archives of this government, your petitioner would be in great perplexity had he not to offer to you the attestation of Don Charles Tayon, captain commanding the village of St. Charles of Missouri, who, at that time, had a perfect knowledge of the original documents here above mentioned, by virtue of which your petitioner was authorized to begin an establishment for which he has made considerable sacrifices.

Full of confidence in the justice and generosity of the government, he hopes that, after the attestation you may be pleased to take from the commandant of St. Charles, you will have the goodness to ratify to him and in the same place the security of a property which he has been enjoying for more than ten years by virtue of the titles to him expedited by your predecessors, and of which he should wish that you would be pleased to order the surveyor of this Upper Louisiana to put him in possession in the following manner: To take two arpents below the creek comprised in his concession and above said creek all the space which is between the said creek and the next plantation by the depth of forty arpents, in order that, being possessed of the certificate of survey which shall be delivered to him, he may, if needed, have recourse to the superior authorities to obtain the ratification of the said title. The petitioner presumes to hope everything of your justice in the decision of the case which he has the honor to submit to your tribunal.

PIERRE CHOUTEAU.

St. Louis of Illinois, *November* 17, 1800.

St. Louis of Illinois, *November* 18, 1800.

Cognizance being taken of the foregoing statement, the sub-lieutenant in the royal army, and captain of militia, commandant of the post of St. Charles, shall give, in continuation, information of all he knows upon what is here asked.

DELASSUS.

In compliance with the foregoing order, I do inform the lieutenant governor that the statement of Don Pierre Chouteau is, in all, conformable to truth, having had a full knowledge of the titles mentioned by him in his petition, as well as of the considerable works he has done on the said land, of which he has always been acknowledged as the proprietor.

CHARLES TAYON.

St. Louis, *November* 25, 1800.

St. Louis of Illinois, *November* 26, 1800.

Having seen the foregoing information, and the just rights stated by Don Pedro Chouteau, to whom an unexpected accident has deprived of his title of concession, and considering that he has been for a long time proprietor of the land in question, the surveyor of this Upper Louisiana, Don Antonio Soulard, shall put him in possession, in the manner solicited, of the tract of land he petitions for, and the survey being executed, he shall draw a plat of said survey which he shall deliver to the interested party, to serve to said party to obtain the title in form from the general intendancy, to which tribunal alone correspond, by royal order, the distributing and granting all classes of lands of the royal domain.

CARLOS DEHAULT DELASSUS.

Registered at the desire of the interested.—(Book No. 2, pages 19, 20 and 21, No. 14.)

SOULARD.

Duly translated. St. Louis, November 3, 1832.

JULIUS DE MUN.

No.	Name of original claimant.	Quantity, in arpents.	Nature and date of claim.	By whom granted.	By whom surveyed, date, and situation.
21	Peter Chouteau, senior.	Not ascert'ed.	Concession, 26th November, 1800.	Carlos Dehault Delassus.	About 20 arpents above St. Charles.

Evidence with reference to minutes and records.

January 25, 1809.—Board met. Present: The Hon. Clement B. Penrose and Frederick Bates.

Pierre Chouteau, claiming a tract of land situate about twenty arpents above the town of St. Charles, commencing two arpents below a small creek on the Missouri, from thence up the river to the first land claimed, and forty arpents back, produces to the board a concession for the same from Don Carlos Dehault Delassus, lieutenant governor, dated 26th November, 1800; this tract including a tract of ten arpents front by ten arpents in depth at the mouth of said creek, formerly granted by François Cruzat, lieutenant governor, to Auguste Chouteau, by concession, bearing date 2d April, 1787, and registered in book of registry No. 4, folio 17, which concession is also produced by claimant. Said land granted for the purpose of building a mill within a year and a day, otherwise to be reunited to the domain.

Noel Mongrain, sworn, says that about twenty years ago claimant commenced the building of a mill-dam upon land about fifteen arpents above St. Charles; that deponent was himself employed by claimant during part of the summer; that he assisted in hauling large pieces of timber for constructing a mill; witness recollects that a great deal of clay was hauled for the making of the dam; that in the spring following said dam was swept away by a large flood. Auguste Chouteau being present declares that he gave all his right (to the one hundred arpents claimed by concession given to him) to his brother, the claimant. Laid over for decision.—(See book 3, page 442.)

July 14, 1810.—Board met. Present: John B. C. Lucas, Clement B. Penrose, and Frederick Bates, commissioners.

Peter Chouteau, claiming —— arpents of land.—(See book No. 3, page 442.) It is the opinion of the board that this claim ought not to be confirmed.—(See book No. 4, page 434.)

October 9, 1832.—The board met pursuant to adjournment. Present: L. F. Linn, W. Updyke, F. R. Conway, commissioners.

Peter Chouteau, sr., claiming a tract of land about twenty arpents above the town of St. Charles, (see book No. 3, page 442; No. 4, page 434; record book B, page 510,) produces a paper purporting to be an original concession from Delassus, dated 26th of November, 1800.

Pascal Cerré, duly sworn, says that the signatures to the above-mentioned concession are the signatures of the respective persons they proffer to be.—(See book No. 6, page 18.)

November 2, 1833.—The board met pursuant to adjournment. Present: L. F. Linn, A. G. Harrison, F. R. Conway, commissioners.

Peter Chouteau, sr., claiming a special location, situate twenty arpents above St. Charles.—(See page 18 of this book.)

The board are unanimously of opinion that this claim ought to be confirmed to the said Peter Chouteau, sr., or to his legal representatives, according to the concession.

The board adjourned until Monday next, at 9 o'clock a. m.—(See book No. 6, page 294.)

L. F. LINN.
F. R. CONWAY.
A. G. HARRISON.

No. 22.—Louis Lorimier, *claiming* 944 *arpents.*

To his Lordship the Governor General:

Don Louis Lorimier, inhabitant of this district, with the utmost respect, represents to your lordship that, wishing to establish himself in said district, he supplicates your lordship to be pleased to grant to him eighty arpents of land in front by one hundred in depth, opposite Cypress island, in Cape Girardeau, bounded on the two extremities by the domain; favor which he hopes to deserve of your lordship.

At the request of the interested party.

JUAN BARNO Y FERRUSOLA.

To his Lordship the Governor General:

I do consider the petitioner worthy of the favor which he solicits, there being united in him all the qualifications called for by the regulations (instruccion.)

THOMAS PONTELL.

New Madrid, *September* 1, 1795.

New Orleans, *October* 26, 1795.

The surveyor, Don Antonio Soulard, shall put the interested party in possession of forty arpents of land in front, of the eighty solicited by him, by one hundred in depth, in the place mentioned in the foregoing memorial, provided they are vacant and do not cause any prejudice to the surrounding neighbors, under the express condition to make the road and regular clearing in the peremptory term of one year, and this concession to be null and void if, at the expiration of the precise term of three years, the land is not settled, and during the said term it shall not be in his power to alienate the same; under which conditions the operations of survey shall be made in continuation, and remitted to me, in order to provide the interested party with the corresponding title in form.

EL BARON DE CARONDELET.

Don Antonio Soulard, surveyor general of the settlements of Upper Louisiana.

I do certify that on the 26th of October, of the present year, (by virtue of the foregoing decree and official letter of his excellency the governor general the Baron de Carondelet,) I have transferred myself on the land of Don Louis Lorimier, in order to survey the same conformably to his demand of eighty arpents in front by one hundred in depth, or eight thousand arpents in superficie, which measurement was made in presence of the proprietor and the adjoining neighbors, with the measure of Paris, of eighteen feet in length, according to the custom adopted in this province of Louisiana, and without regard to the variation of the needle, which is 7° 30′ east, as appears by the preceding figurative plat. Said land is situated at the same place as the village of Cape Girardeau; bounded on the north and west sides by the royal domain; on the south by the lands of the inhabitants, Edward Roberson, James Cox, Andrew Ramsay, and the said royal domain; and in order that it shall be available according to law, I deliver him the present, with the foregoing figurative plat, on which are noted the dimensions and the natural and artificial boundaries of said land.

ANTONIO SOULARD, *Surveyor General.*

ST. LOUIS OF ILLINOIS, *December* 11, 1797.

Truly translated. St. Louis, November 4, 1832.

JULIUS DE MUN.

No.	Name of original claimant.	Quantity, in arpents.	Nature and date of claim.	By whom granted.	By whom surveyed, date, and situation.
22	Louis Lorimer...	944, balance of 8,000.	Order of survey, Oct. 26, 1795.	The Baron de Carondelet.	Antonio Soulard, October 26, 1797; certified by him, December 11, 1797; Cape Girardeau.

Evidence with reference to minutes and records.

May 25, 1809.—Board met. Present: John B. C. Lucas, Clement B. Penrose, and Frederick Bates, commissioners.

Louis Lorimier, claiming 8,000 arpents of land, situate on the Mississippi, district of Cape Girardeau, produces to the board a petition for 80 by 100 arpents; a concession thereon from the Baron de Carondelet, governor general of Louisiana, for 40 arpents front by 100 arpents in depth, dated October 26, 1795; an official letter from the said governor general to Zenon Trudeau, lieutenant governor, ordering him to put claimant in possession of the other 40 arpents front by 100 arpents depth, petitioned for by him, dated January 26, 1797; a certified copy of a plat of survey of 8,000 arpents, taken October 26, 1797, certified December 11, 1797.

ANTOINE SOULARD,
Surveyor General of the Territory of Louisiana.

February 27, 1806.—Laid over for decision.

March 20, 1810.—Board met. Present: John B. C. Lucas, Clement B. Penrose, and Frederick Bates, commissioners.

Louis Lorimier, claiming 8,000 arpents of land.—(See book No. 4, page 73.) The following are translations of the several papers produced by claimant in support of his claim:

To his Lordship the Governor General:

Don Louis Lorimier, inhabitant of this district, with the greatest respect due to your lordship, represents that, wishing to establish himself in the same, petitions your lordship to be pleased to grant him eighty arpents of land in front by one hundred in depth, front to Cypress island, in Cape Girardeau, bounded on its two extremities by the King's domain; favor which he hopes to merit of your justice.

At the request of the party interested.

JUAN BARNO Y FERRUSOLA.

To his Lordship the Governor General:

I consider the petitioner worthy of the favor which he solicits for, being vested with the circumstances required by the instruction.

THOMAS PORTELL.

NEW MADRID, *September* 1, 1795.

NEW ORLEANS, *October* 26, 1795.

The surveyor, Don Anthony Soulard, shall establish the petitioner on forty arpents in front, of the eighty which he demands, by one hundred in depth, on the place mentioned by the above memorial, provided they are vacant, and do not prejudice the neighbors, under the express condition to make the road and regular improvements within the precise term of one year; and this concession to be declared null and void if, at the precise term of three, the said land is not established; and not being in his power to alienate the same within the said term, under which provisions the diligence of survey shall be made at the continuation, which will be remitted to me in order to provide the petitioner with the corresponding title in form.

EL BARON DE CARONDELET.

You will give order to Anthony Soulard to survey for Louis Lorimier the forty arpents more of land which he petitioned for on the place mentioned, and which will complete the eighty he had demanded; after which he is to demand it by memorial, which you will recommend with reference to this official letter, in order to give him the decree of concession. God preserve you many years.

EL BARON DE CARONDELET.

NEW ORLEANS, *January* 26, 1797.

Don ZENON TRUDEAU.—No. 1, Don Louis Lorimier.

Surveyed in virtue of the decree of his lordship the Baron de Carondelet, commandant general of the province, dated October 26, 1795, and of the official letter by him directed to the lieutenant governor, in date of February 26, 1797, by him transmitted to me The said tract surveyed October 26, 1797. The certificate of survey delivered the 11th of December the same year.

I certify the present extract to be faithfully copied and translated from the register A of the surveys in Cape Girardeau district, page 9, No. 1.

ANTOINE SOULARD, *Surveyor General, Territory of Louisiana.*

St. Louis, *February* 26, 1806.

Auguste Chouteau, sworn, says that claimant inhabited and cultivated the land claimed fifteen or twenty years ago, and continued so to do until eight years past; the last time witness saw the place claimed claimant had made considerable improvements on the land.

Marie Philip Le Duc, sworn, says that he saw claimant on the place claimed, inhabiting and cultivating, in 1799; that claimant was then erecting large buildings. Witness has seen the place claimed several times since, the last time in 1808; always found claimant on the land, inhabiting and cultivating and improving the same.

Anthony Soulard, sworn, says that the village of Cape Girardeau is on the tract claimed by Louis Lorimier as proprietor, and that the inhabitants claim after him. The board are unanimously of opinion that this claim ought not to be confirmed. Clement B. Penrose and Frederick Bates, commissioners, declaring that if this claim had not exceeded a league square they would have voted for its confirmation.

John B. C. Lucas, commissioner, states, as reasons of his opinion, that the order of survey or concession under date of October 26, 1795, does not appear to be registered; that the letter of office, under date of January 26, 1797, directed to Don Zenon Trudeau, is not an order directed by said Z. Trudeau to Anthony Soulard; and if it should be construed that the said order is of sufficient authority to make the survey, however, it does not appear that the said order bears registry. He further states that the quantity of land claimed under these two orders is more than the quantity usually allowed, agreeably to the laws, usages, and customs of the Spanish government, and that no ordinance or copy of ordinance has been shown or exhibited authorizing the governor to make decrees or orders for such quantity. Board adjourned till to-morrow nine o'clock, a. m.

JOHN B. C. LUCAS.
CLEMENT B. PENROSE.
FREDERICK BATES.

(See book No. 4, page 299, and following.)

October 10, 1832.—The board met pursuant to adjournment. Present: Lewis F. Linn, W. Updike, F. R. Conway, commissioners.

Louis Lorimier, claiming 8,000 arpents, of which 7,056 arpents have been confirmed; confirmation is prayed for the balance.—(See book No. 4, pages 73 and 299; record book E, pages 22 and 23; for confirmation, see Bates's Decisions, page 67.) Produces a paper purporting to be an original order of survey by the Baron de Carondelet, dated October 26, 1795; also a plat of survey executed October 26, 1797, and certified December 11, 1797, by A. Soulard.—(See book No. 6, page 19.)

November 4, 1833.—The board met pursuant to adjournment. Present: L. F. Linn, A. G. Harrison, F. R. Conway, commissioners.

Louis Lorimier, claiming 944 arpents of land, it being the balance of 8,000 arpents, of which 7,056 have been confirmed.—(See page 19 of this book; for confirmation, see Bates's Decisions, page 67.) The board are unanimously of opinion that 944 arpents of land ought to be confirmed to the said Louis Lorimier, or his legal representatives, according to the concession.—(See book No. 6, page 294.)

L. F. LINN.
F. R. CONWAY.
A. G. HARRISON.

No. 23.—C. D. Delassus, *claiming* 20,000 *arpents.*

To Don Zenon Trudeau, lieutenant colonel in the royal army, captain in the regiment of infantry of Louisiana, and lieutenant governor of the settlements of Illinois and dependencies, &c.:

Don Carlos Dehault Delassus, lieutenant colonel attached to the regiment of infantry of Louisiana, and civil and military commandant of the post of New Madrid, represents to you, that before taking possession of said command, he has come to this place to visit his family, with permission from the governor general of these provinces, El Baron de Carondelet, and at the same time to visit lands, having been apprised by the said governor that he had sent to you the necessary orders to grant lands to him, (to the petitioner,) said orders being dated 8th May, 1793, at the time his family arrived to settle themselves under the dominion of his Majesty.

The petitioner having visited the lands in the royal domain situated upon the waters of the river called De Cobre, (Cuivre river,) which he believes are vacant, and distant six miles to the westward of the river Mississippi, and thirty-nine miles, more or less, to the northwest of this post of St. Louis; and in another place called the *Rio de Sel,* (Salt river,) distant about twelve miles to the westward of the river Mississippi, and one hundred and thirty miles, more or less, to the northwest of this said post; and as these lands appear to him to be of a good quality for cultivation, he begs of you to be pleased to order the surveyor general of this jurisdiction to put him in possession, and to survey for him the quantity of twenty thousand arpents, divided in the two above-mentioned places as much as possible, which quantity is proportionate to one part of his means to improve it, according as the circumstances of the royal service shall permit him.

The petitioner prays God to keep your important life many years.

CARLOS DEHAULT DELASSUS.

St. Louis of Illinois, *June* 17, 1796.

Being certain that the land solicited belongs to the King's domain, the surveyor, Don Antonio Soulard, shall put the interested party in possession of it, and shall make a procès verbal of his survey in continuation to serve in soliciting the concession from the governor general of the province, whom I inform that the petitioner is in circumstances that deserve this favor.

ZENON TRUDEAU.

ST. LOUIS OF ILLINOIS, *June* 18, 1796.

Registered at the desire of the interested, fol. 21, 22, and 23, of book No. 1 of titles of concessions under my charge.

SOULARD.

Registered in our office, under date of 13th of the present month.

NARCISSUS BROUTIN, *Notary Public.*

NEW ORLEANS, *May* 16, 1807.

Don Antonio Soulard, surveyor general of Upper Louisiana.

I do certify that on the 15th of April of the present year (by virtue of the memorial of the interested, and of the annexed decree of the lieutenant governor of this Louisiana, dated June 18, 1796) I have transported myself upon one part of the lands of Don Carlos Dehault Delassus, lieutenant colonel in the royal army, and attached to the stationary regiment of Louisiana, civil and military commandant of the post of New Madrid, to execute the survey, according to one part of his petition, of 13,100 arpents in superficie: said survey was executed without the assistance of the interested, as appears from a letter dated December 17, 1797, which, to this effect, he sent to me from New Madrid, empowering me to represent his person in the surveys. In said letter he offers and promises to approve and confirm all I shall do on the subject, which document remains deposited in the surveyor's archives under my charge. Said survey has been executed in presence of the adjoining neighbor, and with the perch of Paris, of 18 feet in length, conformably to the custom adopted in this province of Louisiana, and without regard to to the variation of the needle, which is 7° 30′ E., as is evident by referring to the foregoing plat. Said land is situated at about six miles west of the river Mississippi, at fifteen to the northeast of the river Missouri, at eighteen miles to the northwest of the post of St. Charles, and thirty-nine miles in the same direction from this town of St. Louis. And to be available according to law, I do give the present, with the preceding figurative plat, in which are designated the dimensions and natural and artificial boundaries that surround said land. Said land is bounded as follows: to the north, by vacant lands of the royal domain; to the south, in part by the same domain cited above, the edge of Cuivre river, and land of Santiago Lewis; to the east and west, by vacant lands of the royal domain, &c.

ANTONIO SOULARD, *Surveyor General.*

ST. LOUIS OF ILLINOIS, *May* 20, 1801.

Truly translated. St. Louis, December 4, 1833.

JULIUS DE MUN.

No.	Name of original claimant.	Quantity, arpents.	Nature and date of claim.	By whom granted.	By whom surveyed, date, and situation.
23	Carlos Dehault Delassus, by his assignee, Madame Delore Sarpy.	*12,944	Concession, June 18, 1796.	Z. Trudeau	Antonio Soulard, 13,100 arpents; April 15, 1801, and certified May 20, 1801; on river Au Cuivre.

* Balance of 20,000 arpents.

Evidence with reference to minutes and records.

September 25, 1807.—The board met agreeably to adjournment. Present: The Hon. John B. C. Lucas' Clement B. Penrose, and Frederick Bates.

Madame Delore Sarpy, widow of John B. Sarpy, claiming 20,000 arpents of land, as assignee of Charles D. Delassus. Produces in support of said claim a concession from Zenon Trudeau, lieutenant governor, to the said Charles D. Delassus, dated June 18, 1796; also a copy of a survey for 13,100 arpents of land, surveyed April 15, 1801, and certified May 16, 1807; also a copy of a survey of 6,900 arpents, surveyed March 30, 1801, and certified May 16, 1807; also a deed of transfer from said Delassus to one John Cortez, attorney in fact for the said John B. Sarpy, dated January 30, 1804. On the objection of the agent, alleging antedate, and the want of being duly registered, and that the quantity is greater than was usually granted by the lieutenant governors, the board require other proof.—(See book No. 3, page 92.)

November 24, 1808.—Board met. Present: The Hon. John B. C. Lucas, Clement B. Penrose, and Frederick Bates.

Auguste Chouteau, attorney of Peter Fouche, attorney of Madame Delore Sarpy, representing Charles Dehault Delassus, claiming 20,000 arpents of land, 13,100 of which are situated on the river Cuivre, and 6,900 on the Saline river, district of St. Charles. Produces to the board a concession from Zenon Trudeau, lieutenant governor, to said Delassus, dated June 18, 1796, and registered with Narcissus Broutin, notary public at New Orleans, May 16, 1807; a plat of survey of 13,100 arpents, dated April 15, 1801, and certified May 20, 1801; also a plat of survey of 6,900 arpents, dated March 30, 1801, and certified May 20, same year; a deed of transfer from said Delassus to Lille Sarpy, dated January 30, 1804. The board in this claim refer to a certified copy of an official letter from the Baron de Carondelet to Zenon Trudeau, May 8, 1793; said copy on file with the recorder. Laid over for decision.—(See book No. 3, page 368.)

July 10, 1810.—Board met. Present: John B. C. Lucas, Clement B. Penrose, and Frederick Bates, commissioners.

Auguste Chouteau, attorney for Peter Foucho, attorney for Madame Delore Sarpy, representing Charles Dehault Delassus, claiming 20,000 arpents of land.—(See book No. 3, pages 92 and 368.) It is the opinion of the board that this claim ought not to be confirmed.—(See book No. 4, page 423.)

October 11, 1832.—The board met pursuant to adjournment. Present: Lewis F. Linn, W. Updike, F. R. Conway, commissioners.

Charles Dehault Delassus, by his assignee, Madame Delore Sarpy, claiming 20,000 arpents of land, of which 7,056 arpents have been confirmed.—(For confirmation see Bates's Decisions, page 40; for record of claim see book No. 6, page 499; minutes, No. 3, pages 93 and 368; book No. 4, page 423.) Produces a paper purporting to be an original concession from Zenon Trudeau, dated June 18, 1796; also a plat of survey executed April 15, 1801, and certified May 20, 1801, for 13,100 arpents. Refers to a letter dated May 8, 1793, purporting to be addressed by the Baron de Carondelet to Zenon Trudeau, already offered in evidence under the claim of P. Delassus Deluziere for 7,056 arpents.—(See book No. 6, page 20.)

November 4, 1833.—The board met pursuant to adjournment. Present: L. F. Linn, A. G. Harrison, F. R. Conway, commissioners.

Charles Dehault Delassus, claiming 12,944 arpents of land, it being the balance of 20,000 arpents, of which 7,056 have been confirmed.—(See page 20 of this book.) The board are unanimously of opinion that 12,944 arpents of land ought to be confirmed to the said Charles Dehault Delassus, or his legal representatives, according to the concession.—(See book No. 6, page 294.)

L. F. LINN.
F. R CONWAY.
A. G. HARRISON.

No. 24.—ANTOINE DUBREUIL, *claiming* 10,000 *arpents.*

To Don Carlos Dehault Delassus, lieutenant governor of Upper Louisiana.

SIR: Antoine Dubreuil, lieutenant of militia, inhabitant of this town, has the honor to state to you that, wishing to form an establishment advantageous to himself as well as to the inhabitants of this Upper Louisiana, in working the saline of the river Aux Bœufs, (Buffalo creek,) situated at about thirty leagues from this town, therefore, sir, the petitioner supplicates you to grant to him one hundred arpents square of lands on the said river, and to place them in such a manner as will appear to him more advantageous to the working of said saline. The petitioner will undertake said works as soon as he can raise the necessary provisions to sustain said works. The petitioner thinks he ought to observe to you that his family, one of the most ancient in this colony, having ever been employed but in a commercial way, has never had any concession of land. The petitioner, knowing the justice of your views, and the pleasure you take in favoring all establishments advantageous to this Upper Louisiana, presumes to hope that you will protect him in this undertaking, and that you will be pleased to grant to him his demand.

ANTOINE DUBREUIL.

ST. LOUIS, *December* 17, 1799.

IN THE TOWN OF ST. LOUIS OF ILLINOIS, *December* 19, 1799.

I, Don Carlos Dehault Delassus, lieutenant colonel in the royal army, lieutenant governor of Upper Louisiana, &c.

Having seen the statement on the other side, and considering the utility which will result to the public by having a saline worked at the above-mentioned place, I do grant to the petitioner the land he solicits; and as it is situated in a desert, where there are no settlements, and distant about thirty leagues from this town, he shall not be compelled to have it surveyed immediately, but as soon as some one will settle in said place, in which case he must have it done without delay; and Don Antonio Soulard, surveyor general of this Upper Louisiana, shall take cognizance of this title for his intelligence and government in what concerns him, that the petitioner may (after the survey is made) solicit the title in form from the governor general of these provinces of Louisiana.

CARLOS DEHAULT DELASSUS.

Registered by order of the lieutenant governor, folios 1 and 2 of book No. 1 of the titles of concessions.

ANTO. SOULARD.

Truly translated. St. Louis, November 21, 1832.

JULIUS DE MUN.

No.	Name of original claimant.	Quantity, arpents.	Nature and date of claim.	By whom granted.	By whom surveyed, date, and situation.
24	Antoine Dubreuil	10,000	Concession, December 19, 1799.	Carlos Dehault Delassus.	Frémon Delauriere, D. S., 24th February, 1806. On Buffalo creek, about 114 miles from St. Louis, on the Mississippi.

Evidence with reference to minutes and records.

November 13, 1811.—Board met. Present: John B. C. Lucas, Clement B. Penrose, and Frederick Bates, commissioners.

Antoine Dubreuil, claiming 10,000 arpents of land, situate on the river Aux Bœufs, district of St. Charles, produces a concession from Charles D. Delassus, lieutenant governor, dated December 19, 1799; a plat of survey of 1,000 arpents, dated February 24, 1806, signed Frémon Delauriere, deputy surveyor. It is the opinion of the board that this claim ought not to be confirmed.

November 21, 1832.—The board met pursuant to adjournment. Present: Lewis F. Linn, F. R. Conway, commissioners.

Antoine Dubreuil, claiming 10,000 arpents of land.—(See book 5, page 403; record book B, page 95; record of survey book B, page 95.)—Produces a paper purporting to be a concession from Charles Dehault Delassus, dated December 19, 1799, registered by Antoine Soulard. Albert Tison, duly sworn, says that the signature to concession is the handwriting of Charles Dehault Delassus; that the signature to the registering is that of Antoine Soulard; that the signature to petition is the handwriting of Antoine Dubreuil. Witness further saith that in December, 1803, he accompanied James Rankin, deputy surveyor, to survey this and other tracts of land; that three tracts were surveyed to the south of the above-mentioned tract, but were prevented of surveying the same, being driven away by a party of Indians. Witness, when he went on said land, saw some kettles which had been used in making salt, and the remains of salt furnaces, and the places where they had been digging for salt water. Witness understood that the said tract was afterwards surveyed by Frémon Delauriere, who resides in this country. David Delaunay, being duly sworn, saith that the signatures to the aforesaid paper are in the respective handwriting of the three individuals who signed it; that, to the best of his recollection, the claimant went, before the change of government, on said land to make an attempt in manufacturing salt, but was driven off by the Indians, and to the best of his belief it was in 1802.—(See book No. 6, pages 31 and 32.)

November 28, 1832.—The board met pursuant to adjournment. Present: Lewis F. Linn, F. R. Conway, commissioners.

To the case of Antoine Dubreuil, claiming 10,000 arpents of land, entered 21st instant, Charles Frémon Delauriere, being duly sworn, saith that in the year 1802, Antoine Dubreuil came to the witness's salt lick, and there made arrangement with him to assist said Dubreuil in settling his salt works on Buffalo creek; that he (witness) furnished said Dubreuil with ten salt kettles, besides oxen, carts, and three of his best men, among them was Benjamin Spencer, now deceased; they built a house for said Dubreuil on his concession at said Buffalo creek; also, erected his furnaces, and actually made salt, and lived on said place till about February, 1803, when they were driven away by the Indians, who killed the oxen, burnt the house, and broke several of the kettles, and the men who were at work there made their escape to said Delauriere's salt works; that several months afterwards said witness went down in a pirogue to have as much as he could of what the Indians left; he found but seven kettles, the others having been broken; saw the remains of the burnt buildings, and the furnaces destroyed. Witness further states that on the 24th February, 1806, he was applied to by Antoine Dubreuil to have his land surveyed, as said Dubreuil had no opportunity to have it surveyed before that time, having been several times driven off by the Indians; that he, said Delauriere, proceeded there, and surveyed said concession. He further saith that having examined the plat of the survey of said land on the record book B, page 95, he finds it to correspond exactly with the plat of his survey, returned to Antoine Soulard, surveyor general, with the exception of the figures 1,000 on the face of said survey and in the certificate, which he is sure is a mistake; that at that time there were in the whole province of Upper Louisiana but three salt works in operation; that salt was then very scarce, and worth six dollars a bushel; that in consequence of his working his saline, salt fell to three dollars a bushel; that the province of Upper Louisiana was dependent mainly on foreigners from the Ohio for their supply of salt. Witness further states that in the year 1805 he was appointed deputy surveyor, and officially acted as such in that year and in 1806.—(See book No. 6, page 62.)

November 4, 1833.—The board met pursuant to adjournment. Present: L. F. Linn, A. G. Harrison, F. R. Conway, commissioners.

Antoine Dubreuil, claiming 10,000 arpents of land.—(See pages 31 and 62 of this book.) The board are unanimously of opinion that this claim ought to be confirmed to the said Antoine Dubreuil, or his legal representatives, according to the concession.—(See book No. 6, page 295.)

Conflicting claims.

By letter dated June 8, 1833, the persons here below named give notice to the board that they hold land lying on the above claim, by purchase of the United States. Alexander Allison, S. ½ section 29, township 54 N., range 1 W., 320 acres. John Jordon, W. ½ of NE. quarter section 31, township 54 N., range 1 W., 301$\frac{8}{10}$ acres. Andrew Jordon, SE. quarter section 31, township 54 N., range 1 W., 160. Robert Jordan, by his administrator, NE. quarter section 36, township 54, range 2 W. William Robert and Joseph McConnel, NW. quarter section 7, township 53 N., range 1 W., 153$\frac{83}{100}$. William Robert and Joseph McConnel, SW. quarter section 7, township 53 N., range 1 W., 150$\frac{88}{100}$. James Templeton, E. half section 5, township 53 N., range 1 W. Andrew Venable, (John Venable,) NE. quarter section 6, township 53 N., range 1 W. Joseph Carroll, (James Templeton,) SW. quarter section 4, township 53 N., range 1 W. David Watson, NE. quarter section 29, township 54 N., range 1 W. John Wamsley and Joseph Burbridge, under Abraham Thomas, SE. quarter section 30, township 54 N., range 1 W. Wm. Parks, under James Jordan, NW. quarter section 29, township 54 N., range 1 W. James Jones, under James Jordan, fractional section 20, township 54 N., range 1 W. Harrison Boothe, under James Boothe, NW. quarter section 6, township 53 N., range 1 W. Harrison Boothe, NE. quarter section 1, township 53 N., range 2 W. Samuel Watson, sen., NW. quarter section 32, and E. ½ NE. quarter section 31, township 54, range 1 W., 240 acres. Robert Kelso, E. ½ of SW. quarter section 36, township 54 N., range 2 W., 80 acres. Robert Kelso, W. ½ of SE. quarter section 36, township 54 N., range 2 W. R. B. Jordan, E. ½ of SE. quarter section 36, township 54, range 2 W. Mijaman Templeton, E. ½ of NW. quarter section 5, township 53 N., range 1 W. Josiah Henry, E., ½ of NE. quarter section 8, township 53 N., range 1 W.

L. F. LINN.
F. R. CONWAY.
A. G. HARRISON.

No. 25.—Mrs. Vallé Villars, *claiming* 7,056 *arpents.*

To the Lieutenant Governor:

Mary Luisa Vallé, widow of the retired lieutenant, Don Luis Villars, in the best form in her power, exposes to you that almost all the lands of this jurisdiction of St. Genevieve, having been divided among the inhabitants to encourage improvements and cultivation, and that the lands which she now solicits for were already granted by the government to her defunct father; and your petitioner wanting at the present to establish a stock farm for the maintenance of her family, which is considerable; for these motives she supplicates you to condescend to grant to her one league square of land of his Majesty's domain in the place called the Grande Glaise, which tract has for principal front, a line running north and south, bounded on one side by the land of the captain of militia, Don Francisco Vallé, and on the other by the domain of his Majesty, and running on both sides towards the westward of Saline river. Favor which she hopes to deserve in consideration of the services of her husband, and being, as already said, overburdened with a numerous family, and also in consideration of the sacrifices made by her late father for the welfare of these settlements.

MARIE LOUISE VALLÉ VILLARS.

St. Genevieve of Illinois, *September* 10, 1796.

St. Genevieve, *September* 11, 1796.

The surveyor, Don Antoine Soulard, shall put the petitioner in possession of the land she solicits, being well understood that it be vacant and does not carry prejudice to any person; and his survey being executed, he shall deliver it to the interested, that she may apply to the governor general to obtain the title of concession which she asks.

ZENON TRUDEAU.

I, the undersigned, curate of St. Genevieve, and vicar general of upper Louisiana, certify that this is a copy of the original which was presented to me by said lady Maria Louisa Vallé. Given at St. Genevieve, February 18, 1806.

DIEGO MAXWELL.

St. Louis, *May* 9, 1806.

Before us, one of the judges of common pleas for the district of St. ————, in the Territory of Louisiana, personally appeared the Rev. Diego Maxwell, who has solemnly sworn that the above copy is of his own handwriting, and in all conformable to the original. In testimony whereof we have signed and sealed the present date as above.

D. DELAUNAY.

Don Antonio Soulard, surveyor general of the settlements of Upper Louisiana.

I do certify that on the 13th of February of last year, conformably to the decree here annexed of the lieutenant governor, Don Zenon Trudeau, dated September 11, of the year 1786,) I transported myself on the land of the widow Maria Louisa Vallé Villars, to survey it according to her petition for 7, 056 arpents in superficie, which survey was made in presence of one son of the proprietor and of the adjoining neighbor, with the perch of Paris, of eighteen feet in length, according to the custom adopted in this province of Louisiana, and without regard to the variation of the needle which is 7° 30′ east, as is evident by the figurative plat here above, which land is situated at about seven miles south of the post of New Bourbon; bounded on the southeast in part by lands of Benjamin Stoddard and vacant lands of the royal domain, and on the other sides, northwest, northeast, and southwest, by the same vacant lands of the said royal domain. And to be available according to law, I do give the present with the figurative plat here above, on which are indicated the dimensions and the natural and artificial bounds which surround said land.

ANTONIO SOULARD.

St. Louis of Illinois, *February* 1, 1799.

Don Antonio Soulard, surveyor general of Upper Louisiana, by desire of the guardian of the children of the late Mrs. Maria Louisa Vallé Villars, Don Bautisia Vallé.

I do certify that the foregoing plat and certificate of survey is in all and every part conformable to the original, which is deposited in the archives under my charge, to which I do refer.

ANTONIO SOULARD.

St. Louis of Illinois, *January* 15, 1804.

A true translation. St. Louis, November 21, 1832.

JULIUS DE MUN.

No.	Name of original claimant	Quantity, arpents.	Nature and date of claim.	By whom granted.	By whom surveyed, date, and situation.
25	Marie Louise Vallé Villars.	7,056	Concession, Sept. 11, 1796.	Z. Trudeau.	Antonio Soulard, February 13, 1798. Certified February 1, 1799. Seven miles south of New Bourbon.

Evidence with reference to minutes and records.

June 21, 1806.—The board met agreeably to adjournment. Present: the honorable C. B. Penrose and James L. Donaldson, esq.

Marie Louise Vallé Villars, claiming 7,056 arpents of land situate on the Grande Glaise waters of the Saline, and district aforesaid, produces a certified copy of a concession from Zenon Trudeau, dated September 11, 1798, and sworn to by James Maxwell; a survey of the same taken February 13, 1798, and certified February 1, 1798.

Batiste Vallé, being duly sworn, says the claimant settled the said tract of land in the year 1799; cleared about 50 acres of the same, and actually inhabited and cultivated it prior to and on the 1st day of October, 1800; that a tan-yard has since been erected on the same; that the said tract of cultivated land has been enlarged, and is still so every year. Claimant claims no other land in her own name in the Territory, and is the mother of eight children.

James Maxwell, vicar general of the province, being also duly sworn, says that, in the year 1799, he took down to New Orleans the original concession, whereof the aforesaid is an exact copy. The board reject this claim for want of a duly registered warrant of survey, and observe that claimant's husband was a captain in the regiment of Louisiana; that he served sometimes as commandant of St. Genevieve, in which capacity he never received any compensation for his service; and that the above concession is the only one ever granted to him or his representatives.—(See book No. 1, page 325.)

December 10, 1811.—Board met. Present: John R. C. Lucas, Clement B. Penrose, and Frederick Bates, commissioners.

Marie Louise Vallé Villars, claiming 7,056 arpents of land situate on the river Saline, district of St. Genevieve, produces record of a copy of concession certified by Diego Maxwell, February 18; concession dated September 17, 1796; record of a plat of survey dated February 3, 1803, certified January 3, 1804. It is the opinion of the board that this claim ought not to be confirmed.—(See book No. 1, page 509.)

November 21, 1832.—The board met pursuant to adjournment. Present: Lewis F. Linn and F. R. Conway, commissioners.

Marie Louise Vallé Villars, by her legal representatives, claiming 7,056 arpents of land.—(See book of record B, page 422; commissioners' minutes, book No. 1, page 325; the same, No. 5, page 509.)

The following additional testimony was taken in the foregoing case, in compliance with a resolution of this board of the 10th of October last:

St. Genevieve, *Missouri*, *October*, 1832.

The heirs and legal representatives of Marie Louise Villars, deceased, claiming 7,056 arpents of land situate on the waters of Saline, in the former district of St. Genevieve, in pursuance of and by virtue of a plat of survey; when Colonel Batiste Vallé, senior, personally appeared before Lewis F. Linn, one of the commissioners appointed finally to settle and adjust the land claims in Missouri, and authorized by the commissioners to receive testimony in this behalf.

Said Vallé, being duly sworn, deposeth and saith that he knew of a concession to Marie Louise Villars for 7,056 arpents of land on the waters of the Saline; that he knew of the intendant or governor of Lower Louisiana sending up instructions to the lieutenant governor of Upper Louisiana directing that the survey of Peyrouse should be run in such a way as to respect the concessions of Marie Louise Villars and François Vallé; that said concessions were given to the Rev. James Maxwell, vicar of Upper Louisiana, to take to New Orleans for the purpose of being laid before the intendant; that he understood and believes that they were either lost by the said Maxwell or left in some of the offices for confirmation.

Question by the commissioner. Do you know or believe that these concessions were antedated?

Answer. No.

Question by the commissioner. Have you any knowledge or reason to believe that any Spanish or French concessions were antedated?

Answer. No; for when I was in New Orleans, during the existence of the Spanish government, the Baron de Carondelet told me that, if I wanted any lands in Upper Louisiana, to make out a list, and he would grant them.

Question by the commissioner. Whilst you were at New Orleans, in your conversations with the Baron de Carondelet, did you understand from him that the power to grant lands by the sub-delegates was denied?

Answer. No; on the contrary, when he pressed me to accept land for myself and family, I informed him that the sub-delegates had given me and my family grants. To which he replied, if you have not enough, ask for more.

J. B. VALLÉ.

Sworn to and subscribed, the day and year first above written, before L. F. Linn, land commissioner.

L. F. LINN.

In behalf of this claim the following papers were produced: A paper purporting to be a copy (certified by D. Maxwell, curate of St. Genevieve) of the claimant's petition to, and concession of, Zenon Trudeau, lieutenant governor; also, a plat and certificate of survey by Antoine Soulard. References as above.—(See book No. 6, page 34.)

November 4, 1833.—The board met pursuant to adjournment. Present: L. F. Linn, A. G. Harrison, F. R. Conway, commissioners.

Marie Louise Vallé Villars claiming 7,056 arpents of land.—(See page 84 of this book.) The board are unanimously of opinion that this claim ought to be confirmed to the said Maria Louisa Vallé Villars, or her legal representatives, according to the concession.—(See book No. 6, page 295.)

L. F. LINN.
F. R. CONWAY.
A. G. HARRISON.

No. 26.—François Vallé, *claiming* 7,046 *arpents.*

To Don Zenon Trudeau, lieutenant governor of the western part of Illinois:

Francis Vallé, captain of militia and commandant of St. Genevieve, believes it is not necessary to recall more particularly to your memory any of his claims to the generous benevolence of the government. He has the honor to supplicate you to have the goodness to grant to him a concession of one league square of land, equal to 7,056 arpents, situated nine miles to the southeast of New Bourbon, of which jurisdiction it will make a part. The numerous family of the petitioner, and the means of farming which he is possessed of, must be to you a sure guaranty that this quantity is even below the one to which he has a right to pretend.

Full of confidence in your justice, he has the honor to be, with great respect,

FRANÇOIS VALLÉ.

St. Louis, *September* 8, 1796.

St. Louis, *September* 9, 1796.

The surveyor, Don Antonio Soulard, shall survey in favor of the captain commandant of St. Genevieve, Don Francisco Vallé, 7,056 arpents of land in superficie, on the vacant lands at about nine miles to the southeast of the town of St. Genevieve, in the manner solicited by the petitioner, to whom he shall deliver a certificate of his survey, in order that the said certificate, added to this decree, shall serve to him (the petitioner) as a title of property until he receives a title in form from the governor general, to whom he must make application in due time.

ZENON TRUDEAU.

Truly translated.

JULIUS DE MUN.

No.	Name of original claimant.	Quantity, arpents.	Nature and date of claim.	By whom granted.	By whom surveyed, date, and situation.
26	François Vallé	7,056	Concession, September 9, 1796.	Zenon Trudeau.	

Evidence with reference to minutes and records.

June 20, 1806.—The board met agreeably to adjournment. Present: The Hon. Clement B. Penrose and James L. Donaldson, esq.

The representatives of François Vallé, claiming 7,056 arpents of land, situated on the waters of the river Saline, district aforesaid, produce a survey and plat of the same, taken September 15, 1797, and a certificate of the same, dated November 15, 1805. A certificate was also produced from Anthony Soulard, stating that he had seen and had in his possession a concession for the aforesaid tract of land, said concession granted by Zenon Trudeau, and bearing date the 9th day of September, 1796.

Batiste Vallé, being duly sworn, says that about the year 1798 or 1799 he saw the aforesaid concession; and further, that the same having been sent down to New Orleans to procure a complete title, he saw the receipt of the person who took the same down to that effect; that about 1798 or 1799 two farms were laid out on said land, and a number of buildings erected on the same.

Israel Dodge, being also duly sworn, says that the said tract of land was settled in the year 1797, forty or fifty arpents cleared, and that the said tract has been actually inhabited and cultivated for the use of the said François Vallé, or his representatives. From that period to this day large stocks have always been kept on the same.—(See book No. 1, pages 321 and 322.)

The board reject this claim for want of a duly registered warrant of survey.

December 1, 1807.—The board met pursuant to adjournment. Present: The Hon. John B. C. Lucas, Clement B. Penrose, and Frederick Bates.

The representatives of François Vallé, sr., claiming 7,056 arpents of land, situated on the river Saline, produce a survey and plat of the same, taken the 15th September, 1797, and a certificate of the same, dated November 16, 1805. A certificate was also produced from Anthony Soulard, stating that he had seen and had in his possession a concession for the aforesaid tract of land, said concession granted by Zenon Trudeau, lieutenant governor, and bearing date the 9th day of September, 1796.

François Vallé, jr., one of the representatives aforesaid, being duly sworn, says that the concession was sent to New Orleans, and that Zenon Trudeau wrote to the deponent's father that he had made a search in the office at New Orleans for the concession, and that it could not be found, and that the said concession is not now in the possession of any of the said representatives, to the best of this deponent's knowledge and belief.

Laid over for decision.—(See book No. 3, page 105.)

April 17, 1810.—Board met. Present: John B. C. Lucas, Clement B. Penrose, and Frederick Bates, commissioners.

François Vallé, sen., the representatives of, claiming 7,056 arpents of land.—(See book No. 1, page 321; book No. 3, page 105.)

It is the opinion of a majority of the board that this claim ought not to be confirmed; Clement B. Penrose, commissioner, voting for the confirmation of one league square; but the said majority declare that if this claim had not exceeded 800 arpents they would have voted for its confirmation.—(See book No. 4, page 325.)

November 22, 1832.—The board met pursuant to adjournment. Present: Lewis F. Linn, F. R. Conway, commissioners.

François Vallé, by his legal representatives, claiming 7,056 arpents of land, (for record of survey, see record book C, page 396; minute book No. 4, page 325,) produces a paper purporting to be the original concession from Zenon Trudeau, dated 9th September, 1796. The following additional testimony was taken in the foregoing case, in compliance with a resolution of this board of the 10th of October last:

St. Genevieve, *Missouri, October* 19, 1832.

The heirs and legal representatives of François Vallé, deceased, claiming seven thousand and fifty-six arpents of land situated on the river Saline, in the former district of St. Genevieve, in pursuance of and by virtue of a concession and survey heretofore filed with the former commissioners. When Bartholomew St. Gemmes personally appeared before Lewis F. Linn, one of the commissioners appointed to finally settle and adjust land claims in Missouri, and authorized by said board of commissioners to receive testimony in this behalf, who, being duly sworn, deposeth and saith: In the year 1798 he, the said St. Gemmes, knew of François Vallé, and by his hands did cultivate the aforesaid tract of land; that the said Vallé had a house and field, and resided on the premises; that the claim existed, and was duly surveyed by Thomas Madden about that time, as he saw the marks made by said Madden when surveying; and that the said Vallé did cultivate the land continually, and held possession during his lifetime; and further knows that the heirs and representatives of said Vallé have continued to hold possession and cultivate said land ever since; that he is well acquainted with the handwriting and signatures of François Vallé and Zenon Trudeau, and has seen them write frequently, and knows the signatures in the original petition and concession are the proper handwriting and signatures of the said François Vallé and Zenon Trudeau, and knows that the said Zenon Trudeau was acting as lieutenant governor at that time; and further this deponent saith not.

B. ST. GEMMES.

Sworn to and subscribed, this day and year first above written, before me.

L. F. LINN, *Land Commissioner.*

(See book No. 6, pages 36 and 37.)

November 27, 1832.—The board met pursuant to adjournment. Present: Lewis F. Linn, F. R. Conway, commissioners.

In the case of François Vallé's legal representatives, claiming 7,056 arpents of land, (entered 22d instant,) M. P. Le Duc, Charles Frémon Delauriere, and Albert Tison, being duly sworn, say that F. Vallé had, at the date of his petition, seven children, and at least from forty to fifty slaves, and that he was then commandant of St. Genevieve. Albert Tison and C. F. Delauriere say that he was then possessed of a great number of cattle.—(See book No. 6, page 53.)

November 4, 1833.—The board met pursuant to adjournment. Present: L. F. Linn, A. G. Harrison, F. R. Conway, commissioners.

François Vallé, claiming 7,056 arpents of land.—(See pages 35 and 53 of this book.) The board are unanimously of opinion that this claim ought to be confirmed to the said François Vallé, or his legal representatives, according to the concession.—(See book No. 6, page 295.)

L. F. LINN.
F. R. CONWAY.
A. G. HARRISON.

No. 27.—Jean Baptiste Labreche, *claiming* 500 *arpents.*

To Don Charles Dehault Delassus, lieutenant colonel, attached to the stationary regiment of Louisiana, and lieutenant governor of the upper part of same province:

Sir: Jean Baptiste Labreche, Canadian, inhabitant of this country for more than forty years, and having never obtained any concession from the government, has the honor to supplicate you to have the goodness to grant to him a concession for five hundred arpents of land in superficie, situated at the mine called A Breton, and adjoining that of Bazile Vallé. For the concession of said five hundred arpents of land the petitioner had obtained, since several years, the promise of your predecessor, Don Zenon Trudeau.

The petitioner, having always lived as a persevering and peaceable cultivator, hopes to deserve the favor he claims from your justice.

his
J. BAPTISTE + LABRECHE.
mark.

St. Louis, *September* 4, 1799.

Witnesses:
Pratte.
A. Choteau.

St. Louis of Illinois, *September* 5, 1799.

Considering that the petitioner has been long settled in this country, and being informed that he has means sufficient to work and to improve the lands he asks, the surveyor of this Upper Louisiana, Don Antonio Soulard, shall put the petitioner in possession of five hundred arpents of land in superficie; after which, the interested shall have to solicit the concession in form from the intendant general of these provinces, to whom, by royal order, corresponds the distributing and granting all classes of land of the royal domain.

CARLOS DEHAULT DELASSUS.

Truly translated. St. Louis, November 24, 1832.

JULIUS DE MUN.

No.	Name of original claimant.	Quantity, in arpents.	Nature and date of claim.	By whom granted.	By whom surveyed, date, and situation.
27	Jean Baptiste Labreche.	500	Concession, September 5, 1799.	Carlos Dehault Delassus.	

Evidence with reference to minutes and records.

June 20, 1806.—The board met agreeably to adjournment. Present: Hon. Clement B. Penrose and James L. Donaldson, esquire.

The widow Moreau, assignee of John B. Labreche, claiming under the 2d section of the act 500 arpents of land situate on the Grand river, joining the Mine à Breton, district aforesaid, (St. Genevieve,) produces, as a special permission to settle, a concession from Charles D. Delassus, dated September 5, 1799; a survey of the same, dated February 10, and certified June 10, 1800; a certificate of public sale before commandant, dated April 15, 1804.

St. Gemme Beauvais, being duly sworn, says that the said Labreche settled the said tract of land in the year 1800, worked the same for mineral in the same year; that in 1801 he raised a crop on the same, and actually inhabited and continued to cultivate and inhabit the same until October 1803; that said Labreche dying in the fall of that year, his widow removed from said land, when the same was sold by commandant, and purchased by claimant, who moved thereon in 1804, and has actually cultivated the same to this day. The board reject this claim for want of actual inhabitation on the 20th day of December, 1803.—(See book No. 1, page 319.)

December 23, 1811.—Board met. Present: John B. C. Lucas, Clement B. Penrose, and Frederick Bates, commissioners.

Widow Moreau, assignee of John Baptiste Labreche, claiming 500 arpents of land situate on the waters of Grand river, district of St. Genevieve, produces a concession from Charles D. Delassus, lieutenant governor, dated September 5, 1799.—(See book No. 1, page 319.) It is the opinion of a majority of the board that this claim ought to be confirmed. Frederick Bates, commissioner, forbears giving an opinion.—(See book No 5, page 536.)

November 24, 1832.—The board met pursuant to adjournment. Present: L. F. Linn, F. R. Conway, commissioners.

Jean Baptiste Labreche, claiming 500 arpents of land, (see book No. 1, page 319; No. 5, page 536; record book C, page 419,) produces a paper purporting to be an original concession from Carlos Dehault Delassus, dated September 5, 1799.

The following additional testimony was taken in the foregoing case, in compliance with a resolution of this board of the 10th of October last:

State of Missouri, *county of St. Genevieve:*

Bazile Mesplais and Therese Rangé, and the heirs and legal representatives of Lambert Rangé, claiming 500 arpents of land, under Baptiste Labreche, situate in the late district of St. Genevieve, now county of Washington, in the State of Missouri, by virtue of a concession, produces the original concession from Charles Dehault Delassus, late the lieutenant governor of Upper Louisiana, to the said Baptiste Labreche, dated the 5th day of September, 1799, for 500 arpents of land. No plat of survey is produced, but reference is made to the records for the same. Whereupon Pascal Detchmendy, aged 71 years, being duly sworn as the law directs, deposeth and saith that he was well acquainted with Charles Dehault Delassus, late lieutenant governor of Upper Louisiana; that he knows he was the lieutenant governor of said Upper Louisiana in the year 1799; he further states that he is well acquainted with the handwriting and signature of the said C. D. Delassus; that he often saw him write, and that the signature and name of said C. D. Delassus to the concession for 500 arpents of land given by him to Baptiste Labreche, dated the 5th day of September, 1799, is in the proper handwriting of the said Charles Dehault Delassus.

P. DETCHMENDY.

Sworn to and subscribed before me, Lewis F. Linn, one of the commissioners appointed to finally settle and adjust the titles and claims to lands in Missouri, this 30th day of October, 1832.

L. F. LINN.

And also personally came François Ogé, aged 85 years, who, being duly sworn, deposeth and saith that he was well acquainted with Baptiste Labreche, named in the aforesaid grant; that he was a residenter of this country at the date of the grant in 1799, and continued a citizen; that about the date of the said concession, in 1799, the said Baptiste Labreche took possession of the land granted; that he settled on the land, built a house, opened a field, and cultivated the same, and that the said tract of land, from about the date of the said concession, has been, by the said Labreche and those claiming under him, actually inhabited and cultivated ever since, and now is inhabited and cultivated.

FRANÇOIS OGÉ, his + mark.

Sworn to and subscribed before me, Lewis F. Linn, one of the commissioners appointed, &c., this 30th of October, 1832.

L. F. LINN.

(See book No. 6, page 46.)

November 4, 1833.—The board met pursuant to adjournment. Present: L. F. Linn, A. G. Harrison, F. R. Conway, commissioners.

Jean Baptiste Labreche, claiming 500 arpents of land.—(See page 46 of this book.) The board are unanimously of opinion that this claim ought to be confirmed to the said Baptiste Labreche, or his legal representatives, according to the concession.—(See book No. 6, page 295.)

L. F. LINN.
F. R. CONWAY.
A. G. HARRISON.

No. 28.—St. Gemme Beauvais, *claiming* 1,600 *arpents*.

To Don Zenon Trudeau, lieutenant colonel, and lieutenant governor of the western part of Illinois:

St. Jayme Beauvais has the honor to state that, wishing to obtain a concession of 40 arpents in front by 40 in depth, situated between the river Au Castor (Beaver creek) and the mine called A la Motte, distant about 15 leagues of the village of the Little Hills of St. Genevieve, he hopes of obtaining this favor of your justice.

J. S. G. BEAUVAIS.

St. Genevieve, *August* 2, 1796.

St. Genevieve, *August* 15, 1796.

Be it forwarded to the lieutenant governor, with information that the land solicited belongs to the royal domain, and will not be prejudicial to any person.

FRANÇOIS VALLÉ.

St. Louis, *September* 2, 1796.

The surveyor, Don Antonio Soulard, shall establish the party upon the land solicited, if belonging to the domain of his Majesty, and does not carry prejudice to any one; and said party shall apply to the governor general of the province for the title of concession which he solicits for.

ZENON TRUDEAU.

Truly translated. St. Louis, November 24, 1832.

JULIUS DE MUN.

No.	Name of original claimant.	Quantity, in arpents.	Nature and date of claim.	By whom granted.	By whom surveyed, date, and situation.
28	St. Gemme Beauvais.	1, 600	Concession, Sept. 2, 1796	Zenon Trudeau.	

Evidence with reference to minutes and records.

June 20, 1806.—The board met agreeably to adjournment. Present: The Hon. Clement B. Penrose and James C. Donaldson, esq.

The same, (St. James Beauvais,) claiming 1,600 arpents of land situated at the Mine à la Motte, district of St. Genevieve, produces a concession from Zenon Trudeau, dated September 2, 1796, and a survey of the same, taken April 25, and certified October 1, 1805.

François Vallé, being duly sworn, says that claimant did, about five or six years ago, being then engaged in working his mines, cut wood on said tract of land for the melting of the mineral.

The board reject this claim, and observe that the above concession is neither antedated nor fraudulent, and that the above claimant had, in 1800, 10 children and 30 slaves.—(See book No. 1, page 316.)

December 30, 1811.—Board met. Present: John B. C. Lucas, Clement B. Penrose, and Frederick Bates, commissioners.

St. James Beauvais, claiming 1,600 arpents of land.—(See book No. 1, page 316.)

It is the opinion of the board that this claim ought not to be confirmed.—(See book No. 5, page 546.)

November 23, 1833.—The board met pursuant to adjournment. Present: Lewis F. Linn and F. R. Conway, commissioners.

St. Gemme Beauvais, claiming 1,600 arpents of land, (book No. 1, page 316; No. 5, page 546; record book C, pages 455 and 456,) produces a paper purporting to be an original concession from Zenon Trudeau, dated September 2, 1796; also a paper purporting to be a copy of a plat of survey by Thomas Madden.

The following additional testimony was taken in the foregoing case, in compliance with a resolution of this board of the 10th of October last:

State of Missouri, *county of St. Genevieve, October* 25, 1832:

St. James Beauvais, the heirs and legal representatives of St. J. Beauvais, claiming 1,600 arpents of land situated in the late district of St. Genevieve, now county of Madison, in the State of Missouri, by virtue and in pursuance of a grant or concession made and given by Zenon Trudeau, formerly lieutenant governor of Upper Louisiana, dated the 2d day of September, 1796, produces the original petition of said St. James Beauvais, dated the 2d August, 1796, and the recommendation of François Vallé, then commandant, of the 15th August, 1796, for the concession; also the concession itself, dated as aforesaid. The claimant produces also a plat of survey, dated, made, and recorded by Antoine Soulard, the former surveyor general of Upper Louisiana, dated the 26th April, 1805, and October 1, 1805; and then the said claimants also produce François C. Lachance, aged sixty-five years, who, being duly sworn as the law directs, deposeth and saith that he is well acquainted with the said St. James Beauvais, and has been from the time he was able to know or recognize any person in the world, and that he has known him as a residenter of this county ever since; that he well knows his children, all of them the present claimants; that they were all born and all natives of this county, where they and him have always resided, and still live, in number ten; that he knows that the land here claimed was and has been in the possession of the said St. James Beauvais from the year 1799; and he further states that the said tract of land has been in the actual possession of the said St. J. Beauvais and his children ever since; and that the same was from the date aforesaid, ever since, and now is, in the possession as aforesaid, and was by the said St. J. Beauvais and his children, and others under him, actually inhabited and cultivated from the year 1799 up to the present date; that houses were built in 1803 or 1804, and rails split, and fields cleared, and actually cultivated for more than twenty years, which houses and fields are still there; that this claim was one of the first grants of the Spanish government in that quarter of the country, and the other grants for Mine à la Motte and the village claim respected and referred to the lines of this grant.

F. CALIOL LACHANCE.

Sworn to and subscribed to before me, Lewis F. Linn, one of the commissioners for settling and adjusting land claims in Missouri, the day and date above.

L. F. LINN.

And personally came John Bte. Vallé, senior, aged seventy-two years, who, being duly sworn as the law directs, deposeth and saith that he was well acquainted with Zenon Trudeau, late lieutenant governor of Upper Louisiana; that he has frequently seen him write, and that he knows that the signature of the said Zenon Trudeau to the concession for 1,600 arpents of land given to St. James Beauvais, dated the 2d day of September, 1796, is in the proper handwriting of the said Zenon Trudeau; and he also knows that the said Zenon Trudeau was, at the date of said grant, the lieutenant governor of Upper Louisiana; and he also personally knows that the signature of F. Vallé, who recommended said grant, is in the proper handwriting of said F. Vallé.

J. BTE. VALLÉ.

Sworn to and subscribed before me, Lewis F. Linn, one of the commissioners appointed to finally settle and adjust the titles and claims of lands in Missouri, this 30th day of October, 1832.

L. F. LINN.

Annexed to the above testimony is an affidavit signed by J. B. Janis and Julien La Breire, proving the cultivation and habitation of said land before the change of government, up to the date of said affidavit, which was sworn to and subscribed on the 30th November, 1818, before M. Amourux, a justice of the peace for the county of St. Genevieve.—(See book No. 6, pages 37, 38, 39, and 40.)

In the case of St. Gemme Beauvais, claiming 1,600 arpents of land.—(See page 37 of this book.)

Peter Ménard, duly sworn, says that he knows St. Gemme Beauvais to be the father of 10 children; that when he first knew him he owned more than forty negroes and a large stock of cattle; that he, the deponent, used to make St. Gemme Beauvais's house his home when at St. Genevieve.—(See book No. 6, page 128.)

November 4, 1833.—The board met pursuant to adjournment. Present: L. F. Linn, A. G. Harrison, F. R. Conway, commissioners.

St. Gemme Beauvais, claiming 1,600 arpents of land.—(See pages 37, 38, 39, 40, and 128, of this book.)

The board are unanimously of opinion that this claim ought to be confirmed to said St. Gemme Beauvais, or his legal representatives, according to the concession.—(See book 6, page 296.)

L. F. LINN.
F. R. CONWAY.
A. G. HARRISON.

No. 29.—Vital St. Gemmes and others, *claiming* 1,600 *arpents.*

To Delassus Deluziere, knight, captain and commandant, civil and military, of the post of New Bourbon:

Sir: The undersigned have the honor of laying before you the present petition, to obtain of your goodness and of the benevolence of the government which you represent, a concession of one hundred and sixty arpents of land in depth by ten arpents in front, situated on the south branch of river Saline, at about six leagues from its mouth, bounded on all sides by lands of the domain. In so doing, the undersigned will never cease to pray for the conservation of your days.

RAPHAEL ST. JEMS.
BATISTE BEQUET.
VITAL ST. JEMS.
BMI. ST. GEMES.

St. Genevieve, *January* 29, 1798.

ST. LOUIS, *February* 1, 1798.

The surveyor of this jurisdiction, Don Antonio Soulard, shall put Messrs. Raphael St. Jayme, Baptist Bequet, Bartelmi St. Jayme, and Vital St. Jayme, in possession of the land solicited for in the present petition; in continuation of which, he shall draw a proces verbal of his survey, for the whole to be returned to us and sent to the governor general of the province, to be definitively determined by him upon the concession of said land.

ZENON TRUDEAU.

Truly translated. St. Louis, November 24, 1832.

JULIUS DE MUN.

No.	Name of original claimant.	Quantity in arpents.	Nature and date of claim.	By whom granted.	By whom surveyed, date, and situation.
29	Raph. St. Gemme, Baptiste Bequet, Vital St. Gemme, Barth. St. Gemme,	1,600	Concession, 1st February, 1798.	Zenon Trudeau.	

Evidence with reference to minutes and records.

December 7, 1807.—The board met agreeably to adjournment. Present: The honorable John B. C. Lucas and Frederick Bates.

Baptiste Bequet, Raphael St. Gemme, Vital St. Gemme, and Barth. St. Gemme, claiming 1,600 arpents of land situated on the north fork of the river Saline, produce, in support of the same, a concession from Zenon Trudeau, lieutenant governor, dated 1st February, 1798, and a plat and certificate of survey for the same by Thomas Maddin, dated 16th February, 1806.

John Mary Legrand, being duly sworn, says that he knows the tract claimed. That in 1805 the same was inhabited and cultivated for the use of the claimants; that he knows that claimants laid a claim to that piece of land five or six years ago. Laid over for decision.—(See book No. 3, page 164.)

June 1, 1810.—Board met. Present: John B. C. Lucas, Clement B. Penrose, and Frederick Bates, commissioners.

Raphael St. Jems, Baptiste Bequet, Vital St. Jems, and Barth. St. Jems, claiming 1,600 arpents of land.—(See book No. 3, page 164.) The paper purporting to be a plat and certificate of survey, signed by Thomas Maddin, is not authenticated by the proper surveyor. It is the opinion of the board that this claim ought not to be confirmed.—(See book No. 4, page 358.)

November 24, 1832.—The board met pursuant to adjournment. Present: Lewis F. Linn, F. R. Conway, commissioners.

Raphael St. Jems, Bequet, and others, claiming 1,600 arpents of land, (see book No. 3, page 164; book No. 4, page 358; record book D, pages 49 and 50,) produce a paper purporting to be an original concession from Zenon Trudeau, dated February 1, 1798. Also a paper purporting to be a plat of survey executed on the 16th of February, 1806, by Thomas Maddin, deputy surveyor.

The following additional testimony was taken in the foregoing case, in compliance with a resolution of this board of the 10th of October last:

STATE OF MISSOURI, *county of St. Genevieve.*

Bartholomew St. Gemme, and Raphael St. Jemmes, and Charles Gregoin, under Vital St. Gemme, deceased, and Thomas Maddin, Richard Maddin, and James Maddin, under Baptiste Bequet and Raphael St. Gemme, claiming 1,600 arpents of land, situate in the late district now county of St. Genevieve, in the State of Missouri, by virtue of concession, produces the original concession from Zenon Trudeau, late lieutenant governor of Upper Louisiana, dated the first day of February, 1798, given to Raphael St. Gemme, Vital St. Gemme, Baptiste Bequet, and Bartholomew St. Gemme, for 1,600 arpents of land, and a plat of the same, surveyed by Thomas Maddin, late deputy surveyor, &c. And thereupon came Paschal Detchmendy, aged seventy-one years, who, being duly sworn as the law directs, deposeth and saith that he was well acquainted with Zenon Trudeau, late lieutenant governor of Louisiana; that he was lieutenant governor of Upper Louisiana in the year 1798, and that he was well acquainted with the handwriting and signature of said Zenon Trudeau, having frequently seen him write, and that the name and signature of said Zenon Trudeau to the concession made by him to Raphael St. Gemme, Vital St. Gemme, Baptiste Bequet, and Bartholomew St. Gemme, for 1,600 arpents of land, dated the first day of February, 1798, is in the proper handwriting of said Zenon Trudeau, and is his signature; and the deponent further says that he was well acquainted with the said Raphael St. Gemme, Vital St. Gemme, Baptiste Bequet, and Bartholomew St. Gemme, the concessioners in the said grant named; and that they and each of them were, at the date of the grant aforesaid, citizens and residents in the county.

P. DETCHMENDY.

Sworn to and subscribed before me, Lewis F. Linn, one of the commissioners appointed to settle and adjust the titles and claims to land in Missouri, this 30th day of October, 1832.

L. F. LINN.

And also, at the same time and place, came Sebastian Butcher, aged fifty-two years, who, being duly sworn as the law directs, deposeth and saith that he was well acquainted with the grantees in the above concession; that they were, in the year 1798, citizens and residents in this county; and he further says that he well knows the land in the above concession named and claimed, having frequently travelled by and through the same about the year 1804, and that he saw one or more men working on the land and making rails, preparing to enclose a field; that there was a considerable quantity of rails.

SEBASTIAN B. BUTCHER, his + mark.

Sworn to and subscribed before me, Lewis F. Linn, one of the commissioners appointed to settle and adjust the titles and claims of land in Missouri, this 30th day of October, 1832.

L. F. LINN.

And also, at the same time and place, came Bazile Mesplas, aged fifty-three years, who, being duly sworn, deposeth and saith that he knows all the grantees named in the aforesaid concession; that they were residents in the county at the date of the concession, in 1798. And he further says he is well acquainted with the land claimed and named in the said concession, and that in the year 1804 he went on the land claimed, by the direction of the grantees, and aided in carrying the chain to survey the same in 1806. That in 1804, when he went on the land, he saw a house and field on the same; that the house was built by one man called Black, and the fields cleared by him. That the said Black was put there by the claimants, who gave him horses, stock, hogs, cattle, &c., on the shares; that said Black remained there for a considerable time, and he believes died there. And that the said land has been cultivated, to the best of his knowledge, ever since, either by the claimants or others under them.

BAZILE MESPLAS.

Sworn to and subscribed before me, Lewis F. Linn, one of the commissioners appointed to finally settle and adjust land claims in Missouri, this 30th day of October, 1832.—(See book No. 6, pages 40, 41, and 42.)

L. F. LINN.

November 5, 1833.—The board met pursuant to adjournment. Present: L. F. Linn, A. G. Harrison, and F. R. Conway, commissioners.

Raphael St. Gemme, Bequet, and others, claiming 1,600 arpents of land.—(See page 40 of this book.)

The board are unanimously of opinion that this claim ought to be confirmed to the said Raphael St. Gemme, Baptiste Bequet, Vital St. Gemme, and Barthemi St. Gemme, or their legal representatives, according to the concession.—(See book No. 6, page 296.)

L. F. LINN.
F. R. CONWAY.
A. G. HARRISON.

No. 80.—Thomas Maddin, *claiming* 1,500 *arpents.*

To Mr. Zenon Trudeau, lieutenant governor of the western part of Illinois:

Supplicates very humbly Thomas Maddin, (King's surveyor, appointed and established for the post and district of St. Genevieve and of New Bourbon, inhabiting since several years the district of the said New Bourbon,) and has the honor to expose that, wishing to construct and build a flour mill, seeing the necessity of such an establishment in this district, being himself destitute of the means to get manufactured the productions of his plântation, and to facilitate to the inhabitants of his neighborhood, and especially to those of the villages of St. Genevieve and New Bourbon, the means of procuring flour easily, there being in those places but horse mills, which make but a small quantity of flour, and of a very inferior quality; which fact is notorious. The petitioner having found a suitable place for the establishment he proposes on the *Glaise à Topois*, which is a branch of the river Aux Vases, distant about two leagues and a half from St. Genevieve, and being in his Majesty's domain, therefore the petitioner has recourse to you, sir, and your authority, that you may be pleased to grant him, his heirs and assignees, the concession for fifteen hundred arpents of land in the above-cited place, the said concession adjoining that of André Deggyre and that of Madame Manuel Joseph Bequette and Joseph Pratte. The petitioner obliging himself to construct his mill and have it completed before the expiration of two years from the time he shall be put in possession of the said concession, under pain, in the contrary case, to be compelled to relinquish all his rights and pretensions on the same, which concession should then be deemed null and void. In so doing, the petitioner will never cease to pray for the conservation of your days.

THOMAS MADDIN.

New Bourbon, *January* 8, 1799.

New Bourbon, *January* 20, 1799.

We, the undersigned, commandant of the post of New Bourbon, do certify to the lieutenant governor of the western part of Illinois, that the statement made in this petition is exact, sincere, and true, and that the petitioner, being an excellent subject, having a numerous family to maintain, also a very good cultivator, who unites to the talent (precious in this country) of surveyor the necessary industry and capacity as a mechanician, and especially for the construction of mills, deserves, in every point of view, to obtain the favor which he solicits of the government.

PIERRE DELASSUS DELUZIERE.

St. Louis of Illinois, *January* 29, 1799.

Having taken cognizance of the present memorial and of the information given by the commandant of the post of New Bourbon, the captain of militia, Don Pedro Delassus Deluziere, and as we are satisfied that the petitioner has sufficient means to improve the lands he solicits, the surveyor of this Upper Louisiana, Don Antonio Soulard, shall put the interested in possession of said land, and, in continuation, shall make a *proces verbal* of his survey, to enable the petitioner to solicit the concession from the governor, who is informed that the petitioner deserves the favor solicited.

ZENON TRUDEAU.

The present original title of concession has been registered, and its collated copy deposited in the archives of the post of New Bourbon, under No. 44.

DELASSUS.

Truly translated. St. Louis, November 24, 1832.

JULIUS DE MUN.

No.	Name of original claimant.	Quantity, in arpents.	Nature and date of claim.	By whom granted.	By whom surveyed, date, and situation.
30	Thomas Maddin.	1,500	Concession, January 29, 1799.	Zenon Trudeau.	

Evidence with reference to minutes and records.

June 23, 1806.—The board met agreeably to adjournment. Present: The Hon. Clement B. Penrose and James D. Donaldson, esq.

Thomas Maddin, claiming 1,500 arpents of land situate on the river Aux Vases, district aforesaid, produces a concession from Zenon Trudeau, dated January 29, 1799, and a survey of the same taken September 23, 1805, and certified February 27, 1806.

Job Westover, being duly sworn, says that he did, some time in August, 1803, begin the building of a mill on the said tract of land; that some time prior to that, to wit, on Ash Wednesday in the year 1800, having gone on said land to seek for a mill seat, he was fired at by a party of Indians; that in consequence whereof the claimant, who had then intended to proceed to the building of said mill, gave up the idea of so doing for some time; that in 1803 he did build said mill; that he had on said land a cabin in which the men engaged in the building as aforesaid then lived; that the said mill was completed in 1809, when he began the cultivating of said land; and that the same has been actually inhabited and cultivated to this day. Claimant was, at the time of obtaining said concession, the head of a family. The board reject this claim, and observe that the aforesaid concession is neither antedated nor fraudulent, but that the same is not duly registered.—(See book No. 1, page 333.)

August 23, 1810.—Board met. Present: John B. C. Lucas and Clement B. Penrose, commissioners.

Thomas Maddin, claiming 1,500 arpents of land.—(See book No. 1, page 333.) It is the opinion of the board that this claim ought not to be confirmed.—(See book No. 4, page 470.)

November 24, 1832.—The board met pursuant to adjournment. Present: Lewis F. Linn and F. R. Conway, commissioners.

Thomas Maddin, by his legal representatives, claiming 1,500 arpents of land, (see book No. 1, page 333; book No. 4, page 470; record book A, pages 514 and 515, and 204 of this book,) produces a paper purporting to be an original concession from Zenon Trudeau, dated January 29, 1799. The additional testimony here below was taken in the foregoing case, in compliance with a resolution of this board of the 10th of October last:

State of Missouri, *county of St. Genevieve:*

Thomas Maddin, now Antoine Janis, the legal representative by regular transfers, claiming one thousand five hundred arpents of land situate in the former district, now county of St. Genevieve, in the State of Missouri, in the county of St. Genevieve, filed with the former board of commissioners, produces the original concession for the same from Zenon Trudeau, late the lieutenant governor of Upper Louisiana, dated January 29, 1799, and refers to the plat of survey heretofore filed and produced to the former board of commissioners; and thereupon the claimant produces Bartholomew St. Gemme, of the age of fifty-eight years, who, being duly sworn as the law directs, deposeth and saith that he is well acquainted with the handwriting and signature of Zenon Trudeau, late lieutenant governor of Upper Louisiana, and that the name and signature of the said Zenon Trudeau to the concession for fifteen hundred arpents of land to Thomas Maddin, dated January 29, 1799, is in the proper handwriting of the said Zenon Trudeau, and that the name of Pierre Delassus Deluziere to the recommendation for said concession is in the proper handwriting of the said Pierre Delassus Deluziere; and this deponent further says that, in the year 1803, he personally saw the said Thomas Maddin and his hands working on the said land and preparing timber to build a mill, and that about the same time said Maddin built a house for the purpose of accommodating himself, his hands, and workmen, and about the same time said Maddin actually cleared and enclosed a small field; and this deponent further says that, at the date of the grant aforesaid, the said Maddin was a residenter in the province, and has continued a residenter ever since; and this deponent further says that the said tract has been actually enclosed, improved, and cultivated ever since, either by the said Maddin or those claiming under him; and this deponent further saith that about that time the settlements distant from the towns were very much retarded by the hostile and repeated depredations of the Indians, who frequently made incursions into the settlements and drove off or frightened the inhabitants.

BARTHOLOMEW ST. GEMMES.

Sworn to and subscribed before me, Lewis F. Linn, one of the commissioners appointed to finally settle and adjust the titles and claims to land in Missouri, this 29th day of October, 1832.

LEWIS F. LINN, *Land Commissioner.*

And also came François Vallé, aged fifty-two years, who, being duly sworn as the law directs, deposeth and saith that, in the latter part of the winter or spring of 1800, he understood that Thomas Maddin was about to commence building a mill on the land mentioned in the concession aforesaid, and that himself or his hands, amongst whom was Job Westover, had gone out to the land for that purpose; that shortly after the same men returned, saying that they had been fired on and driven off by the Indians, (Osage;) that this deponent, with several others, went immediately to the place, and found the facts as above represented, for they saw the balls in the trees where the firing had been, and saw the tracks and signs of the Indians; that this deponent, with the others, followed the Indians all day, without success; and that said Maddin afterwards continued, from time to time, to progress in building the mill, and in 1803 the deponent assisted in building and finishing the mill; that said Maddin built a small house and opened some land, and that he well knows that the said mill has been in operation, generally, ever since, and that the said land was actually inhabited and cultivated from the date aforesaid ever since, and still is; that said Maddin continued to clear and improve the land till, he believes, there were more than one hundred, perhaps one hundred and fifty acres, improved and in cultivation; and that said Maddin, at the date of the grant, and ever since, was, and has been, a residenter of the country.

F. VALLE.

Sworn to and subscribed before me, Lewis F. Linn, one of the commissioners appointed to finally settle and adjust the titles and claims to land in Missouri, this 30th day of October, 1832.

LEWIS F. LINN.

And also came Joseph Vital, about fifty years of age, who, being duly sworn, deposeth and saith that he has been a citizen of this country from since he was eight years of age; that he is well acquainted with the tract of land claimed in the concession aforesaid, as also with Thomas Maddin, who was at the date of the grant, and still is, a citizen and residenter of this country; that he knows that about the year 1800 or 1801 Thomas Maddin went, or took, or sent hands, he does not remember, and begun to prepare to build a mill on the same, and that they were fired on by the Indians and driven off; that this witness was one of the party who went out in pursuit of the Indians, who were then very troublesome at any distance from the villages; and this deponent further says that in 1803, to the best of his recollection, he assisted in person to raise the mill, which was put into operation, and a mill continued on said land ever since; that about that time, or shortly afterwards, said Maddin begun and built a house and opened some land, and continued to improve said land and open more land, till he had from one hundred to one hundred and fifty acres opened; and he further knows that, from about the date of the concession to the present time, the said land has been inhabited, improved, and cultivated.

JOSEPH V. BEAUVAIS.

Sworn to and subscribed before me, Lewis F. Linn, one of the commissioners appointed to finally settle and adjust the titles and claims to land in Missouri, this 30th day of October, 1832.

L. F. LINN.

(See book No. 6, pages 43, 44, 45, and 46.)

November 5, 1833.—The board met pursuant to adjournment. Present: L. F. Linn, A. G. Harrison, F. R. Conway, commissioners.

Thomas Maddin, claiming 1,500 arpents of land.—(See page 43 of this book.) The board are unanimously of opinion that this claim ought to be confirmed to the said Thomas Maddin, or his legal representatives, according to the concession.—(See book No. 6, page 296.)

L. F. LINN.
F. R. CONWAY.
A. G. HARRISON.

No. 31.—William James, *claiming* 600 *arpents*.

To Mr. Zenon Trudeau, lieutenant governor and commander-in-chief of the western part of Illinois, &c.:

William James, inhabitant of New Bourbon, supplicates very humbly, and has the honor to expose to you, that in consequence of the encouragements announced in Kentucky, that should be granted to honest, substantial, and Catholic inhabitants who would emigrate to, and establish themselves in Illinois, on the part belonging to his Majesty the King of Spain, he determined last year to come and settle himself with his family and slaves; that he has already built his dwelling-house upon a piece of land that he has acquired on the right bank of the river Aux Vases; but that land, by the small quantity of it, and its bad quality, (being composed of many unfertile hills,) is not sufficient to occupy his workmen and slaves, nor to furnish to their subsistence and that of his family, neither to maintain his cattle; therefore the petitioner has made researches for a piece of land fit for the cultivation of sundry productions, and has found one near his residence upon the said right side of said river Aux Vases, at about two miles from said river, and towards the concession of Job Westover. This piece of land may have in superficie the quantity of six hundred arpents, which does not exceed his force in family and slaves, neither his means and faculties. In consequence, the petitioner applies to you, sir, that you may be pleased to grant to him, his heirs, and assignees, in full property, the concession of said land such as it is here above described, consisting in six hundred arpents in superficie, in order to cultivate it regularly in divers productions for his subsistence and that of his family and slaves, and for the maintenance of his cattle. In so doing, he will never cease to pray for the conservation of your days.

Done at New Bourbon February 7, 1798.

WILLIAM JAMES.

St. Louis, *February* 20, 1798.

The surveyor of this jurisdiction, Don Antonio Soulard, shall put William James in possession of the land asked for in the present petition, in continuation of which he shall draw a proces verbal of his survey, and the whole returned to us and sent to the governor general of the province, for him to determine definitively upon the concession of said land.

ZENON TRUDEAU.

The present original of the title of concession has been registered, and its collated copy deposited in the archives of the post of New Bourbon, under No. 37.

DELASSUS.

Truly translated. St. Louis, November 24, 1832.

JULIUS DE MUN.

No.	Name of original claimant.	Quantity, arpents.	Nature and date of claim.	By whom granted.	By whom surveyed, date and situation.
31	William James......	600	Concession, January 20, 1798.	Z. Trudeau.	

Evidence with reference to minutes and records.

December 5, 1807.—The board met pursuant to adjournment. Present: the honorable John B. C. Lucas, Clement B. Penrose, and Frederick Bates.

William James, claiming six hundred arpents of land situated on the river Aux Vases; produces in support of said claim, a concession from Zenon Trudeau, lieutenant governor, dated February 20, 1798.

Thomas Maddin, being duly sworn, says that said tract has neither been inhabited nor cultivated, but had the concession either in 1798 or 1799 for the purpose of surveying the same. Laid over for decision.—(See book No. 3, pages 137 and 158.)

May 4, 1810.—Board met. Present: John B. C. Lucas, Clement B. Penrose, and Frederick Bates, commissioners.

William James, claiming 600 arpents of land.—(See book No. 3, page 157.) It is the opinion of the board that this claim ought not to be confirmed.—(See book No. 4, page 350.)

November 26, 1832.—The board met pursuant to adjournment. Present: Lewis F. Linn, F. R. Conway, commissioners.

William James, claiming 600 arpents of land.—(See book No. 3, page 157; record book D, pages 40 and 41.) Produces a paper purporting to be an original concession from Zenon Trudeau, dated February 20, 1798. The following additional testimony was taken in the foregoing case, in compliance with a resolution of this board of the 10th of October last:

STATE OF MISSOURI, *county of St. Genevieve:*

William James, claiming six hundred arpents of land situated in the late district of St. Genevieve, now county of St. Genevieve, in the State of Missouri, on the right bank of the river Aux Vases, by virtue of a concession from Zenon Trudeau, late lieutenant governor of Louisiana, dated the 20th day of February, 1798, made in conformity of a petition of the said James, dated the 7th of February, 1798, and an order of survey to Antoine Soulard, late surveyor general under the Spanish government, of the date first aforesaid. Produces the original concession and order of survey above referred to. When James J. Fenwick, of lawful age, being duly sworn as the law directs, deposeth and saith that he is well acquainted with the claimant in this case, William James; that he came to this country in the year 1797 and settled in the country; that he has remained a residenter of this country from that time to the present moment; that he settled on a tract of land purchased of one Robert Smith, on the river Aux Vases, a few miles from and below the tract claimed; that he has remained in the country and on the land aforesaid ever since.

JAMES F. FENWICK.

Sworn to and subscribed before me, Lewis F. Linn, one of the commissioners for finally settling and adjusting the titles and claims to lands in the State of Missouri, this 26th day of October, 1832.

LEWIS F. LINN.

John Baptiste Vallé, aged seventy-two years, being duly sworn in the case as the law directs, deposeth and saith that he is well acquainted with the handwriting and signature of Zenon Trudeau, who was the lieutenant governor of Louisiana under the late Spanish government; that the signature to the concession of William James for 600 arpents of land, dated February 20, 1798, and an order of survey of the same date, are in the handwriting of the said Zenon Trudeau; and that the memorandum at the bottom of said concession (that the same was duly recorded) is in the proper hand of Charles Dehault Delasssus Deluziere, then commandant; that he knows the said William James came to this country in the year 1797 or 1798, to the best of his recollection, and that he has remained a residenter of the country ever since; that said James settled on the river Aux Vases, a few miles below the land claimed in the concession, where he has remained ever since; that he knows it was considered very dangerous for many years after said James came to the country to make settlements or make surveys at any distance from the towns and settled parts of the country.

BAPTISTE VALLÉ.

Sworn to and subscribed before me, Lewis F. Linn, one of the commissioners for finally settling and adjusting titles and claims to lands in the State of Missouri, this 26th day of October, 1832.

LEWIS F. LINN.

(See book No. 6, pages 48, 49, and 50.)

November 5, 1833.—The board met pursuant to adjournment. Present: L. F. Linn, A. G. Harrison, F. R. Conway, commissioners.

William James, claiming 600 arpents of land.—(See page 48 of this book.) The board are unanimously of opinion that this claim ought to be confirmed to the said William James or his legal representatives, according to the concession.—(See book No. 6, page 297.)

L. F. LINN.
F. R. CONWAY.
A. G. HARRISON.

No. 32.—Charles Frémon Delauriere, by Widow Leclerc, *claiming* 300 *arpents.*

To Mr. Charles Delassus, lieutenant governor and commander-in-chief of the western part of Illinois:

Augustin Charles Frémon Delauriere, &c., residing at St. Genevieve, supplicates very humbly, and has the honor to represent to you, that, wishing to establish a plantation in order to cultivate the soil and raise cattle, to provide for his subsistence and for that of his family, he had asked, by the petition here annexed, dated May 8, 1797, a concession for five hundred and sixty arpents of land in superficie, along the little river Saline; and your predecessor had condescended to promise to the petitioner to deliver to him the title in form, but, unfortunately for the petitioner, it resulted from the survey of the concession before granted to Madame Widow De Villars in this district that the whole of the land asked for by the petitioner was comprised in her concession, as appears by the decree (inserted at the foot of the above-mentioned petition) of the commandant of New Bourbon, dated May 29, 1798, who directs the petitioner to make a new search and petition for other lands belonging to the King's domain; that, in consequence, having visited various parts of the country, he has found a tract of land suitable and convenient to his views, and consisting of three hundred arpents or thereabout in superficie, situated at the mouth of the rivulet ——, distant about one league and a half north of this village on the shore of the Mississippi, which tract has not been granted to any person, and is a part of the King's domain. The petitioner hopes to obtain the concession of said tract, the more so, being a married man, and having with him a sister-in-law and an orphan, slaves, hired hands, and cattle, and besides having, in all the affairs wherein his Catholic Majesty and the public have been interested, employed himself with zeal and gratuitously in his quality of public scrivener; therefore the petitioner applies to you, sir, praying you may be pleased to grant to him, his heirs and assignees, in full property, the concession of the tract here above-mentioned, consisting of about three hundred arpents in superficie, to establish a plantation thereon, to cultivate the land and raise a great quantity of cattle. In so doing, the petitioner shall never cease to pray for the conservation of your days.

FRÉMON DELAURIERE.

St. Genevieve, *December* 4, 1799.

We, commandant of the said post of St. Genevieve, do certify to the lieutenant governor of Louisiana that the land asked for by the petitioner is not granted to any person, and is a part of his Catholic Majesty's domain. Moreover, we do attest that the said petitioner resides in this post since seven years, and that he unites the necessary qualities and circumstances, prescribed by the regulations, to obtain the concession he solicits.

FRANCISCO VALLÉ.

Being convinced, by the information of the commandant of St. Genevieve, Don Francisco Vallé, that the land solicited is vacant, and is not prejudicial to the surrounding neighbors, and considering that the petitioner has been a long time settled in this country, and that his family is sufficiently considerable to obtain the quantity of land which he solicits, the surveyor, Don Antonio Soulard, shall put the interested in possession of said land, and shall make a procès verbal of his survey in continuation, in order to serve in soliciting the concession from the intendant general, to whom alone, by order of his Majesty, corresponds the distributing and granting all classes of the royal domain.

CARLOS DEHAULT DELASSUS.

St. Louis, *December* 10, 1799.

Retroceded the above concession, such as it is, to Madame Widow Leclerc, her heirs or assigns, forever and without any reserve.

FRÉMON DELAURIERE.

Truly translated. St. Louis, December 6, 1832.

JULIUS DE MUN.

No.	Name of original claimant.	Quantity, in arpents.	Nature and date of claim.	By whom granted.	By whom surveyed, date, and situation.
32	Charles Frémon Delauriere, by his legal representatives.	300	Concession, Dec. 10, 1799.	Carlos Dehault Delassus.	

Evidence with reference to minutes and records.

November 25, 1811.—Board met. Present: John B. C. Lucas, Clement B. Penrose, and Frederick Bates, commissioners.

Widow Leclerc, assignee of Charles Frémon Delauriere, claiming 240 arpents of land, situate in Mississippi, district of St. Genevieve, produces record by concession from C. D. Delassus, lieutenant governor, dated December 10, 1799, record of plat of survey, dated 21st, and certified February 26, 1806. It is the opinion of the board that this claim ought not to be confirmed.—(See book No. 5, page 447.)

November 26, 1832.—The board met pursuant to adjournment. Present: Lewis F. Linn, F. R. Conway, commissioners.

Charles Frémon Delauriere, by his legal representatives, claiming 300 arpents of land, (see book No. 5, page, 447; record book C, pages 401 and 402,) produces a paper purporting to be an original concession from Charles Dehault Delassus, dated December 10, 1799. The following additional testimony was taken in the foregoing case, in compliance with a resolution of this board of the 10th of October last.

STATE OF MISSOURI, *county of St. Genevieve:*

The heirs and legal representatives of Marie Louise Leclerc, under Augustin Charles Frémon Delauriere, claiming three hundred arpents of land, situate in the late district of St. Genevieve, now county of St. Genevieve, in the State of Missouri, produce the original concession, dated the 10th day of December, 1799, made to the said Augustin Charles Frémon Delauriere, in his petition, by Charles Dehault Delassus, the late lieutenant governor of Louisiana, together with the original assignment of the said Augustin Charles F. Delauriere to the said Marie Louise Leclerc, when Henry Morris, aged seventy-three, being produced and sworn as the law directs, deposeth and saith that, under and by the orders and directions of the said Marie Louise Leclerc, now deceased, as early as the year 1799 he actually worked on the said land claimed in the concession; that he cut logs and built a house on said land, and made a garden on the land; that the negroes of the said Madame Leclerc were, by her orders and directions, with him, and worked with him; and that in the year 1800 a field was made, and corn planted; and that from the year 1799 up to the present time, the said tract of land has been continually inhabited and cultivated, and that stock were left thereon; that when he worked there in 1799, he understood that the said Madame Leclerc had purchased the said land of the said Delauriere. And further this deponent saith that, at the date of the grant aforesaid, the said Augustin Charles Frémon Delauriere and the said Madame Leclerc were both residenters of the country; that he was well acquainted with them both, and that they continued residenters.

HENRY MORRIS, his x mark.

Sworn to and subscribed before me, Lewis F. Linn, one of the commissioners appointed to finally settle and adjust the titles and claims to lands in Missouri, this 30th day of October, 1832.

LEWIS F. LINN.

And also came F. Vallé, aged fifty-two years, who, being duly sworn as the law directs, deposeth and saith that he was well acquainted with Charles Dehault Delassus; that he was, in the year 1799, the lieutenant governor of Upper Louisiana; that he was well acquainted with the writing of said Dehault Delassus, having seen him write, and that the name and signature to the said concession, dated the 10th day of December, 1799, given by said Charles Dehault Delassus to said Augustin Charles Frémon Delauriere, for 300 arpents of land, is in the proper handwriting of the said Charles Dehault Delassus.

FRANÇOIS VALLÉ.

Sworn to and subscribed before me, Lewis F. Linn, one of the commissioners appointed to finally settle and adjust the titles and claims to lands in Missouri, this 30th day of October, 1832.

LEWIS F. LINN.

(See book No. 6, page 50.)

November 5, 1853.—The board met pursuant to adjournment. Present: L. F. Linn, A. G. Harrison, F. R. Conway, commissioners.

Charles Frémon Delauriere, claiming 300 arpents of land.—(See page 50 of this book.) The board are unanimously of opinion that this claim ought to be confirmed to the said Charles Frémon Delauriere, or his legal representatives, according to the extent of the survey of 402 arpents, unless it conflicts with claims previously granted, and then to the extent that it does not conflict, and in no event under 300 arpents.—(See book No. 6, page 297.)

Conflicting claims.

L. F. Linn states that the said land is covered by an entry made under the United States by Joseph Diel, in consequence of claimant not furnishing a survey of his claim to the United States.

L. F. LINN.
F. R. CONWAY.
A. G. HARRISON.

No. 33.—MANUEL DE LISA, *claiming* 6,000 *arpents.*

To the Lieutenant Governor:

Don Manuel de Lisa, merchant of New Orleans, for the present in this town of St. Louis, with due respect represents to you that it being his intention to establish himself in this country with his family, which is now ascending this river in a boat of his own, therefore the petitioner wishes to obtain a concession for six thousand arpents of land in superficie upon one of the banks of the river Missouri, in a place where may be found some small creek emptying into the said river, in order to facilitate the raising of cattle, and, with time, to be able to make shipments of salted as well as dried meat to the capital; in consequence, the petitioner humbly supplicates you to condescend to admit his petition for the reasons already mentioned, and order to be given to the petitioner the title of property which he solicits, favor which he hopes to receive of your known justice. May God preserve your life many years.

MANUEL DE LISA.

ST. LOUIS, *July* 16, 1799.

ST. LOUIS, *July* 17, 1799.

In a vacant place along the river Missouri, and to the satisfaction of the interested, the surveyor, Don Antonio Soulard, shall put him in possession of the six thousand arpents of land in superficie which he solicits, in order that, according to the procès verbal of survey, the corresponding title of concession may be expedited to him; meanwhile, from this moment, the said interested party is authorized to make use of the tract of land which he has chosen, as being his own property.

ZENON TRUDEAU.

Registered at the demand of the interested, book No. 2, pages 32 and 33 of said book.

SOULARD.

Truly translated. St. Louis, December 25, 1832.

JULIUS DE MUN.

No.	Name of original claimant.	Quantity in arpents.	Nature and date of claim.	By whom granted.	By whom surveyed, date, and situation.
33	Manuel de Lisa, by his legal representatives.	6,000	Concession, July 17, 1799.	Zenon Trudeau.	

Evidence with reference to minutes and records.

August 22, 1806.—(Omitted in their proper place.) Manuel de Lisa, *assignee of Joachin Lisa*, (in his own name, and not as assignee,) claiming 6,000 arpents of land, by virtue of a concession from Zenon Trudeau, duly registered, dated July 17, 1799, *and a deed of transfer of the same, dated July* 8, 1804. (This is an error, the grant being made to Manuel de Lisa himself.)

Jacques Clamorgan, being duly sworn, says that he was present at the lieutenant governor's house when the aforesaid concession was given to claimant; that the same was granted at the time it bears date.—(See book No. 2, page 33.)

November 23, 1808.—Board met. Present: The Hon. John B. C. Lucas, Clement B. Penrose, and Frederick Bates, commissioners.

Manuel de Lisa, claiming 6,000 arpents of land, unlocated, produces to the board a concession from Zenon Trudeau, lieutenant governor, for the same, dated July 17, 1799. Eugenio Alvarez, sworn, says that the father of claimant came to this country with him, the witness, at the time the Spaniards took possession here; that claimant's father was then in the service of Spain, and died in the service; that claimant was born a subject of Spain, in Spanish America, and has resided since his birth, or shortly after, in Louisiana. (Here follows the testimony of Jacques Clamorgan, taken August 22, 1806.) Clamorgan declares that he has no other claim to land in Louisiana in his own name. Laid over for decision.—(See book No. 3, page 365.)

July 9, 1810.—Board met. Present: John B. C. Lucas, Clement B. Penrose, and Frederick Bates, commissioners.

Manuel de Lisa, claiming 6,000 arpents of land.—(See book No. 3, page 365.) It is the opinion of the board that this claim ought not to be confirmed.—(See book No. 4, page 421.)

November 27, 1832.—The board met pursuant to adjournment. Present: Lewis F. Linn, F. R. Conway, commissioners.

Manuel de Lisa, by his legal representatives, claiming 6,000 arpents of land, (see book B, page 91; book No. 2, page 33; No. 3, page 365; and No. 4, page 421,) produces a paper purporting to be an original concession from Zenon Trudeau, dated July 17, 1799. Charles Frémon Delauriere, being duly sworn, saith that the signatures to said concession, and to the registering, are in the proper hadwriting of the said Zenon Trudeau and of Antoine Soulard. M. P. Le Duc, being duly sworn, saith that the signature to the petition is in the proper handwriting of said Manuel de Lisa—(See book No. 6, page 52.)

November 5, 1835.—The board met pursuant to adjournment. Present: L. F. Linn, A. G. Harrison, F. R. Conway, commissioners.

Manuel de Lisa, claiming 6,000 arpents of land.—(See page 52 of this book.) The board are unanimously of opinion that this claim ought to be confirmed to the said Manuel de Lisa, or his legal representatives, according to the concession.—(See book No. 6, page 298.)

L. F. LINN.
F. R. CONWAY.
A. G. HARRISON.

No. 34.—Francis Lacombe, *claiming four hundred arpents.*

To Mr. Charles Dehault Delassus, lieutenant governor of Upper Louisiana:

Sir: Francis Lacombe, residing on the Maramec, has the honor to supplicate you to grant to him a tract of land situated on the hills of the Maramec, containing in all four hundred arpents, to wit: ten arpents in front, east and west, by forty in depth, north and south. The said land (adjoining the bottom land of Nely Gormenie) has been cultivated in 1789 by one Joseph Philippes, who was the last to abandon it; and, inasmuch as no one is in possession of the said land but your petitioner, who has already caused a house to be built thereon, where his family is already settled, the petitioner presumes to hope that his excellency the governor will be pleased to grant to him the said land.

He has the honor to be, with profound respect, sir, your very humble and very obedient servant,

FRANCIS LACOMBE.

St. Louis of Illinois, *August* 1, 1799.

Considering that the petitioner has been a long time residing in this country, and that his family is considerable enough to obtain the quantity of land which he solicits, the surveyor, Don Antonio Soulard, shall put the interested in possession of it, and shall make a procès verbal of his survey in continuation, in order to serve to solicit the concession from the intendant, to whom alone corresponds, by order of his Majesty, the distributing and granting of all classes of lands of the royal domain.

CARLOS DEHAULT DELASSUS.

Truly translated. St. Louis, December 25, 1832.

JULIUS DE MUN.

No.	Name of original claimant.	Quantity, arpents.	Nature and date of claim.	By whom granted.	By whom surveyed, date, and situation.
34	François Lacombe, by Manuel Lisa's legal representatives.	400	Concession, Aug. 1, 1799.	Carlos Dehault Delassus.	

Evidence with reference to minutes and records.

November 23, 1808.—Board met. Present: the honorable John B. C. Lucas, Clement B. Penrose, and Frederick Bates.

Manuel Lisa, assignee of François Lacombe, claiming four hundred arpents of land on the Maramec, district of St. Louis, produces to the board a concession from Charles Dehault Delassus, lieutenant governor, to François Lacombe, for the same, dated February 26, 1800, (August 1, 1799;) a deed of conveyance from said Lacombe to claimant, dated May 14, 1804.

Louis Ménard, sworn, says that in the fall of the year before Adam House was killed on the Maramec that François Lacombe and his wife were residing on the tract claimed; that the whole neighborhood abandoned their land immediately after said House was killed. Laid over for decision.—(No. 3, page 364.)

July 9, 1810.—Board met. Present: John B. C. Lucas, Clement B. Penrose, and Frederick Bates, commissioners.

Manuel Lisa, assignee of François Lacombe, claiming 400 arpents of land.—(See book No. 3, page 364; see also Adam House's claim, book No. 3, page 330.) The concession in this claim is dated August 1, 1799. It is the opinion of the board that this claim ought not to be confirmed.—(See book No. 4, p. 421.)

November 28, 1832.—The board met pursuant to adjournment. Present: Lewis F. Linn, F. R. Conway, commissioners.

François Lacombe, by Manuel Lisa's legal representatives, claiming 400 arpents of land.—(See book C, pages 442 and 443; No. 3, pages 330 and 364; No. 4, page 421.) Produces a paper purporting to be an original concession from Charles Dehault Delassus, dated August 1, 1799.

M. P. Le Duc, only sworn, saith that the signature to the said concession is in the proper handwriting of the said Charles Dehault Delassus.—(See book No. 6, page 61.)

October 27, 1808.—Board met. Present: the honorable Clement B. Penrose and Frederick Bates, commissioners.

The heirs of Adam House, claiming 400 arpents of land, situate on the Fourche à Rénault, district of St. Louis, produces to the board a notice of claim dated June 27, 1808; a certificate from Don Zenon Trudeau, lieutenant governor, of having given to Adam House permission to settle, and also that said House had been settled for two years before, dated June 10, 1799; a concession from Don Carlos Dehault Delassus, lieutenant governor, for the same, dated September 30, 1799.

John Cummins, sworn, says that about eleven years ago Adam House settled on said tract, and inhabited and cultivated the same three years, and was preparing for a fourth crop when himself and son were both killed by the Indians on the tract claimed. Laid over for decision.—(See book No. 3, page 330.)

November 5, 1853.—The board met pursuant to adjournment. Present: L. F. Linn, A. G. Harrison, F. R. Conway, commissioners.

François Lacombe claiming 400 arpents of land.—(See book No. 3, page 364, and No. 4, page 421.) The board are unanimously of opinion that this claim ought to be confirmed to the said François Lacombe, or his legal representatives, according to the concession.—(See book No. 6, page 298.)

L. F. LINN.
F. R. CONWAY.
A. G. HARRISON.

No. 35.—Philip Bacanné, *claiming* 480 *arpents.*

To Don Zenon Trudeau, lieutenant governor of all the western part of Illinois:

Sir: Philip Bacanné, citizen of this town of St. Louis, has the honor to represent, that wishing to form an establishment in order to cultivate the land and raise cattle thereon, in a place situate to his views, therefore he supplicates you to be pleased to grant to him 12 arpents of land in front by 40 arpents in depth, at the place commonly called Portage des Sioux, to be taken on the bank of the Mississippi, by lines which shall be perpendicular to it.

his
PHILIPPE × BACANNÉ.
mark.

St. Louis, *December* 15, 1796.

The surveyor shall place the petitioner upon the quantity of land which he petitions for, at Portage des Sioux, in giving the preference to those who should have solicited any before him; and this he will know by the date and number of the decrees of those to whom lands have been granted.

ZENON TRUDEAU.

St. Louis, *December* 15, 1796.

Truly translated. St. Louis, December 24, 1832.

JULIUS DE MUN.

No.	Name of original claimant.	Quantity, arpents.	Nature and date of claim.	By whom granted.	By whom surveyed, date, and situation.
35	Philippe Bacanné....	480	Concession, Dec. 15, 1796, and a subsequent order of survey, Nov. 18, 1803.	Zenon Trudeau.	

Evidence with reference to minutes and records.

May 8, 1806.—The board met agreeably to adjournment. Present: The Hon. Clement B. Penrose and James L. Donaldson, esq.

The same, Manuel Lisa, assignee of Philippe Bacanné, claiming 4,800 (480) arpents of land, situated in the district of St. Louis, produces a concession from Zenon Trudeau, dated December 14, (15,) 1796, and a certificate and plat of survey, dated February 25, 1806; a deed of transfer of the same, dated August 3, 1804. The above remarks apply to this case. (From the antiquity of the instrument, from its appearance, and from the signature of Zenon Trudeau, the board are satisfied that this is a *bona fide* claim, and that the said concession is neither fraudulent nor antedated.) The board reject this claim, the same being unsupported by actual inhabitation and cultivation on the 1st of October, 1800, and the above concession not being duly registered.—(See book 1, page 285.)

November 24, 1808.—Board met. Present: Hon. John B. C. Lucas, Clement B. Penrose, and Frederick Bates.

Manuel Lisa, assignee of Philippe Bacanné, claiming 480 arpents of land.

Antoine Soulard sworn, says that he had the concession in this claim in his possession, to make a survey, some time in 1797; that it was one of the concessions which interfered with the Portage des Sioux; in consequence of which information the lieutenant governor, Delassus, ordered them to be surveyed on the vacant domain. Order dated November 18, 1803. Laid over for decision.—(See book No. 3, page 368.)

July 10, 1810.—Board met. Present: John B. C. Lucas, Clement B. Penrose, and Frederick Bates, commissioners.

Manuel Lisa, assignee of Philippe Bacanné, claiming 480 arpents of land.—(See book No. 1, page 285; book No. 3, page 268.) It is the opinion of the board that this claim ought not to be confirmed.—(See book No. 4, page 423.)

November 28, 1832.—The board met pursuant to adjournment. Present: Lewis F. Linn, F. R. Conway, commissioners.

Philippe Bacanné, by Manuel Lisa, legal representatives, claiming 480 arpents of land.—(See book C, page 442; No. 1, page 285; No. 3, page 368.) For survey, see book C, page 443; No. 4, page 423. Produces a paper purporting to be an original concession from Zenon Trudeau, dated September 15, 1796. M. P. Le Duc, duly sworn, saith that the signature to the said concession is in the proper handwriting of Zenon Truedeau.—(See book No. 6, page 61.)

November 5, 1833.—The board met pursuant to adjournment. Present: L. F. Linn, A. G. Harrison, F. R. Conway, commissioners.

Philippe Bacanné, claiming 480 arpents of land.—(See page 61 of this book.) It appears from the testimony that the land at the spot indicated in the petition was already occupied, and that a new order of survey, dated November 18, 1803, was issued by Charles Dehault Delassus, for the same quantity of land, to be located in any other vacant place. The board are unanimously of opinion that this claim ought to be confirmed to the said Philippe Bacanné, or his legal representatives, according to the said order of survey, dated November 18, 1803.—(See book No. 6, page 298.)

L. F. LINN.
F. R. CONWAY.
A. G. HARRISON

No. 36.—Baptiste Riviere, *claiming* 400 *arpents.*

To the lieutenant governor of the western part of Illinois:

Baptiste Riviere, inhabitant of the village of Florissant, (St. Ferdinand,) has the honor to represent that, wishing to establish a tract of land of 20 arpents square, situated opposite L'Isle aux Biches, (Elk island,) at about 10 arpents from the river Missouri, to be taken from the foot of the hills, in order to improve it in the time prescribed by the regulations, therefore he supplicates you to grant to him the concession of said tract, favor which he hopes from the protection you have always given to the ancient farmers of this jurisdiction.

his
BAPT. + RIVIERE.
mark.

The surveyor of this jurisdiction, Don Antonio Soulard, in case the land demanded belongs to the King's domain, and is not prejudicial to any one, shall put the said Bapt. Riviere in possession of it, in order that, in continuation of his procès verbal of survey, we may deliver to him the concession in form.

ZENON TRUDEAU.

St. Louis, *October* 17, 1796.

Don Antonio Soulard, surveyor general of this upper Louisiana:

We do inform the interested that the tract of land mentioned in his petition has been surveyed in favor of Mr. William Griffin, by virtue of the decree of the lieutenant governor, Don Zenon Trudeau, bearing date March 2, 1796. Therefore it is necessary that he should obtain an order from the lieutenant governor, in order that the same quantity of land may be surveyed for him in any other vacant place of the domain.

SOULARD.

St. Louis, *January* 3, 1803.

St. Louis of Illinois, *January* 8, 1803.

Cognizance being taken of the foregoing documents, and of the legality of the interested's rights, the proper quantity of land expressed in his memorial may be surveyed for him in any other part of the royal domain, at his choice.

DELASSUS.

Registered at the desire of the interested.—(Book No. 2, page 1.)

SOULARD.

No.	Name of original claimant.	Quantity in arpents.	Nature and date of claim.	By whom granted.	By whom surveyed, date, and situation.
36	Baptiste Riviere.	400	Concession, Oct. 17, 1796. Concession, Jan. 8, 1803.	Zenon Trudeau .... Carlos Dehault Delassus.	James Rankin, deputy surveyor, Feb. 25, 1806.

Evidence with reference to minutes and records.

May 8, 1806.—The board met agreeably to adjournment. Present: Clement B. Penrose and James L. Donaldson, esqrs.

Manuel Lisa, assignee of Bte. Riviere, claiming 400 arpents of land situate in the district of St. Louis, produces a concession from Zenon Trudeau, duly registered, dated October 17, 1796, and a survey and plat of the same, dated February 25, 1806; a deed of transfer of the same, dated August 3, 1804. From the antiquity of the instrument, from its appearance, and from the signature of Zenon Trudeau, the board are satisfied that this is a *bona fide* claim, and that the said concession is neither fraudulent nor antedated.

They reject this claim, the same being unsupported by actual inhabitation and cultivation.—(See book No. 1, page 285.)

November 24, 1808.—Board met. Present: Hon. John B. C. Lucas, Clement B. Penrose, and Frederick Bates.

Manuel Lisa, assignee of Baptiste Riviere, claiming 400 arpents of land situate in the district of St. Louis, produces to the board a certificate from Antoine Soulard, stating that the land claimed is not vacant, and that Baptiste Riviere must obtain a new order of survey from the lieutenant governor before it can be surveyed, dated January 3, 1803; produces also an order of survey from Charles Dehault Delassus, lieutenant governor, dated January 8, 1803.

Antoine Soulard, sworn, says that he knows the concession from Zenon Trudeau, lieutenant governor, was given about the time it bears date, and that he had said concession in his hands to survey some time before his certificate was given, and that said certificate was given at the time it bears date.

Laid over for decision.—(See book No. 3, page 368.)

July 10, 1810.—Board met. Present: John B. C. Lucas, Clement B. Penrose, and Frederick Bates, commissioners.

Manuel Lisa, assignee of Baptiste Riviere, claiming 400 arpents of land.—(See book No. 1, page 285; book No. 3, page 368.)

It is the opinion of the board that this claim ought not to be confirmed. The board refer, as it respects the registry, to the remark in the claim of Jean P. Cabanné.—(Book No. 4, page 386; see book No. 4, page 423.)

November 28, 1832.—The board met pursuant to adjournment. Present: Lewis F. Linn and F. R. Conway, commissioners.

Baptiste Riviere, by Manuel Lisa, legal representatives, claiming 400 arpents of land.—(See book C, pages 442 and 443; No. 1, page 285; No. 3, page 368; and No. 4, page 423.) Produces a paper purporting to be an original concession from Zenon Trudeau, dated October 17, 1796; also a concession from Charles Dehault Delassus, dated January 8, 1803.

M. P. Le Duc, being duly sworn, saith, that the signatures to the above concession are in the proper and respective handwriting of said Zenon Trudeau and said Charles D. Delassus; and that the signature to the report of Soulard, on the first concession, is in the proper handwriting of said Soulard.

Claimant also produces a paper purporting to be a plat of survey executed by James Rankin, deputy surveyor, February 25, 1806.

M. P. Le Duc saith, that the signature to said plat of survey for the above concessions is in the proper handwriting of said Rankin; and that said Rankin was acting as deputy surveyor under Soulard before and after the change of government.—(See book No. 6, pages 61 and 62.)

November 5, 1833.—The board met pursuant to adjournment. Present: L. F. Linn, A. G. Harrison, F. R. Conway, commissioners.

Baptiste Riviere, claiming 400 arpents of land.—(See pages 61 and 62 of this book.)

The board remark that the survey produced in this case is probably the survey of the tract claimed, but it is not so stated in the said plat.

The board are unanimously of opinion that this claim ought to be confirmed to the said Baptiste Riviere, or his legal representatives, according to the concession.—(See book No. 6, page 299.)

L. F. LINN.
F. R. CONWAY.
A. G. HARRISON.

No. 37.—Francis Coleman, *claiming* 2,500 *arpents.*

To Don Henry Peyroux de la Coudreniere, captain in the army, civil and military commandant of the post of St. Genevieve of Illinois:

Sir: Francis Coleman, inhabitant of the Petites Côtes, (New Bourbon,) in the district of this post, has the honor to represent to you that, being always infirm, and having a numerous family to maintain, he would wish to form his children a permanent establishment where he might provide to their wants; in consequence, he supplicates you, sir, to be pleased to grant to him the concession, in full property, for him, his heirs, and assigns, of a tract of land situated on the north side of the river establishment, taking in its width, of about 50 arpents, from the edge of the said river to the foot of the hills, and taking its depth from the plantation of one Thomas Clem, to which it joins, and running 50 arpents in descending along the edge of the said river and following its direction towards the Mississippi. The said tract of land belonging to the King's domain, and upon which the petitioner has begun to work some time since.

The petitioner shall never cease to pray for your conservation.

FRANÇOIS COLEMAN, his ⋈ mark.

St. Genevieve, *February* 4, 1788.

Be the present petition forwarded to Don Manuel Perez, captain of the first stationary battalion of Louisiana, and lieutenant governor of the western part of Illinois, in order that he may be pleased to determine on the subject.

PEYROUX DE LA COUDRENIERE.

St. Genevieve, *February* 20, 1788.

The captain of infantry, Don Henry Peyroux, commandant of the post of St. Genevieve, may grant to Francis Coleman, as being in possession, the arpents of land he solicits for in the foregoing memorial, provided they have not been already granted to another person.

MANUEL PEREZ.

St. Louis of Illinois, *March* 12, 1788.

We, Don Henry Peyroux de la Coudreniere, captain of infantry, civil and military commandant of the post of St. Genevieve of Illinois, having verified that the tract of land asked for by Mr. Francis Coleman, inhabitant of the village *Des Petites Côtes*, (New Bourbon,) belongs to his Majesty's domain, we do grant to the said petitioner, in full property, for him and his heirs, to enjoy forever, a tract of land of fifty arpents in length by fifty arpents in width, situated on the north shore of the river establishment, adjoining to Mr. Thomas Clem's plantation on one side, conformably, in all, to the demand specified in the petition on the other side.

PEYROUX DE LA COUDRENIERE.

St. Genevieve, *March* 15, 1788.

Truly translated. St. Louis, December 22, 1832.

JULIUS DE MUN.

No.	Name of original claimant.	Quantity in arpents.	Nature and date of claim.	By whom granted.	By whom surveyed, date, and situation.
37	François Coleman, by his legal representatives.	2,500	Decree of Manuel Perez, March 12, 15, 1788. Concession, March 15, 1788.	Manuel Perez. Henry Peyroux.	Thomas Maddin, D. S., February 21, 1806. Certified by Soulard, February 28, 1806.

Evidence with reference to minutes and records.

April 11, 1810.—Board met. Present: John B. C. Lucas, Clement B. Penrose, and Frederick Bates, commissioners.

Amable Partinay, assignee of Theresa Colman, claiming 2,500 arpents of land, situate on the river establishment, district of St. Genevieve, produces to the board an order from Manuel Perez, lieutenant governor, to Henry Peyroux, commandant of St. Genevieve, to concede, provided it is vacant, a tract of land 50 arpents square, situated on the river establishment at the side towards the Mississippi, adjoining land of Thomas Clem, to Francis Coleman, dated May 12, 1788; a concession from said Henry Peyroux, for the same, to F. Colman, dated May 15, 1788; a plat of survey, dated February 21, 1806, certified to be received for record February 28, 1806; transfer from Theresa Colman to claimant, dated January 29, 1806. The following testimony in the foregoing claim transcribed from the rough minutes, as perpetuated by the board on the 14th November, 1808:

Baptiste Bequet, sworn, says that twenty years ago Francis Colman had a house built on the tract claimed, and enclosed a field. It is the opinion of the board that this claim ought not to be confirmed.—(See book No. 4, page 316.)

November 29, 1832.—The board met pursuant to adjournment. Present: Lewis F. Linn and F. R. Conway, commissioners.

François Coleman, by his legal representatives, J. P. Cabanné and J. N. Macklet, claiming 2,500 arpents of land, (see book C, pages 121 and 143; No. 4, page 316,) produces a paper purporting to be a decree from Manuel Perez, lieutenant governor, dated March 12, 1788, and also a concession from H. Peyroux, late commandant of St. Genevieve, dated March 15, 1788; also a paper purporting to be a plat of survey executed by Thomas Maddin, deputy surveyor, on the 21st February, 1806; received for record by Antoine Soulard, surveyor general, February 28, 1806.

M. P. Le Duc, duly sworn, saith that the signatures to the foregoing papers are in the proper handwriting of the above-named persons who signed them.—(See book No. 6, page 64.)

November 5, 1833.—The board met pursuant to adjournment. Present: L. F. Linn, A. G. Harrison, F. R. Conway, commissioners.

Francis Coleman, claiming 2,500 arpents of land.—(See page 64 of this book.) The board are unanimously of opinion that this claim ought to be confirmed to the said Francis Coleman, or his legal representatives, according to the concession.—(See book No. 6, page 299.)

L. F. LINN.
F. R. CONWAY.
A. G. HARRISON.

No. 38.—Jean René Guiho de Klegand, *claiming* 500 *arpents.*

To the Chevalier Charles Dehault Delassus, lieutenant colonel in the armies of his Catholic Majesty, lieutenant governor and commander-in-chief of Upper Louisiana, &c.:

Jean René Guiho, Lord of Klegand, native of Nantes, in Brittany, formerly an officer in the navy' supplicates very humbly, and has the honor to represent, that having lost the greatest part of his fortùne in consequence of the French revolution and compelled to emigrate with his family, he landed in the United States of America, where he resided during several years; that having been strongly invited by the Chevalier Deluziere, commandant of New Bourbon, to come and definitively settle himself near him in the vicinity of said New Bourbon, besides being animated by the desire to live and die under the benevolent government of his Catholic Majesty, he had no difficulty to yield to an invitation so congenial to his views; that, in consequence, he sent, since last year, one of his sons to the said New Bourbon to secure a house, which was done by buying that of Mr. Fenwick, situated in the said village, where he has lately arrived with his family, composed of eight persons, his slaves, and cattle of every description; that the lands which he has acquired with said house being little adapted and not near sufficient to provide particularly to the maintenance and feeding of his cattle, he occupied himself, without delay, to the indispensable research of a tract of land convenient to place and raise his cattle thereon, and to make some improvements; that he has found one suitable to his views, situated on the south fork of the river Saline, to the west of the said river, and bounded by the said river, one arpent to the north of a small branch nearly opposite a tract of land belonging to the Chevalier Deluziere, which is on the eastward of the said river, starting from the first boundary and running to the south along the said river, and to the west along the said branch the distance of about one arpent to the hills, and along said hills running in a southerly direction, so as to contain from four to five hundered arpents of land in superficie; that this same tract of land, he has been assured, has not been granted to anybody and is a part of his Catholic Majesty's domain. For these motives the petitioner has recourse to you, sir, hoping that you may be pleased, provisionally and without delay, to grant to him, his heirs or assigns, in full property, the concession here above mentioned, situated on the said south fork of the river Saline, in order to cultivate and raise and maintain a great number of cattle thereon. In so doing he shall never cease to pray for the preservation of your days.

Done at New Bourbon, December 24, 1799.

J. GUIHO DE KLEGAND.

New Bourbon, *January* 9, 1800.

We, commandant of the said post of New Bourbon, do certify to the lieutenant governor of Upper Louisiana that the statement of the petitioner is very exact and true; that the land for which he asks a concession is a part of the King's domain; and that he unites the qualifications and circumstances prescribed by the regulations to obtain this favor from your justice and goodness.

PIERRE DELASSUS DELUZIERE.

St. Louis of Illinois, *January* 15, 1800.

It being obvious that the petitioner has more than the means and number of hands (populacion) necessary to obtain the concession solicited for, according to the tenor of the regulation of the governor general of this province, the surveyor, Don Antonio Soulard, shall put the interested in possession of it, (said land,) and shall make a procès verbal of his survey in continuation, in order to serve in soliciting the concession from the intendant general of these provinces, to whom alone corresponds, by order of his Majesty, the distributing and granting all classes of lands of the royal domain.

CARLOS DEHAULT DELASSUS.

In consequence of the verbal demand made by the daughter of the petitioner in this memorial, it was searched for and found amongst various others, and Don Ramon de Lopez y Angulo said: Be it presented to the fiscal.

[On each side there is a flourish.]

It has been presented to Señor Don Juan Ventura Morales, principal accomptant of the army and intendant *pro tempore* of the royal fisc of these provinces of Louisiana and Western Florida, who has set his paraph to it (que lo rubrico) in accordance with the counsellor general of the intendancy.

In New Orleans, October 22, 1802.

PEDRO PEDESCLAUX, *Public Scrivener.*

On said day I presented it to the intendant of the royal fisc, which I do certify.

PEDESCLAUX, *Scrivener.*

The fiscal having seen the petition presented by Mr. Jean René Guiho de Klegand, soliciting the grant of five hundred arpents of land in the place which he indicates in the district of Illinois, (in order to establish his family, composed of eight persons, and stating that since the year 1799 he went from France to the said post,) says that the said tract of land being vacant and belonging to the royal domain, as by information of the commandant of New Bourbon it appears to be, the fiscal is of opinion that it be granted to him, the plat and certificate of survey, which is to be executed by the surveyor of those settlements, being first presented. The tribunal will determine what shall be judged most conformable to justice, which is asked by the fiscal.

GILBERTO LEONARD.

New Orleans, *October* 23, 1832.

The plat of survey and measurement being presented, let them be brought, in order to determine upon the title.

[On each side a flourish.]

Señor Don Juan Ventura Morales, principal accomptant of the army, intendant *pro tem.* of these provinces of Louisiana and Western Florida, judge sub-delegate of the superintendency general, has given his decree, and set his paraph to it, (lo rubrico,) in accordance with the counsellor of the intendancy.

PEDRO PEDESCLAUX, *Public Scrivener.*

New Orleans, *October* 25, 1802.

On said day I gave notice of it to Miss Klegand, daughter of the petitioner.

PEDESCLAUX, *Scrivener.*

No.	Name of original claimant.	Quantity, in arpents	Name and date of claim.	By whom granted.	By whom surveyed, date, and situation.
38	Jean René Guiho de Klegand, by assignee, Matthew Duncan.	500	Concession, January 15, 1800.	Carlos Dehault Delassus.	Special location.

Evidence with reference to minutes and records.

June 28, 1806.—The board met agreeably to adjournment. Present: Clement B. Penrose and James L. Donaldson, esqs.

The same, (James Maxwell,) assignee of L. G. De Kerlegant, claiming a tract of 500 arpents of land situate on the Saline, district aforesaid, produces a concession from Charles Dehault Delassus, dated January 15, 1800, with a written certificate of reference of Morales to the fiscal and assessor for his opinion, certified by Pedro P. Delaure, notary public, under the date of October 22, 1802, who gives his opinion that the same may be granted by his certificate under his hand, dated October 23, same year, followed by an order of survey from Morales, under promise that upon producing a plat of survey a title or form will be granted, dated October 25, same year. Israel Dodge, being duly sworn, says that when the aforesaid Kerlegand obtained the aforesaid concession his family consisted of himself, wife, five children, and six slaves. The board reject this claim, and observe that they are satisfied that the aforesaid concession was granted at the time it bears date.—(See book No. 1, page 386.)

May 3, 1810.—Board met. Present: John B. C. Lucas, Clement B. Penrose, and Frederick Bates, commissioners.

James Maxwell, assignee of Ecuyer Jean René Guiho Sieur de Kerlegand, claiming 500 arpents of land.—(See book No. 1, page 386; book No. 3, page 149.) It is the opinion of the board that this claim ought not to be confirmed.—(See book No. 4, page 346.)

November 29, 1832.—The board met pursuant to adjournment. Present: Lewis F. Linn and F. R. Conway, commissioners.

Jean René Guiho de Klegant, by his assignee, Matthew Duncan, claiming 500 arpents of land, (see book B, page 500; No. 1, page 386; No. 3, page 346,) produces a paper purporting to be an original concession from Charles Dehault Delassus, dated January 15, 1800; also a deed of conveyance. M. P. Le Duc, duly sworn, saith that the signature to said concession is in the proper handwriting of said Charles Dehault Delassus.—(See book No. 6, page 64.)

November 5, 1833.—The board met pursuant to adjournment. Present: L. F. Linn, A. G. Harrison, and F. R. Conway, commissioners.

René Guiho de Kerlegand, claiming 500 arpents of land.—(See page 64 of this book.) The board are unanimously of opinion that this claim ought to be confirmed to the said René Guiho de Kerlegand, or his legal representatives, according to the concession.—(See book No. 6, page 299.)

L. F. LINN.
F. R. CONWAY.
A. G. HARRISON.

No. 39.—Marie Nicolle Les Bois, *claiming 244 arpents and 50 perches.*

To Don Charles Dehault Delassus, lieutenant colonel, attached to the stationary regiment of Louisiana, and lieutenant governor of the upper part of the same province:

Marie Nicolle Les Bois has the honor of representing to you that having lost her father and mother, since her most tender years, in consequence of a very well known disaster, which alone would be sufficient to render her situation interesting to all men of feelings, and having had for support, since that moment, an uncle and aunt, both respectable, who have taken care of her infancy; considering that time in its flight deprives her every day of some one of her protectors; that her brothers and sisters are all married and loaded with family and without fortune; that she remains as an insulated being, who cannot expect any assistance of any one whomsoever, and who, without fortune, finds herself under several points of view, in a calamitous situation, which appears to her to be worthy to attract the attention of the good heart everybody knows you possess. Full of this idea, and convinced of the generosity of the government, which has never ceased to grant favors to the unfortunate, and to be particularly the protector of orphans, she hopes you will be pleased to grant to her the concession of a tract of land situated to the south of this town, and being vacant lands of his Majesty's domain, and which may contain two hundred and thirteen arpents in superficie, more or less, which land shall be bounded as follows: to the north, south, and west by the vacant lands of the domain, and to the east by a concession of same width belonging to Mr. Antonio Soulard.

Such is the statement of my misfortune and pretensions, and I presume to hope this favor of the generosity of a benevolent and generous government, and of a chief as worthy as you are to fulfil its benevolent intentions.

MARIE NICOLLE LES BOIS.

St. Louis, *May* 10, 1803.

St. Louis of Illinois, *May* 11, 1803.

Having seen the foregoing statement, I do grant to Marie Nicolle Les Bois, for her and her heirs, the land which she solicits, in case it is not prejudicial to any person; and the surveyor of this Upper Louisiana, Don Antonio Soulard, shall put the petitioner in possession of the quantity of land she solicits, in the place designated, of which, when executed, he shall draw out a plat of survey, delivering the same to the party with his certificate, in order to serve to her to obtain the concession and title in form from the intendant general, to whom alone corresponds, by royal order, the distributing and granting of all classes of lands of the royal domain.

CARLOS DEHAULT DELASSUS.

Don Antonio Soulard, surveyor general of Upper Louisiana.

I do certify that I have measured, run the lines, and bounded, in favor of Marie Nicolle Les Bois, a piece of land of two hundred and forty-four arpents and fifty perches in superficie, measured with the perch of the city of Paris, of eighteen French feet in length, lineal measure of the same city, according to the agrarian measure of this province, which land is situated at the distance of about twenty-five arpents to the southwest of this town of St. Louis, and is bounded to the north-northeast by lands of Don Santiago Mackay; to the east-southeast by lands belonging to me; to the south-southwest in part by lands of Don Jh. Brazeau, and by vacant lands of the royal domain, and to the west-northwest by vacant lands; which measurement and survey I took, without regarding the variation of the needle, which is 7° 30′ east, as is evident by the foregoing figurative plat, on which are noted the dimensions, direction of the lines and limits, and other boundaries, &c. Said survey was executed by virtue of the memorial and decree of the lieutenant governor and sub-delegate of the royal fisc, Don Carlos Dehault Delassus, dated May 11, 1803.

In testimony whereof, I do give the present, with the preceding figurative plat, executed by my exertions on the 27th of May of the current year.

ANTONIO SOULARD, *Surveyor General.*

St. Louis, *August* 20, 1803.

Truly translated. St Louis, December 15, 1832.

JULIUS DE MUN.

No.	Name of original claimant.	Quantity, in arpents.	Nature and date of claim.	By whom granted.	By whom surveyed, date, and situation.
39	Marie Nicolle Les Bois, by her legal representatives.	244½	Concession, May 11, 1803.	Carlos Dehault Delassus.	Antonio Soulard, May 27, 1803; certified by him, August 20, 1803; distant about twenty-five arpents south of St. Louis.

Evidence with reference to minutes and records.

October 7, 1808.—Board met. Present: The honorable Clement B. Penrose and Frederick Bates.

Marie Nicolle Les Bois, claiming 244½ arpents of land, situated in the commons of St. Louis, produces to the board a concession from Don Charles Dehault Delassus, lieutenant governor, for the same, dated May 11, 1803; a plat and certificate of survey, dated May 27, 1803, and certified August 20, same year. Laid over for decision.—(See book No. 3, page 282.)

August 21, 1811.—Board met. Present: Clement B. Penrose and Frederick Bates, commissioners.

Marie Nicolle Les Bois, claiming 244½ arpents of land.—(See book No. 3, page 282.)

It is the opinion of the board that this claim ought not to be confirmed.—(See book No. 5, page 328.)

November 29, 1832.—The board met pursuant to adjournment. Present: Louis F. Linn, F. R. Conway, commissioners.

Marie Nicolle Les Bois, by her legal representatives, claiming 244½ arpents of land, (see book C, pages 73, 74, and 75; No. 3, page 282; No. 5, page 328,) produces a paper purporting to be an original concession for 213 arpents of land, more or less, from Charles Dehault Delassus, dated May 11, 1803; also a paper purporting to be a plat and certificate of survey for 244 arpents and 50 perches, taken May 27, and certified August 20, 1803, by Antonio Soulard.

Mr. P. Le Duc, duly sworn, saith that the signature to said concession is in the proper handwriting of the said Charles D. Delassus, and the signature to said certificate of survey is in the proper handwriting of said Soulard.—(See book No. 6, pages 64 and 65.)

November 5, 1833.—The board met pursuant to adjournment. Present: L. F. Linn, A. G. Harrison, F. R. Conway, commissioners.

Marie Nicolle Les Bois, claiming 244½ arpents of land.—(See pages 64 and 65 of this book.)

The board are unanimously of opinion that this claim ought to be confirmed to the said Marie Nicolle Les Bois, or her legal representatives, according to the concession.—(See book No. 6, page 300.)

L. F. LINN.
F. R. CONWAY.
A. G. HARRISON

No. 40.—Jean François Perrey, *claiming* 3,000 *arpents.*

To Don Zenon Trudeau, captain commanding, Upper Louisiana:

Jean François Perrey has the honor to represent that he is a foreigner in this country, and does not possess in it any land on which he might form an establishment; that, at this moment, he is in the pursuit of some small affairs of commerce, which keep him on the other shore. Wishing to put himself in the case to be able to settle himself in a fixed manner, he has recourse to you, sir, and supplicates you to be pleased to grant to him the quantity of three thousand arpents of land, to be taken on the river Aux Bœufs, (Buffalo creek,) or in its vicinity, at the distance of one hundred and thirty miles to the northwest of St. Louis, more or less, and between four and seven from the river Mississippi; supplicating you, also, to be pleased to exempt him from making his establishment in the time prescribed by law, on account of the reasons here above alleged to you; and he shall never cease to pray for the continuation of your government.

PERREY.

St. Louis, *July* 17, 1798.

St. Louis, *July* 18, 1798.

The surveyor, Don Antonio Soulard, shall put the interested party, Don Juan Francisco Perrey, in possession of the three thousand arpents of land which he solicits, in the place mentioned by him, in case they are vacant and belong to the King's domain, delivering to him the *procès verbal* of his survey in continuation of the present, to enable him to have recourse to the governor general of the province to obtain the title of concession in form.

I do inform his lordship that the said Don Juan Perrey is a Frenchman, C. A. R., well educated, and possesses all the other recommendable qualifications which make me desire to see him fix himself in the settlements under my command.

ZENON TRUDEAU.

Truly translated. St. Louis, December 14, 1832.

JULIUS DE MUN.

No.	Name of original claimant.	Quantity, in arpents	Nature and date of claim.	By whom granted.	By whom surveyed, date, and situation.
40	Jean François Perrey.	3,000	Concession, July 18, 1798.	Zenon Trudeau.	

Evidence with reference to minutes and records.

August 23, 1806.—The board met agreeably to adjournment. Present: The honorable Clement B. Penrose and James L. Donaldson, esq.

The same, (J. F. Perrey,) claiming 3,000 arpents of land situate on the river Aux Bœufs, district aforesaid, produces a concession dated July, 1798. Being unsupported by actual inhabitation and cultivation, the board reject this claim, and observe that, from a letter in the possession of claimant, now produced to them, they are satisfied that the said concession was granted at the time it bears date.—(See book No. 1, page 488.)

August 20, 1811.—Board met. Present: Clement B. Penrose and Frederick Bates, commissioners.

John Perrey, claiming 3,000 arpents of land.—(See book No. 1, page 488.) It is the opinion of the board that this claim ought not to be confirmed.—(See book No. 5, page 322.)

November 29, 1832.—The board met pursuant to adjournment. Present: Lewis F. Linn, F. R. Conway, commissioners.

Jean F. Perrey, by his legal representatives, claiming 3,000 arpents of land, (see book B, page 93; No. 1, page 488; No. 5, page 322,) produces a paper purporting to be an original concession from Zenon Trudeau, dated July 18, 1798.

M. P. Le Duc, duly sworn, saith that the signature to said concession is in the proper handwriting of said Zenon Trudeau.—(See book No. 6, page 65.)

November 5, 1833.—The board met pursuant to adjournment. Present: L. F. Linn, A. G. Harrison, F. R. Conway, commissioners.

Jean François Perrey, claiming 3,000 arpents of land.—(See page 65 of this book.) The board are unanimously of opinion that this claim ought to be confirmed to the said Jean François Perrey, or his legal representatives, according to the concession.—(See book No. 6, page 300.)

L. F. LINN.
F. R. CONWAY.
A. G. HARRISON.

No. 41.—WM. LOUGHRY, *claiming* 450 *arpents.*

To Don Carlos Dehault Delassus, lieutenant colonel, attached to the stationary regiment of Louisiana, and commander-in-chief of Upper Louisiana, &c.:

William Loughry, C. R., has the honor to represent that, with permission of the government, he came over on this side, where he has made choice of a piece of land in the domain of his Majesty; therefore, he has the honor to supplicate you to have the goodness to grant to him, at the same place, in full property, four hundred and fifty arpents of land in superficie, the quantity which is necessary to form his establishment. The petitioner having the necessary means, and having no other views but to live as a peaceable cultivator of the soil, hopes to deserve this favor which he solicits of your justice.

WILLIAM LOUGHRY.

ST. ANDRÉ, *March* 12, 1802.

Be it forwarded to the commander-in-chief with information that the statement here above is true, and that the petitioner deserves the favor which he solicits.

SANTIAGO MACKAY.

ST. ANDRÉ, *March* 12, 1802.

ST. LOUIS OF ILLINOIS, *March* 19, 1802.

In consequence of the information from the commandant particular of the post of St. André, I do grant to the petitioner, for him and his heirs, the land which he solicits, in case it is not prejudicial to anybody; and the surveyor, Don Antoine Soulard, shall put the interested in possession of the quantity of land asked for, in the place cultivated by him, if it does not do prejudice to any one; and when this is executed, he shall draw a plat of his survey, delivering the same to the party, with his certificate, [here is an omission,] and title in form from the intendant general, to whom alone corresponds, by royal order, the distributing and granting all classes of lands of the royal domain.

CARLOS DEHAULT DELASSUS.

Truly translated. St. Louis, December 24, 1832.

JULIUS DE MUN.

No.	Name of original claimant.	Quantity, in arpents.	Nature and date of claim.	By whom granted.	By whom surveyed, date, and situation.
41	William Loughry, by his legal representatives.	450	Concession, March 19, 1802	Carlos Dehault Delassus.	Special.

Evidence with reference to minutes and records.

November 25, 1811.—Board met. Present: J. B. C. Lucas, Clement B. Penrose, and Frederick Bates, commissioners.

William Loughry, claiming 450 arpents of land situate on Indian creek, district of St. Genevieve, produces record of concession from Delassus, lieutenant governor, dated March 19, 1802. It is the opinion of the board that this claim ought not to be confirmed.—(See book No. 5, page 450.)

November 29, 1832.—The board met pursuant to adjournment. Present: Lewis F. Linn and F. R. Conway, commissioners.

William Loughry, by his legal representatives, claiming 450 arpents of land, (see book D, page 282; No. 5, page 450,) produces a paper purporting to be an original concession from Charles Dehault Delassus, dated March 19, 1802.

M. P. Le Duc, duly sworn, saith that the signature to said concession is in the proper handwriting of said Charles Dehault Delassus.—(See book No. 6, page 65.)

November 5, 1833.—William Loughry, claiming 450 arpents of land.—(See page 65 of this book.) The board are unanimously of opinion that this claim ought to be confirmed to the said William Loughry, or his legal representatives, according to the possession, as admitted by the lieutenant governor.—(See book No. 6, page 300.)

L. F. LINN,
F. R. CONWAY.
A. G. HARRISON.

No. 42.—Mathias Vanderhider, *claiming* 400 *arpents.*

To Don Zenon Trudeau, lieutenant colonel, lieutenant governor, and commander-in-chief of the western part of Illinois:

Mathias Vanderhider supplicates very humbly, and has the honor to represent, that having the intention of settling himself in this country, and wishing to make a plantation, he has examined a place upon the river Maramec, at a place commonly called La Fourche au Négre, (Negro fork,) at about half a league from the concession of Jaimy Haid; and your petitioner, wishing to secure to himself the property of the said place, claims of your goodness to be pleased to grant to him the concession of it, in order that he may settle himself, and construct thereon the buildings convenient and necessary to his establishment, in the interim that he gets it surveyed by a surveyor, who shall deliver to him the procès verbal and title of property whenever you shall be pleased to order him to do so; in consequence, the petitioner hopes that you will be pleased to grant to him the concession of ten arpents in front by forty arpents in depth, upon the Negro fork, having for the present no nearer neighbor than the said James Haids, and the said tract being in the King's domain. If it pleases your goodness to grant to him his demand, the petitioner shall never cease to pray Heaven for your conservation.

his
MATHIAS + VANDERHIDER
mark.

St. Louis, *March* 15, 1797.

St. Louis, *March* 16, 1797.

The surveyor of this jurisdiction, Don Antonio Soulard, shall put the petitioner in possession of the quantity of land he asks, at the place designated, in case it belongs to the King's domain and does not prejudice any person, and he shall make a procès verbal of his survey at the foot of the present decree, which shall be returned to us to solicit the concession from the governor general of this province.

ZENON TRUDEAU.

Truly translated. St. Louis, December 14, 1832.

JULIUS DE MUN.

No.	Name of original claimant.	Quantity, in arpents	Nature and date of claim.	By whom granted.	By whom surveyed, date, and situation.
42	Mat. Vanderdider.	400	Concession, March 16, 1797.	Z. Trudeau.	

Evidence with reference to minutes and records.

December 10, 1811.—Board met. Present: John B. C. Lucas, Clement B. Penrose, and Frederick Bates, commissioners.

Mathias Vanderhider, representatives of, claiming 400 arpents of land situate on Negro fork of Maramec, district of St. Louis, produce records of concession from Zenon Trudeau, lieutenant governor, dated March 16, 1797. It is the opinion of the board that this claim ought not to be confirmed.—(See book 5, page 511.)

November 29, 1832.—The board met pursuant to adjournment. Present: L. F. Linn, F. R. Conway, commissioners.

Mathias Vanderhider, by his legal representatives, claiming 10 by 40 arpents of land, (see book E, page 17; book No. 5, page 511,) produces a paper purporting to be an original concession from Zenon Trudeau, dated March 16, 1797; also a deed of conveyance.

M. P. Le Duc, duly sworn, saith that the signature to the said concession is in the proper handwriting of the said Zenon Trudeau.—(See book No. 6, page 66.)

November 5, 1833.—The board met pursuant to adjournment. Present: L. F. Linn, A. G. Harrison, F. R. Conway, commissioners.

Mathias Vanderhider, claiming 400 arpents of land.—(See page 66 of this book.) The board are unanimously of opinion that this claim ought to be confirmed to the said Vanderhider, or his legal representatives, according to the concession.—(See book No. 6, page 300.)

L. F. LINN.
F. R. CONWAY.
A. G. HARRISON.

No. 43.—J. B. PRATTE, senior, *claiming* 1,000 *arpents.*

To Don Charles Dehault Delassus, lieutenant colonel, attached to the stationary regiment of Louisiana, and lieutenant governor of the upper part of the same province:

SIR: John Baptiste Pratte, merchant of St. Genevieve, inhabiting this country since nearly fifty years, father of a numerous family, and supporter of several orphans, and owner of a pretty considerable number of slaves, has the honor of observing to you, that to this day he has not obtained a gratuitous concession from the generosity of the government. Considering the lands in the vicinity of the post wherein he lives are daily conceded to foreigners; that the commercial resources are visibly decreasing; and, finally, that those offered by agriculture are, for the present, the only safe ones upon which one may found hopes for the future; considering, besides, that the incursions of the Indians being less frequent, people may, with more confidence, inhabit remote parts of the country, he has begun an improvement, with the verbal permission of your predecessor, upon a tract of land situated upon the *Grand Rivière*, at the same place, where he supplicates you to be willing to grant to him a concession for one thousand arpents of land in superficie.

Confiding in your justice, he hopes to be deserving the favor which he solicits.

PRATTE.

ST. LOUIS, *September* 4, 1799.

ST. LOUIS OF ILLINOIS, *September* 5, 1799.

Considering that the petitioner has been a long time settled in this country, and that his family is sufficiently large to obtain the quantity of land which he solicits, the surveyor of this Upper Louisiana, Don Ant. Soulard, shall put the petitioner in possession of one thousand arpents of land which he solicits, for him to enjoy in the same terms as he solicits; and the operations of survey being executed, he shall make out a corresponding certificate of said survey, with which the interested shall apply to the intendancy general, to which tribunal alone corresponds, by order of his Majesty, the granting of lands and town lots belonging to the royal domain.

CARLOS DEHAULT DELASSUS.

Don Antonio Soulard, surveyor general of Upper Louisiana.

I do certify that on the 5th of November of last year, having taken cognizance of the statement in the petition of the interested, and in consequence of the decree of the lieutenant colonel in the royal army, and lieutenant governor of this Upper Louisiana, Don Carlos Dehault Delassus, which follows the said petition, and bearing date of 5th September, 1799, I went on the land of John Baptiste Pratte, in order to survey it conformably to his demand of one thousand arpents in superficie, which measurement was taken in presence of the proprietor and adjacent neighbors, with the perch of Paris of eighteen feet in length, according to the custom adopted in this province of Louisiana, and without regard to the variation of the needle, which is 7° 30′ E., as it is evinced in the foregoing figurative plat. Said land is situated at about 28 miles N. 78° W. from the post of St. Genevieve, bounded on its four sides as follows: to the north and west by vacant lands of the royal domain; to the east by the land of Abraham Ead; to the south by that of Mr. John Baptiste Pratte, jr. And in order that it may be available according to law, I do give him the present, with the foregoing figurative plat, on which are indicated the dimensions and the natural and artificial limits which surround said land.

ANTONIO SOULARD, *Surveyor General.*

ST. LOUIS OF ILLINOIS, *March*, 5, 1801.

Truly translated from record book C, pages 221, 222, and 223. St. Louis, January 18, 1833.

JULIUS DE MUN.

No.	Name of original claimant.	Quantity, in arpents.	Nature and date of claim.	By whom granted.	By whom surveyed, date, and situation.
43	John Bte. Pratte.	1,000	Concession, September 5, 1799.	Carlos Dehault Delassus.	Antonio Soulard, Nov. 5, 1800; certified March 5, 1801. On the waters of Grand river, 28 miles NW. from St. Genevieve.

Evidence with reference to minutes and records.

August 12, 1806.—The board met agreeably to adjournment. Present: the Hon. John B. C. Lucas, Clement B. Penrose, and James L. Donaldson, esquire.

John B. Pratte, claiming one thousand arpents of land situate on Grand river, district of St. Genevieve, produces a concession from Charles Dehault Delassus, dated September 5, 1799, stating the same to have been granted for the purpose of farming, and declaring claimant to be an ancient inhabitant, with a survey of said land, taken November 5, 1800, and certified March 5, 1801.

Amable Partney, being duly sworn, says that the said tract of land was settled in the year 1798 by claimant, who built two or three cabins on the same, fenced in a field of about twenty-five or thirty acres, and has at this day about one hundred arpents of the same under cultivation, and about twelve houses or out-houses, and that the same was, prior to and on the 1st day of October, 1800, actually inhabited and cultivated for claimant's use; that he had then a wife, nine children, and forty-five slaves, and claims no other lands in his own name. The board, from the testimony of a number of witnesses produced on the part of the United States, by their agent, reject this claim, and require further proof.—(See book No. 1, p. 454.)

John Baptiste Pratte, sr., claiming one thousand arpents of land.—(See book No. 1, page 454.) It is the opinion of a majority of the board that this claim ought not to be confirmed. Frederick Bates, commissioner, forbears giving an opinion.—(See book No. 5, page 537.)

December 13, 1832.—F. R. Conway, esq., appeared, pursuant to adjournment. John B. Pratte, by his legal representatives, claiming one thousand arpents of land.—(See book No. 1, page 454; No. 5, page 537; record book C, page 221, and page 200 of this book.) The following additional testimony was taken in the foregoing case, in compliance with a resolution of this board of the 10th of October last:

St. Genevieve, *October* 25, 1832.

The heirs and legal representatives of John B. Pratte, claiming one thousand arpents of land situated on Grand River waters, in the former district of St. Genevieve, in pursuance of and by virtue of a concession and order of survey, heretofore filed with the former commissioners. When Louis Lasource personally appeared before Lewis F. Linn, one of the commissioners appointed to finally settle and adjust land claims in Missouri, and authorized by the said board of commissioners to receive testimony in this behalf; when said Lasource, after being duly sworn, deposeth and saith, that he knows of the cultivation and habitation of said tract of land by John B. Pratte, in 1800 or 1801; that he has seen said Pratte when residing on the place, where and when he had all his work hands; that his number of hands were very numerous, and that the land under cultivation was quite a large field, how many arpents he does not know.

LOUIS LASOURCE.

Sworn to and subscribed the day and date before written, in presence of—

L. F. LINN.

Colonel Bte. Vallé appeared in behalf of said claimant, and, after being duly sworn, deposeth and saith that the signature to the concession is in the handwriting of Charles Dehault Delassus, and the signature to the petition is in the handwriting of John B. Pratte; and that to the best of his knowledge the land claimed (under said concession, and now before the board of commissioners) was in a state of cultivation in 1801, and that it has always been cultivated and inhabited ever since by Pratte, his heirs or representatives.

J. BTE. VALLÉ.

Subscribed in presence of— L. F. LINN.

(See book No. 6, pages 71 and 72.)

June 27, 1833.—The board met pursuant to adjournment. Present: L. F. Linn and F. R. Conway, commissioners.

John Bte. Pratte, by his heirs and legal representatives, claiming one thousand arpents of land situate on the waters of Big river, county of St. Francis, (see book C, page 221 and following; also page 71 of this book,) produces a paper purporting to be an original concession from Charles Dehault Delassus, dated September 5, 1799; also a plat of survey by Antoine Soulard, dated March 5, 1801.

State of Missouri, *County of Washington:*

Jacob Mostiller, a witness, aged fifty-six years, being duly sworn, deposeth and saith that he was well acquainted with John B. Pratte, sr., and with a tract of land, he thinks about one thousand arpents, claimed by him by concession, on the waters of Big river, in the late district of St. Genevieve, now county of St. Francis; that he knows that in the year 1801 the said John Bte. Pratte had negroes on the land claimed—a man, woman, and children; that some land was cleared and some small houses put up, and he believes some digging was done; that he saw Mr. Monteon there, who said he was there doing business for said Pratte; and that the said tract of land has been inhabited and cultivated by said John Bte. Pratte, or those claiming under him, ever since he had a stock on the farm, and was frequently there in person.

JACOB MOSTILLER.

Sworn to before me, the commissioner, this 9th day of May, 1833.

L. F. LINN, *Commissioner.*

And also came John F. McNeal, a witness, aged about seventy years, who, being duly sworn as the law directs, deposeth and saith that he was well acquainted with Jean Bte. Pratte, the original claimant; he also knows the tract of land claimed; that he understood it was claimed by virtue of a Spanish concession; that in 1802 he saw on the land a white man who was said to be the manager of said Pratte, and some negroes on the land, and some land cleared, say for eight acres at least, and the same was in cultivation; that the houses and field had the appearance of having been of several years' standing; he had oxen at work there, and he saw cattle and hogs there, but does not know whose they were.

JOHN F. McNEAL.

Sworn to and subscribed before me, the commissioner, this 10th day of May, 1833.

L. F. LINN, *Commissioner.*

Also came John Stewart, a witness, aged about sixty-four years, who, being duly sworn, deposeth and saith that he was well acquainted with the said John Bte. Pratte, the original claimant; he also knows the land claimed; that he understood it was claimed under a Spanish grant; that he was there in 1801, and frequently passed there afterwards; that he saw John Bte. Pratte, junior, acting as a manager for the claimant; there were some negroes there, and in 1803 there were two fields, both in cultivation; that he saw a stock of cattle, horses, hogs, &c., at different times as he passed; that he understood the same was inhabited and cultivated ever since.

JOHN STEWART.

Sworn to and subscribed before me, the commissioner, this 10th day of May, 1833.

L. F. LINN, *Commissioner.*

(See book No. 6, pages 200, 201, and 202.)

November 6, 1833.—The board met pursuant to adjournment. Present: L. F. Linn, A. G. Harrison, F. R. Conway, commissioners.

Jean Baptiste Pratte, claiming 1,000 arpents of land.—(See pages 200, 201, and 202, of this book.) The board are unanimously of opinion that this claim ought to be confirmed to the said Jean Bte. Pratte, or his legal representatives, according to the concession.—(See book No. 6, page 301.)

L. F. LINN.
F. R. CONWAY.
A. G. HARRISON.

No. 44.—JOHN COONTZ, *claiming* 450 *arpents.*

To Don Charles Dehault Delassus, lieutenant colonel, attached to the stationary regiment of Louisiana, and commander-in-chief of Upper Louisiana, &c.:

John Coontz, C. R., has the honor to represent that having, with the permission of the government, crossed over this side, where he has made choice of a tract of land in his Majesty's domain to make a plantation thereon; therefore he supplicates you, sir, to have the goodness to grant to him a piece of land of four hundred and fifty arpents in superficie, which quantity is necessary to comprise the water and timber sufficient for the maintenance of his family and cattle.

The petitioner, having no other views but to live as a submissive and peaceable cultivator of the soil, hopes to render himself worthy of the favor which he solicits of your justice.

JOHN COONTZ, (supposed to be.)

ST. ANDRÉ, *May* 29, 1800.

Nota.—The above signature is illegible to the translator.

Be it forwarded to the lieutenant governor, with information that the statement here above is true, and that the petitioner deserves the favor which he solicits.

JAMES MACKAY.

ST. ANDRÉ, *May* 29, 1800.

ST. LOUIS OF ILLINOIS, *May* 30, 1800.

By virtue of the information from the commandant of St. André, Don Santiago Mackay, I do grant to the petitioner the tract of land of four hundred and fifty arpents which he solicits, if it is not prejudicial to any person; and the surveyor, Don Antonio Soulard, shall put the interested in possession of the said quantity of land asked, in the place designated; which having executed, he shall draw a plat of survey, delivering the same to the party, with his certificate, in order to serve to him to obtain the concession and title in form from the intendant general, to whom alone corresponds the distributing and granting all classes of lands of the royal domain.

CARLOS DEHAULT DELASSUS.

Truly translated. St. Louis, December 13, 1832.

JULIUS DE MUN.

No.	Name of original claimant.	Quantity, in arpents	Nature and date of claim.	By whom granted.	By whom surveyed, date, and situation.
44	John Coontz and E. Hempstead.	450	Concession, May 30, 1800.	Carl. Dehault Delassus.	

Evidence with reference to minutes and records.

November 13, 1811.—Board met. Present: John B. C. Lucas, Clement B. Penrose, and Frederick Bates, commissioners.

John Coontz and Edward Hempstead, claiming 450 arpents of land situate in the district of St. Charles, produce the record of a concession from Charles Dehault Delassus, lieutenant governor, to John Coontz, dated 29th (30th) May, 1800; a transfer of one-half of said tract to Edward Hempstead, dated June 18, 1808. Said transfer unauthenticated. It is the opinion of the board that this claim ought not to be confirmed.—(See book No. 5, page 399.)

November 29, 1832.—The board met pursuant to adjournment. Present: L. F. Linn and F. R. Conway, commissioners.

John Coontz and Edward Hempstead, claiming 450 arpents of land, (see book D, page 259; book No. 5, page 399,) produce a paper purporting to be an original concession from Carlos Dehault Delassus, dated May 30, 1800.

M. P. Le Duc, duly sworn, saith that the signature to said concession is in the proper handwriting of said Carlos Dehault Delassus.—(See book No. 6, page 67.)

November 6, 1333.—The board met pursuant to adjournment. Present: L. F. Linn, A. G. Harrison, F. R. Conway, commissioners.

John Coontz and Edward Hempstead, claiming 450 arpents of land.—(See page 67 of this book.) The board are unanimously of opinion that this claim ought to be confirmed to said John Coontz, or his legal representatives, according to the concession.—(See book No. 6, page 302.)

L. F. LINN.
F. R. CONWAY.
A. G. HARRISON.

No. 45.—HENRY DIELLE, *claiming* 400 *arpents, and* 1 *arpent by* 40.

To Mr. Zenon Trudeau, lieutenant governor and commander-in-chief of the western part of Illinois, &c.:

Henry Dielle, residing in St. Genevieve, supplicates very humbly, and has the honor to state, that wishing to establish a farm and a plantation, in order to feed, raise, and fatten cattle, and to cultivate in a manner corresponding to such an establishment, which it is impossible to do with success in the villages or their vicinity, he has found a place quite suitable to form such an establishment, having upon it many sugar maple trees, (avec une sucrerie d'érables,) upon the south fork of the river Saline. This concession would take its beginning from the mouth of a branch of said fork, (on the opposite side of which is such another concession, belonging to Messrs. Parent and Govrot,) and would consist of forty arpents in length of front along the said fork by ten arpents in depth. In consequence, the petitioner applies to you, sir, praying you may be pleased to grant to him, his heirs and assignees, in full property, the concession of the said land, such as it is here above designated and specified, not only to make sugar thereon and to raise and feed cattle, but also to make such cultivation as will be suitable to this land, a great part of it being hilly.

Done at New Bourbon January 30, 1798.

H. DIELLE.

ST. LOUIS, *February* 15, 1798.

The surveyor of this jurisdiction, Don Ant. Soulard, shall put Mr. Henry Dielle in possession of the land asked by him in the present petition, at the foot of which he shall make a proces verbal of his survey, and the whole to be returned to us, to be sent to the governor general of the province, who will definitively determine upon the concession of the said land.

ZENON TRUDEAU.

To Mr. Zenon Trudeau, lieutenant governor and commander-in-chief of the western part of Illinois, &c.:

Henry Dielle, residing in St. Genevieve, supplicates very humbly, and has the honor of representing to you, that having married six years ago, and having built his house at the place called Le Moulin, (The Mill,) he had obtained (upon the hills at the end of the field on the hills of New Bourbon) from Mr. François Vallé one arpent in length of front along the said hills by forty arpents in depth, adjoining the land of Madame Widow Leclerc, which is the last one of the above-mentioned field on the hills of New Bourbon (la dernière du susdit pré des côtes de la Nouvelle Bourbon,) the said F. Vallé being then in the belief that said arpent in front constituted a part of his concession for the mill seat, which arpent the petitioner has enclosed, cleared, and regularly cultivated since five years. But by the survey which the said Mr. Vallé caused to be taken by the King's surveyor having resulted that the concession of the mill seat of the said Vallé does not comprise the said arpent in front of the petitioner by its depth of forty arpents, and is of course a part of the King's domain, and that consequently the petitioner has no more any title to keep possession of it, he applies to you, sir, praying that you may be pleased to grant to him, his heirs and assignees, in full property, the concession of the land, consisting of one arpent in front on the hills of New Bourbon by the depth of forty arpents, adjoining the land of Madame Widow Leclerc, the last one in the field on the hills of the said New Bourbon, and on the opposite side adjoining the King's domain; which arpent in front, containing forty arpents in superficie, the petitioner with his slaves has enclosed with rails, and cultivated in wheat since five years. In so doing, he shall not cease to pray for the conservation of your days.

Done at New Bourbon February 6, 1798.

H. DIELLE.

ST. LOUIS, *February* 15, 1798.

The surveyor of this jurisdiction, Don Antonio Soulard, shall put Mr. Henry Dielle in possession of the land asked for in the present petition; and as the land is a part of the lands comprised in the field of New Bourbon, the said proprietor shall have his name inserted in the certificate of survey for the lands of the said field, and the present document shall serve to prove his right of property in the said lands.

ZENON TRUDEAU.

Truly translated. St. Louis, December 7, 1832.

JULIUS DE MUN.

No.	Name of original claimant.	Quantity, in arpents.	Nature and date of claim.	By whom granted.	By whom surveyed, date, and situation.
45	Henry Dielle....	400 & 40	2 concessions, Feb'ry 15, 1798.	Zenon Trudeau....	400 arpents on the south fork of Saline river. 40 arpents in the field of New Bourbon.

Evidence with reference to minutes and records.

December 7, 1807.—The board met agreeably to adjournment. Present: The honorable John B. C. Lucas and Frederick Bates.

Henry Dielle, claiming four hundred arpents of land, situated on the south fork of the river Saline, district of St. Genevieve, produces, in support of the same, a concession from Zenon Trudeau, lieutenant governor, dated February 15, 1798.

Camille Delassus, being duly sworn, says that in 1798 claimant showed him, the witness, a concession, which is the same as the one above related. Laid over for decision.—(See book No. 3, page 168.)

June 4, 1810.—Board met. Present: John B. C. Lucas, Clement B. Penrose, and Frederick Bates, commissioners.

Henry Dielle, claiming 400 arpents of land.—(See book No. 3, page 168.) It is the opinion of the board that this claim ought not to be confirmed.—(See book No. 4, page 360.)

December 13, 1832.—F. R. Conway, esq., appeared pursuant to adjournment.

Henry Dielle, claiming 400 arpents of land; also one arpent in front by 40 in depth, (book No. 3, page 168; No. 4, page 360; record book D, page 54,) produces a paper purporting to be an original concession from Zenon Trudeau, dated February 15, 1798, for 400 arpents of land; also a paper purporting to be a concession from Zenon Trudeau, dated February 15, 1798, for one arpent in front by forty in depth. The following additional testimony was taken in the foregoing case, in compliance with a resolution of this board of the 10th October last:

St. Genevieve, *November* 2, 1832.

Henry Dielle, claiming 400 arpents of land lying on the waters of the Saline, in the former district of St. Genevieve; when Cathrine Bolduc, after being duly sworn, deposeth and saith that she is acquainted with the handwriting of Zenon Trudeau, and knows that his name attached to the concession here presented is the handwriting of said Trudeau, and she knows that Henry Dielle took possession of the land in 1798.

VE. BOLDUC.

Sworn to and subscribed before me, L. F. Linn, one of the commissioners appointed for the final adjustment of land claims in Missouri.

L. F. LINN.

(See book No. 6, pages 72 and 73.)

November 6, 1833.—The board met pursuant to adjournment. Present: L. F. Linn, A. G. Harrison, F. R. Conway, commissioners.

Henry Dielle, claiming 400 arpents of land and a 40-arpent lot.—(See pages 72 and 73 of this book.) The board are unanimously of opinion that this claim of 400 arpents ought to be confirmed to the said Henry Dielle, or his legal representatives.

The board remark that the 40-arpent lot is, in their opinion, confirmed by the first section of the act of Congress of June 13, 1812; otherwise, it is recommended for confirmation.—(See book No. 6, page 303.)

L. F. LINN.
F. R. CONWAY.
A. G. HARRISON.

No. 46.—Julien Ratté, *claiming* 150 *arpents.*

Don Charles Dehault Delassus, lieutenant colonel in the armies of his Catholic Majesty, and lieutenant governor of Upper Louisiana.

Julien Ratté supplicates very humbly, and has the honor to state, that wishing to make and improve a plantation, and having searched for a piece of land suitable to his views, he has found one situated on the headwaters of Saline river, at a place called Le Rocher à Casetorneau; the said tract of land consisting of 150 arpents in superficie. The petitioner hopes that you will be pleased to grant to him this small quantity of land to make his plantation and raise cattle thereon; in so doing the petitioner shall never cease to pray for the conservation of your days.

Done at New Bourbon October 1, 1799.

JULIEN his ⋈ mark. RATTÉ.

Camille Delassus, *witness to the mark.*

We, captain, civil and military commandant of the post of New Bourbon, of Illinois, certify to Don Charles Delassus, lieutenant colonel in the armies of his Catholic Majesty, and lieutenant governor of Upper Louisiana, that Mr. Ratté, who has presented the foregoing petition, is an ancient and very honest inhabitant of this country, who deserves, under all points of view, to obtain the concession solicited, situated in a vacant place, which has not been granted to any person, and is a part of the King's domain, to make his plantation and raise cattle thereon.

Done at New Bourbon, &c., October 5, 1799.

PEDRO DELASSUS DELUZIERE.

St. Louis of Illinois, *October* 18, 1799.

By virtue of the information from the commandant of the post of New Bourbon, Captain Don Pedro Delassus Deluziere, by which it is notorious that the petitioner has more than the means and the number of hands (populacion) necessary to obtain the concession which he solicits, I do grant to him and his heirs the land solicited by him, if it is not prejudicial to any person. And the surveyor, Don Antonio Soulard, shall put the interested party in possession of the quantity of land he petitions for in the place designated, which, when done, he shall draw a plat of survey, which he shall deliver to the party, with his certificate, to serve in obtaining the concession and title in form from the intendant general, to whom alone corresponds, by royal order, the distributing and granting of all classes of land of the royal domain.

CARLOS DEHAULT DELASSUS.

Truly translated. St. Louis, December 11, 1832.

JULIUS DE MUN.

No.	Name of original claimant.	Quantity, in arpents	Nature and date of claim.	By whom granted.	By whom surveyed, date, and situation.
46	Julien Ratté........	150	Concession, October 18, 1799.	Carl. Dehault Delassus.	On the headwaters of Saline river.

Evidence with reference to minutes and records.

December 13, 1833.—F. R. Conway, esq., appeared pursuant to adjournment.

Julien Ratté, by his heirs and legal representatives, claiming 150 arpents of land, (see book F, pages 127 and 128; Bates's Decisions, page 104, where it is not confirmed,) produces a paper purporting to be an original concession from Charles Dehault Delassus, dated October 18, 1799. The following testimony was taken in the foregoing case, in compliance with a resolution of this board of the 10th of October last:

St. Genevieve, *October* 27, 1832.

Julien Ratté, by his heirs and legal representatives, claiming 150 arpents of land on the waters of the Saline, in this former district of St. Genevieve, in pursuance and by virtue of an original concession. When Pierre Robert and Joseph St. Gemme appeared before L. F. Linn, one of the commissioners appointed for the purpose of settling the private land claims in Missouri.

When the said Robert and St. Gemme, being duly sworn, depose and say that they know that said Ratté occupied and cultivated said land in 1804; had built cabins on it then; that it has been in his possession and occupation and that of his family and representatives ever since.—(See book 6, page 75.)

J. B. ST. GEMME.

PIERRE his ⋈ mark. ROBERT.

L. F. LINN, *Land Commissioner.*

November 6, 1833.—The board met pursuant to adjournment. Present: L. F. Linn, A. G. Harrison, F. R. Conway, commissioners.

Julien Ratté, claiming 150 arpents of land.—(See page 75 of this book.) The board are unanimously of opinion that this claim ought to be confirmed to the said Julien Ratté, or his legal representatives, according to the concession.—(See book No. 6, page 303.)

L. F. LINN.
F. R. CONWAY.
A. G. HARRISON.

No. 47.—Hiacinthe Eglis, *claiming* 800 *arpents.*

To the Lieutenant Governor of Upper Louisiana:

Hiacinthe Eglis, inhabiting this country since nearly ten years and having not yet received any gratuitous concession out of his Majesty's domain, has the honor to supplicate you to have the goodness to grant to him the quantity of 800 arpents of land in superficie, to establish thereon a plantation and raise cattle. The said land is situated in the point formed by the rivers Maramec and Mississippi, and bounded as follows: To the northwest and southwest by the river Maramec, to the southeast by the Mississippi, and to the northeast by the lands of Mr. Philip Fein, distant about sixteen miles to the south of this town.

The petitioner, full of confidence in the generosity of the government, hopes to obtain of your justice the favor which he solicits.

HIACINTHE EGLIS.

St. Louis, *December* 15, 1799.

St. Louis of Illinois, *December* 16, 1799.

The surveyor of this Upper Louisiana, Don Antonio Soulard, shall survey the quantity of land which the petitioner solicits for him to enjoy in the same manner as he asks; and the operation being executed he shall make out a certificate of his survey, which he shall deliver original to the interested, in order that with said certificate he may apply to the intendency general of these provinces, to which tribunal corresponds, by order of his Majesty, the granting of lands and town lots belonging to the royal domain.

CARLOS DEHAULT DELASSUS.

Registered at the demand of the interested, book No. 2, pages 8 and 9.

SOULARD.

Truly translated. St. Louis, January 3, 1833.

JULIUS DE MUN

No.	Name of original claimant.	Quantity, in arpents.	Nature and date of claim.	By whom granted.	By whom surveyed, date, and situation.
47	Hyacinthe Eglis.....	800	Concession, December 16, 1799.	Carlos Dehault Delassus.	James Mackay, deputy surveyor, February 20, 1806; recorded by Soulard, surveyor general, February 26, 1806; at the mouth of Maramec river.

Evidence with reference to minutes and records.

June 14, 1806.—The board met agreeably to adjournment. Present: The honorable John B. C. Lucas, Clement B. Penrose and James L. Donaldson, esqs.

John Mullanphy, assignee of Hyacinthe Eglis, claiming 800 arpents of land, situate at the point of the rivers Mississippi and Maramec, district of St. Louis, produces a concession from Charles D. Delassus, dated December 16, 1799; a certificate of survey of 300 arpents, dated February 20, 1806, and a deed of transfer of the same, dated February 9, 1805.

This claim being unsupportable by actual habitation and cultivation, the board reject the same, and require further proof of the date of said concession; they observe that the same is not duly registered.—(See page 530; B. No. 1, page 311.)

September 6, 1806.—Present: The honorable John B. C. Lucas, Clement B. Penrose, and James L. Donaldson, commissioners.

In the case of John Mullanphy, assignee of Hyacinthe Eglis, page 311. Anthony Soulard, being duly sworn, says that he knows of nothing contradicting the date of the concession; and further that he knows of Zenon Trudeau having promised said Hyacinthe Eglis a concession.—(See book No. 1, page 530.)

November 15, 1809.—Board met. Present: John B. C. Lucas and Clement B. Penrose, commissioners.

John Mullanphy, assignee of Hyacinthe Eglis, claiming 800 arpents of land, situate at the point of the rivers Mississippi and Maramec, in the district of St. Louis.—(See book No. 1, pages 311 and 350.) It is the opinion of the board that this claim ought not to be confirmed.—(See book No. 4, page 194.)

December 19, 1832.—F. R. Conway, esq., appeared pursuant to adjournment.

Hyacinthe Eglis, by his legal representative, John Mullanphy, claiming 800 arpents of land, (see book A, pages 30 and 33; minutes No. 1, pages 311 and 330; No. 4, page 194,) produces a paper purporting to be an original concession from Carlos Dehault Delassus, dated December 16, 1799; also a plat and certificate of survey for 300 arpents, dated February 20, 1806, by James Mackay, and recorded by Antonio Soulard.

M. P. Le Duc, being duly sworn, says that the signature to the concession is in the proper handwriting of said Carlos Dehault Delassus, and that the signatures to the plat and certificate of survey are in the proper handwriting of said Mackay and Soulard.—(See book No. 6, page 87.)

November 7, 1833.—The board met pursuant to adjournment. Present: L. F. Linn, A. G. Harrison, F. R. Conway, commissioners.

Hyacinthe Eglis, claiming 800 arpents of land.—(See page 87 of this book.) The board remark that the survey produced in this case is only for 300 arpents. The board are unanimously of opinion that this claim ought to be confirmed to the said Hyacinthe Eglis, or his legal representatives, according to the concession.—(See book No. 6, page 304.)

A. G. HARRISON.
L. F. LINN.
F. R. CONWAY.

No. 48.—Etienne Pepin, *claiming* 1,600 *arpents.*

To Don Carlos Dehault Delassus, lieutenant colonel, attached to the stationary regiment of Louisiana, and lieutenant governor of the upper part of the same province:

Etienne Pepin, father of a family, Canadian by birth, ancient inhabitant of this country, and residing for the present at Portage des Sioux, has the honor to represent to you that, not having as yet received any concession of consequence from the government, he hopes that you will please to make him enjoy the same favors which you have been pleased to grant to all those who have wished to form plantations; therefore, he has the honor to supplicate you to have the goodness to grant to him, in full property, the concession of a tract of land of sixteen hundred arpents in superficie, to be taken between the river Dardaine and the pond called A Bequet, (Bequet's pond,) at about four or five miles to the northwest of the village of Portage des Sioux.

The petitioner, having always lived as a peaceable and submissive cultivator of the soil, hopes that you will please do justice to his demand in a way favorable to the accomplishment of his views.

St. Louis, *October* 17, 1800.

ETIENNE his ⋈ mark PEPIN.

As witness of the signature:
Antonio Soulard.

St. Louis of Illinois, *October* 18, 1800.

Considering that the petitioner has been a long time in this country, and being assured that he possesses sufficient means to improve the land which he solicits, I do grant to him and his heirs the land which he solicits, if it is not prejudicial to any one; and the surveyor, Don Antonio Soulard, shall put the interested in possession of the quantity of land which he asks, in the place designated; and this being executed, he shall draw a plat of his survey, delivering the same to the party with his certificate, in order to serve to him to obtain the concession and title in form from the intendant general, to whom alone corresponds, by royal order, the distributing and granting all classes of lands of the royal domain.

CARLOS DEHAULT DELASSUS.

Registered the present on book No. 1, pages 1 and 2, No. 1.

F. SAUCIER.

Truly translated. St. Louis, January 4, 1833.

JULIUS DE MUN.

No.	Name of original claimant.	Quantity, in arpents.	Nature and date of claim.	By whom granted.	By whom surveyed, date, and situation.
48	Etienne Pepin......	1,600	Concession, October 18, 1800.	Carlos Dehault Delassus.	

Evidence with reference to the minutes and records.

December 6, 1811.—Board met. Present: John B. C. Lucas, Clement B. Penrose, and Frederick Bates, commissioners.

Etienne Pepin, claiming 1,600 arpents of land situate on the Dardennes, district of St. Charles, produces record of a concession from Delassus, lieutenant governor, dated October 18, 1800.

It is the opinion of the board that this claim ought not to be confirmed.—(See book No. 5, page 477.)

December 19, 1832.—F. R. Conway appeared pursuant to adjournment.

Etienne Pepin, by his legal representative, John Mullanphy, claiming 1,600 arpents of land, (see book B, page 509; minutes No. 5, page 447,) produces a paper purporting to be an original concession from Carlos Dehault Delassus, dated October 18, 1800; also, deed of conveyances.

M. P. Le Duc, duly sworn, saith that the signature to said concession is in the proper handwriting of Carlos Dehault Delassus.—(See book No. 6, page 88.)

November 7, 1833.—The board met pursuant to adjournment. Present: L. F Linn, A. G. Harrison, F. R. Conway, commissioners.

Etienne Pepin, claiming 1,600 arpents of land.—(See page 88 of this book.)

The board are unanimously of opinion that this claim ought to be confirmed to the said Etienne Pepin, or to his legal representatives, according to the concession.—(See book No. 6, page 304.)

L. F. LINN.
F. R. CONWAY.
A. G. HARRISON.

No. 49.—André and J. B. Blondeau Drezy, *claiming* 12 *by* 40 *arpents.*

To Mr. Charles Tayon, captain commandant of St. Charles of Missouri:

Sir: André Blondeau Drezy and Jean Baptiste Blondeau Drezy have the honor of representing to you that, wishing to settle themselves at the place commonly called La Perruque, therefore they supplicate you to have the goodness to grant to them a concession of twelve arpents of land in width by forty in depth, situated on the said Perruque, adjoining on one side to one Louis Marchant and on the other sides to the King's domain. The said petitioners presume to hope, sir, that you will please to grant to them the object of their demand, a favor which they expect of your justice.

ANDRÉ & J. B. BLONDEAU DREZY.

St. Charles, *March* 14, 1799.

Be it forwarded to the lieutenant governor, with information that the land solicited belongs to his Majesty's domain and does not do prejudice to anybody.

CHARLES TAYON.

St. Louis, *March* 18, 1799.

The petitioner may settle himself on the twelve arpents in front by forty in depth at the place where he asks; and as soon as it is possible for the surveyor to go on said place he shall have boundaries fixed for the petitioner, and that will serve to him to solicit the concession of the governor general, to whom alone corresponds the delivering of them.

ZENON TRUDEAU.

Truly translated. St. Louis, January 4, 1833.

JULIUS DE MUN.

No.	Name of original claimant.	Quantity, in arpents	Nature and date of claim.	By whom granted.	By whom surveyed, date, and situation.
49	André and Jean Baptiste Blondeau Drezy.	480	Concession, March 18, 1799.	Zenon Trudeau.	James Mackay, deputy surveyor, April 10, 1805; recorded by Soulard, surveyor general, April 15, 1805; district of St. Charles.

Evidence with reference to minutes and records.

August 25, 1806.—The board met agreeably to adjournment. Present: The Hon. John B. C. Lucas and Clement B. Penrose, commissioners.

The representatives of Charles Tayon, junior, who was assignee of A. and J. Bte. Blondeau, claiming 480 arpents of land situate between the rivers Dardennes and Perruque, district of St. Charles, produce a concession from Zenon Trudeau, for twelve by forty arpents, dated March 18, 1799, under survey of the same, dated April 10, 1805.

Isidore Savoy, being duly sworn, says that the aforesaid J. Bte. Blondeau settled the said tract of land in the beginning of 1796, raised a crop on it, and lived thereon until the fall of that year, when his wife being very ill, he removed to the village of St. Charles, in order to procure that medical assistance which her situation required; that she died some time after, leaving him with a large family of children; that, in that situation, he determined upon remaining in the said village, and gave up the said tract. The board reject this claim.—(See book No. 1, page 490.)

November 15, 1809.—Board met. Present: John B. C. Lucas and Clement B. Penrose, commissioners.

John Mullanphy, assignee of Andrew and Baptiste Blondeau Drezy, claiming 480 arpents of land situate on the waters of the river Dardennes, in the district of St. Charles, produces to the board a concession for the same from Don Zenon Trudeau, lieutenant governor, dated the 18th of March, 1799; also a plat of survey, dated the 10th of April, 1805, signed Mackay. It is the opinion of the board that this claim ought not to be confirmed.—(See book No. 4, page 194.)

December 19, 1832.—F. R. Conway, esq., appeared pursuant to adjournment.

Andrew and J. Bte. Blondeau Drezy, by their legal representative, John Mullanphy, claiming 480 arpents of land, (see book A, page 44; minutes No. 1, 490; No. 4, page 194,) produces a paper purporting to be an original concession from Zenon Trudeau, lieutenant governor, dated 18th of March, 1799; also a plat of survey, certified by James Mackay, deputy surveyor, and recorded by A. Soulard, surveyor general.

M. P. Leduc, being duly sworn, saith that the signature to the concession is in the proper handwriting of the said Zenon Trudeau, and that the signatures to the plat and certificate of survey are in the proper handwriting of the said Mackay and Soulard.—(See book No. 6, page 88.)

November 7, 1833.—The board met pursuant to adjournment. Present: L. F. Linn, A. G. Harrison, and F. R. Conway, commissioners.

André and Jean Baptiste Blondeau Drezy, claiming 480 arpents of land.—(See page 88 of this book.) The board are unanimously of opinion that this claim ought to be confirmed to the said André and John Baptiste Blondeau Drezy, or their legal representatives, according to the concession.—(See book No. 6, page 304.)

L. F. LINN.
F. R. CONWAY.
A. G. HARRISON.

No. 50.—Silvester Labbadie, *claiming eight by forty arpents.*

To the Lieutenant Governor:

Silvester Labbadie, inhabitant and merchant of this town of St. Louis, in the best form possible, in his right, says that, wishing to establish a plantation for cultivation and raising of cattle, to these ends he supplicates you to be willing to grant to him eight arpents of land in front by eight in depth; bounded in front (east) by the road leading to Mr. De Lor's village, and on the north side by that of Maria Borchoa, widow of Augustin Choto, and on the two other sides by his Majesty's domain, and opposite the back part of Don Benito Vasquez's plantation, in the place commonly called the Little Prairie. Favor which he hopes to receive of your equitable justice.

SILVESTER LABBADIE.

St. Louis of Illinois, *August* 5, 1788.

Don Manuel Perez, captain of the regiment of infantry of Louisiana, lieutenant governor and commander of this western part and district of Illinois:

Cognizance being taken of the statement of the foregoing memorial, presented by Mr. Silvester Labbadie, inhabitant and resident of this town, bearing date the 5th of August of the present year, I have granted and do grant to him, his heirs, and others who may represent his right, in fee simple, for the eight arpents of land in front by eight arpents in depth, in order that he may thereon establish the plantation which he solicits; said land being bounded on the front (east) by the road which leads to the small village of Vide Poche and the Prairie à Catalan, (said front being opposite the back part of Don Benito Vasquez's plantation,) on the north side by that of Maria Theresa Borchoa, and on the two other sides by the King's domain, on condition to establish and improve it in the term of one year, to begin from this date; and, on the contrary, to remain incorporated to the royal domain. Said land shall be liable to public taxes and others which it may please his Majesty to impose.

Given in St. Louis of Illinois, August 9 1788.

MANUEL PEREZ.

ORLEANS, *May* 27, 1791.

The surveyor of this province, Don Carlos Trudeau, shall establish the party upon the eight arpents of land in front, which he solicits, by the usual depth of forty, in the place designated in the foregoing petition, provided they are vacant and do not cause any prejudice, under the precise condition to make the road and regular clearing in the peremptory term of one year; and this concession shall be null if at the expiration of the precise time of three years the land should not be improved; and during said time it shall not be alienable. Under which supposition the operations of survey shall be extended in continuation, and remitted to me, in order to provide the interested with the corresponding title in form.

ESTEVAN MIRO.

Registered.

Truly translated. St. Louis, January 14, 1833.

JULIUS DE MUN.

No.	Name of original claimant.	Quantity, in arpents	Nature and date of claim.	By whom granted.	By whom surveyed, date, and situation.
50	Silvester Labbadie.	320	Concession, August 9, 1798; order of survey, May 27, 1791.	Manuel Perez, lieutenant governor; Estevan Miro, governor general.	Prairie à Catalan.

Evidence with reference to minutes and records.

May 13, 1806.—The board met agreeably to adjournment. Present: The Hon. Clement B. Penrose.

The representatives of Silvester Labbadie, claiming eight by forty arpents of land situate on the Mississippi, district of St. Louis, produce a concession from Stephen Miro, dated May 27, 1797, with a proviso that the same does not prejudice any one, and a certificate of survey of 300 arpents, dated June 21, 1806.

Grégoire Sarpy, being duly sworn, says that the said Silvester Labbadie, having obtained the aforesaid concession, proceeded to the improvement and cultivation of said land, but was prevented from so doing by the lieutenant governor, who, upon the remonstrance of the inhabitants of the village, ordered him, the said Silvester Labbadie, to stop any further improvements on the said land until the intendant below should be made acquainted with the circumstances of said claim, and have decreed otherwise.

The board reject this claim for want of actual inhabitation and cultivation on the 1st of October, 1800.—(See book No. 1, page 294.)

November 28, 1808.—Board met. Present: The Hon. John B. C. Lucas, Clement B. Penrose, and Frederick Bates, commissioners.

The representatives of Silvester Labbadie, claiming eight arpents front on the Mississippi by forty arpents in depth, produce to the board a concession from Manuel Perez, lieutenant governor, to Silvester Labbadie, for eight arpents front by eight arpents in depth, back to the road leading from St. Louis to Vide Poche, or Prairie Catalan, dated August 9, 1788; a concession from Estevan Miro, for eight arpents in front by forty arpents in depth, to Silvester Labbadie, dated Orleans, May 27, 1791. A plat of survey of three hundred and twenty arpents, dated January 1, 1806, certified January 27, 1806. Laid over for decision. (At the margin the following: Survey to be ordered on this claim to ascertain the road from St. Louis to Prairie à Catalan.)—(See book No. 3, page 373.)

August 16, 1811.—Board met. Present: Clement B. Penrose and Frederick Bates, commissioners.

Silvester Labbadie, representatives of, claiming eight arpents front by forty in depth of land.—(See book No. 1, page 294; book No. 3, page 373.) It is the opinion of the board that this claim ought not to be confirmed.—(See book No. 5, page 309.)

January 12, 1833.—F. R. Conway, esq., appeared pursuant to adjournment, having been authorized by a resolution of the board of commissioners of the 1st of December last to receive evidence.

Silvester Labbadie, by his heirs and legal representatives, claiming eight arpents of land in front by forty arpents in depth, (see record book A, page 525; minutes No. 1, page 294; No. 3, page 373; and No. 5, page 309,) produces a paper purporting to be an original concession from Manuel Perez, dated August 9, 1788, and an order of survey, dated May 27, 1791, signed by Estevan Miro, governor general of Louisiana.

M. P. Leduc, being duly sworn, saith that, having had many opportunities of seeing the official signatures of the above-named Manuel Perez and Estevan Miro, he is of opinion that the signatures affixed to the said concession and order of survey are in their proper handwriting.

P. Chouteau, sr., being duly sworn, saith that at the date of said concession Manuel Perez was lieutenant governor of Upper Louisiana, and Estevan Miro governor general of the province of Louisiana, and that their signatures affixed to the above-mentioned concession and order of survey are in their proper handwriting. He further saith that, as soon as the said land was surveyed, he often went in company with the said Silvester Labbadie on said piece of land to look at Labbadie's slaves working at the clearing of said land; that said Silvester Labbadie was his brother-in-law, and confided to him all his affairs; and he perfectly knew that the said land was improved by virtue of the concession he obtained at the time of its date.—(See book No. 6, page 94.)

November 7, 1833.—The board met pursuant to adjournment. Present: L. F. Linn, A. G. Harrison, F. R. Conway, commissioners.

Silvester Labbadie claiming eight by forty arpents of land.—(See page 94 of this book.) The board remark that the concession of Manuel Perez, lieutenant governor, is for eight arpents in front by eight in depth; but the order of survey of Estevan Miro, governor general, is for eight arpents in front by forty in depth. The board are unanimously of opinion that this claim ought to be confirmed to said Silvester Labbadie, or his legal representatives, according to the concession made by Miro.—(See book No. 6, page 304.)

L. F. LINN.
F. R. CONWAY.
A. G. HARRISON.

No. 51.—Gabriel Cerré, *claiming an island at the mouth of Cuivre.*

To Don Charles Dehault Delassus, lieutenant colonel, attached to the stationary regiment of Louisiana, and lieutenant governor of the upper part of the same province:

Gabriel Cerré, merchant of this town, and one of the most ancient inhabitants, without speaking of his attachment to the government, nor of the services which he has been happy enough to render on several occasions, which facts must be known to you, has the honor to supplicate you to have the goodness to grant to him, in full property, the island situated across the mouth of Cuivre river, in the Mississippi, at about forty-five miles of this town; the said island being evidently a part of his Majesty's domain, since it is separated from our shore but by a small channel, which is navigable only in the spring freshets. The said island being high and arable land, he would wish to make a plantation thereon, and, after a while, occupy himself in felling building timber and wood for fuel, both of which will soon be very much wanted in this town. The petitioner, full of confidence in your justice, hopes that you will please consider his demand in a manner favorable to the accomplishment of his views, and you will do justice.

CERRÉ.

St. Louis of Illinois, *May* 20, 1800.

St. Louis of Illinois, *May* 25, 1800.

After examining the contents of the foregoing statement, it being manifest to me that the conduct and personal merit of the petitioner make him recommendable among the ancient inhabitants of this country, and that the said island belongs to this side of the river Mississippi, I do grant it to him in all its extents of width, length, and superficie, such as it now stands, for him to possess and enjoy, as well as his heirs, and dispose of it as of a property to him belonging; provided it is not prejudicial to the territorial right of the United States of America, stipulated in article IV of the treaty of amity, navigation, and limits, concluded between both powers on the 27th of October, 1795, and ratified on the 25th of April, 1796.

And Don Antonio Soulard, surveyor general of this Upper Louisiana, shall take cognizance of this title for his intelligence and government in what concerns him; and, afterwards, the interested shall have to solicit the title in form from the intendant general of these provinces of Louisiana, to whom alone corresponds, by royal order, the distributing and granting all classes of lands of the royal domain.

CARLOS DEHAULT DELASSUS.

Registered by order of the lieutenant governor.—(Pages 17 and 18 of book No. 1 of titles of concessions under my charge.)

SOULARD.

Truly translated. St. Louis, January 4, 1833.

JULIUS DE MUN.

No.	Name of original claimant.	Quantity, in arpents.	Nature and date of claim.	By whom granted.	By whom surveyed, date, and situation.
51	Gabriel Cerré.	An island.	Concession, May 25, 1800.	Carlos Dehault Delassus.	An island at the mouth of Cuivre river, in the Mississippi.

Evidence with reference to minutes and records.

July 8, 1806.—The board met agreeably to adjournment. Present: The Hon. Clement B. Penrose and James L. Donaldson, esq., commissioners.

John Mullanphy, assignee of Gabriel Cerré, claiming an island situate at the mouth of the river Cuivre, in the Mississippi, produces a concession from Charles D. Delassus, May 25, 1800, and an act of public sale of the effects and property of said Gabriel Cerré, deceased, dated July 28, 1805.

The board reject this claim, and require further proof, &c.—(See book No. 1, page 394.)

November 15, 1809.—Board met. Present: John B. C. Lucas and Clement B. Penrose, commissioners.

John Mullanphy, assignee of Gabriel Cerré claiming an island of 800 arpents of land at the mouth of the river Cuivre, in the Mississippi, in the district of St. Charles.—(See book No. 1, page 394.)

It is the opinion of the board that this claim ought not to be confirmed.—(See book No. 4, page 194.)

December 19, 1832.—F. R. Conway, esq., appeared pursuant to adjournment.

Gabriel Cerré, by his legal representative, John Mullanphy, claiming an island at the mouth of Cuivre, in the Mississippi.—(See book No. 1, page 394. No. 4, page 194.) Produces a paper purporting to be an original concession from Carlos Dehault Delassus, dated May 25, 1800; also deed of conveyance.

M. P. Leduc, being duly sworn, saith that the signature to the concession is in the proper handwriting of Carlos Dehault Delassus.—(See book No. 6, page 89.)

November 7, 1833.—The board met pursuant to adjournment. Present: L. F. Linn, A. G. Harrison, F. R. Conway, commissioners.

Gabriel Cerré, claiming an island at the mouth of Cuivre, in the Mississippi.—(See page 89 of this book.)

The board are unanimously of opinion that this claim ought to be confirmed to said Gabriel Cerré, or his legal representatives, according to the concession.—(See book No. 6, page 305.)

L. F. LINN.
F. R. CONWAY.
A. G. HARRISON.

No. 52.—Benito Vasquez, *claiming nine arpents of land in front.*

To the Lieutenant Governor:

Benito Vasquez, inhabitant of the town of St. Louis, in the best form possible, in his right, says that wishing to establish a plantation, in order to cultivate it and raise cattle thereon, he supplicates you to be pleased to grant him nine arpents of land of his Majesty's domain, bounded north by the land of Joseph Brazeau, south by that of Mr. Motar, east by the river Mississippi, and to the west by the main road of the Little Prairie. Favor which he expects of your equitable justice.

BENITO VASQUEZ.

St. Louis of Illinois, *November* 18, 1786.

Don Francisco Cruzat, lieutenant colonel of infantry by brevet, captain of grenadiers in the stationary regiment of Louisiana, commander and lieutenant governor of this western part and district of Illinois.

Cognizance being taken of the statement made in the petition presented by Don Benito Vasquez, an inhabitant of this town, bearing date 18th of November of this present year, I have granted and do grant to him, his heirs, or others who may represent his right, in full property, the nine arpents of land which he solicits, which are bounded on one side by the lands of Joseph Brazeau, on the other by those of Joseph Motar, to the east by the edge of the Mississippi, and to the west by the main road which leads to the *Prairie à Catalan*, (Praderia à Catalan,) on condition to establish said land in the term of one year, to begin from this date, and on the contrary the said nine arpents to remain incorporated to the royal domain. Said land shall be liable to all public taxes and others which it may please his Majesty to impose.

Given in St. Louis of Illinois, the 20th day of November of the year 1786.

FRANCO. CRUZAT.

Truly translated. January 16, 1833.

JULIUS DE MUN.

No.	Name of original claimant.	Quantity, in arpents.	Nature and date of claim.	By whom granted.	By whom surveyed, date and situation.
52	Benito Vasquez.	9 in front, depth from the Mississippi to the main road.	Concession, November 20, 1786.	Francisco Cruzat.	Between St. Louis and Carondelet.

Evidence with reference to minutes and records.

July 19, 1806.—The board met agreeably to adjournment. Present: Hon. J. B. C. Lucas, Clement B. Penrose, James L. Donaldson, commissioners.

Joseph Brazeau, assignee of Benito Vasquez, claiming nine arpents of land situate in the district of St. Louis, running north and south, bounded northerly by a tract the property of said claimant, being part of a tract granted said Benito Vasquez, by concession from Francis Cruzat, dated November 20, 1786, produces the said concession, together with an assignment of said land, dated May 26, 1800.

Jacque Clamorgan, being duly sworn, says that the said Benito settled the said tract of land about the year 1788; built a house on the same, and that the same has been actually cultivated, either by the said Benito or his representatives, to this day; and that three crops had been raised on the same prior to the year 1800. The board reject this claim for want of actual inhabitation on the first day of October, 1800; and remark, that the said Benito, having raised three crops on the same, had, by the Spanish laws and usages, acquired the right of domain.—(See book No. 1, page 412.)

August 19, 1811.—The board met. Present: Clement B. Penrose and Frederick Bates, commissioners.

Joseph Brazeau, assignee of Benito Vasquez, claiming nine arpents front, running back to the road leading from St. Louis to Carondelet.—(See book No. 1, page 412.) The board order that this tract be surveyed at expense of claimant.

January 15, 1812.—Board met. Present: John B. C. Lucas, Clement B. Penrose, Frederick Bates, commissioners.

Joseph Brazeau, claiming under Benito Vasquez.—(See book 5, page 319.) A majority of the board declare that they would have confirmed this claim had it been found not to have exceeded twenty arpents. John B. C. Lucas, commissioner, makes the same remarks as in the claim of Auguste Choteau, (p. 559,) to wit: That he cannot give an absolute vote, under the present circumstances, upon the claim, inasmuch as the board has heretofore ordered a survey to be made under the foregoing concession, for the purpose of examining the quantity, and inasmuch as the same reasons which induced the board to make said orders previous to the decision of the claim still exist, and the said order remains in force, not having been rescinded; he further remarks that the claim ought to be confirmed without being able at present to say what quantity.—(See book No. 5, pages 319 and 562.)

January 12, 1833.—F. R. Conway, esq., appeared pursuant to adjournment, having been authorized, by a resolution of the board of commissioners of the 1st of December last to receive evidence.

Benito Vasquez, by his legal representative, Bernard Pratte, claiming nine arpents of land in front, by the depth comprised between the Mississippi and the public road leading to the village of Carondelet.—(See book B, page 417; book D, page 362. Minutes, No. 1, page 412; No. 5, pages 319 and 562. L. T. No. 4, page 15.) Produces a paper purporting to be an original concession from Francis Cruzat, dated November 20, 1786.

M. P. Le Duc, being duly sworn, saith that the signature to the said concession is in the proper handwriting of the said Francisco Cruzat.

Peter Chouteau, senior, being duly sworn, saith that the signature to the said concession is in the proper handwriting of the said Cruzat. He further saith that immediately after getting the said concession the said Benito Vasquez had a house built on said land, and had some of his hands employed in improving the same.—(See book No. 6, page 95.)

November 7, 1833.—The board met pursuant to adjournment. Present: L. F. Linn, A. G. Harrison, F. R. Conway, commissioners.

Benito Vasquez, claiming nine arpents of land in front, by the depth from the Mississippi to the main road leading to Carondelet.—(See page 95 of this book.) The board remark, that in the petition the words *in front* were evidently omitted after the word *nine*. The board are unanimously of opinion that this claim ought to be confirmed to the said Benito Vasquez, or his legal representatives, according to the boundaries asked for in the petition, and expressed in the concession.—(See book No. 6, page 305.)

L. F. LINN.
F. R. CONWAY.
A. G. HARRISON.

No. 53.—Jean Baptiste Pujeol, *claiming* 240 *arpents.*

To Mr. Zenon Trudeau, lieutenant colonel by brevet, captain in the stationary battalion of Louisiana, lieutenant governor of the western part of Illinois, and commander-in-chief of the said part, &c.

Sir: Jean Baptiste Pujeol, inhabitant of the village of Carondelet, has the honor to represent to you that he would wish to establish a plantation on the banks of the river Maramec, on this side, but as he cannot do it without your consent, therefore the petitioner begs of you to grant to him six arpents of land in front, by forty in depth; the upper line of which (tract) is formed by the direction of a branch that comes down from the hills and empties itself into the said Maramec. The petitioner hopes, sir, that you will please to grant to him, conformably to his demand, a concession which shall serve to him as a title of property for him, his heirs or assigns; and he shall never cease to pray for your conservation and prosperity; and you will do justice.

JEAN BAPTISTE PUJEOL.

St. Louis, *November* 11, 1796.

St. Louis, *November* 11, 1796.

The surveyor of this jurisdiction, Don Antonio Soulard, shall put the individual called Jean Baptiste Pujeol in possession of six arpents of land in front by forty in depth, in the place designated, according to his demand, provided that the said land belongs to the King's domain, and be not prejudicial to any one.

ZENON TRUDEAU.

Registered at the demand of the interested—(Book No. 2, pages 7 and 8.)

SOULARD.

Truly translated. St. Louis, January 15, 1833.

JULIUS DE MUN.

No.	Name of original claimant.	Quantity, in arpents.	Nature and date of claim.	By whom granted.	By whom surveyed, date, and situation.
53	Jean Baptiste Pujeol.	240	Concession, 11th November, 1796.	Zenon Trudeau.	On the Maramec.

Evidence with reference to minutes and records.

September 20, 1806—The board met agreeably to adjournment. Present: The honorable John B. C. Lucas, Clement B. Penrose and James L. Donaldson, esquires.

Bernard Pratte, assignee of John B. Pujeol, claiming six by forty arpents of land, situate on the Maramec, district of St. Louis, produces a concession from Zenon Trudeau, dated November 11, 1796, and a deed of transfer of the same, dated the 4th of January, 1804.

Richard Averitt, being duly sworn, says that the said Pujeol settled the said tract of land in 1797 or 1798, and that the same has been actually inhabited and cultivated to this day, with the exception of one or two years.

John James, being also duly sworn, says that the said tract of land was prior to, and on the 1st day of October, 1800, actually inhabited and cultivated.

The board reject this claim for want of a duly registered warrant of survey.—(See book No. 2, page 18.)

November 30, 1808.—Board met. Present: The honorable John B. C. Lucas, Clement B. Penrose and Frederick Bates.

Bernard Pratte, assignee of John Baptiste Pujeol, claiming six by forty arpents of land situate on Maramec river. Laid over for decision. At the margin: Survey to be ordered, there being a natural boundary.—(See No. 3, page 382.)

July 11, 1810.—Board met. Present: Clement B. Penrose and Frederick Bates, commissioners

Bernard Pratte, assignee of Jean Baptiste Pujeol, claiming six by forty arpents of land.—(See book No. 2, page 18; book No. 3, page 382.) The Board order that this claim be surveyed conformably to a concession from Zenon Trudeau, lieutenant governor, to Jean Baptiste Pujeol, dated 11th of November, 1796, and recorded in book C, page 461, of the recorder's office.—(See book No. 4, page 429.)

January 15, 1812.—Board met. Present: John B. C. Lucas, Clement B. Penrose and Frederick Bates, commissioners.

Bernard Pratte, claiming under John Baptiste Pujeol.—(See book No. 4, page 429.) A majority of the board declare that they would have confirmed this claim, had it been found not to have exceeded two hundred and forty arpents. John B. C. Lucas, commissioner, makes the same remarks as in the claim of Auguste Chouteau, page 559, to wit: John B. C. Lucas, commissioner, declares that he cannot give an absolute vote under the present circumstances upon the claim, inasmuch as the board has heretofore ordered a survey to be made under the foregoing concession for the purpose of ascertaining the quantity, and inasmuch as the same reasons which induced the board to make said order, previous to the decision of the claim, still exist, and the said order remains in force, not having been rescinded. He further remarks that the claim ought to be confirmed, without being able at present to say what quantity.—(See book No. 5, pages 561 and 559.)

January 12, 1832.—F. R. Conway, esquire, appeared pursuant to adjournment.

Jean Baptiste Pujeol, by his legal representative, Bernard Pratte, claiming six arpents of land in front by forty in depth.—(See book C, page 462; minutes, No. 2, page 18; No. 3, page 382; No. 4, page 429; No. 5, page 561.) Produces a paper purporting to be an original concession from Zenon Trudeau, dated 11th November, 1796.

M. P. Le Duc, being duly sworn, saith that the signature to the concession is in the proper handwriting of the said Zenon Trudeau.

Peter Chouteau, sr., being duly sworn, saith that the signature to the concession is in the proper handwriting of the said Zenon Trudeau; he further saith that before and about 1800 he bought of said Pujeol, several in succession, the crops of tobacco he raised on said tract of land, whereon said Pujeol resided; that he had a garden, corn-fields, an dlarge tobacco plantations; that he lived many years on said land.—(See book No. 6, page 96.)

November 7, 1833.—The board met pursuant to adjournment. Present: L. F. Linn, A. G. Harrison, F. R. Conway, commissioners.

Jean Baptiste Pujeol, claiming two hundred and forty arpents of land.—(See page 96 of this book.) The board are unanimously of opinion that this claim ought to be confirmed to the said Jean Baptiste Pujeol, or his legal representatives, according to the concession.—(See book No. 6, page 306.)

L. F. LINN.
F. R. CONWAY.
A. G. HARRISON.

No. 54.—James Mackay, *claiming* 200 *and more arpents.*

To Don Charles Dehault Delassus, lieutenant governor and commander-in-chief of Upper Louisiana:

James Mackay, commandant of St. André of Missouri, has the honor to represent that, having often sundry reports to make to the government, on which account his presence is required in this town, he would wish to have a place of residence in the same; therefore, considering that all the town lots are conceded, he has the honor to supplicate you to have the goodness to grant to him, to the south of this town, a vacant tract of land of about two hundred and some arpents in superficie, which tract of land is bounded as follows: to the north by the land of Mr. Auguste Chouteau; to the south by lands of Mr. Ant. Soulard; to the east by the public road going from this town to Carondelet, and to the west by his Majesty's domain.

The petitioner, confiding in your justice, hopes that his zeal for his Majesty's service, and the small salary which he enjoys, will be strong motives in the opinion of a chief who, like you, makes his happiness consist in distributing favors to the officers who have the honor to serve under his orders. In this belief he hopes to obtain of your justice the favor which he solicits.

JAQUE MACKAY.

St. Louis, *October* 9, 1799.

St. Louis of Illinois, *October* 9, 1799.

Cognizance being taken of the foregoing memorial of Mr. James Mackay, and due attention being paid to his merit and good services, the surveyor of this Upper Louisiana, Don Antonio Soulard, shall put the interested party in possession of the land which he solicits in the place designated in this memorial; and this being executed, he shall draw a plat of his survey, delivering the same to the party, with his certificate, in order that it shall serve to him to obtain the concession and title in form from the intendant general, to whom alone corresponds, by royal order, the distributing and granting of all classes of lands of the royal domain.

CARLOS DEHAULT DELASSUS.

Truly translated. St. Louis, February 20, 1833.

JULIUS DE MUN.

No.	Name of original claimant.	Quantity, arpents.	Nature and date of claim.	By whom granted.	By whom surveyed, date, and situation.
54	James McKay.	200 and more.	Concession, October 9, 1799.	Carlos Dehault Delassus.	Antonio Soulard, —— 24, 1802; certified by him Dec. 17, 1802; south of St. Louis, adjoining the commons.

Evidence with reference to minutes and records.

July 22, 1806.—The board met agreeably to adjournment. Present: John B. C. Lucas, Clement B. Penrose, and James L. Donaldson, commissioners.

James Mackay, claiming 200 arpents of land or thereabouts, situate in the field of St. Louis, produces a concession from Charles D. Delassus, dated October 9, 1799, and a survey of the same, dated November 24, and certified December 17, 1802. Auguste Chouteau, being duly sworn, says that the said tract of land was surveyed in 1804 or 1805; that he never heard of a concession having been granted for the same until the survey was taken; that the said tract is adjoining a tract claimed by the witness, and that the same interferes with a tract claimed by the inhabitants of St. Louis as a common. The board, from the above testimony, are satisfied that the aforesaid concession is antedated.—(See book No. 1, page 417.)

St. Louis, *December* 28, 1813.—James Mackay claims about 30 arpents of land near the town of St. Louis; produces a concession from Charles D. Delassus, lieutenant governor, for about 200 arpents, dated October 9, 1799; survey of 288 arpents, December 17, 1802, (certified.) M. P. Le Duc, as agent of claimant, abandons all but about 30 arpents, the part abandoned supposed to be comprehended by the survey of the commons; it appearing from the minutes, book 1, page 417, that no testimony has been introduced on the merits of this claim. A witness now admitted. Antoine Soulard, duly sworn, says that this tract was granted to claimant by C. D. Delassus, lieutenant governor, on the recommendation of his predecessor, Z. Trudeau, who had promised the same. It was surveyed under the Spanish government, and has ever since been considered as property of claimant; that corn was raised on the premises for claimant during three or four of the last years.

Note.—No more abandoned than may fall within the commons, should they be confirmed.

At the margin: confirmed 30 arpents of land.—(See recorder's minutes, page 117; see Bates's Decisions, page 36.)

February 18, 1833.—F. R. Conway, esq., appeared, pursuant to adjournment, having been authorized by a resolution of the board of commissioners of the 1st of December last to receive evidence.

James Mackay, by his legal representative, claiming 200 and more arpents, it being a special location.—(See book B, pages 433 and 434; minutes No. 1, page 417; minutes of recorder, page 117.) The claimant further refers to book B, page 486, in order to show that the claim for the common of St. Louis does not interfere with this claim; also to book No. 5, page 552. Produces a paper purporting to be a concession from Carlos Dehault Delassus, dated October 9, 1799.

M. P. Le Duc, being duly sworn, saith that the signature to the concession is in the proper handwriting of the said Carlos Dehault Delassus. For further testimony of M. P. Le Duc in behalf of this claim, see next claim below, to wit: Deponent further says that he informed Mr. Soulard that in case he would abandon the part of his claim which was included in the common of St. Louis, Mr. Bates would confirm the balance of said claim; thereupon Soulard called on Mr. Bates and made the abandonment, upon which Bates confirmed the part of said claim which lies east of the common, and, at the same time, Soulard, agent for Mackay, made the same abandonment on Mackay's claim; and that, since that time, Soulard told the deponent that Mackey disapproved of said abandonment, and that he, the said deponent, never acted as agent for Mackay in said claim; that he does not know that Soulard ever was authorized by Mackay to make said abandonment; that since the time of said abandonment Mackay remained as ostensible owner and claimant of said land; that he built thereon a house, and lived and died in it.

The deponent further says that what he understands by these claims interfering with the common of St. Louis, is the part of said claim included in the survey of said common, made by Mackay, in 1806, as recorded.

Deponent believes that taxes were paid by Mackay and Soulard on said lands until 1820; and that the part of Mackay's claim which was not confirmed was sold under an execution, as being the property of said Mackay.—(See book No. 6, page 103.)

July 31, 1807.—The board met agreeably to adjournment. Present: The honorable John B. C. Lucas, Clement B. Penrose and Frederick Bates, commissioners. Same (James Mackay) claiming about 282 arpents in the commons of St. Louis, produces a concession from Carlos D. Delassus, dated 9th of October, 1799. Survey and certificate dated the 17th of December, 1802. Laid over for decision.—(See book No. 3, page 21.)

November 4, 1809.—Board met. Present: John B. C. Lucas and Clement B. Penrose, commissioners. James Mackay, claiming 282 arpents of land situate in the commons of St. Louis.—(See book No. 1, page 417; book No. 3, page 21.) It is the opinion of the board that this claim ought not to be confirmed.—(See book No. 4, page 186.)

November 7, 1833.—The board met pursuant to adjournment. Present: L. F. Linn, A. G. Harrison, F. R. Conway, commissioners. James Mackay claiming 200 and more arpents of land.—(See page 103 of this book.) The board, after minutely examining the original papers in this case, see no cause for entertaining even the suspicion of the concession being antedated, as expressed by the former board, and they are unanimously of opinion that this claim ought to be confirmed to the said James Mackay or to his legal representatives, according to the concession.—(See book No. 6, page 306.)

L. F. LINN.
F. R. CONWAY.
A. G. HARRISON.

No. 55.—BERNARD PRATTE, *claiming 7,056 arpents.*

To Don Charles Dehault Delassus, lieutenant colonel of the stationary regiment of Louisiana and lieutenant governor of the upper part of the same province, &c.:

SIR: The undersigned, convinced that the resources of agriculture are the most infallible means to secure to his family an independent existence, and to shelter them hereafter from the disasters of poverty, and wishing to participate in the gratuitous gifts made by the government to the inhabitants of this dependency, has the honor to represent to you that he has the project of forming sundry establishments, as well for agriculture as for the raising of cattle; therefore the undersigned humbly supplicates, and has recourse to your authority, in order to obtain, in full property, one league square of land in superficie, to be taken in any vacant part of his Majesty's domain, in the place which will be found most convenient to the execution of his project, without prejudice to any one. He hopes that you will be pleased to take into consideration the well-grounded motives of his demand, and that your decision will be favorable.

BERNARD PRATTE.

ST. LOUIS, *September* 18, 1799.

ST. LOUIS OF ILLINOIS, *October* 19, 1799.

Having examined the statement on the other side, and considering that the petitioner was born in this country, and that his family is one among the most ancient inhabitants of this country, whose known conduct and personal merit are recommendable, and being satisfied to evidence that he possesses more means than is necessary to improve the land he solicits, I do grant to him and his heirs the land which he solicits, in case it is not prejudicial to any one; and the surveyor, Don Antoino Soulard, shall put the interested party in possession of the land which he asks, in a vacant place of the royal domain, and this being executed, he shall draw a plat of survey, delivering the same to the party, with his certificate, in order to serve to the said party to obtain the concession and title in form from the intendent general, to whom corresponds, by royal order, the distributing and granting all classes of lands of the royal domain.

CARLOS DEHAULT DELASSUS.

Registered at the desire of the interested, (No. 17, pages 26 and 27 of book of registers of memorials, decrees, and titles of concessions, No. 1.)

SOULARD.

Truly translated. St. Louis, February 22, 1833.

JULIUS DE MUN.

No.	Name of original claimant.	Quantity, in arpents.	Nature and date of claim.	By whom granted.	By whom surveyed, date, and situation.
55	Bernard Pratte.	7,056	Concession, October 19, 1799.	Charles Dehault Delassus.	Nathaniel Cook, D. S., 15th February, 1806; certified 20th February, 1806, by A. Soulard; on river St. Francis.

Evidence with reference to minutes and records.

May 5, 1806.—The board met agreeably to adjournment. Present: The honorable Clement B. Penrose and James L. Donaldson, commissioners.

Bernard Pratte, claiming 7,056 arpents of land situate on the river St. Francis, district of St. Genevieve, produces a concession from Charles D. Delassus for the same, not duly registered, and dated October 19, 1799; and a survey of the same, taken 15th and certified 19th February, 1806. No condition inserted in said concession. The board required further proofs of the date of said concession, which were not adduced.

The board reject this claim.—(See book No. 1, page 276.)

December 7, 1807.—The board met agreeably to adjournment. Present: Hon. John B. C. Lucas and Frederick Bates, commissioners.

The same, (James Maxwell,) assignee of Bernard Pratte, claiming 7,056 arpents of land situate on the river St. Francis, district of St. Genevieve, produces a concession from Charles D. Delassus for the same, (not duly registered,) and dated October 19, 1799; and a survey of the same, taken the 15th and certified 19th of February, 1806. No condition inserted in said concession. Also a deed of conveyance from said Pratte to claimant, dated May 8, 1806, and duly acknowledged the 9th of May of the same year. Laid over for decision.—(See book No. 3, page 163.)

May 31, 1810.—Board met. Present: J. B. C. Lucas, Clement B. Penrose, and Frederick Bates, commissioners.

James, Maxwell, assignee of Bernard Pratte, claiming 7,056 arpents of land.—(See book No. 1, page 276; book No. 3, page 163.)

It is the opinion of the board that this claim ought not to be confirmed.—(See book No. 4, page 356.)

February 18, 1833.—F. R. Conway, esq., appeared pursuant to adjournment, having been authorized by a resolution of the board of commissioners of the 1st of December last to receive evidence.

Bernard Pratte, claiming 7,056 arpents of land, (see book C, page 256; No. 1, page 276,) produces a paper purporting to be a concession from Carlos Dehault Delassus, dated October 19, 1799; also a plat of survey, taken 15th and certified 19th February, 1806, by Antonio Soulard.

M. P. Le Duc, duly sworn, saith that the signature to the concession is in the proper handwriting of

Carlos Dehault Delassus, and the signature to the plat of survey is in the proper handwriting of Antoine Soulard.—(See book No. 6, page 104.)

November 7, 1833.—The board met pursuant to adjournment. Present: L. F. Linn, A. G. Harrison, F. R. Conway, commissioners.

Bernard Pratte, claiming 7,056 arpents of land.—(See page 104 of this book.)

The board are unanimously of opinion that this claim ought to be confirmed to said Bernard Pratte, or his legal representatives, according to the concession.—(See book No. 6, page 306.)

Conflicting claims.

Samuel Holstead, by letter addressed to L. F. Linn, commissioner, dated October 9, 1832, states that in 1809 he purchased an improvement of John Murphy, son of William Murphy, senior, south and adjoining a tract confirmed to said W. Murphy. About the year 1805, by order of governor Wilkinson, the said Wm. Murphy had an additional tract surveyed for him, which included the improvement purchased by said Holstead, and on which he now lives. He further states that Pratte's claim was first surveyed in 1806, and the said survey was made to adjoin the south line of the additional tract of Wm. Murphy; but the said additional tract failing of confirmation, said Holstead's improvement was, of course, on public land. In 1821 said Holstead came to St. Louis, and proved his pre-emption right, but could not enter the land, a part being included in Pratte's claim. Said claim was not at that time (1821) designated on the plat, but Pratte forbid the sale of it.

Pratte did not go down to show his lines; they were *guessed* at, and *made* to adjoin the south line of the tract originally granted to William Murphy.

A certificate of Wm. Murphy, saying that Pratte's survey was made to adjoin the south line of his (Wm. Murphy's) additional tract, now the improvement of said Holstead.

Also certificate of Laken Walker, to the same end.

L. F. LINN.
F. R. CONWAY.
A. G. HARRISON

No. 56.—Henry Dielle, *claiming* 5,000 *arpents.*

To Don Charles Dehault Delassus, lieutenant colonel, attached to the stationary regiment of Louisiana, and lieutenant governor of the upper part of the same province:

Sir: Henry Dielle, inhabitant of St. Genevieve, father of a numerous family, owner of slaves, and of all the means necessary for farming on a large scale, having never obtained any concession from the government, has the honor to supplicate you, with all due respect, to be willing to grant to him in full property a tract of land of 5,000 arpents in superficie, to be taken in a vacant part of his Majesty's domain, at his choice, upon the waters of the river St. Francis or thereabouts. The undersigned, full of confidence in the generosity of the government and in your justice, presumes to hope that you will be pleased to do justice to his demand in such a way as to enable him to fulfil his views.

H. DIELLE.

St. Louis, *December* 28, 1799.

We forward the present petition to the lieutenant governor of Upper Louisiana, and do observe to him that the statement of the petitioner is conformable to truth; that by his means, his conduct, and his good morals, he deserves, in every point of view, to obtain of your justice the favor which he solicits from the government.

FRANCISCO VALLÉ.

St. Louis of Illinois, *December* 29, 1779.

Cognizance being taken of the statement on the other side, and of the information given by the commandant of St. Genevieve, Captain Don Francisco Vallé, and considering that the petitioner is one of the most ancient inhabitants of this country, whose known conduct and personal merit are recommendable, and being satisfied to evidence that he possesses sufficient means to improve the land which he solicits, I do grant to him and his heirs the land which he solicits, in case it is not prejudicial to any one; and the surveyor, Don Antonio Soulard, shall put the interested in possession of the quantity of land he asks in one of the places designated; and this being executed, he shall draw a plat of survey, which he shall deliver to the party, with his certificate, in order to serve to him to obtain the concession and title in form from the intendant general, to whom alone corresponds, by royal order, the distributing and granting all classes of lands of the royal domain.

CARLOS DEHAULT DELASSUS.

Truly translated. St. Louis, February 22, 1833.

JULIUS DE MUN.

No.	Name of original claimant.	Quantity, in arpents.	Nature and date of claim.	By whom granted.	By whom surveyed, date and situation.
56	Henry Dielle............	5,000	Concession, February 2?, 1799.	Carlos Dehault Delasus.	Nathaniel Cook, D. S., February 3, 1806; certified by Soulard, February 19, 1806; on St. Francis river.

Evidence with reference to minutes and records.

May 5, 1806.—The board met agreeably to adjournment. Present: The Hon. Clement B. Penrose and James L. Donaldson, commissioners.

The same, (Bernard Pratte,) assignee of Henry Dielle, claiming 5,000 arpents of land, situate as aforesaid. Produces a concession from Charles Dehault Delassus for the same, not duly registered, and dated December 29, 1799; a survey of the same, taken the 3d and certified February 19, 1806; a deed of transfer of the same, dated November 14, 1805. No condition expressed in said concession. The board required further proof of the date of the said concession, which was not adduced. The board reject this claim.—(See book No. 1, page 276.)

December 7, 1807.—The board met agreeably to adjournment. Present: the Hon. John B. C. Lucas and Frederick Bates, commissioners.

The same, (James Maxwell,) assignee of Bernard Pratte, who was assignee of Henry Dielle, claiming 5,000 arpents of land situate on the river St. Francis, district of St. Genevieve. Produces a concession from Charles Dehault Delassus for the same, not duly registered, and dated December 29, 1799; a survey of the same taken the 3d and certified February 19, 1806; a deed of transfer of the same, dated November 14, 1805; also a deed of conveyance from said Pratte to claimant, dated May 8, 1806, and duly acknowledged May 9, of the same year. No condition expressed in said concession. Laid over for decision.—(See book No. 3, page 163.)

May 31, 1810.—Board met. Present: John B. C. Lucas, Clement B. Penrose, and Frederick Bates, commissioners.

James Maxwell, assignee of Bernard Pratte, assignee of Henry Dielle, claiming 5,000 arpents of land.—(See book No. 1, page 276; book No. 3, page 163.) It is the opinion of the board that this claim ought not to be confirmed.—(See book No. 4, page 356.)

February 18, 1833.—F. R. Conway, esq., appeared pursuant to adjournment, having been authorized by a resolution of the board of commissioners of the 1st of December last to receive evidence.

Henry Dielle, by his assignee, Bernard Pratte, claiming 5,000 arpents of land on the waters of the St. Francis.—(See record book C, page 257; minutes No. 1, page 276.) Produces a paper purporting to be a concession from Charles Dehault Delassus, dated February 29, 1799; also a plat of survey taken the 3d and certified February 19, 1806, by Antoine Soulard.

M. P. Le Duc, duly sworn, saith that the signature to the concession is in the proper handwriting of Carlos Dehault Delassus, and the signature to the plat of survey is in the proper handwriting of A. Soulard.—(See book No. 6, page 105.)

November 7, 1833.—The board met pursuant to adjournment. Present: L. F. Linn, A. G. Harrison, F. R. Conway, commissioners.

Henry Dielle, claiming 5,000 arpents of land.—(See page 105 of this book.) The board are unanimously of opinion that this claim ought to be confirmed to said Henry Dielle, or his legal representatives, according to the concession.—(See book No. 6, page 105.)

L. F. LINN.
F. R. CONWAY.
A. G. HARRISON.

No. 57.—Mathieu Saucier, *claiming* 1,200 *arpents.*

To Don Charles Dehault Delassus, lieutenant colonel, attached to the stationary regiment of Louisiana, and lieutenant governor of the upper part of the same province:

Mathieu Saucier, a native of this country, father of eight children, and son of an officer in the French troops of the navy, has the honor of representing to you that he would wish to form an insulated plantation in order to raise cattle thereon, and to establish his numerous family as soon as they shall be of age to work for themselves. Therefore, full of confidence in the generosity of a government which he and those related to him have always served with fidelity, he has the honor respectfully to supplicate you to have the goodness to grant to him, in full property, the quantity of twelve hundred arpents of land in superficie, to be taken in a vacant place of his Majesty's domain on the north side of the Missouri. Full of confidence in your justice, he awaits with hope the good effect thereof; this new favor shall be one more tie which will invariably bind him and his family to the soil which has seen their birth, and to the government which has always treated them as its own subjects.

MATH. SAUCIER.

St. Louis, *November* 25, 1800.

St. Louis of Illinois, *November* 28, 1800.

Considering that the petitioner has grown old in this country, and that his family is sufficiently large to obtain the quantity of land which he solicits, and as we are assured that he possesses sufficient means to improve the land which he solicits, I do grant to him and his heirs the land which he solicits, if it is not prejudicial to anybody; and the surveyor, Don Antonio Soulard, shall put the interested in possession of the quantity of land which he asks, in the place designated, and this being executed, he shall draw a plat of his survey, delivering the same to the party, with his certificate, in order to serve to him to obtain the concession and title in form from the intendant general, to whom alone corresponds, by royal order, the distributing and granting all classes of lands of the royal domain.

CARLOS DEHAULT DELASSUS.

Truly translated. St. Louis, February 22, 1833.

JULIUS DE MUN.

No.	Name of original claimant	Quantity, in arpents.	Nature and date of claim.	By whom granted.	By whom surveyed, date, and situation.
57	Mathew Saucier.....	1,200	Concession, November 28, 1800.	Carlos Dehault Delassus.	

Evidence with reference to minutes and records.

December 9, 1811.—The board met. Present: John B. C. Lucas, Clement B. Penrose, and Frederick Bates, commissioners.

Peter Chouteau, assignee of Mathew Saucier, claiming 1,200 arpents of land situate on the Mississippi, district of St. Charles, produces record of a concession from Delassus, lieutenant governor dated November 28, 1800. It is the opinion of the board that this claim ought not to be confirmed.—(See book No. 5, page 498.)

February 18, 1833.—F. R. Conway, esquire, appeared pursuant to adjournment.

Mathew Saucier, by his legal representative, Pierre Chouteau, senior, claiming 1,200 arpents of land, (see book D, pages 163 and 164; book No. 5 page 498,) produces a paper purporting to be a concession from Carlos Dehault Delassus, dated November 28, 1800. M. P. Le Duc, duly sworn, saith the signature to the concession is in the proper handwriting of Carlos Dehault Delassus.—(See book No. 6, page 105.)

November 7, 1833.—The board met pursuant to adjournment. Present: L. F. Linn, A. G. Harrison, F. R. Conway, commissioners.

Mathew Saucier, claiming 1,200 arpents of land.—(See page 105 of this book.) The board are unanimously of opinion that this claim ought to be confirmed to the said Mathew Saucier, or his legal representatives, according to the concession.—(See book No. 6, page 307.)

L. F. LINN.
F. R. CONWAY.
A. G HARRISON.

No. 58.—Purnel Howard, *claiming* 400 *arpents.*

To Don Charles Dehault Delassus, lieutenant governor and commander-in-chief of Upper Louisiana, &c.:

Purnel Howard, C. R., has the honor to represent to you that, with the permission of the government, he has settled himself on a tract of land in his Majesty's domain, on the north side of the Missouri; therefore he supplicates you to have the goodness to grant to him, at the same place, the quantity of land corresponding to the number of his family, composed of himself, his wife, and four children; the petitioner having sufficient means to improve a plantation, and having no other views but to live as a peaceable and submissive cultivator of the soil, hopes to obtain the favor which he solicits of your justice.

PURNEL HOWARD, + mark.

St. André, *November* 11, 1799.

Be it forwarded to the lieutenant governor, with information that the statement above is true, and that the petitioner deserves the favor which he solicits.

SANTIAGO MACKAY.

St. André, *November* 11, 1799.

St. Louis of Illinois, *November* 25, 1799.

By virtue of the information given by Don Santiago Mackay, commandant of the settlement of St. André, in which he testifies as to the truth of the number of individuals stated to compose the family of the petitioner, the surveyor, Don Antonio Soulard, shall put him in possession of 400 arpents of land in superficie, in the place where asked by him, this quantity corresponding to the number of his family, conformably to the regulation of the governor general of the province; and this being executed, the interested party shall have to solicit the title of concession in form from the intendant general of the same province, to whom, by royal order, corresponds the distributing and granting all classes of lands of the royal domain.

CARLOS DEHAULT DELASSUS.

Don Antonio Soulard, surveyor general of the settlements of Upper Louisiana.

I do certify that a tract of land, of 500 arpents in superficie, has been measured, the lines run and bounded, in favor and in presence of Purnel Howard. Said measurement has been taken with the perch of Paris, of 18 French feet, lineal measure of the same city, according to the agrarian measure of this province. Said land is situated on the north side of the Missouri, at the distance of two miles from said river, and at about sixty miles west of this town of St. Louis, and is bounded on its four sides—north, south, east, and west—by vacant lands of the royal domain. The said survey and measurement was taken without having regard to the variation of the needle, which is 7° 30′ east, as is evinced by the foregoing figurative plat, on which are noted the dimensions, courses of the lines, other boundaries, &c. This survey was taken by virtue of the decree of the lieutenant governor and sub-delegate of the royal fisc, Don Carlos Dehault Delassus, bearing date November 25, 1799, here annexed.

In testimony whereof, I do give the present, with the foregoing figurative plat drawn conformably to the survey executed by the deputy surveyor, Don Santiago Mackay, on the 28th of March, 1804.

ANTONIO SOULRAD, *Surveyor General.*

Truly translated. St. Louis, February 23, 1833.

JULIUS DE MUN.

No.	Name of original claimant.	Quantity, in arpents.	Nature and date of claim.	By whom granted.	By whom surveyed, date, and situation.
58	Purnel Howard.	400	Concession, November 25, 1799.	Carlos Dehault Delassus.	James Mackay, deputy surveyor, March 28, 1804; certified by Soulard, north side of Missouri, 60 miles west of St. Louis.

Evidence with reference to minutes and records.

November 20, 1811.—Board met. Present: John B. C. Lucas, Clement B. Penrose, and Frederick Bates, commissioners.

Joshua Dodson, assignee of Purnel Howard, claiming four hundred arpents of land situate on Smith's creek, district of St. Charles, produces record of a concession from Delassus, lieutenant governor, dated November 25, 1799; record of a plat of survey, dated March 28, 1804; record of a transfer from Howard to claimant, dated March 30, 1804.

It is the opinion of the board that this claim ought not to be confirmed.—(See book No. 5, page 430.)

February 18, 1833.—F. R. Conway, esq., appeared pursuant to adjournment.

Purnel Howard, by his legal representative, claiming four hundred arpents of land, (see record book C, pages 384 and 385; book No. 5, page 430,) produces a paper purporting to be a concession from Carlos Dehault Delassus, dated November 25, 1799; also a plat of survey, dated March 28, 1804, by Soulard.

M. P. Le Duc, being duly sworn, saith that the signature to the concession is in the proper handwriting of Carlos Dehault Delassus, and the signature to the plat of survey is in the proper handwriting of A. Soulard.—(See book No. 6, page 106.)

November 7, 1833.—The board met pursuant to adjournment. Present: L. F. Linn, A. G. Harrison, and F. R. Conway, commissioners.

Purnel Howard, claiming four hundred arpents of land.—(See page 106 of this book.) The board remark that there is evidently a mistake in the certificate of survey, for it is therein stated five hundred arpents, when the survey shows four hundred. The board are unanimously of opinion that this claim ought to be confirmed to the said Purnel Howard, or to his legal representatives, according to the concession.—(See book No. 6, page 307.)

L. F. LINN.
F. R. CONWAY.
A. G. HARRISON.

No. 59.—Pierre François Devolsey, *claiming six by forty arpents.*

On the 15th of September, 1767, on the demand of Mr. Pierre François Devolsey, (ecuyer,) an officer in the troops detached from the marines, residing at the post of St. Louis, who desires to cultivate land we have granted and do grant to him in fee, for him, his heirs, and assigns, a tract of land of six arpents in front, in the prairie which is to the south of the Little river; the said front runs north and south, by the ordinary depth of forty arpents, running east and west, adjoining on the south side to the King's domain or lands not granted, and on the north side to the land conceded to Madame Chouteau, on condition that said land shall be improved in one year and a day, and that it shall be subject to the public charges and others which it may please his Majesty to impose.

Given in St. Louis the day and year as above, and we have signed.

ST. ANGE.
LABUXIERE.

Truly translated from Livre Terrein, No. 1, pages 14 and 15. St. Louis, February 20, 1833.

JULIUS DE MUN.

No.	Name of original claimant.	Quantity, in arpents.	Nature and date of claim.	By whom granted.	By whom surveyed, date, and situation.
59	Pierre François Devolsey	240	Concession, September 15, 1767.	St. Ange.......	In the little prairie, south of St. Louis.

Evidence with reference to minutes and records.

February 15, 1833.—F. R. Conway, esq., appeared pursuant to adjournment, having been authorized by a resolution of the board of commissioners of the 1st of December last to receive evidence.

Pierre François Devolsey, by his legal representative J. P. Cabanné, claiming six arpents of land in front by forty in depth, (see Livre Terrein, No. 1, page 14; record book F, page 152,) produces a paper purporting to be a copy of a concession from St. Ange, lieutenant governor, dated September 15, 1767; also a deed of conveyance from François Dupuis to J. P. Cabanné, dated October 2, 1817; also a copy of Devolsey's last will and testament and a translation of the same; also a paper purporting to be the deposition of Paul Portneuf, alias Ladéroute, before F. M. Guyol, a justice of the peace for the county of St. Louis, on the 10th of March, 1819.

Pierre Chouteau, senior, being duly sworn, saith that Devolsey was a captain in the French service, and had a concession granted to him for the above piece of land; that Devolsey did not settle himself on said land, because at that time no one would have dared to live out of town on account of the Indians, but cut his wood and made his hay on the same; that any one who wanted to cut timber on the same had to ask Devolsey's permission. He says also that the signature affixed to the concession in Livre Terrein, No. 1, pages 14 and 15, which is exhibited to him, is in the true handwriting of St. Ange, then lieutenant governor. He further states that he knew Paul Portneuf, alias Ladéroute; that he was a natural son of a former commandant and a man of good repute; that he, the deponent, having been thirty years among the Indians, he never paid attention, during his short stays in St. Louis, whether there was any field on said land, at least he does not remember of having seen any; that at the time when Theodore Hunt was recorder of land titles, and receiving evidences under the act of Congress, 1824, he, the deponent, went before the said Hunt and gave his testimony in behalf of this claim, and Mr. Rene Paul went with him as his interpreter; that said land is situated immediately south and adjoining Madame Chouteau's land, in the little prairie south of St. Louis, and is bounded east by the road to Carondelet, south and west by lands which were then vacant.

Rene Paul, being duly sworn, saith that, in 1825, he, being then commissioned deputy surveyor, was requested, by Theodore Hunt, to go and identify all the possessions in the little prairie, according to their respective concessions, and conformably to the testimonies given by Baptiste Riviere, alias Bacanné, and Rene Dodier, who had been previously sworn to that effect; that he identified the claim of Cabanné, under Devolsey, to be in the little prairie south of St. Louis, bounded north by lands granted to Madame Chouteau, east by the Carondelet road, south by lands granted to Bacanné, and west by lands said to be the commons of St. Louis, containing six arpents of land in front by forty in depth. The northeast corner thereof being on the west side of the road, and eight linear arpents south of the south boundary line of Soulard's land. He further states that, in 1825, he went with P. Chouteau, sr., before T. Hunt, and served as interpreter to said Chouteau when he gave his testimony in behalf of this claim.

Laurent Reed, being duly sworn, saith that he is seventy-three years of age, and when a boy he knew Devolsey, who then lived in St. Louis, and he continued to know him until his death. He believes that Devolsey died about forty years ago, more or less; that he knew that one of Devolsey's negroes cultivated a small field in the little prairie, but does not remember exactly the place, it being so long since; that said negro cultivated tobacco, melons, and other articles of produce.—(See book No. 6, page 100.)

November 8, 1833.—The board met pursuant to adjournment. Present: L. F. Linn, A. G. Harrison, F. R. Conway, commissioners.

Pierre François Devolsey, claiming six by forty arpents of land.—(See page 100 of this book.) The board are unanimously of opinion that this claim ought to be confirmed to the said Pierre François Dovolsey, or his legal representatives, according to the concession; and they remark that their opinion was formed independently of the deposition of Portneuf, produced in this case.—(See book No. 6, page 307.)

L. F. LINN.
F. R. CONWAY.
A. G. HARRISON.

No. 60.—Gabriel Cerré, *claiming ten by forty arpents*

To Don Manuel Perez, captain of the regiment of infantry of Louisiana, lieutenant governor, &c.:

Having examined the contents of the memorial presented by Don Gabriel Cerré, residing in this town of St. Louis, and bearing date the 11th of March, 1789, I granted and do grant to him in fee, for him, his heirs and assigns, a tract of land of ten arpents in front by forty in depth, situated on river Gravois, which empties into river Des Peres, at the distance of two leagues from this town and about eight arpents from the river Mississippi, bounded on every side by the King's domain, under condition to establish and improve the same in the term of one year from this date; on the contrary, to remain incorporated to the royal domain. The said land to be subject to the public charges and others which it may please his Majesty to impose.

Given in St. Louis of Illinois on the 15th day of March, of the year 1789.

MANUEL PEREZ.

Truly translated from Livre Terrein.—(Book No. 4, pages 21 and 22.) St. Louis, February 10, 1833.

JULIUS DE MUN.

No.	Name of original claimant.	Quantity, in arpents.	Nature and date of claim.	By whom granted.	By whom surveyed, date, and situation.
60	Gabriel Cerré.......	400	Concession, March 15, 1789.	Manuel Perez...	On Gravois, two leagues from St. Louis.

Evidence with reference to minutes and records.

October 18, 1811.—Board met. Present: John B. C. Lucas, Clement B. Penrose, and Frederick Bates, commissioners.

Gabriel Cerré, claiming 400 arpents of land situate on the river Maramec, (Gravois,) district of St.

Louis, produces a concession from Charles D. Delassus, lieutenant governor, dated August 13, 1799. It is the opinion of the board that this claim ought not to be confirmed.—(See book No. 5, page 384.)

February 8, 1833.—F. R. Conway, esq., appeared pursuant to adjournment, having been authorized by a resolution of the board of commissioners of the 1st of December last to receive evidence.

Gabriel Cerré, by his legal representative, Frederic Dent, claiming ten arpents of land in front by forty arpents in depth, (see Livre Terrein, No. 4, pages 21 and 22,) for general notice, see record book F, page 346,) produces a paper purporting to be a certified copy of a concession granted by Manuel Perez, lieutenant governor, dated March 15, 1789.

Pascal Cerré, being duly sworn, saith that he is acquainted with the tract mentioned in the above concession; that it was granted to his father by Manuel Perez in the year 1789; that in the beginning of June, 1789 or 1790, but he rather thinks it was in 1789, his father had two ploughs at work on said land, and planted a cornfield, which was not fenced in; that he had a cabin built and an orchard planted; that he, the said deponent, planted said orchard with his own hands, and had it fenced in, and had grass mowed on said land, and had two haystacks made in the enclosure of said orchard; that his father remained in possession until the deponent's mother died, when a division of the property took place, and the said land fell into the deponent's hands; that now he has no kind of interest in said property, having sold the same to Abraham Gallatin; that said land was surveyed by Antoine Soulard under the Spanish authorities.—(See book No. 6, page 98.)

May 22, 1833.—F. R. Conway, esq., appeared pursuant to adjournment.

In the case of Gabriel Cerré, claiming 10 arpents of land in front by 40 in depth, (see page 98 of this book,) the claimant produces a paper purporting to be a plat of survey, signed by Jos. C. Brown, and dated February 13, 1822.

Joseph C. Brown, duly sworn, says that the plat of survey presented by the claimant was executed by him conformably to the survey he made of said land, and that what is therein stated is true.—(See book No. 6, page 169.)

November 8, 1833.—The board met pursuant to adjournment. Present: L. F. Linn, A. G. Harrison, F. R. Conway, commissioners.

Gabriel Cerré, claiming 400 arpents of land.—(See pages 98 and 169 of this book.)

The board are unanimously of opinion that this claim ought to be confirmed to said Gabriel Cerré, or his legal representatives, according to the concession.—(See page 308, book No. 6.)

L. F. LINN.
F. R. CONWAY.
A. G. HARRISON.

No. 61.—B. Cousin, *claiming* 899 *arpents*.

To Don Charles Dehault Delassus, lieutenant colonel in his Catholic Majesty's armies attached to the stationary regiment of Louisiana, and lieutenant governor of Upper Louisiana:

Bartholomew Cousin humbly supplicates, and has the honor of representing to you, that, since he resided in Cape Girardeau, he has constantly fulfilled the functions of interpreter and writer of Don Lewis Lorimier, commandant of said post—duties which have taken up the best part of his time, and rendered his presence always necessary, in a settlement whose population is considerable, and composed of Americans. Convinced of the equity and beneficence of the government which he has the honor to serve, the petitioner would think he was unjust towards himself if he neglected any longer to represent the need he has of receiving the reward of his services; and, with a confidence inspired by a legitimate demand, he now applies to you, sir, in order that you may be pleased to take his prayer into consideration, and grant him an indemnification proportionate to the length and utility of his services. It is not a pecuniary gratification which the petitioner solicits; his desires are limited to obtain, in the way of salary, a species of property which the government has made, till now, the object of gratuitous liberality. The favor which the petitioner desires is a concession of six thousand arpents in superficie, and he prays you to grant to him, his heirs, or assigns, the said quantity of land, on a vacant part of this district, at the distance of about fifteen miles to the west of this place, on the forks of a river commonly called White Water, and to order that, in surveying this land, there shall be allowed to him three-twentieths on the length of each line, on account of the roads, (les eaux,) creeks, and ponds, the unfertile lands, and the loss in chaining, occasioned by the inequalities of the land.

The petitioner presumes to expect this favor of a just and generous government, which will not leave useful services without their reward; and he shall never cease to pray Heaven for the preservation of your precious life.

B. COUSIN.

Cape Girardeau, *October* 8, 1799.

St. Louis of Illinois, *October* 15, 1799.

In consequence of the foregoing demand made by Don Bartholomew Cousin, of Cape Girardeau, and in consideration of the information given by Don Luis Lorimier, commandant of said post; and, also, in consideration of the services which the petitioner has rendered in fulfilling, with the greatest zeal, the functions of interpreter and writer in the affairs which required a correspondence with the officers of the other side, belonging to the United States of America; and, also, in all the petitions, requests, and other documents in demand of right in justice from the inhabitants of said Cape Girardeau, who are almost all Americans; in which laborious work he has been employed by the said Don Luis Lorimier, all of which is to me evident and notorious, I have determined to grant him the favor which he asks, and I do grant to him and his successors the quantity of six thousand arpents of land in superficie, in the way of reward for the above-mentioned services which he rendered very faithfully, and with the greatest disinterestedness. Therefore, the surveyor of this Upper Louisiana, Don Antonio Soulard, shall put the interested in possession of six thousand arpents in superficie, which he solicits, in the place designated in his demand,

and with the allowance of three-twentieths, *which are to be deducted on the length of each line*, (que han de ser rebajados sobre lo largo de cada linea,) in order that he may enjoy and dispose of this concession as being his own property; and the survey being executed, the corresponding certificate shall be delivered to him, in order to serve to obtain the title of concession in form from the competent authority.

CARLOS DEHAULT DELASSUS.

We, commandant of the post of Cape Girardeau of Illinois, for his Catholic Majesty, have the honor to inform the lieutenant governor that the petitioner, since he has resided in this place, has been constantly employed by us in the capacity of public scrivener and interpreter of the French, English, and Spanish languages—functions which the population of this settlement has rendered indispensable, and which the petitioner has always fulfilled with a great deal of assiduity, faithfulness, and exactness. For these reasons we are led now to recommend him to the beneficence of the government, and do certify that the land for which he asks a concession is a part of his Majesty's domain.

L. LORIMIER.

CAPE GIRARDEAU, *October* 8, 1799.

Truly translated from book D, page 314, of record in this office. St. Louis, November 13, 1833.

JULIUS DE MUN.

No.	Name of original claimant.	Quantity, in arpents	Nature and date of claim.	By whom granted.	By whom surveyed, date, and situation.
61	Bartholomew Cousin.	800, balance of 7,935.	Concession, October 15, 1799.	Carlos Dehault Delassus.	Antonio Soulard, December 8, 1801. Certified by him March 1, 1802. Fourteen miles W.NW. of Cape Girardeau.

Evidence with reference to minutes and records.

August 30, 1806.—The board met agreeably to adjournment. Present: The Hon. John B. C. Lucas Clement B. Penrose, and James L. Donaldson, esq.

Bartholomew Cousin, claiming 6,000 arpents of land situate on the river White Water, district of Cape Girardeau, produces a concession from Charles D. Delassus, dated the 15th of October, 1799, and a survey of the same taken the 8th of December, 1801, and certified the 1st of March, 1802, the same being granted as a compensation to claimant for his service to government. Claimant produces also a letter from Charles D. Delassus, the lieutenant governor, dated the 15th of October, 1799, wherein he acknowledges his claim to the generosity and benevolence of the Spanish government for the many services he had rendered the country since his arrival in the same, showing a disposition to do more for him when occasion should offer, and promising to procure him the appointment of interpreter to the district of Cape Girardeau, with a fixed salary annexed to the same; an official letter from the same to the governor general, dated the 25th June, 1802, wherein, after reciting the service rendered by claimant to government, he recommends him to said governor; and, lastly, another official letter from the same to claimant, wherein he dispenses him (as far as in his power) with a compliance with the fourth article of the regulations, to wit, settlement and inhabitation; said letter dated 20th March, 1803.

Anthony Soulard, being duly sworn, says that the above claimant was employed by government as interpreter of the English language to Louis Lorimier, commandant of that district; that the object of government was to extend the settlement of said district to the river St. Francis; that Zenon Trudeau, whose favorite claimant was, had recommended him to Delassus; that some time after, having shown a desire to move from said district, Delassus persuaded him to remain and promised him an office with some salaries annexed to the same, together with other compensations, for his former service to government. The board reject this claim, and remark that they are satisfied that the said concession was granted at the time the same bears date.—(See book No. 1, page 512.)

May 25, 1809.—Board met. Present: John B. C. Lucas, Clement B. Penrose, and Frederick Bates, commissioners.

Bartholomew Cousin, claiming 6,000 arpents of land situate on White Water, district of Cape Girardeau. Laid over for decision.—(See book No. 4, page 70.)

March 9, 1810.—Board met. Present: John B. C. Lucas, Clement B. Penrose, and Frederick Bates, commissioners.

Bartholomew Cousin, claiming 6,000 arpents of land.—(See book No. 1, page 512; book No. 4, page 70.) On the motion of John B. C. Lucas, commissioner, as follows, to wit: Whereas it appears in the minutes of the former board that the said board have remarked that they are satisfied that the said concession was granted at the time the same bears date, and inasmuch as it does not appear that any suggestion of fraud and antedate was made, either by the agent of the United States or any of the members of the board, which being the case, shows that no question did exist before the said board as to fraud or antedate to which this decision, by way of remark, can apply; and whereas any decision, without question, is in itself preposterous and might be considered as officious: Therefore, resolved, that this remark and decision be rescinded. A question being taken on the motion, it was negatived. And on the question being taken on the claim, it is the unanimous opinion of the board that this claim ought not to be confirmed.

Board adjourned till Monday next, 9 o'clock a. m.

JOHN B. C. LUCAS.
CLEMENT B. PENROSE.

(See book No. 4, page 294.)

October 11, 1832.—The board met pursuant to adjournment. Present: Lewis F. Linn, W. Updyke, F. R. Conway, commissioners.

Bartholomew Cousin, claiming 7,935 arpents of land, of which 7,056 arpents have been confirmed. (For confirmation, see Bates's report, (decision,) page 67. For record of claim, see book B, page 314; minutes, book No. 1, page 512; book No. 4, pages 70 and 299.)

November 8, 1833.—The board met pursuant to adjournment. Present: L. F. Linn, A. G. Harrison, F. R. Conway, commissioners.

Bartholomew Cousin, claiming 899 arpents of land, it being the balance of 7,935 arpents, of which 7,056 have been confirmed.—(See page 20 of this book.) The board are unanimously of opinion that this claim ought to be confirmed to the said Bartholomew Cousin, or his legal representatives, according to the concession.—(See book No. 6, page 308.)

A. G. HARRISON.
L. F. LINN.
F. R. CONWAY.

No. 62.—J. St. Vrain, *claiming* 4,000 *arpents.*

Don Carlos Dehault Delassus, lieutenant governor of Upper Louisiana:

Sir: Don Santiago de St. Vrain, captain of militia, commander of his Majesty's galley Lafleche, has the honor to represent to you that, having a numerous family, he would wish to obtain of the goodness of this government a tract of land upon which he may collect his family and keep it near him, referring you, in this particular, to the orders which my lord the Baron de Carondelet, governor general of these provinces, &c., has passed to the lieutenant governor of this Upper Louisiana, by which he is enjoined to give lands to Mr. Deluziere, and to his children, as soon as they arrive, and according to their means; therefore, sir, the petitioner prays you to grant to him four thousand arpents of land in superficie, to be taken on the vacant lands of the King's domain. The petitioner prays you to permit him to have the said land surveyed in the manner which will appear most advantageous to his interest, and most suitable to his intention of distributing the said land among his children, as soon as they are old enough to settle themselves. The zeal and activity which the petitioner has always shown for the service of his Majesty incline him to hope that he will obtain this favor of your justice.

SANTIAGO DE ST. VRAIN.

St. Louis, *November* 17, 1799.

St. Louis of Illinois, *November* 18, 1799.

Having examined the foregoing petition, and by virtue of the orders of the Baron de Carondelet, formerly governor of these provinces, dated May 8, 1793, who enjoins "to give to each son of Don Pedro Carlos Delassus concessions according to his means."

Being convinced that the quantity which he solicits is in accordance with his means; considering, also, that he is entitled to this favor on account of his good services since he has been employed in his Majesty's small squadron of galleys, I do grant to him the four thousand arpents in superficie, which he solicits for him and his heirs, in order that he may distribute them, as he states, among his children; and the surveyor, Don Antonio Soulard, shall put the party interested in possession of the said quantity, in the place which will be chosen by the petitioner on the domain of his Majesty, without prejudice to anybody; and he shall make a proces verbal of his survey in continuation, in order to serve said petitioner to solicit the title in form from the intendant, to whom corresponds, by royal order, the granting and distributing all classes of lands of the royal domain.

CARLOS DEHAULT DELASSUS.

Don Antonio Soulard, surveyor general of the settlements of Upper Louisiana:

I do certify that a tract of land of four thousand arpents in superficie was measured, the lines run and bounded, in favor and in presence of Don Santiago de St. Vrain. Said measurement was taken with the perch of the city of Paris, of eighteen French feet, lineal measure of the same city, conformably to the agrarian measure of this province. These lands are situated at about fifty miles north of St. Louis, and bounded to the N.NW. by lands of John Baptist Desgroseillers; S.SE. by lands of various proprietors; E.NE. by lands of Albert Tison; and W.SW. by the river Cuivre. Said survey and measurement was executed without regard to the variation of the needle, which is 7° 30′ E., as it is evident by referring to the foregoing figurative plat, on which are noted the dimensions, direction of the lines, and other boundaries, &c. This survey was executed by virtue of the decree of the lieutenant governor and sub-delegate of the royal fisc, Don Carlos Dehault Delassus, dated November 18, 1799, here annexed. In testimony whereof, I do give the present, with the foregoing figurative plat, drawn conformably to the survey executed by the deputy surveyor, Mr. James Rankin, on the 14th February, 1804, who signed on the minutes, which I do certify.

ANTONIO SOULARD, *Surveyor General.*

St. Louis of Illinois, *March* 5, 1804.

Truly translated. St. Louis, January 5, 1833.

JULIUS DE MUN, *T. B. C.*

No.	Name of original claimant.	Quantity, in arpents.	Nature and date of claim.	By whom granted.	By whom surveyed, date, and situation.
62	Jacques St. Vrain, by John Mullanphy, as assignee, and likewise cnt'd by St. Vrain's children, claiming the same as their property under the concession.	4,000	Concession, Nov. 18, 1799.	Carlos Dehault Delassus.	Jas. Rankin, deputy surveyor, Feb. 14, 1804. Certified by Soulard, March 5, 1804. On Cuivre river, 55 miles north of St. Louis.

Evidence with reference to minutes and records.

May 3, 1806.—The board met agreeably to adjournment. Present: The Hon. John B. C. Lucas, Clement B. Penrose, and James L. Donaldson, esq.

John Mullanphy, assignee of Jacque St. Vrain, claiming 4,000 arpents of land situate on the river Cuivre, district of St. Charles, produces a concession from Charles D. Delassus, dated November 18, 1799; a survey of the same, dated February 14, 1804, and certified March 5, 1804; and a deed of transfer of the same, from the said Jacque St. Vrain to the claimant, dated November 12, 1804.

Marie P. Le Duc, being duly sworn, says that the aforesaid concession is his own handwriting; that he arrived at St. Louis on the 22d November, 1799, and was on his way from New Madrid at the time the same bears date; that about eight or ten days after his arrival he entered with Mr. Delassus as his secretary; that, when with Delassus in that capacity, he was in the habit of writing decrees or concessions; that he wrote several in 1800–'1–'2, and was there informed by the lieutenant governor that such had been promised some time towards the latter end of 1799, and they were accordingly dated of that date. Being asked whether he had any decrees or concessions in 1803, bearing date prior to October 1, 1800, answered, he did not recollect he had. He further said that petitions would remain sometimes with the lieutenant governor before he gave his decrees thereon, and that Jacque St. Vrain was for about ten years captain of a galley up the Mississippi.

Lewis Lebeaume, being also sworn, says that he believes the petition annexed to the aforesaid concession to be his handwriting, and that he did, about the time the same bears date, write one for him for the same quantity of arpents; that he saw the aforesaid concession in the possession of the said Jacque St. Vrain some time about October or November, 1800, when he, the said St. Vrain, was preparing to send the same down to New Orleans to have his title completed. St. Vrain is brother to the lieutenant governor, Delassus, and holds no other claim of that quantity of land. The board reject this claim.—(See book No. 1, page 271.)

November 15, 1819.—Board met. Present: John B. C. Lucas, Clement B. Penrose, commissioners.

John Mullanphy, assignee of Jacque St. Vrain, claiming 4,000 arpents of land situate on the Cuivre, in the district of St. Charles:—(See book No. 1, page 271.) It is the opinion of the board that this claim ought to be confirmed.—(See book No. 4, page 193.)

December 19, 1832.—F. R. Conway, esq., appeared pursuant to adjournment.

Jacque de St. Vrain, by his legal representative, John Mullanphy, claiming 4,000 arpents of land, (see book of records A, pages 18 and 19; minutes No. 1, pages 271 and 272; No. 4, page 193,) produces a paper purporting to be an original concession from Dehault Delassus, dated November 18, 1799; also, a plat and certificate of survey, dated March 5, 1804, by A. Soulard; also, deeds of conveyance.

M. P. Le Duc, being duly sworn, saith that the signature to the concession is in the proper handwriting of the said Carlos Dehault Delassus, and that the signature to the plat and certificate of survey is in the handwriting of A. Soulard.—(Book No. 6, page 89.)

April 17, 1833.—The board met pursuant to adjournment. Present: A. G. Harrison, F. R. Conway, commissioners.

In the case of St. Vrain, claiming 4,000 arpents of land, see page 89 of this book.

Albert Tison, duly sworn, says that at the time the concession for the said tract of 4,000 arpents of land was granted to said St. Vrain he had four children living, to wit: Charles, Felix, Odille, and Ceran.

Adjourned until to-morrow, at 10 o'clock a. m.

A. G. HARRISON.
F. R. CONWAY.

(See book No. 6, page 156.)

October 17, 1833.—The board met pursuant to adjournment. Present: A. G. Harrison, F. R. Conway, commissioners.

Jacque de St. Vrain's children, claiming 4,000 arpents of land, under the same concession produced by John Mullanphy, (see page 89 of this book,) it being the same tract of land claimed by said Mullanphy, as assignee.

Albert Tison, duly sworn, says that at the time the concession for the said tract of 4,000 arpents of land was granted to the said St. Vrain he had four children, to wit: Charles, Felix, Odille, and Ceran; that said St. Vrain had altogether nine children, of whom eight are now alive, to wit: Charles, Ceran, Odille, Isabelle, Savigny, Domitille, Emma, and Marcelin, and Felix, who died last year, leaving a widow and four children; that at his death said St. Vrain was insolvent; that said St. Vrain sold said tract of land to John Mullanphy for 12½ cents an arpent, and received in payment goods at an enormous price. The witness verily believes that said Mullanphy did not give more in real value for said land than 2 cents an arpent; that said St. Vrain was not obliged to sell the said tract of land for the support of his children, but did it, unfortunately, to suit his own purposes; that he was not authorized by any authorities to sell said property.

Claimants, for the purpose of showing that the Spanish government had made concessions to the said Jacque de St. Vrain, without any stipulations in favor of his children, refer to the following concessions: One for 3,250 arpents, dated in 1799, surveyed in 1801; another for 900 arpents, being a complete grant made by Morales, dated April 22, 1802; and, thirdly, one for 10,000 arpents, dated in 1796.—(See book No. 6, page 274.)

November 8, 1833.—The board met pursuant to adjournment. Present: L. F. Linn, A. G. Harrison, F. R. Conway, commissioners.

Jacque St. Vrain, claiming 4,000 arpents of land.—(See pages 89, 156, and 274, of this book.) The board are unanimously of opinion that this claim ought to be confirmed to the said Jacque St. Vrain, or his legal representatives, according to the concession.—(See book No. 6, page 308.)

A. G. HARRISON.
L. F. LINN.
F. R. CONWAY.

No. 63.—ANTONIO SOULARD, *claiming* 204 *arpents* 48 *perches.*

To the Lieutenant Governor:

Antonio Soulard, captain of militia, surveyor general of Upper Louisiana, and adjutant interim of this post, has the honor to represent to you that, wishing to increase his means by living in a secure and economical rural way, in order to be able to support his family, he has in view a tract of vacant land of about 14 arpents in front by about 15 in depth, situated to the south of this town, opposite to the piece of land asked for in augmentation by Don Gabriel Cerré, father-in-law of the petitioner, and which you have been pleased to grant him. The said tract of land to be bounded north by lands adjoining this town, south of the mill creek, south and east by vacant lands of the royal domain, and west by a public road of eighty feet in width, which leads from this town to the village of Carondelet, and which divides the land of Gabriel Cerré from that solicited by the petitioner; therefore, the petitioner supplicates you to condescend to grant to him the said tract of land, in remuneration of his zeal and of the services he has rendered with the greatest care and attention for several years without any salary or emolument whatsoever; and, as the enclosing of lands to cultivate in common is abolished, and thereby all right to lands in community annulled, he is confident that there shall be no obstacles to the attainment of the favor which he solicits. And he further prays that you will be pleased to allow him the time necessary (according to the smallness of his means) to effect his settlement on the above-mentioned place.

ANTONIO SOULARD.

ST. LOUIS OF ILLINOIS, *August* 7, 1798.

ST. LOUIS OF ILLINOIS, *August* 7, 1798.

Being convinced of the truth of the inconveniences related by the petitioner, and in consideration of the zeal which he has always manifested for the service of his Majesty, and for which he deserves the greatest consideration, the said surveyor of these settlements, Don Antonio Soulard, shall survey for himself the land which he solicits, giving to the same the boundaries which he asks for; and he shall take his own certificate of the dimensions and boundaries which surround it, in order to serve in soliciting the concession from the governor general of the province.

ZENON TRUDEAU.

Truly translated. St. Louis, February 21, 1833.

JULIUS DE MUN.

Don Antonio Soulard, surveyor general of Upper Louisiana.

ST. LOUIS OF ILLINOIS, *January* 20, 1800.

I do certify that on the 20th of January of this present year, by virtue of the decree, here annexed, of the lieutenant governor, Don Zenon Trudeau, dated 7th August, 1798, I went on my land in order to survey the same, conformably to my petition for 14 arpents and 2 perches in front by 15 arpents in depth, or 204 arpents 48 perches in superficie; which measurement was taken in my presence, as owner, and in the presence of the adjoining neighbors, with the perch of Paris, of 18 feet in length, according to the custom adopted in this province of Louisiana, and without regard to the variation of the needle, which is 7° 30′ E., as it is evinced by the foregoing figurative plat; said land is situated in the part marked A, at about 93 perches to the north, 7½° east of the south tower of this town, and bounded on its four sides as follows: north by the piece of vacant land next to the mill creek; south in part by vacant lands of the royal domain, by a cross road, and by lands of Joseph Brazeau; east by the road going from St. Louis to the village of Carondelet, and by lands of Gabriel Cerré; and west by vacant lands of the royal domain; and in order that it shall be available according to law, I do give myself the present certificate, with the foregoing figurative plat, on which are designated the dimensions and the natural and artificial limits which surround said land.

ANTONIO SOULARD, *Surveyor General.*

Truly translated. St. Louis, February 21, 1833.

JULIUS DE MUN.

No.	Name of original claimant.	Quantity, in arpents.	Nature and date of claim.	By whom granted.	By whom surveyed, date, and situation.
63	Antoine Soulard.....	204 and 48 perches.	Concession, August 7, 1798.	Zenon Trudeau.	Antonio Soulard; surveyed and certified Jan-January 20, 1800; 93 perches south of St. Louis.

Evidence with reference to minutes and records.

December 16, 1813.—Antoine Soulard, claiming 56 arpents 9 perches of land situate below near the town of St. Louis. Produces notice; also concession from Zenon Trudeau, dated August 7, 1798, for 14 by 15 arpents; a plat and certificate of survey of 204 arpents 48 perches, January 20, 1800; a certificate from Carlos Howard, lieutenant colonel of regiment of Louisiana, and military commandant, dated August 1, 1797. The difference between the claim and the concession abandoned, as lying within the claim of the people for commons.

James Mackay, duly sworn, says that the concession alleged as the basis of this claim was made, as stated, by Z. Trudeau, lieutenant governor, to claimant; that some time thereafter witness assisted claimant to run the lines of the said tract.—(See next page.)

December 17, 1813.—Antoine Soulard, claiming 56 arpents of land, as stated yesterday.

Jacque Clamorgan, duly sworn, says that Zenon Trudeau, late lieutenant governor, did grant to claimant a tract of land on the westerly part of claimant's tract, below and near the town of St. Louis, and on the opposite side of the road from the present residence of claimant, but knows not the quantity. Witness knows further, that when Zenon Trudeau came to the country as lieutenant governor, he did promise said tract of land to the present wife of claimant, then unmarried; and it was in fulfillment of this promise that the grant was afterwards made to her husband.—(See recorder's minutes, pages 80 and 81; B.'s Decisions, 33.)

February 18, 1833.—F. R. Conway, esq., appeared pursuant to adjournment, having been authorized, by a resolution of the board of commissioners of the 1st December last, to receive evidence.

Antoine Soulard, by his legal representatives, claiming 204 arpents 48 perches.—(See book F, pages 244, 245, and 256; recorder's minutes, pages 80 and 81.) Claimant further refers to book B, pages 486, 487, and 488, in order to show that the claim for the common of St. Louis does not interfere with this claim. Produces a paper purporting to be a concession from Zenon Trudeau, dated August 7, 1798; also a plat of survey by Antoine Soulard, dated January 20, 1800, and certified same day.

M. P. Le Duc, being duly sworn, saith that the signature to the concession is in the true handwriting of the said Zenon Trudeau; and that the signature to the plat and certificate of survey is the proper handwriting of Antoine Soulard. Deponent further says that he informed Mr. Soulard that in case he would abandon the part of his claim which was included in the common of St. Louis, Mr. Bates would confirm the balance of said claim; thereupon Soulard called on Mr. Bates and made the abandonment, upon which Bates confirmed the part of said claim which lies east of the common; and at the same time Soulard, as agent for Mackay, made the same abandonment on Mackay's claim; and that since that time Soulard told the deponent that Mackay disapproved of the said abandonment, and that he, the said deponent, never acted as agent for Mackay in said claim; that he does not know that Soulard ever was authorized by Mackay to make said abandonment; that since the time of said abandonment Mackay remained as ostensible owner and claimant of said land, that he built thereon a house, and lived and died in it.

The deponent further says that what he understands by these claims interfering with the common of St. Louis, is the part of said claim included in the survey of said common, made by Mackay in 1806, as recorder. Deponent believes that Mackay and Soulard paid taxes on the said lands until 1820, and that the part of Mackay's claim which was not confirmed was sold under an execution as being the property of said Mackay.—(See book No. 6, page 103.)

November 8, 1833.—The board met pursuant to adjournment. Present: L. F. Linn, A. G. Harrison, F. R. Conway, commissioners.

Antoine Soulard, claiming 204 arpents 48 perches of land.—(See page 103 of this book.) The board are unanimously of opinion that this claim ought to be confirmed to the said Antoine Soulard, or his legal representatives, according to the concession.—(See book No. 6, page 309.)

Conflicting claim.—Said to conflict with the commons of St. Louis.

A. G HARRISON.
L. F. LINN.
F. R. CONWAY.

No. 64.—PIERRE DELASSUS DELUZIERE, *claiming* 7,056 *arpents.*

To Don Zenon Trudeau, lieutenant governor of the western part of Illinois, &c.:

Pierre Carlos Dehault, knight, lord of Delassus, Deluzieres, and knight of the great cross of the royal order of St. Michael, residing in New Bourbon, dependency of the post of St. Genevieve, has the honor to represent that when he was at the city of New Orleans in May, 1793, he resolved to come up in the Illinois country, on the positive assurance given to him by his lordship the Baron de Carondelet, governor general of Louisiana, that he would order and authorize you to grant him a tract of land for the exclusive exploration of lead mines, and of a sufficient and convenient extent for said exploration, provided it should not be formally granted to another; which warranty and assurances of the government are to be found formally expressed in a letter here subjoined, and directed to your petitioner by the said baron, under the date of May 8, 1793, and which you have been pleased to assure me was exactly conformable to the official letter you received on that subject from the governor general. The long and cruel disease which your petitioner experienced on his arrival in Illinois, in August, 1793, the hostile threats of an invasion on the part of the French against this country some short time after, the orders you gave to the inhabitants not to go any distance from their post, and the care and trouble which, to your knowledge, I have taken in that time to countenance the wise and efficacious means you had taken so successfully in putting the posts of Illinois in a state of defence in case of an attack, of which care, endeavor, and zeal on my part his lordship Louis de las Casas, captain general of Havana, being informed, I received from him a letter bearing date May 20, 1794, by which he gives me the most honorable evidence of his satisfaction, as appears by copy of said letter here subjoined; that the occurrence of several circumstances having hindered your petitioner to make a search of a tract of land containing lead mineral, he now, with the assistance of his children and son-in-law, and persons acquainted with the country, visited a place situated on one of the branches of river St. François, called Gaboury, in the district of St. Genevieve, and about twelve leagues from this post, which has not been yet granted, makes part of the King's domain, and where it is ascertained some mineral had been anciently dug; besides, the external and internal appearances, according to mineralogical principles, indicate that the spot contains lead mineral, therefore your petitioner has resolved to try in that place a regular exploration of a lead mine; he is so much induced to prosecute such an undertaking, that he expects the arrival of his eldest son, now emigrated in Germany, who is well learned in mineralogy, having studied it particularly, and having been engaged in a similar branch in Europe with your petitioner, and will be very useful in exploring and conducting the one now solicited. Your petitioner flatters himself that you will not refuse to give this concession the extent of a league square, in order to secure the necessary fuel for the melting of the mineral and other necessaries. Under these considerations, your petitioner humbly prays you, sir, that in conformity to the intentions of the government, manifested in the subjoined letter, of which you have been notified by the governor general himself, you will be pleased to grant for himself, his heirs, and assigns, in full property, the concession of a league square of land situated on said branch of river St. François, called Gaboury, in the district of St. Genevieve, with the exclusive right to explore the lead mines in the same, and to cultivate and raise cattle on the said land if necessary; in so doing, your petitioner will ever pray.

DELASSUS DELUZIERES.

New Bourbon, *March* 3, 1795.

St. Genevievve, Illinois, *March* 10, 1795.

We, the commandant of said post, do inform the lieutenant governor that the concession demanded in the within petition is part of the King's domain, and has not been granted to any body, and that its extent, fixed to a league square, is indispensable and necessary to secure the timber for the melting of mineral and other necessary supply.

FRANÇOIS VALLÉ.

[Letter.]

To Zenon Trudeau:

The knight, Don Pierre Dehault Delassus, has entered into a contract with this intendancy to deliver yearly, during the term of five years, thirty thousand pounds of lead in balls or bars. In order that he may comply with his contract, your worship will put him in possession of the land he may solicit for the exploration, benefit, and enjoyment of the mines; for which purpose he is to present a memorial, directed to me, and which your worship will transmit, that I may give him the corresponding decree of concession, being understood that, in the mean time, your worship will put him in possession. God preserve your worship many years.

EL BARON DE CARONDELET.

New Orleans, *May* 7, 1793.

[Letter.]

Mr. Dehault Delassus:

I send you back the primitive titles of the concession granted to Mr. François Vallé, of St. Genevieve, who transferred it to Mr. Dodge, one moiety of which this last ceded to Mr. Tardiveau, who made a gift of it to you, together with the approbation and *visa* you desired. By this opportunity I write to Mr. Zenon Trudeau to grant you the land where you will have made the discovery of lead mines, with adjacent lands of sufficient extent for their exploration: provided, nevertheless, that it should not be conceded to another. Your son-in-law and your sons shall have, also, as you desired, a plantation in any place they will select in Illinois, of an extent proportionate to the establishment and improvement they propose to make. This is my answer to your letter No. 3. God have you in his holy keeping.

EL BARON DE CARONDELET.

New Orleans, *May* 8, 1795.

[Letter.]

Sir Don Peter Dehault Delassus Deluzieres:

The Baron de Carondelet, governor general of this province, has manifested to me, in his letter of the 27th of February last, the zeal and activity with which your worship (although laboring under a weak state of health) has manifested in exciting the inhabitants and Indians to join in the common defence of those settlements, and most particularly the post under your command; I do hope that your worship will continue with the same efficaciousness, in similar circumstances, and give me an opportunity to reward your worship. God preserve your worship many years.

LUIS DE LAS CASAS.

Havana, *May* 20, 1794.

[Decree.]

St. Louis, Illinois, *April* 1, 1795.

Having read the present petition, the subjoined letter of the Baron de Carondelet, directed to the petitioner, under the date of May, 1793, also, the official letter to us directed by said governor general, authorizing and giving us order to grant the petitioner a concession in the spot selected by him, and of a sufficient extent to explore exclusively the lead mines in the same; also, the above information of the commandant of St. Genevieve, by which he testifies that the land petitioned for is of the King's domain, and that it is indispensable that the quantity should be a league square: We, the lieutenant governor, in conformity with said orders and intentions of the government, have granted, and do grant, unto the petitioner, and to his heirs and assigns, in fee, the concession demanded, situate on a branch of the river St. François, called Gaboury, in the place selected by him, the extent of which shall be a league square, to the end that he may explore exclusively the lead mines belonging to the same, and, if necessary, to cultivate and raise cattle; hereby commanding Don Francis Vallé, captain and commandant of St. Genevieve, in whose district the land is situated, to put the petitioner in possession thereof; the regular survey of which will be done as soon as the surveyor will be appointed and commissioned for the Upper Louisiana.

ZENON TRUDEAU.

St. Genevieve, Illinois, *April* 15, 1795.

We, Don Francis Vallé, captain commandant civil and military of the post of St. Genevieve, in compliance with the aforegoing decree of Don Zenon Trudeau, lieutenant governor of the western part of Illinois, bearing date the first instant, have this day, the 15th of the same month, put the knight Peter Delassus Deluzieres in possession of the league square of land, situate on a branch of the river St. François, called Gaboury, as granted to him by the aforesaid decree, conformable to orders, and with the approbation of his lordship, the governor general of this province. The said concession to be in future regularly surveyed by the King's surveyor, who is soon to be named and appointed for this upper colony. *In præmissoram fidem.*

FRANCIS VALLÉ.

To Don Carlos Dehault Delassus, colonel of the royal armies and lieutenant governor of Upper Louisiana.

Humbly petitions Peter Charles Dehault Delassus Deluzieres, knight, &c., residing in New Bourbon, and has the honor to represent that in conformity to the orders of the governor of this province, your predecessor, Don Zenon Trudeau, did grant to your petitioner a concession of a league square of land, situate on a branch of the river St. François, called Gaboury, with the exclusive right to explore the lead mines on the same, as appears by his decree, bearing date April 1, 1795, of which concession and land your petitioner was put in possession by Don Francis Vallé, captain commandant of the post of St. Genevieve, in whose district the land is situated, as appears by his act, bearing date the 15th day of April of said year. And whereas it is mentioned in said decree of Don Zenon Trudeau that said concession will be regularly surveyed by the surveyor who was to be appointed by the government for Upper Louisiana; and whereas Don Antonio Soulard has been commissioned and appointed as such surveyor, therefore, under these considerations, your petitioner requests you, sir, that after mature consideration of the instruments here submitted relating to said concession, you will be pleased to give the necessary orders to Don Antonio Soulard, surveyor of Upper Louisiana, to proceed without delay to the regular survey of said concession of a league square, on the said branch of river St. François, called Gaboury, to explore, exclusively to any other, the lead, &c., and of which land he has already been put in possession by the commandant of St. Genevieve, and has already begun the exploration; he hopes to obtain his demand, inasmuch as he did not hurry the survey, in order to give him the necessary time to attend to the surveying of concessions belonging to other inhabitants who wished to have their surveys quickly executed. In so doing you will do justice.

PETER DELASSUS DELUZIERES.

New Bourbon, *November* 25, 1799.

By virtue of the contents of the above memorial and the accompanying documents, and also from what appears by the official letter of the Baron de Carondelet, late governor of these provinces, bearing date the 7th and 8th of May, 1793, on file in these archives, the surveyor, Don Antonio Soulard, will survey the league square of land which was granted to the party interested by the decree of my predecessor, the lieutenant governor, Don Zenon Trudeau, dated April 1, 1795, conformable to orders of his lordship the governor, and of which land he has been put in possession, as appears by decree of Francis Vallé, commandant of St. Genevieve, bearing date April 15, of the year last mentioned, to be hereafter surveyed by the surveyor of this Upper Louisiana when appointed and commissioned.

CHARLES DEHAULT DELASSUS.

St. Louis, *November* 29, 1799.

Truly translated. St. Louis, November 18, 1833

JULIUS DE MUN.

No.	Name of original claimant.	Quantity in arpents.	Nature and date of claim.	By whom granted.	By whom surveyed, date, and situation.
64	Pierre Delassus Deluziere.	7,056	Concession, April 1, 1795.	Zenon Trudeau...	Antoine Soulard, December 14, 1799; certified March 5, 1800. On the waters of St. Francis, district of St. Genevieve.

Evidence with reference to minutes and records.

June 28, 1806.—The board met agreeably to adjournment. Present: Hon. Clement B. Penrose and James L. Donaldson, esq.

The same (P. D. Deluziere) claiming 7,056 arpents of land situate on the waters of the river St. Francis, district of St. Genevieve, produces a concession from Zenon Trudeau for the same, dated April 1, 1795, stating that in consequence of a letter from the Baron de Carondelet to claimant under, date of May 8, 1793, and also of an office from the said baron to him, the said lieutenant governor, ordering and authorizing him to grant to said claimant, on any spot he might choose, a sufficient extent of land to enable him to work exclusively such mine as might be found on the same; and also in consequence of a certificate from François Vallé, then commandant of St. Genevieve, that the quantity of land petitioned for is vacant, and that it is absolutely necessary that the extent be a league square. He grants and concedes to claimant, in full property, the aforesaid tract, and directs the commandant of St. Genevieve to put him in possession of the same. Said concession bears no terms or conditions. An order of survey from Charles Dehault Delassus, dated November 29, 1799, and a survey of the same, dated December 14, 1799, and certified March 5, 1800. He also produced a certificate from François Vallé, dated March 10, 1795, that the league square petitioned for is vacant, and that quantity absolutely necessary to the working of the mine. A letter from Louis de las Casas, captain general at the Havana, to claimant, dated May 20, 1794, wherein he much approves of the conduct of claimant, and the services he has rendered government in forming the establishment of New Bourbon, and rousing the people and adjacent Indians to the common defence of the country. A certified copy of a letter on file, from the Baron de Carondelet to claimant, dated New Orleans, May 8, 1793, declaring to him that he had given order to Zenon Trudeau, then lieutenant governor, to concede to him a mine which he had discovered, together with as much land as might be necessary for the working of the same; and further to concede to his sons and son-in-law as much land as they might wish to establish. The board reject this claim.—(See book No. 1, pages 387 and 388.)

December 27, 1811.—Board met. Present: John B. C. Lucas, Clement B. Penrose, and Frederick Bates, commissioners.

Pierre Charles Dehault Delassus Deluziere, claiming 7,056 arpents of land.—(See book No. 1, page 387.) It is the opinion of a majority of the board that this claim ought not to be confirmed. Frederick Bates, commissioner, forbears giving an opinion.—(See book No. 5, page 541.)

October 9, 1832.—The board met pursuant to adjournment. Present: L. F. Linn, W. Updyke, F. R. Conway, commissioners.

Pierre Delassus Deluziere, claiming 7,056 arpents of land.—(See book No. 1, page 387; No. 5, page 541; record book C, pages 450 and 451.) Produces a paper purporting to be an original concession from Zenon Trudeau, dated April 1, 1795, to P. D. de Luziere; also a certificate of delivery of property, by François Vallé, dated April 17, 1795; also an order of survey dated November 29, 1799, by Carlos Dehault Delassus; also a plat of survey, executed on the 14th of December, 1799, and certified March 5, 1800, by Antoine Soulard; also an original letter, signed the Baron de Carondelet, and addressed to Don Zenon Trudeau, dated May 7, 1793; also an original letter, purporting to be signed by the Baron de Carondelet, addressed to Dehault Delassus, dated May 8, 1793; also a certificate of William Milburn, of the position of the tract upon the general map.

Pascal Cerré, duly sworn, saith, that the signature to the certificate of delivery is the handwriting of François Vallé; that the signature to the concession is the handwriting of Zenon Trudeau; that the signature to the certificate of survey is the handwriting of Antoine Soulard; that the signatures to the two above-mentioned letters are the handwriting of the Baron de Carondolet.—(See book No. 6, page 14.)

November 27, 1832.—The board met pursuant to adjournment. Present: L. F. Linn and F. R. Conway, commissioners.

In the case of Pierre Delassus Deluziere, claiming 7,056 arpents of land.—(See page 14 of this book, No. 6.)

Albert Tison and Frémon Delaurieré, being duly sworn, prove the signature of said Deluziere to his petition, dated March 3, 1795. They also prove the handwriting of François Vallé to a certificate, dated March 10, 1795; also the handwriting of said Delassus Deluziere to a petition, dated November 25, 1799; also the handwriting of Carlos Dehault Delassus to an order of survey, dated November 29, 1799; also the handwriting of Antonio Soulard to a plat of survey of a league square—(the above-mentioned papers already presented in evidence on the 9th of October last.) Said witnesses also prove the handwriting of François Vallé to a certified copy of a letter of Don Luis de las Casas, captain general of Havana, addressed to the Chevalier Delassus Deluziere, dated May 20, 1794; also the handwriting of Zenon Trudeau to a decree of concession of a league square to Pierre Delassus Deluziere, dated April 1, 1795; also the handwriting of Fränçois Vallé, commandant of St. Genevieve, to a certificate of delivery of possession of a league square, situated on a branch of the St. Francis called Gaboury; also prove the signature of the Baron de Carondelet to a letter, dated May 17, 1793, addressed to Mr. Dehault Delassus.

Albert Tison saith that Pierre Deluziere was known in France and by the Baron de Carondelet by the name of Dehault Delassus, and that during the French revolution he took the name of Deluziere. The above-named witnesses also prove the handwriting of the Baron de Carondelet to an original letter, dated May 7, 1793, addressed to Don Zenon Trudeau; also that said Deluziere had no salary as commandant of New Bourbon; that he enjoyed the confidence and esteem of the governor general and of the lieutenant governor of Upper Louisiana; that he was a personal friend and allied by blood to the Baron de Carondelet.—(See book No. 6, page 54.)

November 8, 1833.—The board met pursuant to adjournment. Present: L. F. Linn, A. G. Harrison, and F. R. Conway, commissioners.

Pierre Delassus Deluziere, claiming 7,056 arpents of land.—(See page 54 of this book.)

The board are unanimously of opinion that this claim ought to be confirmed to the said Pierre Delassus Deluziere, or his legal representatives, according to the concession.—(See book No. 6, page 309.)

A. G. HARRISON.
L. F. LINN.
F. R. CONWAY.

No. 65.—Francis Tayon, *claiming* 2,944 *arpents.*

To Don Charles Dehault Delassus, lieutenant colonel, attached to the stationary regiment of Louisiana, and lieutenant governor of the upper part of the same province

Francis Tayon, jr., a farmer, born on this side of the Mississippi, father of a family, and member of one of the oldest families in this country, has the honor respectfully to supplicate you to have the goodness to assist him in furthering his views of establishing himself, and therefore to be pleased to grant to him, in full property, a concession for a tract of land of ten thousand arpents in superficie, situated in a vacant place of the domain between Mine à Breton and this town, without being prejudicial to the little village of Boyer's family, the petitioner having the project to form on said place a considerable farm for cultivation and a grazing farm—in a word, to employ all the means in his power to give value to said property, in order to secure to his family an independent existence—hopes that, considering the remoteness of the tract of land which he solicits for, and the certainty that the said concession shall not be prejudicial to anybody, you will be pleased to do justice to his demand in a way favorable to the accomplishment of his views; favor which he presumes submissively to expect of your justice.

FRANÇOIS + TAYON. (his mark.)

Anto. Soulard, *witness of the signature.*
St. Louis, *October* 15, 1799.

St. Louis of Illinois, *October* 15, 1799.

Whereas we are assured that the petitioner possesses sufficient means to improve the land which he solicits, I do grant to him and his heirs the land which he solicits, in case it does not cause prejudice to anybody; and the surveyor, Don Anto. Soulard, shall put the interested in possession of the quantity of land which he asks, in the place designated, which being executed, he shall draw a plat of his survey, delivering the same to the party, with his certificate, in order to serve to him to obtain the concession and title, in form, from the intendant general, to whom alone corresponds, by royal order, the distributing and granting all classes of lands of the royal domain.

CARLOS DEHAULT DELASSUS.

Don Antonio Soulard, surveyor general of the settlements of Upper Louisiana.

I do certify that a tract of land of ten thousand arpents in superficie was measured; the lines run and bounded in favor of Francis Tayon, and in presence of Nicholas Boilvin, his agent. The said measurement was taken with the perch of the city of Paris, of eighteen French feet lineal measure of the same city, conformably to the agrarian measure of this province, the said land being situated at about fifty-five miles west-northwest from the post of St. Genevieve, bounded north and west by vacant lands of the royal domain, south by lands belonging to the inhabitants of Mine à Breton, and east by a creek which empties its waters into the river Maramec. The above survey and measurement was taken without regard to the variation of the needle, which is 7° 30′ E., as appears by the foregoing figurative plat, on which are noted the dimensions, courses of the lines, other boundaries, &c. The survey was executed by virtue of the decree of the lieutenant governor and sub-delegate of the royal fisc, Don Carlos Dehault Delassus, dated October 15, 1799, here annexed; and in order that it shall be available according to law, I do give the present with the foregoing figurative plat, drawn conformably to the survey executed by the deputy surveyor, Thomas Maddin, on the 6th of February, 1804, who signed the minutes to which I certify.

ANTO. SOULARD, *Surveyor General.*

St. Louis of Illinois, *February* 25, 1804.

Truly translated. St. Louis, February 26, 1833.

JULIUS DE MUN.

No.	Name of original claimant.	Quantity in arpents.	Nature and date of claim.	By whom granted.	By whom surveyed, date, and situation.
65	Francis Tayon.	*2, 944	Concession, Oct. 15, 1799.	Carlos Dehault Delassus.	Thomas Maddin, deputy surveyor, February 6, 1804; certified by Soulard, February 25, 1804; 55 miles W.NW. of St. Genevieve.

* Being a balance of 10,000, of which a league square has been confirmed.

Evidence with reference to minutes and records.

May 3, 1806.—The board met agreeably to adjournment. Present: The Hon. John B. C. Lucas, Clement B. Penrose, and James L. Donaldson, commissioners.

Peter Chouteau, assignee of Francis Tayon, jr., claiming 10,000 arpents of land situate on the river Renaud, district of St. Charles, (St. Genevieve,) produces a concession from Carlos D. Delassus, without any condition inserted in the same, dated October 15, 1799; a survey of the same, dated February 6, 1804, and certified the 25th of the same month and year, and a deed of transfer of the same from the said

Francis Tayon, jr., to the said Peter Chouteau, dated January 3, 1804. In this case the board required that the age of the claimant at the time of obtaining said concession should be proved, which was refused.

It appeared in testimony by Anthony Soulard and Auguste Chouteau that Mr. Charles Tayon had rendered services to the Spanish government from the year 1770; that he was second in command at the siege of St. Joseph, which he contributed to take; that afterwards, from his merits, he received a commission of second lieutenant; that he was commandant of St. Charles from the year 1792 to the year 1804, during which time he rendered many services to the government in operations against the Indians, training the militia, and protecting the district; that he never received any compensation, except eleven dollars a month as lieutenant and his fees of office, which were trifling, and seldom paid, exclusive of the lands claimed by him and his family; that he spent a great part of his own property in his public employment, and appeared to have devoted himself to the interest of the province. The board was satisfied that Mr. Charles Tayon, the father of the original proprietor, Francis Tayon, jr., was an active and meritorious officer.

The board reject this claim, and are of opinion that although it appears that the decree is antedated, yet, from testimony and circumstances, it had not been antedated from fraudulent designs, but merely to make the date of the decree correspond with the date of the petition; and further, they are satisfied that the said decree or order of survey was issued before the 1st of October, 1800.—(See book No. 1, p. 272.)

August 18, 1810.—Board met. Present: Clement B. Penrose and Frederick Bates, commissioners.

Peter Chouteau, assignee of Charles (Francis) Tayon, jr., claiming 10,000 arpents of land.—(See book No. 1, page 272.) It is the opinion of the board that this claim ought not to be confirmed.—(See book No. 4, page 464.

February 18, 1833.—F. R. Conway, esq., appeared pursuant to adjournment, having been authorized by a resolution of the board of commissioners of the 1st of December last to receive evidence.

Francis Tayon, by his legal representative, Pierre Chouteau, sr., claiming the balance of 10,000 arpents of land, of which a league square has been confirmed, (see book C, pages 379 and 380; minutes No. 4, page 464; No. 3, page 64, wherein a league square has been confirmed,) produces a paper purporting to be a concession from Carlos Dehault Delassus, dated October 15, 1799; also a plat of survey, dated 6th and certified 25th February, 1804, by Anthony Soulard.

M. P. Le Duc, being duly sworn, saith that the signature to the concession is in the proper handwriting of Carlos D. Delassus, and the signature to the plat and certificate of survey the true handwriting of Soulard.—(See book No. 6, page 107.)

November 7, 1833.—The board met pursuant to adjournment. Present: L. F. Linn, A. G. Harrison, and F. R. Conway, commissioners.

Francis Tayon, jr., claiming balance of 10,000 arpents of land.—(See page 107 of this book.) The board are unanimously of opinion that this claim ought to be confirmed to the said Francis Tayon, or his legal representatives, according to the concession.—(See book No. 6, page 309.)

A. G. HARRISON.

No. 66.—Nicholas Barsaloux, *claiming four by forty arpents.*

On the 20th of April, 1768, on the demand of Mr. Nicholas Barsaloux, residing in this post of St. Louis, who wishes to cultivate the soil, taking in consideration the means he is possessed of, we have granted and do grant to him, his heirs or assigns, in fee simple, a tract of land of four arpents in front, in the prairie south of the little creek, said front running north and south by the usual depth of forty arpents, running east and west adjoining on the north side to the land taken by the individual named Bacanné, and on the south side by the land of Mr. Beausoleil, on condition of cultivating the said land in the term of one year and one day, under pain of having said land reunited to the King's domain.

Given in St. Louis the said day and year.

ST. ANGE.
LABUXIERE.

Translated from Livre Terrein, page 17.

On the 29th of May, 1774, I, the undersigned, have baptized with the customary ceremonies of the church, Louis, son of Nicholas Barsaloux, and of Magdalena Lepage; the godfather has been François Lepage, and the godmother, not knowing how to sign, has made her mark.

FRANÇOIS LEPAGE.
Mark of the godmother, +
FR. VALENTIN, *Curate.*

On the 11th of May, 1771, the ceremonies of baptism have been supplied by us, missionary priest, to Marie Archange, legitimate daughter of Nicholas Barsaloux, and of Magdelaine Lepage, his wife. The godfather, Antoine Royer; the godmother, Marie Oubremeau, wife of Lapensée.

PRE. GIBAULT.

I, the undersigned, certify to have faithfully copied the above from the register of the parish of St. Louis, this November 2, 1830.

EDM. SAULNIER.

In the year 1776, on the 10th of August, I, a Capuchin priest, apostolic missionary, curate of St Louis, Illinois, province of Louisiana, have baptized Jean Baptiste, born yesterday, and being legitimate son of Barsaloux and of Magdelaine Lepage, his father and mother. The godfather has been Noël Langlois, and the godmother, Madelaine Barcello, who have signed with me, the day and year as above.

F. BERNARD.
NOEL LANGLOIS.
Godmother, +

In the year 1771, on the 8th of September, there being no curate, I, the undersigned, certify that a girl named Marie Archange, five months old, daughter of Mr. Barsaloux, died in the village of St. Louis of Illinois, province of Louisiana, and was buried in the churchyard of this village.

In testimony whereof I sign.

RENE KIERSERAUX.

In the year 1776, on the 16th of December, I, a Capuchin priest, apostolic missionary, curate of St. Louis, province of Louisiana, bishoprick of Cuba, have buried in the cemetery of this church the body of Nicholas Barsaloux, 40 years of age, to whom had been administered all the sacraments of our mother, the holy church.

In testimony whereof I have signed the day and year as above.

F. BERNARD, *qui supra.*

I, the undersigned, priest, doing the functions of curate, and having in my possession the registers of the parish of St. Louis, do certify to have made researches in the register of baptism for the certificates of Louis, Marie Archange, and Jean Baptiste Barsaloux, and have found no other but the three above mentioned, besides the certificate of burial of Mr. Nicholas Barsaloux and of Marie Archange. And further, I certify that I have faithfully copied all these extracts.

EDM. SAULNIER.

St. Louis, *July* 19, 1831.

Truly translated. St. Louis, March 6, 1833.

JULIUS DE MUN.

No.	Name of original claimant.	Quantity, arpents.	Nature and date of claim.	By whom granted.	By whom surveyed, date, and situation.
66	Nicholas Barsaloux.	160	Concession, April 20, 1768.	St. Ange.	

Evidence with reference to minutes and records.

March 5, 1833.—The board met pursuant to adjournment. Present: F. R. Conway and A. G. Harrison, commissioners.

Nicholas Barsaloux, by his legal representative, claiming four arpents of land in front by forty arpents in depth.—(See Livre Terrein, No. 1, page 16; book F, page 153.)

René Dodier, being duly sworn, saith that he well knew Nicholas Barsaloux; that he died a long time ago, perhaps 47 or 48 years ago; that he, the deponent, will be 71 years of age in June next; that to his knowledge Barsaloux cultivated a piece of land south of the mill creek; that said Barsaloux had a small house built upon wheels, and used to have it hauled on said piece of land when he wanted to work on the same; that he saw said Barsaloux work on said land several years in succession; that he was known as the lawful owner of said land. He further states that the first tract of land south of said mill creek belonged to Ortey; then came Cambas, Jervais, Mad. Chouteau, Devolsey, Bacanné, Barsaloux, Beausoliel, &c. He further says, that when a young man he heard that said Barsaloux was one among the first settlers that came to this place, and that said Barsaloux had a wife and children.

The claimant states that, by referring to Livre Terrein for the concession, it is to be observed that said claim was not reunited to the domain; further, that said Barsaloux, being one of the first settlers, had no other lands granted to him by written concession but a town lot in St. Louis, and no confirmation but for the said town lot.

Adjourned until to-morrow, at 10 o'clock.

F. R. CONWAY.
A. G. HARRISON.

March 6, 1833.—The board met pursuant to adjournment. Present: F. R. Conway and A. G. Harrison, commissioners.

In the case of Nicholas Barsaloux, the claimant produces two papers purporting to be copies of certificates of baptism of Louis and Marie Archange Barsaloux, and of Jean Baptiste Barsaloux; also a certificate of the burial of Marie Archange, and of Nicholas Barsaloux, her father. Certified by E. Saulnier, curate of St. Louis, 19th July, 1831.—(See book No. 6, pages 110 and 111.)

November 8, 1833.—The board met pursuant to adjournment. Present: L. F. Linn, A. G. Harrison, F. R. Conway, commissioners.

Nicholas Barsaloux, claiming 160 arpents of land.—(See pages 110 and 111 of this book.) The board are unanimously of opinion that this claim ought to be confirmed to the said Nicholas Barsaloux or his legal representatives, according to the concession.—(See book No. 6, page 309.)

A. G. HARRISON.
L. F. LINN.
F. R. CONWAY.

No. 67.—Charles Tayon, *claiming* 1,600 *arpents.*

To Don Charles Dehault Delassus, lieutenant colonel, attached to the stationary regiment of Louisiana, and lieutenant governor of the upper part of same province:

Charles Tayon, sub-lieutenant in the army, captain of militia, commandant of the post of St. Charles of Missouri, has the honor to represent to you that he had obtained of Don Francisco Cruzat, lieutenant governor of this part of Illinois, on the 7th June 1786, a tract of land of 40 arpents front by 40 arpents in depth, or 1,600 arpents in superficie, as appears by the original title here annexed. The said land is situated on River Des Peres, at about six or eight miles from this town; and some time after this he received orders of your predecessor, Don Zenon Trudeau, to go and take the command of St. Charles. The little value of land prevented him to sell several properties which he was obliged to leave without cultivating; but when Americans and others were admitted in the country and landed property began to increase in value, and there being a surveyor appointed by the government for this upper part of Louisiana, he wished to have the said land surveyed, but to his great surprise he found that possession had been taken of it by surveys made by virtue of orders given by Don Zenon Trudeau. His love for peace and the consideration which he has for those who, without any bad intentions, have been put in possession of tracts of land over which your petitioner has unquestionable rights by virtue of the title in form with which he is vested and the improvements which he has made on the said lands, he would wish that you would be pleased to grant to him the same quantity of land, to be taken in any other vacant part of the domain at his choice, and that you would give orders to the surveyor of this Upper Louisiana to put him in possession of the said land by surveying the same, after which he would have to deliver to me a figurative plat and certificate of his survey, in order to serve, as it is fit, in support of my original title. The petitioner, full of confidence in your justice, hopes that you will be pleased to approve his views of conciliation, and do justice to his demand in such a way as will prevent him from laying any claims against those who are in actual possession of the tract of land above-mentioned; in doing which you will do justice.

CHARLES TAYON.

St. Louis, *January* 14, 1800.

St. Louis of Illinois, *January* 16, 1800.

Having taken cognizance of the foregoing statement and of the original title annexed thereto, expedited in favor of the interested party by the lieutenant colonel, Don Francisco Cruzat, on the 7th June, 1786, by which he unquestionably appears to be the owner of the land designated, and submitting himself, to avoid difficulties, to lose his rights, as a proof of our approbation of these dispositions, the surveyor of this Upper Louisiana, Don Antonio Soulard, shall survey in favor of Don Carlos Tayon the quantity of land mentioned in his above said title and concession, in any other vacant place of the royal domain, at his will and choice; and this operation being concluded, he shall deliver to the interested the corresponding documents and his original title in support of the same, in order to serve to him as he shall think fit; and this is as a remuneration for the praiseworthy motives which have determined him to make this voluntary sacrifice of his original property.

CARLOS DEHAULT DELASSUS.

Truly translated. St. Louis, February 25, 1833.

JULIUS DE MUN.

No.	Name of original claimant.	Quantity, in arpents.	Nature and date of claim.	By whom granted.	By whom surveyed, date, and situation.
67	Charles Tayon......	1,600	Concession, January 16, 1800.	Carlos Dehault Delassus.	

Evidence with reference to minutes and records.

December 10, 1811.—Board met. Present: John B. C. Lucas, Clement B. Penrose, and Frederick Bates, commissioners.

Peter Chouteau, assignee of Charles Tayon, claiming 1,600 arpents of land situate in the district of St. Louis, produces record of a concession from Delassus, lieutenant governor, dated 16th January, 1800; record of a transfer from Tayon to claimant, dated 17th December, 1803. It is the opinion of the board that this claim ought not to be confirmed.—(See book No. 5, page 506.)

February 18, 1833.—F. R. Conway, esq., appeared pursuant to adjournment, having been authorized by a resolution of the board of commissioners of the 1st of December last to receive evidence.

Charles Tayon, by his legal representative, Pierre Chouteau, senior, claiming 1,600 arpents of land, (see book D, pages 160 and 161; minutes No. 5, page 506,) produces a paper purporting to be a concession from Carlos Dehault Delassus, dated 16th January, 1800.

M. P. Le Duc, duly sworn, saith that the signature to the concession is in the proper handwriting of Charles Dehault Delassus.—(See book No. 6, page 107.)

November 8, 1833.—The board met pursuant to adjournment. Present: L. F. Linn, A. G. Harrison, F. R. Conway, commissioners.

Charles Tayon claiming 1,600 arpents of land.—(See page 107 of this book.) The board are unanimously of opinion that this claim ought to be confirmed to the said Charles Tayon, or his legal representatives, according to the concession.—(See book No. 6, page 309.)

A. G. HARRISON.
F. R. CONWAY.
L. F. LINN.

No. 68.—Antoine Gagnier, *claiming* 1,800 *arpents.*

To Don Carlos Dehault Delassus, lieutenant governor of Upper Louisiana:

Sir: Antoine Gagnier has the honor to represent to you, that wishing to establish himself in this province, wherein he has been residing for some time, therefore he has recourse to the benevolence of this government, praying that you may be pleased to grant to him a tract of land of eighteen hundred arpents in surperficie, to be taken on the vacant lands of his Majesty's domain in the place which will appear most convenient to the interest of your petitioner, who presumes to expect this favor of your justice.

ANTOINE his ⋈ mark. GAGNIER.

St. Louis, *June* 10, 1800.

St. Louis of Illinois, *June* 12, 1800.

Whereas we are assured that the petitioner possesses sufficient means to improve the land which he solicits, I do grant to him and his heirs the land which he solicits, if it is not prejudicial to any person; and the surveyor, Don Antonio Soulard, shall put the interested party in possession of the quantity of land which he asks in a vacant place of the royal domain; and, this being executed, he shall draw a plat of his survey, delivering the same to the party with his certificate, in order to serve him to obtain the title in form from the intendant general, to whom alone corresponds, by royal order, the distributing and granting all classes of lands, &c.

CARLOS DEHAULT DELASSUS.

Truly translated. St. Louis, March 19, 1833.

JULIUS DE MUN, *T. B. C.*

Recorded in book No. 2, pages 65 and 66; No. 7, 1805.

SOULARD, *Surveyor General, District of Louisiana.*

No.	Name of original claimant.	Quantity, arpents.	Nature and date of claim.	By whom granted.	By whom surveyed, date, and situation.
68	Antoine Gagnier....	1,800	Concession, June 12, 1800.	Carlos Dehault Delassus.	R. L. Nash, deputy surveyor, February, 1804. Recorded by Soulard, February 28, 1806. On the Missouri, 120 miles above its mouth.

Evidence with reference to minutes and records.

November 19, 1811. Board met. Present: John B. C. Lucas, Clement B. Penrose, and Frederick Bates, commissioners.

Albert Tison, assignee of Antoine Gagnier, claiming 1,800 arpents of land situate on the Missouri, district of St. Charles. Produces a record of concession from Charles D. Delassus, surveyor general, dated January 12, 1800; record of a plat of survey, dated February, 1804, certified February 28, 1806; record of a transfer from Gagnier to claimant, dated January 11, 1805.

It is the opinion of the board that this claim ought not to be confirmed.—(See book No. 5, page 426.)

March 12, 1833.—The board met pursuant to adjournment. Present: L. F. Linn, A. G. Harrison, commissioners.

Antoine Gagnier, by Albert Tison, claiming 1,800 arpents of land on the Missouri, Howard county.—(See book B, pages 463 and 464. Minutes No. 5, page 426.) Produces a paper purporting to be a concession from Carlos Dehault Delassus, dated June 12, 1800; also a plat and certificate of survey received for record by Antoine Soulard, February 28, 1806; also a deed from said Gagnier to A. Tison, dated January 11, 1805.

Frémon Delauriere, duly sworn says that the signature to the concession and to plat of survey are in the respective handwriting of said Delassus and Soulard.—(See book No. 6, page 114.)

November 8, 1833.—The board met pursuant to adjournment. Present: L. F. Linn, A. G. Harrison, F. R. Conway, commissioners.

Antoine Gagnier, claiming 1,800 arpents of land.—(See page 114 of this book.)

The board are unanimously of opinion that this claim ought to be confirmed to said Antoine Gagnier, or his legal representatives, according to the concession.—(See book No. 6, page 310.)

A. G. HARRISON.
L. F. LINN.
F. R. CONWAY.

No. 69.—John Watkins, *claiming* 7,056 *arpents.*

To Mr. Zenon Trudeau, lieutenant colonel and lieutenant governor of the western part of Illinois:

John Watkins, residing in this part of Illinois, has the honor to represent that there being in this part of the country a great scarcity of horned cattle and hogs, and the petitioner having the means of bringing a certain quantity of them from the American settlements on the Ohio, which importation he thinks would be advantageous to the general welfare of the community, inasmuch as most of the inhabitants are in need of those animals so necessary to farmers, and the scarcity of which has prevented, to this day, to have a well regulated meat market, and has been the cause that St. Louis and other places have often been without meat; he is confident that you will consider in a favorable way the plan which he has formed to establish an extensive stock farm, (*vacherie,*) which may in a few years provide for the urgent need already stated. In this consideration, and, as the petitioner believes, having been recommended to you by the governor general, in order to obtain lands in your jurisdiction, he, in the most humble manner, has recourse to you, praying that you will be pleased to grant to him one league square of land in the place commonly known by the name of Richland, comprising in the said league square the branch called Rivière Sauvage, which empties itself in the river Maramec, about ten leagues above Renaud's fork. In so doing the petitioner shall never cease to pray for the conservation of your days.

JOHN WATKINS.

St. Louis of Illinois, *July* 23, 1797.

Zenon Trudeau, lieutenant colonel of infantry and lieutenant governor of the western part of Illinois.

The surveyor, Don Antonio Soulard, shall survey for the petitioner the league square of land which he petitions for in the place designated by him; the said petitioner being from this day empowered to take possession of the said land, the present decree serving to him as a title of concession (having been particularly ordered by the governor general of this province, the Baron de Carondelet, to grant land to him) until he presents himself to the general government with this document, in order that conformably to the survey he may obtain one in due form and have it recorded.

ZENON TRUDEAU.

St. Louis of Illinois, *July* 24, 1797.

Recorded book No. 1, folios 29, 30, and 31. No. 20.

SOULARD.

Truly translated. St. Louis, March 20, 1833.

JULIUS DE MUN.

I declare that I have had in my hands, during the government of the Lieutenant Governor Don Zenon Trudeau, the concession by him made to the late Doctor John Watkins, bearing date July 24, 1797, which said concession was registered at the survey office under my care; I declare, also, that said Doctor John Watkins made several applications to me, as well in my public capacity of surveyor of the province as that of his private agent, to have the lands included in said concession surveyed, which survey I deferred making upon the principle that the affairs of Doctor Watkins were in some measure my own, and as such I was in the habit of postponing them to the claims and interests of absolute strangers, which postponement was the cause of said survey not having been sooner effected. I certify further that I saw and read an official letter of the Baron de Carondelet, governor general of Louisiana, for his Catholic Majesty, addressed to the said lieutenant governor, Don Zenon Trudeau, which directed him to grant to the said Doctor John Watkins that quantity of land which would correspond to his wishes and to his means of establishment in this country.

ANTONIO SOULARD.

St. Louis, *December* 6, 1817.

Territory of Missouri, *county and township of St. Louis:*

Be it remembered, that on the 19th day of December, A. D. 1817, before me, the undersigned, F. M. Guyol, one of the justices of the peace in and for the county and township aforesaid, personally came and appeared Antoine Soulard, who, being duly sworn according to law, made oath and declareth that this foregoing affidavit by him made contains the truth, the whole truth, and nothing but the truth.

[L. S.] Given under my hand and seal this day, month, and year above written.

F. M. GUYOL, *J. P.*

Frederick Bates, secretary, exercising the government of the Territory of Missouri, to all whom it may concern:

Be it known that F. M. Guyol is and was, on the 19th instant, a justice of the peace within and for the county of St. Louis, in the Territory of Missouri, regularly commissioned. In testimony whereof I have hereunto affixed the seal of the Territory.

[L. S.] Given under my hand, at St. Louis, the 23d day of December, A. D. 1817, and of the independence of the United States the forty-second.

FREDERICK BATES.

A true copy. St. Louis, November 23, 1833.

JULIUS DE MUN, *T. B. C.*

No.	Name of original claimant.	Quantity, arpents.	Nature and date of claim	By whom granted.	By whom surveyed, date, and situation.
69	John Watkins.	7, 056	Concession, July 24, 1797.	Zenon Trudeau.	James Mackay, D. S., February 18, 1805; recorded by Soulard Feb. 27, 1806; on the Maramec.

Evidence with reference to minutes and records.

September 17, 1806.—The board met agreeably to adjournment. Present: the honorable John B. C. Lucas and James Donaldson, commissioners.

The same, (John Watkins,) claiming a league square, or 7,056 arpents, situate on the Maramec, district of St. Louis, produces a duly registered concession from Zenon Trudeau, dated July 24, 1797, and a survey of the same taken the 18th, and certified February 27, 1806.

Anthony Soulard, being duly sworn, says that when the said claimant left this place for New Orleans, he, the witness, received from him, among other papers left to his charge, the aforesaid concession; that he does not know whether it was granted at the time it bears date, but that he has seen among the official papers of Zenon Trudeau an order from the Baron de Carondelet, to said Zenon Trudeau, to grant said claimant a league square. The board reject this claim, and are satisfied that the same was granted at the time it bears date.—(See book No. 2, page 10.)

September 22, 1808.—Board met. Present: The Hon. John B. Lucas, Clement B. Penrose, and Frederick Bates, commissioners.

John Watkins, claiming 7,056 arpents of land situate on the river Maramec, district of St. Louis. Laid over for decision.—(See book No. 3, page 262.)

June 12, 1810.—Board met. Present: John B. C. Lucas, Clement B. Penrose, Frederick Bates, commissioners.

John Watkins, claiming 7,056 arpents of land—(See book No. 2, page 10; book No. 3, page 262.) It is the opinion of the board that this claim ought not to be confirmed. Clement B. Penrose and Frederick Bates, commissioners, declare that the opinion of the former board, as to the date of the concession in this claim, must be an error, as the said concession bears no date. John B. C. Lucas, commissioner, declares that he does not concur with the opinion of the former board, so far as it appears by their minutes that they are satisfied that the concession was granted at the time it bears date.—(See book No. 4, page 376.)

March 12, 1833.—The board met pursuant to adjournment. Present: L. F. Linn, A. G. Harrison, commissioners.

John Watkins, claiming 7,056 arpents of land situate on the Maramec.—(See book C, pages 367 and 368; minutes, No. 2, page 10; No. 3, page 262; No. 4, page 376.) Produces a paper purporting to be an original concession from Zenon Trudeau, dated July 24, 1797; also, a plat and certificate of survey, received for record by A. Soulard, February 27, 1806.

Albert Tison, being duly sworn, saith that the signatures to the above papers are in the respective handwriting of said Zenon Trudeau and said Soulard. He further says that to his knowledge the above land was inhabited and cultivated in about 1802 or 1803.—(See book No. 6, page 114.)

November 8, 1833.—The board met pursuant to adjournment. Present: L. F. Linn, A. G. Harrison, F. R. Conway, commissioners.

John Watkins, claiming 7,056 arpents.—(See page 114 of this book.) The board, upon a careful examination of the original concession, find that there is a date to the same in Zenon Trudeau's own handwriting, and they are unanimously of opinion that this claim ought to be confirmed to the said John Watkins, or to his legal representatives, according to the concession.—(See book No. 6, page 310.)

A. G. HARRISON.
L. F. LINN.
F. R. CONWAY.

No 70.—Esther, *claiming* 80 *arpents.*

To Don Zenon Trudeau:

Esther, a free mulatto woman, residing in this town of St. Louis, humbly supplicates, and has the honor of representing to you, that she would wish to obtain, in the part north of this town, a piece of land situated on the borders of the Mississippi, bounded on three sides by his Majesty's domain, and on the other side by the banks of the Mississippi. The northern part of the concession, now petitioned for, to be situated between the mound commonly called *La Grange de Terre* and the banks of the Mississippi, having at its two ends four arpents in front, running about from east-northeast to west-southwest, by twenty arpents in length or depth, running about from north-northwest to south-southeast, in order that the petitioner may enjoy the same in full property for her, her heirs or assigns, to make hay, pasture her cattle, or for any other purpose suitable to her interest; and the petitioner shall never cease to render thanks to your goodness.

One cross for Esther's mark.

St. Louis, *October*, 1793.

We, lieutenant governor, after having ascertained that the land petitioned for belongs to his Majesty's domain, and that it is not prejudicial to any person, I certify to have put in possession the free mulatto woman named Esther, residing in this town of St. Louis, according to her petition, dated 2d instant, [+] And after having put her in possession ourselves, as appears by the document which we have drawn the next day, we have granted and do grant to the said Esther, in fee simple, for her, her heirs or assigns, or any other who may represent her rights, the piece of land here above designated, having four arpents in width at its two extremities, running from about east-northeast to west-southwest, by 20 arpents in length running from about north-northwest to south-southeast, situated to the north of this town; and the north end of the present concession shall be situated between the mound called La Grange de Terre and the Mississippi, and thence descending the said river until the complement of the above-mentioned 20 arpents in depth. The north-northwest, south-southeast, and west-southwest, which are about the courses of the lines, shall be bounded by his Majesty's domain, and the east-northeast side, which is the side facing the Mississippi, shall be bounded by the edge of its banks, in order that the said Esther may gather thereon the forage she requires, pasture her cattle, and for such other purposes as may suit her interest, remaining subject to the laws, taxes, and impositions which it may please his Majesty hereafter to impose. Given in the town of St. Louis of Illinois, this 5th day of October, 1793.

Approved thirty-two lines written at the margin here behind, and marked by a cross on the decree of delivery of possession.

ZENON TRUDEAU.

Nota.—The following is written at the margin:

[×] Of the piece of land described in her petition, having four arpents in front, running from about east-northeast to west-southwest, by twenty arpents in depth, running from about north-northwest to south-southeast, situated in the northern part of this town, between the mound called La Grange de Terre and the banks of the Mississippi, descending the said river. Three sides of the land petitioned for are bounded by his Majesty's domain, and the other side, which is to the east-northeast, is bounded by the banks of the Mississippi, as appears by the plat.

In testimony whereof, we have given the present in the town of St. Louis, this day, October 3, 1793.

ZENON TRUDEAU.

Don Zenon Trudeau, lieutenant governor of the western part of Illinois.

In consequence of the demand to us made by the free mulatto woman named Esther, residing, &c.

Truly translated from Livre Terrein, book 5, pages 10 and 11. St. Louis, March 7, 1833.

JULIUS DE MUN.

No.	Name of original claimant.	Quantity, arpents.	Nature and date of claim.	By whom granted.	By whom surveyed, date, and situation.
70	Esther, free mulatto woman.	80	Concession, October 5, 1793.	Z. Trudeau.....	Zenon Trudeau; October 3, 1793; north of St. Louis.

Evidence with reference to minutes and records.

August 22, 1806.—The board met agreeably to adjournment. Present: The honorable John B. C. Lucas, Clement B. Penrose, and James L. Donaldson, commissioners.

The same, (Jacque Clamorgan,) assignee of Esther, a mulatto woman, claiming four by twenty arpents of land, situate in the prairie of St. Louis, produces a duly registered warrant of survey from Zenon Trudeau, dated the 2d October, 1798, granted for the purpose of cutting hay, and a deed of transfer of the same dated the 2d September, 1794.

Joseph Brazeau, being duly sworn, says that to his knowledge claimant did make hay on said land, but cannot say positively when.

The board reject this claim.—(See book No. 1, page 485.)

March 6, 1833.—The board met pursuant to adjournment. Present: F. R. Conway, A. G. Harrison, commissioners.

Esther, free mulatto woman, claiming eighty arpents of land.—(See Livre Terrein, No. 5, pages 10 and 11; book C, pages 159 and 160.)

René Dodier, being duly sworn, says that he knew Esther, a free mulatto woman, who lived with Clamorgan; that she had a grant of land near the mound commonly called La Grange de Terre; that she lived with Clamorgan as if she had been his wife; that Clamorgan had several children by her; that Esther had cattle which were sent to pasture, along with Clamorgan's cattle, on said piece of land, and that she was generally known as being the lawful owner of said land; that said land was comprised in the common field of St. Louis, the fence of said field running on this side of where now lives Mr. John Mullanphy. Witness further says that he thinks Esther's land extended to the bank of the Mississippi, as it did not run west of the road going to Bellefontaine.—(See book No. 6, page 111.)

April 26, 1833.—The board met pursuant to adjournment. Present: A. G. Harrison, F. R. Conway, commissioners.

In the case of Esther, claiming eighty arpents of land.—(See page 111 of this book.)

Jean Baptiste Riviere, dit Bacanné, duly sworn, says he knew Esther, a free mulatto woman, who lived with Clamorgan; that to his knowledge said Esther had to the north of St. Louis a small piece of land which had been given to her by the public at the end of their common fields, and that Esther made use of said piece of land as a pasture for her calves and cows; that the said land was situated between the mound commonly called La Grange de Terre and the next mound south of the Grange de Terre, and running from the descent of the hill between the above said two mounds to the Mississippi; that he does not know exactly how long she possessed the said land. He further says that when he said that the said land had been given to Esther by the public he meant the government.

François Duchouquette, duly sworn, says he knows that Esther owned a piece of land situated at the foot of the Grange de Terre, and running thence to the Mississippi, but does not know what quantity of land; that said Esther was the reputed owner of said land for more than ten years.

Elizabeth Hortez, duly sworn, said that she heard her husband and others say that Esther had a piece of land situated about the Grange de Terre, and running towards the Mississippi; that she always understood that Esther was the reputed owner of said land; that the cows which were at Clamorgan's were always called Esther's cows.—(See book No. 6, page 160.)

November 8, 1833.—The board met pursuant to adjournment. Present: L. F. Linn, A. G. Harrison, F. R. Conway, commissioners.

Esther, free mulatto woman, claiming eighty arpents of land.—(See pages 111 and 160 of this book.)

The board are unanimously of opinion that this claim ought to be confirmed to the said Esther or her legal representatives, according to the concession.—(See book No. 6, page 310.)

A. G. HARRISON.
L. F. LINN.
F. R. CONWAY.

No. 71.—John Neybour, *claiming* 8 *by* 40 *arpents.*

To Don Zenon Trudeau, lieutenant governor, and commander-in-chief of the western part of Illinois:

John Neybour, residing on the river Maramec, humbly supplicates, and has the honor to represent to you that he would wish to obtain of your goodness the quantity of eight arpents of land (in front) by forty arpents in depth, situated on the said river, and distant an arpent and a half from the small house belonging to Mr. Clamorgan, in ascending on the right shore of the said Maramec.

The said land now petitioned for having its front on the said Maramec, and its depth running in a northeast direction, in the same manner as other lands have been heretofore granted in said place. The petitioner shall never cease to render thanks to your goodness.

JOHN NEYBOUR, his + mark.

St. Louis, *October* 19, 1795.

Don Zenon Trudeau, lieutenant governor, and commander-in-chief of the western part of Illinois, having ascertained that the eight arpents of land in front, situated on the banks of the Maramec, by the depth of forty arpents in a northeast direction, and distant an arpent and a half from the land of Mr. Clamorgan, belonging to his Majesty's domain, and shall not cause prejudice to anybody, Mr. Clamorgan shall put the said John Neybour in possession of the said tract, in order, afterwards, to deliver to him the concession for the same.

ZENON TRUDEAU.

St. Louis, *October* 20, 1795.

By virtue of the lieutenant governor's decree, bearing date 20th instant, we do certify to have put Mr. John Neybour in possession of the tract of land here above petitioned for, situated on the river Maramec, consisting of eight arpents in front on the banks of the river Maramec, one arpent and a half above the house of Mr. Clamorgan, which is situated near the cart road leading to the Saline. The said four arpents in front shall extend in depth to the northeast, and shall be bounded south by the tract of one arpent and a half of said Clamorgan, and north by his Majesty's domain.

The present grant being prejudicial to no person. In testimony whereof, we have given the present in St. Louis, this 21st of October, 1795.

J. CLAMORGAN.

Don Zenon Trudeau, lieutenant governor, and commander-in-chief of the western part of Illinois.

In consequence of the demand to us made by Mr. John Neybour, a German by birth, and inhabitant of this dependency, whom we have caused to be put in possession by Mr. Clamorgan, under date of 21st of the present month, we have granted and do grant to the said John Neybour, in fee simple, to him, his heirs or assigns, or any other representing his rights, the tract of land above described, consisting of eight arpents in front by forty in depth; the said eight arpents being situated on the banks of the Maramec, bounded on the south side by a small tract of land of one arpent and a half, on which there is a house belonging to Mr. Clamorgan, and on the north side by his Majesty's domain, and running parallel in depth in a northeast direction.

The said concession not being prejudicial to any person, we do grant it to him, under charge and condition that he shall form an establishment thereon in one year from this day, under pain to have the same reunited to his Majesty's domain; and it shall be subject to the laws, taxes, and impositions which it may please his Majesty hereafter to impose.

Given in St. Louis, this 22d day of October, of the year 1795.

The word eight, erased, to stand good.

ZENON TRUDEAU.

Nota.—In the original, where the word eight (*huit*) is used, the word four (*quatre*) has been first written, and afterwards altered into eight, except in the fourth line from the top, in Clamorgan's certificate, where the word four (*quatre*) stands as first written.

At the foot of the concession, which was written by Clamorgan, the approval of the word eight is in Zenon Trudeau's own handwriting.

Truly translated. St. Louis, March 25, 1833.

JULIUS DE MUN.

John Watkins, *claiming* 800 *arpents.*

To Don Charles Dehault Delassus, lieutenant colonel, attached to the stationary regiment of Louisiana, and lieutenant governor of the upper part of the same province:

Doctor John Watkins has the honor of representing to you that, having purchased of John Neybour (as is evinced by the certified copy of the deed of sale, executed July 12, 1799, here annexed) a tract of land of eight arpents in front by forty in depth, situated on the river Maramec, such as it is designated in the title of concession which it has pleased your predecessor, Don Zenon Trudeau, to expedite in favor of the proprietor, the said John Neybour, under date of October 22, 1795, also here annexed for the better intelligence of your petitioner's demand, which is to supplicate your justice to be pleased to grant to him an augmentation of about six or seven arpents in front, it being the space comprised between the above-mentioned land and the land belonging to Mr. Gabriel Cerré, by the depth already mentioned. The petitioner has the honor to observe to you that he is owner of a very large number of cattle of all kinds; that the quantity of land contained in his purchase aforesaid has but a small part of it fit for cultivation, the depth being hilly and sterile land. The quantity of land which he claims of your justice will enable him to extend his fields, and will give him a greater range for the pasture of his cattle; favor which the petitioner hopes to deserve from the generosity of the government and of your justice.

ST. LOUIS, *October* 30, 1799.

ST. LOUIS OF ILLINOIS, *October* 30, 1799.

In consequence of the authenticity of the documents annexed to the foregoing memorial, in which said documents are mentioned, and taking into consideration the just demand of the interested, the surveyor, Don Antonio Soulard, shall measure and set boundaries to the land purchased by the petitioner according to the tenor of the concession produced by him, including in said measurement the augmentation solicited in the foregoing memorial, provided it does not exceed six or seven arpents in front, conformably to what is expressed above. And this operation being executed, he shall deliver a certificate to the interested, in order to enable him, with the same, to obtain the confirmation of the primitive title, and the delivery of the concession in form from the intendancy general of these provinces, to which tribunal alone corresponds the granting of lands and town lots belonging to the royal domain.

CARLOS DEHAULT DELASSUS.

Don Antonio Soulard, surveyor general of Upper Louisiana.

I do certify that on the 5th of October of last year, (by virtue of the decree, here annexed, of the lieutenant colonel, Don Carlos Dehault Delassus, lieutenant governor of this Upper Louisiana, under date of 30th of October of the aforesaid year, and of other documents mentioned in the said memorial, and all annexed to the same,) I went on the land of John Watkins in order to survey the same, conformably to his demand of 613 arpents in superficie, which measurement has been taken in presence of the proprietor and of the adjoining neighbors, with the perch of Paris, of 18 feet in length, according to the custom adopted in this province of Louisiana, and without regard to the variation of the needle, which is 7° 30′ east, as is evinced by the foregoing figurative plat. The said land is situated at about sixteen miles to the southwest of this town of St. Louis, and bounded as follows: northeast by vacant lands of the royal domain, southwest by the margin of the river Maramec, southeast by land of Santiago Clamorgan, and northwest by lands of Don Gabriel Cerré; and that it shall be available according to law, I do give the present, with the foregoing figurative plat, on which are designated the dimensions and natural and artificial boundaries of said land.

ANTONIO SOULARD, *Surveyor General.*

ST. LOUIS OF ILLINOIS, *December* 7, 1800.

Truly translated. St. Louis, March 27, 1833. JULIUS DE MUN.

No.	Name of original claimant.	Quantity, in arpents.	Nature and date of claim.	By whom granted.	By whom surveyed, date, and situation.
71	John Watkins, for himself, and as assignee of J. Neybour.	800	Concession for 320 to John Neybour, October 22, 1795.	Zenon Trudeau.	J. Clamorgan, October 21, 1795.
			Concession for augmentation, October 30, 1799.	Carlos Dehault Delassus.	Antoine Soulard, December 7, 1800; 16 miles from St. Louis, on the Maramec.

Evidence with reference to minutes and records.

October 6, 1808.—Board met. Present: The Hon. Clement B. Penrose and Frederick Bates, commissioners.

John Watkins, assignee of Joseph Neybour, claiming eight arpents front by forty arpents deep, situate on the river Maramec, district of St. Louis, produces to the board a concession from Zenon Trudeau, lieutenant governor, for the same, to Joseph Neybour, dated October 22, 1795, and registered in book of register No. 5; No. 29, a certified copy of a deed of transfer from said Neybour to claimant, dated July 12, 1798, and certified October 31, 1803; a plat and certificate of survey of 613 arpents, dated November 5, 1799, and certified October 6, (December 7,) 1800.

Pierre Tournat, alias Lajoy, sworn, says that Joseph Neybour settled on said land fourteen years ago, and inhabited and cultivated the same from that time until about 1801 or 1802, and that the same has been inhabited and cultivated ever since for claimant.

Same, claiming six or seven arpents front by forty arpents deep, as an augmentation of the foregoing claim, produces to the board, in support thereof, a concession from Don Carlos Dehault Delassus, lieutenant governor, to claimant for the same, dated October 30, 1799, and also the above-mentioned plat and certificate of survey.

Antoine Soulard sworn, says that he knows that before Zenon Trudeau, lieutenant governor, left this country, he did actually grant to claimant the aforesaid augmentation, but on a search made for the same it could not be found; says that he wrote the petition and concession signed by Delassus, lieutenant governor, now produced; but on being interrogated as to the date thereof, referred the board to a former answer made by him before this board on a similar question, May 2, 1806, page 270, book No. 1, to wit:

Question. Do you recollect when that was written, and is it your belief that it was written at the time it bears date?

Here the witness refused to answer; whereupon he was asked by the board whether he meant to give similar answers to the questions in all similar cases, and answered yes.—(See book No. 3, page 278.)

January 16, 1809.—Board met. Present: John B. C. Lucas and Frederick Bates, commissioners.

John Watkins, assignee of Joseph Neybour, a claim for eight arpents front by forty in depth, situate on the river Maramec, district of St. Louis.—(See book No. 3, page 278.) The board examining the original concession in this claim are satisfied that the quantity originally granted was four arpents front, and that the alteration made in said quantity is spurious. Confirmed to John Watkins 160 arpents, and order that the same be surveyed so as to include the improvement of Joseph Neybour, four arpents in front on the Maramec by forty arpents in depth, on any land not heretofore legally surveyed, that may be found vacant there, except the survey heretofore made for claimant. Certificate to issue on return of survey.—(See book No. 3, page 430.)

March 12, 1833.—The board met pursuant to adjournment. Present: L. F. Linn and A. G. Harrison, commissioners.

John Watkins, for self, and as assignee of John Neybour, claiming 800 arpents of land situate on the Maramec.—(See book C, page 536, and following; minutes, No. 3, pages 278 and 430; Livre Terrein, No. 5, page 29.) Produces a paper purporting to be a concession from Zenon Trudeau, dated 22d October, 1795, to John Neybour, for 400 arpents, an order of survey to John Watkins for 800 arpents, said survey taken 5th November, and certified by Antoine Soulard 7th December, 1800; a deed from John Neybour to John Watkins; a notice of A. Soulard to said Watkins; copy of a petition from said Soulard, certified by Frederick Bates, recorder of land titles; affidavit of A. Soulard and James Mackay; affidavit of Jacque Clamorgan, and a plat and certificate of survey for 613 arpents, taken 9th November, and certified by Soulard the 7th December, 1800.

M. P. Leduc, C. F. Delauriere, and A. Tison, being duly sworn, certify to the signature of all the above papers. A. Tison further states that to his knowledge the said tract of land was inhabited and cultivated in about 1802 or 1803.—(See book No. 6, page 114.)

November 8, 1833.—The board met pursuant to adjournment. Present: L. F. Linn, A. G. Harrison, and F. R. Conway, commissioners.

John Watkins, in his own name, and as assignee of John Neybour, claiming 800 arpents of land.—(See page 114 of this book.) The board observe that after a minute examination of John Neybour's concession they see no good reasons for believing with the former board that the alteration mentioned was spurious, as the word *four*, altered into *eight*, was sanctioned by the lieutenant governor in the following, in his own handwriting, to wit: "The word eight, erased, to stand good;" immediately under which follows his own signature, making the quantity of arpents granted eight in front by forty in depth. The board are unanimously of opinion that 160 arpents (being the balance claimed by John Neybour) should be confirmed, the former board having already confirmed the other 160. The board are also of opinion that six or seven arpents in front by forty in depth, granted to John Watkins, should also be confirmed.—(See book No. 6, page 311.)

A. G. HARRISON.
L. F. LINN.
F. R. CONWAY.

No. 72.—J. M. Papin, *claiming* 8 *by* 25 *arpents.*

To the Lieutenant Governor:

Joseph Marie Papin, an inhabitant of this town of St. Louis, in the most respectful manner, in his right says, that wishing to form a plantation for the purpose of cultivation and raising of cattle, he supplicates you to grant to him 8 arpents of land of his Majesty's domain adjoining north to the land of Mr. Motard, east to the Mississippi, south to the land of Mr. Tayon, and west to the main road, (Camino Real,) leading to Mr. Delor's village; subjecting himself to leave a sufficient road between his concession and that of said Motard to enable people and cattle to pass; and also to leave vacant the Indian village near the river Mississippi, which is bounded north by Mr. Motard's plantation. Favor which the petitioner expects of your equitable justice.

J. M. PAPIN.

St. Louis of Illinois, *March* 28, 1787.

Don Francisco Cruzat, lieutenant colonel of infantry by brevet, captain of grenadiers in the stationary regiment of Louisiana, commandant and lieutenant governor of the western part and district of Illinois.

Having examined the statement in the above memorial, dated 28th March of this present year, presented by Mr. John Marie Papin, inhabiting and residing in this town, I have granted and do grant in fee simple to him, his heirs, and others who may represent his right, the eight arpents of land solicited by him, and which shall begin from the plantation of Joseph Motard, (leaving free all the space contained in the prairie called the Little Indian village, in order that the animals belonging to the public may pass freely and go down to the Mississippi, as they have been and are yet accustomed to do,) until it reaches the plantation of Joseph Tallon; on condition to establish and improve the said tract of land in the term of one year, to begin from this date, and on the contrary to be reunited to the royal domain. And it shall be liable to public charges and others which it may please his Majesty to impose.

Given in St. Louis of Illinois, the 30th of March, 1787.

FRANCO. CRUZAT.

Registered at the desire of the interested. (Book No. 2, pages 12 and 13.)

SOULARD.

To Don Charles Dehault Delassus, lieutenant colonel, attached to the stationary regiment of Louisiana, and lieutenant governor of the upper part of the same province:

Joseph Marie Papin has the honor to represent to you, in support of the title of concession which it has pleased the lieutenant governor, Don Francisco Cruzat, to grant to your petitioner under date of 30th March, 1787, which original document is here annexed, that the want of a surveyor appointed by the government having prevented him to have boundaries set to the said land up to this day, and in consequence of this operation not having heretofore been executed, he has the honor to supplicate you to have the goodness to order the surveyor of this Upper Louisiana to measure the said land when the petitioner shall require it, with the particular observation to give to the said land a depth of about twenty-five arpents, in order to avoid hereafter the difficulties which might result in accomplishing literally what is expressed in his petition, which says that the said land shall be bounded in the depth *by the road leading to Mr. Delor's village.* As a road is always subject to alterations which might increase or lessen his property, he wishes to have it invariably fixed to 25 arpents in depth. Favor which he hopes to obtain of your justice.

JN. PAPIN.

St. Louis of Illinois, *December* 28, 1802.

St. Louis of Illinois, *December* 29, 1802.

By virtue of the title of concession granted to the interested, under date of March 30, 1787, by the lieutenant governor, Don Francisco Cruzat, and in consideration of the survey which is solicited, the surveyor of this Upper Louisiana, Don Antonio Soulard, shall measure the land designated in the primitive title here annexed, and also conformably to his demand in the foregoing memorial, in order that, being vested with the necessary documents, the petitioner may apply to the general intendancy of this province, and solicit the ratification and title of property in form from the same tribunal.

CARLOS DEHAULT DELASSUS.

Registered at the desire of the interested. (Book No. 2, pages 13, 14, and 15.)

SOULARD.

Truly translated. St. Louis, March 28, 1833.

JULIUS DE MUN.

I do certify to all whom it may concern that I have been several times requested by Mr. M. Papin to survey for him a concession near this town, conformably to his titles; one from Don Francisco Cruzat, under date of March 30, 1787, and the other from Charles Dehault Delassus, of December 29, 1802; which survey I was obliged to delay on account of various occupations of my office, and at other times when said survey might have been made the proprietor was absent.

ANTOINE SOULARD, *Surveyor General Territory Louisiana.*

St. Louis, *February* 22, 1806.

Truly translated. November 22, 1833.

JULIUS DE MUN, *T. B. C.*

No.	Name of original claimant.	Quantity, arpents.	Nature and date of claim.	By whom granted.	By whom surveyed, date, and situation.
72	Joseph M. Papin.....	8 by 17	First concession, March 30, 1787. Second concession, December 29, 1802.	Francisco Cruzat. Carlos Dehault Delassus.	Special location.

Evidence with reference to minutes and records.

December 6, 1811.—Board met. Present: John B. C. Lucas, Clement B. Penrose, and Frederick Bates, commissioners.

Jos. M. Papin, claiming 8 by 25 arpents of land situate on the commons of St. Louis, produces record of a concession from Delassus, lieutenant governor, dated December 29, 1802. It is the opinion of the board that this claim ought not to be confirmed.—(See book No. 5, page 479.)

March 12, 1833.—The board met pursuant to adjournment. Present: L. F. Linn, A. G. Harrison, commissioners.

Joseph M. Papin's legal representatives, claiming 8 by 17 arpents of land, situated south of Little river or Mill creek, on the west side of the road leading from St. Louis to Carondelet, which separates the same from the arsenal, about two and a half miles from St. Louis.—(See book C, pages 434 and 435, for first and second concessions, and certificate of Soulard, Livre Terrein, No. 4, page 16.) Produces a paper purporting to be a concession from Francisco Cruzat, dated March 30, 1787; also an additional concession from Carlos Dehault Delassus, dated December 29, 1802; a certificate of A. Soulard, surveyor general, dated February 2, 1806; a plat of survey, signed M. P. Le Duc, dated August 27, 1823.

Albert Tison, being duly sworn, says that the signatures to the above papers are in the respective handwriting of the above-named persons who signed them, except the signature of Francisco Crozat, with which he is not acquainted.—(See book No. 6, page 115.)

November 8, 1833.—The board met. Present: L. F. Linn, A. G. Harrison, F. R. Conway, commissioners.

Joseph Marie Papin, claiming 200 arpents of land.—(See page 115 of this book.) The board are unanimously of opinion that this claim ought to be confirmed to the said Joseph Marie Papin, or to his legal representatives, according to Charles Dehault Delassus's concession.—(See book No. 6, page 311.)

A. G. HARRISON.
L. F. LINN.
F. R. CONWAY.

No. 73.—A. SAUGRAIN, *claiming* 20,000 *arpents.*

To Don Zenon Trudeau, lieutenant colonel, captain in the stationary regiment of Louisiana, and lieutenant governor of the western part of Illinois:

Ant. Saugrain, a Frenchman, has the honor to represent to you that, after having resided in several parts of the United States, he heard such advantageous reports of the assistance given by the Spanish government to foreigners who came to settle in this Upper Louisiana, that he conceived the project to come and settle himself in this province. In consequence, he had the honor of writing to you on the subject, and your answer, dated September 12, 1797, which he received, was so congenial to his wishes that from that moment he considered himself as a subject of his Majesty, and came to St. Louis, expecting, when it was in his power, to send for his family. The petitioner will not enter into a minute detail of the manner in which he has been formerly employed in the service of his Majesty by his excellency Count Galvez, governor general of this province, in the department of natural history, &c., as these particulars have come to your knowledge; but, according to your written promise, he has the honor to supplicate you to have the goodness to grant to him, in full property, twenty thousand arpents of land in superficie, four thousand arpents to be taken at about four miles southwest of the river Mississippi, and at fifty-seven miles from this town, and the remaining sixteen thousand arpents to be taken as follows: ten thousand arpents in a vacant place of the domain, at the petitioner's choice, and finally the other six thousand arpents in two different tracts of three thousand arpents each, in situations suitable to the accomplishment of his contemplated enterprises, without being prejudicial to the pretensions of any one whomsoever. And the petitioner, having in view the establishment of mills of various kinds, of a distillery, stock farm, &c., hopes that you will please to authorize him to have the right to choose the said tracts of land above mentioned, in all the extent of the district of St. Louis, and on the left side of the Missouri.

Your petitioner, having no other view but employing his industry in accordance with the fidelity which is due to the government, hopes to obtain the favor which he claims of your justice.

A. SAUGRAIN.

ST. LOUIS, *November* 8, 1797.

Don Zenon Trudeau, lieutenant governor of the western part of Illinois, &c.

The surveyor, Don Antonio Soulard, shall survey in favor of the interested party the twenty thousand arpents of land which he solicits in the place above cited, and shall deliver to the same the proces verbal of his survey, in order that with this decree it shall serve to him as a title of property until the corresponding title in form be expedited by the governor general.

ZENON TRUDEAU.

ST. LOUIS, *November* 9, 1797.

St. Louis, March 23, 1833. Truly translated.

JULIUS DE MUN.

No.	Name of original claimant.	Quantity, in arpents.	Nature and date of claim.	By whom granted.	By whom surveyed, date, and situation.
73	Antoine Saugrain..	20,000	Concession, Nov. 9, 1797.	Z. Trudeau ...	7,000 arpents. Frémon Delauriere, deputy surveyor, January 1, 1806; 3,000 arpents by same, January 5, 1806; 3,000 arpents by same, January 7, 1806; received for record by Soulard, March 8, 1806; on Salt river.

Evidence with reference to minutes and records.

May 10, 1806.—The board met agreeably to adjournment. Present: Hon. Clement B. Penrose.

Anthony Saugrain, claiming 20,000 arpents of land situate in the district of St. Charles, produces a concession from Zenon Trudeau to claimant, dated November 9, 1797; a survey of 4,006 arpents, situate on the waters of the Missouri, dated December 27, 1803, and certified January 28, 1804; and another survey of 3,000 arpents, situate on the waters of the Mississippi, dated January 7, and certified February 15, 1804. Claimant produced a letter from Zenon Trudeau to him, inviting him to the country, dated September 12, 1797. The board reject this claim, and observe that they are satisfied that the above concession was granted at the time it bears date, and is *bona fide*, but not duly registered.—(See book No. 1, page 289.)

August 18, 1810.—Board met. Present: Clement B. Penrose, Frederick Bates, commissioners.

Antoine Saugrain, claiming 20,000 arpents of land.—(See book No. 1, page 289.) It is the opinion of the board that this claim ought not to be confirmed.—(See book No. 4, page 465.)

March 12, 1833.—The board met pursuant to adjournment. Present: L. F. Linn, A. G. Harrison, commissioners.

Antoine Saugrain, by his heirs, claiming 20,000 arpents of land, of which a league square has been confirmed, (see book C, pages 252 and 253; minutes No. 1, page 289; No. 4, page 465,) produces a paper purporting to be a concession from Zenon Trudeau, dated November 9, 1797; three plats of surveys, one of which is for 7,000 arpents, and the two others for 3,000 arpents each.

M. P. Le Duc, duly sworn, says that the decree of concession, and the signature to it, are in the handwriting of Zenon Trudeau, and the signature to the petition is in the handwriting of A. Saugrain.

C. Frémon Delauriere, duly sworn, says that the three above plats of survey were executed by him, being at the time commissioned deputy surveyor.—(See book No. 6, page 116.)

November 8, 1833.—The board met pursuant to adjournment. Present: Lewis F. Linn, A. G. Harrison, F. R. Conway, commissioners.

Antoine Saugrain, claiming 20,000 arpents of land.—(See page 116 of this book.) The board are unanimously of opinion that this claim ought to be confirmed to the said Antoine Saugrain, or his legal representatives, according to the concession.—(See book No. 6, page 312.)

A. G. HARRISON.
L. F. LINN.
F. R. CONWAY.

No. 74.—The sons of J. M. Papin, *claiming* 5,600 *arpents.*

To Don Charles Dehault Delassus, lieutenant colonel, attached to the regiment (stationary) of Louisiana, and lieutenant governor of the upper part of the same province:

Joseph Papin, Hipolite Papin, Pierre Papin, Silvestre Papin, Didier Papin, Theodore Papin, Alexander Papin, brothers, and sons of Mr. J. M. Papin, all of them born under the domination of his Majesty, and accustomed to the generosity and goodness of his government, hope that you will be pleased to take into consideration their situation, and assist them in their intention of procuring to themselves an independent existence and help their parents who are living, since a long time, in unfortunate circumstances, unable to give them the necessary education, and render them fit to provide for thei r own wants. All your petitioners being of the same mind, have determined to supplicate you to grant them your protection, and, consulting only the goodness of your heart, to concede to each of them 800 arpents of land, or 5,600 arpents, to be taken in one or several vacant places of his Majesty's domain. The petitioners presume to expect this favor of your justice; they only regret to have nothing else to offer in return for so much goodness but the assurance of their devotedness and sincere and constant fidelity to the benevolent government under which they are born, and of which they hope to remain all their lives faithful subjects.

HIPOLITE PAPIN.
PIERRE PAPIN.
THEODORE PAPIN.
ALEXANDER PAPIN.
JOSEPH PAPIN.
DIDIER PAPIN.
SILVESTRE PAPIN.

St. Louis, *January* 19, 1800.

St. Louis of Illinois, *January* 21, 1800.

Cognizance being taken of the foregoing statement and of the praiseworthy motives which influence the petitioners, and considering that their family is one of the most ancient in the country, and deserving the favors of the government, I do grant to the petitioners, to them and their heirs, the land they solicit, provided it is not to the prejudice of any one; and the surveyor, Don Antonio Soulard, shall put the parties interested in possession of the quantity of land they ask for, in one or two vacant places of the royal domain; which being executed, he shall make out a plat of his survey, delivering the same to said parties, with his certificate, in order to serve to them to obtain the concession and title in form from the intendant general, to whom alone corresponds, by royal order, the distributing and granting all classes of lands of the royal domain.

CARLOS DEHAULT DELASSUS.

Truly translated from Spanish record of concessions, (book No. 2, pages 15 and 16.) St. Louis, August 12, 1833.

JULIUS DE MUN

No.	Names of original claimants.	Quantity, in arpents	Nature and date of claim.	By whom granted.	By whom surveyed, date, and situation.
74	Joseph Papin, Didier Papin, Alexander Papin, Hipolite Papin, Silvestre Papin, Theodore Papin, and Pierre Papin	5,600	Concession, January 21, 1800.	Carlos Dehault Delassus.	

Evidence with reference to minutes and records.

October 10, 1808.—Board met. Present: The honorable Clement B. Penrose and Frederick Bates, commissioners.

Joseph, Alexander, Hipolite, Pierre, Silvestre, Didier, and Theodore Papin—sons of Joseph M. Papin—claiming 800 arpents of land each, on any vacant land, produce to the board a concession from Charles Dehault Delassus, lieutenant governor, for the same, dated 21st January, 1800. Laid over for decision.—(See book No. 3, page 286.)

June 18, 1810.—Board met. Present: John B. C. Lucas, Clement B. Penrose, and Frederick Bates, commissioners.

Joseph Papin, claiming 800 arpents of land.—(See book No. 3, page 286.) It is the opinion of the board that this claim ought not to be confirmed.

Alexander Papin, claiming 800 arpents of land.—(See book No. 3, page 286.) It is the opinion of the board that this claim ought not to be confirmed.

Hipolite Papin, claiming 800 arpents of land.—(See book No. 3, page 286.) It is the opinion of the board that this claim ought not to be confirmed.

Pierre Papin, claiming 800 arpents of land.—(See book No. 3, page 286.) It is the opinion of the board that this claim ought not to be confirmed.

Silvestre Papin, claiming 800 arpents of land.—(See book No. 3, page 286.) It is the opinion of the board that this claim ought not to be confirmed.

Didier Papin, claiming 800 arpents of land.—(See book No. 3, page 286.) It is the opinion of the board that this claim ought not to be confirmed.

Theodore Papin, claiming 800 arpents of land.—(See book No. 3, page 286.) It is the opinion of the board that this claim ought not to be confirmed.—(See book No. 4, page 386.)

March 12, 1833.—The board met pursuant to adjournment. Present: L. F. Linn, A. G. Harrison, commissioners.

The sons of Joseph M. Papin, to wit, Joseph, Didier, Alexander, Hipolite, Silvestre, Theodore, and Pierre, claiming 800 arpents of land each, under the same concession.—(See book C, page 485; minutes No. 3, page 286; No. 4, pages 386 and 387; Spanish record of concession, No. 2, page 15, No. 11; see book No. 6, page 117.)

November 9, 1833.—The board met pursuant to adjournment. Presen: L. F. Linn, A. G. Harrison, F. R. Conway, commissioners.

The sons of Joseph M. Papin, claiming 5,600 arpents of land.—(See page 117 of this book.) The board are unanimously of opinion that this claim ought to be confirmed to the said sons of Joseph M. Papin, to wit, Joseph, Didier, Alexander, Hipolite, Silvestre, Theodore, and Pierre Papin, or their legal representatives, according to the concession.—(See book No. 6, page 312.)

A. G. HARRISON.
L. F. LINN.
F. R. CONWAY.

No. 75.—Bernard Pratte, *claiming* 800 *arpents.*

To Mr. Zenon Trudeau, lieutenant colonel and governor of the western part of Illinois, &c.:

Sir: The undersigned has the honor to represent to you that, having formed the project of making a plantation in this neighborhood, he wishes to obtain a piece of land on the river Des Peres, adjoining, south, the line of Mr. Papin, and bounded north by the St. Charles road, by forty arpents in depth. Favor which he expects of your justice.

BERNARD PRATTE.

St. Louis, *May* 24, 1799.

St. Louis, *May* 24, 1799.

Being satisfied that the land solicited is vacant, and of the domain of his Majesty, and that the granting of the same prejudices nobody; that the petitioner is in such circumstances as to enable him to form an establishment on a large scale, the surveyor, Don Antonio Soulard, shall put him in possession of 800 arpents of land in superficie, in the manner most convenient to the party interested, and advantageous for the location of other settlers; and afterwards he shall make out his plat of survey to enable him to solicit the concession of the governor general, who, knowing personally the petitioner and his family, has no need of a recommendation.

ZENON TRUDEAU.

I, the undersigned, transfer to Madame Beral Sarpy, and abandon to her, the above title of concession, as being her own and irrevocable property, and to enjoy the same as such.

BERNARD PRATTE.

St. Louis, *October* 17, 1800.

I notify the party interested that the present petition having not been presented to me at the time, the place designated in the same has been taken by other surveys, and I must have an order from the lieutenant governor to be able to place the same quantity of land on any other vacant place which shall be chosen.

SOULARD.

St. Louis, *May* 5, 1803.

On account of the above information, and of the authenticity of the title, the proprietor may take the same quantity of land on any other vacant part of the domain, and this to be executed by the surveyor without objections, provided the place chosen shall not be prejudicial to anybody.

CARLOS DEHAULT DELASSUS.

St. Louis, *May* 6, 1803.

Truly translated. St. Louis, March 6, 1833.

JULIUS DE MUN.

Don Antonio Soulard, surveyor general of Upper Louisiana.

I do certify that a tract of land of 800 arpents in superficie was measured, the lines run and bounded, in favor of Mrs. Pelagie Sarpy, and in presence of the deputy surveyor, her agent; which concession was abandoned and ceded by the original owner, Bernard Pratte, to the said Pelagie Sarpy, as is evinced by the transfer inserted below the memorial here annexed. Said measurement was taken with the perch of Paris, of 18 French feet lineal measure of the same city, conformably to the agrarian measure of this province; which land is situated at about 30 miles southwest of St. Louis, bounded on the four sides by vacant lands of the royal domain. The said survey and measurement were executed without regard to the variation of the needle, which is 7° 30′ E., as is evinced by the foregoing figurative plat, on which are designated the dimensions, courses of the lines, other boundaries, &c. Said survey was executed by virtue of the decree of the lieutenant governor, Don Zenon Trudeau, to which is adjoined that of the lieutenant governor and sub-delegate of the royal treasury, Don Carlos Dehault Delassus, under dates of May 24, 1799, and of May 6, 1803, here annexed. And, in order that all here above cited be available according to law, I do give the present, with the foregoing figurative plat, drawn conformably to the survey executed by the deputy surveyor, John Terrey, on the 4th of January, 1804, and who signed on the minutes, which I certify.

ANTONIO SOULARD, *Surveyor General*

St. Louis of Illinois, *April* 15, 1804.

Truly translated. St. Louis, April 8, 1833.

JULIUS DE MUN, *T. B. C.*

No.	Name of original claimant.	Quantity, in arpents.	Nature and date of claim.	By whom granted.	By whom surveyed, date, and situation.
75	Bernard Pratte..	800	Concession, May 24, 1799. Concession, May 6, 1803.	Zenon Trudeau.. Carlos Dehault Delassus.	John Terry, deputy surveyor, January 4, 1804. Certified by Soulard April 15, 1804. Thirty miles SW. of St. Louis.

Evidence with reference to minutes and records.

December 6, 1811.—Board met. Present: John B. C. Lucas, Clement B. Penrose, and Frederick Bates, commissioners.

Madame Barraul Sarpy, assignee of Bernard Pratte, claiming 800 arpents of land situate on the Maramec, district of St. Louis, produces record of a concession from Zenon Trudeau, lieutenant governor, dated May 24, 1799, and a certificate from the surveyor that the land is not vacant; record of an order from Delassus, lieutenant governor, to survey the same on vacant lands, dated May 6, 1803; record of a plat of survey dated January 4, and certified April 15, 1804; record of a transfer from Pratte to claimant, dated October 17, 1800.

It is the opinion of the board that this claim ought not to be confirmed.—(See book No. 5, page 478.)

March 12, 1833.—The board met pursuant to adjournment. Present: L. F. Linn and A. G. Harrison, commissioners.

Bernard Pratte, by his assignee, Pelagie Sarpy, claiming 800 arpents of land, (see book C, pages 363 and 366; No. 5, page 478,) produces a paper purporting to be an original concession from Zenon Trudeau, dated May 24, 1799; also a plat of survey taken January 4, and certified April 15, 1804; a deed of conveyance, dated October 11, 1819, and a concession from C. D. Delassus, dated May 6, 1803.

M. P. Le Duc, duly sworn, says that the signatures to the concessions are in the proper handwriting of the said Zenon Trudeau and C. D. Delassus.—(See book No. 6, page 117.)

November 9, 1833.—The board met pursuant to adjournment. Present: L. F. Linn, A. G. Harrison, F. R. Conway, commissioners.

Bernard Pratte, claiming 800 arpents of land —(See page 117 of this book.)

The board are unanimously of opinion that this claim ought to be confirmed to the said Bernard Pratte, or to his legal representatives, according to the concession.—(See book No. 6, page 312.)

A. G. HARRISON.
L. F. LINN.
F. R. CONWAY.

No. 76.—Charles Gratiot, jr., *claiming* 2,500 *arpents.*

To Don Charles Dehault Delassus, lieutenant colonel, attached to the stationary regiment of Louisiana, and lieutenant governor of the upper part of the same province:

Charles Gratiot, junior, has the honor to represent to you that, being of an age at which he ought to think of procuring to himself an independent existence, he hopes that you will be pleased to assist him in his views, and grant to him the same favor which the government diffuses upon all his Majesty's subjects; therefore, having formed the project of establishing a farm on a large scale, he has the honor to supplicate you to have the goodness to grant to him, in full property, 2,500 arpents of land in superficie, to be taken in a vacant place of the King's domain, on the left bank of the Maramec, between the river called *A Calvé* and the Little Maramec, so as to include the bottom, situated at about fifty-four or sixty miles from the mouth of the said river Maramec, one of its branches, or thereabout.

The petitioner hopes that the numerous family of his father, the length of time they have been in the country, and their constant fidelity to the government, will have acquired to him, in your opinion, the right to obtain the favor which he presumes to expect of your justice.

CHARLES GRATIOT, Jr.

St. Louis, *December* 15, 1802.

St. Louis of Illinois, *December* 16, 1802.

Whereas it is evident that the petitioner possesses more than sufficient means to improve the lands which he solicits, I do grant to him and his heirs the land which he solicits, provided it is not prejudicial to any person; and the surveyor, Don Antonio Soulard, shall put the party interested in possession of the quantity of land he asks, in the place designated; and this being executed, he shall draw a plat of his survey, delivering the same to the party, with his certificate, in order to enable him to obtain the concession and title in form from the intendant general, to whom alone corresponds, by royal order, the distributing and granting all classes of lands of the royal domain.

CARLOS DEHAULT DELASSUS.

Registered at the desire of the party interested, pages 18 and 19, in book No. 1 of titles of concessions, No. 11.

SOULARD.

Truly translated. St. Louis, April 2, 1833.

JULIUS DE MUN.

No.	Name of original claimant.	Quantity, in arpents.	Nature and date of claim.	By whom granted.	By whom surveyed, date, and situation.
76	Charles Gratiot, jr.	2,500	Concession, December 16, 1802.	Carlos Dehault Delassus.	On the Maramec, 54 or 60 miles from its mouth.

Evidence with reference to minutes and records.

November 20, 1811.—Board met. Present: John B. C. Lucas, Clement B. Penrose, and Frederick Bates, commissioners.

Charles Gratiot, jr., claiming 2,500 arpents of land situate on the Maramec, district of St. Louis, produces record of concession from Charles D. Delassus, lieutenant governor, dated 16th December, 1802. It is the opinion of the board that this claim ought not to be confirmed.—(See book No. 5, page 427.)

March 13, 1833.—The board met pursuant to adjournment. Present: Lewis F. Linn, A. G. Harrison, commissioners.

Charles Gratiot, jr., claiming 2,500 arpents of land on the left bank of the river Maramec, between the river commonly called Cavé and Little Maramec, so as to include the bottom, and situated about 54 or 60 miles from the mouth of the river Maramec (see book D, page 119; book No. 5, page 427,) produces a paper purporting to be a concession from Carlos Dehault Delassus, dated 16th December, 1802.

M. P. Le Duc, duly sworn, says that the signature to the concession is in the proper handwriting of said Carlos Dehault Delassus.—(See book No. 5, page 119.)

November 9, 1833.—The board met pursuant to adjournment. Present: L. F. Linn, A. G. Harrison, F. R. Conway, commissioners.

Charles Gratiot, jr., claiming 2,500 arpents of land.—(See page 119 of this book.) The board are unanimously of opinion that this claim ought to be confirmed to the said Charles Gratiot, jr., or to his legal representatives, according to the concession.—(See book No. 6, page 313.)

A. G. HARRISON.
L. F. LINN.
F. R. CONWAY.

No. 77.—Levy Theel, *claiming* 200 *arpents.*

To Don Charles Dehault Delassus, lieutenant colonel, attached to the stationary regiment of Louisiana, and lieutenant governor of the upper part of the same province:

Levy Theel, R. C., has the honor to represent to you that he settled, about two years ago, (with the consent of Mr. Zenon Trudeau,) on a piece of land situated on the north side of the river Maramec, which land he has ever since continued to cultivate with success, without giving cause to anybody to complain about his conduct. Various circumstances have prevented him to present his petition to Mr. Trudeau in order to obtain the fulfilment of his promise; but, full of confidence in your justice, he hopes that you will be pleased to grant to him on the said river Maramec, and at the place which he cultivates, the quantity of two hundred arpents of land in superficie, which shall be bounded on one side by the plantation formerly belonging to Thos. Tyler, and now the property of Mr. Gabriel Cerré. Favor which he presumes to expect of your justice.

LEVY THEEL.

St. Louis, *December* 15, 1799.

St. Louis of Illinois, *December* 15, 1799.

Whereas we are informed that the petitioner possesses sufficient means to work and improve the land which he is cultivating since two years, by virtue of the permit of our predecessor, and considering that he bears a good character, the surveyor, Don Antonio Soulard, shall put the party interested in possession of the same, and shall make out a plat and certificate of his survey, in order to serve to solicit the concession from the intendant general of these provinces, to whom alone corresponds, by order of his Majesty, the distributing and granting all classes of lands of the royal domain.

CARLOS DEHAULT DELASSUS.

Truly translated. St. Louis, April 2, 1833.

JULIUS DE MUN.

No.	Name of original claimant.	Quantity, in arpents.	Nature and date of claim.	By whom granted	By whom surveyed, date, and situation.
77	Levy Thiel...............	200	Concession, December 15, 1799.	Carlos Dehault Delassus.	

Evidence with reference to minutes and records.

December 10, 1811.—Board met. Present: John B. C. Lucas, Clement B. Penrose, and Frederick Bates, commissioners.

Charles Gratiot, assignee of Levy Thiel, claiming 200 arpents of land situate on the Maramec, district of St. Louis, produces record of a confirmation from Delassus, lieutenant governor, dated December 15, 1799.

It is the opinion of the board that this claim ought not to be confirmed.—(See book No. 5, page 507.)

March 13, 1833.—The board met pursuant to adjournment. Present: L. F. Linn and A. G. Harrison, commissioners.

Levy Thiel, by Charles Gratiot, senior's, representatives, claiming 200 arpents of land, (see book D, page 120; No. 5, page 507,) produces a paper purporting to be an original concession from Carlos D. Delassus, dated December 15, 1799, and an agreement between C. Gratiot and Thiel, dated January 13, 1811.

M. P. Le Duc, duly sworn, says that the signature to the concession is in the proper handwriting of said Delassus.—(See book No. 6, page 119.)

November 9, 1833.—The board met pursuant to adjournment. Present: L. F. Linn, A. G. Harrison, F. R. Conway, commissioners.

Levy Thiel, claiming 200 arpents of land.—(See page 119 of this book.)

The board are unanimously of opinion that this claim ought to be confirmed to the said Levy Thiel, or his legal representatives, according to the concession.—(See book No. 6, page 313.)

A. G. HARRISON.
L. F. LINN.
F. R. CONWAY.

No. 78.—Mathurin Bouvet, *claiming* 20 *arpents square.*

To Mr. Zenon Trudeau, captain in the stationary regiment of Louisiana, lieutenant governor, and commander-in-chief of the western part of Illinois:

Sir: Mathurin Bouvet humbly supplicates, and has the honor to represent to you, that three years ago he went to a river known by the name of river Auhaha, the mouth of which is at the distance of about thirty-four leagues from St. Louis; that, having ascended sixteen leagues in the said river, he penetrated half a league inland in order to look at a saline, which he found to suit his wishes; and having worked the same in different places he settled himself at the place called Le Bastion; and having tried the water of the said saline he succeeded in making salt. This experiment being made, he came down with the intention of returning there with men and all necessary utensils for the said manufacture; but when he got back to the said place, he saw, with pain, that Indians of the Sac nation had been there in his absence and had taken away all his effects, tools, and kettles, which he had left, and also three valuable mares which they had stolen. The petitioner was not discouraged, and, considering the actual state of his affairs, had considerable work done; he had a furnace erected, a warehouse of thirty-five feet, a dwelling-house, and other small buildings, and cleared a pretty large field. After sometime he sent down his three men in search of provisions; but they, having fallen sick, would not come up again, so he found himself compelled to winter there alone, and as soon as the weather permitted, he hid (en cache) all his effects and came down by land. The Indians of the same nation, knowing of his absence, have taken advantage of it, and have robbed all he had left behind, to the value of upwards of twelve hundred dollars. The petitioner presumes to flatter himself that, taking into consideration all these losses and expenses, you will be pleased to grant to him a concession of the said place, in order that he may indemnify himself, and to encourage him in his intention of having thereon his manufactory of salt. He claims of your goodness that you will condescend to grant to him the concession of the said saline and twenty arpents square, (of which the said Bastion shall be the centre, the said twenty arpents running from north to south and from east to west,) in order that he may, with security, have the necessary works and buildings done, and secure the surrounding timber for the use of his said manufactory, and continue to make the roads which he has already begun from the river Auhaha to the said saline, and thence to the Mississippi, for the effectuation of his undertaking. The petitioner shall never cease to pray for your conservation in acknowledgment of your goodness.

M. BOUVET.

St. Louis, *March* 17, 1795.

Don Zenon Trudeau, lieutenant governor and commander-in-chief of the western part of Illinois, after having examined the demand made in Mr. Bouvet's petition, we have granted to him the concession of twenty arpents square, situated on the river Auhaha, at fifteen leagues from its mouth, which falls into the Mississippi at the distance of about thirty-four leagues from this town; the survey of said land shall be at his charge.

Done at St. Louis, June 1, 1795.

ZENON TRUDEAU.

Truly translated. St. Louis, April 1, 1833.

JULIUS DE MUN.

CHARLES GRATIOT, *claiming 7,056 arpents.*

To Don Carlos Dehault Delassus, lieutenant colonel, attached to the stationary regiment of Louisiana, and lieutenant governor of the upper part of the same province:

Charles Gratiot, merchant of this town, father of a very numerous family, has the honor to represent to you that on the 30th of November, in the year 1800, he bought at a public sale, of which a copy certified by yourself is here annexed, and which sale took place in your presence, a property, consisting in a saline, situated on the river Auhaha, and granted, with 20 arpents of land on each side, to Mathurin Bouvet, deceased, his creditor, by virtue of a petition which he presented to the lieutenant governor, Don Zenon Trudeau, under date of March 17, 1795, and of the decree of concession of the lieutenant governor above named, dated June 1, 1795, all said documents being here annexed. In consequence of the said titles, he has the honor to represent to you that, wishing to work the said saline, and determined to make all the sacrifices which such an enterprise carries along with it, he lays the foundation of his hopes of obtaining the augmentation of land which is necessary to an establishment requiring such a consumption of wood, on the generosity of a government of which he has always experienced the liberality and kindness; confiding in this opinion, he has the honor to supplicate you to have the goodness to grant to him, at the place purchased by him, an augmentation to the original concession of the late Mathurin Bouvet, which will complete one league square of land in superficie, or 7,056 arpents, and refers to the original title for the situation of the same.

The difficulty of raising cattle in the vicinity of this town made him have in contemplation the project of making a stock farm on the said land, which he hopes to do with advantage; and, as the above-named establishments always require a great extent of land, and that the government has never refused, in such cases, to grant similar concessions, he expects of your generosity that you will be pleased to assist him in his project, and that you will do justice to the favor which he hopes to obtain of your justice.

C. GRATIOT.

ST. LOUIS, *January* 5, 1801.

ST. LOUIS OF ILLINOIS, *January* 6, 1801.

Having examined the contents of the foregoing statement, and in consideration of the undertakings which the petitioner has in contemplation, and for the success of which he requires a great consumption of fuel and a considerable extent of land; considering, also, that if he succeeds in his projects it will be very advantageous to these settlements, I do grant to the petitioner the land which he solicits; and as it is situated in a desert where there are no establishments, and thirty or forty leagues, more or less, distant from this town, he shall not be obliged to have it surveyed immediately, but as soon as any settler shall appear in the vicinity of the above-mentioned place, in this case he must have it surveyed without delay; and Don Antonio Soulard, surveyor general of this Upper Louisiana, shall take cognizance of this title for his intelligence and government in what concerns him, in order that the party interested may, after the survey is made, solicit the title in form from the intendant general of these provinces of Louisiana.

CARLOS DEHAULT DELASSUS.

Registered, by order of the lieutenant governor, pages 5, 6, and 7 of book No. 1 of titles of concessions No. 3.

SOULARD.

ST. LOUIS, *April* 10, 1803.

No.	Name of original claimant.	Quantity, in arpents.	Nature and date of claim.	By whom granted.	By whom surveyed, date, and situation.
78	Mathurin Bouvet, 400; his assignee, Charles Gratiot, 6,656.	7, 056	Concession, June 1, 1795; concession, January 6, 1801.	Zenon Trudeau and C. Dehault Delassus.	Frémon Delauriere, deputy surveyor, Feb. 20, 1806. Recorded April 15, 1806, by Soulard. On Salt river.

Evidence with reference to minutes and records.

ST. LOUIS, *July* 8, 1806.

Charles Gratiot, assignee of Mathurin Bouvet, claiming 20 square arpents of land, on which there is a salino, situate on the river Auhaha, district of St. Charles, produces a concession, duly registered, from Zenon Trudeau, dated June 1, 1795, and an act of public sale of the effects and property of said Bouvet, dated December 7, 1800.

Francis M. Benoist, being duly sworn, says that he has known a saline established on said land for eleven or twelve years since; that the same was established by said Bouvet; that he died about five years ago by fire; that his house was then destroyed; and that he worked said mine to the last moment.

The board reject this claim; they observe that the aforesaid concession is duly registered; that the conditions on which said concession was granted have been complied with; but that the same was not actually inhabited and cultivated prior to and on the 1st day of October, 1800.—(See book No. 2, recorder's minutes, page 27.)

November 29, 1808.—Board met. Present: The Hon. John B. C. Lucas, Clement B. Penrose, and Frederick Bates, commissioners.

Charles Gratiot, assignee of Mathurin Bouvet, claiming twenty arpents square, situate on the river Auhaha. Laid over for decision.—(See book No. 3, page 379.)

July 11, 1810.—Board met. Present: Clement B. Penrose and Frederick Bates, commissioners.

Charles Gratiot, claiming 7,056 arpents of land.—(See book No. 3, page 379.) It is the opinion of this board that this claim ought not to be confirmed.—(See book No. 4, page 428.)

January 9, 1812.—Board met. Present: John B. C. Lucas, Clement B. Penrose, Frederick Bates, commissioners.

Charles Gratiot, assignee of Mathurin Bouvet.—(See book No. 2, page 27; book No. 3, page 379.) It is the opinion of a majority of the board that this claim ought not to be confirmed.

Frederick Bates, commissioner, forbears giving an opinon.—(See book No. 5, page 556.)

March 18, 1833.—The board met pursuant to adjournment. Present: L. F. Linn, A. G. Harrison, commissioners.

Mathurin Bouvet, by Charles Gratiot's representatives, claiming 7,056 arpents of land, (see book A, page 534; minutes No. 2, page 27; No. 3, page 379; No. 4, page 428; No. 5, page 556; Livre Terrein, No. 5, page 14,) produces a paper purporting to be a concession from Zenon Trudeau, dated June 1, 1795; also an additional concession from C. D. Delassus, dated January 5, 1801; also a plat of survey for 400 arpents, certified by Frémon Delauriere, deputy surveyor, dated February 19, 1806; also a plat and certificate of survey for 7,056 arpents, including the above 400, made by C. F. Delauriere, deputy surveyor; received for record by Soulard April 15, 1806.

M. P. Le Duc, duly sworn, says that the signature to the concession is in the proper handwriting of Zenon Trudeau; that the signature to the additional concession is in the handwriting of C. D. Delassus; and the signatures to the plat of survey are in the respective handwriting of C. F. Delauriere and Antoine Soulard.

Charles F. Delauriere, duly sworn, says that in 1800 or 1801 he was on said tract, and saw a well and the remains of a house and furnace, and several broken kettles, and, by appearances, it was evident salt had been manufactured there, and had often heard that salt had been manufactured there. As to the survey, witness states as follows: that the survey already produced is one of those included among the surveys mentioned in the above letter; that the survey was executed at the time it bears date; that there was great difficulty and danger in executing surveys; that he was twice repulsed by the Indians; and that the third time he went up he could not execute several of the surveys, being prevented by Indians of the Sac and Fox nations, although he and his companions were well armed; that surveyors were very scarce, and it was difficult to procure any one to take a survey; that there was not half the number of surveyors necessary to execute the surveys that were then to be made. Claimant produces a copy of a public sale to C. Gratiot.—(See book No, 5, page 119.)

November 9, 1833.—The board met pursuant to adjournment. Present: L. F. Linn, A. G. Harrison, F. R. Conway, commissioners.

Mathurin Bouvet and Charles Gratiot, claiming 7,056 arpents of land.—(See page 119 of this book.) The board are unanimously of opinion that this claim ought to be confirmed to the said Mathurin Bouvet and Charles Gratiot, or their legal representatives, according to the concession.—(See book No. 6, page 313.)

Conflicting claim.

J. D. Caldwell, by letter dated ———, gives notice to the board that he has purchased of the United States the southwest quarter of section thirty-two, township fifty-six, range five; also, the southeast fractional quarter of section thirty, township fifty-six north, range five, within the above-mentioned claim.

A. G. HARRISON.
L. F. LINN.
F. R. CONWAY.

No. 79.—Mathurin Bouvet, *claiming* 84 *arpents in length.*

To Mr. Zenon Trudeau, captain in the stationary regiment of Louisiana, lieutenant governor, and commander-in-chief of the western part of Illinois:

Mathurin Bouvet humbly supplicates, and has the honor to represent that, having obtained of your goodness the concession of the saline *Du Bastion*, on the river Auhaha, it becomes indispensable for him to have an establishment on the Mississippi, in order to raise buildings thereon to deposit the salt manufactured at his works, on account of the difficulty of navigation in the said river Auhaha; and to obviate these difficulties, he contemplates to make an establishment and improve a plantation at the foot of the hills of the bay De Charles, which hills run along the Mississippi at the distance of about three leagues from the said saline Du Bastion. The said hills are at the unequal distance of from one half arpent in the least to two arpents in the greatest width from the banks of the said bay; therefore the petitioner claims your authority, in order that you may be pleased, sir, to grant to him the concession for eighty-four arpents in length, to be taken six arpents below the outlet of the said bay De Charles, ascending eighty-four arpents along the said bay and from the hills to the margin of said bay De Charles, in order that he may build thereon suitable buildings for the storage of his salt and improve a plantation; and the petitioner shall never cease to pray Heaven for the conservation of your days.

M. BOUVET.

St. Louis, *June* 6, 1795.

Don Zenon Trudeau, lieutenant governor and commander-in-chief of the western part of Illinois, after having examined the demand made in Mr. Bouvet's petition, we have granted to him the concession of eighty-four arpents in length, to be taken six arpents below the outlet of the bay De Charles, distant about forty leagues from this village, ascending along the said bay; the width to be the space comprised along the eighty-four arpents between the hills and the said bay, in order that he may locate his concession and build thereon. The said Mr. Bouvet shall cause the said concession to be surveyed and bounded.

ZENON TRUDEAU.

St. Louis, *June* 12, 1795.

Truly translated. St. Louis, March 29, 1833.

JULIUS DE MUN.

Charles Gratiot, *claiming* 84 *by* 40 *arpents.*

To Don Charles Dehault Delassus, lieutenant colonel, attached to the stationery regiment of Louisiana, and lieutenant governor of the upper part of the same province:

Charles Gratiot, merchant of this town, and father of a very numerous family, has the honor to represent to you that, having acquired at a juridical sale, executed before you, under date of November 30, 1800, of which a certified copy is here annexed, the lands belonging to Mr. Mathurin Bouvet, deceased, whose original petition, dated June 6, 1795, to which is subjoined the decree of concession from the lieutenant governor, Don Zenon Trudeau, under date of 12th of the same month and same year, is here also annexed, the petitioner supplicates you to have the goodness to observe that the manner in which the demand is worded makes it liable to difficulties which are offered by the locality itself. It is therein said that the proprietor shall possess, on the said bay De Charles, eighty-four arpents in length by the depth comprised between the hills and the river; but as those hills are in places very near and at other places at a very great distance from the said river, it would give to the said land very irregular boundaries, and more liable to bring on difficulties than lines whose courses would be fixed and bounded in all their length. In consequence of the above observations, the petitioner hopes that you will be pleased to grant to him the favor to take the land conformably to the foregoing plat, by which you will see that the petitioner desires that a line A B be drawn from the bottom of the bay, where the hills come nighest to the river; that the said line be run as perpendicular to the river as possible, forty arpents in depth; that from the said point B a line of forty-two arpents be drawn on the right to C; from this point a parallel to the line A B to the river, at D; the same operation being executed on the left, as it is indicated by the letters E F. This will give to the petitioner the extent of eighty-four arpents as expressed in the title purchased by him, and also all the space contained between his lines, which space cannot be determined until after a regular survey be made. The petitioner takes the liberty to assure you that in this manner of fixing limits to his property, he shall have a superficie not so considerable as he should have had in following what is expressed in the petition of Mathurin Bouvet, deceased. Your petitioner hopes that his demand not comprehending any augmentation, you will do it justice, inasmuch as he has no other views but that of attaining to have his property circumscribed in the most regular manner possible, and the least liable to difficulties which might accrue hereafter.

CHARLES GRATIOT.

St. Louis, *January* 5, 1801.

St. Louis of Illinois, *January* 8, 1801.

Having examined the contents of the petitioner's statement, and considering the just reasons which he alleges, in order to obtain that the land which he purchased at the juridical sale of the property of the late Mathurin Bouvet be surveyed conformably to the figurative plat which precedes his memorial; considering also that he does not contemplate any augmentation of land, and that the said concession is not prejudicial to any body, since it is situated in a place remote from any other establishments, I do grant to him what he solicits, without his being obliged to have the survey taken immediately; but as soon as any neighbor shall present himself in the said place, he shall cause it to be surveyed without any delay; and Don Antonio Soulard, surveyor general of this Upper Louisiana, shall take cognizance of this title for his intelligence and government in what concerns him, in order that the interested, after the survey is made, and being vested with the primitive title and with the copy of the juridical sale, may solicit the formal ratification of the title from the intendant general of these provinces of Louisiana.

CARLOS DEHAULT DELASSUS.

Registered by order of the lieutenant governor, pages 7, 8, and 9, in book No. 1 of the titles of concessions No. 4.

SOULARD.

St. Louis, *April* 10, 1803.

Truly translated. St. Louis, March 30, 1833.

JULIUS DE MUN.

No.	Name of original claimant.	Quantity, in arpents.	Nature and date of claim.	By whom granted.	By whom surveyed, date, and situation.
79	Mathurin Bouvet.	84 by 40	First concession, June 12, 1795; second concession, January 5, 1801.	Zenon Trudeau and Carlos Dehault Delasus.	Frémon Delauriere; February 17, 1806; recorded by Soulard 15th April, 1806; on Bay Charles.

Evidence with reference to minutes and records.

September 22, 1806.—The board met agreeably to adjournment. Present: The Hon. John B. C. Lucas, Clement B. Penrose, and James L. Donaldson, commissioners.

The same, (Charles Gratiot,) assignee of the same, (Mathurin Bouvet,) claiming 84 arpents situate on Baye de Charles, district of St. Charles, fronting on the Mississippi, beginning six arpents below the emptying of said bayou and ascending 84 arpents bordering said bay, by such width as may be found on said 84 arpents from the hills to said bay, the same being granted for the establishing a place of deposit for the salt manufactured at the saline of Bastion, and also for cultivation, produces a duly registered concession from Zenon Trudeau, dated June 12, 1795, and the public sale as aforesaid.

Francis M. Benoist, being duly sworn, says that the said Mathurin Bouvet begun the settling of said land about ten years ago; that he built houses on the same, had a garden and a large field fenced in, and actually inhabited and cultivated the same prior to and on the first day of October, 1800; that he was an ancient inhabitant, and a notary public under the Spanish government. The board confirm this claim, provided said tract does not exceed eight hundred arpents, reserving the right of ordering a new survey.—(See book No. 2, page 27.)

November 29, 1808.—Board met. Present: The Hon. John B. C. Lucas, Clement B. Penrose, and Frederick Bates, commissioners.

Charles Gratiot, assignee of Mathurin Bouvet, claiming 84 arpents front on the Mississippi, in depth from the river to the hills, produces to the board a supposed plat of said land, together with a petition of Charles Gratiot to Delassus, lieutenant governor, dated January 5, 1801, and an order by said lieutenant governor, dated January 8, 1801, (date appears to have been altered,) by which the said lieutenant governor directs that the measurement of the land shall take place according to the supposed plan.

Antoine Cheney, sworn, says that about fourteen or fifteen years ago he saw Mathurin Bouvet on a piece of land situate two or three arpents in the Bay Charles, on the Mississippi; that he inhabited and cultivated the same during three years from that time; that there were about three arpents under fence; that he had no family, but had hired hands; and that said Bouvet was burnt in the house on said land. Laid over for decision.—(See book No. 3, page 379.)

July 10, 1810.—Board met. Present: John B. C. Lucas, Clement B. Penrose, and Frederick Bates, commissioners.

Charles Gratiot, assignee of Mathurin Bouvet, claiming 84 arpents of land front on the Mississippi, and in depth from the river back to the hills, in the district of St. Charles.—(See book No. 2, page 27; book No. 3, page 379.) The board order that this claim be surveyed (provided it is not situated above the mouth of the river Jeffrion) conformably to the possession of Mathurin Bouvet.—(See book No. 4, page 427.)

January 9, 1812.—Board met. Present: John B. C. Lucas, Clement B. Penrose, and Frederick Bates, commissioners.

Charles Gratiot, assignee of Mathurin Bouvet.—(See book No. 2, page 27; No. 3, page 379; No. 4, page 427.) It is the opinion of a majority of the board that this claim ought not to be confirmed. Frederick Bates, commissioner, forbears giving an opinion.—(See book No. 5, page 556.)

March 13, 1833.—The board met pursuant to adjournment. Present: L. F. Linn and A. G. Harrison, commissioners.

Mathurin Bouvet, by Charles Gratiot's representatives, claiming 7,056 arpents of land situated on Bay de Charles, (see book C, pages 230 and 231; minutes No. 2, page 27; No. 3, page 279; No. 4, page 427; No. 5, page 556; Livre Terrien, No. 5, page 16,) produces a paper purporting to be a concession from Zenon Trudeau, dated June 12, 1795; also a concession from C. D. Delassus to Charles, dated January 8, 1801; a plat and certificate of survey, taken by C. F. Delauriere, deputy surveyor, dated February 17; received for record by Soulard April 15, 1806.

M. P. Le Duc, duly sworn, says that the signatures affixed to the aforesaid papers are in the respective handwriting of Zenon Trudeau, C. D. Delassus, Charles F. Delauriere, and A. Soulard.

Charles Frémon Delauriere, being duly sworn, says that, in the fall of 1805 and spring of 1806, he went on said land and saw an old field and garden, and the remains of old houses which had been burnt by the Indians, and in which old Bouvet was burnt to death. For survey witness states as follows: that the survey already produced is one of those included among the surveys mentioned in the above letter; that the survey was executed at the time it bears date; that there was great difficulty and danger in executing surveys; that he was twice repulsed by the Indians, and that the third time he went up he could not execute several of the surveys, being prevented by Indians of the Sac and Fox nations, although he and his companions were well armed; that surveyors were very scarce, and it was difficult to procure any one to take a survey; that there was not half the number of surveyors necessary to execute the surveys that were then to be made.—(See book No. 6, page 120.)

November 9, 1833.—The board met pursuant to adjournment. Present: L. F. Linn, A. G. Harrison, F. R. Conway, commissioners.

Mathurin Bouvet, claiming 84 by 40 arpents of land.—(See page 120 of this book.) The board remark that the alteration of the date of the concession consists in altering the two into one, but they think that nothing is to be inferred against this claim by said alteration, and they are unanimously of opinion that this claim ought to be confirmed to the said Mathurin Bouvet, or his legal representatives, according to Delassus's concession.—(See book No. 6, page 314.)

A. G. HARRISON.
L. F. LINN.
F. R. CONWAY.

No. 80.—Benito Vasquez, *claiming* 7,056 *arpents.*

Don Francisco Cruzat, lieutenant colonel of infantry by brevet, commander-in-chief, and lieutenant governor of the western part and district of Illinois:

Having examined the memorial presented by Don Benito Vasquez, lieutenant in one of the companies of the militia in this town, I have granted, and do grant to him in fee simple, for him, his heirs, and others who may represent his right, one league square of land, in order that he may establish the stock farm (baqueria) he solicits, in the place called La Salina à Catalan, on the south side of the river Maramec, (Barameca,) at four leagues from its mouth, on condition to establish and improve the same in one year from this date; and on the contrary, said land to be reunited to the royal domain; and it shall be liable to public charges and others which it may please his Majesty to impose.

Given in St. Louis of Illinois the 8th day of the month of September, 1784.

FRANCISCO CRUZAT.

Truly translated from Livre Terrein, No. 4, page 10. St. Louis, March 28, 1833.

JULIUS DE MUN.

No.	Name of original claimant.	Quantity, in arpents.	Nature and date of claim.	By whom granted.	By whom surveyed, date, and situation.
80	Benito Vasquez	7,056	Concession, September 8, 1784.	Francisco Cruzat.	On the south side of Maramec, four leagues from its mouth.

Evidence with reference to minutes and records.

August 29, 1806.—The board met agreeably to adjournment. Present: The Hon. John B. C. Lucas and Clement B. Penrose, commissioners.

Charles Gratiot, assignee of Pierre Chouteau, who was assignee of Benito Vasquez, claiming 7,056 arpents of land, situate on the river Maramec, district of St. Louis, produces a duly registered concession from Francis Cruzat for the same, dated September 8, 1784, and certified by Charles D. Delassus, March 9, 1803; the same granted for a vacherie, and on the condition of establishments within a year and a day. A survey of the same, dated the 15th, and certified February 15, 1806, together with a deed of transfer of said land, executed by Victoire, the wife of said Benito Vasquez, dated September 26, 1785, and passed before the commandant, Francis Cruzat; a ratification of said transfer by said Benito Vasquez, dated January 31, 1805; and also a deed of transfer from the said Peter Chouteau to claimant, dated May 4, 1804.

Louis Bouri, being duly sworn, saith that he has known the said tract of land established as a farm; that it was settled under Francis Cruzat by the said Benito Vasquez, who made a park on the same; that there is on said tract a salt spring, distant from said park about three arpents; that he went through said land at two different times; that the same was then actually inhabited and cultivated; saw a great number of cattle, but could not say to whom they did belong.

Hyachinthe St. Cyr, being also duly sworn, said that he was on said tract of land about 21 years ago; that the same was then actually inhabited and cultivated for the use of said Benito Vasquez, who then had salt works established at the aforesaid salt springs; and further, that it was prior to and on the 1st day of October, 1800, actually inhabited and cultivated for the said Peter Chouteau.—(See book No. 1, page 506.)

October 25, 1808.—Board met. Present: The Hon. Clement B. Penrose and Frederick Bates, commissioners.

Charles Gratiot, assignee of Peter Chouteau, assignee of Benito Vasquez, claiming 7,056 arpents of land situate on river Maramec, district of St. Louis.

Pierre Lajoy, sworn, says that claimant made an establishment on the land claimed about 12 years ago, when it was inhabited and cultivated for him, and that the same has been inhabited and cultivated for him ever since. Laid over for decision.—(See book No. 3, page 322.)

December 27, 1811.—Board met. Present: John B. C. Lucas, Clement B. Penrose, and Frederick Bates, commissioners.

Charles Gratiot, assignee of Pierre Chouteau, assignee of Benito Vasquez, claiming 7,056 arpents of land situate near river Maramec.—(See book No. 1, page 506; book No. 3, page 322.) It is the opinion of Clement B. Penrose, commissioner, that one league square ought to be confirmed. It is the opinion of John B. C. Lucas, commissioner, that this claim ought not to be confirmed Frederick Bates, commissioner, forbears giving an opinion.—(See book No. 5, page 544.)

March 13, 1833.—The board met pursuant to adjournment. Present: L. F. Linn, A. G. Harrison, commissioners.

Benito Vasques, by Charles Gratiot's representatives, claiming 7,056 arpents of land on the Maramec, (see book C, page 229; book F, page 192; minutes No. 1, page 506; No. 3, page 322; No. 5, page 544; Livre Terrein, No. 4, page 10,) produces a paper purporting to be a copy of a concession, certified by C. D. Delassus. Said certificate dated March 3, 1803; also said Livre Terrein, on which said grant bears date September 8, 1784.

Albert Tyson, duly sworn, says that in 1800 or 1801 he saw ground fenced in and a large quantity of stock; that they were then making salt, and, by appearances, had been making salt for some years prior to that time; and that the works continued in operation long afterwards, as said witness went occasionally on said place to procure salt.

Charles Frémon Delauriere, deputy surveyor, being duly sworn, says that in 1799, for the first time, he passed through said place, and saw fields, furnaces, people at work—in fact, it was a pretty large establishment; that he saw the same for several years in succession in operation, and that the first time he saw said place it had all the appearance of having been settled several years prior to that time.—(See book No. 6, page 121.)

November 9, 1833. The board met pursuant to adjournment. Present: L. F. Linn, A. G. Harrison, F. R. Conway, commissioners.

Benito Vasquez, claiming 7,056 arpents of land.—(See page 121 of this book.) The board are unanimously of opinion that this claim ought to be confirmed to the said Benito Vasquez, or to his legal representatives, according to the concession.—(See book No. 6, page 314.)

A. G. HARRISON.
L. F. LINN.
F. R. CONWAY.

No. 81.—John Hilderbrand, *claiming* 320 *arpents.*

We, Don Fernando de Leyba, captain in the regiment of Louisiana, commander-in-chief, and lieutenant governor, &c.:

On the demand of John Albrane, who has represented to us, in his petition dated 23d instant, that he had come over from the American side in order to fix his residence on this side, and become a subject of his Catholic Majesty, provided we would receive him as such; that he would wish to cultivate the soil and form a permanent establishment, and supplicates us to grant to him a title of concession for eight arpents of land in width by forty arpents in length, situated at about four leagues from the mouth of the river Maramec, on the right side of the said river in descending the stream, and at half a league from the banks of the said river. Through the said eight arpents in width passes a bayou or branch, which, after having run through the land of John Senders, crosses this said tract from one end to the other. The two extremities of the said land run north and south, and the two sides east and west; and having offered to take the oath of fidelity to his Catholic Majesty, and declared that he was of the Catholic Apostolic and Roman religion, therefore, after the said John Albrane had sworn to be faithful to the King and to his government, we have granted and do grant to him in fee simple, as well as to his heirs or assigns, the eight arpents of land in width by forty arpents in length, in all their extent of length and width, such and according as they are designated in his said petition, which we have returned to him on condition to establish himself thereon, and improve the said land in one year from this day under pain to have the same reunited to the King's domain, and regranted. And the said land to be liable to the public charges, and others which it may please his Majesty to impose, forbidding all persons, of whatever rank they may be, to trouble the said John Albrane in his present grant, and to cause him any damage, under pain of punishment.

Given in St. Louis, November 24, 1779.

FERNANDO DE LEYBA.

Truly translated from Livre Terrein, No. 3, page 31. St. Louis, April 3, 1833.

JULIUS DE MUN, *T. B. C.*

No.	Name of original claimant.	Quantity, in arpents.	Nature and date of claim.	By whom granted	By whom surveyed, date, and situation.
81	John Hilderbrand, alias Albrane.	320	Concession, Nov. 24, 1799.	Fernando de Leyba.	James Rankin, deputy surveyor, February 28, 1806; received for record February 29, 1806. On the Maramec.

Evidence with reference to minutes and records.

July 30, 1806.—The board met agreeably to adjournment ¹⁄₁₈₇. Present: The honorable John B. C. Lucas, Clement B. Penrose, and Jas L. Donaldson, commissioners.

The same, (Jacque Clamorgan,) assignee of Thomas Tyler, who was assignee of John Albrane, claiming eight by forty arpents of land, situate as aforesaid, produces a duly registered concession, signed and dated as aforesaid, together with a survey taken and certified as aforesaid, and two deeds of transfer, the one from said Albrane to Tyler, dated November 22, 1788, and another from said Tyler to claimant, dated September 17, 1791.

John Boli, being duly sworn, says that about 18 or 19 years ago, the time at which he arrived in this country, the aforesaid Thomas Tyler lived about one mile below the fork of a run on said land, and had then about 80 arpents of the same under fence; 40 of which were then planted in tobacco and corn, and then considered the largest farm in the country; that he remained on it about six or seven years; that about two years after this, the witness's arrival, the settlers being obliged on account of the Indians to fortify themselves, they chose the middle of the settlement; in consequence of which, the said Tyler moved up to the fork; that about four or five years afterwards he moved again, and settled himself at about two miles from the aforesaid place, down the creek towards the saline, made a field and garden, built a house; and that the said tracts have been actually cultivated to this day, either by the said Tyler for his use, or for claimant's use by his agents; and that the said last tract was actually inhabited and cultivated prior to and on the first day of October, 1800. The board confirm this claim to the said claimant, as per his concession.—(See book No. 1, page 438.)

November 29, 1808.—Board met. Present: John B. C. Lucas, Clement B. Penrose, and Frederick Bates, commissioners.

Jacque Clamorgan, assignee of Thomas Tyler, who was assignee of John Albrane, claiming eight by forty arpents of land situate near river Maramec, district of St. Louis.

Peter Chouteau, sworn, says that John Hilderbrand inhabited and cultivated the land claimed in 1774, and that he found him still inhabiting and cultivating the same in 1780, when deponent, by order of the lieutenant governor, went on the premises to warn said Hilderbrand to abandon the same on account of Indian depredations; this order was obeyed by Hilderbrand, as well as all the inhabitants of the settlement of the Maramec.

Charles Gratiot produces to the board a deed of conveyance from Jeremiah Connor, sheriff of St. Louis district, for the above land, to Edward Hempstead, dated June 11, 1808, but stating in the body of the same to have been sold by said sheriff to said Hempstead on the 7th day of July, same year; same deed afterwards acknowledged in open court on the 11th July, 1808; produces also an acknowledgment from Edward Hempstead and wife that said property was purchased by him for Charles Gratiot, and by said Hempstead and wife conveyed to said Gratiot, dated November 25, 1808.

It is acknowledged by Charles Gratiot that there is a saline on this claim which has been worked for many years. Laid over for decision.—(See book No. 3, page 377.)

December 27, 1811.—The board met. Present: John B. C. Lucas, Clement B. Penrose, and Frederick Bates, commissioners.

Jacque Clamorgan, assignee of Thomas Tyler, assignee of John Hilderbrand, claiming eight by forty arpents of land situate near Maramec.—(See book No. 1, page 488; book No. 3, page 377.) It is the opinion of a majority of the board that this claim ought to be confirmed. Frederick Bates, commissioner, forbears giving an opinion.—(See book No. 5, page 544.)

March 13, 1833. The board met pursuant to adjournment. Present: L. F. Linn and A. G. Harrison, commissioners.

John Hilderbrand, by the heirs of Charles Gratiot, claiming 320 arpents of land on the Maramec, (see book C, page 146; minutes, No 1, pages 438 and 439; No. 8, pages 377 and 378, for concession by Leyba, dated November 24, 1779; see Livre Terrein, No. 3, page 31,) produces a survey of the same, received for record by Soulard February 29, 1806.

Albert Tison, duly sworn, says: That from between 1795 and 1804 and 1805 he saw said land inhabited and cultivated, and that it has been inhabited and cultivated ever since. He further says that the signature to receipt of survey is in the handwriting of Antonio Soulard.

November 9, 1833.—The board met pursuant to adjournment. Present: L. F. Linn, A. G. Harrison, and F. R. Conway, commissioners.

John Hilderbrand, claiming 320 arpents of land.—(See page 121 of this book.) The board are unanimously of opinion that this claim ought to be confirmed to the said John Hilderbrand, or his legal representatives, according to the concession.—(See book No. 6, page 114.)

A. G. HARRISON.
L. F. LINN.
F. R. CONWAY.

No. 82.—CHARLES GRATIOT, *claiming five hundred arpents.*

To Don Charles Dehault Delassus, lieutenant colonel attached to the stationary regiment of Louisiana and lieutenant governor of the upper part of the same province:

SIR: Charles Gratriot, a merchant of this town, and one of its most ancient inhabitants, and father of a very numerous family, has the honor to represent to you that the land (situated a few miles from this town) which he owns by virtue of the titles which have been made out and delivered to him by his excellency the governor general of these provinces, Don Manuel Gayoso de Lemos, on account of their vicinity to this place, and of the indulgence which the petitioner has had for those who cut wood on the said land, being now in part destitute of timber; considering that the establishment of the saw-mill which he has constructed would become a loss to him if he failed to take measures to provide himself with timber, has the honor to supplicate you to have the goodness to grant to him, to the west of his concession, the quantity of 500 arpents of land in superficie, adjoining on three sides the land of John Ball, and to be taken on the vacant lands of his Majesty's domain. The petitioner presumes to flatter himself that the knowledge you have of the above-cited facts, and of the establishments he has made, shall be strong claims to obtain of your justice the same protection which you have always granted to industrious people, and to those who have formed useful establishments.

CHARLES GRATIOT.

ST. LOUIS, *January* 15, 1800.

ST. LOUIS OF ILLINOIS, *January* 18, 1800.

Having examined the foregoing statement, and considering that the petitioner has inhabited this country many years, and has a large family, I do grant to him and his heirs the land which he solicits, provided it is prejudicial to nobody; and the surveyor of this Upper Louisiana, Don Antonio Soulard, shall put the party interested in possession of the quantity of land which he asks in the place designated; and this being executed, he shall draw a plat of his survey, delivering the same to the party, with his certificate, to enable him to obtain the concession and title in form from the intendant general, to whom alone corresponds, by royal order, the distributing and granting all classes of lands of the royal domain.

CARLOS DEHAULT DELASSUS.

Don Antonio Soulard, surveyor general of the settlements of Upper Louisiana.

I do certify that a tract of land, of five hundred arpents in superficie, was measured, the lines run and bounded, in favor and in presence of Don Carlos Gratiot. Said measurement was taken with the perch of the city of Paris, of eighteen French feet lineal measure of the same city, conformably to the agrarian measure of this province; which land is situated on the road to Crevecœur, at about nine miles west from this town of St. Louis, and bounded on its four sides as follows: to the north by lands of James Mackay, to the south and west by vacant lands of the royal domain, and to the east in part by the same royal domain above cited, and by land of John Ball. Said survey and measurement were taken without regard to the variation of the needle, which is 7° 31′ east, as evinced by the foregoing figurative plat, on which are designated the dimensions, courses of the lines, and other boundaries, &c. The said survey was executed by virtue of the decree of the lieutenant governor of this Upper Louisiana, Don Carlos Dehault Delassus, under date of January 18, 1800, here annexed And in order that all the above be available according to law, I do give the present, with the foregoing figurative plat, drawn conformably to the survey executed by the deputy surveyor, Don Santiago Mackay, under date of November 28 of last year, who signed the minutes, of which I do certify.

ANTONIO SOULARD, *Surveyor General.*

ST. LOUIS OF ILLINOIS, *January* 5, 1803.

Truly translated from book A, page 541, and book C, page 229. St. Louis, April 6, 1833.

JULIUS DE MUN, *T. B. C.*

No.	Name of original claimant.	Quantity, in arpents.	Nature and date of claim.	By whom granted.	By whom surveyed, date, and situation.
82	Charles Gratiot..	500	Concession, Jan. 18, 1800.	Carlos Dehault Delassus.	James Mackay, deputy surveyor, Nov. 28, 1802; certified by Soulard Jan. 5, 1803; nine miles west of St. Louis.

Evidence with reference to minutes and records.

September 20, 1806.—The board met agreeably to adjournment. Present: The honorable John B. C. Lucas, Clement B. Penrose, James L. Donaldson, commissioners.

Charles Gratiot, claiming 500 arpents of land situate adjoining the land of one John Ball, district of St. Louis, produces a concession from Charles D. Delassus, dated January 18, 1800, and a survey of the same taken November 20, 1802, and certified January 5, 1803.

The board require further proof; whereupon Anthony Soulard, being duly sworn, says that he cannot say when the said concession was granted, but sees nothing that contradicts the date thereof.—(See book No. 2, page 18.)

October 26, 1808.—Board met. Present: The honorable Clement B. Penrose and Frederick Bates, commissioners.

Charles Gratiot, claiming 500 arpents of land adjoining the foregoing tract, conceded as an augmentation of wood for the use of claimant's saw-mill on an adjoining tract.

James Green, sworn, says that claimant built a saw-mill in the year 1800 on the river Des Peres. Laid over for decision.—(See book No. 3, page 327.)

June 26, 1810.—Board met. Present: John B. C. Lucas, Clement B. Penrose, and Frederick Bates, commissioners.

Charles Gratiot, claiming 500 arpents of land.—(See book No. 2, page 18; book No. 3, page 327.)

It is the opinion of the board that this claim ought not to be confirmed.—(See book No. 4, page 408.)

March 13, 1833.—The board met pursuant to adjournment. Present: L. F. Linn, A. G. Harrison, commissioners.

Charles Gratiot, by his heirs, claiming 500 arpents of land on river Des Peres, (see book A, page 541; minutes No. 2, page 18; No. 3, page 327; No. 4, page 408,) being a concession granted by Charles Dehault Delassus to said Gratiot, dated January 18, 1800. Survey taken November 28, 1802; certified by A. Soulard January 5, 1803.—(See book No. 6, page 123.)

November 9, 1833.—The board met pursuant to adjournment. Present: L. F. Linn, A. G. Harrison, F. R. Conway, commissioners.

Charles Gratiot, sr., claiming 500 arpents of land.—(See page 122 of this book.)

The board are unanimously of opinion that this claim ought to be confirmed to the said Charles Gratiot, or to his legal representatives, according to the concession.—(See book No. 6, page 314.)

A. G. HARRISON.
L. F. LINN.
F. R. CONWAY.

No. 83.—Peter Chouteau, sr., *claiming* 30,000 *arpents.*

To Don Charles Dehault Delassus, lieutenant colonel, attached to the stationary regiment of Louisiana, and lieutenant governor of the upper part of said province:

Peter Chouteau, lieutenant of militia, and commandant of the fort of Carondelet, in the nations of the Great and Little Osages, has the honor of representing to you that, being often stopped in his travels for the want of water in the Osage river, he has formed, in consequence, the project of a considerable establishment, to serve him as a place of deposit, at 60 miles below the said river, on the south side of the Missouri; at which place he supplicates you to have the goodness to grant to him, in full property, the quantity of thirty thousand arpents of land in superficie, in which quantity shall be comprised the river A la Mine, and also the salt springs which the petitioner has the intention of working and improving at such time when, less troubled by the Indian nations, he may give more extension to his industry. The great quantity of timber necessary for the fabrication of salt and to maintain a considerable stock farm, are the reasons which have determined the petitioner to ask for a quantity of land that may correspond to his views.

The petitioner, full of confidence in your justice, hopes that you will be pleased to take into consideration the confidence which it has pleased the government to place in him, as also the daily troubles he has taken to maintain good order among the Osage nations, and the multiplied sacrifices which he and his brother, Don Auguste Chouteau, proprietor of the exclusive trade with the above-mentioned nations of Indians, have made in all cases wherein it has been necessary to give to the government proofs of their zeal and attachment. These will be sufficient considerations to determine you to grant to him the favor which he claims of your justice and of the generosity of the government.

PIERRE CHOUTEAU.

St. Louis, *November* 19, 1799.

St. Louis of Illinois, *November* 20, 1799.

Having seen the statement in the foregoing memorial, and being convinced of the truth of what is alleged by the interested, who is worthy of the favors and benevolence of the government, in consideration of his services, and the zeal with which he has conducted himself in his employments, and his activity among the Indian nations of the Great and Little Osages; and adverting that the tract of land which he solicits is situated at too great a distance from these settlements to be prejudicial to any person; that his projects of improvement must have a result beneficial to all this country; and inasmuch as, for the manufacture of salt as well as for the establishment of a large stock farm, a considerable extent of land is needed, and a great quantity of timber and fuel is consumed; for these motives I have determined to grant to him the thirty thousand arpents of land in the place solicited by him, in order that he enjoys and disposes of them as a property to him lawfully belonging. And as it is situated at a great distance from this post, he will have it surveyed when convenient to his interests, unless some person presents himself with a concession, in the vicinity of this, who wishes to have it surveyed; in which case, the petitioner must have his concession surveyed also, without delay; and Don Antonio Soulard, surveyor general of this Upper Louisiana, shall take cognizance of this title for his intelligence and government in what concerns him, in order that after the survey is executed the interested party may ask the title in form from the intendancy.

CARLOS DEHAULT DELASSUS.

Registered by order of the lieutenant governor.—(Folios 13, 14, 15, of book No. 1 of titles of concessions.)

SOULARD.

Truly translated. St. Louis, December 8, 1832.

JULIUS DE MUN.

Brother: As thou hast, since a long time, fed our wives and our children; and that thou hast always been good for us; and that thou hast always assisted us with thy advices, we have listened with pleasure to thy words; therefore take thou, on the river A la Mine, the quantity of land which may suit thee, and anywhere thou pleaseth. This land is ours; we do give it to thee; and no one can take it from thee, neither to-day nor ever. Thou mayest remain there, and thy bones shall never be troubled. Thou askest a paper from us, and our marks. Here it is. If our children do trouble thine, they have but to show this same paper; and if some nation disturbs thee, we are ready to defend thee.

At the Fort of Grand Osages, this 19th March, 1792.

Cheveux Blank, his x mark.
Robfol, his x mark.
Clermont, chief of Great Osages, his x mark.
La Bombarde, his x mark.
Voihahan, his x mark.
Vent, chief of the Little Osages, his x mark.
Tonner Foux, his x mark.
Bel Oiseau, his x mark.
Plumme Blanche, his x mark.
Cahigue Voitaninguex, his x mark.
Petit Chef, his x mark.
Saldat du Chennefils, his x mark.

As witnesses:
St. Michel, his x mark.
Joseph Hebert, his x mark.
Andre Bisonette, his x mark.
Jacques Sonde.

Truly translated. December 8, 1832.

JULIUS DE MUN.

No.	Name of original claimant.	Quantity, in arpents.	Nature and date of claim.	By whom granted.	By whom surveyed, date, and situation.
83	Pierre Chouteau, sr..	30,000	Concession, Nov. 20, 1799.	Carlos Dehault Delassus.	South side of Missouri, on river A la Mine.

Evidence with reference to minutes and records.

December 27, 1811.—Board met. Present: John B. C. Lucas, Clement B. Penrose, and Frederick Bates, commissioners.

Pierre Chouteau, claiming 30,000 arpents of land situate on the Saline river, district of St. Louis, produces a concession from Charles D. Delassus, lieutenant governor, dated November 20, 1799; a paper purporting to be a gift from sundry Indians to claimant, dated March 19, 1792.

It is the opinion of a majority of the board that this claim ought not to be confirmed.

Frederick Bates, commissioner, forbears giving an opinion.—(See book No. 5, page 545.)

March 14, 1833.—The board met pursuant to adjournment. Present: L. F. Linn, A. G. Harrison, F. R. Conway, commissioners.

Pierre Chouteau, senior, claiming 30,000 arpents of land on the river A la Mine, (see book B, page 509; minutes No. 5, page 545,) produces a paper purporting to be an original concession from Carlos Dehault Delassus, dated November 20, 1799; also assent of the Osage Indians to Chouteau's taking as much land as he pleased on said spot, registered by Soulard.

Pascal L. Cerré, duly sworn, says that the signature to the concession is in the proper handwriting of C. D. Delassus, and the signature to the registering that of Soulard.—(See book No 6, page 123.)

November 9, 1833.—The board met pursuant to adjournment. Present: L. F. Linn, A. G. Harrison, F. R. Conway, commissioners.

Pierre Chouteau, claiming 30,000 arpents of land.—(See page 123 of this book.)

The board are unanimously of opinion that this claim ought to be confirmed to the said Pierre Chouteau, or his legal representatives, according to the concession.

The board have decided upon this claim without any reference to the assent of the Osage nation to Chouteau's taking any quantity of land he pleased on the river A la Mine.—(See book No. 6, page 314.)

A. G. HARRISON.
L. F. LINN.
F. R. CONWAY.

No. 84.—Joseph Brazeau, *claiming* 347 *arpents.*

To Don Charles Dehault Delassus, lieutenant colonel, attached to the stationary regiment of Louisiana, and lieutenant governor of the upper part of same province:

Joseph Brazeau, native of Illinois, and one of the most ancient inhabitants of this town, has the honor of representing to you that, having obtained of Don François Cruzat, lieutenant governor of this Upper Louisiana, (during the year 1786,) the concession of a piece of land of ten arpents in front, upon the depth comprised between the river and the main road, (chemin royal,) the said piece of land being situated in the small prairie adjoining this town, as it is proven by the original title of concession here annexed. Considering that the said quantity is insufficient for his means of cultivation, and is entirely destitute of timber, the petitioner hopes that, taking into consideration the length of time he has been in the country, you may be pleased to grant to him an augmentation of twelve arpents in front, to be taken from the main road, by such depth as will complete to him thirty arpents, to be taken from the primitive point of his first concession, said point being the edge of the river Mississippi, and comprising in the survey that shall take place his primitive concession, according to the tenor of his title of concession. As the said land has not any known proprietors, and that the establishment he (the petitioner) proposes himself to make shall be rather advantageous than prejudicial to the adjacent parts of this town, which are covered with shrubby places, serving to the wolves as places of refuge during the night, the petitioner hopes to obtain of your justice the favor which he solicits.

JOSEPH BRAZEAU.

St. Louis, *November* 19, 1799.

St. Louis of Illinois, *November* 19, 1799.

Considering that the petitioner is one of the most ancient inhabitants of this country, whose known conduct and personal merits are recommendable, and being satisfied to evidence as to the truth of his statement in his petition, the surveyor of this Upper Louisiana, Don Antonio Soulard, shall survey for him the quantity of land granted to him by the late Don Francisco Cruzat, who was lieutenant governor of these settlements, as is notorious, reference being had to the original concession here annexed; and he shall survey, also, the portion of land solicited for in augmentation; and this being executed, he shall draw a plat of survey, which he shall deliver to the party, with his certificate, to enable him to obtain the concession and title in form from the intendant general of these provinces, to whom alone corresponds, by royal order, the distributing and granting all classes of lands of the royal domain.

CARLOS DEHAULT DELASSUS.

Don Antonio Soulard, surveyor general of Upper Louisiana.

I do certify that a tract of land of three hundred and forty-seven arpents in superficie, was measured, the lines run and bounded, in favor and in presence of Don Joseph Brazeau; said measurement was done with the perch of the city of Paris, of 18 French feet in length, lineal measure of the same city, conformably to the agrarian measure of this province. The said land is situated at 25 or 30 arpents to the south of this town, bounded west by lands of the royal domain; east by the river Mississippi; north by lands of Don Antonio Soulard and Donna Maria Nicol, and south by lands of various inhabitants, which surveys and measurements were executed without any regard to the variation of the needle, which is of 7° 30′ east, as is evident by referring to the foregoing figurative plat, in which are noted the dimensions, the directions of the lines, and other boundaries, &c. Said survey was executed by virtue of the petitions and decrees of the lieutenant governor and sub-delegate of the royal fisc, Don Carlos Dehault Delassus, dated November 19, 1799, and June 17, 1800, as it is evident by referring to the juridical pieces here annexed. In testimony whereof, I do give the present with the foregoing figurative plat, drawn conformably to the survey executed by the deputy surveyor, Don Santiago Mackay, on the 28th of May, 1803, which I do certify.

ANTONIO SOULARD, *Surveyor General.*

St. Louis of Illinois, *August* 21, 1803.

Truly translated. St. Louis, December 5, 1832.

JULIUS DE MUN.

To the Lieutenant Governor:

Joseph Brazeau, an inhabitant of this town of St. Louis, in the best manner possible, in his right says that, wishing to establish a plantation, in order to improve the same and raise cattle thereon, he supplicates you to be willing to grant to him ten arpents of land, from north to south, on his Majesty's domain, and which are bounded to the east by the river Mississippi, to the west by the main road of the little province. Favor which he expects of your equitable justice.

BRAZEAU.

St. Louis, *November* 18, 1786.

Don Francisco Cruzat, lieutenant colonel of infantry by brevet, captain of grenadiers in the stationary regiment of Louisiana, commandant and lieutenant governor of the western part and district of Illinois.

Cognizance being taken of the memorial presented by Joseph Brazeau, inhabiting and residing in this town, under date of 18th November of this present year, I have granted and do grant in fee, to him, his heirs, or others who may represent his right, a tract of land of ten arpents, from north to south, and bounded on one side by the bank of the Mississippi river, and on the other by the main road which leads to the Prairie à Catalan, on condition to establish and improve the same in one year from this date; and, on the contrary, said land shall be reunited to the King's domain, and it shall be liable to public charges and others which it may please his Majesty to impose.

Given at St. Louis of Illinois, November 20, 1786.

FRANCISCO CRUZAT.

Truly translated. St. Louis, November 1[illegible], 1833.

JULIUS DE MUN.

No.	Name of original claimant.	Quantity, in arpents.	Nature and date of claim.	By whom granted.	By whom surveyed, date, and situation.
84	Joseph Brazeau.....	360	Concession, November 19, 1799.	Carlos Dehault Delassus.	James Mackay, deputy surveyor, May, 1803; certified by Soulard, August 21, 1803; 25 or 30 arpents south of St. Louis.

Evidence with reference to minutes and records.

July 19, 1806.—The board met agreeably to adjournment. Present: The Hon. John B. C. Lucas, Clement B. Penrose, and James L. Donaldson, commissioners.

The same, Joseph Brazeau, claiming 12 arpents front, joining his former concession, and granted him as a compensation, the same being of the depth of 30 arpents, beginning at the aforesaid tract granted him by Cruzat, produces a concession from Charles D. Delassus, dated November 19, 1799, and a survey of 347 arpents, forming the whole of the above tract claimed by him, and dated the 28th May, and certified the 21st of August, 1803. This claim being unsupported by actual inhabitation and cultivation, the board reject the same. They remark that they are satisfied that the aforesaid concession was granted at the time it bears date, but that the same interferes with a tract of land claimed by the inhabitants of the town of St. Louis as commons.—(See book No. 1, page 413.)

August 19, 1811.—Board met. Present: Clement B. Penrose and Frederick Bates, commissioners.

Joseph Brazeau, claiming 347 arpents of land.—(See book No. 1, page 413.) It is the opinion of the board that this claim ought not to be confirmed.—(See book No. 5, page 320.)

March 14, 1833.—The board met pursuant to adjournment. Present: L. F. Linn, A. G. Harrison, F. R. Conway, commissioners.

Joseph Brazeau, by his legal representatives, claiming 12 arpents front on the river Mississippi, running back 30 arpents, (see book B, page 416; minutes No. 1, page 413; No. 5, page 320,) produces a paper purporting to be an original concession from Carlos Dehault Delassus, dated November 19, 1799; also, a plat and certificate of survey, dated May 28, 1803.

Pascal L. Cerré, duly sworn, says that the signature to the concession is in the proper handwriting of Carlos D. Delassus, and the signature to the certificate of survey is in the proper handwriting of A. Soulard. He further states that Joseph Brazeau, to his knowledge, inhabited and cultivated the land embraced in the concession of 1799, which land so cultivated was the same as contained in the concession of 1786, and which inhabitation and cultivation has continued from 1799 to the present time by him or his legal representatives. He believes that the land so cultivated was the whole embraced in the concession of 1786.—(See book No. 6, page 123.)

November 11, 1833.—The board met pursuant to adjournment. Present: Lewis F. Linn, A. G. Harrison, F. R. Conway, commissioners.

Joseph Brazeau, claiming 360 arpents of land.—(See page 123 of this book.) The board are unanimously of opinion that this claim ought to be confirmed to the said Joseph Brazeau, or to his legal representatives, according to the concession.—(See book No. 6, page 315.)

A. G. HARRISON.
L. F. LINN.
F. R. CONWAY.

No. 85.—Newton Howell, *claiming* 350 *arpents*.

To Mr. Charles Dehault Delassus, lieutenant colonel, attached to the stationary regiment of Louisiana, and commander-in-chief of Upper Louisiana:

Newton Howell, Roman Catholic, has the honor to represent to you that he has, with the permission of the government, made choice of a piece of land, in order to make a farm, on the domain of his Majesty, and on the north side of the Missouri; therefore he supplicates you to have the goodness to grant to him, in the same place which he has chosen, the quantity of 350 arpents of land in superficie. The petitioner, having sufficient means to improve a farm, and no other views but to live as a peaceable and submissive cultivator of the soil, hopes to obtain the favor which he solicits of your justice.

NEWTON HOWELL

St. André, *May* 17, 1801.

Be it forwarded to the lieutenant governor, with information that the above statement is true, and that the petitioner deserves the favor which he solicits.

SANTIAGO MACKAY.

St. André, *May* 17, 1801.

St. Louis of Illinois, *May* 25, 1801.

In consequence of the information given by the commandant of the settlements of St. André, Don Santiago Mackay, I do grant to the petitioner the 350 arpents of land in superficie which he solicits, provided it shall not be prejudicial to anybody; and the surveyor, Don Antonio Soulard, shall put the party interested in possession of the above-mentioned quantity of land which he asks in the place designated; and, this being executed, he shall make out a plat of his survey, delivering the same to the said party, with his certificate, in order to enable him to obtain the concession and title in form from the intendant general, to whom alone corresponds, by royal order, the distributing and granting all classes of lands of the royal domain.

CARLOS DEHAULT DELASSUS.

Recorded, No. 36.

MACKAY.

Truly translated. St. Louis, April 9, 1833.

JULIUS DE MUN, *T. B. C.*

No.	Name of original claimant.	Quantity, in arpents.	Nature and date of claim.	By whom granted.	By whom surveyed, date, and situation.
85	Newton Howell .	350	Concession, May 25, 1801.	C. Dehault Delassus. .	Nathan Boone, deputy surveyor, August 23, 1823; on the Missouri, district of St. Charles.

Evidence with reference to minutes and records.

October 19, 1808.—Board met. Present: Hon. John B. C. Lucas, Clement B. Penrose, and Frederick Bates, commissioners.

Newton Howell, claiming 350 arpents of land below the mouth of Femme Osage river, district of St. Charles, produces to the board a notice to the recorder and a concession for the same from Don Carlos Dehault Delassus, lieutenant governor, to claimant, dated May 25, 1801. Claimant was not of age at the time the grant was given.

William Stewart, sworn, says that in 1804 he, witness, by permission from claimant, had a camp on the tract claimed, and made sugar; and that sugar has been made on the same by or for claimant ever since.

James Mackay, sworn, says that in the fall of 1803 he run a line between claimant and Arund Rulgers, and that he saw claimant with several other persons working on the place at the same time. Laid over for decision.—(See book No. 3, page 301.)

June 19, 1810.—Board met. Present: John B. C. Lucas, Clement B. Penrose, and Frederick Bates, commissioners.

Newton Howell, claiming 350 arpents of land.—(See book No. 3, page 301.) It is the opinion of the board that this claim ought not to be confirmed.—(See book No. 4, page 393.)

March 14, 1833.—The board met pursuant to adjournment. Present: L. F. Linn, A. G. Harrison, F. R. Conway, commissioners.

Newton Howell, claiming 350 arpents of land, (see book D, page 37; minutes No. 3, page 301; No. 4, page 393,) produces a paper purporting to be an original concession from Carlos Dehault Delassus, dated May 25, 1801; also a plat of survey, dated August 23, 1823, by Nathaniel Boone, deputy surveyor.

Pascal L. Cerré, duly sworn, says that the signature to the concession is in the proper handwriting of Carlos Dehault Delassus, and the signature at the margin is in the handwriting of James Mackay.

William Milburn, duly sworn, says that the signature to the plat of survey is in the proper handwriting of Nathaniel Boone, at the time deputy surveyor.—(See book No. 6, page 124.)

November 11, 1833.—The board met pursuant to adjournment. Present: L. F. Linn, A. G. Harrison, F. R. Conway, commissioners.

Newton Howell, claiming 350 arpents of land.—(See page 124 of this book.) The board are unanimously of opinion that this claim ought to be confirmed to the said Newton Howell, or to his legal representatives, according to the concession.—(See book No. 6, page 315.)

A. G. HARRISON.
L. F. LINN.
F. R. CONWAY.

No. 86.—Mackay Wherry, *claiming* 1,600 *arpents.*

To Don Charles Dehault Delassus, lieutenant colonel in the armies of his Catholic Majesty and lieutenant governor of Upper Louisiana:

Mackay Wherry, having for a long time inhabited this part of Illinois, has the honor very humbly to represent to you that he had formerly obtained of your predecessor, Don Zenon Trudeau, a small concession of four hundred arpents of land in superficie. Since that time, his family having much increased, and the number of his cattle especially having grown considerably larger, this small quantity of land is not now sufficient to maintain them. This being considered, he supplicates you, sir, to be pleased to grant to him and his heirs a concession of 1,600 arpents of land, in superficie, or thereabout, situated near the rivers Dardenne and the Mississippi, on the vacant lands of his Majesty, and which he will indicate when the survey shall be made. The petitioner presumes to expect of you this favor, which he believes he deserves on account of his conduct and devotedness to the Spanish government.

MACKAY WHERRY.

St. Louis, *April* 15, 1802.

St. Louis of Illinois, *April* 18, 1802.

Considering that the petitioner has been a long time settled in this country, and that his family is sufficiently numerous to obtain the quantity of land which he solicits, I do grant to him and his heirs the land which he solicits, provided it is not prejudicial to any one; and the surveyor, Don Antonio Soulard, shall put the party interested in possession of the quantity of land which he asks, in a vacant place of the royal domain; and this being executed, he shall make out a plat of his survey, delivering the same to the said party, with his certificate, to enable him to obtain the concession and title in form from the intendant general, to whom alone corresponds, by royal order, the distributing and granting all classes of lands of the royal domain.

CARLOS DEHAULT DELASSUS.

Truly translated. April 9, 1833.

JULIUS DE MUN.

No.	Name of original claimant.	Quantity, in arpents.	Nature and date of claim.	By whom granted.	By whom surveyed, date, and situation.
86	Mackay Wherry.	1, 600	Concession, April 18, 1802.	Carlos Dehault Delassus.	Nathan. Boone, deputy surveyor, May 15, 1826. On the Dardenne, district of St. Charles.

Evidence with reference to minutes and records.

November 18, 1808.—Board met. Present: The honorable John B. C. Lucas, Clement B. Penrose, and Frederick Bates, commissioners.

Mackay Wherry, claiming 1,600 arpents of land, unlocated, in the district of St. Charles, by virtue of a concession said to be lost, produces to the board a notice of claim, dated 24th June, 1808.

Pierre Probenché, sworn, says that about the spring or summer of 1801, when he, witness, resided with Charles D. Delassus, lieutenant governor, he saw a concession from said Delassus to Mackay Wherry, and had the same in his possession, for 1,600 arpents of land lying in the district of St. Charles, on the river Dardenne, or river Cuivre. Claimant at that time resided in this country with his family.

Antoine Soulard, sworn, says that about the year 1800 he had a concession in his hands for the purpose of making a survey, from Charles D. Delassus, lieutenant governor, to claimant, for 600 or 800 arpents; that he, witness, gave the said concession to some of the deputy surveyors, since when he has not seen it, nor does he know what has become of it. Laid over for decision.—(See book No. 3, page 356.)

July 9, 1810.—Board met. Present: John B. C. Lucas, Clement B. Penrose, and Frederick Bates, commissioners.

Mackay Wherry, claiming 1,600 arpents of land.—(See book No. 3, page 356.) It is the opinion of the board that this claim ought not to be confirmed.—(See book No. 4, page 420.)

March 14, 1833.—The board met pursuant to adjournment. Present: L. F. Linn, A. G. Harrison, F. R. Conway, commissioners.

Mackay Wherry, by his legal representatives, claiming 1,600 arpents of land, (see minutes No. 3, page 356; No. 4, page 420,) produces a paper purporting to be an original concession from Carlos Dehault Delassus, dated 18th of April, 1802; also a plat of survey, dated 15th May, 1826, by Nathaniel Boone.

Pascal L. Cerré, duly sworn, says that the petition is in the handwriting of Provenchère, the concession in the handwriting of Antoine Soulard, and the signature to said concession is in the handwriting of Carlos Dehault Delassus.

William Milburn, duly sworn, says that the signature to the plat of survey is in the proper handwriting of Nathaniel Boone, and the signature to the certificate is in the deponent's own handwriting.—(See book No. 6, page 124.)

November 11, 1833.—The board met pursuant to adjournment. Present: L. F. Linn, A. G. Harrison, F. R. Conway, commissioners.

Mackay Wherry, claiming 1,600 arpents of land.—(See page 124 of this book.) The board are unanimously of opinion that this claim ought to be confirmed to the said Mackay Wherry, or to his legal representatives, according to the concession.—(See book No. 6, page 316.)

A. G. HARRISON.
L. F. LINN.
F. R. CONWAY.

No. 87.—Louis Lorimier, *claiming* 30,000 *arpents.*

To Don Charles Dehault Delassus, lieutenant colonel in the armies of his Catholic Majesty, and lieutenant governor of Upper Louisiana:

Louis Lorimier, captain of militia, and commandant of the post and district of Cape Girardeau of Illinois, has the honor very respectfully to represent to you, that since he has become a subject of his

Catholic Majesty, he has been employed in superintending the Indian nations living in this vicinity, and in maintaining peace and order, as well among themselves as between them and the whites; in consequence of which he has often been called near the lieutenant governors and commandants of this Upper Louisiana, to serve not only as interpreter between them and the chiefs of the different nations, but also as mediator and conciliator near those chiefs on various critical occasions, on which the petitioner has made use, with success, of the influence and ascendency which he has acquired among those nations, in order to bring them, without violence, to determinations advantageous to the general welfare, and to the tranquillity of the country. The cares and troubles which the petitioner experienced in fulfilling the various missions with which he was charged; the frequent voyages he was obliged to make to the injury of his private interest, which suffered during his absence, and even at the peril of his health and life; the numerous and importunate visits of those same Indians, to whom he was obliged to furnish lodgings, provisions, ammunition, and to which he has often added considerable presents; a thousand other inconveniences and expenses, which it would take too long to enumerate, have remained to this day without reward or indemnification from the govenment. And although at all times his conduct has procured to him the approbation of his superiors, and even that of the government of the United States, these honorable attestations are, as yet, the only fruits he has reaped for his services during upwards of fifteen years.

Founded upon such strong pretensions the petitioner applies now to your lordship and solicits, with confidence, a reward or indemnification adequate to the importance and extent of his services, and to the great sacrifices which they obliged him to make, praying you to grant to him, in full property, as well for himself as for his heirs or assigns, a tract of land of 30,000 arpents in superficie on his Majesty's domain, with the liberty to have it surveyed when he will find it convenient, in such place or places which he may choose, without prejudice to anybody.

The petitioner hopes to obtain this favor of your justice and of the generosity of this government; and, full of gratitude for the same, he will pray Heaven for the conservation of your days.

L. LORIMIER.

CAPE GIRARDEAU, *December* 18, 1799.

ST. LOUIS OF ILLINOIS, *January* 15, 1800.

I, Don Carlos Dehault Delassus, lieutenant colonel in the royal armies, lieutenant governor of Upper Louisiana, and sub-delegate of the intendancy general of these provinces, having examined the statement made in the foregoing memorial, and being convinced of the truth of all therein alleged by Captain Louis Lorimier, commandant of Cape Girardeau, who is worthy of the favors and beneficence of the government in consideration of his very important services, and of the zeal, prudence, activity, and great disinterestedness with which he has used his known influence over the Indian nations of Delawares, Shawnees, &c., in order to adjust their differences and for the maintenance of peace and good order, which have occasioned to the petitioner great expenses and inconveniences, and from which have resulted great advantages to the whole country; for these motives I have come to the determination to grant to the said Don Louis Lorimier, for him and his successors, the quantity demanded of 30,000 arpents of land in superficie, in the place or places and in the manner he desires, in order that he may enjoy and dispose of this concession as of a property to him belonging, which he will have surveyed when convenient to his interest. And Don Antonio Soulard, surveyor of this Upper Louisiana, shall take cognizance of this title for his intelligence and government in what concerns him; and, at the request of the (party) interested, he shall put him in possession of the aforementioned quantity of land, delivering to him the corresponding certificate or certificates of survey; after which said party shall have to solicit the title in form from the intendancy general of these provinces.

CARLOS DEHAULT DELASSUS.

Recorded by order of the lieutenant governor, book No. 2, folios 39, 40, and 41, No. 28.

SOULARD.

Truly translated. St. Louis, June 3, 1833.

JULIUS DE MUN.

ST. LOUIS OF ILLINOIS, *August* 2, 1803.

Under date of 3d of last May his lordship, Don Manuel de Salcedo, governor of these provinces, tells me what follows, and which I translate: "The merit of Don Louis Lorimier is of the most distinguished character and is worthy of the greatest notice of the government, which at all times has shown it to him, soliciting even for him the favor of the sovereign in order to obtain the grade of captain, which your lordship asks in his favor; but I do not know why the rumors of war have put all kinds of business to a stand, which is the more to be lamented as this misfortune falls upon a person who, by his good services, deserves with justice the price and reward which are his due under so many heads. Now, when we are on the point of delivering up the province, we cannot do else but recommend him to the French government, and this we shall do efficaciously. It is all I can say to your lordship in answer to your official note No. 174, &c.," which I transcribe for your knowledge.

May God have you in his holy keeping.

CHARLES DEHAULT DELASSUS.

Don LOUIS LORIMIER, *Commandant of Cape Girardeau.*

Truly translated from book E, page 24. St. Louis, November 12, 1833.

JULIUS DE MUN.

No.	Name of original claimant.	Quantity, in arpents.	Nature and date of claim.	By whom granted.	By whom surveyed, date, and situation.
87	Louis Lorimier.	30, 000	Concession, January 15, 1800.	Carl. Dehault Delassus.	Unlocated.

Evidence with reference to minutes and records.

May 25, 1809.—Board met. Present: John B. C. Lucas, Clement B. Penrose, and Frederick Bates, commissioners.

Louis Lorimier, claiming 30,000 arpents of land, produces to the board a concession for the same from Don Carlos Dehault Delassus, lieutenant governor, dated 15th January, 1800; also an official letter from said lieutenant governor to claimant, dated 2d August, 1803. Laid over for decision.—(See book No. 4, page 74.)

March 22, 1810.—Board met. Present: John B. C. Lucas, Clement B. Penrose, and Frederick Bates, commissioners.

Louis Lorimier, claiming 30,000 arpents of land.—(See book No. 4, page 74.) It is the opinion of the board that this claim ought not to be confirmed.—(See book No. 4, page 302.)

March 16, 1833.—The board met pursuant to adjournment. Present: L. F. Linn, A. G. Harrison, and F. R. Conway, commissioners.

Louis Lorimier, sr., by his legal representatives, claiming 30,000 arpents of land for services.—(See book E, pages 23 and 24; minutes, No. 4, page 302.) Produces a paper purporting to be an original concession from Don Carlos Dehault Delassus, dated January 15, 1800.

Pierre Menard, duly sworn, says that the signature to petition is the handwriting of L. Lorimier, sr., that the signature to the concession is the handwriting of Carlos Dehault Delassus, and the signature to the registering is in the handwriting of Antoine Soulard. Lecture being made of the aforesaid petition, deponent states that it is a true statement of the petitioner's services; that he was well acquainted with said Lorimier since the year 1788 until his death, which happened, he believes, in 1815; that, at the solicitation of the Spanish government, said Lorimier brought a number of Shawnee and Delaware Indians to settle in the vicinity of Cape Girardeau, and they served as a guard to the country against the depredations committed by the Osages; that the Shawnees and Delawares had six villages between Cape Girardeau and Cape St. Come.—(See book No. 6, page 127.)

November 11, 1833.—The board met pursuant to adjournment. Present: L. F. Linn, A. G. Harrison, and F. R. Conway, commissioners.

Louis Lorimier, claiming 30,000 arpents of land.—(See page 127 of this book.) By order of the board, the letter produced to the former board, and which is of record in the recorder's office, is to be translated, and attached to the concession. The board are unanimously of opinion that this claim ought to be confirmed to the said Louis Lorimier, or to his legal representatives, according to the concession.—(See book No. 6, page 316.)

A. G. HARRISON.
L. F. LINN.
F. R. CONWAY.

No. 88.—François Berthiaume, *claiming* 420 *arpents.*

To Don Charles Dehault Delassus, lieutenant colonel attached to the stationary regiment of Louisiana, and lieutenant governor of Upper Louisiana.

The undersigned, a Roman Catholic, and the father of four children, has the honor to represent to you that being, since a number of years, a resident of this colony, and having followed farming for a long time, he would wish to partake of the generosity of this government, and secure to himself and his children a landed property. In this intention the petitioner applies now to your lordship, hoping that you will be pleased to grant to him, in the district of Cape Girardeau, a quantity of land proportional to the number of persons composing his family, which is as follows: himself, his wife, four children, and one slave. Favor which the petitioner presumes to expect of your justice, and for which he shall not cease to pray heaven for your conservation.

FRANÇOIS BERTHIAUME.

Cape Girardeau, *September* 11, 1799.

We, captain commandant of Cape Girardeau, do inform the lieutenant governor that the statement of the petitioner is true; that the land he asks belongs to his Majesty's domain, and that the concession of the same shall not be prejudicial to anybody; and that the petitioner, having the qualifications required by the law, deserves the favor which he solicits.

L. LORIMIER.

Cape Girardeau, *September* 13, 1799.

St. Louis of Illinois, *December* 28, 1799.

In consequence of the information here above from the commandant of Cape Girardeau, Don Louis Lorimier, the surveyor, Don Antonio Soulard, shall put the party interested in possession of 420 arpents of land in superficie in the place where he asks the same, this quantity being proportionate to the number composing his family conformably to the regulations of the governor general of this province. And after this is executed, the said party shall have to solicit the title of concession in due form from the intendant general of these provinces, to whom alone corresponds, by royal order, the granting of lands and town lots.

CARLOS DEHAULT DELASSUS.

Truly translated. St. Louis, April 9, 1833.

JULIUS DE MUN.

No.	Name of original claimant.	Quantity, in arpents.	Nature and date of claim.	By whom granted.	By whom surveyed, date, and situation.
88	François Berthiaume.	420	Concession, Dec. 28, 1799	Carlos Dehault Delassus.	Cape Girardeau.

Evidence with reference to minutes and records.

May 25, 1809.—Board met. Present: John B. C. Lucas, Clement B. Penrose, and Frederick Bates, commissioners.

Louis Lorimier, assignee of François Berthiaume, claiming 420 arpents of land, produces to the board a concession from Don Carlos Dehault Delassus, lieutenant governor, to the said Berthiaume, for the same, dated December 28, 1799, and a deed of transfer from Berthiaume to claimant, dated December 5, 1804. Laid over for decision.—(See book No. 4, page 74.)

March 22, 1810.—Board met. Present: John B. C. Lucas, Clement B. Penrose, and Frederick Bates, commissioners.

Louis Lorimier, assignee of François Berthiaume, claiming 420 arpents of land.—(See book No. 4, page 74.) It is the opinion of the board that this claim ought not to be confirmed.—(See book No. 4, page 302.)

March 16, 1833.—The board met pursuant to adjournment. Present: L. F. Linn, A. G. Harrison, and F. R. Conway, commissioners.

François Berthiaume, by his legal representatives, claiming 420 arpents of land, (see book E, pages 24 and 25; No. 4, pages 74 and 302,) produces a paper purporting to be an original concession from Carlos Dehault Delassus, dated December 28, 1799.

Pierre Ménard, duly sworn, says that the signature to the concession is in the proper handwriting of Carlos Dehault Delassus.—(See book No. 6, page 128.)

November 11, 1833.—The board met pursuant to adjournment. Present: L. F. Linn, A. G. Harrison, F. R. Conway, commissioners.

François Berthiaume claiming 420 arpents of land.—(See page 128 of this book.) The board are unanimously of opinion that this claim ought to be confirmed to the said François Berthiaume, or his legal representatives, according to the concession.—(See book No. 6, page 316.)

A. G. HARRISON.
L. F. LINN.
F. R. CONWAY.

No. 89.—B. Cousin, *claiming* 10,000 *arpents.*

To Don Charles Dehault Delassus, lieutenant colonel in the armies of his Catholic Majesty, lieutenant governor of Upper Louisiana, &c.:

Bartholomew Cousin humbly supplicates, and has the honor of representing to you that, since he has been residing at Cape Girardeau, besides the functions of interpreter and public scrivener, which he has constantly exercised, and on account of which you have been pleased to grant to him a gratification in lands, he has morever been employed by the commandant of said post in sundry other public and extraordinary services, which are in no manner whatsoever connected with the functions hereafter cited, such as taking the annual census and various missions and express voyages, as well in the interior of the settlement as in the adjoining districts, and other public services, which it would be too long to enumerate, and which are mostly known by your excellency. These said services, besides the loss of time, have occasioned to the petitioner inconveniences and expenses for which he has not, as yet, received any indemnification. For these reasons, he is induced now, sir, to present himself before you, hoping that you will be pleased to grant to him, in full property, as well for himself as for his heirs or assigns, under the title of reward and compensation for the services and expenses above mentioned, the quantity of ten thousand arpents of land in superficie, to be taken off such parts of the domain which the petitioner will choose upon the lands to him awarded and reserved by your decree, dated March 5, 1800, inserted below his petition under date of February 27 of the same year. The petitioner, full of gratitude for this favor, shall never cease to pray for the preservation of your days.

B. COUSIN.

Cape Girardeau, *December* 15, 1802.

Cape Girardeau, *December* 17, 1802.

Being convinced, in consequence of the verbal declaration of Don Louis Lorimer, commandant of this post, and also by my own experience, that the foregoing statement of Don Bartholomé Cousin is true, and considering the public advantages which have resulted from his services, as also the expenses and the many inconveniences which said services have occasioned to him, paying due attention also to the merit, activity, fidelity, and good qualities of the petitioner, I have concluded to concede and grant to him the quantity demanded of ten thousand arpents of land in superficie in the places and according to the terms expressed in his petition, in order that he shall enjoy and dispose of this concession, as being his lawful property. And the surveyor general of this Upper Louisiana, Don Antonio Soulard, shall put him in possession of the same, and shall deliver to him the corresponding certificate or certificates of survey, in order to serve to him to obtain the title of concession in form from the competent authority.

CARLOS DEHAULT DELASSUS.

Truly translated. St. Louis, May 29, 1833.

JULIUS DE MUN.

No.	Name of original claimant.	Quantity, arpents.	Nature and date of claim.	By whom granted.	By whom surveyed, date, and situation.
89	Bartholomew Cousin . .	10,000	Concession, December 17, 1802.	Carlos Dehault Delassus.	

Evidence with reference to minutes and records.

May 25, 1809.—Board met. Present: John B. C. Lucas, Clement B. Penrose, and Frederick Bates, commissioners.

Bartholomew Cousin, claiming 10,000 arpents of land, produces to the board a concession from Don Carlos Dehault Delassus, lieutenant governor, dated November 17, 1802. Laid over for decision.—(See book No. 4, page 70.)

March 13, 1810.—Board met. Present: John B. C. Lucas, Clement B. Penrose, and Frederick Bates, commissioners.

Bartholomew Cousin, claiming 10,000 arpents of land, produces to the board a pre-emption right for 50,000 arpents, granted by Charles D. Delassus, lieutenant governor, dated March 5, 1800; said land to be paid for in services or otherwise. Also a concession from Don Carlos D. Delassus, lieutenant governor, dated December 17, 1802, for 10,000 arpents as compensation for services rendered, being part of the above 50,000 arpents.—(See book No. 4, page 70.) It is the opinion of the board that this claim ought not to be confirmed.—(See book No. 4, page 295.)

March 16, 1833.—The board met pursuant to adjournment. Present: L. F. Linn, A. G. Harrison, F. R. Conway, commissioners.

Bartholomew Cousin, by his legal representatives, claiming 10,000 arpents of land for services.—(See book E, page 21; No. 4, pages 70 and 295.)

Pierre Ménard, duly sworn, says that he knew Cousin; that he was acting as secretary to Commandant Lorimier; that said Cousin was a man of great talents, who rendered important services to the government, and was held in great consideration by said government.—(See book No. 6, page 129.)

November 11, 1833.—The board met pursuant to adjournment. Present: L. F. Linn, A. G. Harrison, and F. R. Conway, commissioners.

Bartholomew Cousin, claiming 10,000 arpents of land.—(See page 129 of this book.) The board are unanimously of opinion that this claim ought to be confirmed to the said Bartholomew Cousin, or his legal representatives, according to the concession.—(See book No. 6, page 316.)

A. G. HARRISON.
L. F. LINN.
F. R. CONWAY.

No. 90.—Bartholomew Cousin, *claiming* 8,000 *arpents.*

To Don Charles Dehault Delassus, lieutenant colonel in the armies of his Catholic Majesty, attached to the stationary regiment of Louisiana, lieutenant governor of Upper Louisiana, &c.:

Bartholomew Cousin, inhabitant of Cape Girardeau of Illinois, has the honor to represent to you that in the year 1799 your excellency was pleased to grant to him a concession of land in the said district as a reward, or in the way of salary, for his services in the capacity of interpreter and public scrivener until the 15th October of the aforesaid year. Encouraged by the justice and beneficence of this government, and in the hope of assuring to himself an honorable living in serving the same, the petitioner has always continued since then to fulfil the same functions, which have become every day more laborious and more indispensable on account of the rapid increase of the population of this settlement. And as he has not received, since the 15th of October, 1799, any gratification for his services up to this day, he hopes that the reasons which have induced you to do justice to his first demand will have with you, in the present circumstance, a new degree of force and justice. In this confidence the petitioner applies to you, sir, praying that you will be pleased to grant to him, on the domain of his Majesty, a concession of 8,000 arpents of land in superficie as a reward, and in way of salary, for his services aforesaid, and to order that this quantity be measured for him in such place or places, and in the manner most convenient to him, namely, on the lands formerly occupied by Messrs. Benjamin Rose and M. Williams & Co., at Tewapity and Cape à la Cruche, and since a long time abandoned and reunited to the domain.

The petitioner demands also to have allowed to him in the survey three-twentieths on the length of the lines, to compensate for the roads, (les eaux) the creeks and ponds, barren lands, and the loss in chaining.

Full of gratitude for this favor, the petitioner shall never cease to pray for your conservation.

BART. COUSIN.

Cape Girardeau, *March* 22, 1803.

St. Louis of Illinois, *March* 31, 1803.

In consequence of the foregoing demand of Don Bartholomew Cousin, inhabitant of Cape Girardeau, and in consideration of the services which the petitioner has rendered in continuing to employ himself with much zeal in the discharge of the duties of interpreter of the English language since the 15th of October, 1799, to this day, as also in the affairs requiring a correspondence with the civil officers on the side of the United States of America, and in all the solicitations, demands, and other requests in right of justice, from the inhabitants of said Cape Girardeau, of whom the greatest part are Americans, in which laborious work he has been employed by Don Lowis Lorimier, commandant of the aforesaid settlement, the whole of which being evidently and notoriously obvious to me, and the known merit and services of the petitioner being also supported by the said Don Lowis Lorimier, in his official letters, numbered 39, 51, and 52, dated March 17 and December 11 of last year, and January 20, of the present year, I have determined to grant to him the favor which he solicits, in the way of compensation for the aforesaid services which he faithfully rendered, with the greatest disinterestedness and without interruption, abandoning his private business, particularly since he has been proposed (to the general government) as interpreter for said district, to which proposal I have not as yet received any answer from the governor general, to whom I have forwarded the same, under date of May 16, 1802. Therefore the surveyor of this Upper Louisiana, Don Antonio Soulard, shall put him (the petitioner) in possession of the 8,000 arpents of land in superficie which he solicits, with the allowance stated, and in the places designated in his petition or certificate or certificates shall be remitted to him, in order that they serve to him to obtain the title of concession in form from the intendancy general of these provinces, to which belongs the right of making such distribution.

CARLOS DEHAULT DELASSUS.

Registered, at the request of the proprietor, in book No. 2, pages 41, 42, and 43, No. 29.

SOULARD.

Truly translated. St. Louis, May 30, 1833.

JULIUS DE MUN.

No.	Name of original claimant.	Quantity, in arpents.	Nature and date of claim.	By whom granted.	By whom surveyed, date, and situation.
90	Bartholomew Cousin.	8,000, with an allowance of $\frac{3}{20}$.	Concession, March 31, 1803.	Carlos Dehault Delassus.	Antoine Soulard, February 27, 1806. Three different tracts, district of Cape Girardeau.

Evidence with reference to minutes and records.

May 25, 1809.—The board met. Present: John B. C. Lucas, Clement B. Penrose, and Frederick Bates, commissioners.

Bartholomew Cousin, claiming 8,000 arpents of land, with allowance of three-twentieths for roads, &c., produces to the board a concession from Don Carlos Dehault Delassus, lieutenant governor, for the same, dated March 31, 1803; a plat of survey of 1,000 arpents, situate on the river Mississippi and Cape La Cruche creek, district of Cape Girardeau, dated March 5, 1800, and certified February 27, 1806; a plat of survey of 1,113 arpents 39 perches, situated on the Mississippi, district aforesaid, dated March 5, 1800, countersigned Antoine Soulard, surveyor general of Louisiana; a plat of survey of 4,700 arpents of an island in the Mississippi, district aforesaid, dated March 5, 1800, and certified February 27, 1806; a plat of survey of 3,350 arpents, situate on the forks of White Water creek, district aforesaid, certified February 26, 1806, by Antoine Soulard, surveyor general of the Territory of Louisiana; a plat of survey of 1,082 arpents 41 perches, claimed partly as assignee of Baptiste Godair, to wit: for 175 arpents, situate on the Big Swamp, district aforesaid, certified February 27, 1806, by Antoine Soulard, surveyor general; a deed of transfer from John Baptiste Godair for said 175 arpents, dated July 28, 1804. The grant in this claim stated to have been given as a compensation for services rendered by claimant as interpreter and public writer, for which he is said never to have received any other compensation. Produces also to the board a petition from William Smith to the commandant of Cape Girardeau, for the sale of certain property left by Benjamin Rose, in August, 1799, together with the order of said commandant for the sale thereof, dated May 7, 1802; a paper signed William Smith and Edward Hogan, dated October 16, 1802, purporting to be a valuation and arbitration of labor done by Stephen Quimby on said survey; also Stephen Quimby's receipt for the amount of the award; also a paper purporting to be the conditions by which a certain Thomas Welburn rented premises of B. Cousin; and an order from Louis Lorimier to prevent Daniel Sexton from trespassing on the premises, dated September 26, 1804; a petition of B. Cousin, and a decree of Don Carlos Dehault Delassus, lieutenant governor, for annulling the concession and warrant of survey of Benjamin Rose and Morris Williams, dated December 12, 1803.

The following acknowledgment was made before Frederick Bates, commissioner at Cape Girardeau, June 4, 1808: B. Cousin acknowledges that he surveyed this tract for B. Rose, April 12, 1799, by decree of Zenon Trudeau, lieutenant governor. Laid over for decision.—(See book No. 4, pages 68 and 69.)

November 26, 1810.—Board met. Present: John B. C. Lucas, Clement B. Penrose, and Frederick Bates, commissioners.

Bartholomew Cousin, claiming 8,000 arpents of land.—(See book No. 4, page 68; see also James Brady's claim, assignee of Benjamin Rose, book No. 4, pages 69, 79, and 84.)

It is the opinion of the board that this claim ought not to be confirmed.—(See book No. 5, page 14.)

March 16, 1833.—Board met pursuant to adjournment. Present: L. F. Linn, A. G. Harrison, and F. R. Conway, commissioners.

Bartholomew Cousin, by his legal representatives, claiming 8,000 arpents of land, (see book B, pages 219, 317, 318, and 319; minutes, No. 4, page 68; No. 5, page 14,) produces a paper purporting to be an original concession from Carlos Dehault Delassus, dated March 31, 1803; also three plats of surveys.

Pierre Ménard, duly sworn, says that the signature to the concession is in the proper handwriting of Carlos Dehault Delassus, to the surveys the handwriting of Soulard, and the signature to the petition in the handwriting of B. Cousin.—(See book No. 6, page 129.)

November 11, 1833.—The board met pursuant to adjournment. Present: L. F. Linn, A. G. Harrison, and F. R. Conway, commissioners.

Bartholomew Cousin, claiming 8,000 arpents of land.—(See page 129 of this book.)

The board are unanimously of opinion that this claim ought to be confirmed to the said Bartholomew Cousin, or to his legal representatives, according to the concession.—(See book No. 6, page 216.)

Conflicting claim.

Said to interfere with James Brady's claim of two hundred and forty arpents.

A. G. HARRISON.
L. F. LINN.
F. R. CONWAY.

No. 91.—Louis Reed, *claiming* 240 *arpents.*

We, Don Fernando de Leyba, captain in the regiment of infantry of Louisiana, commander-in-chief and lieutenant governor of the western part of Illinois.

In consequence of the demand to us made by Louis Ride, in his petition of this day, representing that he has no land to cultivate, and is reduced, with a numerous family, to the impossibility of sowing any grain, the land he had having fallen in share to his children; and there being a prairie at about one and a half league to the north of this village which has never been cultivated nor conceded to anybody, he supplicates you, sir, to be pleased to grant to him, in the said prairie, six arpents of land in width by the ordinary depth of forty arpents; which six arpents of land, in front, are bounded on the east by the river called River à Gingras; on the other end, west, by the King's domain; on the south side, towards the village of St. Louis, by a branch coming down from the hills and emptying into the said River à Gingras, said branch being the boundary between the land of Mr. Belestre, in Prairie Lajoie, and the six arpents herein demanded, and designating the said south side of the same; and on the other side, north, by what remains of the prairie or the King's domain. The petitioner intends, sir, if you have the goodness to grant his demand, to settle himself thereon, raise cattle, and cultivate the soil, to which he will apply himself with all his might.

[*One cross for said Ride's mark.*]

St. Louis, *May* 12, 1779.

Therefore, wishing to favor the petitioner in his establishment, and give him the means of making a plantation which cannot be but advantageous to the public good, we have granted and do grant to him, in fee-simple, for him, his heirs or assigns, the six arpents of land by him demanded in his petition, by the ordinary depth of forty arpents, such as it is described and bounded in his petition, on condition to settle and improve the same in one year and one day, and that the said land shall be liable to public charges and others which it may please his Majesty to impose.

Given in St. Louis, May 12, 1779.

FERNANDO DE LEYBA.

Truly translated from the Spanish record of concessions, book No. 3, page 25. St. Louis, August 12, 1833.

JULIUS DE MUN.

No.	Name of original claimant.	Quantity, in arpents.	Nature and date of claim.	By whom granted.	By whom surveyed, date, and situation.
91	Louis Reed, *alias* Ride.	240	Concession, May 12, 1797.	F. de Leyba ..	On river Gingras.

Evidence with reference to minutes and records.

March 18, 1833.—The board met pursuant to adjournment. Present: L. F. Linn, A. G. Harrison, and F. R. Conway, commissioners.

Louis Reed, by his legal representatives, claiming six arpents of land in front by forty in depth situate on White Ox prairie.—(For concession by Leyba, dated May 12, 1779, see Livre Terrein, No. 3, page 25; record book F, page 187.)

Baptiste Riviere, *alias* Bacanné, being duly sworn, says that he is eighty-six years of age; that he was the first who ever ploughed the land above mentioned, having been hired by said Louis Reed for that purpose; he thinks it is about forty-four or forty-six years ago, more or less; that he believes the said Reed cultivated the said land all his lifetime, but to his certain knowledge he cultivated the same for eight or ten years in succession.—(See book No. 6, page 129.)

November 11, 1833.—The board met pursuant to adjournment. Present: L. F. Linn, A. G. Harrison, and F. R. Conway, commissioners.

Louis Reed, claiming two hundred and forty arpents of land.—(See page 129 of this book.) The board are unanimously of the opinion that this claim ought to be confirmed to the said Louis Reed, or to his legal representatives, according to the concession.—(See book No. 6, page 316.)

A. G. HARRISON.
L. F. LINN.
F. R. CONWAY.

No. 92.—GABRIEL NICOLLE, *claiming* 608 *arpents.*

To Don Peter Charles Dehault Delassus Deluziere, knight grand cross of the royal order of St. Michael and commandant, civil and military, of New Bourbon, &c.:

SIR: Gabriel Nicolle has the honor very humbly to supplicate you to grant to him the concession of a piece of land situated on the river St. Francis, upon a fork of the said river called Grand river, to the south of the said fork, twenty arpents in front by thirty arpents in length, adjoining north to Antoine Lachance and south to the King's domain, and without prejudice to any one whomsoever, upon the said river. The petitioner expects this favor of your goodness, and shall not cease to pray for your prosperity and conservation.

GABRIEL NICOLLE.

NEW BOURBON, *January* 22, 1798.

ST. LOUIS, *February* 1, 1798.

The surveyor of this jurisdiction, Don Antonio Soulard, shall put Gabriel Nicolle in possession of the land which he demands in the above petition, and afterwards shall make out a plat and certificate of his survey, and the whole shall be returned to us to be sent to the governor general of the province, who shall determine definitively upon the concession of the said land.

ZENON TRUDEAU.

Truly translated. St. Louis, April 8, 1833.

JULIUS DE MUN.

No.	Name of original claimant.	Quantity, in arpents.	Nature and date of claim.	By whom granted.	By whom surveyed, date, and situation.
92	Gabriel Nicolle.	608	Concession, February 1, 1798.	Zenon Trudeau.	Nathaniel Cook, deputy surveyor, January 7, 1806; on the St. Francis river, 37 miles S.SW. from St. Genevieve.

Evidence with reference to minutes and records.

March 20, 1833.—The board met pursuant to adjournment. Present: L. F. Linn and F. R. Conway, commissioners.

Gabriel Nicolle, by his legal representative, G. A. Bird, claiming six hundred arpents of land, (see book C, page 386,) produces a paper purporting to be an original concession from Zenon Trudeau, dated February 1, 1798; also a plat of survey, dated January 7, 1806; also a deed of conveyance, dated February 22, 1812.

L. F. Linn, being duly sworn, says that he knows that C. L. Bird resided on a piece of land which deponent is confident was said Bird's property, situate at about thirty-seven miles in a south-southwest direction from St. Genevieve, on the main branch of the river St. Francis and near Mine à la Motte and St. Michael; that he was on said piece of land in the spring of 1813, and that C. L. Bird had then fifty or sixty acres in cultivation and was preparing to build a mill, and that he lived on said place until his death.

Antoine Chénier, being duly sworn, says that the signature to the concession is in the proper handwriting of Zenon Trudeau, lieutenant governor.—(See book No. 6, page 131.)

November 11, 1833.—The board met pursuant to adjournment. Present: L. F. Linn, A. G. Harrison, F. R. Conway, commissioners.

Gabriel Nicolle, claiming 608 arpents of land.—(See page 131, of this book.) The board are unanimously of opinion that this claim ought to be confirmed to the said Gabriel Nicolle, or to his legal representatives, according to the concession.—(See book No. 6, page 316.)

Conflicting claim.

This land, it is said by the present claimant, has been sold by the United States.

A. G. HARRISON.
L. F. LINN.
F. R. CONWAY.

No. 93.—Michel Lachance, *claiming 72 arpents.*

To Don Peter Charles Dehault Delassus Deluziere, knight grand cross of the royal order of St. Michael, and civil and military commandant of New Bourbon and dependencies:

Sir: Michel Lachance has the honor to supplicate you very humbly to grant to him the concession of a piece of land situated on the river St. Francis, on the north side of the said river, in the first fork below the road leading to Mine à la Motte, six arpents in front by twelve in depth. The petitioner expects this favor of your goodness, and shall not cease to pray for your conservation.

New Bourbon, January 7, 1800. Stamped M. L.

MICHEL LACHANCE.

New Bourbon, *January* 10, 1800.

We, commandant of the post above named, refer the present petition to the lieutenant governor of the western part of Illinois, to whom we do certify that the said Michel Lachance is a very ancient settler in this district, in which he was born; being on the eve of marrying, and having a very great number of cattle, he is vested with all the qualifications necessary to obtain a concession for the tract of land demanded, and which does consist only of seventy-two arpents in superficie. Moreover, we do attest that it is evident, from the surveys already taken of the adjacent lands, that the said seventy-two arpents are not comprised in them, and are a part of the King's domain.

P. DELASSUS DELUZIERE.

St. Louis of Illinois, *January* 24, 1800.

Being convinced by the information given by the commandant of the post of New Bourbon, Don Pedro Delassus Deluziere, that the land which he solicited is vacant and does not do prejudice to any of the adjacent neighbors, and that the petitioner has sufficient means to improve the land which he solicits, in the term fixed by the regulations of the governor general of this province, the surveyor, Don Antonio Soulard, shall put the party interested in possession of the same; and afterwards he shall make out a plat and certificate of his survey, in order to serve (said party) to solicit the concession from the intendant general of these provinces, to whom alone corresponds, by royal order, the distributing and granting all classes of lands of the royal domain.

CARLOS DEHAULT DELASSUS.

Truly translated. St. Louis, April 8, 1833.

JULIUS DE MUN.

No.	Name of original claimant.	Quantity, in arpents.	Nature and date of claim.	By whom granted.	By whom surveyed, date, and situation.
93	Michel Lachance	72	Concession, January 24, 1800.	Carlos Dehault Delassus.	Thomas Maddin, deputy surveyor, recorded by Soulard, Oct. 1, 1805, on the waters of the St. Francis.

Evidence with reference to minutes and records.

June 25, 1806.—The board met agreeably to adjournment. Present: The Hon. Clement B. Penrose and James L. Donaldson, commissioners.

Michael Lachance, claiming seventy-two arpents of land situate on the waters of the river St. Francis, district aforesaid, produces a concession from Charles D. Delassus, dated January 24, 1800, and a survey of the same, certified October 1, 1805. This claim being unsupported by actual inhabitation and cultivation, the board reject the same, and are satisfied that it was granted at the time the said concession bears date.—(See book No. 1, page 349.)

August 28, 1810.—Board met. Present: John B. C. Lucas, Clement B. Penrose, and Frederick Bates, commissioners.

Michael Lachance, claiming seventy-two arpents of land.—(See book No. 1, page 349.) It is the opinion of the board that this claim ought not to be confirmed.

John B. C. Lucas, commissioner, declares that he does not concur in opinion with the former board in the present case, respecting the satisfaction which the said former board expresses that the concession was issued at the time it bears date.—(See book No. 4, page 478.)

March 20, 1833.—The board met pursuant to adjournment. Present: L. F. Linn, F. R. Conway, commissioners.

Michael Lachance, by G. A. Bird, his legal representative, claiming seventy-two arpents of land, (see book C, pages 386 and 387; minutes, No. 1, page 349; No. 4, page 478,) produces a paper purporting to be an original concession from Carlos Dehault Delassus, dated January 24, 1800; also a plat of survey, dated April 30, 1805, recorded by Antoine Soulard.—(See book No. 6, page 132.)

November 11, 1833.—The board met pursuant to adjournment. Present: L. F. Linn, A. G. Harrison, F. R. Conway, commissioners.

Michael Lachance, claiming 72 arpents of land.—(See page 182 of this book.) The board are unanimously of opinion that this claim ought to be confirmed to the said Michael Lachance, or to his legal representatives, according to the concession.—(See book No. 6, page 816.)

A. G. HARRISON.
L. F. LINN.
F. R. CONWAY.

No. 94.—Manuel Gonzalez Moro, *claiming* 7,056 *arpents.*

To his excellency the lieutenant governor of Upper Louisiana:

Don Manuel Gonzalez Moro, for the present in this city, most humbly and respectfully represents and says, that having returned here from Illinois in order to join my regiment, after having been for a long time garrisoned at said place, for just reasons I have left the royal service, with the intention of going to Europe; but as this could not be effected, on account of this port being continually blockaded by the enemy, I have determined to go back to Illinois by the first opportunity, intending to establish myself and marry in St. Louis. Consequently, wishing to secure my subsistence, and that of my children, in such a way as to shield them hereafter from the unfortunate events which so often take place, and seeing that agriculture in that country gives a prospect of sure and progressive increase, I am inclined to devote myself to it, and am induced to undertake the erection of considerable buildings, having around them an extent of land sufficient to keep grazing thereon a number of breeding mares and cows, along with sheep, hogs, goats, &c., (una yéguada, una vaqueria...... y otros ganados tanto tanares como de cerda, cabrios, &c.,) and adding to this a water saw-mill, besides the sowings which I intend to make, and the planting of orchards of various kinds of fruit trees; the whole shall form a mass of rural industry which will diffuse a spirit of emulation, so necessary in new settlements. Therefore, and in consideration of the merit which I have acquired in the royal service during fifteen consecutive years that I have remained in the same, in the character of *distinguido*, (this is a title given in the Spanish service to soldiers and non-commissioned officers distinguished for their exemplary conduct,) fulfilling all the orders and commissions with which I was charged to the satisfaction of my superiors, from whom I obtained the most satisfactory approbations and praises, I am induced to believe, with confidence, that I am one among the meritorious, and, consequently, worthy of the favors with which our beneficent government rewards the zeal of his Majesty's subjects.

I humbly supplicate you to condescend to grant to me a league square of land in superficie, or the same quantity of 7,056 arpents of land in the place commonly called River au Cuivre, situated between the two rivers Missouri and Mississippi, or else in their vicinity, at my choice, which location I shall make myself as soon as I shall return to Illinois, wherever I shall meet with a vacant place belonging to the royal domain, and which I shall indicate to the surveyor of that place, in order to have it surveyed and bounded regularly. I hope to deserve of you this favor, as you have been vested by the superior authority with the power to grant such to the meritorious, and to people of good morals. For which favor I shall always be grateful, and seek opportunities of giving you manifest proofs of my everlasting gratitude.

MANUEL GONZALEZ MORO.

New Orleans, *June* 18, 1799.

St. Louis of Illinois, *September* 16, 1799.

Being fully satisfied as to the services here stated by Don Manuel Gonzalez Moro, as also of the commendable personal qualities which adorn him, besides his good lineage; and considering the intentions manifested by him of establishing himself in this country, and to contribute to its improvement, I do grant to him in fee-simple, for him, his heirs, or whatever other person who may represent his right, the 7,056 arpents of land which he asks, or one league square of land in superficie, in the place mentioned by him, at his choice, on a vacant place belonging to the King's domain, which shall not be prejudicial to any other proprietor. And the surveyor of this Upper Louisiana, Don Antonio Soulard, shall make the survey and shall run the corresponding lines as soon as he shall be required to do so by the (party) interested; and the survey being executed, he shall deliver to him the documents in support of the same, in order that it may avail where convenient, and may serve to him to solicit and obtain the title of concession in due form from the intendancy general, to which tribunal alone corresponds the distributing and granting lands and town lots belonging to the royal domain.

CARLOS DEHAULT DELASSUS.

Registered, at the request of the interested, No. 2, pages 2, 3, 4, and 5.

SOULARD.

Truly translated. St. Louis, April 9, 1833.

JULIUS DE MUN.

No.	Name of original claimant.	Quantity, in arpents.	Nature and date of claim.	By whom granted.	By whom surveyed, date, and situation.
94	Manuel Gonzalez Moro.	7,056	Concession, September 16, 1799.	Carlos Dehault Delassus.	On Cuivre river.

Evidence with reference to minutes and records.

November 27, 1811.—Board met. Present: John B. C. Lucas, Clement B. Penrose, and Frederick Bates, commissioners.

Manuel Gonzalez Moro, claiming 7,056 arpents of land situate on the river Cuivre, district of St. Charles, produces record of a concession from Delassus, lieutenant governor, dated September 16, 1799. It is the opinion of the board that this claim ought not to be confirmed.—(See book No. 5, page 459.)

March 21, 1833.—F. R. Conway, esq., appeared pursuant to adjournment, being authorized to receive evidence by a resolution of this board, taken 8th instant.

Manuel Gonzalez Moro, by his legal representatives, claiming 7,056 arpents of land, (see record book D, page 127; minutes, No. 5, page 459,) produces a paper purporting to be an original concession from Carlos Dehault Delassus, dated September 16, 1799.

M. P. Le Duc, duly sworn, says that the said M. G. Moro was an officer under the Spanish government, employed in the treasury department, but had a very small salary. He further says that the signature to the petition is in the proper handwriting of said Moro, and the signature to the concession is in the proper handwriting of Carlos D. Delassus.—(See book No. 6, page 182.)

November 11, 1833.—The board met pursuant to adjournment. Present: L. F. Linn, A. G. Harrison, F. R. Conway, commissioners.

Manuel Gonzalez Moro, claiming 7,056 arpents of land.—(See page 132 of this book.) The board are unanimously of opinion that this claim ought to be confirmed to the said Manuel Gonzalez Moro, or to his legal representatives, according to the concession.—(See book No. 6, page 317.)

A. G. HARRISON.
L. F. LINN.
F. R. CONWAY.

No. 95.—Manuel Gonzalez Moro, *claiming* 800 *arpents.*

To his excellency the lieutenant governor of Upper Louisiana:

I, Don Manuel Gonzalez Moro, inhabitant of this place, with all the respect due to you, represent and say that having married here lately with the intention of settling permanently and prosper in this country, I wish to rely on some landed property in order to procure my subsistence and that of my children. In this view, and in consideration of the merit which I have acquired in the service of his Majesty, during a permanency in the same of just fifteen consecutive years, I most humbly supplicate you to condescend to grant me the usual quantity of 800 arpents of land, in a vacant place belonging to the royal domain, at my choice, where I intend to make what is commonly called here a plantation, on which I think of cultivating several kinds of grain and fruit trees, and raise poultry and cattle; which favor I hope to deserve of your justice, considering it, in part, as a reward for my above-mentioned services, and for which bounty I shall always give you proofs of my unbounded gratitude.

MANUEL GONZALEZ MORO.

St. Louis of Illinois, *June* 17, 1800.

St. Louis of Illinois, *June* 20, 1800.

As he asks; and the surveyor of this Upper Louisiana, Don Antonio Soulard, shall take the survey and run the corresponding lines as soon as he shall be required to do so, and these operations being executed, he shall deliver to him the documents in proof of the same, in order to serve to him (the petitioner) to solicit and obtain the title of concession in form from the intendancy general of these provinces, to which tribunal alone corresponds the granting of lands and town lots of the royal domain.

CARLOS DEHAULT DELASSUS.

Registered, book No. 2, page 2, at the request of the party interested.

SOULARD.

Ne varietur (by request) from an instrument recorded in my office, under date of this day.

LOUIS LA CAIRE, *Notary Public.*

New Orleans, *February* 25, 1833.

Witnesses:
Charles Barcantel
Phi. Lacoste.

Truly translated. St. Louis, April 12, 1833.

JULIUS DE MUN.

No.	Name of original claimant.	Quantity, in arpents.	Nature and date of claim.	By whom granted.	By whom surveyed, date, and situation.
95	Manuel Gonzalez Moro.	800	Concession, June 22, 1800.	Carlos Dehault Delassus.	

Evidence with reference to minutes and records.

November 27, 1811.—Board met. Present: John B. C. Lucas, Clement B. Penrose, and Frederick Bates, commissioners.

Manuel Gonzalez Moro, claiming 800 arpents of land, situate in district of St. Charles, produces record of a concession from Delassus lieutenant governor, dated June 20, 1800. It is the opinion of the board that this claim ought not to be confirmed.—(See book No. 5, page 459.)

March 21, 1833.—F. R. Conway, esq., appeared pursuant to adjournment, being authorized to receive evidence by a resolution of this board taken 9th instant.

Manuel Gonzalez Moro, by his legal representatives, claiming 800 arpents of land, (see book D, page 127; minutes, No. 5, page 459,) produces a paper purporting to be an original concession from Charles Dehault Delassus, dated June 20, 1800.

M. P. Le Duc, duly sworn, says the same as in the above case, and that the signature to the concession is in the handwriting of said Delassus.—(See book No. 6, page 133.)

M. P. Le Duc, duly sworn, further says that the said M. G Moro was an officer under the Spanish government, employed in the treasury department, and highly considered by said government, but had a very small salary.—(See book No. 6, page 133.)

November 11, 1833.—The board met pursuant to adjournment. Present: L. F. Linn, A. G. Harrison, and F. R. Conway, commissioners.

Manuel Gonzalez Moro, claiming 800 arpents of land.—(See page 133 of this book.) The board are unanimously of opinion that this claim ought to be confirmed to the said Manuel Gonzalez Moro, or to his legal representatives, according to the concession.—(See book No. 6, page 317.)

A. G. HARRISON.
L. F. LINN.
F. R. CONWAY

No. 96.—William Lorimier, *claiming* 1,000 *arpents.*

To Don Charles D hault Delassus, lieutenant colonel in the armies of his Catholic Majesty attached to the Louisiana, and lieutenant governor of Upper Louisiana:

William Lorimier humbly supplicates, and has the honor to represent to you, that wishing to settle in the district of Cape Girardeau, and employ the resources and means in his possession in cultivating the soil, besides, being of age, to establish himself and work for his own benefit, and having spent a part of his youth employed in the different kinds of works needed in husbandry, with the intention to become one day a useful member of society in contributing as much as in his power lies to the prosperity of the settlement in which he intends to reside, therefore, the petitioner applies to you, sir, praying that you will be pleased to grant to him, on his Majesty's domain in the district of Cape Girardeau, a concession of 1,000 arpents of land, and to order that it be measured in the place which he will think most convenient, without prejudice to any other person—favor which the petitioner presumes to expect of your justice, and of the encouragement which you give to industry.

W. LORIMIER.

Cape Girardeau, *December* 18, 1799.

We, Don Louis Lorimier, captain commandant of the post of Cape Girardeau of Illinois, for his Catholic Majesty, have the honor to inform the lieutenant governor that the petitioner's statement is candid and true; that being provided with sufficient means to improve the 1,000 arpents of lands which he asks, we judge him worthy to obtain them, and as such we do recommend him to the beneficence of the government.

L. LORIMIER.

Cape Girardeau, *December* 18, 1799.

St. Louis of Illinois, *December* 28, 1799.

In consequence of the information here above from the commandant of Cape Girardeau, Don Louis Lorimier, and whereas we are assured that the petitioner possesses sufficient means to improve the lands which he solicits in the term fixed by the regulations of the governor general of this province, the surveyor of this Upper Louisiana, Don Antonio Soulard, shall put the petitioner in possession of 1,000 arpents of land in superficie, which he solicits, in order for him to enjoy the same in the same manner as he asks; and the operation of survey being executed, he shall make out the corresponding certificate of said survey, with which the (party) interested shall have to apply to the intendancy general of these provinces, to which tribunal alone corresponds, by order of his Majesty, the granting of lands and town lots belonging to the royal domain.

CARLOS DEHAULT DELASSUS.

Truly translated. St. Louis, May 31, 1833.

JULIUS DE MUN.

No.	Name of original claimant.	Quantity, in arpents.	Nature and date of claim.	By whom granted.	By whom surveyed, date, and situation.
96	William Lorimier.	1,000	Concession, Dec. 28, 1799.	Carlos Dehault Delassus.	District of Cape Girardeau.

Evidence with reference to minutes and records.

May 25, 1809.—Board met. Present: John B. C. Lucas, Clement B. Penrose, and Frederick Bates, commissioners.

William Lorimier, claiming 1,000 arpents of land situate on forks of Cape la Cruche, district of Cape Girardeau, produces to the board a concession for the same from Don Carlos Dehault Delassus, lieutenant governor, dated December 28, 1799. Laid over for decision.—(See book No. 4, page 74.)

March 22, 1810.—Board met. Present: John B. C. Lucas, Clement B. Penrose, and Frederick Bates, commissioners.

William Lorimier, claiming 1,000 arpents of land.—(See book No. 4, page 74.) It is the opinion of the board that this claim ought not to be confirmed.—(See book No. 4, page 302.)

March 21, 1833.—F. R. Conway, esq., appeared pursuant to adjournment, being authorized to receive evidence by a resolution of this board taken 9th instant.

William Lorimier, by his legal representatives, claiming 1,000 arpents of land, (see book D, pages 25 and 26,) produces a paper purporting to be an original concession from Carlos Dehault Delassus, dated December 28, 1799.

M. P. Le Duc, duly sworn, says that the signature to the concession is in the proper handwriting of Carlos Dehault Delassus.—(See book No. 6, page 133.)

November 11, 1833.—The board met pursuant to adjournment. Present: L. F. Linn, A. G. Harrison, and F. R. Conway, commissioners.

William Lorimier, claiming 1,000 arpents of land.—(See page 133 of this book.) The board are unanimously of opinion that this claim ought to be confirmed to the said William Lorimier, or to his legal representatives, according to the concession.—(See book No. 6, page 318.)

A. G. HARRISON.
L. F. LINN.
F. R. CONWAY.

No. 97.—FRANÇOIS NORMANDEAU, *claiming* 2,500 *arpents.*

Don Carlos Dehault Delassus, lieutenant governor of Louisiana :

SIR : François Normandeau, alias Delauriere, sub-lieutenant of militia of St. Ferdinand, has the honor to represent to you, that residing in this province since a long time, and wishing to form an establishment in order to maintain his family in a suitable manner, the petitioner having never possessed any lands, claims of the goodness of this government, and prays you to grant him, 2,500 arpents of land in superficie, for the purpose of cultivating and raising cattle of all kinds; the said tract to be taken on the vacant lands of his Majesty's domain, in a place convenient to the interest of your petitioner, who presumes to expect this favor of your justice, having always shown the greatest zeal for the service of his Majesty, and he shall continue to do so all his lifetime.

FRANÇOIS his ⋈ mark. NORMANDEAU.

ST. LOUIS, *November* 18, 1799.

ST. LOUIS OF ILLINOIS, *November* 20, 1799.

Cognizance being taken of the statement presented by the sub-lieutenant of the militia of the village of St. Ferdinand, Mr. F. Normandeau, alias Delauriere, and considering that he is one of the old settlers of this country, whose known conduct and personal merit are recommendable, I do grant to him and his heirs the land he solicits, provided it is not to the prejudice of any one; and the surveyor, Don Antonio Soulard, shall put the party interested in possession of the quantity of land he asks for, in a vacant place of the royal domain; and this being executed, he shall make out a plat of his survey, delivering the same to said party, with his certificate, to serve to him to obtain the concession and title in form from the intendant general, to whom alone corresponds, by royal order, the distributing and granting all classes of lands of the royal domain.

CARLOS DEHAULT DELASSUS.

Truly translated from Spanish record of concessions, book No. 2, pages 51 and 52. St. Louis, August 13, 1833.

JULIUS DE MUN.

No.	Name of original claimant.	Quantity, in arpents.	Nature and date of claim.	By whom granted.	By whom surveyed, date, and situation.
97	François Normandeau.	2, 500	Concession, November 20, 1799.	Carlos Dehault Delassus.	

Evidence with reference to minutes and records.

November 27, 1811.—Board met. Present: John B. C. Lucas, Clement B. Penrose, and Frederick Bates, commissioners.

Jacques St. Vrain, assignee of François Normandeau, claiming 2,500 arpents of land situate on river Loutre, district of St. Charles, produces record of concession from Delassus, lieutenant governor, dated November 20, 1799; record of plat of survey, signed Frémon Delauriere.

It is the opinion of the board that this claim ought not to be confirmed.—(See book No. 5, page 465.)

March 21, 1833.—F. R. Conway, esq., appeared pursuant to adjournment, being authorized to receive evidence by a resolution of this board taken 9th instant.

François Normandeau, by Albert Tison, claiming 2,500 arpents of land.—(See book B, page 94; minutes, No. 5, page 465.) Claimant refers also to the testimony given by Charles Frémon Delauriere, in F. Saucier's case, to wit: that the signatures to the receipt are in the respective handwriting of A. Soulard and B. Cousins.

Charles Frémon Delauriere, duly sworn, says that the survey already produced is one of those included among the surveys mentioned in the above letter; that the survey was executed at the time it bears date; that there was great difficulty and danger in executing surveys; that he was twice repulsed by the Indians, and that the third time he went up, he could not execute several of the surveys, being prevented by Indians of the Sac and Fox nations, although he and his companions were well armed; that surveyors were very scarce, and it was difficult to procure any one to take a survey; that there was not half the number of surveyors necessary to execute the surveys that were then to be made.—(See page 118 of this book; Spanish record of concession, No. 2, page 51. See book No. 6, page 133.)

November 11, 1833.—The board met pursuant to adjournment. Present: L. F. Linn, A. G. Harrison, F. R. Conway, commissioners.

François Normandeau, claiming 2,500 arpents of land.—(See page 133 of this book.)

The board are unanimously of opinion that this claim ought to be confirmed to the said François Normandeau, or to his legal representatives, according to the concession.—(See book No. 6, page 318.)

A. G. HARRISON.
L. F. LINN.
F. R. CONWAY.

No. 98.—Andrew Kinaird, *claiming* 600 *arpents.*

To Don Charles Dehault Delassus, lieutenant colonel, attached to the stationary regiment of Louisiana, and commander-in-chief of Upper Louisiana, &c.:

Andrew Kinaird, Roman Catholic, has the honor to represent to you that, with the consent of the government, he settled himself in the district of St. Charles; therefore he has the honor to supplicate you to have the goodness to grant to him, in the same place, the quantity of land corresponding to the number of his family, consisting of himself, his wife, and eight children. The petitioner, possessing the means necessary to improve a farm, and having no other views but to live as a peaceable and submissive cultivator of the soil, hopes to deserve the favor which he solicits of your justice.

his
ANDREW + KINAIRD,
mark.

St. André, *January* 21, 1800.

Be it forwarded to the commander-in-chief, with the information that the above statement is true and that the petitioner is worthy of the favor which he solicits.

SANTIAGO MACKAY.

St. André, *January* 21, 1800.

St. Louis of Illinois, *January* 28, 1800.

In consequence of the information given by the commandant of the settlement of St. André, Captain Don Santiago Mackay, I do grant to the petitioner, for him and his heirs, the quantity of 600 arpents of land in superficie, quantity corresponding to the number of his family, provided it is not prejudicial to anybody; and the surveyor, Don Antonio Soulard, shall put the party interested in possession of the quantity of land he asks in the same place he cultivates, if it is not prejudicial to any person. And this being executed, he shall make out a plat of survey, delivering the same to said party, with his certificate, in order to enable him to obtain the concession and title in form from the intendant general, to whom alone corresponds, by royal order, the distributing and granting of all classes of lands of the royal domain.,

CARLOS DEHAULT DELASSUS.

Recorded, No. 67. MACKAY.

Truly translated. St. Louis, April 11, 1833.

JULIUS DE MUN.

No.	Name of original claimant.	Quantity, in arpents.	Nature and date of claim.	By whom granted.	By whom surveyed, date, and situation.
98	Andrew Kinaird.....	600	Concession, January 28, 1800.	Carlos Dehault Delassus.	District of St. Charles.

Evidence with reference to minutes and records.

November 20, 1811.—Board met. Present: John B. C. Lucas, Clement B. Penrose, Frederick Bates, commissioners.

James Mackay, assignee of John Long, assignee of Andrew Kincaid, (Kinaird,) claiming 600 arpents of land situate in the district of St. Charles, river Tucque, produces record of concession from Charles D. Delassus, lieutenant governor, dated 28th January, 1800; record of transfer from Kincaid to Long, dated 4th February, 1802; record of transfer from Long to claimant, dated 8th February, 1805. It is the opinion of the board that this claim ought not to be confirmed.—(See book No. 5, page 440.)

March 21, 1833.—F. R. Conway, esq., appeared pursuant to adjournment, being authorized to receive evidence by a resolution of this board taken 9th instant.

Andrew Kincaid, (Kinaird,) by his legal representatives, claiming 600 arpents of land, (see book C, page 480; minutes, No. 5, page 440,) produces a paper purporting to be an original concession from Carlos Dehault Delassus, dated 28th January, 1800.

M. P. Le Duc, duly sworn, says that the signature to the concession is in the proper handwriting of Carlos Dehault Delassus.—(See book No. 6, page 133.)

November 11, 1833.—The board met pursuant to adjournment. Present: L. F. Linn, A. G. Harrison, F. R. Conway, commissioners.

Andrew Kinaird, claiming 600 arpents of land.—(See page 133 of this book.) The board are unanimously of opinion that this claim ought to be confirmed to the said Andrew Kinaird, or to his legal representatives, according to the concession.—(See book No. 6, page 318.)

A. G. HARRISON.
L. F. LINN.
F. R. CONWAY.

No. 99.—John Henry, *claiming* 900 *arpents.*

Don Zenon Trudeau, lieutenant governor and commander-in-chief, civil and military, of Upper Louisiana:

Sir: John Henry, petitioner, has the honor to represent to you with all the respect due, that he has been residing for two years in these parts, and that since last year he settled, with your permission, on the river Bonne Femme. The petitioner having worked on a piece of land, and wishing to settle permanently, prays you to grant to him the concession of 30 arpents of land in front on the Missouri by 30 arpents in depth, (here a piece of the paper is torn and missing,) and to the west by Mr. Mackay and Belle Pointe; the petitioner, having settled himself with his family upon this piece of land, presumes to expect this favor of your justice.

JOHN HENRY, his + mark.

Recorded, No. 5. MACKAY.

St. Louis, *February* 7, 1798.

The surveyor of this jurisdiction shall set limits to the land of the petitioner in the shape demanded, provided that in such a shape it shall not be prejudicial to the surrounding neighbors; and the said surveyor shall make out, here below, a map and certificate of his survey, in order to serve in soliciting the concession of the governor general.

ZENON TRUDEAU.

Truly translated. St. Louis, April 11, 1833.

JULIUS DE MUN.

No.	Name of original claimant.	Quantity, in arpents.	Nature and date of claim.	By whom granted.	By whom surveyed, date, and situation.
99	John Henry.....	900	Concession, February 7, 1798.	Zenon Trudeau....	On river Bonne Femme.

Evidence with reference to minutes and records.

November 20, 1811.—Board met. Present: John B. C. Lucas, Clement B. Penrose, and Frederick Bates, commissioners.

James Mackay, assignee of John Long, assignee of John Henry, claiming 900 arpents of land situate on river Bonne Femme, district of St. Charles, produces record of a concession from Zenon Trudeau, lieutenant governor, dated February 7, 1798; record of transfer from Henry to Long, dated June, 1801; record of transfer from Long to claimant, dated February 8, 1805.

It is the opinion of the board that this claim ought not to be confirmed.—(See book No. 5, page 433.)

March 21, 1833.—F. R. Conway, esq., appeared pursuant to adjournment, being authorized to receive evidence by a resolution of this board taken 9th instant.

John Henry, by his legal representatives, claiming 900 arpents of land, (see book C, page 479; minutes No. 5, page 433,) produces a paper purporting to be an original concession from Zenon Trudeau, dated February 7, 1798.

M. P. Le Duc, duly sworn, says that the signature to the concession is in the proper handwriting of said Zenon Trudeau.—(See book No. 6, page 134.)

November 11, 1833.—The board met pursuant to adjournment. Present: L. F. Linn, A. G. Harrison, F. R. Conway, commissioners.

John Henry, claiming 900 arpents of land.—(See page 134 of this book.) The board are unanimously of opinion that this claim ought to be confirmed to the said John Henry, or to his legal representatives, according to the concession.—(See book No. 6, page 318.)

A. G. HARRISON.
L. F. LINN.
F. R. CONWAY.

No. 100.—Edward Bradley, *claiming* 500 *arpents.*

To Don Charles Dehault Delassus, lieutenant governor and commander-in-chief of Upper Louisiana, &c.:

The petitioner, Edward Bradley, a Roman Catholic, has the honor to represent to you that, with the permission of the government, he crossed over to this side, where he has made choice of a piece of land on the north side of the Missouri; therefore, he has the honor to supplicate you to have the goodness to grant to him, at the same place he has chosen, the quantity of land corresponding to the number of his family, which is composed of himself, his wife, and six children. The petitioner, possessing all the means necessary to improve a farm, and having no other views but to live as a peaceable and submissive cultivator of the soil, hopes to render himself worthy of the favor which he solicits of your justice.

St. André, *June* 18, 1800.

Be it forwarded to the commander-in-chief, with information that the above statement is true, and that the petitioner deserves the favor which he solicits.

SANTIAGO MACKAY.

St. André, *June* 19, 1800.

St. Louis of Illinois, *June* 25, 1800.

In consequence of the foregoing information from the commandant of St. André, Captain Don Santiago Mackay, the surveyor, Don Antonio Soulard, shall put the party interested in possession of 500 arpents of land in superficie in the place demanded, said quantity corresponding to the number of his family, conformably to the regulation of the governor general of this province; and this being executed, he shall make out a plat of his survey, delivering the same to said party, with his certificate, in order to enable him to obtain the concession and title in form from the intendant general of the provinces, to whom alone corresponds, by royal order, the distributing and granting all classes of lands of the royal domain.

CARLOS DEHAULT DELASSUS.

Recorded, No. 9.

MACKAY.

Truly translated. St. Louis, April 11, 1833.

JULIUS DE MUN.

No.	Name of original claimant.	Quantity, in arpents.	Nature and date of claim.	By whom granted.	By whom surveyed, date, and situation.
100	Edward Bradley.	500	Concession, June 25, 1800.	Carlos Dehault Delassus.	James Mackay; November 8, 1803; north side of Missouri.

Evidence with reference to minutes and records.

October 18, 1811.—Board met. Present: John B. C. Lucas, Clement B. Penrose, and Frederick Bates, commissioners.

Edward Bradley, claiming 500 arpents of land situate on the Missouri, district of St. Louis, produces a concession from Charles D. Delassus, lieutenant governor, dated June 25, 1800. It is the opinion of the board that this claim ought not to be confirmed.—(See book No. 5, page 375.)

March 21, 1833.—F. R. Conway appeared pursuant to adjournment, being authorized to receive evidence by a resolution of this board taken 9th instant.

Edward Bradley, by his legal representatives, claiming 500 arpents of land, (see book D, page 199; minutes No. 5, page 375,) produces a paper purporting to be an original concession from Carlos Dehault Delassus, dated June 25, 1800; also a plat of survey, dated November 8, 1803.

M. P. Le Duc, duly sworn, says that the signature to the concession is in the proper handwriting of said Carlos D. Delassus, and the signature to plat of survey is in the proper handwriting of James Mackay.—(See book No. 6, page 134.)

November 12, 1833.—The board met pursuant to adjournment. Present: L. F. Linn, A. G. Harrison, F. R. Conway, commissioners.

Edward Bradley, claiming 500 arpents of land.—(See page 134 of this book.) The board are unanimously of opinion that this claim ought to be confirmed to the said Edward Bradley, or to his legal representatives, according to the concession.—(See book No. 6, page 319.)

A. G. HARRISON.
L. F. LINN.
F. R. CONWAY.

No. 101.—George Crump, *claiming* 450 *arpents.*

To Don Charles Dehault Delassus, lieutenant colonel, attached to the stationary regiment of Louisiana, and commander-in-chief of Upper Louisiana:

George Crump, a Roman Catholic, has the honor to represent to you that, with the permission of the government, he came over to this side with his family, and having made choice of a piece of land on the domain of his Majesty, on which he is established, he supplicates you to have the goodness to grant to him, in the same place, the quantity of land corresponding to the number of his family. The petitioner, having no other views but to live as a cultivator of the soil for the support of his family, conforming himself with submission to the laws, and having the necessary means to establish a farm, hopes that you will be pleased to grant to him the favor which he solicits of your justice.

St. André, *May* 4, 1800.

Be it forwarded to the lieutenant governor, with information that the above statement is true, and that the petitioner deserves the favor which he solicits.

SANTIAGO MACKAY.

St. André, *May* 4, 1800.

We do certify that the family of the petitioner is composed of himself, his wife, and five children.

MACKAY.

St. Louis of Illinois, *May* 9, 1800.

In consequence of the information given by Don Santiago Mackay, commandant of the settlement of St. André, by which the number of individuals composing the family of the petitioner is evidently ascertained, the surveyor, Don Antonio Soulard, shall put him in possession of 450 arpents of land in superficie in the place demanded, said quantity corresponding to the number composing his family, conformably to the regulation of the governor general of the province; and afterwards the party interested shall have to solicit the title of concession in form from the intendant general of the same province, to whom alone corresponds, by royal order, the distributing and granting all classes of lands of the royal domain.

CARLOS DEHAULT DELASSUS.

Recorded, No. 17.

MACKAY.

Truly translated. St. Louis, April 10, 1833.

JULIUS DE MUN.

No.	Name of original claimant.	Quantity, in arpents.	Nature and date of claim.	By whom granted.	By whom surveyed, date, and situation.
101	George Crump..	450	Concession; May 9, 1800.	Carlos Dehault Delassus.	James Mackay; February 14, 1804; about two miles west of St. Charles.

Evidence with reference to minutes and records.

September 28, 1810.—Board met. Present: John B. C. Lucas, Clement B. Penrose, commissioners.

James Mackay, assignee of George Crump, claiming 450 arpents of land.—(See book No. 2, page 32, as follows:) James Mackay, assignee of George Crump, claiming 450 arpents of land situate on the river Gingras, district of St. Louis, produces a concession from Charles D. Delassus, dated May 9, 1800, and a deed of transfer of the same, dated January 8, 1802.

Hyacinthe St. Cyr, duly sworn, says that about three years ago he saw a house on said land, but could not tell whether it was inhabited. Saw no marks of cultivation. It is the opinion of the board that this claim ought not to be confirmed.—(See book No. 4, page 517.)

March 21, 1833.—F. R. Conway, esq., appeared pursuant to adjournment, being authorized to receive evidence by a resolution of this board taken 8th instant.

George Crump, by his legal representatives, claiming 450 arpents of land, (see book C, page 477; minutes No. 4, page 517,) produces a paper purporting to be an original concession from Carlos D. Delassus, dated May 9, 1800; also a plat of survey, dated February 14, 1804, by Mackay.

M. P. Le Duc, duly sworn, says that the signature to the concession is in the proper handwriting of said Delassus, and the signature to the plat of survey the true signature of said Mackay.—(See book No. 6, page 135.)

November 12, 1833.—Board met pursuant to adjournment. Present: L. F. Linn, A. G. Harrison, F. R. Conway, commissioners.

George Crump, claiming 450 arpents of land.—(See page 135 of this book.) The board remark that, in the entry of this claim in the minutes of the former board, there is a mistake, probably made by their clerk, stating this land to lie on the river Gingras, district of St. Louis; this land being evidently in the district of St. Charles.

The board are unanimously of opinion that this claim ought to be confirmed to the said George Crump, or to his legal representatives, according to the concession.—(See book No. 6, page 319.)

A. G. HARRISON.
L. F. LINN.
F. R. CONWAY.

No. 102.—John Long, *claiming* 10,000 *arpents.*

To Don Zenon Trudeau, lieutenant governor of this western part of Illinois:

John Long, father of a numerous family and owner of several slaves, member of a family which has been protected by the government on account of the useful settlement it has made in this country, himself having views of aggrandizement, and the project of forming useful establishments, and particularly that of improving a considerable stock farm, considering the first concession which he has obtained of you as very insufficient for his views, he hopes that the generosity of the government and your particular goodness will be pleased to grant to him, in fee simple, the quantity of 10,000 arpents of land in superficie, to be taken, 5,000 arpents in a place convenient to the interest of your petitioner, and the 5,000 arpents remaining in another place at his choice, on vacant parts of his Majesty's domain, and without prejudice to the pretensions of any one whomsoever. The petitioner, having no other views but to live as a peaceable and submissive cultivator of the soil, hopes to deserve this favor of your justice.

JOHN LONG.

St. Louis, *August* 28, 1797.

Don Zenon Trudeau, captain of grenadiers, and lieutenant governor of Upper Louisiana.

The ten thousand arpents of land in superficie which are solicited, being found vacant, the surveyor, Don Antonio Soulard, shall put the party interested in possession of the said quantity of 10,000 arpents, and shall deliver to him a plat and certificate of survey, in order to serve to said party as a title of property; meanwhile the corresponding title in form be made out and delivered by the governor general, to whom he must apply in due time.

ZENON TRUDEAU.

St. Louis, *September* 1, 1797.

Truly translated. St. Louis, April 10, 1833.

JULIUS DE MUN.

No.	Name of original claimant.	Quantity, in arpents.	Nature and date of claim.	By whom granted.	By whom surveyed, date, and situation.
102	John Long...	10,000	Concession, September 1, 1797.	Zenon Trudeau.	James Mackay, deputy surveyor, 5,050 arpents, March 21, 1805, 55 miles west of St. Louis; 5,000 arpents, January 20, 1806, on the Missouri 50 miles west of St. Louis; both surveys received for record by Soulard February 27, 1806.

Evidence with reference to minutes and records.

November 23, 1811.—Board met. Present: John B. C. Lucas, Clement B. Penrose, and Frederick Bates, commissioners.

John Long, claiming 10,000 arpents of land situate on the rivers Dubois and St. John, district of St. Louis, produces record of a concession from Zenon Trudeau, lieutenant governor, dated September 1, 1797, record of a plat of survey on river St. John for 5,000 arpents, dated 20th January, and certified February 27, 1806; record of a plat of survey on river Dubois for 5,050 arpents, dated March 21, 1805, certified February 27, 1806. It is the opinion of the board that this claim ought not to be confirmed.—(See book No. 5, page 444.)

March 21, 1833.—F. R. Conway, esq., appeared pursuant to adjournment, being authorized to receive evidence by a resolution of this board taken 9th instant.

John Long, by his legal representatives, claiming 10,000 arpents of land, (see book B, page 442; No. 5, page 444,) produces a paper purporting to be an original concession from Zenon Trudeau, dated September 1, 1797; also, two plats of survey—one for 5,000 arpents, dated January 20, 1806, the other for 5,050 arpents, dated March 21, 1805—by James Mackay.

M. P. Le Duc, duly sworn, says that the signature to the concession is in the true handwriting of Zenon Trudeau, and the signatures to the surveys are in the proper handwriting of James Mackay and Anthony Soulard.—(See book No. 6, page 136.)

November 12, 1833.—The board met pursuant to adjournment. Present: L. F. Linn, A. G. Harrison, F. R. Conway, commissioners.

John Long, claiming 10,000 arpents of land.—(See page 136 of this book.) The board remark that the survey exceeds the quantity granted by 50 arpents. The board are unanimously of opinion that this claim ought to be confirmed to the said John Long, or to his legal representatives, according to the concession.—(See book No. 6, page 319.)

A. G. HARRISON.
L. F. LINN.
F. R. CONWAY.

No. 103.—Charles Roy, *claiming 2 by 40 arpents.*

We, Don Fernando de Leyba, lieutenant governor, &c., on the demand to us made by Charles Roy, inhabitant of this post, in his petition dated 20th March, (the present month,) in which he represents to us that he would wish to establish himself in the new settlement called the river Des Peres, adjoining the grand prairie, and praying us to be pleased to grant to him a tract of land of 2 arpents in front, by 40 arpents in depth, contiguous to the other inhabitants of the said place, and, on one side, adjoining the land of François Hebert, and on the other side, the King's domain—the south end fronting the Little river, and the north end fronting the King's domain. Therefore, wishing to favor the said Charles Roy, we have granted to him the said land in all its width and length, such as it is described in the said petition, on condition to establish the same in one year from this day, and that it shall be liable to the public charges, and others which it may please his Majesty to impose.

Given in St. Louis, March 25, 1780.

FERNANDO DE LEYBA.

Truly translated from Livre Terrein, No. 4, page 2. St. Louis, April 10, 1833.

JULIUS DE MUN.

No.	Name of original claimant.	Quantity, in arpents.	Nature and date of claim.	By whom granted.	By whom surveyed, date, and situation.
103	Charles Roy....	80	Concession March 25, 1780.	Fernando de Leyba.	On river Des Peres.

Evidence with reference to minutes and records.

March 21, 1833.—F. R. Conway, esq., appeared pursuant to adjournment, being authorized to receive evidence by a resolution of this board taken 9th instant.

Charles Roy, by his legal representative, J. P. Cabanné, claiming 2 arpents of land in front by 40 arpents in depth, (see book F, page 190; Livre Terrein, No. 4, page 2,) produces said Livre Terrein, on which there is a decree of concession to Charles Roy by Fernando de Leyba, dated March 25, 1780; and deed of conveyance from Charles Roy to Charles Gratiot, and from Charles Gratiot and wife to J. P. Cabanné, for said land.—(See book No. 6, page 135.)

July 8, 1833.—L. F. Lynn, esq., appeared pursuant to adjournment.

Charles Roy, by John P. Cabanné, claiming 2 by 40 arpents of land.—(See Livre Terrein, No. 4, page 2; book F, page 190.)

Peter Chouteau, sen., being duly sworn, says that he has perfect knowledge of this tract; that about the year 1780, or thereabout, it was cultivated by said Roy, and was so cultivated for four or five consecutive years, till the time of his death.—(See book No. 6, page 218.)

November 12, 1833.—The board met pursuant to adjournment. Present: L. F. Linn, A. G. Harrison, F. R. Conway, commissioners.

Charles Roy, claiming 80 arpents of land.—(See page 218 of this book.) The board are unanimously of opinion that this claim ought to be confirmed to the said Charles Roy, or his legal representatives, according to the concession.—(See book No. 6, page 320.)

A. G. HARRISON.
L. F. LINN.
F. R. CONWAY.

No. 104.—Seneca Rawlins, *claiming* 400 *arpents.*

To Don Charles Dehault Delassus, lieutenant governor, and commander-in-chief of Upper Louisiana, &c.

Seneca Rawlins, a Roman Catholic, has the honor to represent to you that, with the consent of the government, he came over to this side, where he has made choice of a piece of land on the domain of his Majesty, in order to make a farm; therefore he supplicates you to have the goodness to grant to him the quantity of land corresponding to the number of his family, which is composed of himself, his wife, and four children. The petitioner, having the means to improve a farm, and no other views but to live as a peaceable and submissive cultivator of the soil, hopes that you will be pleased to grant to him the favor which he solicits of your justice.

St. André, *December* 17, 1802.

Be it forwarded to the lieutenant governor, with information that the above statement is true, and that the petitioner deserves the favor which he solicits.

SANTIAGO MACKAY.

St. André, *December* 17, 1802.

St. Louis of Illinois, *December* 22, 1802.

In consequence of the information given by Don Santiago Mackay, commandant of the settlement of St. Andrew, concerning the number of individuals, composing the family of the petitioner, the surveyor, Don Antonio Soulard, shall put him in possession of four hundred arpents of land in superficie, in the place where he asks the same, said quantity corresponding to the number of his family, according to the regulation of the governor general of the province. And this being executed, the party interested shall have to solicit the title of concession in form from the intendant general of the same province, to whom alone corresponds, by royal order, the distributing and granting all classes of lands of the royal domain.

CARLOS DEHAULT DELASSUS.

Recorded, No. 33.

MACKAY.

Truly translated. St. Louis, April 10, 1833.

JULIUS DE MUN.

No.	Name of original claimant.	Quantity, in arpents.	Nature and date of claim.	By whom granted.	By whom surveyed, date, and situation.
104	Seneca Rollins.	400	Concession, Dec. 22, 1802.	Car. Dehault Delassus.	

Evidence with reference to minutes and records.

December 6, 1811.—Board met. Present: John B. C. Lucas, Clement B. Penrose, and Frederick Bates, commissioners.

James Mackay, assignee of Seneca Rollins, claiming 400 arpents of land situate in the district of St. Charles, produces record of a concession from Delassus, lieutenant governor, dated December 22, 1802; record of a transfer from Rollins to Mackay, dated May 1, 1804. It is the opinion of the board that this claim ought not to be confirmed.—(See book No. 5, page 486.)

March 21, 1833.—F. R. Conway, esq., appeared pursuant to adjournment, being authorized to receive evidence by a resolution of this board taken the 9th instant.

Seneca Rollins, by his legal representatives, claiming 400 arpents of land, (see book C, page 477; minutes No. 5, page 486,) produces a paper purporting to be an original concession from Charles D. Delassus, dated December 22, 1802.

M. P. Le Duc, duly sworn, says that the signature to the concession is in the proper handwriting of said C. D. Delassus.—(See book No. 6, page 135.)

November 12, 1833.—The board met pursuant to adjournment. Present: L. F. Linn, A. G. Harrison, F. R. Conway, commissioners.

Seneca Rollins, claiming 400 arpents of land.—(See page 135 of this book.) The board are unanimously of opinion that this claim ought to be confirmed to the said Seneca Rollins, or to his legal representatives, according to the concession.—(See book No. 6, page 320.)

A. G. HARRISON.
L. F. LINN.
F. R. CONWAY.

No. 105.—Joachin Roy, *claiming* 400 *arpents.*

To Don Zenon Trudeau, lieutenant colonel by brevet, lieutenant governor, and commander-in-chief of the western part of Illinois:

Joachin Roy supplicates humbly, and has the honor to represent to you, that he would wish to make a plantation on the river Maramec, and that having found a piece of bottom land which is for the greatest part subject to inundation, nevertheless he would wish to improve the small piece of land next to the hills, where he might build his house on this same piece of land which is well timbered. The petitioner claims of your customary goodness that you would be pleased to grant to him what remains of the bottom of the great swamp, (or pond,) to be taken from the line of Widow Boly, and to run to the foot of the hills which are close to the river Maramec, and running forty arpents in depth, on which tract the great swamp is situated; and wishing to secure to himself the property of the said land, to have it surveyed, and the certificate of survey delivered in due form, before he makes any improvement on the same. Therefore, sir, may you be pleased to grant to the petitioner the said bottom of the great swamp, to be taken from the Maramec, running forty arpents in depth, adjoining on the eastern side the line of Widow Boly, and to the westward running to the hills which are close to the said river Maramec. The petitioner shall never cease to be thankful for your goodness.

JOACHIN his + mark ROY.

St. Louis, *January* 30, 1797.

St. Louis, *February* 3, 1797.

In case the land demanded does belong to the King's domain, and does not exceed ten arpents in front by the customary depth of forty, the surveyor of this jurisdiction shall put the petitioner in possession of the same, and shall make out a plat and certificate of his survey, which shall be remitted to us, in order to solicit the concession of the governor general.

ZENON TRUDEAU.

Truly translated. July 18, 1833.

JULIUS DE MUN.

No.	Name of original claimant.	Quantity, in arpents.	Nature and date of claim.	By whom granted.	By whom surveyed, date, and situation.
105	Joachin Roy	400	Concession, Feb. 3, 1797.	Zen. Trudeau......	On the Maramec.

Evidence with reference to minutes and records.

March 21, 1833.—F. R. Conway, esq., appeared pursuant to adjournment, being authorized to take evidence by a resolution of this board taken the 9th instant.

Joachin Roy's legal representatives, claiming four hundred arpents of land on the river Maramec, under a concession from Zenon Trudeau, dated February 3, 1797, it being a special location, (see book F, page 138,) as claimed by Pierre Tournot's representatives.—(See book No. 6, page 136.)

June 26, 1833.—The board met pursuant to adjournment. Present: L. F. Linn, F. R. Conway, commissioners.

Joachin Roy, by his legal representatives, claiming four hundred arpents of land, (see book F, page 138; Bates's Decisions, No. 5, page 104,) produces a paper purporting to be a concession from Zenon Trudeau, dated 3d February, 1797.—(See book No. 6, page 189.)

November 12, 1833.—The board met pursuant to adjournment. Present: L. F. Linn, A. G. Harrison, F. R. Conway, commissioners.

Joachin Roy, claiming four hundred arpents of land.—(See page 189 of this book.) The board are unanimously of opinion that this claim ought to be confirmed to the said Joachin Roy, or to his legal representatives, according to the concession.—(See book No. 6, page 320.)

A. G. HARRISON.
L. F. LINN.
F. R. CONWAY.

No. 106.—William L. Long, *claiming* 400 *arpents.*

To Don Charles Dehault Delassus, lieutenant colonel, attached to the stationary regiment of Louisiana, and lieutenant governor of Upper Louisiana:

William Long, a Roman Catholic, has the honor to represent to you that he wishes to obtain of your goodness the property of four hundred arpents of land in superficie, in the district of St. Louis, the above quantity being indispensable in order to comprise the water and timber necessary to form a good plantation. The petitioner, possessing sufficient property to be able to improve a plantation, and having no other views but to live as a peaceable and submissive cultivator of the soil, hopes to obtain the favor which he solicits of your justice.

WILLIAM L. LONG.

St. André, *October* 5, 1799.

Be it forwarded to the lieutenant governor, with information that the above statement is true, and that the petitioner deserves the favor which he solicits.

SANTIAGO MACKAY.

St. André, *October* 5, 1799.

St. Louis of Illinois, *October* 10, 1799.

In consequence of the foregoing information from the commandant of St. Andrew, Captain Don Santiago Mackay, and being assured that the petitioner possesses sufficient means to improve the lands which he solicits in the term fixed by the regulation of the governor general of this province, the surveyor, Don Antonio Soulard, shall put the party interested in possession of the four hundred arpents of land in superficie, in the same place designated in this petition. And this being executed, he shall make out a plat of his survey, delivering the same to the party, with his certificate, in order to enable him to obtain the concession and title in form from the intendant general of these provinces, to whom alone corresponds, by royal order, the distributing and granting all classes of lands of the royal domain.

CARLOS DEHAULT DELASSUS.

Registered, No. 45.

MACKAY.

Truly translated. St. Louis, April 10, 1833.

JULIUS DE MUN.

No.	Name of original claimant.	Quantity, in arpents.	Nature and date of claim.	By whom granted.	By whom surveyed, date, and situation.
106	William Long.......	400	Concession, October 10, 1799.	Carlos Dehault Delassus.	

Evidence with reference to minutes and records.

November 25, 1811.—Board met. Present: John B. C. Lucas, Clement B. Penrose, and Frederick Bates, commissioners.

William Long, claiming four hundred arpents of land situate in the district of St. Louis, produces record of concession from Charles D. Delassus, lieutenant governor, dated 10th of October, 1799. It is the opinion of the board that this claim ought not to be confirmed.—(See book No. 5, page 448.)

March 21, 1833.—F. R. Conway, esq., appeared pursuant to adjournment, being authorized to receive evidence by a resolution of this board taken 9th instant.

William Long, by his legal representatives, claiming four hundred arpents of land, (see book C, page 510; minutes No. 5, page 448,) produces a paper purporting to be an original concession from Carlos Dehault Delassus, dated 10th of October, 1799.

M. P. Le Duc, duly sworn, says that the signature to the concession is in the proper handwriting of said Delassus.—(See book No. 6, page 136.)

November 12, 1833.—The board met pursuant to adjournment. Present: L. F. Linn, A. G. Harrison, F. R. Conway, commissioners. William Long, claiming four hundred arpents of land.—(See page 136 of this book.) The board are unanimously of opinion that this claim ought to be confirmed to the said William Long, or to his legal representatives, according to the concession.—(See book No. 6, page 320.)

A. G. HARRISON.
L. F. LINN.
F. R. CONWAY.

No. 107.—Edward Young, *claiming* 800 *arpents*.

To Don Carlos Dehault Delassus, lieutenant governor, and commander-in-chief of Upper Louisiana, &c.:

Edward Young, a Roman Catholic, and father of a family, has the honor to represent to you that, with the permission of the government, he came over to this side, where he made choice of a tract of land on the north side of the Missouri, at the place called the Saline, near the river A Manitie, at about 50 leagues of St. André; which, being considered, he has the honor to supplicate you to have the goodness to grant to him, in full property, and including the said saline, the quantity of 800 arpents of land in superficie. The petitioner, possessing the means to improve the said land, and no other views but to live peaceably and support his family by his industry, hopes to obtain the favor which he solicits of your justice.

St. André, *January* 3, 1800.

Be it forwarded to the commander-in-chief, with information that the above statement is true, and that the petitioner deserves, in every point of view, the favor which he solicits.

SANTIAGO MACKAY.

St. André, *January* 3, 1800.

St. Louis of Illinois, *January* 15, 1800.

In consequence of the information given by the commandant of the post of St. André, I do grant to the petitioner, for him and his heirs, the land which he solicits, provided it is not prejudicial to anybody; and the surveyor, Don Antonio Soulard, shall put the party interested in possession of the quantity of land which he asks in the same place where he solicits; and this being executed, he shall make out a plat of his survey, delivering the same to the said party, with his certificate, [here is an omission,] and title in form from the intendant general, to whom alone corresponds, by royal order, the distributing and granting of all classes of lands of the royal domain.

CARLOS DEHAULT DELASSUS.

Recorded, No. 6.

MACKAY.

Truly translated. St. Louis, April 9, 1833.

JULIUS DE MUN.

No.	Name of original claimant.	Quantity, in arpents.	Nature and date of claim.	By whom granted.	By whom surveyed, date, and situation.
107	Edward Young......	800	Concession, Jan. 15, 1800.	Carlos Dehault Delassus.	

Evidence with reference to minutes and records.

December 10, 1811.—Board met. Present: John B. C. Lucas, Clement B. Penrose, and Frederick Bates, commissioners.

Edward Young, claiming 800 arpents of land on Manitie saline, district of St. Louis, produces record of a concession from Charles D. Delassus, lieutenant governor, dated January 15, 1800. It is the opinion of the board that this claim ought not to be confirmed.—(See book No. 5, page 514.)

March 21, 1833.—F. R. Conway, esq., appeared pursuant to adjournment, being authorized to receive evidence by a resolution of this board taken 9th instant.

Edward Young, by his legal representatives, claiming 800 arpents of land at a place called Manitie saline, (see book D, page 199; minutes No. 5, page 514,) produces a paper purporting to be an original concession from Carlos Dehault Delassus, dated January 15, 1800.

M. P. LeDuc, duly sworn, says that the signatures to the concession is in the proper handwriting of Carlos Dehault Delassus.—(See book No. 6, page 137.)

November 12, 1833.—The board met pursuant to adjournment. Present: L. F. Linn, A. G. Harrison, F. R. Conway, commissioners.

Edward Young, claiming 800 arpents of land.—(See page 137 of this book.) The board are unanimously of opinion that this claim ought to be confirmed to the said Edward Young, or to his legal representatives, according to the concession.—(See book No. 6, page 320.)

A. G. HARRISON.
L. F. LINN.
F. R. CONWAY.

No. 108.—JAMES MACKAY, *claiming* 400 *arpents.*

To Don Zenon Trudeau, lieutenant governor of all the western part of Illinois:

SIR: James Mackay, an inhabitant of this village, wishing to establish himself on this side, (of the Mississippi,) has the honor to supplicate you to be willing to grant to him a concession for a tract of land of ten arpents in front by forty arpents in depth, on the saline of the river, called river Bonne Femme, in the domain of his Catholic Majesty, promising to establish himself thereon in the time prescribed by you—favor which he expects of your justice.

JAMES MACKAY.

ST. LOUIS, *May* 31, 1797.

ST. LOUIS, *May* 31, 1797.

The surveyor of this jurisdiction, Don Antonio Soulard, shall put Mr. James Mackay in possession of the land which he solicits, provided it belongs to the King's domain, and is not prejudicial to anybody; and he shall make out a plat of his survey, with his certificate here below, and shall remit the whole to us, in order to solicit the title of concession for the same, in form, from the governor general of the province.

ZENON TRUDEAU.

Signed (at the margin) Antonio Soulard. No. 30, recorded.

MACKAY.

Truly translated. April 16, 1833.

JULIUS DE MUN.

No.	Name of original claimant.	Quantity, in arpents.	Nature and date of claim.	By whom granted.	By whom surveyed, date, and situation.
108	James Mackay..	400	Concession, May 31, 1797.	Zenon Trudeau..	James Mackay, deputy surveyor, December 2, 1804. On river Bonne Femme.

Evidence with reference to minutes and records.

July 31, 1807.—The board met agreeably to adjournment. Present: John B. C. Lucas, Clement B. Penrose, and Frederick Bates, commissioners.

James Mackay, claiming 10 by 40 arpents of land situate on the Saline "la rivière Bonne Femme," produces a concession from Zenon Trudeau, dated May 31, 1797.

It appears to the board that, on the petition of the aforesaid concession, the name of the claimant, the place of his residence, the quantity granted, and the situation of the land, has been altered and written on erasure; and that the concession refers to the petition, especially as to the situation, name, and quantity granted; and, also, the aforesaid petition declares that the land prayed for is situated on a saline; which part of said petition appears to be altered and written on erasure.

The agent of the United States objects to the aforesaid concession, on the ground of its being antedated and otherwise fraudulent. Further proof is required of the party.—(See book No. 3, page 21.)

November 4, 1809.—Board met. Present: John B. C. Lucas, Clement B. Penrose, commissioners.

James Mackay, claiming 10 by 40 arpents of land, situate on the saline and river Bonne Femme, (see book No. 3, page 21,) produces to the board a plat dated December 2, 1804, signed "Mackay."

It is the opinion of the board that this claim ought not to be confirmed.—(See book No. 4, page 186.)

March 22, 1833.—F. R. Conway, esq., appeared pursuant to adjournment.

James Mackay, by his legal representatives, claiming 10 arpents of land in front, by 40 in depth, on the saline of the river called river Bonne Femme, (see book C, page 476; minutes, No. 3, page 21; No. 4, page 186,) produces a paper purporting to be an original concession from Zenon Trudeau, dated May 31, 1799; also a plat of survey, dated December 2, 1804, by Mackay, and certified on oath by Antoine Soulard.

M. P. Le Duc, duly sworn, says that the signature to the concession is in the proper handwriting of Zenon Trudeau; and the signature to the plat of survey and certificate in the respective handwriting of James Mackay and Antoine Soulard.—(See book No. 6, page 137.)

November 12, 1833.—The board met pursuant to adjournment. Present: L. F. Linn, A. G. Harrison, F. R. Conway, commissioners.

James Mackay, claiming 400 arpents of land.—(See page 137 of this book.)

The board, after a minute examination of the original concession, are of opinion that the paper on which it is written is in places defective, but they see nothing to indicate fraudulent erasures, as suggested by the agent of the United States before the former board. They are unanimously of opinion that this claim ought to be confirmed to the said James Mackay, or to his legal representatives, according to the concession.—(See book No. 6, page 321.)

A. G. HARRISON.
L. F. LINN.
F. R. CONWAY.

No. 109.—ANTOINE GAUTIER, *claiming* 4,000 *arpents.*

To the lieutenant governor of the western part of Illinois:

Don Ante. Gautier, lieutenant of militia, inhabitant of St. Charles, on the Missouri, has the honor to represent to you that now that the Indians appear to be peaceable enough to give sufficient security to form insulated establishments, remote from the villages, he wishes to make one at about two leagues from the said village of St. Charles, at the place called Le Marais de Temps Clair, (Clear Weather swamp,) which, being continually overflowed, is good only for the timber which is found thereon, and to raise cattle; therefore, sir, besides the concession of the said swamp which he has the honor to ask of you, he supplicates you to grant to him also a concession of ten arpents in front, on the dry prairie situated on the margin of said swamp, by fifteen (arpents) in depth, so as to join the Marais Croche, it being about the distance which separates the two, (swamps;) a favor which he expects from the encouragement you have always given to new establishments, and he shall not cease to pray for your happiness and prosperity.

+

St. Louis, *November* 29, 1796.

St. Louis, *November* 29, 1796.

The surveyor of this jurisdiction, Don Anto. Soulard, shall put Mr. Gautier in possession of ten arpents of land in front, on the Clear Weather swamp, (Marais de Temps Clair,) by such a depth as to join the Crooked swamp, (celui nommé Croche,) and after his survey is executed, the concession for the said land, as also that for the swamp above demanded by the said Mr. Ante. Gautier, shall be immediately granted to him.

ZENON TRUDEAU.

Whereas the tract of land mentioned in the present petition would lead into difficulties with the whole of the inhabitants of St. Charles and Portage des Sioux, conformably to the official authority with which we have been vested by the lieutenant governor, Don Charles Dehault Delassus, under date of 20th February, 1802, the deputy surveyor, Mr. James Mackay, or any other that has been appointed by us, may measure the same quantity of land mentioned in the petition of Mr. Antoine Gautier on any other vacant part of his Majesty's domain; and whereas the said quantity is not sufficiently expressed in the petition or decree, by the knowledge we have of the tract demanded, we do estimate the totality of said land to be about four thousand arpents.

ANTONIO SOULARD.

St. Louis, *January* 17, 1803.

Truly translated. St. Louis, May 21, 1833.

JULIUS DE MUN.

No.	Name of original claimant.	Quantity, in arpents.	Nature and date of claim.	By whom granted.	By whom surveyed, date, and situation.
109	Antoine Gautier.	4,000	Concession, November 29, 1796.	Zenon Trudeau..	Jas. Mackay, deputy surveyor, December 3, 1804; received for record by Soulard, February 15, 1806; on the Missouri, between Bonne Femme and Pierre à la Fleche.

Evidence with reference to minutes and records.

September 17, 1806.—The board met agreeably to adjournment. Present: The Hon. John B. C. Lucas, Clement B. Penrose, and James L. Donaldson, commissioners.

The same, (James Mackay,) assignee of Antoine Gautier, claiming ten arpents of land in front, on Marais Temps Clair, by such quantity as may be found between the aforesaid Marais Temps Clair and the Crooked Pond, produces a concession from Zenon Trudeau, dated the 29th of November, 1796, and a deed of transfer of the same, dated 1st of July, 1804. The board reject this claim.—(See book No. 2, page 32.)

September 28, 1810.—Board met. Present: John B. C. Lucas and Clement B. Penrose, commissioners.

James Mackay, assignee of Antoine Gautier, claiming ten arpents front, &c.—(See book No. 2, p. 32.) It is the opinion of the board that this claim ought not to be confirmed.—(See book No. 4, page 517.)

March 21, 1833.—F. R. Conway, esq., appeared pursuant to adjournment, being authorized to receive evidence by a resolution of this board taken 9th instant.

Antoine Gautier, by his legal representatives, claiming 4,000 arpents of land, (see book C, page 478; minutes, No. 2, page 32; No. 4, page 17,) produces a paper purporting to be an original concession from Zenon Trudeau, dated November 29, 1796; also a plat of survey by Soulard, dated December 3, 1804.

M. P. Le Duc, duly sworn, says that the petition, decree, and the signature affixed thereto, are in the proper handwriting of said Zenon Trudeau, and the signature to the plat of survey in the proper handwriting of Antonio Soulard.—(See book No. 6, page 137.)

November 12, 1833.—The board met pursuant to adjournment. Present: L. F. Linn, A. G. Harrison, and F. R. Conway, commissioners.

Antoine Gautier, claiming 4,000 arpents of land.—(See page 137 of this book.) The board remark that, by the petition, the Clear Weather swamp is asked for, but the surveyor general, Antoine Soulard, says, at the foot of the concession, that the granting of said swamp would lead into difficulties with the inhabitants of St. Charles and Portage des Sioux, and therefore, being vested with the proper authority, he gives order that this claim is to be surveyed in any other part of the King's domain. The board are unanimously of opinion that this claim ought to be confirmed to the said Antoine Gautier, or to his legal representatives, according to the concession.—(See book No. 6, page 321.)

A. G. HARRISON.
L. F. LINN.
F. R. CONWAY.

No. 110.—John McMillan, *claiming* 650 *arpents.*

To Don Charles Dehault Delassus, lieutenant colonel attached to the stationary regiment of Louisiana, and lieutenant governor of Upper Louisiana, &c.:

John McMillan, saddler by trade, and Roman Catholic, being settled, with the permission of the government, on the north side of the Missouri, supplicates you to grant to him, in the same place which he cultivates, the quantity of 650 arpents of land in superficie; said quantity being needed to include the water and timber necessary for the establishment of his plantation. The petitioner, being useful, on account of his trade, to the settlements on the north side of the Missouri, is inclined to hope that you will be pleased to grant to him the favor which he solicits of your justice, and he shall try to render himself worthy of it by his submission and fidelity to the kind government which has admitted him among the number of his Majesty's subjects.

JEAN + McMILLAN. (his mark)

St. André, *September* 14, 1799.

Be it forwarded to the lieutenant governor, with information that the statement above is true, and that the petitioner deserves, in every point of view, the favor which he solicits.

SANTIAGO MACKAY.

St. André, *September* 14, 1799.

St. Louis of Illinois, *September* 21, 1799.

In consequence of the foregoing information from the commandant of St. André, Captain Don Santiago Mackay, and being assured that the petitioner possesses sufficient means to improve the lands which he solicits, in the term prescribed by the regulation of the governor general of this province, the surveyor, Don Antonio Soulard, shall put the party interested in possession of the 650 arpents of land in superficie, in the same place indicated in his memorial; and this being executed, he shall make out a plat of his survey, delivering the same to the party, with his certificate, in order to enable him to obtain the concession and title in form from the intendant general of these provinces, to whom alone corresponds, by royal order, the distributing and granting all classes of lands of the royal domain.

CARLOS DEHAULT DELASSUS.

Recorded, No. 55.

MACKAY.

Truly translated. St. Louis, April 16, 1833.

JULIUS DE MUN.

No.	Name of original claimant.	Quantity, in arpents.	Nature and date of claim.	By whom granted.	By whom surveyed, date, and situation.
110	John McMillan......	650	Concession, September 21, 1797.	Carlos Dehault Delassus.	On the north side of the Missouri.

Evidence with reference to minutes and records.

September 28, 1810.—Board met. Present: John B. C. Lucas and Frederick Bates, commissioners.

James Mackay, assignee of John McMillan, claiming 650 arpents of land.—(See book No. 2, page 33.)

It is the opinion of the board that this claim ought not to be confirmed.—(See book No. 4, page 517.)

March 22, 1833.—F. R. Conway, esq., appeared pursuant to adjournment.

John McMillan, by his legal representative, claiming 650 arpents of land, (see book C, pages 476 and 477; minutes, No. 4, page 517,) produces a paper purporting to be a concession from Carlos Dehault Delassus, dated September 21, 1799.

M. P. Le Duc, duly sworn, says that the signature to the concession is in the proper handwriting of Carlos Dehault Delassus.—(See book No. 6, page 138.)

November 12, 1833.—The board met pursuant to adjournment. Present: L. F. Linn, A. G. Harrison, F. R. Conway, commissioners.

John McMillan, claiming 650 arpents of land.—(See page 138 of this book.)

The board are unanimously of opinion that this claim ought to be confirmed to the said John McMillan, or to his legal representatives, according to the concession.—(See book No. 6, page 322.)

A. G. HARRISON.
L. F. LINN.
F. R. CONWAY.

No. 111.—John Colligan, *claiming* 1,200 *arpents.*

To Mr. Zenon Trudeau, lieutenant governor and commander-in-chief of Upper Louisiana, &c.:

John Colligan, inhabiting the district of St. André of Missouri, has the honor to represent to you, that having given up a part of his plantation in order to establish a village thereon, in the said district of St. André, he would wish to obtain from you, for the purpose of improving a new plantation, the property of twelve hundred arpents of land in a vacant place on the south side of the Missouri—favor which he expects of your justice.

St. André, *December* 13, 1798.

I have the honor to inform the lieutenant governor that the above statement is conformable to truth, and therefore the petitioner deserves to obtain what he asks.

SANTIAGO MACKAY.

St. Louis, *December* 14, 1798.

Being satisfied that the party interested has voluntarily abandoned the land which he had improved, in order that a village should be formed in the most advantageous place for that purpose, in the jurisdiction of St. André, the surveyor shall put him in possession of the twelve hundred arpents in superficie, which he solicits, as corresponding to what had been offered to him by the commandant of said jurisdiction, Don Santiago Mackay, in case he abandoned his first establishment, for which he deserves the concession which he solicits.

ZENON TRUDEAU.

Recorded, No. 1.

MACKAY.

Truly translated. St. Louis, April 16, 1833.

JULIUS DE MUN.

No.	Name of original claimant.	Quantity, in arpents.	Nature and date of claim.	By whom granted.	By whom surveyed, date, and situation.
111	John Colligan.......	1,200	Concession, December 14, 1798.	Zenon Trudeau.	South side of the Missouri.

Evidence with reference to minutes and records.

November 2, 1811.—Board met. Present: John B. C. Lucas, Clement B. Penrose, and Frederick Bates, commissioners.

James Mackay, assignee of John Colligan, claiming 1,200 arpents of land situate in St. André, district of St. Louis, produces a concession from Zenon Trudeau, lieutenant governor, dated December 15, 1798, to John Coligan. It is the opinion of the board that this claim ought not to be confirmed.—(See book No. 5, page 395.)

March 22, 1833.—F. R. Conway, esq., appeared pursuant to adjournment.

John Colligan, by his legal representative, claiming 1,200 arpents of land, (see book C, page 479; minutes, No. 5, page 395,) produces a paper purporting to be an original concession from Zenon Trudeau, dated December 14, 1798.

M. P. Le Duc, duly sworn, says that the decree, and signature thereto affixed, are in the proper handwriting of Zenon Trudeau.—(See book No. 6, page 138.)

November 12, 1833.—The board met pursuant to adjournment. Present: L. F. Linn, A. G. Harrison, F. R. Conway, commissioners.

John Colligan, claiming 1,200 arpents of land.—(See page 138 of this book.)—The board are unanimously of opinion that this claim ought to be confirmed to the said John Colligan, or to his legal representatives, according to the concession.—(See book No. 6, page 322.)

A. G. HARRISON.
L. F. LINN.
F. R. CONWAY.

No. 112.—John Bishop, *claiming* 350 *arpents.*

To Don Carlos Dehault Delassus, lieutenant colonel attached to the stationary regiment of Louisiana, and lieutenant governor of Upper Louisiana:

John Bishop, a German, of the Roman Catholic religion, and father of a family, has the honor to represent to you, that, with the consent of Mr. Mackay, he has made choice of a convenient spot, on the south side of the Missouri, district of St. André, and he expects of your justice that you will be pleased to grant to him, in the same place, a tract of land proportionate to the number of individuals in his family, which consists of himself, his wife, and three children. The petitioner, having no other views but to live as a peaceable and submissive cultivator of the soil, hopes to deserve this favor of your justice.

JEAN his + mark BISHOP.

St. Louis, *November* 14, 1799.

St. Louis of Illinois, *November* 14, 1799.

In consequence of the official note sent to us by Don Santiago Mackay, commandant of the settlements of St. André, dated November 13 of this present year, by which the number of persons composing the family of the petitioner is proven, the surveyor, Don Antonio Soulard, shall put him in possession of 350 arpents of land in superficie, in the place where he asks, which quantity is corresponding to the number of his family, according to the regulations of the governor general of these provinces; and afterwards the (party) interested shall have to solicit the title of concession in due form from the intendant general of these provinces, to whom alone corresponds, by order of his Majesty, the distributing and granting all classes of lands of the royal domain.

CARLOS DEHAULT DELASSUS.

Don Antonio Soulard, surveyor general of the settlements of Upper Louisiana.

I do certify that a tract of land of 350 arpents in superficie was measured, the lines run and bounded, in favor and in presence of John Bishop; said measurement was made with the perch of Paris, of 18 French feet lineal measure of the same city, according to the agrarian measure of this province. This land is situated at twenty miles northwest of this town, and bounded north by vacant lands of the royal domain, south by the lands of Joseph Chartran; southeast by lands of Robert Yock and Emilian Yosty; and northeast by the river Missouri. Which survey and measurement were executed without regard to the variation of the needle, which is 7° 30′ east, as is obvious by referring to the foregoing figurative plat, on which are noted the dimensions, courses of the lines, and other boundaries, &c. This survey was executed by virtue of the decree of the lieutenant governor and sub-delegate of the royal treasury, Don Carlos Dehault Delassus, under date of November 14, 1799, here annexed; and in order that all here above-mentioned be available according to law, I do give the present, with the preceding figurative plat, drawn conformably to the survey executed by the deputy surveyor, Don Santiago Mackay, on December 1, 1802, who signed on the minutes, of which I do certify.

ANTONIO SOULARD, *Surveyor General.*

St. Louis of Illinois, *August* 23, 1803.

Truly translated. May 8, 1833.

JULIUS DE MUN.

No.	Name of the original claimant.	Quantity, in arpents.	Nature and date of claim.	By whom granted.	By whom surveyed, date, and situation.
112	John Bishop.......	350	Concession, November 14, 1799.	Carlos Dehault Delassus.	James Mackay, deputy surveyor, December 1, 1802; certified by Soulard, August 22, 1803. 20 miles N. W., of St. Louis.

Evidence with reference to minutes and records.

July 22, 1806.—The board met agreeably to adjournment. Present: John B. C. Lucas, Clement B. Penrose, and James L. Donaldson, commissioners.

The same, (James Mackay,) assignee of John Bishop, claiming 350 arpents of land situated on the Missouri, district of St. Louis, produces a concession from Charles D. Delassus, dated November 14, 1799, and a survey of the same, dated December 1, 1802, and certified August 23, 1803; a deed of sale, dated February 2, 1801.

John Tayon, being duly sworn, says that he, the witness, did, in the year 1804, build a house on said tract of land, made a field, and raised a crop, and that the same has been actually cultivated to this day. The board reject this claim.—(See book No. 1, page 417.)

September 8, 1810.—Board met. Present: John B. C. Lucas, Clement B. Penrose, and Frederick Bates, commissioners.

James Mackay, assignee of John Bishop, claiming 350 arpents of land, (see book No. 1, page 417.) It is the opinion of the board that this claim ought not to be confirmed.—(See book No. 4, page 489.)

March 22, 1833.—F. R. Conway, esq., appeared pursuant to adjournment.

John Bishop, by his legal representatives, claiming 350 arpents of land, (see book B, page 439; minutes, No. 1, page 417; No. 4, page 489,) produces a paper purporting to be an original concession from Carlos Dehault Delassus, dated 14th November, 1799; also a plat of survey, dated 23d August, 1803, by Antoine Soulard.

M. P. Le Duc, duly sworn, says that the signature to the concession is in the proper handwriting of said Delassus; and the signature to the plat of survey in the handwriting of Antoine Soulard.—(See book No. 6, page 138.)

November 12, 1833.—The board met pursuant to adjournment. Present: L. F. Linn, A. G. Harrison, F. R. Conway, commissioners.

John Bishop, claiming 350 arpents of land.—(See page 138 of this book.)

The board are unanimously of opinion that this claim ought to be confirmed to the said John Bishop, or to his legal representatives, according to the concession.—(See book No. 6, page 322.)

A. G. HARRISON.
L. F. LINN.
F. R. CONWAY.

No. 113.—Charles F. Delauriere, *claiming* 10,000 *arpents.*

To Don Zenon Trudeau, lieutenant governor of the western part of Illinois, and commander-in-chief of St. Louis, &c.:

Charles Frémon Delauriere has the honor to humbly represent that having been sent to this colony for services relative to this government, and having served his Catholic Majesty in the militia volunteers, which he has had the honor to command in the expedition made in the Mississippi in 1795, he would wish to establish himself in this province, and to have a property on which he might settle permanently, and make thereon, as soon as his means and circumstances will permit, useful establishments, advantageous to his fortune, of which he has been in part deprived by the French revolution; therefore he has recourse to your justice, and to the generosity of this government, hoping that, after taking in consideration the foregoing statement, you will be pleased, sir, to grant to him in full property a concession of ten thousand arpents of land in superficie, to be taken near the Prairie à Rondo, in the district of St. Genevieve, and to give orders to the surveyor general of Upper Louisiana to put him in possession, as soon as he shall be required to do so by your petitioner, who shall never cease to pray for the conservation of your days.

FRÉMON DELAURIERE.

St. Louis, *January* 15, 1797.

Don Zenon Trudeau, lieutenant governor of Upper Louisiana, &c.:

The surveyor, Don Antonio Soulard, shall put the (party) interested in possession of the ten thousand arpents of land in superficie which he solicits, in the place above mentioned, provided it be vacant and belonging to his Majesty's domain; and his survey being executed, he shall deliver (a plat of) it to him, (the petitioner,) in order that, along with this decree, it shall serve to him as a title of property, until the corresponding title in form be delivered to him by the general government, to which he must apply in due time.

ZENON TRUDEAU.

St. Louis, *January* 17, 1797.

Truly translated. St. Louis, May 1, 1833.

JULIUS DE MUN.

No.	Name of original claimant.	Quantity, in arpents.	Nature and date of claim.	By whom granted.	By whom surveyed, date, and situation.
113	Charles Frémon Delauriere.	10,000	Concession, January 17, 1797.	Zenon Trudeau.	John Ferrey, deputy surveyor, Jan. 9, 1804. In Richwood, 50 miles southwest of St. Louis.

Evidence with reference to minutes and records.

December 24, 1811.—The board met. Present: John B. C. Lucas, Clement B. Penrose, and Frederick Bates, commissioners.

Louis Labeaume and Charles Frémon Delauriere, claiming 10,000 arpents of land situate near Prairie à Rondo, district of St. Genevieve, produce record of a concession from Zenon Trudeau, lieutenant governor, dated 17th January, 1797; certificate of a plat of survey, signed and sworn to by Anthony Soulard, and dated 15th March, 1808. The board remark that no kind of testimony suggests or makes it appear that the land claimed includes a lead mine. It is the opinion of the board that this claim ought not to be confirmed.—(See book No. 5, page 539.)

March 25, 1833.—F. R. Conway, esq., appeared pursuant to adjournment.

Charles Frémon Delauriere, by Louis Labeaume's representatives, claiming 10,000 arpents of land situate near Prairie Rondeau, now Richwood, (see record book D, pages 300 and 301; minutes, No. 5, page 539,) produces a paper purporting to be an original concession from Zenon Trudeau, dated 17th January, 1797; also a deed between said Delauriere and Labeaume, dated July 15, 1806.

Albert Tison, duly sworn, says that the signature to said concession is in the proper handwriting of Zenon Trudeau; that said land was surveyed in 1803; that it was settled by Labeaume in 1806; and possessed, cultivated, and inhabited ever since by or through him.

Charles F. Delauriere, being duly sworn, says that in the spring of 1800 he engaged and hired two men to go on said land, in order to build a house and make what improvements they could; that in the fall of the same year he sent another man on said land; but circumstances turning out differently to his expectations, he discontinued improving said land. The deponent further declares that he is in no way whatsoever interested in the above-mentioned tract of land.—(See book No. 6, page 139.)

November 13, 1833.—The board met pursuant to adjournment. Present: L. F. Linn, A. G. Harrison, F. R. Conway, commissioners.

Charles Frémon Delauriere, claiming 10,000 arpents of land.—(See page 139 of this book.) The board are unanimously of opinion that this claim ought to be confirmed to the said Charles Frémon Delauriere, or to his legal representatives, according to the concession.—(See book No. 6, page 323.)

A. G. HARRISON
L. F. LINN.
F. R. CONWAY.

No. 114.—J. Bte. Tison, *claiming* 7,056 *arpents.*

Don Carlos Dehault Delassus, lieutenant governor of Upper Louisiana:

Sir: Jean Bte. Tison has the honor to represent to you that he would wish to form an establishment for the support of his numerous family, composed of eight children; the petitioner has been inhabiting this province for upwards of fifteen years, and has never possessed any land; therefore, sir, the petitioner, in order to be able to raise his family and keep it near him, prays you to grant to him a tract of land of seven thousand and fifty-six arpents in superficie, to be taken on the vacant lands of his Majesty's domain, and that he be permitted to take the said land in the manner which will appear most convenient and most advantageous to the end which he proposes to himself—favor which the petitioner presumes to expect of your goodness and justice.

JEAN BAPTISTE TISON.

St. Louis, *November* 16, 1799.

St. Louis of Illinois, *November* 19, 1799.

Whereas it is notorious that the petitioner possesses more than the means and number of hands necessary to obtain the concession which he solicits, I do grant to him and his heirs the land he solicits, provided it is not prejudicial to any person; and the surveyor, Don Antonio Soulard, shall put the (party) interested in possession of the quantity of land he asks, in a vacant place of the royal domain; which being executed, he shall make a plat of (his) survey, delivering the same to said party, with his certificate, in order to enable him to obtain the concession and title in form from the intendant general, to whom alone corresponds, by royal order, the distributing and granting all classes of lands of the royal domain.

CARLOS DEHAULT DELASSUS.

Registered at the request of the interested.—(Book No. 2, page 50, No. 86.)

SOULARD.

Truly translated. May 1, 1832.

JULIUS DE MUN.

No.	Name of original claimant.	Quantity, in arpents.	Nature and date of claim.	By whom granted.	By whom surveyed, date, and situation.
114	Jean Baptiste Tison..	7,056	Concession, Nov. 19, 1799.	Carlos Dehault Delassus.	Frémon Delauriere, deputy surveyor, Jan. 31, 1806. On the waters of Grand Glaise.

Evidence with reference to minutes and records.

December 10, 1811.—Board met. Present: John B. C. Lucas, Clement B. Penrose, and Frederick Bates, commissioners.

Louis Labeaume, assignee of Jean Baptiste Tison, claiming 7,056 arpents of land situate on Salt river, district of St. Charles, produces record of a concession from Delassus, lieutenant governor, dated November 19, 1799; record of a transfer from Tison to claimant, dated May 20, 1803. It is the opinion of the board that this claim ought not to be confirmed.—(See book No. 5, page 507.)

March 25, 1833.—F. R. Conway, esq., appeared pursuant to adjournment.

Jean Baptiste Tison, by Louis Labeaume's legal representatives, claiming 7,056 arpents of land.—(See book No. 6, page 301; No. 5, page 507.) For survey claimant refers to the testimony given by Charles Frémon Delauriere, in the case of F. Saucier, (see page 118 of this book,) to wit: That the survey already produced is one of those included among the surveys mentioned in the above letter; that the survey was executed at the time it bears date; that there was great difficulty and danger in executing surveys; that he was twice repulsed by the Indians, and that the third time he went up he could not execute several of the surveys, being prevented by the Indians of the Sac and Fox nations, although he and his companions were well armed; that surveyors were very scarce, and it was difficult to procure any one to take surveys; that there was not half the number of surveyors necessary to execute the surveys that were then to be made. Produces a paper purporting to be a concession from Charles Dehault Delassus, dated November 19, 1799; a certified copy of a deed from Tison to Labeaume; also a deed of partition between said Tison and Labeaume.

M. P. Le Duc, duly sworn, says that the signature to the concession is in the proper handwriting of said Carlos Dehault Delassus.—(See book No. 6, page 140.)

November 13, 1833.—The board met pursuant to adjournment. Present: L. F. Linn, A. G. Harrison, F. R. Conway, commissioners.

Jean Baptiste Tison, claiming 7,056 arpents of land.—(See page 140 of this book.) The board are unanimously of opinion that this claim ought to be confirmed to the said Jean Baptiste Tison, or to his legal representatives, according to the concession.—(See book No. 6, page 323.)

A. G. HARRISON.
L. F. LINN.
F. R. CONWAY.

No. 115.—Louis Delille, *claiming* 2,500 *arpents.*

Don Charles Dehault Delassus, lieutenant governor of Upper Louisiana:

Sir: Louis Delille, one of the ancient inhabitants of this town, having a very numerous family, and several slaves, wishes to make an establishment in this Upper Louisiana; therefore he has recourse to your goodness, praying that you will be pleased to grant to him 2,500 arpents of land in superficie, to be taken on the vacant lands of the King's domain, in a convenient place, where he may with advantage occupy himself in agriculture, and in raising all kinds of cattle—favor which the petitioner presumes to expect of your justice.

LOUIS his + mark DELILLE.

St. Louis, *November* 2, 1799.

St. Louis of Illinois, *November* 6, 1799.

Considering that the petitioner is one of the most ancient inhabitants of this country, whose known conduct and personal merit are recommendable, and being satisfied to evidence as to the truth of what he states in his petition, and that his family is sufficiently considerable to obtain the quantity of land which he solicits, I do grant to him and his heirs the land he solicits, provided it is not prejudicial to anybody; and the surveyor, Don Antonio Soulard, shall put the (party) interested in possession of the quantity of land he asks, in a vacant place of the royal domain; which being executed, he shall make out a plat of (his) survey, delivering the same to said party with his certificate, in order to enable him to obtain the concession and title in form from the intendant general, to whom alone corresponds, by royal order, the distributing and granting all classes of lands of the royal domain.

CARLOS DEHAULT DELASSUS.

Don Antonio Soulard, surveyor general of the settlements of Upper Louisiana.

I do certify that a tract of land of 2,500 arpents in superficie was measured, the lines run and bounded, in favor of Don Louis Labeaume, and in presence of Albert Tison, his agent; which land was originally granted to Louis Delille, who sold it to the above-named Labeaume, the present owner, as it is proven by the deed of sale executed by him, and deposited in the archives of this government. The said land was measured with the perch of the city of Paris, of eighteen French feet lineal measure of the same city, conformably to the agrarian measure of this province. This land is situated at about sixty-two miles north of St. Louis, bounded N.NW. by the lands of Philip Le Duc and Don Louis Brazeau, S.SE. by vacant lands of the royal domain, W.SW. by lands of Pedro Janin, and E.NE. by lands of Aristide Augustin Chouteau. These surveys and measurements were executed without regard to the variation of the needle, which is of 7° 30′ east, as it is evinced by the foregoing figurative plat, on which are noted the dimensions, courses of the lines, other boundaries, &c. This survey was made by virtue of the power and decree of the lieutenant governor and sub-delegate of the royal treasury, Don Carlos Dehault Delassus, under date of November, 6, 1799, here annexed. And in order that the whole may be available according to law, I do give the present, with the foregoing figurative plat, drawn conformably to the survey executed by the deputy surveyor, James Rankin, under date of February 14, 1804, who signed the minutes, to which I do certify.

ANTONIO SOULARD, *Surveyor General.*

ST. LOUIS OF ILLINOIS, *March* 20, 1804.

Truly translated. St. Louis, May 2, 1833.

JULIUS DE MUN.

No.	Name of original claimant.	Quantity, in arpents	Nature and date of claim.	By whom granted.	By whom surveyed, date, and situation.
115	Louis Delille......	2,500	Concession, Nov. 6, 1799.	Carlos Dehault Delassus.	James Rankin, deputy surveyor, Feb. 14, 1804; certified by Soulard, March 20, 1804. 62 miles north of St. Louis.

Evidence with reference to minutes and records.

November 14, 1811.—Board met. Present: John B. C. Lucas, Clement B. Penrose, and Frederick Bates, commissioners.

Louis Labeaume, assignee of Louis Delille, claiming 2,500 arpents of land situate in the district of St. Charles, produces the record of a concession from Charles D. Delassus, lieutenant governor, dated November 6, 1799; a plat of survey dated February 14 and certified March 20, 1804; a certified extract of a sale made by Delille to claimant, dated October 7, 1803. It is the opinion of the board that this claim ought not to be confirmed.—(See book No. 5, page 407.)

March 25, 1833.—F. R. Conway, esq., appeared pursuant to adjournment.

Louis Delille, by Louis Labeaume's representatives, claiming 2,500 arpents of land, (see book C, pages 340 and 341; minutes, No. 345, page 407,) produces a paper purporting to be an original concession from Carlos Dehault Delassus, dated November 6, 1799; a plat of survey, taken February 14, and certified March 20, 1804, by Soulard; also a certificate of transfer, signed M. P. Le Duc, recorder.

M. P. Le Duc, sworn, says that the signature to the concession is in the proper handwriting of Carlos D. Delassus; and the signature to plat and certificate of survey is in the proper handwriting of said Soulard.—(See book No. 6, page 141.)

November 13, 1833.—The board met pursuant to adjournment. Present: L. F. Linn, A. G. Harrison, F. R. Conway, commissioners.

Louis Delille, claiming 2,500 arpents of land.—(See page 141 of this book.) The board are unanimously of opinion that this claim ought to be confirmed to the said Louis Delille, or to his legal representatives, according to the concession.—(See book No. 6, page 323.)

A. G. HARRISON.
L. F. LINN.
F. R. CONWAY.

No. 116.—JOSEPH MORIN, jr., *claiming* 160 *arpents.*

To Don Zenon Trudeau, lieutenant colonel, captain in the stationary regiment of Louisiana, and lieutenant governor of the western part of Illinois:

Joseph Morin, jr., being at the eve of establishing himself, and wishing to continue to live near his family, in order to be at hand to help his father in his works, has the honor to supplicate you to be willing to grant to him the quantity of four arpents of land in front by forty arpents in depth, situated at six or seven miles north of this town, and bounded as follows: north by vacant lands of his Majesty's domain; south by lands of Antoine Morin, his father; east by the river Mississippi, and west by lands of the domain; observing to you that the said piece of land crosses the little river A Gingras at the distance from the Mississippi of about nine or ten arpents. The petitioner hopes to deserve this favor of your justice and of the encouragement you give to industry.

JOSEPH his + mark MORIN, JR.

ST. LOUIS OF ILLINOIS, *September* 7, 1796.

ST. LOUIS, *September* 9, 1797.

The surveyor, Don Antonio Soulard, shall put the party interested in possession of the land he solicits, *and shall make out a plat of his survey, with his certificate, which shall be here annexed,* (y formalisara su apeo á continuacion,) in order to serve to solicit the concession from the governor general of the province, who is informed that the said land solicited is vacant, and that the petitioner is a native of this town, having no land, and whose conduct deserves the favor which he solicits.

ZENON TRUDEAU.

At the request of Mr. Louis Labeaume, I do certify to all whom it may concern that the above plat of survey is a true copy of a plat recorded in page 28 of the book entitled as follows: "*Register of Surveys, St. Louis, A,*" which survey was executed by me on the 16th November, 1799, by virtue of a decree of the lieutenant governor, Don Zenon Trudeau, under date September 9, 1797, in favor of Joseph Morin, jr., for the quantity of 162 arpents 48 perches, as above described. In testimony whereof, I have delivered the present to the party interested, in order that it may serve to him in proving his claims.

ANTONIO SOULARD, *Surveyor General Louisiana Territory.*

ST. LOUIS, *February* 20, 1806.

Truly translated. St. Louis, April 17, 1833.

JULIUS DE MUN.

No.	Name of original claimant.	Quantity, in arpents	Nature and date of claim.	By whom granted.	By whom surveyed, date, and situation.
116	Joseph Morin, jr.	160	Concession, September 9, 1797.	Zen. Trudeau...	Antonio Soulard, surveyor general, Nov. 16, 1799; certified Feb. 20, 1806; on river Gingras.

Evidence with reference to minutes and records.

November 27, 1811.—Board met. Present: John B. C. Lucas, Clement B. Penrose, and Frederick Bates, commissioners.

Louis Labeaume, assignee of Baptiste Pacquette, assignee of Joseph Morin, claiming 160 arpents of land situate in White Ox prairie, district of St. Louis, produces record of a concession from Zenon Trudeau, lieutenant governor, dated September 9, 1797; record of a plat of a survey certified February, 1806; record of a transfer from Morin to Pacquette, dated May 8, 1804; record of a transfer from Pacquette to claimant, dated May 8, 1804. It is the opinion of the board that this claim ought not to be confirmed.—(See book No. 5, page 458.

March 25, 1833.—F. R. Conway, esq., appeared pursuant to adjournment.

Joseph Morin, by Louis Labeaume's legal representatives, claiming 160 arpents of land, (see book D, pages 303, 304, and 305; minutes No. 5, page 458, (produces a paper purporting to be a concession from Zenon Trudeau, dated September 9, 1797; a plat and certificate of survey, signed A. Soulard, said survey taken November 16, 1799, and certificate, dated February 20, 1806; also deed from said Morin to J. B. Pacquette, dated March 13, 1804, and deed from Pacquette to Labeaume, dated May 8, 1804.

M. P. Le Duc, duly sworn, says that the signature to the concession and the concession itself are in the proper handwriting of Zenon Trudeau, and the signature to the plat of survey is in the proper handwriting of A. Soulard.

Albert Tison, duly sworn, says that about twenty-eight years ago he went on said land, built a house, dug a well, and fenced in a field; that he resided on the same near two years, and about ten years after he left said place the claimant went on said land, and by or through him it has been inhabited and cultivated ever since.—(See book No. 6, page 149.)

April 3, 1833.—F. R. Conway, esq., appeared pursuant to adjournment.

In the case of Joseph Morin, jr., claiming 160 arpents of land.—(See page 149 of this book.)

Joseph Hebert, duly sworn, says that to his knowledge the said land was inhabited and cultivated thirty-two or thirty-three years ago by or through Joseph Morin, jr., and has been inhabited and cultivated ever since.—(See book No. 6, page 152.)

November 13, 1833.—The board met pursuant to adjournment. Present: L. F. Linn, A. G. Harrison, F. R. Conway, commissioners.

Joseph Morin, jr., claiming 160 arpents of land.—(See pages 149 and 152 of this book.) The board remark that the concession is for 160 arpents, and the survey 162 48 perches. The board are unanimously of opinion that this claim ought to be confirmed to the said Joseph Morin, jr., or to his legal representatives, according to the concession.—(See book No. 6, page 323.)

A. G. HARRISON.
L. F. LINN.
F. R. CONWAY.

No. 117.—James Williams, *claiming 400 arpents.*

To Don Carlos Dehault Delassus, lieutenant colonel, attached to the stationary regiment of Louisiana, and lieutenant governor of the upper part of the same province:

James Williams, inhabiting this side of the Mississippi since several years, has the honor to represent to you that in the year 1796 he obtained of your predecessor, Don Zenon Trudeau, a tract of land of 400 arpents in superficie, situate near the lands of the village of St. Ferdinand, which was surveyed, as it is proven by the certificate of survey delivered to him by the surveyor of this Upper Louisiana, and which is here annexed. Family affairs having required his presence in the United States, and those same affairs having retained him there longer than he would have wished, his absence has been looked upon as a tacit abandonment of the land which had been granted to him, and the said land was included in other surveys which have been made on the same place. It being his intention to have difficulties with nobody, he has recourse to your justice, in order that you will be pleased to have the goodness to indemnify him for the loss of a piece of land which he thought (and justly) of importance to him, and that you will grant him a concession, in full property, of the same quantity of 400 arpents, to be taken in a vacant place of his Majesty's domains. The petitioner, full of confidence in your justice, and having always had a conduct exempt of reproaches, hopes that you will be pleased to do justice to his demand in a manner satisfactory to the accomplishment of his wishes.

his
JAMES + WILLIAMS.
mark.

St. Louis of Illinois, *April* 15, 1803.

St. Louis of Illinois, *April* 15, 1803.

Having examined the statement in the foregoing petition, and paying due attention to the just reasons alleged by the petitioner, who has always continued to be a subject of his Majesty since the time that the first concession was granted by my predecessor, Don Zenon Trudeau, which is evident by referring to the certificate of survey here annexed, I do grant to him and his heirs the land which he solicits, provided it is not prejudicial to any person; and the surveyor, Don Antonio Soulard, shall put the party interested in possession of the quantity of land he asks in the place designated; which being executed, he shall make out a plat of his survey, delivering the same to said party with his certificate, in order to enable him to obtain the concession and title in form from the intendant general, to whom alone corresponds, by royal order, the distributing and granting all classes of lands of the royal domain.

CARLOS DEHAULT DELASSUS.

We, the undersigned, surveyor, commissioned by the government, do certify to all whom it may concern that this day, 14th of December, 1796, by virtue of the order of the lieutenant governor, under date of November 6 of this present year, we have been on the land of Mr. James Williams, in order to measure and survey a tract of land to him granted, of 10 arpents in front by 40 in depth, or 400 arpents in superficie; which measurement was made in presence of the proprietor and of the adjoining neighbors with the perch of the city of Paris, of 18 French feet in length, conformably to the usage and custom of this colony. This land is situated at the distance of about three miles, nearly in a NE. direction from the village of St. Ferdinand, and at 15 arpents from the little river of the same name; bounded on one side by the land of John Herben, and on the others adjoining vacant lands of his Majesty's domain. And in order that it may be available according to law, I do give the present, with the figurative plat annexed to it, on which we have marked the natural and artificial boundaries, &c.

ANTONIO SOULARD.

St. Louis of Illinois, *December* 20, 1796.

Truly translated. St. Louis, May 6, 1833.

JULIUS DE MUN.

No.	Name of original claimant.	Quantity, in arpents.	Nature and date of claim.	By whom granted.	By whom surveyed, date, and situation.
117	James Williams..	400	Concession, April 15, 1803.	Carlos Dehault Delassus.	The first grant said to have been made by Zenon Trudeau was surveyed by Soulard December 14, 1796. Near St. Ferdinand.

Evidence with reference to minutes and records.

December 10, 1811.—Board met. Present: John B. C. Lucas, Clement B. Penrose, and Frederick Bates, commissioners.

Albert Tison, assignee of Louis Labeaume, assignee of James Williams, claiming 400 arpents of land situate in the district of St. Louis, produces record of a concession from Delassus, lieutenant governor, dated April 15, 1803; record of a transfer from Williams to Labeaume, dated April 29, 1806. It is the opinion of the board that this claim ought not to be confirmed.—(See book No. 5, page 513.)

March 25, 1833.—F. R. Conway, esq., appeared pursuant to adjournment.

James Williams, by L. Labeaume's legal representatives, claiming 400 arpents of land, (see book D, pages 310, 311, and 312; minutes, book No. 5, page 513,) produces a paper purporting to be an original concession from Carlos Dehault Delassus, dated April 15, 1803; also, a deed from said Williams to Labeaume, dated April 29, 1806; also, assignment by Labeaume to A. Tison, and release from said Tison to Labeaume; also, a survey in support of said claim, as an evidence of the same not claiming the land contained in the survey, but only produces it in support of the grant made in lieu thereof.

M. P. Le Duc, duly sworn, says that the signature to the concession is in the proper handwriting of said Delassus, and the signature to the survey in the proper handwriting of Antonio Soulard.—(See book No. 6, page 150.)

November 13, 1833.—The board met pursuant to adjournment. Present: L. F. Linn, A. G. Harrison, F. R. Conway, commissioners.

James Williams, claiming 400 arpents of land.—(See page 150 of this book.) The board are unanimously of opinion that this claim ought to be confirmed to the said James Williams, or to his legal representatives, according to the concession.—(See book No. 6, page 324.)

A. G. HARRISON.
L. F. LINN.
F. R. CONWAY.

No. 118.—Josiah McClenahan, under Gabriel Cerré, *claiming* 300 *arpents.*

To Don Charles Dehault Delassus, lieutenant colonel, attached to the stationary regiment of Louisiana, and lieutenant governor of the upper part of the same province:

Gabriel Cerré, father of a family, owner of slaves, and one of the most ancient inhabitants of this country, has the honor to supplicate you to have the goodness to grant to him, to the north of this town, on the *Ruisseau de Pierre*, (Stony creek,) an augmentation of three hundred arpents of land in superficie to a tract of land he purchased several years ago, so as to give him the enjoyment of a spring, the owning of which he thinks very important, according to his views of improvement. The said augmentation to be bounded as follows: On the north by the line of the land I purchased, the title of which, with the ratification in form, has been delivered to me; on the south and east by the lines of Mr. Labeaume's land, and on the west by the vacant lands of the domain. The petitioner hopes so much the more to obtain the favor which he claims of your justice, because the public road passes now on his first piece of land through a hilly and difficult place for carting, and that he intends, as soon as he obtains the augmentation solicited, to make the said road pass in a more suitable place, but this will require the construction of a bridge, which he shall cause to be built immediately over the said creek. The petitioner, full of confidence in your justice, hopes that you will be pleased to do justice to his demand in such a manner as to fulfil his views.

CERRÉ.

St. Louis, *January* 3, 180, (1800.)

St. Louis of Illinois, *January* 3, 1800.

Considering that the petitioner is one of the most ancient inhabitants of this country, whose known conduct and personal merit are recommendable, and being satisfied to evidence as to the truth of what he states in his petition, the surveyor of this Upper Louisiana, Don Antonio Soulard, shall put the interested party in possession of the three hundred arpents of land in superficie which he solicits, for him to enjoy the same under the same boundaries that he asks; and the survey being executed, he (the surveyor) shall make out the corresponding certificate of the same, with which the interested party shall apply to the intendancy general of these provinces, to which alone corresponds, by order of his Majesty, the granting of lands and town lots belonging to the domain.

CARLOS DEHAULT DELASSUS.

Registered at the request of the interested in book No. 2, pages 28 and 29.

SOULARD.

Truly translated from book B, page 389.

JULIUS DE MUN.

No.	Name of original claimant.	Quantity, in arpents.	Nature and date of claim.	By whom granted.	By whom surveyed, date, and situation.
118	Gabriel Cerré.......	300	Concession, January 3, 1800.	Carlos Dehault Delassus.	

Evidence with reference to minutes and records.

July 7, 1806.—The board met agreeably to adjournment. Present: The Hon. Clement B. Penrose and James L. Donaldson. Josiah McLanahan claiming, as aforesaid, 800 arpents of land situate in the district of St. Louis, produces a concession from Charles Dehault Delassus, dated January 5, (3,) 1800. A survey of the same, dated 27th, and certified February 28, 1806, together with the act of public sale aforesaid.

Antoine Soulard, duly sworn, says that he wrote the decree of the lieutenant governor to the said concession; that he does not recollect whether it was granted at the time it bears date; that it was granted for the building of a bridge, which was completed by the said Gabriel Cerré about five years ago. The board reject this claim; they are satisfied it was granted at the time it bears date.—(See book No. 1, page 393.)

September 1, 1810.—Board met. Present: John B. C. Lucas, Clement B. Penrose, and Frederick Bates, commissioners.

Josiah McLanahan, assignee of the representatives of Gabriel Cerré, deceased, claiming 800 arpents of land.—(See book No. 1, page 393.) It is the opinion of a majority of the board that this claim ought not to be confirmed. Clement B. Penrose, commissioner, voting for the confirmation of 300 arpents of land.—(See book No 4, page 484.)

March 29, 1833.—F. R. Conway, esq., appeared pursuant to adjournment. Gabriel Cerré, by Josiah McLanahan, claiming 300 arpents of land.—(See book B, pages 258 and 389; minutes No. 1, page 393; No. 4, page 484.)

Pascal L. Cerré, duly sworn, says that Gabriel Cerré was his father; that he knows the conditions of said grant to have been, on the part of his father, to build a bridge over the Ruisseau de Pierre; that his said father having gone to Canada previous to Delassus's signing the grant, he, the deponent, remained charged with his business in this country, when Delassus, who had not yet signed the grant, hurried him to go on with the bridge, but the deponent would not do it until the grant was signed; which Delassus having done, he sent his hands immediately to work, having already all the materials on the spot, and soon completed the bridge.—(See book No. 6, page 151.)

August 7, 1833.—The board met pursuant to adjournment. Present: L. F. Linn, A. G. Harrison, F. R. Conway, commissioners.

In the case of Gabriel Cerré, by Josiah McLanahan, claiming 300 arpents of land.—(See page 151 of this book.)

André Landreville, being duly sworn, says that, under the Spanish government, he knows that Gabriel Cerré, at his own expense, made and built a bridge over the Ruisseau de Pierre; that said bridge was of great public utility, and that he, the deponent, passed many a time over said bridge.—(See book No. 6, page 241.)

October 31, 1833.—The board met pursuant to adjournment. Present: L. F. Linn, A. G. Harrison, F. R. Conway, commissioners.

In the case of Gabriel Cerré, claiming 300 arpents of land.—(See pages 251 and 241 of this book.)

Hyacinthe Lecompte, duly sworn, says that he is about fifty-eight years of age; that he knows perfectly well that Gabriel Cerré caused a bridge to be built at his own expense over the Ruisseau de Pierre. Witness says, further, that said bridge was of the greatest utility to the public; that by the old road there was almost an impossibility of passing with loaded carts; that himself had had his cart, loaded with hay, very often overturned on said old road; that, when said bridge was built, the Spaniards had possession of the country, and that as soon as said bridge was erected all the inhabitants abandoned the old road; that it was built some time before the Americans took possession of the country, but cannot recollect how long before.—(See book No. 6, page 286.)

November 13, 1833.—The board met pursuant to adjournment. Present: L. F. Linn, A. G. Harrison, F. R. Conway, commissioners.

Gabriel Cerré, claiming 300 arpents of land.—(See pages 151, 241, and 286, of this book.) The board are unanimously of opinion that this claim ought to be confirmed to the said Gabriel Cerré, or to his legal representatives, according to the concession.—(See book No. 6, page 324.)

A. G. HARRISON.
L. F. LINN.
F. R. CONWAY.

No. 119.—Charles Frémon Delauriere, *claiming* 10,000 *arpents.*

To Don Zenon Trudeau, lieutenant governor of Illinois, and commander-in-chief in St. Louis:

Sir: Louis Labeaume and Charles Frémon Delauriere have the honor to state to you that, wishing to work some saline, they claim of your justice, and of the benevolence of the government which you represent, the permission to go to visit and examine the places which will appear to them the most convenient to their project, and to take there the quantity of land which they will think necessary to make this establishment, so that when their choice is made, and the locality determined, they may apply to you, sir, or to your successor, to obtain the concession and title of property. It is a favor which the petitioners presume to hope from your goodness and justice.

L. LABEAUME.
FRÉMON DELAURIERE.

St. Louis, *May* 12, 1799.

Be it done as is required. St. Louis, May 13, 1799.

TRUDEAU.

To Don C. Dehault Delassus, lieutenant governor of Upper Louisiana:

Sir: Charles Frémon Delauriere and Louis Labeaume have the honor to state to you that, in consequence of the demand which they made to the intendant general of this province, dated November 22,

1800, and in virtue of your official letter to the said intendant, dated 28th of same month, by which you authorize the petitioners to begin their works, and to explore the salines which they have solicited, the petitioners have immediately transported themselves on said place, with the cattle, kettles, and other utensils necessary to said employment, and have succeeded in making very fine and very good salt, and up to this day preferable to all the salt made at the several salines worked in this Upper Louisiana.

The petitioners, encouraged by your approbation, sir, and by the preference which the public has given to their salt, continue their works, and are going to ameliorate them as much as possible, although they are at considerable expenses, and they find great obstacles to the importation of their salt to the centre of the population.

The petitioners, persuaded that the beauty and richness of the lands of the river Ohaha must soon attract the attention of this government, not willing in any way to be prejudicial, or constrain the population which will necessarily carry itself there, having, moreover, fulfilled the conditions which they had proposed, and having transported on their place the kettles necessary to erect four or five furnaces, supplicate you to grant to them at the place called La Saline Ensanglantée (the Bloody Saline) the quantity of one hundred arpents square of land, making a superficie of ten thousand arpents, and to order the surveyor general of this jurisdiction to transport himself on the place for the purpose of measuring said land, so that the limits of the petitioners being known, persons to whom lands might be conceded in that part of the country may place themselves without encroaching on the rights of the petitioners, who hope to be every day more deserving your favors and the protection which you have been pleased to grant to their establishment.

L. LEBEAUME.
FRÉMON DELAURIERE.

St. Louis, *March* 25, 1801.

St. Louis of Illinois, *March* 26, 1801.

Being satisfied that the interested have fulfilled what they state, having already brought here samples of the salt, which is a great deal preferable to the other salt made in small quantity and of a bad quality in the other salines, and of the expenses occasioned to them by this difficult enterprise in a place so distant from the settlements, and being convenient to the general welfare that that place should be established to enable the interested to find men for the improvement of said salt works, which is beneficial to the public, I do grant to them the quantity of land solicited by them as their property, that they may dispose of it to facilitate in that remote place a settlement necessary to their operations; and the surveyor, Don Antonio Soulard, shall put them in possession of said quantity without being prejudicial to any person, and shall make a proces verbal of his survey, to serve to them in soliciting the title in form from the intendant, to whom correspond the granting and distributing by royal order all classes of lands of the royal domain.

CARLOS DEHAULT DELASSUS.

Registered, at the desire of the interested, book No. 2, pages 35, 36, 37, and 38.

SOULARD.

Surveyed by virtue of the decree of the lieutenant governor, Colonel Don Carlos Dehault Delassus, dated March 26, 1801.

In my former quality of surveyor general I do certify that the foregoing plat of survey is a true copy of the original which is in my hands, signed by my ex-deputy, Mr. James Rankin, which survey has been taken by virtue of the title here above mentioned, and at the request of Messrs. Charles Frémon Delauriere and L. Labeaume, under the former authorities, and could not be entered, by various reasons of delay, on the books (record) of plats of surveys under my charge, and that the certificate could not be expedited in the form heretofore customary.

ANTONIO SOULARD.

St. Louis, *November* 15, 1807.

Truly translated. St. Louis, December 17, 1832.

JULIUS DE MUN.

No.	Names of original claimants.	Quantity, in arpents.	Nature and date of claim.	By whom granted.	By whom surveyed, date, and situation.
119	Charles Frémon Delauriere and Louis Lebeaume.	10,000	Concession, March 26, 1801.	Carlos Dehault Delassus.	James Rankin, deputy surveyor; Jan. 2, 1804; on Salt river.

Evidence with reference to minutes and records.

December 27, 1811.—Board met. Present: John B. C. Lucas, Clement B. Penrose, and Frederick Bates, commissioners.

Charles Frémon Delauriere and Louis Labeaume, claiming ten thousand arpents of land situate on Salt river, district of St. Charles, produces record of permission from Zenon Trudeau, lieutenant governor, to choose a salt spring, dated May 13, 1799; record of a concession from Charles D. Delassus, lieutenant governor, dated March 26, 1801; record of a plat of survey, signed Antonio Soulard, dated November 15, 1807.

It is the opinion of a majority of the board that this claim ought not be confirmed. Frederick Bates, commissioner, forbears giving an opinion.—(See book No. 5, page 545.)

November 21, 1832.—The board met pursuant to adjournment. Present: Lewis F. Linn, F. R. Conway, commissioners.

Charles F. Delauriere, for himself and as assignee of Louis Labeaume, by his legal representatives, claiming ten thousand arpents of land, (see record book D, pages 287, 288, 289, and 290; book No. 5, page 545,) produces a paper purporting to be the petition of Louis Labeaume and Frémon Delauriere, dated May 7, 1799, to Don Zenon Trudeau, lieutenant governor, and the concession of said Trudeau, dated May 131, 799; also, a paper purporting to be the petition of said Labeaume and Frémon Delauriere, dated March 25, 1801, to Don Charles Dehault Delassus, lieutenant governor of Louisiana; also, the concession of said Delassus, dated March 26, 1801; registered by Soulard, record book D, pages 288 and 289; also, a plat and certificate of survey, signed by Antoine Soulard.—(See book D, page 288.)

Albert Tison, being duly sworn, saith that the signatures to petition are in the respective handwriting of Louis Labeaume and Frémon Delauriere; that the signature to first concession is in the handwriting of Zenon Trudeau; that the signatures to second petition are in the respective handwriting of Louis Labeaume and Frémon Delauriere; and the signature to second concession is in the handwriting of Charles Dehault Delassus.

David Delaunay, being duly sworn, saith that the signatures to second petition and concession are in the respective handwriting of the three individuals who signed them; that the signature to plat and certificate of survey is in the handwriting of Antoine Soulard; and that the signature to the affidavit by James Rankin, on the back of said plat of survey, is in the handwriting of said Rankin.

Claimant produces, also, a paper purporting to be a deed of conveyance from Louis Labeaume to Frémon Delauriere.—(Recorded book D, pages 289 and 290.)

David Delaunay saith that the signatures to said deed are in the handwriting of Louis Labeaume and Frémon Delauriere.

Albert Tison saith that he was present when James Rankin surveyed the said 10,000 arpents of land at the time stated in the affidavit; that he saw the salt furnaces in operation by Frémon Delauriere; that the family of said Delauriere had been residing on said saline since either 1801 or 1802, in fact, a long time before the land was surveyed, at least two years before; that they made a great quantity of salt at said works for the supply of inhabitants; that they sustained losses by boats upsetting in the Mississippi, and more yet in Salt river itself; that at the beginning of their undertaking there was great danger on account of the Indians; that they were obliged to fortify themselves; had a piece of cannon, and were several times threatened of being attacked; that the place where they made salt was the extreme frontier of the settlements; that by this undertaking Frémon Delauriere was reduced to poverty.—(See book No. 6, pages 32 and 33.)

November 18, 1833.—The board met pursuant to adjournment. Present: L. F. Linn, A. G. Harrison, F. R. Conway, commissioners.

Charles Frémon Delauriere, for himself and as assignee of Louis Labeaume, claiming 10,000 arpents of land.—(See page 32 of this book.)

The board are unanimously of opinion that this claim ought to be confirmed to the said Charles Frémon Delauriere and Louis Labeaume, or to their legal representatives, according to the concession.—(See book No. 6, page 324.)

Conflicting claims.

James Hurley and James Small, by letter dated May 16, 1833, inform the board that James Hurley owns 80 acres of land, lying on said claim, by purchase from the United States, as per patent dated June 1, 1829. The said 80 acres is lot No. 5 in northeast fractional quarter of section 3, township 55, range 5 west; and that James Small is also owner of 80 acres of land, lot No. 4, in northeast quarter of section 3, township 55, range 5 west, as per certificate of the land office at Palmyra, dated December 10, 1828, No. 1065. Both lots of 80 acres each said to lie on the above claim.

James Emison and John Krigbaum, by letter dated May 29, 1833, state to the board that they have purchased of the United States the following tracts of land, said by them to lie on the above-named C. F. Delauriere's claim, to wit: southeast quarter of section 3, township 55, range 5, 160 acres; east half of the southwest quarter of section 3, township 55, range 5, 80 acres; lot No. 1 in the northwest quarter of section 3, township 55, range 5, 80 acres; the west half of the southwest quarter of section 3, township 55, range 5, 80 acres; and the west half of the southeast quarter of section 4, township 55, range 5, 80 acres.

A. G. HARRISON.
L. F. LINN.
F. R. CONWAY.

No. 120.—James Richardson, *claiming* 400 *arpents.*

To Don Charles Dehault Delassus, lieutenant colonel, attached to the stationary regiment of Louisiana, and lieutenant governor of Upper Louisiana:

James Richardson, inhabitant of the Marias des Liards, father of a numerous family, and owner of several slaves, settled for more than twelve years on this side of the Mississippi, and one of those who cultivate on the largest scale in this country, having always experienced, since his settling in the same, difficulties in disposing of his produce, for which one can get in exchange (on account of there being no way of exportation) but goods at exorbitant prices, he had formed the project under your predecessor, Don Zenon Trudeau, to establish a distillery, and by virtue of his verbal promise to grant to the petitioner a tract of land suitable to the execution of his undertaking, he procured the stills and all the apparatus necessary to the erection of a distillery on a large scale, but a serious disease prevented him from soliciting of Don Zenon Trudeau before his departure the fulfilment of his promise.

As the industry of the petitioner is known to you, and that the truth of the difficulties above mentioned is notorious, he has the honor to supplicate you to have the goodness to grant to him a concession for a tract of land of 400 arpents in superficie, situated on the river Maline at the end of the concessions of Messrs. John Brown and Alexander Clark, between the said lands and the road leading to St. Ferdinand, at about 12 or 15 miles in a N.NW. direction from this town, pledging himself to establish the said distillery and improve the land in the term prescribed by law. The petitioner confiding in your justice, hopes to deserve this favor as a new encouragement to his industry.

JAMES RICHARDSON.

St. Louis, *December* 15, 1799.

St. Louis of Illinois, *December* 16, 1799.

Having paid due attention to the just motives alleged by the petitioner, and being convinced that what he states in the present petition is true, the surveyor, Don Antonio Soulard, shall put the party interested in possession of the four hundred arpents of land in superficie in the place where he asks; and afterwards he shall make out the plat of survey with his certificate, in order to serve to solicit the concession from the intendant general of these provinces, to whom alone corresponds, by order of his Majesty, the distributing and granting all classes of lands of the royal domain.

CARLOS DEHAULT DELASSUS.

Registered at the request of the interested.—(Book No. 2, folios 5 and 6.)

SOULARD.

Truly translated. St. Louis, May 23, 1833.

JULIUS DE MUN.

No.	Name of original claimant.	Quantity, in arpents	Nature and date of claim.	By whom granted.	By whom surveyed, date, and situation.
120	James Richardson	400	Concession, 16th December 1799.	Carlos Dehault Delassus.	Special location 12 or 15 miles N.NW. from St. Louis.

Evidence with reference to minutes and records.

January 30, 1809.—Board met. Present: John B. C. Lucas, Clement B. Penrose, and Frederick Bates, commissioners.

James Richardson, claiming 400 arpents of land situate on the river Maline, district of St. Louis, produces to the board a concession from Don Carlos Dehault Delassus, lieutenant governor, for the same, dated December 16, 1799; a plat of survey taken February 20, 1806, and certified February 24, same year.

David Musick, sworn, says that about nine or ten years ago claimant built a still-house on the land claimed, and distilled in it about three years, and fenced in about one and a half acre of ground.

Laid over for decision.—(See book No. 3, page 454.)

July 14, 1810.—Board met. Present: John B. C. Lucas, Clement B. Penrose, and Frederick Bates, commissioners.

James Richardson, claiming 400 arpents of land.—(See book No. 3, page 454.)

It is the opinion of the board that this claim ought not to be confirmed.—(See book No. 4, page 435.)

April 9, 1833.—F. R. Conway, esq., appeared pursuant to adjournment.

James Richardson, by his legal representatives, claiming 400 arpents of land, situate on the river Maline, (see record book B, pages 304 and 404; minutes No. 3, page 454; No. 4, page 435,) produces a paper purporting to be an original concession from Carlos Dehault Delassus, dated December 16, 1799; also a copy of the survey.

William Campbell, duly sworn, says that he knows the tract of land here above mentioned; that, in 1799 or 1800, deponent helped Richardson to raise a building intended for a distillery; that, to his knowledge, the said Richardson distilled liquors there for three seasons in succession from the time he built the said house; that, in 1802 or 1803, deponent saw corn growing in a small lot; that the said Richardson kept his stock, hogs, &c., on said place; and that from the time it was first settled it has been inhabited or held by or through said Richardson ever since.

M. P. Le Duc, duly sworn, says that the signature to the concession is in the proper handwriting of Carlos Dehault Delassus.—(See book No. 6, page 153.)

November 13, 1833.—The board met pursuant to adjournment. Present: L. F. Linn, A. G. Harrison, F. R. Conway, commissioners.

James Richardson, claiming 400 arpents of land.—(See page 153 of this book.)

The board are unanimously of opinion that this claim ought to be confirmed to the said James Richardson, or to his legal representatives, according to the concession.—(See book No. 6, page 324.)

A. G. HARRISON.
L. F. LINN.
F. R. CONWAY.

No. 121.—Pierre Delor, *claiming* 400 *arpents.*

To Don Zenon Trudeau, captain in the stationary regiment of Louisiana, lieutenant governor, and commander-in-chief of the western part of Illinois:

Pierre Delor, captain commanding the militia of the village of Carondelet, supplicates very humbly, and has the honor to represent to you, that he would wish to make an establishment near the river Aux Gravois, on the road leading from St. Louis and the village of Carondelet to the saline of the Maramec;

and having found a place corresponding to his wishes, he claims of your goodness that you will grant to him the concession of the said place, having ten arpents in front by forty arpents in depth; the said tract being situated at a turn of the said river Aux Gravois, on the side of the village of Carondelet, which turn runs for the space of about ten arpents from east to west, and forty arpents from north to south. The petitioner, desiring to secure to himself the property of the said tract, has recourse to your goodness, praying that you will be pleased to grant the concession, and secure to him the property of the same by giving him titles in due form, in order that he may, with security, make thereon the improvements required, according to custom, as he wishes to begin to work as soon as you will please grant him the concession.

This considered, may you be pleased, sir, to grant to him the aforesaid concession of ten arpents in front by forty arpents in depth, such as it is here above designated. The petitioner shall never cease to pray Heaven for your conservation.

PIERRE his + mark. DELOR.

St. Louis, *December* 4, 1796.

St. Louis, *December* 6, 1796.

The surveyor of this jurisdiction shall put Mr. Delor de Treget in possession of the land which he asks in the place and in the shape designated, provided it belongs to the King's domain, and is not prejudicial to any other concession heretofore granted.

ZENON TRUDEAU.

Truly translated. St. Louis, May 24, 1833.

JULIUS DE MUN.

No.	Name of original claimant.	Quantity, in arpents.	Nature and date of claim.	By whom granted.	By whom surveyed, date, and situation.
121	Pierre Delor.	400	Concession, December 6, 1796.	Zenon Trudeau.	Jos. C. Brown, deputy surveyor; May, 1821; township 44 north, range 6 east.

Evidence with reference to minutes and records.

April 12, 1833.—The board met pursuant to adjournment. Present: F. R. Conway, A. G. Harrison, commissioners.

Pierre Delor, claiming ten arpents of land in front by forty arpents in depth, on the river Aux Gravois, a special location, (see record book F, page 96; Bates's Decisions, No. 5, page 102,) produces a paper purporting to be an original concession from Zenon Trudeau, dated 6th December, 1796; also a plat of survey, dated May, 1821, by Jos. C. Brown.

John Boli, duly sworn, says that he was present when Jos. C. Brown surveyed a tract of land from Pierre Delor, on river Aux Gravois; that near the main road he was several times shown a tree said to be the corner of said land as before surveyed, and that in running the lines he saw trees marked with old blazes; and he heard of said Delor and others that these old lines were run by Bouvet, who was commissioned surveyor at the date of the concession; that said Delor was a Spanish officer, and acted as commandant at his father's decease, and he (the deponent) served under him.—(See book No. 6, page 154.)

April 17, 1833.—The board met pursuant to adjournment. Present: A. G. Harrison, F. R. Conway, commissioners.

In the case of Pierre Delor, claiming ten by forty arpents of land.—(See page 154 of this book.)

Joseph C. Brown, duly sworn, says that he made the survey of the land above mentioned; that John Boli was along, with several other neighbors, for the purpose, he thinks, of showing the land as claimed by the proprietor.—(See book No. 6, page 156.)

November 13, 1833.—The board met pursuant to adjournment. Present: L. F. Linn, A. G. Harrison, F. R. Conway, commissioners.

Pierre Delor, claiming 400 arpents of land.—(See page 156 of this book.) The board are unanimously of opinion that this claim ought to be confirmed to the said Pierre Delor, or to his legal representatives, according to the concession.—(See book No. 6, page 325.)

A. G. HARRISON.
L. F. LINN.
F. R. CONWAY.

No. 122.—St. Vrain, by Ch. Gregoire, jr., *claiming* 25 *by* 60 *arpents.*

To Mr. François Vallé, captain, civil and military commandant of the post of St. Genevieve of Illinois and dependencies:

Jacques Marcelin Cerand Dehault Delassus de St. Vrain, inhabitant of Illinois, supplicates very humbly, and has the honor of representing to you, that having attentively and carefully visited and travelled over the lands in the vicinity of St. Genevieve, and particularly that part called the sugar maple groves, (les sucreries,) distant about four leagues from the said St. Genevieve, he has made the discovery of a place abundant enough in pine trees, with a creek emptying (abordant) into the river Aux Vases, and suitable to erect a saw-mill thereon; that this same place having never been granted to any person whatsoever, not being susceptible of any kind of cultivation, and being distant from the usual place from which the inhabitants habitually draw the pine timber for their use, and the petitioner intending to begin, in a short time, the works relative to his improvement and to the said mill, the completion of which shall be of the most precious utility to the public, he flatters himself, with confidence, that you will not refuse to him, sir, the concession of this tract of land. Therefore, he applies to you, sir, praying you may be pleased, for the object here above-mentioned, to grant to him, and beginning at the northwest angle, or thereabout, of Mr. St. James Beauvais' sugar camp, (sucrerie,) twenty-five arpents in front, running towards the north, by sixty arpents in depth. In so doing, &c.

DE ST. VRAIN, *D. L. S.*

ST. GENEVIEVE, *February* 12, 1797.

ST. LOUIS, *November* 22, 1797.

The surveyor of this jurisdiction, Don Antonio Soulard, shall put Mr. De St. Vrain in possession of the land demanded by him in the present petition, at the foot of which he shall make out a procès verbal of his survey, and the whole to be returned to us and forwarded to the commandant general of the province, who will determine definitively upon the concession of said land.

ZENON TRUDEAU.

Registered at the desire of Don Pascual Detchmendy, proprietor of said concession, as it is notorious by the juridical documents annexed to said memorial.

SOULARD.

Truly translated. St. Louis, December 11, 1832.

JULIUS DE MUN.

No.	Name of original claimant.	Quantity, in arpents	Nature and date of claim.	By whom granted.	By whom surveyed, date, and situation.
122	St. Vrain..........	1,500	Concession, Nov. 22, 1797	Zenon Trudeau..	Special.

Evidence with reference to minutes and records.

December 9, 1811.—Board met. Present: John B. C. Lucas, Clement B. Penrose, and Frederick Bates, commissioners.

Pascual Detchmendy, assignee of Jacque St. Vrain, claiming 25 by 60 arpents of land situate on Mud river, district of St. Genevieve, produces notice to the recorder. It is the opinion of the board that this claim ought not to be confirmed—(See book No. 5, page 498.)

December 14, 1832.—F. R. Conway, esquire, appeared pursuant to adjournment.

St. Vrain, by his legal representative, Charles Gregoire, claiming 1,500 arpents of land, (see book No. 5, page 498; record D, page 360,) produces a paper purporting to be an original concession from Zenon Trudeau, dated November 22, 1797.

The following additional testimony was taken in the foregoing case, in compliance with a resolution of this board of the 10th of October last:

ST. GENEVIEVE, MISSOURI, *November* 1, 1832.

Jacques Marcelin Cerand Dehault Delassus de St. Vrain, by his legal representative, Charles Gregoire, junior, claiming 1,500 arpents of land situated on the waters of the river Aux Vases, in the former district of St. Genevieve, in pursuance of and by virtue of a concession heretofore filed with the former commissioners; when Bartholomew St. Gemme personally appeared before Lewis F. Linn, one of the commissioners appointed to finally settle and adjust land claims in Missouri, and authorized by the said board of commissioners to receive testimony in this behalf, who, being duly sworn, deposes and saith that, in the year 1797, he, the said deponent, was making sugar at a sugar orchard belonging to his father; that then and there the above-named Jacques M. C. Dehault Delassus came and requested to know where the lines of his said father's claim were run, as he wanted to examine the creek in and about that neighborhood, to see if he could not find a suitable place for a mill-seat; that he proceeded on that examination, (after he had been shown the supposed lines of said deponent's father,) and deponent understood that said Delassus obtained a grant or concession of a tract adjoining that of deponent's father from Zenon Trudeau, said Trudeau being then governor of Upper Louisiana, and that it was well understood at that time, and always has been, that said tract was claimed under said grant by the said Delassus De St. Vrain and his legal representatives. This deponent further saith that he is well acquainted with the handwriting of Zenon Trudeau, late governor of Upper Louisiana; that he has often seen him write, and that the concession here shown for 1,500 arpents of land, dated November 22, 1797, and the signature thereto, are in the proper handwriting of said Zenon Trudeau; that he is also well acquainted with the handwriting of Antonio Soulard, late surveyor general of Upper Louisiana; that he has often seen him write, and that the signature to the certificate annexed to said concession is in the proper handwriting of said Soulard.

B. ST. GEMME.
L. F. LINN.

(See book No. 6, pages 75 and 76.)

November 13, 1833.—The board met pursuant to adjournment. Present: L. F. Linn, A. G. Harrison F. R. Conway, commissioners.

Jacque St. Vrain, claiming 1,500 arpents of land.—(See pages 75 and 76 of this book.) The board are unanimously of opinion that this claim ought to be confirmed to the said Jacque St. Vrain, or to his legal representatives.—(See book No. 6, page 325.)

A. G. HARRISON.
L. F. LINN.
F. R. CONWAY.

No. 123.—Louis Courtois, jr., *claiming 7,056 arpents.*

To Don Charles Dehault Delassus, lieutenant colonel, attached to the stationary regiment of Louisiana, and lieutenant governor of the upper part of the same province:

Louis Courtois, jr., has the honor to submit that, being on the eve of establishing himself, he would wish to obtain the concession of a sufficient quantity of land for the cultivation he intends to do, and the settling of a grazing farm. Therefore, and not to be prejudicial to, or prejudiced by, any person, he has made choice, with the verbal consent of your predecessor, of a tract of land situated on the left shore of Maramec, at 69 miles of its mouth, in which place he has the honor to supplicate you, with all due respect, to have the goodness to grant to him one league square of land in superficie, or 7,056 arpents, to be taken from the river Aux Gravois, ascending Maramec as far as the land of Louis Courtois, senior; so that said tract will be bounded on the lower part by the river Aux Gravois, and on the upper part by the land of the above-named L. Courtois, sen. Your petitioner hopes that you will have the goodness to consider that the tract of land he solicits is entirely insulated, and can offer him hopes of utility only at a very remote time. Besides, that it is advantageous to the government to have settlements on the upper part of the river, to give notice to the settlers on the lower part when the parties of Indians of the Osage nations do scatter themselves in the country. Your petitioner, full of confidence in your justice, hopes that you will be pleased to take in consideration the great length of time since his family has been settled in the country, and that all of them have rendered themselves worthy of the benevolence of the government by their fidelity and submission; particulars which cause him to believe that you will be pleased to do justice to his demand in a manner favorable to the accomplishment of his views.

DE COURTOIS, Jr., his + mark.

St. Louis, *December* 15, 1799.

St. Louis of Illinois, *December* 15, 1799.

Having seen the foregoing statement, and being informed that the petitioner has sufficient means to work and make use of the land he solicits, and that he is considered as a man of good character, I do grant to him and his heirs the tract of land which he solicits, if it is not prejudicial to anybody, and the surveyor, Don Antonio Soulard, shall put the party interested in possession of the quantity of land he asks for, in the place indicated; after which he will draw a plat, which he shall deliver to the said interested party, with his certificate, to serve to him to obtain the concession and title in form from the intendant general, to whom alone corresponds, (belongs,) by royal order, the distributing and granting all classes of lands belonging to the royal domain.

CARLOS DEHAULT DELASSUS.

A true translation. St. Louis, October 20, 1832.

JULIUS DE MUN.

No.	Name of original claimant.	Quantity, in arpents.	Nature and date of claim.	By whom granted.	By whom surveyed, date, and situation.
123	Louis Courtois, jr..	7, 056	Concession, December 15, 1799.	Carlos Dehault Delassus.	On the Maramec, 69 miles from its mouth. A special location.

Evidence with reference to minutes and records.

October 8, 1832.—The board met pursuant to adjournment. Present: L. F. Linn, William Updyke, F. R. Conway, commissioners.

Louis Courtois, jr., claiming 7,056 arpents of land, (see record book E, pages 217 and 218, it being a special location,) produces a paper purporting to be a concession from C. D. Delassus, dated December 15, 1799.

Pascal Cerré, duly sworn, saith that the signature to the concession is the handwriting of Carlos D. Delassus, and that the signature to the certificate of record of said concession is the handwriting of Antoine Soulard. (This claim has not been acted upon by the former board.)—(See book No. 6, page 13.)

November 13, 1833.—The board met pursuant to adjournment. Present: L. F. Linn, A. G. Harrison, F. R. Conway, commissioners.

Louis Courtois, jr., claiming 7,056 arpents of land.—(See page 13 of this book.) The board are unanimously of opinion that this claim ought to be confirmed to the said Louis Courtois, or to his legal representatives, according to the concession.—(See book No. 6, page 325.)

A. G. HARRISON.
L. F. LINN.
F. R. CONWAY.

No. 124.—François Moreau and Antoine Marechal, *claiming 300 arpents.*

To the lieutenant governor of the western part of Illinois:

Sir: François Moreau and Antoine Marechal have the honor to represent that, having under their charge several old men who are unable to cultivate the soil, but are yet strong enough to take care of cattle, they would wish to place them upon a vacant piece of land, at about one league to the eastward of the village of St. Ferdinand, adjoining the land granted to Mr. François Duncgan; therefore they supplicate you to grant to them fifteen arpents in front from east to west, by twenty arpents in depth, in order that they may immediately form their establishment. Favor which they hope of your protection.

† †

St. Louis, *November* 20, 1796.

The surveyor of this jurisdiction shall put the petitioners in possession of the fifteen arpents of land in front by twenty in depth, in the place demanded by them, and shall remit to us his procès verbal of survey, to be able to deliver the concession in form to the interested.

ZENON TRUDEAU.

Recorded, No. 23.

MACKAY.

Truly translated. St. Louis, December 14, 1832.

JULIUS DE MUN.

No.	Names of original claimants.	Quantity, in arpents.	Nature and date of claim.	By whom granted.	By whom surveyed, date, and situation.
124	François Moreau and Antoine Marechal.	300	Concession, Nov. 20, 1796.	Zenon Trudeau..	Special.

Evidence with reference to minutes and records.

September 29, 1808.—Board met. Present: The honorable J. B. C. Lucas, Clement B. Penrose, and Frederick Bates.

Edward Heamstead, assignee of Antoine Marechal, and Mary Catherine Tibeau, his wife, for himself and the heirs of François Moreau, deceased claiming 300 arpents of land situate near the village of St. Ferdinand, district of St. Louis, produces to the board an order of survey for the same from Don Zenon Trudeau, lieutenant governor, to Antoine Marechal and François Moreau, dated November 20, 1796; also a deed of conveyance from Antoine Marechal and Mary Catherine Tibeau, his wife, to Edward Heamstead, one of the claimants, for their part of said claim, dated February 7, 1805.

Antoine Soulard, sworn, says that he knew Antoine Marechal and François Moreau; that they resided in the village of St. Ferdinand from the year 1796 to 1803, and were the heads of families, and were farmers. Laid over for decision.—(See book No. 3, page 271.)

June 14, 1810.—Board met. Present: John B. C. Lucas, Clement B. Penrose, and Frederick Bates, commissioners.

Edward Heamstead, assignee of Antoine Marechal and Mary Catherine Tibeau, his wife, for himself, and the heirs of François Moreau, claiming 300 arpents of land.—(See book No. 3, page 271.) It is the opinion of the board that this claim ought not to be confirmed.—(See book No. 4, page 381.)

November 29, 1832.—The board met pursuant to adjournment. Present: Lewis F. Linn, F. R. Conway, commissioners.

François Moreau and Antoine Marechal, by their legal representatives, Edward Heamstead's heirs and devisees, claiming 15 by 20 arpents of land, (see book D, page 228; No. 3, page 271, and No. 4, page 381,) produces a paper purporting to be an original concession from Zenon Trudeau, lieutenant governor, dated November 20, 1796; also a deed of conveyance.

M. P. Le Duc, duly sworn, saith that the signature to said concession is in the handwriting of the said Zenon Trudeau.—(See book No. 6, page 66.)

November 13, 1833.—The board met pursuant to adjournment. Present: L. F. Linn, A. G. Harrison, F. R. Conway, commissioners.

François Moreau and Antoine Marechal, claiming 300 arpents of land.—(See page 66 of this book.) The board are unanimously of opinion that this claim ought to be confirmed to the said François Moreau and Antoine Marechal, or to their legal representatives, according to the concession.—(See book No. 6, page 326.)

A. G. HARRISON.
L. F. LINN.
F. R. CONWAY.

No. 125.—François Lacombe, *claiming* 400 *arpents.*

Don Carlos Dehault Delassus, lieutenant governor of Upper Louisiana:

Sir: François Lacombe has the honor to represent to you that he wishes to establish himself in the upper part of this province, where he has been residing for some time; therefore the petitioner has recourse to your goodness, praying that you may be pleased to grant to him a tract of land of four hundred arpents in superficie, to be taken on the vacant lands of the King's domain, in the place which will appear most convenient to the interests of your petitioner, who presumes to hope this favor of your justice.

FRANÇOIS LACOMBE.

St. Louis, *February* 24, 1800.

St. Louis of Illinois, *February* 26, 1800.

Being assured that the petitioner has sufficient means to improve the lands petitioned for, I do grant to him and his heirs the land which he solicits, in case it is not prejudicial to any one; and the surveyor, Don Antonio Soulard, shall put the interested in possession of the quantity of land which he asks, in a vacant place of the royal domain; and this being executed, he shall draw a plat of survey, delivering the same, with his certificate, to the party, in order to serve to him to obtain the title in form from the intendant general, to whom alone corresponds, by royal order, the distributing and granting all classes of lands of the royal domain.

CARLOS DEHAULT DELASSUS.

Truly translated. St. Louis, December 22, 1832

JULIUS DE MUN.

No.	Name of original claimant.	Quantity, in arpents.	Nature and date of claim.	By whom granted.	By whom surveyed, date, and situation.
125	François Lacombe.	400	Concession, Feb. 26, 1800.	Carlos Dehault Delassus.	

Evidence with reference to minutes and records.

November 28, 1832.—The board met pursuant to adjournment. Present: L. F. Linn, F. R. Conway, commissioners.

François Lacombe, by Manual Lisa's representatives, claiming 400 arpents of land, (see record book D, page 232,) produces a paper purporting to be an original concession from Carlos Dehault Delassus, dated February 26, 1800; also a deed of conveyance for same.

M. P. Le Duc, duly sworn, says that the signature to said concession is in the proper handwriting of Carlos Dehault Delassus.—(See book No. 6, page 60.)

November 13, 1833.—The board met pursuant to adjournment. Present: L. F. Linn, A. G. Harrison, F. R. Conway, commissioners.

François Lacombe, claiming 400 arpents of land.—(See page 60 of this book.) The board are unanimously of opinion that this claim ought to be confirmed to the said François Lacombe, or to his legal representatives, according to the concession.—(See book No. 6, page 326.)

A. G. HARRISON.
L. F. LINN.
F. R. CONWAY.

No. 126.—James Journey, *claiming* 400 *arpents.*

To Don Carlos Dehault Delassus, lieutenant colonel, attached to the stationary regiment of Louisiana, and lieutenant governor of Upper Louisiana, &c.:

James Journey, C. R., a good farmer and an honest man, has the honor to represent to you that he is settled in the district of St. Charles, of Missouri, with the permission of the government; he supplicates you (considering the means with which he is provided, as well in cattle as in implements of husbandry and other goods,) to grant to him a piece of land of 400 arpents in superficie, at the same place which he has chosen. The petitioner, having no other views but to live as a peaceable and submissive cultivator of the soil, hopes of your justice the favor which he solicits.

JAMES JOURNEY.

St. André, *September* 14, 1799.

Be it forwarded to the lieutenant governor, with information that the statement here above is true, and that in every point of view the petitioner deserves the favor he solicits.

SANTIAGO MACKAY.

St. André, *September* 14, 1799.

St. Louis of Illinois, *September* 21, 1799.

By virtue of the foregoing information from the commandant of St. André, the Captain Don Santiago Mackay, and as we are assured that the petitioner possesses sufficient means to improve the lands which he solicits in the time prescribed by the regulation of the governor general of this province, the surveyor, Don Antonio Soulard, shall put the interested party in possession of the 400 arpents of land in superficie, in the same place indicated in this petition; which being done, he shall draw a plat, delivering the same to the party, with his certificate, to serve to the said party to obtain the concession and title in form from the intendant general of these provinces, to whom alone belongs, by royal order, the distributing and granting of all classes of lands of the royal domain.

CARLOS DEHAULT DELASSUS.

Truly translated. St. Louis, December 5, 1832.

JULIUS DE MUN.

No.	Name of original claimant	Quantity, arpents.	Nature and date of claim.	By whom granted.	By whom surveyed, date, situation.
126	James Journey	400	Concession, September 21, 1799.	Carlos Dehault Delassus.	

Evidence with reference to minutes and records.

October 15, 1832.—The board met pursuant to adjournment. Present: W. Updyke, F. R. Conway, commissioners.

James Journey, claiming 400 arpents of land, (see book F, page 104; Bates's report, page 103,) produces a paper purporting to be a concession from Carlos Delassus, dated September 21, 1799; also a translation of said concession signed by said Delassus.

M. P. Le Duc, duly sworn, saith that the signature to said concession is the handwriting of Carlos D. Delassus, and that the signature to the recommendation attached to said concession is that of James Mackay.—(See book No. 6, page 22.)

November 13, 1833.—The board met pursuant to adjournment. Present: L. F. Linn, A. G. Harrison, F. R. Conway, commissioners.

James Journey, claiming 400 arpents of land.—(See page 22 of this book.)

The board are unanimously of opinion that this claim ought to be confirmed to the said James Journey, or to his legal representatives, according to the concession.—(See book No. 6, page 326.)

A. G. HARRISON.
L. F. LINN.
F. R. CONWAY.

No. 127.—Louis Bissonet, *claiming* 2 *by* 20 *arpents.*

To the lieutenant governor of Illinois:

Sir: Louis Bissonet, an inhabitant of this town, with due respect appears before you, and says that not having a sufficient quantity of land to maintain his family he has recourse to you, in order to obtain the concession for a tract of land of 2 arpents in width by 20 arpents in length, situated in the prairie called the White Ox prairie, (Prado del Buey Blanco,) and bounded on one side by the river Gingras, behind by a creek which comes down from the hills, and on the other two sides by lands which are not yet conceded; observing to you that he will leave between his land and the trees which cover the river Gingras an arpent of land, and on the side of the creek two arpents, as being entirely unfit for cultivation. Favor which he expects of your equitable justice.

LOUIS BISSONET, his + mark.

In St. Louis, *August* 27, 1777.

Having examined the contents of the foregoing petition, dated August 27, 1777, and the demand made by Louis Bissonet, an inhabitant of this town of St. Louis, who has stated that he has not land in sufficient quantity to make the sowings necessary for the support of his family, I have granted and do grant to him in full property, for him and his heirs, a piece of land of 2 arpents in width by 20 in length, situated in the prairie called the White Ox prairie, and bounded on one side by the river Gingras, behind by a creek coming down from the hills, and on the two other sides by lands not yet conceded, on condition of improving said land in one year from this day, his Majesty reserving to himself to dispose of it as being his domain in case of utility to his royal service.

Given in St. Louis of Illinois on the 28th of August, 1777.

FRANCISCO CRUZAT.

We, Amos Stoddard, captain of artillery and first civil commandant of Upper Louisiana, for the United States of America, do certify to all whom it may concern, that Mr. Auguste Chouteau, merchant of this town, has acquired at the third public sale (adjudication) of the property of the late Genevieve Routier, (who died widow of Louis Bissonet,) at the door of the church of this town, sundry properties as follows:

One piece of land of two arpents and a half in front by forty in depth, situated in the grand prairie of the Great Pond, (Grand Marais,) which had been bid off to Michel Fortin, for the sum of $51, and has been bid off this time to Mr. Auguste Chouteau for the sum of $52. His security, Regis Loisel.

Another detached arpent (arpent détaché) of land, in the said prairie, which had been bid off to Mr. Joseph Lacroix for $15, and has been at this last sale adjudged to Mr. Auguste Chouteau, for the sum of $51. His security, Mr. Regis Loisel.

Another piece of land of two arpents in front, conformably to the decree of Mr. Francis Cruzat, dated August 28, 1777, containing two arpents in front by twenty in depth, situated in the White Ox prairie, which had been bid off to Mr. Joseph Lacroix for $40, and has been at this last sale adjudged to Mr. A. Chouteau for $180. His security, Mr. Regis Loisel.

The above sales, made in favor of Mr. Auguste Chouteau, have taken place at the door of the church of this town, after the saying of the parochial mass, at which there was a great assembly of people, on the 22d day of July last.

In testimony whereof we, commandant, have signed the present document, in order that it shall be available according to law.

AMOS STODDARD, *Civil and Military Commandant, Upper Louisiana.*

St. Louis of Illinois, *September* 28, 1804.

Truly translated.

JULIUS DE MUN.

No.	Name of original claimant.	Quantity, arpents.	Nature and date of claim.	By whom granted.	By whom surveyed, date, and situation.
127	Louis Bissonet, by the heirs of Auguste Chouteau.	40	Concession, 28th August, 1777.	Francisco Cruzat.	James Mackay. Certified by him 28th February, 1806. White Ox prairie.

Evidence with reference to minutes and records.

May 1, 1806.—The board met agreeably to adjournment. Present: The honorable John B. C. Lucas, Clement B. Penrose, and James L. Donaldson, commissioners.

Auguste Chouteau, assignee of Genevieve, widow of Louis Bissonet, claiming two by twenty arpents of land, situate at the Prairie du Bœuf Blanc, produces a concession from Francis Cruzat, dated August 28, 1777, and a certificate of survey of the same, dated February 28, 1806. A certificate of public sale of the effects and property of the said Genevieve, widow as aforesaid, dated July 22, 1804.

Emilieu Yostie, being duly sworn, says that the aforesaid Bissonet settled the said tract of land in the year 1798, by building a cabin thereon; that the same never was inhabited, but served as a shelter when the said Bissonet went on the said land to make hay; that the said land never was cultivated nor under fence, but was appropriated and granted for the sole purpose of cutting hay, which was done every year by the owner.

The following being the condition on which the aforesaid tract was granted in the words of the concession: "*Con condicion de establecer dha. tierra en el espacio de un año de este dia.*" The board applied to the interpreter, who translated the same as follows: "On condition to settle the said land within the term of one year from this date."

The board reject this claim, the said tract not having been settled within the time prescribed by the said concession, and for non-inhabitation and cultivation prior to and on the 1st day of October, 1800.—(See book No. 1, page 258.)

September 16, 1808.—Board met. Present: The honorable John B. C. Lucas, Clement B. Penrose, and Frederick Bates, commissioners.

Auguste Chouteau, assignee of Genevieve, widow of Louis Bissonet, claiming two by twenty arpents of land, situate in the Prairie Bœuf Blanc, district of St. Louis, produces to the board a concession for the same from François Cruzat, lieutenant governor, to Louis Bissonet, dated August 28, 1777, and registered in book of registry No. 3, folio 12. Laid over for decision.—(See book No. 3, page 252.)

February 21, 1809.—Board met. Present: John B. C. Lucas, Clement B. Penrose, and Frederick Bates, commissioners.

The claim of Auguste Chouteau, assignee of Genevieve, widow of Louis Bissonet, being taken up by the board and a vote being taken thereon, it is the opinion of the board that said claim ought not to be confirmed. This claim for the major part included within the claim of the widow and representatives of Antoine Morin this day. Confirmed.—(See book No. 3, page 485.)

October 9, 1832.—The board met pursuant to adjournment. Present: L. F. Linn, W. Updike, F. R. Conway, commissioners.

Louis Bissonet, by the heirs of Auguste Chouteau, claiming 40 arpents.—(See record, book D, page 119; book B, page 75. See minutes, No. 1, page 258; No. 3, pages 252 and 485.)

Produces a paper purporting to be an original concession from Francisco Cruzat to Louis Bissonet, dated August 28, 1777; also a document purporting to be an adjudicated sale, certified by Amos Stoddard, commandant of Upper Louisiana, of said tract of land, among others, to Auguste Chouteau, dated September 28, 1804; also a certificate, with a plat of survey, dated February 28, 1806, signed by John Mackay.

Pascal Cerré, duly sworn, saith that the signature to the concession is the handwriting of Francisco Cruzat. He believes the signature to said document is the handwriting of Stoddard, but is not very sure that the signature to the survey is the handwriting of James Mackay.—(See book No. 6, page 16.)

November 13, 1833.—The board met pursuant to adjournment. Present: L. F. Linn, A. G. Harrison, F. R. Conway, commissioners.

Louis Bissonet, claiming 40 arpents of land.—(See page 16 of this book.) The board remark that, in the minutes of the former board, it is there stated that this claim interferes with the claim of the widow and representatives of Antoine Morin. The board are unanimously of opinion that this claim ought to be confirmed to the said Louis Bissonet, according to the concession.—(See book No. 6, page 326.)

Conflicting claim.

Conflicts with the confirmed claim of the representatives of Antoine Morin, deceased.

A. G. HARRISON.
L. F. LINN.
F. R. CONWAY.

No. 128.—Etienne St. Pierre.

To Don Charles Dehault Delassus, lieutenant colonel, attached to the stationary regiment of Louisiana, and lieutenant governor of the upper part of the same province:

Etienne St. Pierre, having for a long time resided in this country, has the honor to represent to you that wishing to form an insulated plantation, in order to cultivate the several kinds of grains which this country is susceptible to produce, and establishing also a stock farm, he has made choice, with the consent of your predecessor, Don Zenon Trudeau, of a tract of vacant land on the right bank of the Missouri, at 66 miles from its mouth, which tract is to be bounded as follows: 1st. The first line shall begin at the foot of the hills which are lower down than the mouth of Berger river, running parallel to said river to about a league, more or less, from the point of departure; thence, by another line which shall be run to the foot of the hills which are opposite Maline island, so as to comprise a part of the course of the river and the bottom. The superficie of this said tract shall be contained in an obtuse angle, formed by the two above-mentioned lines, and the third side of the triangle by the river Missouri, and cannot be determined but after the legal survey, which will result from the orders which you will be pleased to give on this subject.

Your petitioner respectfully claims of your justice that you will grant him your protection in the furtherance of his views, and that you will make him enjoy the same favors which the government generously grants to all his Majesty's subjects. Having no other views but to live as a peaceable and submissive cultivator of the soil, he hopes that you will be pleased to do justice to his demand in a way favorable to his views.

ETIENNE ST. PIERRE, his + mark.

As witness to the signature: ANTONIO SOULARD.
ST. LOUIS, *October* 7, 1799.

ST. LOUIS OF ILLINOIS, *October* 8, 1799.

Being assured that the petitioner possesses sufficient means to improve the land which he solicits, I do grant to him and his heirs the land which he solicits, if it is not prejudicial to anybody; and the surveyor, Don Antonio Soulard, shall put the interested party in possession of the land he asks, in the place designated; and this being executed, he shall draw a plat of his survey; delivering the same to the party, with his certificate, in order to serve to him to obtain the concession and title in form from the intendant general, to whom alone corresponds, by royal order, the distributing and granting all classes of lands of the royal domain.

CARLOS DEHAULT DELASSUS.

Truly translated. St. Louis, February 25, 1833.

JULIUS DE MUN.

No.	Name of original claimant.	Quantity, in arpents.	Nature and date of claim.	By whom granted.	By whom surveyed, date, and situation.
128	Etienne St. Pierre.	Special location.	Concession, October 8, 1799.	Carlos Dehault Delassus.	Special location.

Evidence with reference to minutes and records.

December 9, 1811.—Board met. Present: John B. C. Lucas, Clement B. Penrose, and Frederick Bates, commissioners.

Pierre Chouteau, assignee of Etienne St. Pierre, claiming a tract of land, beginning at the foot of the hills below the mouth of River à Berger, and ascending said river one league, and including the Pointe basse (bottom) opposite (Maline) Mill island, district of St. Charles, produces record of concession from Delassus, lieutenant governor, dated October 8, 1799; record of a transfer from St. Pierre to claimant, dated January 3, 1804. It is the opinion of the board that this claim ought not to be allowed.—(See book No. 5, page 495.)

February 18, 1833.—F. R. Conway, esq., appeared pursuant to adjournment.

Etienne St. Pierre, by his assignee, Pierre Chouteau, senior, claiming a special location, of which a league square has been confirmed.—(See record, book B, page 510; minutes, No. 5, page 495; Bates's Decisions, book No. 3, page 59, wherein a league square is confirmed.) Produces a paper purporting to be a concession from Carlos Dehault Delassus, dated October 8, 1799.

M. P. Le Duc, being duly sworn, saith that the signature to the concession is in the true handwriting of Carlos D. Delassus.—(See book No. 6, page 106.)

November 15, 1833.—The board met pursuant to adjournment. Present: L. F. Linn, A. G. Harrison, and F. R. Conway, commissioners.

In the case of Etienne St. Pierre, claiming a special location on River à Berger, François Boucher, being duly sworn, says he is 56 years of age; that he has travelled up and down the Missouri since he was a young man; that he has ascended said river perhaps forty times; that he believes the distance from the hills below Berger river to the hills opposite Maline island to be three leagues in following the turn of the Missouri, which makes a great bend at that place. Witness further says that he never crossed Berger bottom by land, and cannot say what is the distance in a straight line.

James Gunsolis, being also duly sworn, says that he has often ascended the Missouri in keelboats and steamboats, and that he believes the distance to be, from the hills below Berger river to the hills opposite Maline island, 9 miles more or less.

Peter Chouteau, the present claimant, personally appeared before the board, and states that the line beginning at the foot of the hills below Berger river has always been understood to be one league in length, although the petition expresses one league, more or less, and the said line is to run parallel with the general course of said Berger river; and from the end of the said line of one league in length another straight line is to be run, to strike the foot of the hills opposite Maline island, which foot of said hills is washed by the Missouri, and the quantity comprised between the said two lines and the Missouri is the quantity claimed, of which the number of arpents contained in a league square has been confirmed.—(See Bates's Decisions, page 59.)

The board is unanimously of opinion that the balance of this claim ought to be confirmed to the said Etienne St. Pierre, or to his legal representatives, according to the concession.—(See book No. 6, page 327.

A. G. HARRISON.
L. F. LINN.
F. R. CONWAY.

No. 129.—JOHN ST. CLAIRE, jr., *claiming* 640 *acres.*

No.	Name of original claimant.	Quantity, in arpents.	Nature and date of claim.	By whom granted.	By whom surveyed, date, and situation.
129	John St. Claire, jr.........	640	Settlement right.		

Evidence with reference to minutes and records.

November 13, 1833.—The board met pursuant to adjournment. Present: L. F. Linn, F. R. Conway, and A. G. Harrison, commissioners.

John Sinclaire, jr., otherwise called John St. Claire, otherwise John Senclare, otherwise called John St. Clare, claiming 640 acres of land situate on the waters of St. Francis, in the late district of St. Genevieve, now county of Madison.—(See record, book F, page 13; Bates's Decisions, page 97.) The following testimony was taken before L. F. Linn, commissioner:

STATE OF MISSOURI, *county of Madison:*

Thompson Crawford, a witness aged about forty-seven years, who being duly sworn as the law directs, deposeth and saith that he is well acquainted with the original claimant; that he came to this country, then the province of Upper Louisiana, in the fall of the year 1803; that he was then a young man grown, and made his home at his father's, whose name was also John St. Claire. Witness also knows the land claimed, and that, in the early part of the year 1804, the claimant made some improvements on the land, and he knows cultivated land that year, but whether the cultivation was on the land claimed or not, witness does not recollect; and that the land claimed has been inhabited, improved, and cultivated ever since.

THOMPSON CRAWFORD.

Sworn to and subscribed before me, L. F. Linn, commissioner, this 22d October, 1833.

LEWIS F. LINN, *Commissioner.*

And, also, came John Reaves, a witness aged about seventy-three years, who, also, being duly sworn, deposeth and saith that he well knew John St. Claire, the claimant; that he came with the claimant to the country in 1803; that they lived a while together; witness knows the land claimed, and knows that the claimant settled on, improved, and cultivated the same in 1803 and 1804; that the Osage Indians, in 1804, drove the inhabitants together, where they made a common defence and common crop in that year; and witness further knows that the land has been actually inhabited, improved, and cultivated ever since.

his
JOHN + REAVES,
mark.

Sworn to and subscribed before me, L. E. Linn, commissision, this 23d October, 1833.

L. F. LINN, *Commissioner.*

The board are unanimously of opinion that 640 acres of land ought to be granted to the said John St. Claire, or to his legal representatives —(See book No 6, page 328.)

A. G. HARRISON.
L. F. LINN.
F. R. CONWAY.

No. 130.—DANIEL KRYTZ, *claiming* 234 *arpents and* 36 *perches.*

No.	Name of original claimant.	Quantity, in arpents.	Nature and date of claim.	By whom granted.	By whom surveyed, date, and situation.
130	Daniel Krytz..........	234 36 p.	Settlement right.	....	B. Cousin, D. S., 7th January, 1806, countersigned Antonio Soulard, S. G.; on waters of Bird's creek, district of Cape Girardeau.

Evidence with reference to minutes and records.

May 1, 1809.—Board met. Present: Clement B. Penrose and Frederick Bates, commissioners.

Peter Krytz, legatee of Dawalt Krytz, (Daniel Crites,) claiming two hundred and thirty-four arpents thirty-six perches of land situate on waters of Bird's creek, district of Cape Girardeau, produces to the board, as a special permission to settle, list B, on which Dawalt Krytz is No. 28, for two hundred arpents; a plat of survey, dated January 7, 1806, signed B. Cousin and countersigned Antonio Soulard, surveyor general.

The following testimony in the foregoing claim was taken as aforesaid at Cape Girardeau, June 2, 1808, by Frederick Bates, commissioner:

George F. Bollinger, duly sworn, says that this land was improved in the year 1804, in October or November; cabin built; a few acres, about twelve or fourteen, cleared, enclosed, and cultivated; constantly inhabited and cultivated to this day. Board adjourned till Friday next, 9 o'clock a. m.—(See book No. 4, page 36.)

February 19, 1810.—Board met. Present: John B. C. Lucas, Clement B. Penrose, and Frederick Bates, commissioners.

Peter Krytz, legatee of Dawalt Krytz, (Daniel Crites,) claiming two hundred and thirty-four arpents thirty-six perches.—(See book No. 4, page 36.) It is the opinion of the board that this claim ought not to be granted.—(See book No. 4, page 280.)

November 15, 1833.—The board met pursuant to adjournment. Present: L. F. Linn, A. G. Harrison, and F. R. Conway, commissioners.

Daniel Crites, claiming six hundred and forty acres of land situate in the late district of Cape Girardeau, now county of Cape Girardeau.—(See book No. 4, pages 36 and 280.)

The following testimony was taken before L. F. Linn, commissioner:

STATE OF MISSOURI, *county of Madison:*

Daniel Bollinger, aged about eighty years, who, being duly sworn as the law directs, deposeth and saith that he is well acquainted with the original claimant, Daniel Crites or Crits; that said claimant came to this country, then the province of Upper Louisiana, in the fall of the year 1802; witness also knows the land claimed, and knows that the claimant got permission of Louis Lorimier, then commandant at Cape Girardeau, to settle lands, and witness also knows that the claimant settled on said land claimed, in 1803 or early in 1804, and then built a good house, a good barn, and stables, with kitchen and out-houses; fenced in and cleared, in 1803 and 1804, some ten acres or more, and cultivated the same in corn and other things necessary for a family. Claimant also at that time planted an orchard; claimant had a wife and seven or eight children; claimant had a good stock of horses, cattle, hogs, &c., and the claimant has actually continued to inhabit, improve, and cultivate the said land from the time of the original settlement to the present day, and still actually resides on and cultivates the same, being his only home from the time he came to the country to the present day, himself and such of his family as remain with him at home.

DANIEL his + mark. BOLLINGER.

Sworn to and subscribed before me, L. F. Linn, commissioner, this 23d day of October, 1833.

L. F. LINN, *Commissioner.*

(See book No. 6, page 330.)

The board are unanimously of opinion that two hundred and thirty-four arpents thirty-six perches of land, being the quantity originally claimed, ought to be granted to the said Daniel Krytz, or to his legal representatives.—(See book No. 6, page 331.)

A. G. HARRISON.
L. F. LINN.
F. R. CONWAY.

No. 131.—JACOB WALKER, *claiming* 982 *arpents* 65 *perches.*

No.	Name of original claimant.	Quantity, in arpents.	Nature and date of claim.	By whom granted.	By whom surveyed, date, and situation.
131	Jacob Walker.	982 arpents 65 perches.	Settlement right.	....	B. Cousin, deputy surveyor; received for record February 27, 1806, by A. Soulard, surveyor general; district of Cape Girardeau.

Evidence with reference to minutes and records.

April 21, 1809.—Board met. Present: John B. C. Lucas, Clement B. Penrose, and Frederick Bates, commissioners.

Jacob Welker, (Walker,) claiming nine hundred and eighty-two arpents sixty-five perches of land situate on the waters of Caney creek, district of Cape Girardeau, produces to the board, as a special permission to settle, list A, on which claimant is No. 109, for three hundred arpents; a plat of survey signed B. Cousin, and certified to be received for record February 27, 1806, by Antoine Soulard, surveyor general.

The following testimony in the foregoing claim, taken as aforesaid by Frederick Bates, commissioner, at Cape Girardeau, June 1, 1808:

Leonard Walker, duly sworn, says that claimant settled in 1804, in November, and moved his family on in the spring following; built a cabin and cultivated about six acres of ground; premises constantly inhabited and cultivated to this time.

Laid over for decision.—(See book No. 4, page 12.)

January 23, 1810.—Board met. Present: John B. C. Lucas, Clement B. Penrose, and Frederick Bates, commissioners.

Jacob Walker, claiming nine hundred and eighty-two arpents sixty-five perches of land.—(See book No. 4, page 12.)

It is the opinion of the board that this claim ought not to be granted.—(See book No. 4, page 264.)

November 15, 1833.—Board met pursuant to adjournment. Present: L. F. Linn, A. G. Harrison, and F. R. Conway, commissioners.

Jacob Walker, by his heirs and legal representatives, claiming nine hundred and eighty-two arpents sixty-five perches of land.—(See book No. 4, pages 12 and 264.)

The following testimony was taken before L. F. Linn, commissioner:

State of Missouri, *county of Cape Girardeau:*

George T. Bollinger, aged about sixty years, and Joseph Neswonger, aged nearly fifty-four, being severally duly sworn as the law directs, depose and say, that they were well acquainted with Jacob Walker, the original claimant; that he came to this country, then the province of Upper Louisiana, now State of Missouri, in the year 1799; that he obtained a grant or permission to settle from Louis Lorimier, the then Spanish commandant of this post; they also knew that he built a house on the land claimed in the year 1801, and cultivated the same land; and that the said land has been both inhabited and cultivated ever since.

GEORGE T. BOLLINGER.
JOSEPH his + mark NESWONGER.

Sworn to and subscribed, October 19, 1833.

L. F. LINN, *Commissioner.*

The board are unanimously of opinion that six hundred and forty acres of land ought to be granted to the said Jacob Walker, or to his legal representatives.—(See book No. 6, page 332.)

A. G. HARRISON.
L. F. LINN.
F. R. CONWAY.

No. 132.—Thomas Caulk, *claiming* 400 *arpents.*

To Don Charles Dehault Delassus, lieutenant governor and commandant-in-chief of Upper Louisiana, &c.:

The petitioner, Thomas Caulk, has the honor of representing to you that he is inhabiting this side (of the Mississippi) since some time, and has settled himself, with the permission of the government, in the district of St. Charles, and farming the land of Richard Caulk; and having made choice of a piece of land, therefore he has the honor to supplicaté you to have the goodness to grant to him, at the same place, the quantity of four hundred arpents of land in superficie, a quantity which is necessary to comprehend the wood and water necessary. The petitioner, having the means of improving a farm, and having no other view but to live in submission to the laws and gain honestly his livelihood, hopes to render himself worthy of the favor which he solicits of your justice.

St. André, *March* 3, 1800. [No signature.]

Be it transferred to the commandant-in-chief, with information that what is here alleged is true, and that the petitioner is worthy of the favor which he solicits.

SANTIAGO MACKAY.

St. André, *March* 4, 1800.

St. Louis of Illinois, *March* 10, 1800.

In virtue of the information here above of the commandant of St. André, Captain Don Santiago Mackay, the surveyor, Don Antonio Soulard, shall put the interested in possession of four hundred arpents of land in superficie in the place he asks for; this quantity is corresponding to the number of individuals composing his family, according to the regulation made by the governor of this province; and when this is done, he will draw a plat, which he shall deliver to the party, with his certificate, to serve him in obtaining the concession and title in form from the intendant general of these provinces, to whom alone corresponds the distributing and granting all classes of lands of the royal domain.

CARLOS DEHAULT DELASSUS.

Don Antonio Soulard, surveyor general of the settlements of Upper Louisiana.

I do certify that a tract of land of four hundred arpents in superficie was measured, the lines run and bounded, in favor and in presence of Thomas Caulk, jr.; this measurement was done with the perch of Paris, of eighteen feet lineal measure of the same city, according to the agrarian mode of measurement in this province, which land is situated three miles from the river Missouri, one mile and a half below the river Aux Calumets and about eighty miles to the northwest of this town of St. Louis; bounded on its four sides as follows: northwest with land of Richard Caulk, northeast by land of Don Antonio Saugrin, southwest by land of Richard Caulk, and southeast by vacant lands of the royal domain; which survey and measurement were executed without regard to the variation of the needle, which is 7° 30′ E., as is evident by the figurative plat here above, in which are noted the dimensions, directions of the lines, other boundaries, &c. This survey was executed by virtue of the decree of the lieutenant governor and sub-delegate of the fiscal department, Don Carlos Dehault Delassus, dated March 10, 1800, which is here annexed. In testimony whereof I do give the present with the figurative plat here above, in conformity with the survey executed by the deputy surveyor, Don Santiago Mackay, dated the 19th of February of this present year, and which he signed on the minutes, all which I do certify.

ANTONIO SOULARD, *Surveyor General.*

ST. LOUIS OF ILLINOIS, *March* 28, 1804.

A true translation. St. Louis, October 17, 1832.

JULIUS DE MUN.

No.	Name of original claimant.	Quantity, in arpents.	Nature and date of claim.	By whom granted.	By whom surveyed, date, and situation.
132	Thomas Caulk...	400	Concession, Mar. 10, 1800.	Carlos Dehault Delassus.	James Mackay, Feb. 19, 1804; certified by Soulard, March 28, 1804; 3 miles from the Missouri and 1½ mile below the river Calumet.

Evidence with reference to minutes and records.

October 5, 1832.—The board met pursuant to adjournment. Present: Lewis F. Linn and F. R. Conway, commissioners.

Thomas Caulk, claiming 400 arpents of land.—(See record, book D, page 368.) This claim has not been acted upon by the former board. Produces a paper purporting to be a concession from Carlos Dehault Delassus, dated March 10, 1800, and a paper purporting to be a survey, taken on the 19th of February, and certified the 28th of March, 1804, by Antoine Soulard, surveyor general.

M. P. Le Duc, duly sworn, saith that the signature to the said concession is the handwriting of Carlos Dehault Delassus, and that the signature to the survey is the handwriting of Antoine Soulard, surveyor general. The claimant refers to the affidavits of James Mackay and Antoine Soulard, taken in the above case of Richard Caulk; also, to the affidavit of Martin Wood, taken before Benjamin Cottle, justice of the peace, dated September 28, 1819.—(See book No. 6, page 7.)

November 13, 1833.—The board met pursuant to adjournment. Present: L. F. Linn, A. G. Harrison, F. R. Conway, commissioners.

Thomas Caulk claiming 400 arpents of land.—(See page 7 of this book.) The board are unanimously of opinion that this claim ought to be confirmed to the said Thomas Caulk, or to his legal representatives, according to the concession.—(See book No. 6, page 325.)

A. G. HARRISON.
L. F. LINN.
F. R. CONWAY.

No. 133.—JOACHIN LISA, *claiming* 6,000 *arpents.*

To the lieutenant governor:

Don Manuel de Lisa, inhabitant and merchant of New Orleans, for the present in this town of St. Louis, with great respect represents to you that his eldest brother, Don Joachin de Lisa, wishing to follow the petitioner and settle himself in the same place where the petitioner's residence has to be, implores your justice, in order to obtain a concession for 6,000 arpents of land in superficie, on the domains of his Majesty, that by this means his brother may dispose of and sell the plantation which he owns in New Orleans, and come up with his family and slaves to this jurisdiction. For these motives the petitioner supplicates you to condescend to grant to his said brother the concession which he solicits, and to order that the place where you shall be pleased to grant be designated—favor which your petitioner and his brother expects of your well known justice. May God preserve your life many years.

MANUEL DE LISA.

ST. LOUIS, *July* 16, 1799.

ST. LOUIS, *July* 17, 1799.

In a vacant place, on the banks of the river Missouri, and to the satisfaction of Don Manuel de Lisa, the surveyor, Don Antonio Soulard, shall put him in possession of 6,000 arpents of land in superficie, in favor of Don Joachin de Lisa, his brother, in order that, according to the procès verbal of survey, the title of concession in form can be expedited to him; in the meanwhile the interested party, from this time, may dispose of the tract of land which is chosen as being his own property.

ZENON TRUDEAU.

Truly translated. St. Louis, December 25, 1832.

JULIUS DE MUN.

No.	Name of original claimant.	Quantity, arpents.	Nature and date of claim.	By whom granted.	By whom surveyed, date, and situation.
133	Joachin Lisa........	6,000	Concession, July 17, 1799.	Zenon Trudeau.	

Evidence with reference to minutes and records.

August 22, 1806.—Manuel Lisa, assignee of Joachin Lisa, claiming 6,000 arpents of land by virtue of a concession from Zenon Trudeau, (duly registered,) dated the 17th of July, 1799, and a deed of transfer of the same, dated the 8th of July, 1804.

Jacque Clamorgan, being duly sworn, says that he was present at the lieutenant governor's house when the aforesaid concession was given to claimant; that the same was granted at the time it bears date. They reject this claim.

November 23, 1811.—Board met. Present: John B. C. Lucas, Clement B. Penrose, and Frederick Bates, commissioners.

Manuel Lisa, assignee of Joachin Lisa, claiming 6,000 arpents of land unlocated.

Eugenio Alvarez, sworn, says that the father of Joachin Lisa came to this country with him (the witness) at the time the Spaniards took possession here; that said Joachin Lisa's father was then in the service of Spain and died in the service; that Joachin Lisa was born a subject of Spain, in Spanish America, and has resided since his birth, or shortly after, in Louisiana. Laid over for decision.—(See book No. 3, page 365.)

July 9, 1810.—Board met. Present: John B. C. Lucas, Clement B. Penrose, and Frederick Bates, commissioners.

Manuel Lisa, assignee of Joachin Lisa, claiming 6,000 arpents of land.—(See book No. 2, page 33; book No. 3, page 365.) It is the opinion of the board that this claim ought not to be confirmed.—(See book No. 4, page 421.)

November 28, 1832.—The board met pursuant to adjournment. Present: Lewis F. Linn, F. R. Conway, commissioners.

Joachin Lisa, by Manuel Lisa's legal representatives, claiming 6,000 arpents of land.—(See book B, page 91; minutes, No. 2, page 33; No. 3, page 365; No. 4, page 421.) Produces a paper purporting to be an original concession from Zenon Trudeau, dated July 17, 1799, and a deed of conveyance for the same.

M. P. Le Duc, duly sworn, saith that the signature to said concession is in the proper handwriting of the said Zenon Trudeau, lieutenant governor.—(See book No. 6, page 61.)

November 6, 1833.—The board met pursuant to adjournment. Present: L. F. Linn, A. G. Harrison, F. R. Conway, commissioners.

In the case of Joachin Lisa, claiming 6,000 arpents of land.—(See page 61 of this book.)

John P. Cabanné, duly sworn, says that, to the best of his knowledge, Joachin Lisa came to this country in the year 1800; that he resided in this town with his family, consisting of his wife and four or five children; that he thinks said Lisa had several slaves, but cannot say how many; that said Lisa resided in this place from 1800 to the fall of 1804, at which time said Lisa went down to New Orleans with him, the deponent. He further says that in 1792, when deponent arrived in New Orleans, said Lisa was then employed in the custom-house in said place; that at that time all the family of said Lisa was living in New Orleans; that he had a plantation near Bayou St. John, and that he sold said plantation before he came to this country, with the intention of settling himself as a farmer; that he, the deponent, first came to this country in 1799, and was married in 1800, and has resided in this country ever since.

The deponent further says that he knew that Manuel Lisa, brother of claimant, was in St. Louis in the summer of 1799, and that the signature to the petition asking 6,000 arpents of land for the said Joachin Lisa is in the proper handwriting of the said Manuel Lisa; that the claimant, Joachin Lisa, was the elder brother of said Manual Lisa.—(See book No. 6, page 301.)

November 15, 1833.—The board met pursuant to adjournment. Present: L. F. Linn, A. G. Harrison, F. R. Conway, commissioners.

Joachin Lisa, claiming 6,000 arpents of land.—(See pages 61 and 301 of this book.) The board are unanimously of opinion that this claim ought to be confirmed to the said Joachin Lisa, or to his legal representatives, according to the concession.—(See book No. 6, page 333.)

A. G. HARRISON.
L. F. LINN.
F. R. CONWAY.

No. 134.—Melchior Aman Michau, *claiming* 600 *arpents.*

To Don Carlos Dehault Delassus, lieutenant governor of Upper Louisiana:

Sir: Victor St. Amant has the honor to represent to you that he would wish to make an establishment in the upper part of this province; therefore he prays you to grant to him a tract of land of 600 arpents in superficie, to be taken on the vacant lands of the King's domain, in the place which shall be most advantageous to the interest of your petitioner, who presumes to expect this favor of your justice.

MELCHIOR AMAN MICHAU.

St. Louis, *May* 14, 1800.

ST. LOUIS OF ILLINOIS, *May* 16, 1800.

Whereas we are assured that the petitioner possesses sufficient means to improve the land which he solicits, I do grant to him and his heirs the land which he solicits, provided it is not prejudicial to anybody; and the surveyor, Don Antonio Soulard, shall put the party interested in possession of the quantity of land he asks, in a vacant place of the royal domain; which being executed, he shall make out a plat of his survey, delivering the same to the party, with his certificate, in order to serve to him to obtain the title in form from the intendant general, to whom alone corresponds, by royal order, the distributing and granting all classes of lands, &c.

CARLOS DEHAULT DELASSUS.

I, the undersigned, certify that on the 16th of May, in the year 1800, it is to Melchior Michau, as it is specified in my foregoing decree, that I have granted the tract of land of 600 arpents in superficie which he asked for in his petition, under date of May 14, of the same year.

Given in St. Louis, July 14, 1818.

CHS. DEHAULT DELASSUS.

Truly translated. St. Louis, May 24, 1833.

JULIUS DE MUN.

No.	Name of original claimant.	Quantity, in arpents.	Nature and date of claim.	By whom granted.	By whom surveyed, date, and situation.
134	Melchior Aman Michau.	600	Concession, May 16, 1800.	Carlos Dehault Delassus.	John Harvey, deputy surveyor. January 15, 1803. Received for record by Soulard, surveyor general, February 28, 1806. District of St. Charles.

Evidence with reference to minutes and records.

April 13, 1833.—The board met pursuant to adjournment. Present: F. R. Conway, A. G. Harrison, commissioners.

Melchior Aman Michau, claiming 600 arpents of land, (see book B, page 238,) produces a plat of survey received for record by Antonio Soulard, February 28, 1806; and as evidence in support of said claim produces a concession purporting to be from Carlos Dehault Delassus, dated 16th May, 1800, at the foot of which there is a certificate of said Delassus, dated July 14, 1818, by which it appears that the land was granted to claimant, and not to J. Michau, as appears by minutes, book 5, page 454.

November 25, 1811.—Board met. Present: John B. C. Lucas, Clement B. Penrose, and Frederick Bates, commissioners.

James Michau, claiming 600 arpents of land situate in the district of St. Charles, produces record of a plat of survey, dated 15th January, and certified 28th February, 1806. It is the opinion of the board that this claim ought not to be granted.—(See book No. 5, page 454.)

M. P. Le Duc, duly sworn, says that the signature to the plat of survey is in the proper handwriting of Antonio Soulard, and that the signatures to the concession and to the certificate are in the proper handwriting of said Carlos Dehault Delassus.—(See book No. 6, page 155.)

November 15, 1833.—The board met pursuant to adjournment. Present: L. F. Linn, A. G. Harrison, F. R. Conway, commissioners.

Melchior Aman Michau, claiming 600 arpents of land.—(See page 155 of this book.) The board are unanimously of opinion that this claim ought to be confirmed to the said Melchior Aman Michau, or to his legal representatives, according to the concession.—(See book No. 6, page 333.)

A. G. HARRISON.
L. F. LINN.
F. R. CONWAY.

No. 135.—AUGUSTE CHOUTEAU, *claiming* 1,281 *arpents.*

To Mr. Charles Dehault Delassus, lieutenant colonel in the army and lieutenant governor of Upper Louisiana, &c.:

SIR: Auguste Chouteau humbly prays, and has the honor to represent to you, that wishing to establish in this town a manufactory suitable to distill the different kinds of grain that are raised in this dependency, in order to supply the wants of the place, whose remote distance from the capital renders the importation too expensive to draw therefrom, annually, the quantity necessary for its consumption; therefore, sir, the petitioner, before he enters into the great expenses necessary to form such an establishment, would wish to obtain the honor of your consent, in order that hereafter he may not be subjected to any alteration prejudicial to his interest, and the petitioner shall return thanks to your goodness in granting his demand.

AUGUSTE CHOUTEAU.

ST. LOUIS OF ILLINOIS, *November* 5, 1799.

ST. LOUIS OF ILLINOIS, *January* 3, 1800.

Considering the establishment which the petitioner proposes to form as useful to the public and to commerce, seeing that there does not exist any of this kind, and that he shall procure liquors in greater abundance and at a more reasonable price than those that come from New Orleans, and in very small quantity, we do grant his demand.

CHARLES DEHAULT DELASSUS

To Mr. Charles Dehault Delassus, lieutenant colonel, attached to the stationary regiment of Louisiana, and lieutenant governor of the upper part of the same province:

Auguste Chouteau, merchant of this town, has the honor to represent to you that the lands in the vicinity of this town being partly conceded, and timber becoming every day more scarce, he finds himself much embarrassed in the carrying on of the considerable distillery which you have permitted him to establish by your decree, dated 5th November of last year; therefore he hopes you will be pleased to assist him in his views, and have the goodness to grant to him the concession of a tract of land of twelve hundred and eighty-one arpents in superficie, situated upon the fourth concession in depth, (beginning from the lands which are adjoining this town,) bounded north by land belonging to Don John Watkins; to the south and west by the lands of the third concession. The petitioner, besides having the intention to improve the said land, hopes to be deserving the favor which he solicits of your justice.

AUGUSTE CHOUTEAU.

St. Louis, *January* 5, 1800.

St. Louis of Illinois, *January* 5, 1800.

Whereas we are assured that the petitioner possesses sufficient means to improve the land which he solicits, within the term fixed by the regulation of the governor general of this province, the surveyor of this Upper Louisiana, Don Antonio Soulard, shall put him in possession of the twelve hundred and eighty-one arpents of land in superficie, in the place where he asks them; and this being executed, the interested shall have to solicit the title of concession in due form from the intendant general of these provinces, to whom alone corresponds, by order of his Majesty, the distributing and granting of all classes of lands of the royal domain.

CARLOS DEHAULT DELASSUS.

Don Antonio Soulard, surveyor general of Upper Louisiana.

I do certify that on the 5th of March of the present year, (by virtue of the decree here annexed of the lieutenant governor and lieutenant colonel in the royal army, Don Carlos Dehault Delassus, dated 5th January of the last year,) I went on the land of Mr. Auguste Chouteau, to survey it conformably to his demand of twelve hundred and eighty-one arpents in superficie, which measurement was executed in presence of the proprietor and adjoining neighbors, with the perch of Paris, of eighteen feet in length, according to the custom adopted in this province of Louisiana, and without regard to the variation of the needle, which is 7° 30′ E., as it is evinced by the foregoing figurative plat. The said land is situated at about four miles N. 56½° W. from this town, and bounded as follows: to the north, in part by lands belonging to Messrs. John Watkins, Philip Riviere, and by vacant lands of the royal domain; to the south and west by the same above-mentioned vacant lands; and to the east by the lands of divers inhabitants of this town of St. Louis; and, that it may be available according to law, I do give the present, with the foregoing figurative plat, on which are noted the dimensions and the natural and artificial limits which surround said land.

ANTONIO SOULARD, *Surveyor General.*

St. Louis of Illinois, *April* 10, 1801.

New Orleans, *May* 20, 1799.

My Dear Friend: In order not to miss any opportunity of expressing my esteem for you, I merely assure you of my esteem, promising to you to answer your letter by the boat which has just now arrived, and which will depart next week.

In my instructions to Mr. Delassus, I particularly recommend to him to favor all your undertakings, &c.

Adieu—I am in such a haste that I have only time to tell you that I am your sincere friend and very humble servant.

MANUEL GAYOSO DE LEMOS.

Mr. Auguste Chouteau.

Truly translated. St. Louis, January 24, 1833.

JULIUS DE MUN.

No.	Name of original claimant.	Quantity, arpents.	Nature and date of claim.	By whom granted.	By whom surveyed, date, and situation.
135	Auguste Chouteau, by his heirs.	1,281	Concession, January 5, 1800.	Carlos Dehault Delassus.	Antonio Soulard, March 5, 1801; 4 miles N. 56½° W. of St. Louis.

Evidence with reference to minutes and records.

July 26, 1806.—The board met agreeably to adjournment. Present: The Hon. John B. C. Lucas, Clement B. Penrose, and James L. Donaldson, esqs.

Auguste Chouteau, claiming 1,281 arpents of land, situate on Beaver pond, district of St. Louis, produces a concession from Charles D. Delassus, dated January 5, 1800, and a survey of the same, taken March 5, and certified April 10, 1801; the aforesaid concession granted for the purpose of procuring fuel for a distillery established by claimant, and which could not be kept in operation without fuel. He further produces a permission from Charles D. Delassus to build the aforesaid distillery, the same being then considered by government as an establishment of public utility and benefit; said permission dated January 3, 1800.

Gabriel Dodié, being duly sworn, says that claimant, having purchased the said tract of land, built a house on the same in the year 1800.

Myers Michael, being also duly sworn, says that claimant had a distillery built prior to October, 1800.

A. Soulard, being also duly sworn, says that, to his knowledge, claimant did procure from the aforesaid tract of land the fuel necessary for the said distillery.

The board reject this claim.—(See book No. 1, page 427.)

September 14, 1808.—Board met. Present: The Hon. John B. C. Lucas, Clement B. Penrose, and Frederick Bates.

Auguste Chouteau, claiming 1,281 arpents of land, situate on Beaver pond, district of St. Louis.

David Delauney, sworn, says that he wrote the petition for the permission to build a distillery, dated November 5, 1799; that the same was written at the time the permission bears date, to wit, January 3, 1800.

Laid over for decision.—(See book No. 3, page 245.)

June 8, 1810.—Board met. Present: John B. C. Lucas, Clement B. Penrose, and Frederick Bates, commissioners.

Auguste Chouteau, claiming 1,281 arpents of land.—(See book No. 1, page 427; No. 3, page 245.)

It is the opinion of the board that this claim ought not to be confirmed.—(See book No. 4, page 370.)

October 8, 1832.—The board met pursuant to adjournment. Present: Lewis F. Linn, Wm. Updyke, and F. R. Conway, commissioners.

Auguste Chouteau, by his heirs, claiming 1,281 arpents of land, (see record, book B, pages 58 and 59; minutes, book No. 1, page 427; No. 3, page 245; and No. 4, page 370,) produces a paper purporting to be a concession from Carlos Dehault Delassus, dated January 5, 1800, to Auguste Chouteau; also a plat of survey, executed March 5, 1801, and certified April 10, 1801; also a paper purporting to be a petition, dated November 5, 1799, signed by A. Chouteau, and addressed to C. D. Delassus, lieutenant governor, together with the answer of said Delassus to said petition; also a letter from Manuel Galloso de Lemos, dated May 20, 1799, to A. Chouteau.

Pascal Cerré, duly sworn, saith that the signature to the petition is the handwriting of A. Chouteau, and the signature to the concession is the handwriting of C. D. Delassus; that the signature to the abovementioned letter is the handwriting of said Galloso; that the signature to the plat of survey and certificate is the handwriting of A. Soulard, surveyor general; that the signature to the petition, dated November 5, 1799, is the handwriting of A. Chouteau, and that the signature to the decree is the handwriting of C. D. Delassus; knows that A. Chouteau had a distillery in operation several years before 1800; believes said distillery was in operation twelve or fifteen years; that to his knowledge Chouteau cut the wood for his distillery on said tract of land; that the Côte Brillante tract was generally known by the inhabitants of St. Louis to be the property of said Chouteau.—(See book No. 6, page 12.)

November 19, 1833.—The board met pursuant to adjournment. Present: L. F. Linn, A. G. Harrison, and F. R. Conway, commissioners.

Auguste Chouteau, claiming 1,281 arpents of land.—(See page 11 of this book, No. 6.)

The board are unanimously of opinion that this claim ought to be confirmed to the said Auguste Chouteau, or to his legal representatives, according to the concession.—(See page 143, No. 6.)

A. G. HARRISON.
F. R. CONWAY.
L. F. LINN

No. 136.—James McDaniel, *claiming* 800 *arpents*.

No.	Name of original claimant.	Quantity, arpents.	Nature and date of claim.	By whom granted.	By whom surveyed, date, and situation.
136	James McDaniel ..	800	Settlement right.	....	James Mackay, February 14, 1806; received for record by Soulard, February 26, 1806; three or four miles above Belle Fontaine, district of St. Louis.

Evidence with reference to minutes and records.

January 2, 1812.—Board met. Present: John B. C. Lucas, Clement B. Penrose, and Frederick Bates, commissioners.

James McDaniel, claiming 800 arpents of land situated on the Missouri, district of St. Louis, produces record of a plat of survey, dated 14th and certified 26th February, 1806. It is the opinion of the board that this claim ought not to be granted.—(See book No. 5, page 552.)

May 23, 1833.—F. R. Conway, esq., appeared, pursuant to adjournment.

James McDaniel, by his legal representatives, claiming 800 arpents of land under settlement right, situated three or four miles above Belle Fontaine.—(See book B, page 262; minutes, No. 5, page 552.)

Albert Tison, duly sworn, says that he saw the said McDaniel living and residing on said land in 1801 and 1802; that he had a cabin and field of about five or six acres; that in 1805 or 1806 the said

McDaniel resided yet on said place; that when he first saw it he judged that it had been settled a few years before.—(See book No. 6, page 170.)

November 15, 1833.—The board met pursuant to adjournment. Present: L. F. Linn, A. G. Harrison, and F. R. Conway, commissioners.

James McDaniel, claiming under settlement right 800 arpents of land.—(See page 170 of this book.) The board are unanimously of opinion that 640 acres of land ought to be granted to the said James McDaniel, or to his legal representatives.—(See book No. 6, page 333.)

A. G. HARRISON.
L. F. LINN.
F. R. CONWAY.

No. 137 —EDMUND CHANDLER, *claiming* 640 *acres.*

No.	Name of original claimant.	Quantity, in acres.	Nature and date of claim.	By whom granted	By whom surveyed, date, and situation.
137	Edmund Chandler.	640	Settlement right.		

Evidence with reference to minutes and records.

February 3, 1809.—Board met. Present: the honorable John B. C. Lucas, Clement B. Penrose, and Frederick Bates, commissioners.

Arthur Burns, jr., assignee of Edmund Chandler, claiming 640 acres of land situate on river Sandy, district of St. Charles, produces to the board a notice to the recorder and a deed of conveyance from said Chandler to claimant, dated December 30, 1805.

(For permission to settle, see Mackay's list.)

Claibourne Rhodes, sworn, says that Edmund Chandler fenced in a piece of ground on the land claimed, but resided in the neighborhood with witness; planted watermelons and potatoes on the same in 1803; in 1804 claimant ploughed a piece of land, and planted corn, which was never gathered in; said Chandler was a single man in 1803. Laid over for decision.—(See book No. 3, page 460.)

July 16, 1810.—Board met. Present: John B. C. Lucas, Clement B. Penrose, Frederick Bates, commissioners.

Arthur Burns, jr., assignee of Edmund Chandler, claiming 640 acres of land.—(See book No. 3, page 460.) It is the opinion of the board that this claim ought not to be granted.—(See book No. 4, page 439.)

May 22, 1833.—F. R. Conway, esq., appeared, pursuant to adjournment.

Edmund Chandler, by Arthur Burns, jr., claiming 640 acres of land under settlement right.—(See record, book D, page 340; minutes, No. 3, page 460; No. 4, page 439.) Produces original deed of conveyance from Chandler to Burns.—(See book No. 6, page 170.)

May 23, 1833.—F. R. Conway, esq., appeared, pursuant to adjournment.

In the case of Edmund Chandler, claiming 640 acres of land.—(See the beginning of this claim.) Albert Tison, duly sworn, says that in the winter of 1803 and 1804 he saw said Chandler, with his family, residing on said land; that he had a house and field.—(See book No. 6, p. 170.)

November 15, 1833.—The board met pursuant to adjournment. Present: L. F. Linn, A. G. Harrison, and F. R. Conway, commissioners.

Edmund Chandler, claiming under settlement right 640 acres of land.—(See page 170 of this book.) The board are unanimously of opinion that 640 acres of land ought to be granted to the said Edmund Chandler, or to his legal representatives.—(See book No. 6, page 334.)

A. G. HARRISON.
L. F. LINN.
F. R. CONWAY.

No. 138.—WILLIAM DILLON, *claiming* 640 *acres.*

No.	Name of original claimant.	Quantity, acres.	Nature and date of claim.	By whom granted.	By whom surveyed, date, and situation.
138	William Dillon.	640	Settlement right.		

Evidence with reference to minutes and records.

November 30, 1808.—Board met. Present: John B. C. Lucas, Clement B. Penrose, and Frederick Bates, commissioners.

William Dillon, claiming 640 acres of land situate on the west side of the river St. François, opposite a concession claimed by James Dodson, produces to the board a notice of claim.

Samuel Campbell, sworn, says that in 1803 claimant built a cabin on the tract claimed, moved on it, and continued to reside on it that winter. Laid over for decision.—(See book No. 3, page 386.)

July 12, 1810.—Board met. Present: John B. C. Lucas, Clement B. Penrose, and Frederick Bates, commissioners.

William Dillon, claiming six hundred and forty acres of land.—(See book No. 3, page 386.) It is the opinion of the board that this claim ought not to be granted.—(See book No. 4, page 431.)

November 15, 1833.—Board met pursuant to adjournment. Present: L. F. Linn, A. G. Harrison, F. R. Conway, commissioners.

William Dillon, heirs and legal representatives of, now the heirs of William Crawford, claiming six hundred and forty acres of land.—(See book No. 3, page 386; No. 4, page 431.) The following testimony was taken before L. F. Linn, commissioner:

STATE OF MISSOURI, *county of Madison:*

Samuel Campbell, aged about sixty-eight years, who, being duly sworn, deposeth and saith that he was well acquainted with the original claimant; that the witness became acquainted with him in the spring of 1803, and understood the claimant had been here for some years before; witness also knows the land claimed, and knows that the claimant was settled on the same, and living thereon, in the spring of 1803, and the place had the appearance of having been settled for several years, for there were then two houses, a dwelling-house and kitchen, and several acres of land under fence and cleared, and appeared to have been in cultivation up to that time, and that he knows the claimant actually inhabited and cultivated the same in 1803, and that the same tract of land has been continually inhabited and cultivated by either the claimant or some other person ever since, till within a few years past, and may have been for those few years, but the witness cannot positively say, as he removed to another part of the State.

SAMUEL CAMPBELL.

Sworn to and subscribed before me, the subscriber, L. F. Linn, commissioner, this 22d October, 1833.

L. F. LINN, *Commissioner.*

Also came John Clements, a witness, aged about fifty-three years, who, being duly sworn as the law directs, deposeth and saith that he was well acquainted with William Dillon, the original claimant; that he found him in this country, then the province of Upper Louisiana, in the spring of the year 1802; the witness also knows the land claimed, and knows that the claimant was then settled on and living on the land claimed; that claimant had then a dwelling-house, and in the same year built a kitchen; that claimant had in 1802 some three or four acres under fence and cleared, which land was actually cultivated, in the year 1802, in corn and other things; claimant also had a garden; claimant continued to inhabit and cultivate the land during that year, and the witness understood that he had afterwards remained there for some time, but witness went away in the fall of 1802, and cannot say positively; witness lived with claimant, and helped him to build the house, and attend the same at the time.

JOHN his × mark. CLEMENTS.

Sworn to and subscribed before me, L. F. Linn, commissioner, this 22d October, 1833.

L. F. LINN, *Commissioner.*

Also came John Reaves, a witness, aged about seventy-three years, who, being duly sworn as the law directs, deposeth and saith that he knew the original claimant; that he found him a citizen and residenter of this county in 1803, when the witness came to the country; witness also knew the land claimed. Claimant was settled on the same in 1803, had a house in which he lived, and had several acres in actual cultivation, cleared and under fence, and the same tract of land has been actually inhabited, continually improved, and cultivated ever since.

JOHN his + mark. REAVES.

Sworn to and subscribed before me, L. F. Linn, commissioner, this 23d October, 1833.

L. F. LINN, *Commissioner.*

The board are unanimously of opinion that six hundred and forty acres ought to be granted to the said William Dillon, or to his legal representatives.—(See book No. 6, page 334.)

L. F. LINN.
F. R. CONWAY.
A. G. HARRISON.

No. 139.—ROBERT GIBONEY, *claiming* 348 *arpents and* 42 *perches.*

No.	Name of original claimant.	Quantity, in arpents.	Nature and date of claim.	By whom granted.	By whom surveyed, date, and situation.
139	Robert Giboney.	348 arpents 42 perches.	Settlement right.	....	B. Cousin, deputy surveyor, 24th December, 1805; countersigned Ant. Soulard, surveyor general. On Giboney's creek, district of Cape Girardeau.

Evidence with reference to minutes and records.

March 6, 1809.—Board met. Present: John B. C. Lucas, Clement B. Penrose, and Frederick Bates, commissioners.

Robert Giboney, claiming three hundred and forty-eight arpents and forty-two perches of land situate on Giboney's creek, district of Cape Girardeau, produces to the board, as a special permission to settle, list

A, on which claimant is No. 46, a plat of survey, dated 24th December, 1805, countersigned Antoine Soulard, surveyor general. The following testimony in the above claim taken by Frederick Bates, commissioner, at Cape Girardeau, by authority from the board, May 31, 1808:

Andrew Ramsey, sr., sworn, says that the claimant came to the country last of the year 1797, or beginning of the year 1798; that he has continued in the country ever since, and performed all those duties usually enjoined on subjects during the continuance of that government; that claimant followed the business of a blacksmith, which witness presumes prevented a more early application for a concession.

Samuel Bradley, duly sworn, says that he has seen claimant working on the tract claimed; that several acres, perhaps 10, were cleared, and a sufficiency of rails mauled to enclose it; claimant also occupied a sugar camp on said land. Laid over for decision.—(See book No. 3, page 507.)

January 16, 1810.—Board met. Present: John B. C. Lucas, Clement B. Penrose, and Frederick Bates, commissioners.

Robert Giboney, claiming 348 arpents 42 perches of land.—(See book No. 3, page 507.) It is the opinion of the board that this claim ought not to be granted.—(See book No. 4, page 255.)

November 13, 1833.—The board met pursuant to adjournment. Present: L. F. Linn, A. G. Harrison, and F. R. Conway, commissioners.

Robert Giboney, claiming 348 arpents 42 perches of land.—(See book No. 3, page 507; book No. 4, page 255.) The following testimony was taken by L. F. Linn, commissioner:

State of Missouri, *county of Cape Girardeau, sct:*

This day personally appeared before me, Lewis F. Linn, one of the commissioners appointed under an act of Congress to settle and adjust the unconfirmed land claims in the State of Missouri, Alexander Summers, of lawful age, who, being sworn, deposeth and saith that he emigrated to the district of Cape Girardeau in the year 1798, the district being then under the Spanish government; that in the year 1800 this affiant knows that Robert Giboney made a settlement and improvement on the waters of Giboney's creek, in said district; this affiant knows that the said improvement has always been claimed by said Robert Giboney; that the same has been ever since improved and cultivated; that this affiant has lived here, and still resides here.

ALEX. SUMMERS.

Sworn and subscribed October 15, 1833.

L. F. LINN, *Commissioner.*

State of Missouri, *county of Cape Girardeau, sct:*

This day personally appeared before me, Lewis F. Linn, one of the commissioners appointed under an act of Congress to settle and adjust the unconfirmed land claims in the State of Missouri, William Williams, of lawful age, who, being sworn according to law, deposeth and saith that he emigrated to the district of Cape Girardeau under the Spanish government, A. D. 1799. This affiant recollects that as early as the year A. D. 1802 he saw an improvement made and claimed by Robert Giboney, in the district of Cape Girardeau; and this affiant recollects that, from his frequently having passed the said improvement since that time, the same appears to have been improved and cultivated up to the present time.

WM. WILLIAMS.

Sworn to and subscribed October 15, 1833.

L. F. LINN, *Commissioner.*

(See book No. 6.)

November 15, 1833.—The board met pursuant to adjournment. Present: L. F. Linn, A. G. Harrison, F. R. Conway, commissioners.

The board are unanimously of opinion that 348 arpents 42 perches of land, it being the quantity originally claimed, ought to be granted to the said Robert Giboney, or to his legal representatives.—(See book No. 6, page 336.)

L. F. LINN.
F. R. CONWAY.
A. G. HARRISON.

No. 140.—Jacob Wickerham, *claiming* 800 *arpents.*

No.	Name of original claimant.	Quantity, in arpents.	Nature and date of claim.	By whom granted.	By whom surveyed, date, and situation.
140	Jacob Wickerham.....	800	Settlement right.		

Evidence with reference to minutes and records.

June 6, 1833.—F. R. Conway, esq., appeared pursuant to adjournment.

Jacob Wickerham, by his legal representative, William Drennen, claiming 800 arpents of land situated on Balew's creek.—(See record, book F, page 142; Bates's Decisions, page 104.)

William Moss, duly sworn, says that he is settled in this country since the year 1795, and knows the tract now claimed; that in 1803 he went to the farm of Jacob Wickerham's father to buy corn, and having lost his way, he met with the said Jacob Wickerham, who took him through a piece of land on which he had about 500 peach trees he had planted the year before and was then hoeing; the said trees were enclosed with a strong fence, and that the said Wickerham proposed to sell his improvements to him, the said deponent.—(See book No. 6, page 173.)

November 15, 1833.—The board met pursuant to adjournment. Present: L. F. Linn, A. G. Harrison, F. R. Conway, commissioners.

Jacob Wickerham, claiming 800 arpents of land.—(See page 173 of this book.) The board are unanimously of opinion that 640 acres of land ought to be granted to the said Jacob Wickerham, or to his legal representatives.—(See book No. 6, page 338.)

L. F. LINN.
F. R. CONWAY.
A. G. HARRISON.

No. 141.—Jacob Collins, *claiming* 890 *arpents.*

No.	Name of original claimant.	Quantity, in arpents.	Nature and date of claim.	By whom granted.	By whom surveyed, date, and situation.
141	Jacob Collins........	890	Settlement right.....	....	John Stewart, June 21, 1808; on Negro Fork of the river Maramec, district of St. Louis.

Evidence with reference to minutes and records.

October 22, 1808.—Board met. Present: The Hon. Clement B. Penrose and Frederick Bates, commissioners.

Jacob Collins, claiming 890 arpents of land situate on the Negro Fork of the river Maramec, district of St. Louis, produces to the board a notice of claim to the recorder, dated June 25, 1808; a plat of survey, dated June 21, 1808, signed by John Stewart, surveyor.

John Wideman, sworn, says that claimant built a cabin on the place in 1802, and raised a crop; one Charles Pruitt cultivated the same in 1803, but does not know for whom; that three years ago claimant inhabited and cultivated the same, and ever since; that claimant was one of the families that came to the country with him, the witness.

John Pruitt, sworn, says that claimant, in 1803, had a wife and one child.

Laid over for decision (in the margin—for permission to settle, see John Wideman's claim, book No. 1, page 390,) to wit:

Michael Horine, being also duly sworn, says that Francis Vallé, when commandant of St. Genevieve informed him, the witness, that he had permitted the Widemans and their families (consisting then of eight or ten families) to settle on vacant lands.—(See book No. 3, page 315.)

June 21, 1810.—Board met. Present: John B. C. Lucas, Clement B. Penrose, and Frederick Bates, commissioners.

Jacob Collins claiming 890 arpents of land.—(See book No. 3, page 315.)

It is the opinion of the board that this claim ought not to be granted.—(See book No. 4, page 399.)

June 18, 1833.—F. R. Conway, esq., appeared, pursuant to adjournment.

Jacob Collins, claiming 890 arpents of land situate on Big river, Maramec, bounded on one side by the said Big river, on the upper side by Hugh McCullick, on the lower side by Mark Wideman, and back by public land, by virtue of a settlement right.—(See minutes, No. 4, page 399.)

James Rogers, duly sworn, says that he is about fifty-two years of age; that some time in May, 1802, he came on to this country in company with the claimant; that they arrived time enough to raise a crop of corn; that he, the deponent, worked a few days for the claimant; that, in that same year, the claimant raised corn; that they made a camp, it being too late to build a house; that in 1803, claimant got one Charles Pruitt to work said place for him, and said Pruitt sowed flax and planted some corn; that said place is under cultivation now, and deponent thinks it has ever been so since the first settling of it; that there are now about forty acres under cultivation, and never heard that any body claimed it but the aforesaid Jacob Collins; that he never knew of Jacob Collins laying any claims to any other lands; that when claimant first moved to this country he had a wife and three children; that at present there is on the place a hewn two story log-house with shingle roof, a barn, two stables, a well, &c. The deponent further says that he was absent two years at Natchez and the Walnut hills; his absence embracing the time when said Collins presented his claim before the former board of commissioners.—(See book No. 6, page 176.)

November 15, 1833.—The board met pursuant to adjournment. Present: L. F. Linn, A. G. Harrison, F. R. Conway, commissioners.

Jacob Collins, claiming under settlement right 890 arpents of land.—(See page 176 of this book.)

The board are unanimously of opinion that 640 acres of land ought to be granted to the said Jacob Collins, or to his legal representatives.—(See book No. 6, page 333.)

A. G HARRISON.
L. F. LINN.
F. R. CONWAY.

No. 142.—SEBASTIAN BUTCHER AND PETER BLOOM, *claiming* 1,600 *arpents.*

To his lordship the intendant general of the province of Louisiana, in his mansion in New Orleans:

Michael Butcher, Bartholomew Butcher, Bastian Butcher, and Peter Bloom, supplicate very humbly, and have the honor to represent that having resided since several years under the domination of his Catholic Majesty, and having never obtained any land from the government, they would wish to make and improve a plantation as well as a grazing farm. To this effect they have made researches for a tract of land suitable to their views, and they have found one situated at about six miles from Mine à la Motte, on the road which leads to St. Genevieve and New Bourbon, at a place where there is a spring, which is at about a half mile from the land of Mr. Robert Friend, the said tract consisting of sixteen hundred arpents in superficie. For these motives the said petitioners apply to your lordship, praying that you may be pleased to grant to them the above-mentioned tract of land, consisting of sixteen hundred arpents in superficie, at the place above described, for them, their heirs and assigns; and in case the aforesaid quantity of arable land was not to be found in the place here above described, to authorize them to take what would be wanting in a vacant place of the King's domain; the said land now solicited for not being granted to any person, which fact can be certified, if needed, by the nearest neighbors, as well as by the surveyor of this district. In so doing the petitioners shall never cease to pray for the conservation of your days.

Done at New Bourbon, June 11, 1802.

BARTHOLOMEW BUTCHER.
MICHAEL BUTCHER.
BASTIAN BUTCHER, his + mark.
PETER BLOOM, his + mark.

We, captain, civil and military commandant of the post of New Bourbon, of Illinois, do certify to my lord the intendant of Louisiana that the petitioners are very honest individuals, exercising in a perfect manner the profession of masons, who have been of the most precious utility to the inhabitants of these districts since their arrival, as much for the construction of houses and chimneys free of catching fire, *(à l'abry du feu,)* as for the erecting of furnaces to smelt lead. We do certify, besides, that the greatest part of the said mason work being finished, and the said petitioners having the intention of leaving this country, we have united our endeavors to those of Don François Vallé, commandant at St. Genevieve, to prevail upon them to remain, to which they have consented, upon the promise we have made them to employ ourselves near his lordship the intendant, in order to have the concession which they solicit granted to them to form thereon a plantation. The said land has not been granted to any person, and is evidently a part of the King's domain.

Done at New Bourbon, June 15, 1802.

PIERRE DELASSUS DELUZIERE.

A true translation. St. Louis, December 12, 1832.

JULIUS DE MUN.

No.	Name of original claimant.	Quantity, arpents.	Nature and date of claim.	By whom granted.	By whom surveyed, date, and situation.
142	Sebastian Butcher and others.	1, 600	Petition and recommendation, June 15, 1802.		

Evidence with reference to minutes and records.

October 3, 1811.—Board met. Present: John B. C. Lucas, Clement B. Penrose, and Frederick Bates, commissioners.

Michael Butcher, Bartholomew Butcher, Bastian Butcher, and Peter Bloom, claiming 400 arpents of land situate on the waters of the river St. Francis, district of St. Genevieve, produce a petition to the intendant, together with a recommendation from Pierre D. Delassus Deluziere, commandant of New Bourbon, dated December 15, 1802. A plat of survey, dated February 23, 1806, certified February 23, 1806. It is the opinion of the board that this claim ought not to be granted.

Michael Butcher, Bartholomew Butcher, Bastian Butcher, and Peter Bloom, claiming 1,200 arpents of land situate on the waters of Big river, district of St. Genevieve, produce to the board the petition and recommendation, as in the foregoing claim. A plat of survey, dated February 25, 1806; certified February 28, 1806. It is the opinion of the board that this claim ought not to be granted.—(See book No. 5, page 352.)

December 14, 1832.—F. R. Conway, esq., appeared, pursuant to adjournment.

Sebastian Butcher, and the heirs and legal representatives of Bartholomew Butcher, Michael Butcher, and Peter Bloom, claiming 1,600 arpents of land.—(See book No. 5, page 352; record, book D, pages 46 and 47.) Produces a paper purporting to be their petition to the intendant general of Louisiana, and a recommendation to the same of Pierre Delassus Deluziere, commandant of New Bourbon, dated June 15, 1802; also a paper purporting to be a plat and certificate of survey, dated February 25, 1806, by Nathaniel Cook, deputy surveyor.

The following additional testimony was taken in the foregoing case, in compliance with a resolution of this board of the 10th of October last:

The claimants state that, by virtue of their said claim, they located 400 arpents thereof about six miles from Mine à la Motte, as in their petition prayed for; that finding no other vacant land at that place of value for cultivation, they located the remaining 1,200 arpents at a place on the waters of Grand or Big river, agreeably to the tenor of their said petition and the plat of survey herewith shown to the board of commissoners. The petitioners further state that the plat of survey for the said 400 arpents, so located near Mine à la Motte, is now in the land office at Jackson, so that they can now produce it, but believe the same is on record in the office of the recorder of land titles in St. Louis.

Joseph Pratte, being duly sworn in this behalf, deposeth and saith that he has seen the recommendation of the said Deluziere, late commander of the post of New Bourbon, annexed to the petition of the said claimants for a grant or concession of 1,600 arpents of land; that he is well acquainted with the handwriting of said Deluziere, and the said recommendation, dated June 15, 1802, and the signature thereunto affixed, are in the handwriting of the said Deluziere. This deponent further saith that he is well acquainted with the handwriting of Antoine Soulard, late surveyor general of Upper Louisiana, and that his signature to the plat of survey here shown is, as this deponent verily believes, genuine, and written by himself. This deponent further saith that he is fifty-seven years of age, and has resided in St. Genevieve and vicinity, in what was formerly Upper Louisiana, all his life; that he is well acquainted with the nature of Spanish concessions and requests, and recommendations of commandants of posts, of which latter class the claim here shown appears to be; that after the year 1799 or 1800 (as near as he can recollect) the commandants did not give concessions, but recommendations to the intendant general at New Orleans, (as in this case,) and that said recommendations were uniformly considered of equal validity with concessions, and were passed and transferred from hand to hand as such, and that it was the uniform custom of the intendant general at New Orleans to grant and confirm all such claims. This affiant further saith that he has no doubt that the claim here shown would have been confirmed by the said intendant, under the usages and custom of the Spanish government; that he has known the said Sebastian, (or Bastian,) Michael, and Bartholomew Butcher, and Peter Bloom, to have come to the country in the year 1797, and that it was the custom of the government to give lands to persons of their description, when applied for, and he has never heard that they received any other lands than those in the present claim mentioned.

JOSEPH PRATTE,
L. F. LINN,
Land Commissioners.

John Baptiste Vallé, sen., being duly sworn in this behalf, deposeth and saith that he has seen the recommendation of the said Deluziere, late commandant of the post of New Bourbon, annexed to the petition of the said claimants for a grant and concession of sixteen hundred arpents of land; that he is well acquainted with the handwriting of the said Deluziere, and that the said recommendation to the intendant general, and the signature thereunto affixed, are in the handwriting of the said Deluziere. This deponent further says that he was well acquainted with Antoine Soulard, late surveyor general of Upper Louisiana, and that his signature to the plat of survey here shown this deponent believes to be genuine, and written by said Soulard. This deponent further says that he is now seventy-two years of age, and has resided in St. Genevieve, in the district (now county) of St. Genevieve, all his life, and is well acquainted with the manner of granting concessions by the Spanish government in Louisiana, and he always considered incipient titles of the kind here shown as much entitled to a confirmation as any other, and that frequently lands granted by the said Spanish government were not surveyed until several years after they were granted and confirmed.

J. BAPTISTE VALLÉ.

And as a witness in this behalf, Mary Ann Laplante personally appeared before Lewis F. Linn, one of the commissioners appointed to settle and finally adjust the land claims in Missouri, and authorized by the said board of commissioners to receive testimony in this behalf, who, being duly sworn, deposeth and saith that she is about fifty-eight years of age; that she came from France to Upper Louisiana in the family of Mr. Deluziere, late commandant of the post of New Bourbon, and has resided in St. Genevieve and New Bourbon ever since the said Deluziere came to the country; that some time before the change of government, (she thinks about the year 1802,) she was in the office of the said Deluziere, (he being then commandant of the post of New Bourbon,) and saw Mr. Deluziere writing a paper, which said Deluziere then told her was a concession or grant of land to Bartholomew Butcher, Michael Butcher, Sebastian (or Bastian) Butcher, and Peter Bloom, which grant or concession said Deluziere informed the witness was for four hundred arpents for each of said persons, for that, as those persons were such good stone-masons, it was a great object to the people and the government of the country to have such good workmen and peaceable subjects retained in the country. This affiant, being now blind, cannot, of course, say whether the grant or concession or recommendation now shown to the commissioner is the same she saw Mr. Deluziere write.

MARY ANN LAPLANTE, her + mark.
L. F. LINN.

(See book No. 6, page 76.)

November 17, 1833.—The board met pursuant to adjournment. Present: L. F. Linn, A. G. Harrison, F. R. Conway, commissioners.

Sebastian Butcher, Bartholomew Butcher, Bastian Butcher, and Peter Bloom, claiming 1,600 arpents of land. The board, although not considering themselves authorized by the provisions of the act of Congress to take cognizance of this claim, regarding it to be a meritorious claim, respectfully recommend it to the examination of Congress for confirmation.

L. F. LINN.
F. R. CONWAY.
A. G. HARRISON.

-R-

-S-

www.ingramcontent.com/pod-product-compliance
Lightning Source LLC
Chambersburg PA
CBHW080421270326
41929CB00018B/3108
* 9 7 8 0 7 8 8 4 9 4 0 2 4 *